The Scottish Islands

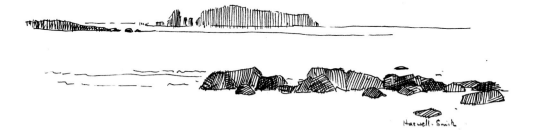

The Scottish

The bestselling guide to

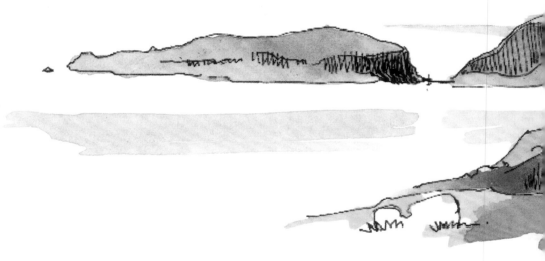

Islands

HAMISH HASWELL-SMITH

every Scottish Island

FULLY REVISED EDITION

CANON ‖ GATE

Edinburgh · London

First published in Great Britain

in 1996 by Canongate Books Ltd

14 High Street, Edinburgh EH1 1TE

Fully revised second edition 2004

Fully revised and updated 2015

1

ISBN 978 1 78211 678 3

British Library Cataloguing-in-Publication Data

A catalogue record for this book is available on

request from the British Library

Art Direction by James Hutcheson

Design and Layout by Barrie Tullett

Set in Photina MT and Gill Sans

Printed in China on acid-free paper by C&C Offset Printing Co., Ltd

To Jean

Author's Note

My original intention was merely to compile, for my personal satisfaction, a list of the Scottish islands equivalent to 'Munro's Tables of the 3000ft Mountains of Scotland' (published by the Scottish Mountaineering Trust). This factually interesting little book satisfies the aspirations of 'Munro-baggers' and I considered that, as someone who enjoyed landing on islands, to grade islands by size instead of mountains by height, would be an interesting exercise and serve me well.

It was during the long labour of calculation that I realised that, like most island-collectors, the pleasure of landing on 'new' territory becomes secondary to the desire to explore and appreciate the island for itself alone. The research became more and more absorbing as the years rolled by. My original simple statistical database of island names and areas grew into an amorphous mass of information from many sources. In the end I had to call a halt and try to return to the logical structure with which I began the quest.

I am only too aware that the information contained here will always be incomplete. Sometimes it has been abbreviated for reasons of space; more often the scarce facts have had to be wrested with difficulty from diverse sources. I have endeavoured to check them assiduously and where possible referred back to original records but, even so, I know there will be errors and omissions. If you are an island resident or owner, I apologise if I have omitted something of particular interest, and if you are a specialist (and in Scotland we are particularly fortunate in having experts in every conceivable field) your comments and corrections would be appreciated for the next edition.

It is quite astonishing how many of our islands were still populated a few decades ago and whose inhabitants are no longer easily traced. All their unrecorded wisdom will vanish with them and so, with every passing year, more and more of our common heritage is being forgotten or lost by neglect.

Edinburgh 1996

Since writing the above note in the first edition of this book, I have come to realise that it has been assumed that all the material needed to list our islands was already available. This was not the case. Because there was no exact and universally applied definition of an island there were two problems:
1) NO ONE KNEW HOW MANY SCOTTISH ISLANDS THERE WERE,
and there was
2) NO ACCURATE RECORD OF THE AREAS OF OUR ISLANDS.

This meant that, unlike Munro, who at least had contour maps showing all the separate regions which were above 3000ft and no need to calculate them, I had to start from scratch. And I had to solve these problems in sequence, i.e. until I had a definition I couldn't work out how many islands there were, and until I had established the individual islands I couldn't work out what their areas were. Needless to say, if there are any errors they are entirely mine.

Edinburgh 2008

Contents

Acknowledgements

This book would not have been possible without *Jandara* – a 41' Moody sloop – who, like every woman, has few faults and many virtues. She possesses four of us – a farmer, a baker, a quantity-surveyor, and me. Three of our wives are called Jean and one is called Ann so, by convoluted reasoning in kitchen Gaelic, her name derives from 'Jean-Ann-andara' – the second wife.

Our partnership has survived for more than twenty years and its success is probably due to our diverse personalities. The farmer, Craig Hutcheson, has a boyish sense of humour, a healthy appetite, and a considerable practical aptitude when he cares to apply it. He plays the 'daft laddie' to perfection but is nobody's fool. The baker, Ian Terris, is a business man and world traveller who wakens everyone at five in the morning and doesn't know the meaning of sotto voce. But he is a competent seaman, a genuine friend, and always steady and reliable in a crisis. Peter Crabb, the quantity-surveyor, is a meticulous handyman who has a steady and considered approach to every problem and a love of the great outdoors. Being 6'5" tall, he is also our spare mast. Peter shares my star-sign – if one accepts such nonsense – and coughs discreetly at our occasional minor divergences of opinion. My only comment on my own personality is to thank my partners for their indulgence.

I am fortunate that my partners share my enthusiasm for exploring islands and that my other sailing friends also accept the challenge wholeheartedly. Among the latter I must particularly mention Harry Holmes, an energetic Yorkshireman and erstwhile Commodore of the Royal Forth Yacht Club, and his wife Brenda, a marvellous cook among her many other attributes; George Steedman, a fellow architect, and steadfast crew on some memorable voyages; and my cousin, Dr Ronald Howie, who has recently taught me a thing or two.

We try to explore every island 'in depth' but conditions are sometimes difficult. A heavy swell and seaweed on the rocks can be a considerable hazard but a conquest doesn't 'count' unless one has truly landed, even if detailed exploration in such cases has to await the next favourable opportunity.

I would like to thank the many kind people who have been so generous with their help. In particular, I wish to record my appreciation for the invaluable information given to me by:

Kenneth John Smith of Earshader, Mrs Anna Mackinnon of Ardroil, Angus McLean of Brenish, Norman Buchanan and his son of Valtos, Uig, and D Murdie of Bernera, all of the Isle of Lewis; Donald Macdonald of Lingerbay, Isle of Harris; Donald MacKillop of Berneray, Sound of Harris; D J Campbell of Lochmaddy, Isle of North Uist; Dorota Rychlik of Vaila (No.11.10); Margaret Wilkes, Head of the Map Library of the National Library of Scotland, and members of staff; Dr David H Caldwell, National Museums of Scotland; the Census Division of the General Register Office of Scotland; Anne Taylor of Scottish Natural Heritage; Mary Miers of South Uist; Nancy Scott of Westray; E Mairi MacArthur (author of *Columba's Island*); Stephen P Newall DL LLD of Shuna (No.3.12); Alan C Millar of Tighnabruaich; Richard Fresson of the

CCC; Angus Duncan; R A Ingham Clark; Major B E Sykes; Dr John Holden; A S Halford-MacLeod of Mulag (No.8.14); Torquil Johnson-Ferguson of Lunga (No.2.12); Jeff Harris of Pabay (No.5.2); Alasdair MacEachen, whose great-grandfather occupied Wiay (No.7.15) for three decades and whose ancestor Neil MacEachen guided Bonnie Prince Charlie through the Hebrides, and was the boatman when Flora MacDonald and the Prince sailed to Skye.

My sincere thanks also to:
Betty Kirkpatrick, Albert Morris, Norman G Masson, and Barbara MacLeod for their encouragement and friendly advice; Kenneth Mackenzie for his information on Scottish birdlife; the late Bobby Tulloch of Yell for his vast knowledge of Shetland, which he divulged so generously, and the late Norman MacCaig for his ready support and permission to include some lines from his poems.

AWESOME LOCH CORUISK, SKYE

Preface

There are few parts of the world which possess such magic and mystery as the seas around Scotland. Some six thousand miles of contorted coastline (69% of the total United Kingdom coastline) create a wonderland of islands and mountains and rocks and stacks and secret inlets and remote, uninhabited places. This is an area of breathtaking beauty with a character formed not only by the proximity of mountains and sea but also by the complexity of the geography and the geology, of the climate and the social history. It is a serene yet chaotic landscape in which every isle has a distinct personality. Each is an individual entity with differences so remarkable that the mere crossing of a short stretch of water can be like visiting another continent.

What is the fascination of an island?

Why do we experience such a thrill at being surrounded by water, cut off from the rest of mankind, imprisoned on a miniature world? Is it because an island is of human scale, easy to comprehend, safe and defensible when the world beyond is big and terrifying? Who hasn't dreamed of being marooned on the proverbial desert island? For generations islands have been a theme of literature and poetry and, more recently, of radio and film. Utopia, Atlantis, *Robinson Crusoe*, *Treasure Island*, *Desert Island Discs* – to name a few. It is a long list.

I have found Scottish islands so intriguing that the lack of a ready source of information on them has been a great frustration. The sheer excitement of landing on – and exploring – another island can be tempered by having little fore-knowledge of what to look for and where to go. Is there an archaeological ruin worth seeing? – a cave worth visiting? – uncommon birdlife? It is the '– you mean to say you were in Venice and you didn't even see St Marks?!' syndrome. This is particularly true as the available time ashore is usually severely limited.

Reach for a book on Scottish islands – there are any number of excellent ones – and time after time the same subjects turn up: Mull, Arran, Lewis, Islay, mainland Orkney or Shetland (because they are large), Staffa (because of Fingal's Cave), Iona (for its history and mystery) . . . and so on: possibly thirty or forty islands in all.

But what about the rest?

What about Hellisay or Killegray? Fuday or Fuiay? Uyea or Wiay? Hascosay or Mingulay?

Scotland has 168 islands of forty hectares and over (i.e. approximately one hundred acres), a figure I arrived at after many months of measurement and classification of each and every separate land mass. My very restrictive rules of classification will be explained later but they don't include 'bridged' islands like Skye, or Seil; they count linked islands like the Uists and Benbecula as only one island; they exclude the hundreds of islands which are less than forty hectares (even islets like the Bass Rock and Staffa); and, yet, they still produce a list of *168 islands* to be described in greater detail and, hopefully, visited?

Islandeering' isn't easy anywhere but Scottish islands present a particularly difficult, but exciting, challenge – arguably more difficult than the collection of mountains. Most of the large islands are well-served with transport and accommodation but it's a different matter for the smaller or more remote islands and almost impossible to plan in advance. How will you get there and back? Are weather and tides suitable for landing and re-embarking? How long can you stay ashore?

However, taking each island one at a time one can still build up a handsome score. A few general statistics may highlight how easy it is to start. Of my 168 listed islands: sixty-one are still populated and many others have at least one part-time resident; (the 2011 census lists ninety-three inhabited 'islands' in the everyday use of the word), forty-six have scheduled ferry services (and at least fourteen more provide informal services on request or by agreement); twenty-seven have airstrips or airfields, and twenty-one have scheduled air services; about thirty-four of the populated islands provide hotel, hostel, or bed-and-breakfast accommodation and many more provide campsites and holiday cottages.

When the first edition of this book was published in 1996 I challenged anyone to land on every one of my listed islands. Well, in 2014 I learned that Donald Thomson, chairman of the North-East Sea Kayaking Club, had just completed the challenge after thirty years. To the best of my knowledge he is the first person ever to do so.

The problem with writing about remote and uninhabited places is that doing so can destroy just what we find so attractive. I remember meeting a couple on an island visit who were from the south coast of England. 'We sail and explore these waters every year,' they said, 'but we don't tell anyone about it. These are secret places, far away from people. Why attract the crowds?'

I understand this viewpoint, yet I am taking a calculated risk that newcomers will visit these secret places, not just to chalk up another conquest, but because they have poetry in their souls and a true love of islands; that they will appreciate that it takes only one castaway beer can or crisp packet to destroy the next visitor's pleasure; and that they will understand that it is common courtesy to respect the privacy of the island's inhabitants, avoid causing damage, and when possible ask permission to land and explore.

Before I could start collating information about islands I was faced with a difficult problem of definition.

What, exactly, is an island? The dictionary says it is 'a mass of land, but not a continent, surrounded with water'. That defines maximum size, but do remember that size changes with every ebb and flow of the tide. The 1861 Census defined an island as 'any piece of solid land surrounded by water which affords sufficient vegetation to support one or two sheep, or is inhabited by man'. That is not a very scientific definition for minimum size – if one is needed – but it again confirms that an island must be surrounded by water. But does this mean

permanently surrounded by water? What if there is a linking sandbank when the tide is out? The definition also seems to allow a bridge or tunnel connection whilst definitely precluding a causeway because that would interrupt the surrounding ring of water.

In the end I had to arrive at my own definition: *An island is a piece of land or group of pieces of land which is entirely surrounded by seawater at Lowest Astronomical Tide and to which there is no permanent means of dry access.*

This satisfies my belief that the quality of insularity requires isolation.

In other words, if you can walk across to a piece of land without wading through seawater, even if it is only at the time of the lowest of tides, then that piece of land is not an island. And, similarly, land accessible by bridge, causeway or tunnel is not an island.

Likewise, if a number of 'islands' are accessible to each other at low water, or by bridge, tunnel or causeway, they should be considered one, single island.

By this definition the Uists, Benbecula, Berneray, Eriskay and their many adjoining satellites ('drying' or 'tidal' islands) count as one large island. And Skye, with a bridge to the mainland, no longer counts as an island. Although some, I know, will disagree with this definition because it may seem unduly restrictive, loosening the parameters leads to so many unresolvable situations that the exercise becomes pointless. Take a close look at the coast of Benbecula to see what I mean.

One requirement in my definition, however, is quite arbitrary: 'seawater'. I have restricted myself to ocean islands. There are plenty of Scottish islands which meet the above definition in every other respect but happen to be surrounded by fresh loch or river water. Maybe, someone someday will want to list them. My only excuse for not doing so is that there is already more than a lifetime's interest in the seaward islands.

In the earlier editions of this book I stated

that I had used averaged planimeter readings to estimate all the island areas. This was a long, monotonous and wearisome task so I also added: 'With digitised map data it will soon be possible to programme a computer to provide this information'.

Happily, at the 2013 Inverness Book Festival I met Jon Metcalf, a BP negotiator, who had devised a program for computing the area by a pixel count of digitised map data within the Mean High Water Springs line (MHWS) on the Ordnance Survey maps. Still fairly labour-intensive, it has nevertheless allowed Jon to check the areas of islands of approximately 40 hectares much more accurately. This has resulted in seven extra islands joining my over-40-hectare classification – Nave Island, Eilean Dubh in the Summer Isles, Trodday, Eilean an Roin Mor, Flodday in Loch Maddy, Muckle Skerry, and Linga in the Yell Sound – and one of my original over-40-hectare islands – Fiaray in the Outer Hebrides – being dropped from the list. Jon had his work laboriously checked by his friend Alan Holmes who had previously drawn up his own revised list using an arduous fine mesh grid count method.

It's amazing how many different groups have diverse interests in the islands. The kayakers, for instance, are a large group with the advantage of being able to reach places which are virtually inaccessible to others. Jon and Alan are part of another group, the Marilyn Baggers, for want of a better name. The Marilyns (the 'Munro' connection is obvious) are listed in Alan Dawson's book The Relative Hills of Britain. Marilyns are of any height, but they must have a minimum drop of 150 metres on all sides of the summit. There are 1557 Marilyns in Britain at the last count and over 200 of these are on Scottish islands so informal groups of enthusiasts jointly hire a boat to take them to these sites. They happily tick another Marilyn off their list and enthusiastically look for more islands regardless of height.

I am particularly indebted to Jon and Alan for their invaluable help.

Hamish Haswell-Smith 2015

Format and Overview

The Scottish islands have been divided into twelve geographical areas or sections.

Every island of forty or more hectares in area (i.e. approximately 100 acres or more) has been separately classified and tabulated.

On each island map:

The sea area is overlaid with a grid of 5-cable squares (i.e. half a nautical mile or nearly one kilometre) to allow instant comparison of scale and distance.

Darker blue colour indicates approximate sea areas of less than 2m depth or areas of potential risk.

Grey-blue colour indicates tidal areas of rock, sand, or foreshore which cover at high water.

The scale shows kilometres and statute miles (– not nautical miles).

Every piece of land which is less than the minimum area for classification but which could still justifiably be called an island or an islet is at least mentioned somewhere together with any information of interest. If there is a lot of interesting information then this is either given in the introduction to the section or put in a separate appendix. Occasionally, some of the 'drying' or 'tidal' islands have also merited this treatment.

Information for each of the 168 classified islands has been presented in the following manner:

NAME

There were four main language groups from which Scottish place-names have evolved:

Brythonic (or P-Celtic). This was probably an older Celtic language than Gaelic. It was spoken by the ancient Britons of the Clyde valley and the Picts may also have spoken it, or a language closely allied to it. It is represented today by the Welsh, Cornish and Breton languages.

Gaelic (or Q-Celtic). This is the Celtic language still spoken today in Scotland and Ireland, although in many different forms. It originated in Ireland, came over with the Scottish settlers and Christian missionaries, and by the 9th century was spoken in much of Scotland.

Norse. Many Viking invaders settled in the Western Isles bringing their language with them and these islands eventually came within the dominion of Norway in or about the 9th century. Even after the Lord of the Isles took control, the Norse language lingered on for a considerable time. The Orkney and Shetland Islands had been part of Norway from a much earlier date and only became part of Scotland when they were annexed by the Scottish Crown in 1471. The vast majority of Scottish island names end in '-ay', which means 'island' (-øy in Norse) and tends to illustrate the strong historical influence of this language.

English. Although English (or a Scottish form of it) is the language of most of Scotland today, having been widely established since the 12th century, there are areas of the Western Isles where Gaelic is still the native tongue and the language of choice. The English language was late in reaching the islands and it has had very little influence on most Scottish island names.

Many of the Western Isles have a local Gaelic name as well as the normal Norse-derived or Anglicised-Gaelic name. The Gaelic names are

CANNA'S CELTIC CROSS (4.4)

usually, but not always, closely related to the common-usage name given on the Ordnance Survey maps. I have for simplicity given only the 'Ordnance Survey' name (with occasional necessary corrections such as Rum instead of Rhum) but the Gaelic or Norse name is sometimes referred to in the notes on derivation.

The following abbreviations have been (loosely) applied:

B	Brythonic	E	English
EI	Early Irish	G	Gaelic
OE	Old English	S	Scottish
Sc	Scandinavian		
ON	Old Norse, Norse, Norn.		

PRONUNCIATION

In a few cases pronunciation is given in square brackets after a name. There are wide variations so this is no more than a very rough guide to normal-usage.

The following simple key has been used:

Pronunciation of Vowels

ë=the, mother	o=lot
a=sat	u=hut
a:=father	oa=boat
ay=day	oo=school
e=fed	aw=crawl
ee=week	ow=fowl
i=fit	a-oo=as ow but longer
Y=isle or by	oy=boy

oe=approximately French oeufs or German Goethe

Pronunciation of Consonants

Most consonants similar to the English but for Gaelic pronunciation there are the following approximations:

s=see	b=nearly p
g=get but nearly ket	d=nearly t
ch=German Bach or ich	l=variable
gh=as ch but voiced	

When an island's name ends in '-ay' the ending is often pronounced either as [-ay] or as [-ë]. For example, Berneray is either Berneray [-ay] or Bernera [-ë], and usually the latter. This may have originated because the Old Norse '-øy' was a sound which was neither [-ay] nor [-ë].

An exception is Islay which is always [Y-lë], and never [Y-lay].

MAP REFERENCES

References are given for the Landranger series of maps at a scale of 1:50,000 (2cm to 1km) and the Explorer series at a scale of 1:25,000 (4cm to 1km), both published by the Ordnance Survey and readily available. References are also given for the applicable Admiralty Charts.

AREA

Shakespeare defined England as 'this scepter'd isle . . . this precious stone set in a silver sea, which serves it . . . as a moat defensive'. This is inspiring stuff, but untrue because the moat is interrupted when it reaches Scotland. England is not an island and nor is Scotland. Britain is an island.

Scotland is for our purposes here, the mainland. It has an overall area of roughly 4,800,000 hectares (30,000 square miles).

How big is an island? As the tide goes in and out, an island varies in size, which leads to many wild suppositions and few hard facts. So, once again, a definition is required but the requirement here is different from the definition of an island given in the Preface. The part of the island that matters is the part that is more-or-less always dry land. Quoting an overall area which included vast tracts of sand, mud and rocks only accessible at low tide would not be realistic. So I have come up with an arbitrary restriction:

An island's area is the total surface area lying above sea-level at Mean High Water Springs.

In the 1990s I used averaged planimeter readings to estimate the area of each and every island within its MHWS perimeter as there was no consistent record elsewhere. I have been as accurate as possible but it was a laborious task and I certainly do not plead infallibility!

In the Preface to this edition I have stated how Jon Metcalf has now devised a means of computing the area by pixel-count of digitised map data. This is still fairly labour intensive, but it has allowed the areas of the islands to be checked much more accurately and corrected as required and this has resulted in several changes.

The tables include every Scottish island (or linked group of islands) which totals forty hectares or more in size. Not only is this a nice round figure, as forty hectares is roughly equivalent to one hundred old-fashioned acres, but if this limit is lowered the number of islands requiring inclusion grows rapidly out-of-control. The disadvantage in being so definitive is that it leads to the omission of some very small islands which are of notable interest: Staffa for instance. Such islets have therefore been included as appendices or within the foreword to the relevant Section.

Where applicable the areas of small tidal islands have been included in the total area for the main island even where these are not specifically mentioned.

HEIGHT
I have included a separate table of heights for interest. The Admiralty and the Ordnance Survey use different sea-level data to suit their differing requirements and even these can change as surveying techniques improve. For example my old edition of the Admiralty Pilot quotes Holy Island as 312.4m in height, the latest Admiralty metric chart shows 311m height whilst the latest edition of the Ordnance Survey gives 314m as the correct height. I have used the most up-to-date Ordnance Survey heights for consistency. There is, in any case, a large margin of error as all the heights are in round-figure metres without decimal fractions.

OWNERSHIP
Some islands have been under one ownership for generations but many change hands with astonishing frequency.

Islands are often bought on impulse. They come on the market. The sun is shining, the seas are calm. This brings out three main categories of buyer: those who buy, visit a few times, intend to return, but never do; those who are hooked and change their lifestyle to suit the island; and those who get bored and quickly trade on to the next impulsive dreamer.

As there is a fairly quick turnover of some Scottish islands it is impossible to keep up to date on ownership. Furthermore, some islands are bought relatively incognito under a company name or that of a bank, or owned as an unspecified small part of a large estate. However, ownership is obviously of interest for a variety of reasons and I have tried to establish it where I can. As the information has come from a variety of sources its accuracy cannot be guaranteed.

THE GREAT STACK OF HANDA (6.9)

POPULATION
Historic figures – pre-1830 – have been gleaned from a number of sources such as travellers' accounts and old gazetteers. These are therefore uncertain and unreliable. More recent figures are taken from the ten-yearly National Census. Some of the small 'uninhabited' islands are still occupied occasionally during the summer by herdsmen or fishermen or, in a few cases, by an owner.

GEOLOGY
Although matters of individual interest have been covered in the text a general history of island formation gives a better overall picture. Most of the life-forms of today only appeared on the islands after the last ice-age, a mere 10,000 years ago. Prior to this, Scottish island development was almost entirely a geological phenomenon.

The First Three Thousand Million Years. . .
About 2500 million years ago, in an area of the earth which is now the far South Atlantic, there was a large slab of proto-continent. The Earth was no longer molten but its crust was still hot and in a state of violent geological upheaval. Great tectonic plates ground against each other

and parts of them, often composed of common rocks rich in quartz and feldspar and mica, were forced deep down beneath the crust and subjected to enormous pressures and intense heat. The rocks folded and melted and twisted, separated into layers and were intruded by other igneous rocks. After a long time the activity slowly subsided and the metamorphosis was complete. The reconstituted rock started to cool down, taking æons to do so, and forming a coarsely crystalline structure. We call this rock – gneiss (pronounced, nice [nYs]. It comes from an old German word meaning 'sparkling').

Through most of the subsequent 2500 million years the gneiss stayed deep beneath the crust, almost undisturbed, until it surfaced in comparatively recent times in the middle of the Outer Hebrides (**North Uist**, **Benbecula** and part of **South Uist**). This partially explains why the rocks there, although ancient, look so freshly scrubbed and clean: they have been kept under wraps until now. They have no fossils because they were formed before there was any recognisable life on earth.

There was a further similar period of upheaval in an adjacent part of the proto-continent about 2000 million years ago. This created gneiss of a different composition which forms the rest of the Outer Hebrides and patches of the Inner Hebrides. It is generally referred to as Lewisian gneiss.

The chunk of proto-continent was on the move, sliding slowly over the Earth's mantle in a northerly direction. By some 800 million years ago it had reached the latitude of what is now South Africa. It had an upland region (which was eventually to become part of Greenland) eroded by rivers which spread alluvial deposits over a plain and into a shallow sea. These deposits built up increasing layers of red and grey sandstones, conglomerates, and shales. They are to be found today in the Torridon district of Wester Ross after which they have been named. Micro-fossils show that plankton and minute primitive life-forms were present in the shallow sea. Islands such as **Handa**, the **Summer Isles**, **Scalpay**, **Soay**, and parts of **Skye**, **Rum** and **Raasay** have all been sculpted from this dull red Torridonian sandstone.

The shallow sea grew and became the Cambrian Sea and the land which contained Scotland and its islands sank beneath it and lay there for 150 million years. During this time the north-western seashore suffered further deformation and metamorphosis due to the vast weight of some five kilometres thickness of sand and mud which was deposited over it. Siltstone became schist, mudstone became slate, limestone became marble and quartz sandstones became quartzites. The crushing and overlapping of strata formed a zone which runs from the north coast of Sutherland to the Sleat peninsula on **Skye** and forced outcropping on **Jura**, **Islay** and in the **Shetland Isles**. There were small outcrops on **Arran**, **Gigha**, **Skye** and **Mull** and, possibly, **Colonsay**. Much of Jura still has 5 kilometres thickness of quartzite which was laid down at this time in the form of clean river sand. Large extrusions of granite also occurred, particularly in Shetland and the Ross of Mull.

During at least one stage, while still far south of the Equator, the land and sea were covered with ice which deposited a bed of glacial boulders. Part of this bed can be clearly seen today at Port Askaig on **Islay**.

The remorseless northern movement of the plate of proto-continent continued until, about 490 million years ago, it came up against another rigid plate. The collision squeezed up a colossal mountain range which equalled the present-day Andes in size. This was the Caledonian Mountain Chain. It extended across the continental slab from the area which was to become Scandinavia, through Scotland and Greenland, into Newfoundland and southwards down the east coast of North America. Only remnants of this chain still exist, as erosion, continental drift and old age have steadily worn it down so that it no longer has the height and grandeur of the more recently formed mountain ranges – the Himalayas, the Andes and the Alps.

As the sliding plate approached the equator the violent upheavals caused by the collision waned, although volcanic activity was widespread. A huge lake stretched over the area of the future Orkneys and Caithness, sometimes extending as far north as Shetland. Layers of sand and limey mud were deposited in this lake forming sandstone strata. Fossils in the sandstone show that the lake was well stocked with fish. This Old Red Sandstone, as it is known, is particularly thick on **Hoy**. forming sea cliffs 350m high. The Old Red Sandstone of the Old Man of Hoy sits on top of a layer of volcanic ash and basalt.

A split in the plate similar to the San Andreas Fault in California started to form at this time, part of which eventually became the Great Glen.

About 350 million years ago the plate crossed the equator. Desert sand was compressed into sandstone on **Arran**. There was volcanic activity along an incipient rift zone forming between Great Britain, Norway and Denmark, which was eventually to become the North Sea. The North Atlantic started to open up, causing a number of rifts, one of which started to split the British Isles away from Greenland and North America. As the gap between Greenland and Europe opened up at the rate of about 2cm per year there was intense igneous activity down the west coast of Scotland. Vast quantities of basalt lava poured out of fissures and volcanoes and piled up at intervals along the centre line between the two plates. This is still going on today but the centre of activity has now moved over to Iceland.

Basaltic lava poured out and rapidly cooled on **Canna**, **Eigg**, **Muck**, **Skye**, **Raasay** and **Mull**. On Mull the lava layer is 1.8 kilometres thick! As the magma reached the surface it cooled fairly quickly forming the well-known columns to be seen at their best on **Staffa** or the **Shiant Isles**. Other activity became concentrated around intrusive centres on **Skye**, **Rum**, **Mull**, **Arran**, the **St Kilda** group and **Rockall**. These centres often have nearly circular outlines of 10–15km diameter. Most of them are of gabbro and peridotite, but some are of granite. Coarse crystalline gabbro is formed from magma which has cooled slowly deep in the earth's crust. Other intrusions into cracks were later eroded to form dykes, stone 'walls' which can look almost man-made and maintain a constant thickness over long distances. There are dykes crossing Mull which continue all the way to the north-east coast of England.

All this violent

THE BRESSAY STONE (11.8)

volcanic activity died down about fifty-five million years ago as the fault centres moved elsewhere. It was at this time that another plate collision started the formation of the Alps in Europe, which tended to uplift Scotland.

For most of geological time the earth has been ice-free, even at the poles. There have been three major exceptions. There was the Ice Age in Precambrian times, which incidentally formed the boulder bed on Islay. Then there was an Ice Age during the Carboniferous period, but as Britain was near the equator at the time she was unaffected. It is the most recent Ice Age which has had a profound influence. Ice sheets formed over the whole country, and glaciers carved out many features in the landscape. For example, Loch Coruisk on Skye was gouged out to a depth of 30m below present sea-level.

The last glaciation finished about 15,000 years ago, a mere blink of the eye in geological time. The immense weight of ice had squeezed the land downwards. When it melted the land rebounded raising beaches and sea-caves far above sea level. Particularly on **Jura** which is still rising at about 2mm per year, but throughout the Inner Hebrides, the effect of this change of level is very obvious. It is as though a giant has pulled the plug and partly drained the sea. The Outer Hebrides and Orkney differ as very little ice covered these areas.

HISTORY. . . or the Last Ten Thousand Years
After the great glaciers of the last Ice Age had receded about 15,000 years ago and while Britain was still linked to the European land-mass, the forests moved north with the improving climate. By about 14000BC at least one small Palæolithic kinship group of hunter-gatherers had settled in the Central Belt and some more settled later in Argyll. By 8000BC there were Mesolithic settlements in the area south of Oban. They spread from there to **Arran**, **Jura**, **Oronsay**, **Rum**, **Skye** and **Lewis**. Evidence of their settlements are to be found in shell heaps, and the remains of their tools – antler mattocks, arrowheads and fish-hooks, stone hammers and flints. Although the number of settlers at this time must have been very small they left a remarkable range and variety of artefacts. Some show possible cultural links with earlier relics from the Basque and Baltic regions.

About 4000BC immigrants arrived in Scotland in larger numbers. These were Neolithic farmers and fishermen. They were skilled seamen who brought their seed-grain, planted crops and kept domestic livestock. They spread up the west coast using the sea and lochs as their highway to the Great Glen, on through the Glen to the north-east and across the sea to **Orkney**. Later they reached **Shetland**. They were an intelligent and hard-working people and their way of life was so successful that they found time to build communal and religious structures. These became progressively more sophisticated. There were chambered cairns and communal tombs of a variety of types and complexity culminating in the splendour of Maes Howe in Orkney. The spectacular village remains at Skara Brae with canopied beds and stone cupboards show how advanced even their domestic structures were. It should be remembered that the best-preserved and largest number of Neolithic remains in the whole of Europe are to be found on the Scottish islands and many of these structures predated the Egyptian pyramids.

Soon after Maes Howe was completed work began on the henges of Brodgar and Stenness. Hundreds of standing stones and stone circles were erected at this time to various mathematical models and apparently using a standard unit of measurement. Their purpose is still a matter of conjecture, probably religious, possibly astronomical, possibly both, but the engineering and geometric skills are clear to see. Callanish on **Lewis** is, of course, a supreme example.

By 2500BC new groups of people had arrived. They are called the Beaker people because of their distinctive pottery but their area of origin is uncertain. For some time they maintained a separate culture but eventually we find them adapting the tombs and structures of the earlier settlers for their own requirements. They introduced basic metallurgy, stone-carving, textiles and new concepts of social structure and political power. One of their prime settlements was the Crinan Plain in Argyll which strangely enough is also where the very first incomers to Scotland are thought to have settled. In due course the Beaker people introduced techniques for working in bronze, probably learnt from Southern Europe, heralding the demise of the Stone Age.

TEAMPULL NA TRIANAID. NORTH UIST (7.15)

Between 1500BC and 700BC the climate, which had been mild and pleasant for many centuries, deteriorated. Wet, cold weather made arable farming less productive, causing economic and social change. In due course the old religions were abandoned and cremation became favoured instead of burial of the dead. Peat moss accumulated around the deserted monuments. The people had attractive jewellery but bronze weaponry and the building of hill-forts indicate that these were troubled times. Jarlshof in **Shetland** has the best-preserved example of a Bronze Age settlement dating from about 1000BC, long before Vikings. There was also the development of timber-reinforced structures. Forts were built with timber posts sandwiched between stone skins (sometimes leading to vitrification) and timber, stone and soil were employed to build crannogs – artificial islands – in the lochs.

The strange and beautiful buildings called brochs were built between c.200BC and 100AD. Fine examples are on Mousa and at Carloway on Lewis. There are hundreds of them and they are found nowhere else in the world. Little is known about their purpose – were they really fortresses or watch-towers as has been claimed? – and, anyway, who built them? The Picts?

This mysterious race produced a wealth of beautiful stone-carvings with many strange, repetitive symbols. For a few centuries they dominated Scotland north of the central belt, but were eventually engulfed by the Scots and the Norsemen and disappeared from the world stage. Where they came from, what they looked like and what language they spoke is all conjecture. They are still one of the mysteries of our past although recent research has begun to produce a few answers.

MIDHOWE BROCH. ROUSAY (10.20)

About this time there was a great influx of newcomers from the south of Britain. Between 600BC and 500AD Celts came over the Channel in large numbers and steadily drifted northwards, bringing their language and culture with them. They had a stratified matriarchal society and a great love of warfare. The Romans said that in spite of cold, wet weather the Celts always fought stark naked, wearing only golden ornaments and a sword belt and sporting an elaborate hair arrangement. Because they were so quarrelsome among themselves they were often easily outwitted by a disciplined force. The Romans also said that even the women enjoyed a fight and were built like Amazons. Celtic priests, the druids, held great authority in society. They worshipped in oak groves and had no connection whatsoever with ancient Neolithic stone circles. Celts were skilled craftsmen who understood the technology of iron-working and were adept at carving stone. The Romans suppressed them in the south of Britain but they held their own elsewhere. Generally speaking, the Roman occupation of Britain had little or no influence on any of the Scottish islands or their inhabitants.

The pre-Celtic or Brythonic or, maybe, Pictish language which was prevalent at the time was displaced in northern Ireland – Dalriada – by the Celtic-speakers that settled there. These were Gauls, or Gaels, of Indo-Aryan origin fleeing from the Roman invasion of Central Europe. Modern Welsh is derived from the earlier tongue (known as P-Celtic) whilst modern Gaelic as spoken in the Western Isles is derived from the Irish version (Q-Celtic).

In the 4th century AD the Romans adopted Christianity and about the 5th century, after the legions had left Britain, a mission was set up by Ninian in the kingdom of Strathclyde. He had studied in Rome and he was followed by Patrick, another Romanised Briton from Ayrshire. Patrick could write Latin and spoke Brythonic (or Welsh). He went to Ireland where he learnt Gaelic and then spread the word in western Scotland. He was followed by Colum Cille O'Neill – the Dove of the Church and prince of the royal Irish house of O'Neill – better known as St Columba. Concurrently, Fergus Mòr, king of the Scots of Dalriada moved the seat of his kingdom from Antrim to Dunadd on the Crinan Plain of Argyll. In this way the Gaelic language, the Scottish name and the Christian religion were introduced to the islands of **Arran**, **Bute**, **Islay**, **Jura** and mainland Argyll. Incidentally, the name of the Scots kingdom of Dalriada came from Cairbre Ruadh (G. – red-haired Cairbar), nicknamed 'Red', who slew Oscar son of Ossian, and became king. Dal-ruaidh means the land of 'Red'.

In 563AD St Columba landed on Iona and founded the famous monastery which gained international recognition. Missionaries from Iona spread the Christian faith to many of the most remote islands, and scholars came from far across Europe to study at this famous seat of learning.

Around the year 800AD, the murderous Viking invasions began. The Danes mainly concentrated on England, but Norsemen could reach Shetland in thirty-six hours, or less, and spread south from there. The first Vikings were wealthy adventurers, expert seamen with good ships, weapons made of the finest Swedish iron, no respect for culture and an interest only in piracy. They plundered the monasteries including Iona and destroyed most of the historical records of the time. Where there was no treasure they could always carry the people off to slavery or hold them to ransom. The tender Scoto-Irish civilisation centred on Iona and recognised by Charlemagne as one of the most learned in Europe was virtually destroyed. Following the first waves of pure piracy a few of the marauders chose to stay and the Norse settlers who followed were better behaved. In due course this brought a modicum of peace to some areas.

In Orkney and Shetland the Pictish culture was all but wiped out before the islands gained a new economic significance as a springboard for Norse raiding parties travelling south. In 1098 another wealthy adventurer, King Magnus, sailed over from Norway on a campaign to plunder

EARL PATRICK'S PALACE, ORKNEY MAINLAND (10.10)

to the throne of Argyll. He first drove the Vikings out of Morvern and in due course outmanoeuvred and defeated them in a brilliant sea-battle in 1156. He then set about restoring the monastery at Iona and founded the House of Islay. He, and the next five generations of his family called themselves 'King of the Isles', but changed this to 'Lord of the Isles' in deference to the King of the Scots. Somerled had three sons. He gave the Lordship of Bute and Arran to his son Angus, Kintyre and the Isles to Ranald, and Lorn to Dughall. His grandson, Donald, gave his name to the Clan Donald which became the most powerful clan in Scottish history. The MacDonalds supported Bruce and the victory at Bannockburn confirmed their powerful position in Argyll and the Isles. In the end however they overplayed their hand and after repeated rebellions they had their inheritance forfeited in 1493. The Campbells then took over.

The Norwegians did not give up easily. They still held the **Northern Isles**, **Lewis**, **Skye**, and the Isle of Man. A son of the King of Man, Leod, inherited Lewis, Harris and Skye and made his home on Dunvegan rock. The King of Scots offered to purchase the Hebrides from King Haakon of Norway but he refused to sell. Furthermore, in 1248, Haakon shrewdly invited Ewen, Somerled's descendant, to Norway and formally accepted his status as King of the Isles. He thus gained Ewen's allegiance, but the Scots started raiding the Hebrides, which put Ewen in a difficult position as he also owed allegiance to the King of Scots for his lands in Argyll.

In 1263, King Haakon IV, an old man by then, decided to demonstrate his authority. He gathered a large fleet and sailed down the west coast of Scotland. Ewen refused to join him, but to be honourable he relinquished his Norwegian title of King of the Isles. There was an inconclusive Scottish-Norwegian skirmish between Largs and the Cumbraes when bad weather persuaded the Norwegians to withdraw. This was a disastrous decision and returning northwards their ships were battered by severe storms. Soon after they reached the haven of **Orkney** King Haakon died and, within two years, sovereignty of all the Western Isles and the Isle of Man had passed to

Lewis, the Uists, Skye, Mull, Iona, Tiree, Islay and the mainland of Argyll. He obtained an agreement from the King of the Scots confirming his ownership of all the islands. An island was defined as any piece of land which a boat could circumnavigate so he gained the Kintyre peninsula by having his men carry him across the Tarbert isthmus sitting in a boat.

He went on to pillage Ireland and came to a violent end in 1103.

In 1117 on the island of Egilsay, a different Magnus, Earl Magnus of Orkney, grandson of Thorfinn the Mighty, was murdered by his cousin, Earl Haakon. Earl Magnus was something of a pacifist and pilgrims to his tomb later claimed they had experienced miracles, so he was canonised and Kirkwall's beautiful cathedral was dedicated to him.

Although Shetland was under direct Norwegian rule and Orkney was a Norse earldom, all the Western Isles were a Norse sub-kingdom controlled from the Isle of Man by a king who was subordinate to the Norwegian sovereign. A Scots prince of the kingdom of Argyll, Somerled (the derogatory name means 'summer-sailor' in Norse), married a daughter of King Olaf, King of Man. In 1130, Somerled, who had built a fleet of ships of improved design and shown himself to be much more than a 'summer-sailor', succeeded

the Scottish Crown.

Alexander III of Scotland offered his daughter's hand in marriage to the new Norwegian King as a diplomatic gesture of friendship which was accepted. But twenty years later Alexander died in an accident with the result that the sole direct heir to the Scottish throne was the King of Norway's baby daughter, Margaret – the Maid of Norway. Unfortunately, on her way to Scotland in 1290, she died at **Orkney**, just as King Haakon had done, and this gave Edward I of England an excuse to claim the vacant Scottish throne. The consequence was Scotland's lengthy war to maintain its independence.

Shetland and **Orkney** remained Norwegian possessions for two more centuries until Margaret, daughter of King Christian of Denmark and Norway, was betrothed to James III, King of Scots, in 1468. The islands were pledged as security for an agreed dowry of 60,000 golden florins. Christian could not find the dowry money so the Scottish Crown foreclosed and took over the islands instead.

Although the Lord of the Isles lost his mini-kingdom during the Haakon intervention the MacDonald clan continued to exercise a powerful and peaceful influence on island affairs from **Islay** where they held councils of Hebridean chieftains

once a year. Their territory encompassed the **Uists**, **Benbecula**, and Sleat on **Skye**. The complex history of the isles at this time saw the formation of vassal clans through marriages and treaties which eventually became interlaced with skirmishes and treachery. The Clan Iain held most of **Jura** and part of **Islay** and **Mull**; the McLeans of Duart held **Coll**, **Tiree** and most of **Mull**; Clan Neil held **Barra**, **South Uist** and **Gigha**; the McPhees held **Colonsay**; the MacLeods held **Lewis**, **Harris** and a large part of **Skye**; the MacKinnons also held parts of **Skye** and **Mull**. All these clans disliked and often disobeyed the Norman feudal system of lords and vassals which was being imposed by the Scottish kings; they preferred the Celtic (and Norse) system of lords and freemen. Eventually an exasperated Stewart King, James IV, broke the last remnants of Donald overlordship: but this only resulted in a lack of adequate leadership and a widespread breakdown of law and order. Clan fought clan, churches were burnt down, and many islanders suffered appalling cruelty and hardship.

James VI was ashamed of his lack of control of this troublesome territory when he succeeded to the English throne in 1603 and decided to prove his authority. So he invited the Hebridean chiefs to a friendly meeting on Mull, imprisoned them all on his flagship and brought them to Edinburgh. They were released a year later but only after having agreed to specific conditions of behaviour. Remarkably, this rough and ready method worked. Relative peace returned to the islands although there were still some minor feuds, in one of which the Campbells wrested control of **Islay** from the MacDonalds. Generally speaking, however, this was a time of reasonable prosperity.

Many of the clans joined forces in a common cause in 1745 when Prince Charles Edward Stewart landed on **Eriskay** to lay claim to the British throne. By the following year, the collapse of his cause at Culloden effectively broke the power, and the wealth, of the clans for ever. Some distressed clan chiefs sold land which in ancient Celtic terms had belonged communally to the members of the clan as a whole, others looked to other means of raising money. By the early 19th century new absentee landlords, and some of the less scrupulous chieftains, were turning their land over to the new, profitable business of sheep-farming. The crofters, who had occupied their own land for centuries but held no written title, were mercilessly evicted. The Clearances had begun and huge areas, and many islands, were depopulated.

Crofters' rights of tenancy were only safeguarded by law in 1886 – too late – for by this time thousands of families had emigrated or been shipped off to Canada, Australia and the United States. Further depopulation was caused by potato blights, the decline of the fishing industry, two world wars and mainland attractions for the young.

WILDLIFE

The Scottish islands have a particularly interesting and diverse natural history mainly due to wide variations in climate and geology. Lime-rich alkaline soils occur on areas of calciferous rocks and acidic soils are found with granite and gneiss. The soil and the climate dictate the plantlife and the ground cover – moorland, meadow, woodland, peat bog, bare rock or sand – and the ground cover dictates the wildlife habitat.

These are the main considerations but there are other factors such as the influence of man or the geographical position of the island. Most islands have the same common plant forms as the nearest mainland regions but islands which lie in the warmth of the Gulf Stream and which are well sheltered, like **Gigha** or **Arran**, have varieties of primula normally only found in the south of Britain and other unusual plants such as the rare whitebeam of Arran.

Scottish islands have few endemic plant species but there are a number of interesting sub-species or specialities. The Hebridean orchid, a sub-species of the common spotted orchid *Dactylorhiza fuchsii*, is found in the **Outer Hebrides**, **Coll**, **Tiree** and **Shetland**, and there is a unique sub-species of the heath spotted orchid *Dactylorhiza maculata* found on **Rum**. One of the few endemic species is the gold and orange flowered hawkweed found only in **Shetland** in a number of varieties.

The outlying islands have the most difficult climatic conditions, yet **Hirta** has around 140 different botanical species and even **Rona** in the far north has nearly fifty species. This can be contrasted with Shetland which has over a hundred times the land area of Hirta yet supports only three times the number of native species. This is partly due to the presence of man, as grazing and burning of the scrub have been going on for over 5000 years. Peat digging has also had a serious effect on many Scottish islands as the top layer is rarely replaced and in the end the

TIGH AN QUAY, 1938 (FROM A FRASER DARLING PHOTOGRAPH)

TIGH AN QUAY, TANERA MOR, 1994 (6.7)

landscape is reduced to bog or bare rock. After the Ice Age most of the islands acquired woodland cover. Even storm-ridden St Kilda had sparse birch and alder scrub. Subsequent climatic changes upset the balance but man was the greatest culprit as trees were cut for buildings or fuel, land was cleared for planting, and overgrazing and erosion then took over.

Atlantic gales have been a mixed blessing to the west side of the 'Long Island', as the almost continuous line of islands in the **Outer Hebrides** is known. They flatten and tear up any vegetation which dares to stand above the rest but they also scatter shell sand from the beaches – a valuable lime fertiliser. Interestingly, early records show much of the west coast of the Long Island as a sandy desert. It was by ploughing in seaweed to bind the sand and provide potash that man created the machair, welcome evidence that our species is not always destructive! In spring and summer the machair is a carpet of tiny wildflowers and particularly in the areas which have not been grazed by sheep this creates an unrivalled spectacle. Level as a billiard table and framed by pink thrift, white sand and deep turquoise sea the colours change with each passing week – daisies, buttercups, silverweed, birdsfoot trefoil, kidney vetch, white and red clover, wild pansies, corn marigold, spotted orchids, purple-tufted vetch and yellow pepperwort. And beyond the machair in the desolate peat bogs are butterfly orchids, bogbeam,

pink ragged robin, mare's tail, marsh cinquefoil, kingcups and cotton grass. Contrast all this colour with the east coast which has little else but sedges, grass, heather and sphagnum moss in peat pockets on the bare rock.

Behind the sand dunes of **Orkney Mainland** there are great drifts of white clover, eyebright and birdsfoot trefoil. There are Arctic alpines in the Cuillin of **Skye** and in some of the nearby islands such as **Soay** and **Raasay** which are to be found nowhere else in Britain; while **Mull**, **Orkney** and **Shetland** and the **St Kilda** archipelago have examples of mountain sorrel, mountain everlasting catsfoot, white globe flower, purple saxifrage, meadow rue, roseroot and moss campion. **Rum** has a rare alpine saxifrage and both **Orkney** and **Shetland** support the unique purple-flowering Scottish primrose. In the peaty lochans of **Jura**, the **Uists**, and some of the smaller islands a distinctive and beautiful subspecies of the white waterlily *Nymphaea alba* can be seen. Unfortunately, such plants are at serious risk from thoughtless collectors and common thieves.

The remaining natural woodlands are mainly thickets of oak, hazel, birch, willow, pine, alder and rowan. Examples can be found on **Soay**, **Raasay**, **Ulva** and (south) **Rona** to name a few. Cultivated woodland in limited areas can also be found on **Canna**, **Gigha**, and **Lewis**, and **Arran** has large tracts of planted imported conifers.

In some ways animal life on the islands is as

Skaw. The last house

varied as the plantlife which supports it. Most of the island mammals were first introduced by man. The Soay sheep of the **St Kilda** group have been there for at least a thousand years. They were domesticated by Neolithic man but their place of origin is unknown. Their population fluctuations are the subject of scientific study at present. There is another Neolithic strain of short-tailed sheep, also of unknown origin, to be found on **North Ronaldsay**. This breed lives mainly on seaweed. Many islands have feral goats which have been traced back to Middle Eastern stock but how they were introduced to the Scottish islands is entirely speculative. Red deer are fairly widespread and as they can swim a considerable distance they may have colonised some of the inshore islands by their own effort. The original population was almost exterminated by destruction of the forests and by hunting. But in the 19th century landlords encouraged their reintroduction for sporting purposes and the deer themselves have learned to adapt to the lack of forest cover. On **Rum** the deer are carefully protected and studied for ecological research. Rum's own breed of ponies is used to bring the deer carcasses in for examination. The breed is the result of the islanders crossing Highland mares with Arab sires. Both the **Shetland** and the **Eriskay** ponies are also the result of selective breeding in the distant past.

The common fox *Vulpes vulpes* has never been native to the Outer Hebrides although a few misguided people still defy common sense by introducing the occasional specimen. Foxes would have a devastating effect if they gained a foothold, particularly on communities of ground-nesting birds such as greenshank, dunlin and tern. These have already suffered from the deliberate introduction of mink, hedgehogs, ferrets, and domestic cats.

There are no frogs or adders in the **Northern Isles** but the adder is very common in parts of the Inner Hebrides such as **Jura.**

Rabbits were first introduced to some of the islands as a source of meat and Boswell mentions in particular the warren on **Coll** in 1773. Rabbits are not indigenous to the British Isles and were originally imported by the Normans who enjoyed their tasty meat. They posed no problem initially as they were kept successfully in defined warrens, culled and savagely guarded by the gentry. Then came the Industrial Revolution and the Clearances; the warrens were left to fall into disrepair and the rabbits were left in peace to do what rabbits do best. Strangely, there are no rabbits on Coll's near neighbour, **Tiree** and thankfully **St Kilda**, **North Rona** and **Berneray** in the Sound of Harris are bunny-free.

Among the other small mammals there are a number of unique sub-species such as the **St Kilda** mouse, the **Rum** mouse, and the **Bute** mouse. Short-tailed voles are a general Hebridean sub-species and there is also an **Orkney** vole but bank voles are only found on **Mull** and **Raasay**. Otters are common in most of the islands and especially on some of the **Northern Isles**.

Many grey or Atlantic seals frequent the west coast of the **Outer Hebrides** and the Scottish Islands generally are home to about half the world's population of this species. The common seal is less common and tends to prefer east-facing coasts. Numbers of porpoises and dolphins were in decline for many years but quite recently there seems to have been some recovery and it is rare to sail any distance in these waters without seeing them. The same goes for the basking shark and schools of killer or minke whales may also be seen.

Insect life is probably no more and no less varied on the islands than it is on the mainland but thanks to a lack of use of insecticides on many of the islands some of the less common species have had a better survival rate. This is particularly true of butterflies. Tiny **Flodday** near **Sandray**, south of Barra for example, boasts a unique sub-species of the dark green fritillary, **Rum** and **Eigg** have a number of species, and the **Northern Isles** also have a good assortment.

THE ORKNEY VOLE

Without doubt, though, the most memorable island insect is the midge. There are thirty-four known species in the UK but only the females of five species bite and the worst belong to just one species, *Culicodes impunctatus*. It has been suggested that the forced depopulation of the islands in the 19th century may have been partly responsible for an increase in these tiny, voracious creatures which can make life so miserable in the mid-summer months. Discounting chemical insect repellents, which are only effective for a very short time, there are only two recognised antidotes – wind and whisky. The former blows them away and the latter makes them bearable. It is probable that, when the population was removed and the land reverted to rough grazing and sporting estates, midges would have found the change to their liking. Bracken, for example, protects them from the wind while cultivation destroys their breeding grounds. Compare well-managed and relatively midge-free **Canna** with the clouds of man-eating midges on wild and boggy **Rum** or **Jura.**

For the birdwatcher the islands are unsurpassed. For seabirds in particular, the remote or uninhabited islands are perfect sanctuaries. About 70% of the world's entire population of razorbills nest on the Scottish islands. In the **St Kilda** group, Stac Lee is home to some 100,000 pairs of gannets, which is probably the biggest gannetry in the world. And this particular island archipelago has a greater number and more species of seabirds than any other island group in Europe. Runners-up on a smaller scale are the **Treshnish** archipelago off Mull and the **Shiant** Islands north of Skye. Apart from also having magnificent seabird communities, the **Northern Isles** are the birdwatchers' finest hunting-ground for rare migrants blown there from far-off places.

Two of Britain's rarest indigenous birds, the corncrake and the chough, are now only to be found in the Western Isles: proof, if such were needed, that this is a last corner of paradise.

ACCESS
Where there is any regular form of public transport to an island, general information is given based on summer schedules but all details should be verified before use. There are a number of excellent annual guides which give more detail than there is room for here

and VisitScotland (the Scottish Tourist Board) can also be of assistance (0131-332 2433). Although all the larger and more populated islands are served by public transport my main interest is with the smaller, and mainly uninhabited, islands. These are never easy to visit and means of access are not covered by the normal tourist guides.

Most hotels and guest-houses on the larger islands, or the adjacent mainland, are very willing to make arrangements with a local boat-owner. But even if weather conditions are suitable be prepared for some uncertainty.

Anchorages
It is, of course, much easier to arrange an island visit if you have your own boat. For this reason I have tried to provide a comprehensive list of all recognised (and some unrecognised) island anchorages with a brief note of their advantages or shortcomings. This is intended solely as an aid to pre-planning. It provides a simple means of selecting an anchorage to suit one's purpose – a quiet night with the family aboard, a visit to some particular site, a quick run ashore, a sketch, photography, a stop for lunch or a safe haven. Difficulty of access, poor holding, or excessive exposure, will all influence one's choice.

In my attempt to be comprehensive I have compiled the list from a variety of sources – from the authority of Admiralty Pilots to the comments of local fishermen. ***Neither these notes, nor the illustrative maps in this publication, should be used for navigation – they are intended only for passage-planning.*** Where anchorages are indicated on the maps in this book by an anchor-symbol it is usually because they are well-recognised anchorages for that island. Most of the listed anchorage positions are described but not shown for reasons of scale. The navigation charts should always be consulted.

British Admiralty Charts and the sailing directions of the CCC, which include the Northern Isles (Clyde Cruising Club Publications Ltd, Suite 101, The Pentagon Centre, 36 Washington Street, Glasgow G3 8AZ (0141-221 2774)) are virtually essential. The CCC also supplies the FYCA sailing directions for the East Coast, Martin Lawrence's excellent West Coast Pilots which I highly recommend, and Imray Yachting Charts (Imray Laurie Norie & Wilson Ltd, St Ives, Cambridgeshire).

Where an anchorage is labelled 'temp' or 'temporary' it must be approached with caution and only used in daylight and under ideal conditions (slack tides, gentle winds, etc). Always maintain an anchor watch and normally use a tripping line.

An 'occasional' anchorage is slightly better and in ideal conditions could be used overnight. However it may only offer shelter from a limited wind direction and if conditions change should be vacated promptly.

The Geographical Sections

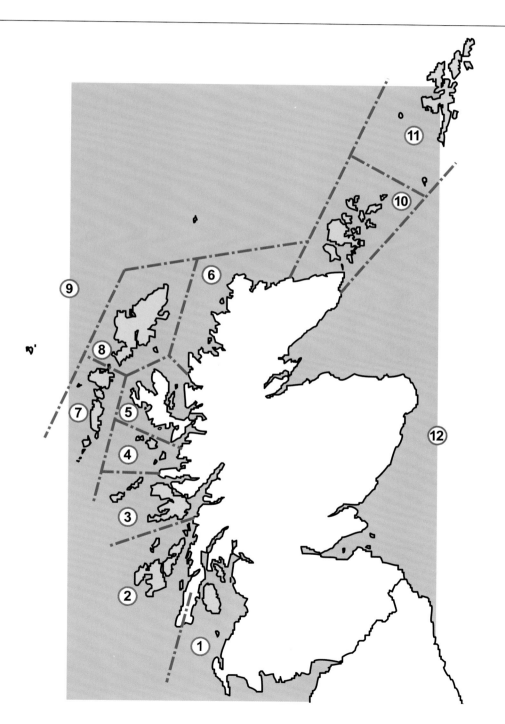

The Solway Firth to the Firth of Clyde

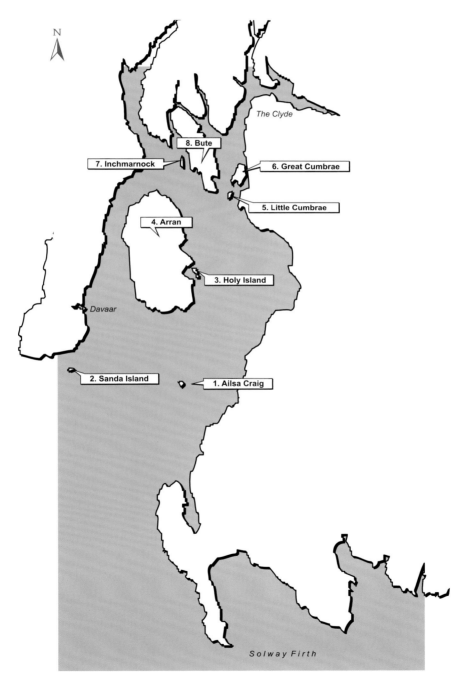

Section 1, Table 1: Arranged according to geographical position

				Table 2*	Table 3**		
No.	Name	Latitude	Longitude	No.	No.	Area in Acres	Area in Hectares
1.1	Ailsa Craig	55° 15N	05° 07W	111	19	245	99
1.2	Sanda	55° 17N	05° 35W	93	54	373	151
1.3	Holy Island	55° 32N	05° 04W	75	20	625	253
1.4	Arran	55° 35N	05° 15W	7	2	106750	43201
1.5	Little Cumbrae Island	55° 43N	04° 57W	64	53	773	313
1.6	Great Cumbrae	55° 46N	04° 55W	39	49	2886	1168
1.7	Inchmarnock	55° 47N	05° 09W	73	106	657	266
1.8	Bute	55° 49N	05° 06W	11	24	30188	12217

*Table 2: The islands arranged in order of magnitude
**Table 3: The islands arranged in order of height

Introduction

Here, within a short distance of Scotland's greatest conurbation, are eight fascinating and diverse islands. Turn left on the Clyde at Cloch Point and travel 'doon the watter' to Bute, guard of the western entrance, with Inchmarnock tucked behind it. The eastern sentinels are the Cumbraes, Great and Little. Ahead and beyond, the towering serrated ridge of Arran dominates the entire Firth, dwarfing even the high peak of Holy Island. Further out, lonely and conspicuous in the southern reaches of the Firth, stands Ailsa Craig – familiarly referred to as Paddy's Milestone and on the horizon, a speck at the foot of the Mull of Kintyre, is mysterious Sanda Island.

This area, with its long sea-lochs, offers a marvellous environment for inshore sailing. The longest of these lochs – longer than Loch Long – is Loch Fyne, stretching from the north of Arran to well beyond Inveraray. The fishing town of Tarbert is the main port on this loch and source of the world-famous Loch Fyne kippers. The larger 'islands' in the vicinity, Barmore and Eilean Aoidhe, are in fact peninsulas and the only islets possibly worthy of the name are **Eilean Buidhe** and **Eilean a' Bhuic** opposite Tarbert and **Eilean a' Chromhraig** just south of the entrance.

Halfway up the loch in Loch Gilp is **Duncuan Island** with, to the east of it, another drying island – Eilean Mór. However, alongside Eilean Mór is the strip of **Liath Eilean** with a pleasant anchorage in between.

In the upper reaches there is **Glas Eilean** off Port Ann with **Eilean Aoghainn** in the centre of the loch and overlooked by Minard Castle.

The islets of the Kilbrannan Sound are equally insignificant – two tiny islets on the coast of the Mull of Kintyre – **Thorn Isle** and **Island Ross**. **Davaar**, which guards the entrance to Campbeltown Loch and issues its own postage stamps, is not by definition a true island as it can be reached at low water over a shingle causeway (dangerous when the tide comes in). It is worth a visit because there are seven caves and the fifth conceals a famous mural of Christ crucified which was painted in secret by a local artist, Alexander MacKinnon in 1887.

On the Ayrshire coast by Ardrossan harbour five species of gull nest on low-lying **Horse Island** and, likewise, colonies of common, sandwich and arctic tern nest on **Lady Isle** off Troon. There are no other islets on this coast and the Solway Firth is also short of islands. The largest group is at Fleet Bay – **Murray's Isles**, **Ardwall Island** and **Barlocco Island**. At Kirkcudbright Bay **Little Ross** is off the Ross headland and **Hestan Island** is in the centre of shallow, tidal Auchencairn Bay. Little Ross supports a Stevenson lighthouse which has been automatic since 1961. Two lighthouse-keepers' houses are owned by Dr S R Wild of Edinburgh. The islet was the scene of a nasty murder in 1960: but that's another story.

1.1 Ailsa Craig

(G. aillse creag – fairy rock). Referred to locally as Paddy's Milestone but sometimes known as creag Ealasaid (G. – Elizabeth's rock). In the old Irish tale of 'Buioe Suibne' it is called carraig Alastair (G. – Alastair's rock).

OS Maps: 1:50000 Sheet 76 1:25000 Sheet 326 1:10000 (NX 09)
Admiralty Chart: 1:75000 No.2126

Area: 99ha (245 acres)
Height: 338m (1109 ft)

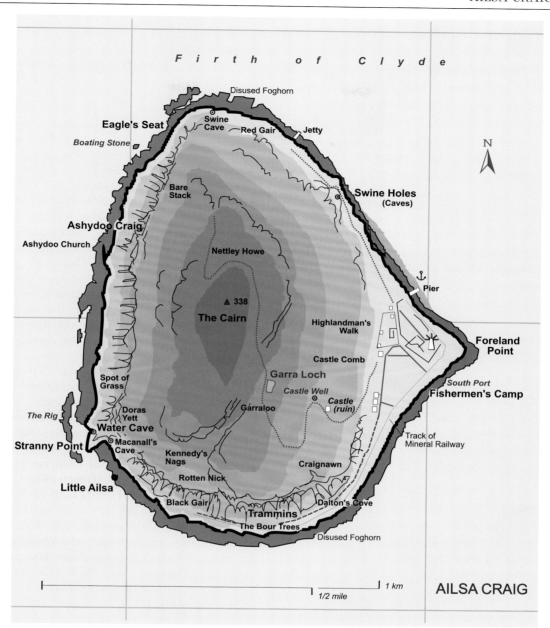

AILSA CRAIG

Firth of Clyde

1 km
1/2 mile

N

Owner: Sold by Cassilis Estates (Marquess of Ailsa) in 2013 for a reputed £1.5 million. The lighthouse property with four houses is owned by Bobby Sandhu.

Population: From 19th century to mid-20th century a small population of quarrymen and families. 1881–29. 1891–27. 1931–11. 1961–10. 1971–3 (lighthouse keepers). 1981–2. 1991–0 (lighthouse automatic). 2011–0.

Geology: Mainly an acid igneous rock containing fine-grained crystals of quartz, mica and feldspar, known as microgranite. In the north-east there is a seam of reibickite, a particularly fine-grained micro-granite, from which 70% of the world's curling stones are made. These were cut on the island and polished on the mainland, but the quarries are now mostly disused even for building stone. The floor of the Chapel of the Thistle in St Giles Cathedral, Edinburgh, is made of this beautiful Ailsa Craig granite. Much of the island is columnar basalt, sometimes forming columns 120 metres (400ft) in height.

AILSA CRAIG FROM DUNURE CASTLE, SEAT OF THE KENNEDYS

History: An old square peel-tower on the island was almost certainly built by the Hamiltons to prevent Phillip II of Spain taking the island in support of the Catholics during the Reformation.

The lighthouse was built in 1868 by the Stevensons.

Wildlife: In 2004 the island became an RSPB Reserve by invitation of the Marquess. It was already a Site of Special Scientific Interest and a European Special Protection Area.

At one time some Soay sheep from St Kilda (neolithic, dark-brown, small and hardy) were bred here. Rabbits were said to have been brought in by the quarrymen to supplement their diet. These have not been as big a problem, however, as the brown rats which arrived in 1889 when ships were ferrying materials and supplies to the newly built lighthouse. (The quarrymen later claimed that the rats and rabbits were interbreeding!)

Before the brown rats moved in there were at least 250,000 pairs of puffins on the island. An ornithologist, Robert Gray, reported in the 1860s that when he disturbed the puffins 'for a time their numbers seemed so great as to cause a bewildering darkness.'

By 1990 the rats had successfully driven many birds off the island and not a single puffin had been seen since 1984. So in 1991 a rat eradication programme was instituted by the Marquess of Ailsa, Glasgow University and Scottish Natural Heritage. Poison to kill the rats, three tons of Warfarin, was airlifted by helicopter from *HMS Gannet*, Prestwick, and distributed on the island in the Spring. 'Some of it was put in bait boxes and a lot went straight into the rat holes,' said Dr Zonfrillo, a leading ornithologist member of the working group. The rats died in their burrows so there were no rat carcasses strewn about. The treatment seems to have worked and it

has also (temporarily?) reduced the rabbit population.

By 1996 black guillemots and shelduck had returned to nest and occasional puffins had been seen, but it was not until 2002 that it was certain that a few puffins had at last established nest-burrows on the island and started breeding again.

Ailsa Craig is noted for its immense gannet colony which has been there since at least 1526. Recently nearly 40,000 breeding pairs of gannets were reported which is about 5% of the gannet population of the world. They are mainly on the south-west side. Numerous guillemots, kittiwakes and gulls are also to be found and blackbirds, song-thrushes, wheatears and willow warblers have been seen. Pipits may be found on the steep slopes above the smooth rock walls.

The island's slow worms, which hide under the rocks, are considered the largest in Europe and there is a wide variety of plant life. In places the cliffs are white with the scented flowers of scurvy grass spotted here and there with red lychnis. The rose-coloured flowers of the tree mallow, *Lavatera arborea*, can be seen growing 2–3m high near the buildings but warmer weather is now unfortunately encouraging this plant to spread across the island and block the puffins' nesting holes (See Bass Rock, Section 12-Appendix).

* * *

AILSA CRAIG is the Lowlands' answer to the Hebridean and Orcadian stacks, those great chunks of rock rearing out of the sea. Its basalt and columnar trap rises abruptly from sea level and soars to a height of nearly 340m – over 1100 feet. When its ethereal shape materialises out of the mist one can understand it being

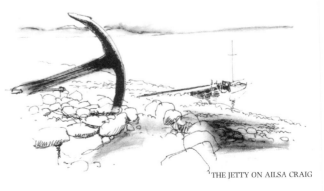

THE JETTY ON AILSA CRAIG

named fairy rock by some ancient Celt. Except on the east side which has an accessible slope it is so precipitous that even the seabirds are unable to nest on some of the cliffs. Wordsworth and Keats were impressed by it, but Burns' only comment (in 'Duncan Gray') was that 'Meg was deaf as Ailsa Craig'!

Twenty-five thousand years ago when Scotland lay smothered under a thick sheet of ice a glacier flowing down the Clyde valley broke off pieces of Ailsa Craig granite and carried them south to the English Midlands where they still lie around today scattered between Wales and the Pennines. Much more recently the same fine-grained granite was again distributed widely, but this time in the form of curling stones. For many years there was no other source.

An old anchor bedded in the pebble beach by the broken jetty marks the path to the group of buildings clustered round the lighthouse.

A rusty narrow-gauge railway line runs from the pier and past the quarrymen's cottages to the abandoned quarry on the south side. A forge and disused foghorns are also in evidence and there are heaps of waste granite pieces from which the spheroidal curling stones have been cut leaving fascinating shapes like miniature Henry Moore sculptures. I am told the heaps are dwindling as the offcuts are being sold as curios. The Andrew Kay company still has the sole quarrying rights on Ailsa Craig.

A well-defined zig-zag path climbs to the top, starting near the lighthouse and passing the old square **peel-tower** about 100m up the slope [NX023995]. The three stars of the Hamilton coat of arms are carved on a stone set in the walls.

Further up, the path passes over the shallow valley of Garraloo and beside the tiny **Garra Loch** with the cleft of Rotten Nick below before making its way to the top. Here the precipice plunges straight to the sea; **Bare Stack**, in the north-west, with two ferocious brown overhangs and **Ashydoo** cliff lying just south. Far below to the south-west is Spot of Grass, Doras Yett and the outcrop of Kennedy's Nags. And beyond the white lace of the surf lie the wide stretches of the Firth of Clyde with the long dark shape of Ulster on the south-western horizon.

It is possible to make an exciting and relatively easy two-mile circumnavigation of the island beneath these cliffs. The only minor obstruction is at **Water Cave** in the south-west cleft. The

exposed corner of Stranny Point has to be negotiated to reach this mini Fingal's Cave when coming from the east around the shore, past **Little Ailsa**. Try and time it for low water.

Climbers may prefer to go directly up the slope from the landing place on the east shore. There is no difficulty in the ascent but in places the route leads over steeply inclined slabs. No rock-climbing routes on any of the dramatic cliffs have been recorded but this is just as well as the island is a bird-sanctuary.

* * *

Access: Crossing time approx. 1 hour. Boat trips from Girvan by arrangement, Mark McCrindle, 01465-713219 or ASW Charters *Rachel Clare*, 01465-715934.

Anchorage:
1. A deteriorating timber jetty or pier in the north-east beside the lighthouse at Foreland Point has only 0.6m at its head. Temp anchorage possible close N of jetty but beware remains of an older jetty close NW of existing jetty. Bottom of granite boulders shelves steeply. Use tripping line and do not leave craft unattended.

1.2 Sanda Island

(ON. sandtange – sand spit) island. There is a large sand spit near the harbour called Oitir Buidhe (G. – yellow sand spit). According to the Ordnance Gazetteer Sanda was called 'Avona Porticosa' by the Vikings and known as 'Aven' in Gaelic (?G. abhainn – river). But Dean Munro says the Danes called it 'Havin', i.e. anchorage – which makes much more sense.

OS Maps: 1:50000 Sheet 68   1:25000 Sheet 356
Admiralty Charts: 1:75000 Nos. 2126 or 2199

Area: 127ha (314 acres)
Height: 123m (403 ft)

Owner: Former owners were, 1969, Jack Bruce of the band Cream and, 1976, James Gulliver. Bought in 1989 by Dick and Meg Gannon for a reported £250,000 including the Barony title. Marketed at £3.2 million but sold to Swiss millionaire Mr Michi Meir for a reported £1.2 million in 2010.

Population: 1841–11 (1 house). 1871–32. 1881–14. 1891–36 (7 houses). 1931–14. 1961–7. 1981–0. 1991–0. 2011–1.

Geology: Lower Old Red Sandstone in red and yellow varieties, and undifferentiated schists.

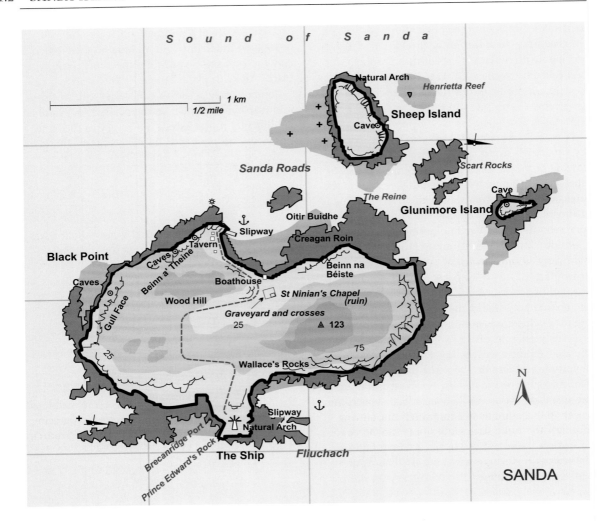

History: In 1306 Bruce may have landed here. Angus II, fifth King of the Isles, sheltered him at Dunaverty Castle which stood on the headland at Southend overlooking Sanda Island [NR688076]. When the English fleet drew closer he slipped away to Ireland.

The end of the lighthouse promontory on the south of the island is called Prince Edward's Rock after Edward Bruce, Robert the Bruce's impulsive brother, who was, very briefly, King of Ireland.

At this time Sanda was part of the lands of the Priory of Whithorn in Galloway and remained so until the late 16th century, when it became the property of the MacDonalds of Sanda with the Earl of Argyll holding the superiority.

In 1647, Dunaverty Castle again entered the history books when 300 MacDonalds of Kintyre, Catholic royalists and supporters of Montrose, made their last stand against the Covenanter

general, Leslie. Among them were Archibald Mor, chief of the MacDonalds of Sanda and his son and heir Archibald Og. Sir Alexander MacDonald had left them to defend the castle when he withdrew to Ireland but they were besieged and short of drinking water. Leslie offered to spare them should they surrender. They did so whereupon he had every one of them massacred. The castle was razed to the ground, never rebuilt, and from then on it has been known as Bloody Castle.

The MacDonalds' estates were forfeited but in 1661 they were restored by Act of Parliament. Ronald MacDonald inherited Sanda but died in 1679 when his son, Archibald, became the 6th Laird of Sanda.

In 1946 the Campbeltown lifeboat *The Duke of Connaught* (brought out of retirement as the new boat was under repair) went to the assistance of the 7000-ton *Byron Darnton* stuck on a reef on the south of Sanda. The skipper of the wrecked ship apparently considered it safer to stay aboard and keep below decks, but the lifeboatmen knew that the ship was bound to break up before long with the almost inevitable death of everyone on board. Unfortunately the old lifeboat had no radio. Conditions were appalling and communication with the ship was impossible as no one was on deck so the lifeboat sailed back round the island to the north harbour, where one of the crew ran overland to the south side. There was a radio transmitter at the lighthouse by which he eventually persuaded the captain of the stricken ship to allow those aboard to be taken off. Once again the lifeboat set out into the violent storm, rounded the island, and in spite of a very unreliable engine risked going into the chaotic sea among the rocks. It took eighteen long hours of almost foolhardy bravery but all fifty-four passengers and crew (and even a dog) were saved. Just as the lifeboat pulled clear of the rocks the ship finally disintegrated. But all was not over for while struggling home the old engine at last sputtered out. It seemed a losing battle as they were blown out to sea but after an hour they coaxed her into life again and at last reached the safety of the harbour.

Wildlife: Two of Sanda's small neighbouring islands, Sheep Island and Glunimore Island, are important breeding grounds for puffins in the Clyde area but many seabirds also breed on Sanda Island's crags. The converted boatshed is a visitors' centre.

* * *

Although **SANDA ISLAND** is a useful stopping-off point for a yacht waiting for the tide to round the Mull of Kintyre the present owner 'banned' all visitors, following a barn fire in 2010. The farmhouse, which was restored by the previous owner for his own occupation, is just beside the jetty and slipway. There is also an old schoolhouse and various farm buildings which he converted in 2003 for letting as holiday cottages and as a popular licensed restaurant, the Byron Darnton tavern. Sanda is a Site of Scientific Interest (SSI) and also an RSPB Reserve since 2005 and the

'THE SHIP' LIGHTHOUSE, SANDA

Nature Conservancy Council have the seabirds monitored and ringed both on Sanda and on its two little neighbours, **Sheep Island** and **Glunimore Island**. Glunimore is a tiny lump of rock but Sheep Island is large enough to provide some grazing for sheep. It has a cave on it and a natural stone arch at its north end.

The road which runs round the bay and across the island to the lighthouse had been macadamed in the past and there are still patches of tar lying in the ruts. The roofless ruin of little **St Ninian's Chapel**, about 10.3m by 6.3m, is on the south side of a knoll within the burial enclosure [NR727046]. Fordun noted this building in the second half of the 14th century. The side walls, of local rubble dressed with local sandstone, are still standing to roof level, but the gables have partly collapsed. There is an intact wooden lintel over the entrance doorway. One of the three window embrasures is still in reasonable condition and it has a stone basin or piscina set in the wall beside it. A matching basin has not been seen since 1873. There is a stone altar slab with a rectangular slot in it – possibly used for relics and an inscription on a grave slab set in the floor refers to 'Archibald – son to MacDonald of Sanda' and 'Cirstin Stewart'. Cirstin Stewart was the widow of Archibald Mor MacDonald who died in the Dunaverty Massacre.

By the north-west corner of the chapel a worn Early Christian slab is incised with a cross and near the centre of the burial ground there is a large much-eroded cruciform-shaped stone nearly 2m high and a few scattered headstones. Heraldic memorials to the MacDonald lairds show that Archibald, the sixth laird, was alive in 1731.

Just west of the chapel are the footings of a small square structure. A 1630 record states – 'at the syde of that Chappell there is a litle well or compass of stones. . . And they say that the bones of certaine holie men that lived in that Illand is buried within that place.' The same record also refers to a 'spring of fresh water called St Ninian's Well' which had therapeutic powers but this has not been identified.

In the past there was an active fishing community living on Sanda. Apparently, by tradition, if there was a severe storm and the men were still at sea, the families would gather in the burial ground by a particular unmarked grave, say a prayer for the fishermen, and then solemnly pour a cup of fresh water on the grave. The origin of this ceremony is unknown.

Legend has it that St Ninian himself is buried on Sanda and that anyone who steps on his grave will die within a year. This dangerous spot once had an alder tree marking its whereabouts but that has long since disappeared.

The island had not been farmed since 1946 but after 1989 the Gannons worked hard repairing the fences and stocking the farm with sheep and poultry. There are no trees but this was not always the case; the hill above the farmhouse is still called Wood Hill. The lighthouse, on a promontory on the south shore (called **The Ship** because it has that appearance from the sea), was built in 1850 by Alan Stevenson and altered in 1881. The skerries here are littered with the wrecks of ships. There is a striking wide-span natural stone arch alongside the lighthouse and many cave-riddled crags and rock formations in the vicinity. On a sunny summer day there are few more enjoyable experiences than a walk across Sanda. The central valley traps the heat as it is sheltered from all the prevailing winds.

*   *   *

Access: Kintyre Marine Charters sails from the Old Quay, Campbeltown, Kintyre (01586-554667) daily throughout the summer, weather (and owners) permitting.
From Girvan, ASW Charters. 01465-715934.

Anchorages:
1. Off Sanda Roads just NE of slipway/jetty, 4–5m, sand. Strong nearby tidal stream requires care. On W side of anchorage a reef extends about ¾c N from Beinn a Theine marked by a perch. Note sunken rocks in centre of the Roads. Some swell likely but well-protected from SW.
2. South Bay, small bight on S side of Sanda. Temporary anchorage and shelter from NW winds about 3c ENE of The Ship light-tower. Rocks dry up to 2.5c E of SW point of the lighthouse promontory.

1.3 Holy Island

First noted as Inis Stroin, later as eilean Molaise (G. – Mo Las' island) corrupted to Lamlash. Also known as Holy Island which became its official name in 1830 when the township on Arran adopted the name of Lamlash.

OS Maps: 1:50000 Sheet 69   1:25000 Sheet 361
Admiralty Charts: 1:20000 No.1864

Area: 253ha (625 acres)
Height: 314m (1030 ft)

Owner: At one time part of the estates of the Duke of Hamilton. Bought in 1991 by a group of Scottish Buddhists, the Samyé Ling Buddhist Centre, for about £350,000 from Mrs Catherine Morris. The price was agreed on the understanding that there would be no commercial exploitation and that the archaeological and spiritual amenities, and the distinctive flora and fauna would be protected.

Population: 1841–no separate record. 1881–15. 1891–16 (3 houses). 1931–19. 1961–7. 1971–10. (These figures include the lighthouse keepers.) 1981–0. 1991–0. 2001–13. 2011–31. A Buddhists community.

Geology: Mainly igneous rock of a rhyolite type in the north and basalt in the south. The steep patches on the west slopes are of porphyry and claystone.

History: The island's one-time resident and patron saint, St Mo Las, was born in Ireland in 566 AD, became bishop of Leighlin, Ireland c.610 and may have died c.640.

In the 12th century Somerled established a monastery on the island and it was visited by King Haakon's Norsemen before and probably also after the Battle of Largs in 1263.

In 1548 the ship carrying the five-year-old child who was to become Mary Queen of Scots sheltered here on its way to France.

Wildlife: The island is a nature reserve. It was once covered with trees and the present owners, following their passionate interest in the environment, have already planted more than

35,000 native species at the north end.

Wild Saanen goats, once common on Arran but now extinct there, still roam free on the island. In Victorian times it was fashionable to drink their milk which was thought to bestow longevity.

There is also a flock of Soay sheep, a herd of Eriskay ponies and, of course, thousands of rabbits on the island. All roam free, forage for themselves in peaceful co-existence with humans and are left to their own devices. Feeding or disturbing them is forbidden. Peregrines breed on the rocky cliffs and many birds, including eider duck, nest on the shores.

The 18th century traveller, Thomas Pennant,

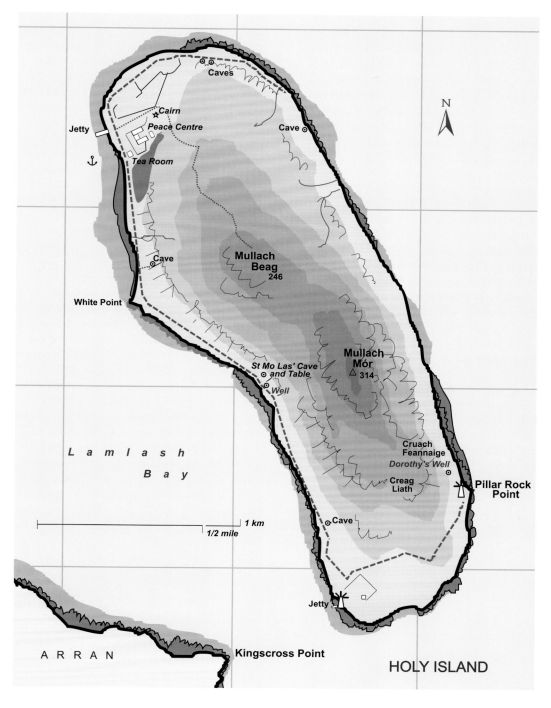

said that the island was 'infested with vipers' but this is certainly not true today.

* * *

HOLY ISLAND shelters one of the finest of naval anchorages and for many years had the large mooring buoys used by the great warships of the Royal Navy in the First World War still in place. This was the home in the 7th century of St Mo Las, or St Molias (or St Luserian in some accounts). The saint lived and meditated comfortably in **St Mo Las' Cave** [NS059297] well-furnished with every 'mod. con.', – a fireplace, a fresh water supply from a nearby spring, drainage carved out of the rock and, beside the front door, a large stone dining-table with stone seats which is known as the Judgement Stone because he sat there to settle local disputes. The saint was said to be a strict disciplinarian. The spring is called **St Mo Las' Well** and the cave contains runic and early Christian inscriptions. The former are thought to have been carved by King Haakon's defeated followers returning home after the Battle of Largs. The latter is a 'signature' thought to refer to Nicholas the 11th century Bishop of Man. It is marked with an episcopal cross. In the 1990s there was an iron grille protecting the cave entrance and the (absent) owners' assistance was required to obtain access to the interior. In view of the damage that vandals have done to the King's Cave on Arran this was a sensible precaution.

Legend claims that St Mo Las lived to the ripe old age of 120 in spite of deliberately contracting thirty nasty diseases to expiate his sins. It is also said that his bones were brought back to Arran from Ireland, carried through the central valley and buried under a rough stone in a wall of the church at Shiskine, near Blackwaterfoot.

There are supposed to be a few traces of a 12th-century fortress built by Somerled, Lord of the Isles, and in the 13th century a monastery was established in a position south-east of the present Peace Centre. The small chapel was used for burials until 1790. The monastery is said to have been founded by Ranald, son of Somerled, but it was in a ruinous state by 1594.

Mullach Mór (G. - big top) is the descriptive name of the central peak and summit of the island at 314m, with Mullach Beag (G. - little top) to the north of it. This is the easiest route for a scramble up the mountain but avoid the precipitous east flank. Apart from the two lighthouses in the south of the island the Peace Centre, outbuildings and known archaeological remains are all in the north beside a mature woodland copse. The plan, however, is to build a Retreat Centre recessed into the southern hillside by Dorothy's Well and overlooking the sea. This will be a 'simple wall of rooms, Potala-like' and will accommodate a community of about 200 adherents looking for 'inner peace'. Meanwhile the renovated lighthouse-keepers' cottages serve as a Retreat.

This is part of the Samyé Ling Buddhist Order's plan to create Europe's biggest non-denominational spiritual sanctuary on the island. Their Peace Centre, which incorporates the original farmhouse, was opened in 2003 with accommodation for 60 people, dining room, library, and multi-purpose Peace Hall. The old boathouse is now an Information Centre and tea room and the existing lighthouse-keepers' cottages have been renovated. Dry-stone dykes have been repaired, the one-time orchard has been replanted with traditional varieties, and there is an extensive vegetable garden as all meals served on the island are strictly vegetarian. Environmental considerations have been paramount: springs supply the fresh water, heating is by solar panels, sewage is treated in state-of-the-art reed beds and a large portion of the island has been reforested with native species.

HOLY ISLE FARMHOUSE – BEFORE THE EXTENSION

A coastal circuit, half by path and dirt road, makes an interesting and not too demanding walk. I have been unable to discover the significance of the name of **Dorothy's Well** which is in the south-east [NS068292].

On the way back from such a walk, if the sun is setting over Goat Fell and Mullach Mór brooding in the evening light, rest for a while by the dry stone dyke and admire the view. Once upon a time, it is said, there was a farmer living in the original farmhouse whose wife bore him fifteen daughters. He was so disgusted at not having a son that he murdered her and buried her body under the stone-flagged kitchen floor.

Access: There is a regular private ferry service (01770-601100) to Holy Island from Lamlash pier (weather and tide permitting). Lamlash is 10 minutes' bus ride from Brodick. The crossing takes 10 minutes. Accommodation and meals available on Holy Island (01770- 601100) for persons of all Faiths but visitors are asked to respect and abide by the Five Golden Rules of Buddhism.

Anchorage:
1. Opposite the Peace Centre in 6m to 8m, well SW of the jetty and as near the shore as reasonable. Weed on pebbles. Check that anchor well bedded. Good shelter.

1.4 Arran

(B. aran – high place).

O S Maps: 1:50000 Sheet 69 1:25000 Sheet 361
Admiralty Charts: 1:75000 Nos.2126 and 2131 1:36000
No.2220 Pladda to Brodick and No.2221 Brodick to Cock of Arran 1:25000 No.1864 Brodick 1:20000 No.1864 Lamlash

Area: 43,201ha (106,750 acres) **Height:** 874m (2867 ft)

Owner: Multiple ownership but the principal owners are the heirs of the Duchess of Montrose, the Forestry Commission, the National Trust for Scotland (NTS), Stephen Gibbs (Dougarie) and J K & C Bone (Glenkiln). The Duchess of Montrose's inheritance came when the direct line of the Hamiltons ceased in 1895. Mary, Duchess of Montrose died in 1957 and in 1958 her daughter, Lady Jean Fforde gifted Goatfell and the neighbouring mountains to the NTS while Brodick Castle was accepted in lieu of estate duty by the Inland Revenue and transferred to the NTS.

Arran, oddly enough, appears to have three earldoms: Earl of Arran (No 1), is the Duke of Hamilton – title granted in 1389; Earl of Arran (No 2), title granted in 1467 and including 1000 acres and Lochranza Castle was sold by Lady Jean Fforde to an anonymous purchaser in 1994; Earl of Arran (No 3), is actually of the Aran Islands on the Irish Atlantic coast and not the Scottish Island.

Population: 1755–3646. 1792–5804. 1821–6600. 1841–6241. 1881–4730. 1891–4824. 1931–4506. 1961–3700. 1971–3564. 1981–3845. 1991–4474. 2001–5045. 2011–4629.

Geology: Arran is a geologist's paradise. It was described by the eminent geologist Sir Archibald Geikie as a complete synopsis of Scottish geology and it was here that James Hutton in the 18th century confirmed his theories of igneous geology. It is regularly visited by parties of students to study the rock formations. Goat Fell is an igneous intrusion into the surrounding Devonian sandstones and schists giving a ring of upturned strata around a granite core – the dramatic high peaks and corries are a direct result of this. The early settlers used local pitchstone for their artefacts and Cruttwell (18th century) claimed that topaz was to be found in the area.

In the north-east of Arran there is a region of carboniferous limestone whilst the south is composed of new red sandstone. Where there is hard granite the many basaltic dykes have eroded to form fissures but in the softer rock in the south of the island the dykes form conspicuous ridges. There are many erratics – boulders which have been moved a considerable distance from their source by Ice Age glaciers, particularly in the south. In the west below Dougarie Lodge there are interesting terraces of glacial material while in the north great rockfalls on the coast date back to the Mesozoic and Palaeozoic periods. The northern tip is a large sandstone outcrop called the Cock of Arran. A raised beach almost 8m above sea level virtually encircles the island.

History: Whoever the first inhabitants may have been several thousand years ago, Arran was probably invaded in 200BC by Britons speaking a Celtic language (Brythonic) related to present-day Welsh. (Dumbarton, meaning Fort of the Britons, was another similar enclave left by the Romans when they departed in 400AD.) Scots arrived from Ireland in the 6th century and included

Arran in the Kingdom of Dalriada (roughly the extent of present-day Argyll, but for a time stretching further south). Norsemen then moved in about the 9th century and separated the island from Dalriada but Somerled, when founding the monastery at Saddell in Kintyre where he was eventually buried, took it from the Norse in 1156. After the Battle of Largs in 1263 Arran (still under the dominion of the Lord of the Isles) became part of the Scottish Kingdom but, as with Bute, it was considered the personal property of the Stewart kings – not Crown property. It was eventually awarded to the Hamiltons by Royal Charter in 1503 and at the end of the 18th century the Duke of Hamilton was still sole proprietor except for five small farms. After 1745 villages and crofts were deserted through massive emigration and large areas were later laid waste by the introduction of sheep farming. The Gaelic life and culture of the island was shattered. James Hogg wrote: 'Ah! Wae's me, I hear the Duke of Hamilton's crofters are a' gaun away, man and mither's son, frae the Isle o' Arran. Pity on us!'

Wildlife: Palm-lilies, a sub-tropical native tree of New Zealand, grow in the mild climate of the south and west. Most types of deciduous trees can be found with two unique species of whitebeam found nowhere else: *Sorbus arranensis*, and, with only two known specimens, *Sorbus pseudomeinichii*.

Some less common species of wildflowers flourish on Arran – alpine enchanter's nightshade in areas of deep shade and alpine lady's mantle which grows in Glen Sannox.

Arran is a red squirrel refuge as there are, thankfully, no grey squirrels on the island. At present there are about 2000 wild red deer, a recovery from near extinction 200 years ago, and a small number of adders and badgers. There are no foxes, stoats, weasels or moles.

The mountains are the domain of golden eagles and most of the characteristic moorland birds are to be found.

*   *   *

Sheltering behind the Mull of Kintyre and sitting snugly in the busy Firth of Clyde, **ARRAN** has the blessing of a mild climate and easy access to populous Glasgow. There is an average annual rainfall of 1250mm (50 ins) in the west, and double that figure up in the mountains. This has been a popular holiday resort since the early 18th century – and tourism is still the main industry, but agriculture and a whisky distillery play their part. This is also an island steeped in legends and ghosts, folklore and fairy tales.

A circuit of the island is about 92 Km (55 miles). The **Isle of Arran Heritage Museum** at Brodick is in an 18th-century croft farm, complete with smiddy, stables, bothy and coach house. It has a tea room and demonstrations of local crafts.

To the north of Brodick Bay (ON *breidr vik* – broad bay) and beneath the highest mountain, Goat Fell (G. *gaoth* – wind, ON *fjeld* – mountain) (874m) stands **Brodick Castle**. The walled garden was started in 1710 and the woodland garden, with one of Europe's finest collections of rhododendrons including some propagated from the plants at Achamore Gardens on Gigha (No.2.3), was started in 1923. Both castle and mountain belong to the National Trust for Scotland.

Part of the Round Tower at Brodick Castle dates from the 13th century but the main building was constructed by the Hamiltons who started the work in 1558. In 1652 Cromwell's forces, normally renowned for destruction, built the Battery and an extra wing but the troops were later massacred by the islanders. In 1844 Gillespie Graham was the architect for the final work including the Great West Tower. He was commissioned by William, son of the tenth Duke of Hamilton, and his wife, Princess Mary of Baden, who was a great-niece of the Empress Josephine. The castle is worth visiting as a fine

BRODICK CASTLE

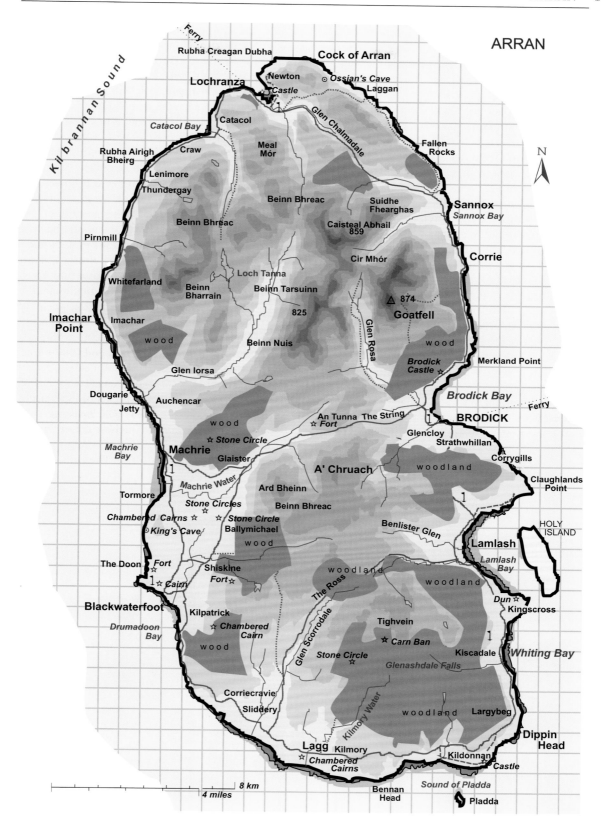

ARRAN

Kil brannan Sound

Ferry
Rubha Creagan Dubha
Cock of Arran
Newton
Ossian's Cave
Lochranza
Castle
Laggan
Catacol Bay
Catacol
Glen Chalmadale
Fallen Rocks
Rubha Airigh Bheirg
Craw
Meal Mór
Lenimore
Thundergay
Beinn Bhreac
Suidhe Fhearghas
Sannox
Sannox Bay
Beinn Bhreac
Caisteal Abhail 859
Pirnmill
Corrie
Cir Mhór
Loch Tanna
Whitefarland
Beinn Bharrain
Beinn Tarsuinn
△ 874
Goatfell
825
Imachar Point
Imachar
Glen Rosa
wood
Beinn Nuis
wood
Brodick Castle ☆
Merkland Point
Glen Iorsa
Dougarie Jetty
Auchencar
An Tunna The String
Brodick Bay
Ferry
☆ Fort
1
BRODICK
wood
Glencloy
Machrie Bay
☆ Stone Circle
Machrie
Strathwhillan
Glaister
A' Chruach
woodland
Corrygills
1
Machrie Water
Claughlands Point
Tormore
Stone Circles
Ard Bheinn
HOLY ISLAND
Chambered Cairns ☆
☆ Stone Circle
Beinn Bhreac
Ballymichael
Benlister Glen
Lamlash
☆ King's Cave
wood
woodland
Lamlash Bay
The Doon
☆ Fort
Shiskine
woodland
woodland
Dun ☆
1 ☆ Cairn
Fort ☆
The Ross
Kingscross
Blackwaterfoot
Kilpatrick
Tighvein
1
Drumadoon Bay
☆ Chambered Cairn
Glen Scorrodale
☆ Carn Ban
Kiscadale
Whiting Bay
wood
Stone Circle ☆
Glenashdale Falls
Corriecravie
Sliddery
woodland
Largybeg
Kilmory Water
Dippin Head
Lagg
Kilmory
☆ Chambered Cairns
Kildonnan
Castle
8 km
4 miles
Bennan Head
Sound of Pladda
Pladda

example of Scottish baronial architecture with richly designed interiors, many art treasures, and a restored Victorian kitchen. The grounds are open throughout the year and the castle is open from Easter until late September.

There is a superb scenic hill-walk of 18km (11 miles) which starts near Brodick [NS004368] and goes up Glen Rosa, across the saddle at 460m (1500 ft) by Cìr Mhór (G. – big comb) then down through the wild landscape of Glen Sannox and the remains of old barytes mines (abandoned 1938) to **Sannox Bay** [NS016454].

North of Brodick is the pretty village of **Corrie** (G. *coire* – a cauldron-shaped hollow) with two tiny harbours. The quarry in the hills behind provided stone for the construction of the Crinan Canal. The road continues through Sannox to Lochranza but, if the weather's good, there is a fine 15km (9 mile) walk along the shoreline passing Ossian's Cave and, the most northerly point, the **Cock of Arran**. The mountain side here once resembled an enormous crowing cock with its wings spread but its head has now eroded away. There is an alternative path at the mid-point, Laggan [NR979508], which goes over the hill ridge. Daniel MacMillan, founder of the publishing empire, spent his childhood here.

The little village of **Lochranza**, home of Arran's only, but renowned, distillery spreads along the southern shore under the ramparts of ruined Lochranza Castle standing in the centre of the loch on a shingle spit. This is where Bruce is reputed to have landed in 1306 or 1307 on his return from Rathlin Island. Fragments of Lochranza Castle are from an early fortification mentioned by Fordun in the 14th century but most of the existing ruin dates from the 16th century. In the early 15th century it belonged to John de Mentieth and it was then granted by James II to Alexander Lord Montgomery.

For the yachtsman the delightful anchorage of Loch Ranza has something of a reputation for anchor-dragging. I can recall one evening when the wind picked up to gale force and swung into the north-east and sudden violent squalls came down the glen. By midnight every one of the nine boats anchored in the loch was playing ring-a-ring-a-roses in the dark as they tried to find a sound bottom. We missed our normal visit to the excellent pub!

At **Catacol** (ON – *ravine of the wildcat*) south of Lochranza the terrace of cottages at the mouth of the glen is known as the Twelve Apostles [NR911497]. Loch Tanna, the largest loch

LOCHRANZA CASTLE

on Arran, is at the summit of Glen Catacol in the wild landscape beneath Beinn Bhreac (G. – speckled mountain) – 711m high (2332 ft). Further south by the fine beach at Pirnmill [NR873445] pine bobbins or 'pirns' were made for the Paisley mills – until there were no more pines.

The road runs on past the palm trees of Whitefarland and Imachar to **Dougarie Lodge** where Iorsa Water tumbles into the sea. The lodge [NR884371] was built by the Hamiltons and the first island telephone was installed here in 1891.

At Machrie Moor (G. *machair* – low, level land) where the central valley opens out there is a feast of archaeological remains. Some of the standing stones were unfortunately turned into millstones but many undamaged stones remain as well as chambered tombs and cairns (3500BC–1000BC) both here and in the southern coastal areas [eg. NR9032 and 9132]. Bronze Age burial chambers or cists have been found inside one of the many stone circles on Machrie Moor and there is a 15-stone circle round a burial cairn in the woods above the road at Auchagallon [NR908351]. Arran has no less than ten such henges or stone circles.

An interesting walk above the shore from **Tormore** leads to the **King's Cave**, a large, dry, sandstone cave, 30m deep and level with the raised beach [NR884309]. In the 18th century the Kirk Session met here and in the 19th century it was used as a school. The cave entrance (protected by a grille in 1995) can be seen when sailing in the Kilbrannan Sound. It was said to have been occupied by Fingal, Fionn MacCaul, the legendary Irish King, who, to prove his manhood, rebuffed a Viking raid by Manos, heir to the Swedish King. The cave was excavated in 1902 exposing early Christian or Viking wall-carvings of hunting scenes but vandals have now covered these with graffiti and caused a lot of damage. Incidentally, this cave is also supposed to have been lived in by Robert the Bruce when he was inspired by the well-kent spider but the cave on Rathlin Island off the north-east corner of Ireland has better credentials.

In 1817 Thomas Telford built the road (B880) which crosses the island to Brodick Bay. It was named 'The String' by sailors because from the sea it looks like a piece of string laid across the bare moorland. South of Machrie Moor the village of **Shiskine** [NR913299] is reputed to be the

MONOLITHS AT MACHRIE MOOR

burial place of St Mo Las of Holy Island (No.1.3).

A large cairn [NR891288] at **Blackwaterfoot**, which was pillaged during the 19th century, contained relics including a dagger and this was thought to show a link with the culture of Stonehenge. The double ramparts of an iron-age fortress, Drumadoon (G. – fort on a ridge) are on a steep slope west of the village [NR886294].

In the south-east, a picturesque minor road called The Ross, follows Sliddery Water and the Green Glen to Lamlash.

Arran's oldest hotel, an 18th-century coaching inn, stands among the trees at **Lagg** (G. – a hollow) [NR956216]. It is haunted by a laird who sold his soul to the devil. Below the village and by the sea is the ruin of a prehistoric tomb which once held the remains of four adults and two children [NR955211].

Torrylin by **Kilmory** is the home of Arran cheese. The whole of this rocky south coast was once the haunt of smugglers from Ireland and wandering through the woods above the village are the ghosts of a young couple who were mistaken for smugglers and shot by coastguards. There is extensive forestry in the area with many interesting woodland walks. **Carn Ban**, a well-preserved Neolithic chambered cairn measuring 30m x 18m [NR991262] is by a burn in a high wooded valley – Allt an t-Sluice. It is 6½km (4 miles) up a forest track which starts just east of Kilmory and the site is 291m above sea level.

In the extreme south-east are the limited ruins of 14th-century **Kildonan Castle** [NS036209], which was granted by King Robert III to his bastard son, John, in 1406.

Kildonan, a place reputedly visited by St Donan after his training at Whithorn, overlooks the small tear-shaped island of **Pladda** (ON – flat isle). Owned by Arran Estate, it was up for sale in 1990 for £80,000, its first time ever on the market. Originally granted to the Hamiltons, the lighthouse was built in 1790 to Thomas Smith's design and was manned until 1990. In spite of being only 11ha in area, Pladda is lucky to have its own fresh water supply.

Glenashdale Burn enters the sea by the youth hostel at **Whiting Bay**. There is an easy walk [NS046252] through the woods one mile up the glen to see the dramatic waterfalls which have a 30m drop over a lava sill. Nearby are the ruins of a fort, two chambered cairns and the 'Giants' Graves'.

The substantial remains of a Viking burial mound and fort [NS056283] are at **Kingscross Point**, south of Lamlash Bay. It was here that Robert the Bruce waited for a bonfire to be lit on the Ayrshire coast as the prearranged signal that his supporters were ready for his final attempt to claim the crown. There was a false alarm and he arrived too early, but his claim was successful nevertheless.

The High School at **Lamlash** [NS024307] stands on the ground where Donald 'Tattie' MacKelvie developed the world renowned seed potatoes, *Arran Chief, Arran Pilot* and *Arran Banner*.

For anglers the salmon and trout fishing in both the Machrie and Iorsa Waters has a high rating and, for general recreational activities, Arran provides swimming, boating, pony-trekking, and seven golf-courses.

For the mountaineer Arran is noted for its four 'Corbetts': Goatfell, 874m; Beinn Tarsuinn (G. – transverse hill), 825m; Cir Mhor [keer vor] (G. – big comb), 798m; and, Caisteal Abhail (G. – Castle ptarmigan), 859m.

It is, I am reliably told, possible to traverse all the main tops in the east and central groups in one day – 'as the going is so easy'. This amounts to a total height of about 2600m to be climbed. Many of the excellent climbs, ridge-walks and hill-walks of Arran are listed in the publications of the Scottish Mountaineering Club.

Incidentally, the name of the mountain called Suidhe Fhearghas (G. – seat of Fergus) [NR990455] recalls a day when the Fianna of Ireland were hunting red deer on Arran. They took time off to meet for a banquet on the mountain and to listen to their bard, Fergus of the True Lips.

Access: Car ferry: Ardrossan/Brodick daily, takes one hour, 08000-66-5000. Train connections with Glasgow. Advance booking usually essential. Tourist Information Office near Brodick pier, 01770-302140. Car ferry: Lochranza/Claonaig Kintyre, summer only and subject to reasonable weather, 30 min. trip. There is a bus service on Arran, 0871-200-2233, and bicycles and cars can be hired. Local companies operate coach tours.

Anchorages:
Note: All anchorages except Lochranza and Lamlash Bay are exposed and only tenable in settled conditions.
1. North Sannox, between the southernmost measured-mile posts. Exposed temp. anchorage in 3m, sand, close inshore just N of the burn. Outstanding views.
2. Sannox Bay, sandy bay at entrance to the Sannox river. Temp anchorage off old stone pier in 6–12m. Beware Sannox rock near centre of bay. Very exposed NE to SE. Beautiful view.
3. Corrie. Exposed temp. anchorage in 4–8m off either of the old stone harbours N and S of Corrie Point.
4. Brodick bay. Visitors' moorings or good anchorage in light W'lies in 3–5m, sand, about 2c W of the pier. Anchor well off-shore to avoid moorings and ferry or, in NW winds, anywhere between Merkland Point and the Old Quay. Restricted temp. shelter within inner pier subject to HM's agreement. (*Access to Brodick Castle and grounds*).
5. Clauchlands Point. Anchor in Lamlash Bay 4c W of the Point. Exposed to E.
6. Lamlash. There are visitors' moorings operated by Holy Isle Ferry, 07970-771960, VHF 37. Or anchor in 4–6m, NE of stone pier but many moorings and bottom steep. Swell in E winds. Squalls in strong NW winds.
7. Cordon to Kingscross. Anchor anywhere from SE of the Cordon shoal to Kingscross avoiding moorings and fish cages. In S'ly gales best NW of old ferry pier.
8. Whiting Bay, between Largybeg and Kingscross Points, sheltered from W'lies only. Temp anchorage in 4–8m, well off-shore.
9. Pladda. Anchor on E side of island close in-shore just N of lighthouse jetty, in 5–8m, sand with thick weed. Sheltered N to W and partly from SW. Many dangers in channel between Pladda and Arran.
10. Blackwaterfoot (Drumadoon Bay), very exposed to S and W. Anchor in 4m near burn mouth but beware many rocks.
11. Machrie bay, mid-W side, temp. anchorage in 3–7m anywhere in bay but avoid Iorsa Patch at N end. Depths increase suddenly. At Machrie burn the shore shoals out for about 1c for 1M on either side. Exposed SW to NW.
12. Whitefarland bay, temp. anchorage in 6–12m,

protected from S and E winds. Bay shoals for 2c off shore
for about ½M N.

13. Catacol bay, temp anchorage at S of bay S of Catacol
burn in 12m, some shelter from S.

14. Lochranza, small sea loch which dries about 2c from
head. Ferry pier extends N from Coillemore point (the S
entrance point). Exposed W through N to NNE. NE to NW
winds cause considerable swell and there can be violent
squalls. Enter closer to ferry pier. Visitors' moorings or
anchor in centre of loch, N of the ruined castle. Bottom
soft mud with poor holding.

1.5 Little Cumbrae

*Probably (B. cymri – Brythonic Gaelic people) i.e. the place of
the Brythonic or Welsh-speaking Gaels. Also known as Little,
Lesser or Wee Cumray.*

OS Maps: 1:50000 Sheet 63   1:25000 Sheet 341
Admiralty Chart: 1:25000 1907 or 1:36000 2221

Area: 313ha (773 acres)
Height: 123m (403ft)

Owner: Property of the Earl of Eglington prior to
1913. Purchased in 1960 by Mr & Mrs Peter Kaye

for £24,000 from the trustees of Ian Robertson Parker. Bought by Stephen Worrallo in 2005. Sold in 2008 for £2.5m to Sam and Sunita Poddar and blessed my Yogrushi Swami Ramdev as 'Shanti Dwipam' (Peace Island) in 2009.

Population: 1841–8. 1881–23. 1891–17. 1931–21. 1961–8. 1991–6. 2001–0. 2011–0.

Geology: Mainly Carboniferous basalt and spilite.

History: Until 1515 the hereditary keepers of the island were the Hunters of Hunterston. During the 14th century Kings Robert II and Robert III used the island as a deer forest.

Cromwell's men landed and caused some damage to the castle in 1653.

Wildlife: In the 19th century over 5000 rabbits a year were 'harvested' and rabbits are still numerous. The Kayes maintained the island as a nature reserve to be visited by occasional university study groups.

* * *

Attractive twelve-bedroom **Cumbrae House** overlooks the castle ruin and a bay with rocky outcrops to the north known as **Broad Islands**.

Castle Island is linked by a drying strand to Little Cumbrae's east coast with **Trail Island** lying alongside like a moored ship. The original castle was possibly built by Bruce's son-in-law. A Royal Charter was signed there in 1375. The present square keep on Castle Island [NS152513] was erected in 1527, apparently to control deer poaching. It was wrecked by Cromwell's army but still stands as an imposing ruin. It is a twin to the keep on the mainland at Portencross. A short distance north of it [NS148518] are the remains of **St Veya's Chapel** and various antiquities which are worth inspection. St Veya (or St Beya) was a 7th-century nun.

The ancient lighthouse tower at the summit of the island [NS143515] is the type that had a fire of coals, or 'cresset', burning in an open grate. Presumably a fairly large fire had to be maintained. Imagine the effort of shipping coal to the island, carrying it up the hillside, hoisting it onto the open platform and keeping it burning during gale-lashed rainstorms! This particular light-tower was built in 1757 and is similar to the original design on the Isle of May (See No.12-1). The modern lighthouse (now automatic solar-powered) and landing place stands below it on the west shore. There is a path leading over 'Rest and Be Thankful' and skirting Tom's Loch before descending to Cumbrae House on the east side by the castle.

The island, which is easily accessible but infrequently visited, is rugged, with many rock outcrops and caves on the raised beach at the south end.

* * *

Access: Try Cumbrae Voyages, Largs Yacht Haven, 0845-257-0404 or a Largs or Millport boat owner.

Anchorages:
1. Give N end of island a wide berth because of shoals. Anchor on E coast in 2–4m between Castle Island and Broad Island or to the N of Broad Island. Avoid moorings and jetty. Uncomfortable in S and E winds.
2. There is a landing place for the lighthouse on the W shore.

1.6 Great Cumbrae

Probably (B. cymri – Brythonic Gaelic people) i.e. the place of the Brythonic or Welsh-speaking Gaels. Formerly known as Great or Greater Cumray.

O S Maps: 1:50000 Sheet 63   1:25000 Sheet 341
Admiralty Charts: 1:25000 No.1907 or 1:36000 No.2221

Area: 1,168ha (2886 acres)
Height: 127m (417ft)

Owner: Owned by the Marquess of Bute's family since the 12th century when King Malcolm reputedly awarded it to their ancestor, Walter Fitzalan, for defeating a mini-invasion of the Clyde. It was sold by the Marquess to his tenants in 1999.

Population: 1793–509. 1841–1413. 1881–1856. 1891–1784. 1931–2144. 1961–1638. 1981–1300. 1991–1393. 2001–1434. 2011–1376. This is the most densely populated of the listed Scottish islands.

Geology: Most of the island is Old Red Sandstone but the area round Millport is Carboniferous limestone. There are many igneous dykes such as 'The Lion' near the south-east corner opposite Largs.

History: King Haakon is reputed to have set up his camp at Tomont End, the northern tip of Great Cumbrae, before the Battle of Largs in 1263.

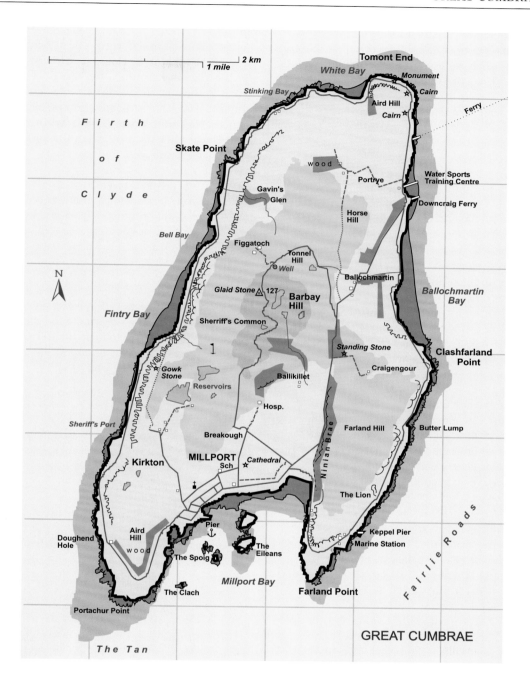

GREAT CUMBRAE

Millport was popular with trippers in the heyday of holidays on the Clyde but in 1906 the steamer companies boycotted the island because of excessive harbour dues. The island nearly died until Lloyd George stepped in and settled the dispute – just in time for the annual Glasgow Fair holiday.

Wildlife: The marine life round the island is very rich and has been studied since the 1840s. At that time David Robertson, the 'Cumbrae Naturalist', after many visits to the island, established a floating laboratory. In 1896 the headquarters of the Scottish Marine Biological Association were built to the east of the town at Kepple Pier but this was transferred to Dunstaffnage near Oban in 1970. The Marine

Biological Station at Millport is now run by the Feild Studies Council. They have diving facilities, research vessels, a decompression chamber and a well-stocked aquarium which is open to the public.

The roseate tern, *Sterna dougallii*, was first identified here as a separate species by Dr MacDougal in 1812.

* * *

At the start of the 19th century the Rev James Adam, a local minister, always prayed for the people of **GREAT CUMBRAE** and 'the adjacent islands of Great Britain and Ireland' – which gives some indication of this island's importance in the eyes of its inhabitants.

A ridge of green hills stippled with rose-red rocks runs down the centre with the highest point (127m) marked by the **Glaid Stone** [NS167570]. Alongside this ridge is a hill road with unrivalled views over the Clyde and, below it, a coastal road of about 20km (12 miles) which encircles the island. In summer it can almost rival Amsterdam with numerous holidaymakers on hired cycles in search of exercise and fun.

Millport spreading round the south-facing bay is a typical small seaside resort with fun-fair, cinema, museum and sandy beaches. It was developed as a resort by the Victorians before they turned their attention to Rothesay. The solid residences look out on the bay to one of the loveliest views of Arran. The rocky islets in the middle of the bay are known simply as **The Eileans** (G. – islands).

The 'city' boasts the smallest cathedral in Britain – the **Episcopal Cathedral of Argyll and the Isles**. It was started in the 1840s by the 6th Earl of Glasgow under the influence of the Oxford Movement and the stone was quarried from the site, forming terraced gardens. The architect was William Butterfield. The mini-cathedral has a 37m spire, a starkly simple nave and a highly ornate brightly-coloured tiled chancel. One feels it has a foot in both camps, Presbyterian and Catholic. The Earl ran out of funds but the project was completed and consecrated in 1886 by Bishop Chinnery-Haldane of Argyll and the Isles.

The village of **Kirkton** in the south-west, which is now almost a suburb of Millport, was the first centre of population on the island. There has been a chapel there since the 13th century or earlier.

Norsemen who died in the Battle of Largs in 1263 are thought to be buried at **Tomont End** which is the northern tip of the island.

Both freshwater and sea fishing can be arranged from Millport and the Scottish Sports Council's **National Water Sports Training Centre** near the ferry terminal in the north-east teaches sailing, sub-aqua and canoeing.

The golf course on Sheriff's Common, near the reservoirs, provides spectacular views as well as a stimulating game and for climbers the rock outcrops on the hill behind Millport and the basaltic dykes of Lion Rock and The Deil's Dyke near Keppel Pier can be fun. Millport also has facilities for bowling and horse riding.

* * *

Access: Car ferry: Largs (10-min crossing time)/ Cumbrae Slip, 08000-66-5000. Round island bus service to Millport timed to meet the ferry, 08712-002233. Train connections: Glasgow/ Largs. Tourist information, 01475-689962.

Anchorages:
1. Millport Bay. Visitors' moorings in the anchorage near the pier or anchor clear of the moorings E of the northmost of The Eileans in a suitable depth. Millport pier leading lights bearing 333deg between the Eileans and The Spoig leads to the W anchorage. Bottom shelves gradually. Occasional berth end of pier.
2. Keppel pier with a T-head, on SE coast about 4c NE of Farland point, the SE extremity. Least depth of 4.9m alongside head of pier.
3. Ballochmartin or Balloch Bay N of Clashfarland Point on E coast has a T-headed pier at the N entrance point of bay. Anchor near Grey House in 8m.
4. National Water Sports Training Centre at N end of Balloch Bay. Suitable moorings may be available. If not anchor N of the slip but well off-shore.
5. Tomont End (Monument), White Bay. Good holding and well-sheltered from SW winds, 5–9m, sand. Bay dries out 1c.

1.7 Inchmarnock

(G. innis Marnoc – island of Marnoc)

OS Maps: 1:50000 Sheet 63   1:25000 Sheet 362
Admiralty Charts: 1:25000 No.2383 or 1:36000 No.2221

Area: 266ha (657 acres)
Height: 60m (197 ft).

MILLPORT

Owner: Bought in 1999 from Sir Richard Branson's brother by Lord (Robert Haldane) Smith, a Scottish merchant banker and BBC governor for, reportedly, £800,000.

Population: 1871–30. 1881–17. 1891–10 (3 houses). 1931–14. 1961–6. 1971–6. 1981–5. 1991–0. 2001–0. 2011–0.

Geology: Mainly Dalradian schistose grit similar to north Bute.

History: After the days of St Marnoc the Cistercians of Saddell in Kintyre owned the island.

  There was a widely held belief that, in the 19th century, the people of Bute left their alcoholics here to cure them 'by deprivation and isolation' but this is doubtful and has not been verified.

Wildlife: Inchmarnock has the largest herring-gull colony on the Clyde and there is prolific birdlife. It is a popular wintering haven for greylag geese.

*   *   *

A derelict 'landing-craft' for ferrying material across to the island is beached beside the anchorage off Midpark Farm on **INCHMARNOCK**. The farm buildings are picturesque with hawthorn hedges on each side of the farm road and bluebells in the long grass verges. The view from the low ridge running down the centre of the island is panoramic, encompassing a great sweep of water stretching from the lower reaches of Loch Fyne to the high peaks of Arran. The hazy blue hills of the Mull of Kintyre are the backdrop. There is an overwhelming sense of peace and it is almost impossible to believe that the great city of Glasgow is only a few miles away as the crow flies.

  Legend has it that there was a cheeky young Scots lad who pestered and interrupted St Columba with questions when he was preaching on the mainland. The monks were irritated and tried to silence him but St Columba chided them and prophesied that young Marnoc would become a great teacher. He had recognised a lively mind. The prophecy came true and Marnoc, later St Marnoc, settled on this island and built himself a chapel. People came from near and far to hear him preach.

A very few remains of the ancient **Chapel of St Marnoc**, probably from a later building of the 12th or 13th century, can be seen just north of the **Midpark** farm buildings [NS024596]. Several stone fragments of Celtic crosses have been uncovered near it and also other sculpted stones including one commemorating the Viking, Gutlief. These are now in Bute Museum. The church existed until the 18th century but a farmer, Alexander McDonald, used the stone from it to build Midpark farmhouse in 1718. Only when the work was complete did he decide to play safe with eternity so he sent £10 to the Church Session and asked for atonement.

A century later the gravestones from the cemetery were used by another farmer to build a

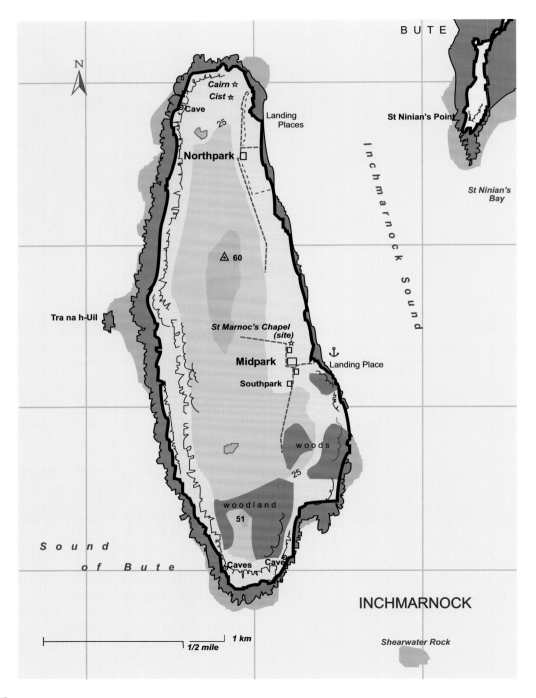

MIDPARK, INCHMARNOCK

cowhouse. No Christian atonement was requested in this case but it is recorded that his cattle all died. The farmer decided the devil was to blame so he made a burnt offering of one of the carcasses on the beach at dead of night.

The farmyard is reputed to have been laid out over the burial ground which was adjacent to the chapel, but **The Women's Burial Place** could still be distinguished in 1860 in a field adjoining the church.

In the extreme north of the island the skeleton of a young woman was found in one of three stone burial cists which were uncovered during archaeological excavation of a Bronze Age cairn [NS020612]. She was wearing a necklace consisting of 139 jet (lignite) beads, which can be seen in Bute Museum, and at her hand lay a flint knife. The tomb of the **Queen of the Inch**, as she is known, is close to Northpark, the owner's house. After the 3500-year-old skeleton had been radiocarbon-dated it was returned to its original tomb with a glass panel fitted to allow it to be seen. This was considered the best way to preserve the remains, rather than letting them moulder in a museum store. But walking past the tomb by torchlight at night requires a very steady nerve, said the previous owner. It is dark, it is quiet, it is lonely, and the shadows in the skull's eye-sockets follow every movement.

The island is divided into three farms – Northpark, Midpark and Southpark – although the latter buildings are now untenanted. The semi-derelict **Southpark** farm buildings adjoin Midpark.

Towards the end of the 19th century a tenant of Southpark was draining a 'moss' when he found in the peat a layer of preserved hazelnuts three feet thick. Investigation showed that although the island had been farmed for over a thousand years, at one time it was covered with luxuriant oak and hazel forest.

The Inchmarnock islanders were evacuated during the Second World War to enable a commando training area to be created. A considerable amount of damage was done and a large area is still covered with craters. The land is generally fertile but largely uncultivated. Visitors to the island should try to obtain permission first or at least keep to the shoreline as the owner is understandably keen that the island should be disturbed as little as possible.

Inchmarnock issued its own first distinctive postage stamp in July 1999.

Access: Try Don Clark, MFV *Morag*, Tighnabruaich, ring 01700-811538 or Cumbrae Voyages, Largs Yacht Haven, 0845-2570404.

Anchorage:
1. Anchor near the middle of the E side of island off Midpark Farm in 5m sand. Sheltered from NW and W but subject to swell.

1.8 Bute

Probably (B. budh – corn, Sc. -aer – island), or, less likely, (ON bot – patch of land). For centuries, however, the island was called Rothes-ay (Roth's or Roderick's island) and the main town was called Baile Bhoid (G. – the town of corn). The Chronicle of the Scots, 1482–1530, says Bute is named after St Brandan but this is doubtful.

O S Maps: 1:50000 Sheet 63 1:25000 Sheet 362
Admiralty Charts: 1:75000 No.2131 1:25000 Nos.1906 and 2383

Area: 12,217ha (30,188 acres)
Height: 278m (912 ft)

Owner: Principal owner – Bute Estate (John Colum Crichton-Stuart, The 7th Marquess of Bute, who prefers to be known as Johnny Dumfries, or Johnny Bute. He was a world championship Grand Prix driver, who won the 24-hour race at Le Mans in 1988).
Sir Richard Attenborough's 600ha of forest at Rudhabodach were the subject of a community buyout in 2010.

Population: 1755–3220. 1792–4759. 1841–7147. 1881–10998. 1891–11735. 1931–12112. 1961–9793. 1971–8423. 1981–7306. 1991–7354. 2001–7228. 2011–6498. There are about one million visitors each year.

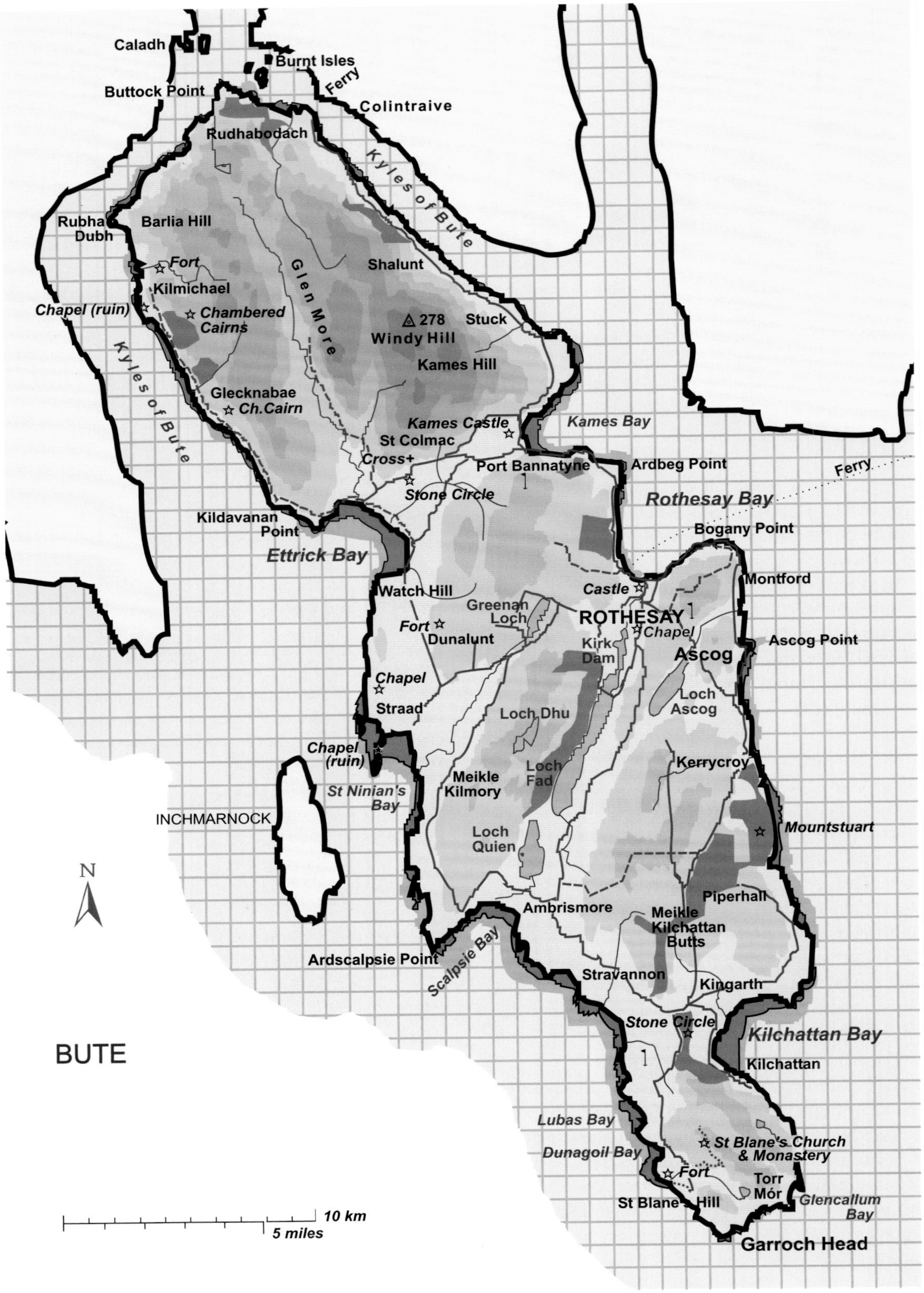

Caladh

Burnt Isles

Buttock Point

Ferry

Colintraive

Rudhabodach

Kyles of Bute

Rubha Dubh

Barlia Hill

Glen More

Shalunt

☆ *Fort*
Kilmichael

Chapel (ruin)

☆ *Chambered Cairns*

Kyles of Bute

△ 278
Windy Hill

Stuck

Kames Hill

Glecknabae
☆ *Ch.Cairn*

Kames Castle ☆

Kames Bay

St Colmac
Cross +

Port Bannatyne

Ardbeg Point

Ferry

☆ *Stone Circle*

Rothesay Bay

Kildavanan Point

Ettrick Bay

Bogany Point

Watch Hill

Castle ☆

Montford

Greenan Loch

Fort ☆
Dunalunt

ROTHESAY

Chapel

Ascog Point

Kirk Dam

Ascog

Chapel
☆
Straad

Loch Dhu

Loch Ascog

Chapel (ruin) ☆

Kerrycroy

St Ninian's Bay

Meikle Kilmory

Loch Fad

INCHMARNOCK

Loch Quien

☆ *Mountstuart*

N

Ambrismore

Piperhall

Meikle Kilchattan Butts

Ardscalpsie Point

Scalpsie Bay

Stravannon

Kingarth

BUTE

Stone Circle
☆

Kilchattan Bay

Kilchattan

Lubas Bay

Dunagoil Bay

☆ *St Blane's Church & Monastery*

☆ *Fort*

Torr Mór

Glencallum Bay

St Blane's Hill

Garroch Head

├────────────┼────────────┤ 10 km
├──────┼──────┤ 5 miles

Geology: Loch Fad, which cuts across the centre of the island, is a continuation of the Highland Boundary Fault. To the south is Old Red Sandstone ('red pudding rock'), some basaltic lavas, and fertile undulating arable land; to the north is Dalradian schistose grit and hilly terrain.

A fine example of a raised beach can be seen from the road at Tormore Hill.

History: Bute has been continuously inhabited for at least 6000 years.

After the Roman period Bute and Arran may still have been Brythonic (Welsh-type language) kingdoms. Nearby Dumbarton means the 'Fort of the Britons'. Later, the Erse, or Gaelic language of the Scots spread into Bute.

How early Bute was personally acquired by the Stewart family is uncertain. Steward Walter married the daughter of Robert the Bruce and fathered Robert II, the first Stuart king, in 1316. The royal Stewarts were known as Sheriffs of Bute and Keepers of Rothesay Castle. Roberts II and III used the castle as a holiday home and Robert the High Steward owned the island in 1334. Rothesay became a Royal Burgh in 1403 with a further charter by James VI in 1584. Many of the Provosts of the Burgh have been members of the Bute family and much of the island's history centres on Rothesay Castle.

In the 19th century before the advent of tourism herring-fishing brought prosperity to the island and as far back as 1779 the first cotton mill was built in Rothesay. Robert Thom, an early mill-owner, realised that more water was needed for the cotton mills and built a canal to bring water from the west side of the island to Rothesay. The dry canal can still be seen below the road at Tormore Hill.

The island peaked in popularity in the Victorian and Edwardian era as a tourist centre providing holidays 'doon the watter' from Glasgow.

Wildlife: Bute has a unique long-tailed field-mouse which is a sub-species of the mainland variety. A trial reintroduction of the European beaver (extinct in Britain since the 13th century) took place on Bute in 1875 but the animals only survived until the 1890s.

Birdlife is not particularly noteworthy due to the amount of cultivation but there are some areas of pleasant mixed woodland habitat which encourage a variety of species.

With bog cotton in the marshes and heather on the upper slopes, all the common botanical species are in evidence but there is little in the way

MOUNTSTUART – ERSTWHILE HOME OF THE MARQUESS OF BUTE

of distinctive plant life. However, Bute Natural History Society in the Bute Museum, Rothesay provides excellent information on nature trails, paths, plants and birdlife, and there is much of interest.

* * *

BUTE is first and foremost an island catering for the needs of visitors and there are many recreational facilities. Coarse fishing for pike and perch, sea angling, cycling, sailing and pony trekking are only a few of the many popular diversions.

The existence of **Rothesay Castle** was first recorded in 1230 when it was besieged and taken by the Norsemen. The breached east wall can still be seen in the massive, circular sandstone structure surrounded by a moat. The English took the castle on one occasion and it was taken in about 1334 by Sir Colin Campbell for Edward Balliol. It was also attacked by the Lord of the Isles in the 15th century. James IV and James V used it as a base for their campaigns to subdue the Hebrides and it was then that the great tower was built (1541). In 1498 the Bute family were appointed hereditary keepers of the castle and the present Marquess still holds that office. The rebel Master of Ruthven attacked the castle in 1527 but failed to take it so he destroyed the surrounding burgh. In 1544 the Earl of Lennox had more success when he took it for the English. Cromwell kept a garrison here but when it withdrew in 1659 much of the building was dismantled and during the Duke of Monmouth's rebellion in 1685 the rest of the castle was burned down by the Duke of Argyll.

The story goes that shortly after this the Duke of Argyll married off one of his daughters to a Bute. When the newly-wed bride reached the island the first thing she did was to complain bitterly to her husband that he did not have a castle fit for her to live in.

The 2nd Marquess of Bute began restoring the castle in 1816 and further work was done by the 3rd Marquess. The great hall was renovated by the 6th Marquess in 1970 and the government now maintains the property. The castle is open daily and well worth a visit.

The harbour at Rothesay was constructed in the 17th century and eventually rebuilt and extended during the heyday of holidays 'doon the watter' from Glasgow. The bay was a naval anchorage

from 1940 to 1957. Nearby, the Victorian Winter Garden on the sea front, at one time the haunt of music hall performers and comedians, has recently been restored.

This is the only Scottish island which had a tram service. This was electrified in 1902 but buses eventually took over in 1936.

The ancient **Church of St Mary's**, which was once part of the Bishopric of Man, is on the road just south of Rothesay at the foot of Loch Fad [NS086637]. It contains two canopied tombs.

Most of the north of the island is wild, hilly and unpopulated. The road runs up the east side to **Rhubodach** with its ferry to Colintraive on the mainland. It passes Kames Bay where there is a tower house, **Kames Castle**, which had its origins in the 14th century [NS064675]. And sitting below Kames Hill, is **Wester Kames**, a 17th-century keep which has been restored [NS062680]. A scramble up Kames Hill (267m) is rewarded by a striking view across to Arran, and a short distance further to the north-west is **Windy Hill** (278m), Bute's highest point.

The bare northern tip of Bute which divides the Kyles is aptly named **Buttock Point** with, opposite it, the delightful little anchorage of Caladh Bay (G. *caladh* – haven) tucked behind **Eilean Dubh** (G. – black isle). On this islet [NS006757], which has been owned by the family of Ingham-Clark for over a century, is the family graveyard. The Stephenson family of locomotive fame owned Caladh before the Ingham-Clarks. Loch Riddon to the north has one tiny islet, **Eilean Dearg**. Its castle was blown up by the English fleet in 1685. There is a sheltered anchorage between it and the shore.

At the head of the East Kyle are three more attractive islets, the **Burnt Islands**, one of which has the remains of a vitrified fort on it.

At the north-west extremity and south of Rubha Dubh there is a fort [NR995713], the ruins of little **Kilmichael Chapel** which was destroyed by the Norsemen [NR993706], and the chambered burial cairn of Glenvoidean in the hills above [NR997706]. Further south there are two more chambered cairns.

All these can be seen on a pleasant but long walk (about 20km total, there and back) along the quiet and narrow coastal road from **Ettrick Bay**. There are beautiful views down the Kyles, and mature woods of birch and oak below the shapely ridge of Barlia Hill (105m).

EILEAN DUBH AND CALADH BAY IN THE KYLES OF BUTE

Near Ettrick Bay there is a stone circle [NS044668] about 1km north-east of the shore and a Celtic cross near St Colmac [NS045672]. At the bridge over Glenmore burn concrete frames built for the army exercises on Inchmarnock (See No.1.7) represented practice landing craft for D-day.

A ruined chapel [NS035613] just north of St Ninian's Point was excavated in 1953. Standing stones can be seen in the north-west corner of St Ninian's Bay with another chapel 1km north of them [NS036626].

Tourism is the main industry but dairy farming and cheese-making are also of major economic importance. The agricultural part of the island is south of the 'rift valley' between Rothesay Bay and **Scalpsie Bay**. This valley is partly filled by **Loch Fad** (G. – long loch) with its wooded shores, and Loch Quien which has a crannog in it. Several duns and forts are near Scalpsie Bay and where the road winds round Tormore there are some of the finest viewpoints on the island.

A stone circle stands starkly on the narrow neck of land near Kingarth [NS092556] beyond the cemetery on the south side of the road. Across the golf links on the other side a row of standing stones looks like stunted exclamation marks [NS084553].

At the extreme south of the island, which culminates in Garroch Head, St Blane's Hill rises steeply 124m (403ft) above the shore. Here a path leads to **St Blane's Chapel**, a 12th-century Norman church [NS095534]. Its green garth is set in a wooded glade amid the well-preserved ruins of a 6th-century Celtic monastery established by St Catan but named after his nephew St Blane who died in 590. The circular stone building is known as the Devil's Cauldron. Remains of the monks' cells are still visible. On a promontory to the west and above a secluded cove with a beach of clean sharp sand is the vitrified Dunagoil fort dating from about 100BC [NS086531]. The whole of this area of tumbled landscape, bristling with antiquities and surrounded by the great expanse of the Firth of Clyde, is a rambler's delight.

On the east coast, approaching Rothesay and the rustic-English-style 19th century village of Kerrycroy from the south, the road passes **Mountstuart**, traditional home of the Bute family for over 250 years. This magnificent building, the first house in Scotland to be lit by electricity, is open to the public, full of surprises and well worth visiting. The wonderful subtropical sunken fernery at nearby Ascog Hall should also be seen. Ascog church and cottages [NS108633], were designed by David Hamilton in 1845.

* * *

Access: Car ferry: Wemyss Bay/ Rothesay (30 mins), 08000-66-5000. Train connections: Glasgow Central/ Wemyss Bay 08457-484950. Also car ferry: Colintraive/ Rhubodach (5 mins), 08000-66-5000. Tourist information, 08707-200619 or 0845-2255-121.

Anchorages:

1. Rothesay bay. Visitors' moorings (pay) off sailing club or anchor anywhere in bay, clear of moorings, holding generally good. W side of bay is best. Considerable swell with NE winds.
2. Rothesay outer harbour. Visitors' pontoon berths (pay, 07799-724225) VHF Ch.37.
3. Kames Bay, Port Bannatyne. Marina with visitors' berths 01700-503116. Or anchor N of marina in 5–7m. E gales can cause heavy swell.
4. Eilean Mór, Burnt Islands. Good anchorage E of S extremity of En Mór in 4m, sand. Avoid rocky patch to N.
5. Balnakailly Bay. Anchor S of Eilean Mór and clear of Wood Farm Rock in 3m to 4m.
6. Wreck Bay. Anchor between Beere Rock (off Bear Craig) and Buttock Point in 3–4m.
7. Blackfarland bay, about 1½M SW of Buttock Point, good anchorage about midway between entrance points in 4–7m. Protected from S

winds. The coast on both sides of entrance to bay is foul.
8. Ettrick Bay is seldom used as open SW and W Head dries out 2c and depths of less than 5.5m extend about 2c farther off-shore. Underwater obstructions reported.
9. St Ninian's Bay, well sheltered except SW. Head of bay dries out 3½c. There is a broad sandy beach. Avoid spit S of St Ninian's Point. Anchor in 6–8m.
10. Scalpsie Bay. Give Ardscalpsie Point a very wide berth. Anchor near centre of bay and well offshore. Sheltered for all points N.
11. Dunagoil Bay. Clear sandy bay. Exposed, but occasional anchorage in light E'lies. (*Useful for visit to Dunagoil fort and St Blane's*).
12. Glencallum Bay (Callum's Hole). NE entrance marked by white beacon. Avoid rocks slightly NE of centre of bay. Occasional anchorage at head or clear of SW shore in 2m to 6m. Exposed to S winds.
13. Kilchattan Bay. Moorings for hotel patrons or anchor NW of disused pier in 4m to 6m. Head of bay dries out about 4c. Exposed SE to NE.

Haswell-Smith

WESTER KAMES – A 17TH CENTURY KEEP

The Mull of Kintyre to the Firth of Lorn

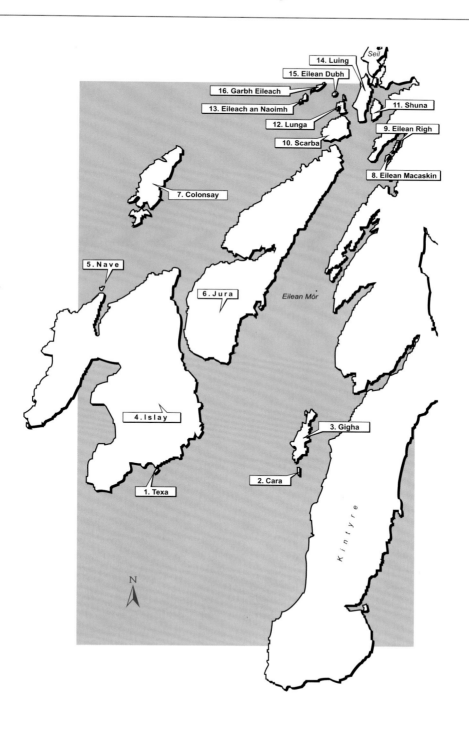

Section 2, Table 1: Arranged according to geographical position

No.	Name	Latitude	Longitude	Table 2* No.	Table 3** No.	Area in Acres		Area in Hectares
2.1	Texa	55° 37N	06° 08W	151	123	119		48
2.2	Cara	55° 38N	05° 45W	134	111	163		66
2.3	Gigha	55° 41N	05° 45W	35	69	3447		1395
2.4	Islay	55° 45N	06° 16W	5	7	153093		61956
2.5	Nave Island	55° 54N	06° 20W	168	147	100		40
2.6	Jura	55° 58N	05° 50W	8	5	90666		36692
2.7	Colonsay	56° 04N	06° 12W	21	45	10067	4074	
	Oronsay	56° 01N	06° 14W			1342	543	4617
2.8	Eilean Macaskin	56° 08N	05° 33W	137	98	158		64
2.9	Eilean Righ	56° 09N	05° 33W	116	113	213		86
2.10	Scarba	56° 11N	05° 43W	34	10	3642		1474
2.11	Shuna	56° 13N	05° 36W	55	77	1114		451
2.12	Lunga	56° 13N	05° 42W	74	71	628		254
2.13	Eileach an Naoimh	56° 13N	05° 48W	143	83	138		56
2.14	Luing	56° 14N	05° 38W	32	75	3534	1430	
	Torsa	56° 16N	05° 37W			279	113	1543
2.15	Eilean Dubh Mór	56° 14N	05° 43W	136	114	161		65
2.16	Garbh Eileach	56° 15N	05° 46W	97	60	351		142
2.A	Seil	56° 18N	05° 37W			3283		1329

*Table 2: The islands arranged in order of magnitude
**Table 3: The islands arranged in order of height

Introduction

The islands to the west and north of the Mull of Kintyre have a long history as they were possibly the very first Scottish islands to be colonised by man. (In fact they may have been settled before anyone dared to colonise the mainland.) In medieval times the area gained particular importance when the Lord of the Isles established the 'capital' of his island empire at Finlaggan on Islay.

The Sound of Jura is a natural highway up the west coast as it is protected from the worst fury of the Atlantic gales. After passing Gigha on the route north, the Kintyre peninsula is broken by a succession of sea-lochs which give some shelter even although they are aligned to the prevailing wind coming from the south-west. The first of these – West Loch Tarbert – has an islet at its head, **Eilean dà Ghallagain**, and likewise the second, Loch Caolisport, has **Eilean Fada**. The latter loch also has two islets nearer the entrance – **Liath Eilean** (G. – grey island) and **Eilean nam Muc** (G. – isle of the pigs).

It is the next loch north, Loch Sween, which has more of interest. Long and narrow, it runs past forbidding Castle Sween and into the wooded hills of Argyll. Here in the creeks among the trees beyond an inhabited islet called **Eilean Loain** (G. – pack-of-hounds isle), are some colourful patches of mossy rock known affectionately as the **Fairy Isles**.

Apart from **Taynish Island** halfway up Loch Sween, all the islets are gathered around the entrance to the loch and the large bridged and tidal island of **Danna**. They are known as the MacCormaig Isles and consist of **Carraig an Daimh** (G. – isle connected to the rock), **Liath Eilean**, **Eilean nan Leac** (G. – island of the grave), **Eilean Gamhna** (G. – island of the farrow cow), **Corr Eilean** (G. – tapering island) with a prehistoric cairn, and the most important island in the group, **Eilean Mór** (G. – big island) which is owned by the Scottish National Party.

Scots-born John Paul Jones sailed in these waters during the American War of Independence and visited Eilean Mór. In ancient times this holy island was the retreat of St Abban mac ui Charmaig, otherwise known as St Cormac, who founded a monastery at Keills and who died in 640. It is worth exploring. A tiny inlet on the north side still has parts of a submerged rock in it, despite army 'exercises' to blow it up in 1996, but is a well-sheltered anchorage in all but northerlies.

The medieval chapel, dedicated to St Cormac, is close to the anchorage. It is relatively well preserved although it was used as an ale-house and illicit still in the 1600s. The saint was buried nearby. To the south beyond the two standing crosses, one of which is a replica, there is a cave which was an anchorite's retreat. This deep, damp

EILEAN MOR

½ km
1/4 mile

grotto has two 8th-century crosses incised on its rock walls. Outside are the ruins of a second chapel proving the veneration in which this little island was held.

North again past **Eilean nan Coinean**, another rabbit island, **Eilean Fraoch**, another heather island, and **Eilean Dubh**, another dark island, brings one to **Carsaig Island** with a delightful anchorage behind it. On a visit there, while a young seal was showing off in front of its admiring elders, I was lucky to see a chough. This area is possibly the last Scottish home of the chough, an attractive member of the crow family – rather like a raven with a red beak. It is thought that there are only about one hundred breeding pairs left.

Eilean da Mhèinn sits in the centre of crowded Crinan Harbour surrounded by so many moorings that it is no longer possible to

anchor to the south or east of it, but Crinan is such a pleasant spot that one can understand its popularity.

2.1 Texa

(EI tech – house, ON -øy – island). Thought to have been the island referred to as Oidecha insula by Abbot Adomnan. An alternative possibility is a monastic seminary – (G. oideachd – instruction).

OS Maps: 1:50000 Sheet 60   1:25000 Sheet 352
Admiralty Chart: 1:75000 No.2168

Area: 48ha (119 acres)
Height: 48m (157ft)

Owner: In 1614 'Ilantasson' (Island Texa) was chartered by the crown to Sir John Campbell of Cawdor (see No.2.4). The Ramsays of Kildalton had ownership from 1855 to 1915, Philip Morel from 1915 to 1951, followed by Ian Hunter and Elizabeth Williamson of Laphroaig. The island was sold in 1983, resold in 1995 to Mr & Mrs Bolmeijer of Chevy Chase, USA, and up for sale again in 1999 for £120,000.

Population: 1625–29. Late 18th century–8. Still populated in early 19th century but uninhabited since then.

Geology: Mainly interstratified quartzose-mica-schist, grit, and some hornblende.

History: Adomnan refers to the 'island of Oidech' as a stopping place for St Cainnech on his journey from Iona to Ireland in the 6th century and most scholars think that this refers to Texa. Cainnech, or Kenneth, was said to have left his pastoral staff on Iona. Columba found it, blessed it, and cast it into the sea and Kenneth later discovered it washed up on the shore of Texa.

It is assumed that Texa's present chapel, which may be on the site of an earlier one, was built in the late 14th century by Reginald, son of John of Islay. It was dedicated to St Mary the Virgin and generously endowed and the well, Tobar Moireig, was similarly dedicated.

The earliest sculptured stone portrait of a member of the house of Somerled was part of the shaft of a 14th-century cross which stood east of the chapel. It was removed in the early 1900s for safe keeping and can be seen in the National Museum of Scotland in Edinburgh. It is of Ragnald, eldest son of John the Good and progenitor of the MacDonalds of Clanranald. The inscription reads, 'This is the cross of Reginald, son of John, of Islay'. It was Ragnald's younger brother, Donald, who succeeded his father as Lord of the Isles. Ragnald inherited some of the Western Isles and also Castle Tioram beside Loch Moidart and it was there that he died. About the same time (1385) Fordun mentioned 'the monks' chapel' on 'Helan ttexa'. Early 16th-century records show that the church was generously endowed with the lands of Texa, Cragabus and 'two Kilbrides'.

In 1608, Andrew Knox, Bishop of the Isles, wrote from 'Ilintexa' to King James VI asking to be retired – '. . .seeing my ould aige dayle crepis on. . . .'

Strangely, a report dated 1614–15 lists only six active churches in the parishes of Islay and there is no mention of Texa. In 1625 Father Cornelius Ward, a Franciscan missionary, also fails to mention the church when he landed on Texa and found that most of the inhabitants were Catholic. He converted the six who were not.

A century and a half later the *Statistical Account 1791–99* records that the inhabitants were 'formerly wont to bury those who were of the popish religion' in the chapel, '. . .but the whole inhabitants now belong to the Established Church, so that there are none now buried. . .'. But, even so, there is a burial enclosure beside the chapel which appears to date from the 19th century.

Wildlife: In early summer the rough ground is so covered with bluebells that it is like a mist collecting in the hollows. Groups of the eighty or so feral goats watch visitors warily and woodmice and otters are other resident mammals.

* * *

TEXA is a wee rocky hump of an island with many caves, good pasturage and a small white concrete beacon at the highest point, Ceann Garbh (48m) (G. – rough headland). It is part of the Islay parish of Kildalton. The traditional monastic islands sited round Islay are thought to have been – Texa to the south, **Nave** with **Eilean Beag** to the north (See No. 2.5) and **Orsay** to the west. All three are tiny in size, Texa being the largest, but they all have religious relics.

On the slope overlooking **Caolas an Eilean** (G. – the island channel, or kyle) and some distance beyond the jetty there is a renovated cottage. On terraced ground about 100m north-

WILD GOATS BY THE RUINED CHAPEL

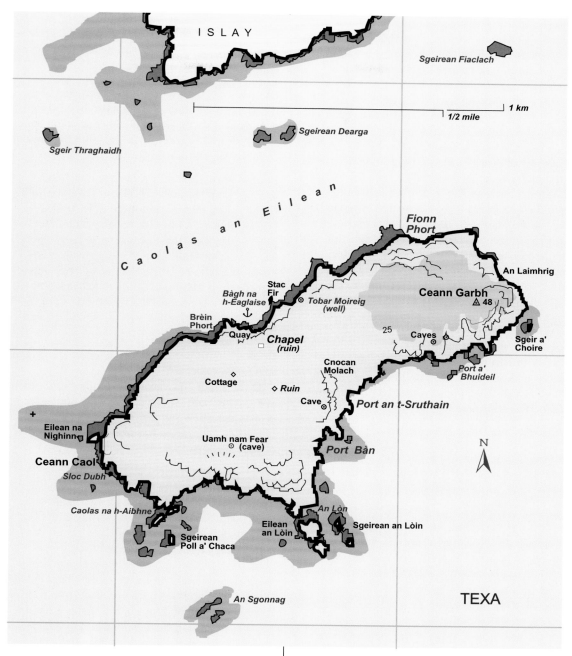

east are the walls of an ancient chapel, built
of rubble but with ashlar sandstone trimmings
[NR391438]. There is evidence that this formed
the centre of an area of continuous agricultural
settlement. There is also a burial ground with the
footings of at least five buildings and an enclosure
to the south and another structure to the north.
None of these buildings is thought to be of an
early date but they have not been examined in
detail. Detailed investigation is needed to establish
whether or not a monastery or seminary ever
existed but at least this tiny island could support
a population for it is fortunate in having its own
water supply, **Tobar Moireig** (G. – Mary's well).

The early Celtic church had no parochial
organisation. Any small Christian community
could build a chapel for the purpose of communal
worship. There would be a lay custodian, but
no resident priest, although occasionally one
might attend from a neighbouring monastery.

It is possible that this was no more than just a primitive 'clachan' church, although it seems unlikely that Texa would support a large enough lay community of farmers and fishermen to undertake such a building.

There are some minor landing places – An Laimhrig (G. – the landing place) in the east, and Port an t-Sruthain (G. – tidal port) and Port Ban (G. – fair port) in the south-east bay. Texa also has a number of caves including Uamh nam Fear (G. – the men's cave).

Across Caolas an Eilean at the entrance to Port Ellen on Islay is tiny **Eilean nan Caorach** (G. – sheep island). In the 12th century Somerled's fleet anchored in nearby Lagavulin Bay beside Dunyvaig Castle. Loch an t-Sàilein provides a better anchorage beyond Lagavulin Bay. It is sheltered by tidal **Eilean Imersay** and the rocks of **Iseanach Mór** while, standing well out to sea like a sentinel, is **Iomallach**. Further up the coast are the lovely Ardmore Islands. They are treeless **Eilean Craobhach** (G. – tree-covered island), **Eilean a' Chuirn** (G. – heap-of-stones island) with a light beacon on it, **Eilean Bhride** (G. – Bridget's isle), and the long reef of **Eilean Mhic Mhaolmhoire**.

* * *

Access: No regular access but Islay Sea Safari at Port Ellen (01496-840510) may be able to help

Anchorages:
Note: Approach with caution, preferably 1½c clear of E end of island, and then keep nearer to S side of the Kyle. Note submerged rock about 3c WNW of En na Nighinn off W extremity of island. All anchorages are exposed.
1. Fionn Phort on the N face of the NE extremity in 5m.
2. Bàgh na h-Eaglaise (G. – Church Bay). Off the quay and chapel ruins near the centre of the N coast in 5–6m, sand. This is the traditional anchorage.
3. Port an t-Sruthain, in centre of open bay on SE coast. There are a number of off-shore rocks and a large 7c reef extending S from the SW extremity. Best avoided.

2.2 Cara

Various possible derivations. (G. carr ON -øy – island of the projecting rock or rock ledge) or (G. cor ON -øy – island of the rounded hill) or (ON Kari-øy – Kari's island), Kari was a Norse hero. A (B. caer – fort) derivation is improbable.

OS Maps: 1:50000 Sheet 62   1:25000 Sheet 357
Admiralty Chart: 1:25000 No.2475

Area: 66ha (163 acres)
Height: 56m (184 ft)

Owner: For centuries Cara has been part of the Macdonald estate of Largie on the Kintyre peninsula. The Macdonalds of Largie claim direct descent from the Lord of the Isles and the present owner is Mr Macdonald Lockhart of Kintyre.

Population: Alexander Macdonald of Largie married Jane McNeill in 1798 on Cara according to the parish register and there were several families living on the island at that time. 1881–4. 1891–3. 1931–3. Last person to be born on the island was Mrs Charlotte McAlister who was living on Gigha in 1991. Last farmed by Angus McGuigan in 1932 and uninhabited since the 1940s but a Londoner was renovating Cara House in 1991, possibly with a view to living on the island.

Geology: Cara is a continuation of the geology of Gigha (No.2.3).

At the south end, below the Mull of Cara, there are two interconnecting caves each about 12m deep which show signs of human – and goat – habitation. The strata has also created a number of rock shelters under overhangs, such as at Poll an Aba.

History: As King Haakon's huge fleet was anchored in Gigalum Sound for two or three weeks in 1263 it would be surprising if the Norsemen had not landed on Cara Island. But no definite evidence has been found.

In 1615 Sir James Macdonald escaped from a Crown prison and enlisted many islanders to help him free his lands from Campbell (Argyll) control. Hector MacNeill of Taynish and Gigha, Chief of the Southern Clan Neill, was thirled to Argyll and the rebels were keen to capture him. The rebels set up their base on Cara as this belonged to their ally, Macdonald of Largie, whilst their army of about 1000 men camped on the Kintyre coast opposite Gigha. MacNeill sent a raiding party to Cara but the Largie servants warned the rebels by beacon and they thwarted the attack. They were however generally undisciplined and Argyll's forces soon had them all in retreat. An uncorroborated story says that the MacNeill and Campbell lords then had a dinner in the Cara mansion-house and finished it by hanging eight captured rebels in front of the house. The corpses were later buried in the chapel.

These were strange times, for only three years later, in 1618, it was Argyll who was disgraced 'for open defection from the true religion' and 'suspicious dealings' with Sir James Macdonald. He was proclaimed a traitor whereas Sir James Macdonald was pardoned and given a pension.

Flora Macdonald was related to the Macdonalds of Largie and some time after the events of 1745 she stayed at Largie for a year before emigrating to Carolina. Her brother was also a guest at Largie but he was mortally wounded in a shooting accident on Cara.

Wildlife: Rabbits (particularly noted for their numbers by Dean Monro), otters, goats, nesting seabirds and peregrine falcons are Cara's specialities. In the days of falconry the Macdonalds would collect chicks from the cliff nests – 'but never more than one chick from a nest having two or more' according to an octogenarian whose grandfather used to collect them. Shags, guillemots and terns with a few

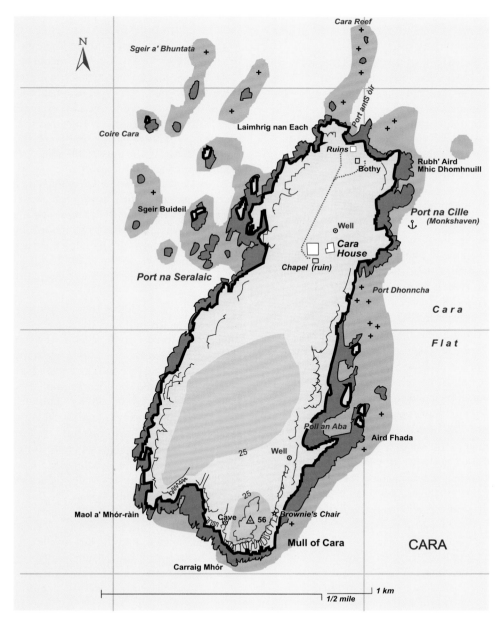

Hesuell Smith

CARA HOUSE – LONELY AND CONSPICUOUS

razorbills, and herring, common and great black-backed gulls breed on the coasts. Elsewhere are nests of ringed plovers, rock and meadow pipits, mute swans and buzzards.

The herd of wild goats is quite large and a considerable number of goat skeletons are scattered about, but the goats themselves can be difficult to see when the bracken is high.

There are many wildflowers but no trees.

Poll an Aba 'is always good for a sea trout near the white shore' says a local man.

* * *

The peaty ground below the house on **CARA** in the month of June is a sea of wildflowers. The marshy nature of the soil here keeps the bracken at bay. Cara House itself is a dour two-storey stone building with a slated roof standing lonely and conspicuous, staring across the Sound towards Kintyre. It was built about 1733 as a residence for the tacksman. There is a well-preserved corn-drying kiln close by.

Behind the house is the ruined chapel which could easily be mistaken at first for a sheep pen [NR640443]. It is about 9m long by 5m broad. It originally had a lancet-shaped window with splayed ingoes near the east end of each side wall as well as the west gable, and the door on the north side was Gothic-arched. It is said that the chapel was used for burials and that a priest is buried in the north-east corner where there is a broken greenish stone slab which was originally part of the pulpit. There is no record of a burial ground. The chapel fell into disuse in the late 18th century and was used for a time as a kitchen for the house.

According to a record dated 14 June 1456 it was called 'the chapel of St Finla in the island of Kara beside the Monkshaven'. St Finlay (G. *Fionnlugh* – fair hero) was a contemporary of

St Columba and evidently the patron saint of the House of Islay. It appears that the chapel was built about this time by the Macdonalds although in the Latin 'Scotia Sacra' there is the entry – 'Insula Carray, where there is a shrine of the Most Holy Trinity. It is doubtful who first founded it.' Dean Monro said the chapel belonged to Icolmkill (Iona) with the island being used as a monks' retreat. This may be corroborated by there being a pleasant round pool on the south-east shore called Poll an Aba (G. – the pool of the abbot) and an anchorage called Monkshaven.

It was at Poll an Aba in later times that the Macdonalds rolled their fishing boats up the beach during the winter months as there was no shelter for them over on Kintyre. The men would stay in huts below the brow of the hill while carrying out maintenance work on the boats. The Brownie's Well close by provided fresh water and it has never run dry.

East of the main house there is another well which serves the house. A track leads from the chapel ruin to Port an Stòir (G. – stormy port) at the north extremity where there are some ruined enclosures. About two hundred years ago the track also extended southwards to a large building of unknown purpose according to an old map.

In 1940 during the Second World War, Aska, a newly-built P & O ship was hit by a German bomb which went straight down its funnel. The blazing hulk drifted for two days before coming to rest in the bay on the west side of Cara where she burned for a further six weeks.

At the south-west corner, Maol à Mhór-ràin, a cleft in the rock conceals part of a lifeboat and an embedded anchor, and the bay on the south side seems to attract all the flotsam and jetsam in the area. This was the area that was always searched first for the bodies of sailors drowned in the vicinity.

In the autumn of 1756 there was, according to the *Statistical Account of Scotland – 1791–99*, a great storm in this area. Lightning struck the southern headland called the Mull of Cara breaking off large pieces of rock, 'which has a lot of iron ore in it', and the shock was felt in all the islanders' houses. The sea rose so high on the west side that the waves swept right across the island. All the houses – which may have been of turf construction – were severely damaged and stacks of corn were ruined. The people 'were obliged to take shelter in the only slated house on the island, which fortunately suffered no damage.' Other reports claim that it was not lightning but a meteorite which struck just below the southern cliff on the Mull of Cara. This seems more probable. If the bulk of the meteorite hit the sea to the south-west, this could account for the freak wave. The broken cliff face can still be seen.

The Brownie's Chair is a huge stone 'armchair', with only one arm, set on a ledge above the sea on the east side of the highest point – the Mull of Cara [NR639434].

The Brownie of Cara is said to be the ghost of a Macdonald murdered by a Campbell. Tradition says that he inhabits an attic room in Cara House, and that the laird and minister have always raised their hats to him when they step ashore on Cara, and so should everyone else. The Macdonald's gallery in the church at Ardminish on Gigha built in 1780 was known as 'the Broonie's gallery'. The *Observer* reported in 1909 that Morton Macdonald of Largie claimed that the Brownie was often seen, or heard, moving about in his room, – 'A neat little man, dressed in brown, with a pointed beard.'

The Brownie has a characteristically impish sense of humour. One story tells how the Laird of Largie sent two of his men over to fetch a cask of wine from the big cellar in Cara House. Whilst they were arranging a gangplank to roll the cask up from the cellar they were joking about the Brownie. They then found they were unable to move the barrel so, in the end, they offered a sincere apology for the remarks they had made. Suddenly the barrel ran up the plank by itself, bounced and rolled across the ground to the sea and came to a stop beside their boat.

There are many stories telling how the Brownie would wash the dishes and tidy up the kitchen to help the housewife and maids – yet couldn't resist an occasional practical joke.

It was essential that the main house had a good view of the mainland because Cara was the centre of smuggling activity for Gigha, Jura and Islay. In 1786 the *Prince of Wales* revenue cutter dug up eighteen casks of foreign spirits at Poll an Aba. No wonder that twinkling lights were often to be seen on dark nights in the window of the Brownie's room!

* * *

Access: Boat trips may be arranged with a local fisherman through the hotel or store at Ardminish on Gigha (but not for anyone with Campbell blood in their veins!).

Anchorages: There are no permanent anchorages but Gigalum Sound is fairly close and sheltered from the E by Gigalum Island (see Gigha No.2.3).
1. Port na Cille or Monkshaven on E coast. Temp. anchorage. in 9m sand, with the house bearing approximately 240deg. Exposed NNE to SSW.
2. Port an Stòir at the N extremity. Used as a landing place but local knowledge essential.

2.3 Gigha

[gee-ë:] (ON Gud-øy – God's island or the good island) This is the normally accepted derivation but possible alternatives are (ON gja-øy – island of creeks or geos) or (ON – Gydha's isle). Gydha was a woman's name.

O S Maps: 1:50000 Sheet 62   1:25000 Sheet 357
Admiralty Charts: 1:75000 No. 2168 or 1:25000 No. 2475

A GABLE OF OLD KILCHATTAN

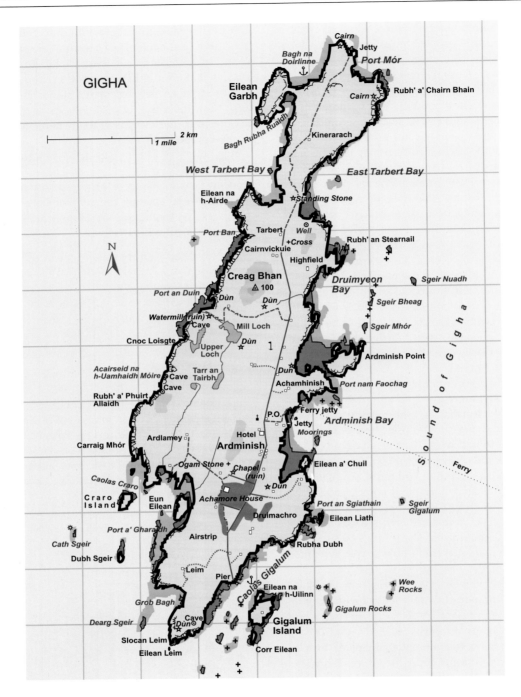

GIGHA

Area: 1,395ha (3447 acres)
Height: 100m (328ft)

Owner: Bought from David W Landale by English property developer Malcolm Potier's company, Tanap Investments, for £5.4m in 1989. This purchase included all Gigha's main businesses and a fish farm. In 1992 it was attached for debts by Interallianz Bank of Zürich and then sold to Holt Leisure Group (owners of Kip and Craobh Marinas) for a reported £2.3m. As is always the case, however, these continual changes of ownership were most unsettling for the islanders so in 2001, when Mr Holt chose to put the island – but not the fish farm – back on the market, he accepted the islanders' bid of £4,000,250 (reported to be £1 million less than the best offer). Unlike the island of Eigg (No.4.2) where there was an anonymous donation of £1 million towards the cost, the islanders' bid broke new ground by being almost entirely paid by Scottish taxpayers (£500,000 from Highlands and Islands Enterprise) and the National Lottery (£3,500,000 from the Lottery-based Scottish Land Fund subject to £1 million being repaid within two years). One million pounds was repaid on time partly financed by the sale of Achamore House in 2003 for a reported £640,000 to Mr Don Dennis, an American. Present indications are that the island's rather idealistic form of collective ownership is succeeding well, the islanders are prospering and the outlook is encouraging.

ACHAMORE HOUSE

Population: Including Cara: 1755–514. 1792–614. 1801–556. 1841–550. Gigha only: 1881–378. 1891–398. 1911–326. 1931–240. 1951–190. 1961–163. 1981–153. 1991–143. 2001–110. 2011–163.

Geology: Some of the best examples of glaciated rock in Scotland are on Creag Bhan (G. – white or sacred rock). The summit appears to have escaped being covered with ice during the Ice Age. The island has a long spinal ridge and hummocky hills of epidiorite with basalt intrusions. In the north and west the rock is clean and less riven – like the Cuillin – and there are many caves along the coast, some at sea level, some at old raised beaches. Sloc an Leim (G. – squirting pit) is a long subterranean passage through which the sea rushes violently during westerly gales and jets up to a great height. The south and east coast are of quartzite and grit and this stratum continues through Gigalum and Cara.

History: Occupancy stretches back five thousand years as proven by the archaeological remains. Gigha's key position on the sea route along the Kintyre peninsula had a profound influence on its history.

One of the earliest recorded visits was in the autumn of 1263 when King Haakon's fleet of more than one hundred ships anchored in Gigalum Sound on the way to the Battle of Largs and were delayed there for some time by bad weather. On board the King's longship was Ewin, Lord of the Isles (called King John in the Haakon Saga). He had come on board at Oban to ask to be excused taking up arms against the Scots' King Alexander. Haakon eventually agreed and Ewin returned to the north. While on the island Haakon received the allegiance of Murdoch and Angus of Kintyre – the Lairds of Gigha, a peace mission from the Abbot of Saddell, and a request from the Irish for his assistance against the English. He sent a cutter to Ireland to investigate.

The King's return to Gigalum Sound after his defeat was not so triumphant. He still considered assisting the Irish but his men wanted to return home to Norway without further delay.

In 1309 the 'island of Gug' was made over by Bruce to the Earl of Mar. In 1335 Edward Balliol formally granted Gigha to John, Lord of the Isles and this grant was 'confirmed' by Edward III when he occupied Scotland in 1336. When the Kings of Scotland had regained their position in 1343 David II also confirmed the grant of the 'island of Githey' to John, Lord of the Isles and Chief of the Macdonalds. In 1449 Alexander, Earl of Ross and Lord of the Isles died having granted part of the island to Torquil MacNeill of Taynish and 'two merklands' to the Monks of Paisley. In 1493 the whole island came into the hands of the MacNeills of Taynish, but a pirate, Allan McLean (Allan-na-Sop), plundered Gigha in 1530 and slew Neil MacNeill of Taynish and many of the inhabitants. However, James V conferred the title on MacNeill's son, also called Neil, and elevated Gigha to a Barony. In 1542 the title deeds of the Thaindom of Gigha were 'lost' when eleven Gigha gentlemen were slain by unknown assailants. Dean Munro wrote in 1549 that 'the auld thane of Gigay should be Laird of the same, call it MacNeill of Gigay and now it is possessed by Clan Ranald' (i.e. the Macdonalds). Sure enough, by 1554 the deeds had reappeared in Macdonald hands. The following year Neil MacNeill was restored as Lord of Gigha by Mary, Queen of Scots, but he then sold the island to the Macdonalds of Islay. They in turn sold Gigha to Sir John Campbell of Calder but McNeill of Taynish repurchased most of it in 1590 for 3000 merks (£170 sterling).

William of Orange landed on Gigha in 1689 and had the support of MacNeill of Gigha. MacNeill also remained loyal during the 1745 uprising but this is not altogether surprising as the Duke of Argyll was his overlord.

About 1779 MacNeill of Taynish sold out to John MacNeil of Colonsay, probably a relation, who became the first resident owner. The remaining part of Gigha was owned by another member of the MacNeill family of Taynish.

In 1865 Captain William Scarlett of Thrybergh in Yorkshire, the third Lord Abinger, bought Gigha for £49,000 and built a mansion at Achamore. This was the first time that the entire island had been under single ownership and it remained in the Scarlett family until 1919 when it was bought by Major John Allen. He sold it to R J A Hamer in 1937 and his son-in-law Somerset de Chair sold it to Sir James Horlick in 1944. David W Landale purchased it from the Horlick estate in 1973.

Wildlife: Gigha has an abundance of wildflowers. In late spring the Achamore woods are a sea of bluebells and the rocks and ridges are crowded with dwarf whin scented like honey and competing with the honey-scented flowers of the Grass of Parnassus. Apart from the main woodland at Achamore, Gigha has more trees than many small Scottish islands, with scrub willow, prostrate juniper, sycamore, thorn, alder, birch and hazel.

When the Scarletts were the proprietors from 1870 to 1919 they regularly stocked the Mill and Upper Lochs with trout – but these are now very scarce. Deer, weasels, stoats, moles and foxes apparently never reached the island but there are many rabbits. There were hares but they became extinct in the 19th century, probably due to the great black-backed gulls.

Over 70 species of bird have been recorded on Gigha, including great northern and black-throated divers, mute and whooper swans, snipe, eider, fulmar, and shelduck by Eun Eilean in Craro Bay on the west coast. There is a gullery on Eilean Garbh in the north-west with eider and guillemot nesting on the western ledges. Hen harrier nest in the central moorland.

*   *   *

GIGHA is a fertile and hospitable island with good arable land on 25% of its surface area and a mild climate. In fact the rich soil produced such beautiful potatoes that the Irish used to buy them to place on top of their own potatoes on the way to market. This wonderful island supports a stable community and a relaxed way of life. Electricity is supplied by three second-hand wind turbines with the surplus sold to the Grid.

When William James Yorke Scarlett, owner in the 1890s, was away on the mainland and his servants were taking time off for a round of golf on the island's course, a fire unfortunately burned down most of the Mansion House. It was eventually rebuilt and renamed **Achamore House** [NR642479].

Sir James Horlick (of the well-known beverage) purchased Gigha in 1944 and is remembered by the islanders as a very fine and generous benefactor who did a lot to make the island viable and stop depopulation. He modernised the farms, built-up dairy production to 250,000 gallons of milk a year and created the Achamore Creamery. He converted some deciduous woodland around Achamore House into one of the finest gardens on the west coast of Scotland planted with many rare species which he had collected for his garden near Ascot. Apart from the varied deciduous trees there are rhododendron (including the famous Horlick hybrids), azalea, laburnum, *Primula candelabra*, and various sub-tropical plants such as palm lilies (*Cordyline australis*), palm-tree – shaped New Zealand cabbage trees and flame-trees (*Embothrium longifolium*). Sir James used to drive through his gardens in a dragon-caparisoned motorised tricycle. He died at Achamore House in 1972.

The beautiful gardens of Achamore (the plants were gifted to the National Trust in 1962), are open to the public from April to September inclusive. May is probably the best month to see them.

In the scattered little village of Ardminish there is an attractive hotel (which won an architectural award), about eighteen new houses built by the Island Trust – 'for people with special needs' – and the award-winning Boathouse Café Bar. The well-known local resident, Mr Seumas McSporran, who, with his wife, ran the island's only general store and post office, was also the postman,

Registrar of Births, Marriages and Deaths, coastguard, fireman, policeman, and holder of numerous other official duties before enjoying a well-earned partial retirement.

The parish church, whose congregation includes all denominations, has several good stained-glass windows, one dedicated to Kenneth MacLeod who was born in 1872 on Eigg (No.4.2). He composed, among many other songs, the 'Road to the Isles'.

The red and yellow sandstone ruins of the 13th-century **Kilchattan** (St Catan's Chapel) are south of Ardminish [NR643481]. St Catan was an Irish missionary of the 6th century who settled in Bute but travelled widely. There are a number of interesting carved grave-slabs in the churchyard dating back to the 14th century. The original octagonal stone font has been moved into the Parish Church at Ardminish for safe-keeping. Opposite the lower end of the graveyard and south of the road is St Catan's Well.

The ogam stone above the church ruins is the only example of its kind in the west of Scotland. Ogam is an ancient Celtic writing which is still largely undeciphered. There are also some unusual standing stones and 'cup-marked' stones at different parts of the island.

The beaches at Ardminish and in the many attractive coastal bays and inlets are of fine white sand. The pier in the south-east corner at Caolas Gigalum was the only ferry pier until the ro-ro ferry access was constructed at Ardminish in the 1980s. Gigalum Island, which gives its name to the kyle, is tiny but has a modern house in the dead centre. The two largest lochs, **Mill Loch** and the **Upper Loch**, are very ancient artificial lochs and the small islands in the latter may be crannogs.

Gigha is rich in folklore. At the north end of the island is Raven's Rock where it is believed that Noah's raven (not a dove) landed after the Flood. Just south of East Tarbert Bay, where a Viking burial is said to have taken place, is Tobar a' Bheathaig (G. – Beathag's well). If a sailor wants a fair wind he must throw the well-water in the required direction and leave some payment by the well. The very narrow loch west of and above North Ardminish, Tarr an Tairbh (G. – the tail of the bull), hides a shy bull-like monster reputedly seen by the islanders.

There are a number of interesting caves around the coastline. **Uamh Mhor** (G. – big cave)

[NR633495] is on the coast to the west of Tarr an Tairbh and difficult to approach from the land. It was probably occupied in prehistoric times and was also a favourite hide for smugglers. It has the same well-worn legend as other Hebridean islands; that a dog disappeared down it and reappeared, not as usual on the other side of the island, but on the mainland. This cave has never been fully explored. South of it is a large bay, full of rocks, skerries, and two islets, **Craro Island** in the centre which now belongs to Mr Don Dennis – the new owner of Achamore House, and tidal **Eun Eilean** (G. – bird island). Mr Dennis runs several small businesses producing flower essences, boat tours and bed and breakfast at Achamore House, all of which have provided useful employment.

In 1991 the Russian factory ship *Kartli* was hit by a freak wave off Islay. Her crew was rescued but the wreck drifted on to the rocks off the coast of Gigha. Although the islanders had to live with the smell of rotting fish for several months after the disaster, with their customary generosity they collected a substantial sum to assist the injured captain.

* * *

Access: Every day frequent ro-ro ferry from Tayinloan, Kintyre (20 mins), 0990-650000 or 08000-66-5000. Caravans not permitted. Cycles can be hired from the store near the ferry pier and also from the hotel. Tourist info. 08707-200600

Anchorages:

1. Gigalum Sound (Caolas Gigalum). Approach is easy provided all visible rocks are identified and given a reasonable berth but best avoid S approach in fresh S'lies. The shore is foul. Anchor off the pier, sand.

2. Ardminish Bay. The most popular anchorage. Extensive reefs on both sides of the bay. Kiln rock, 1c off the jetty covers. 23 visitors' moorings available (pay, 01583-505390) with pontoon and jetty or anchor clear of the moorings, sand. Can be unpleasant in E'lies.

3. Drumyeon Bay. Has been much obstructed by a fish farm. Sand and weed.

4. East Tarbert Bay. Occasional anchorage avoiding rocks and shellfish floats in middle of the bay.

5. Port Mor. Pleasant occasional anchorage if breeze is southerly and weather settled.

6. Eilean Garbh. Good anchorage N or S of the sand spit as close as depth permits, sand. Exposed N or SW respectively.

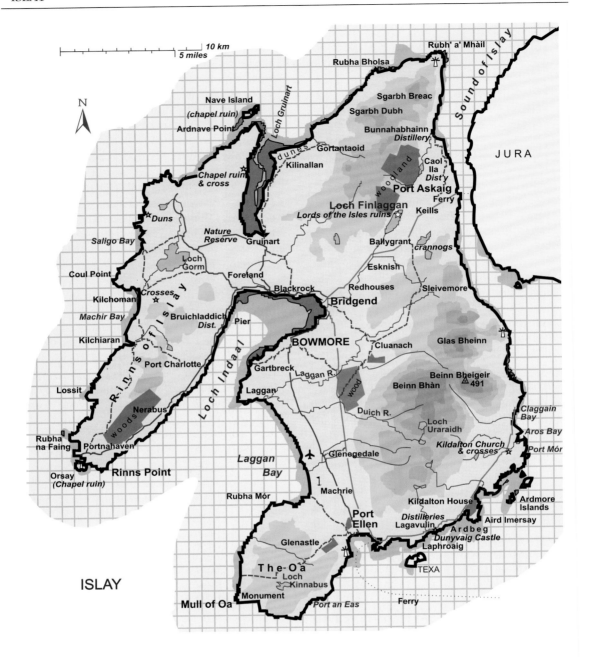

10 km
5 miles

N

Nave Island
(chapel ruin)
Ardnave Point

Chapel ruin
& cross

dunes

Loch Gruinart

Gortantaoid

Kilinallan

Rubha Bholsa

Rubh' a' Mhàil

Sgarbh Breac

Sgarbh Dubh

Bunnahabhainn
Distillery

woodland

Caol
Ila
Dist'y

JURA

Sound of Islay

Port Askaig

Ferry

Keills

woodland

Loch Finlaggan
Lords of the Isles ruins

Duns

Saligo Bay

Nature
Reserve

Gruinart

Loch
Gorm

Coul Point

Foreland

Blackrock

Ballygrant

crannogs

Esknish

Redhouses

Sleivemore

Kilchoman

Crosses

Bridgend

Machir Bay

Bruichladdich
Dist.

Pier

Kilchiaran

Port Charlotte

Rinns of Islay

Loch Indaal

BOWMORE

Gartbreck

Laggan R.

Cluanach

wood

Glas Bheinn

Beinn Bheigeir
△ 491

Lossit

Nerabus

woods

Laggan

Beinn Bhàn

Duich R.

Claggain
Bay

Aros Bay

Rubha
na Faing

Portnahaven

Loch
Uraraidh

Kildalton Church
& crosses

Port Mór

Orsay
(Chapel ruin)

Rinns Point

Laggan
Bay

Glenegedale

Machrie

Kildalton House

Ardmore
Islands

Rubha Mór

Distilleries
Lagavulin

Aird Imersay

Port
Ellen

Ardbeg
Dunyvaig Castle
Laphroaig

Glenastle

TEXA

ISLAY

The Oa

Loch
Kinnabus

Mull of Oa

Monument

Port an Eas

Ferry

N side was favourite picnic stop for *RY Britannia*.

7. West Tarbert Bay. Approach is clear. Exposed W. Reasonable in E'lies but swell likely. Anchor in 4–8m, sand and shingle.

8. Craro Bay. Temp. anchorage in settled weather, best approached from due W. Anchor about 2½c E of the centre of Craro Island in 8m.

2.4 Islay

*[**Y**-lĕ] Possibly, (ON Yula-øy or Jle-øy – Yula's isle). Yula was a Norse princess who is reputed to be buried under a standing stone on the east side of Port Ellen.*

OS Maps: 1:50000 Sheet 60 1:25000 Sheets 352 and 353
Admiralty Charts: 1:75000 No.2168 Sound of Islay
1:25000 No.2481 Port Ellen 1:15000 No.2474

Area: 61956ha (153,093 acres)
Height: 491m (1610 ft)

Owner: Multiple ownership. Robert Fleming & Trusts, the Duke of Argyll and Lord Margadale have the largest holdings but the RSPB reserves take up a substantial area including the Oa (purchased 2003).

Population: 1755–5344. 1792–9500. 1841–15772. 1881–7559. 1891–7375. 1931–4970. 1961–3860. 1981–3792. 1991–3538. 2001–3457. 2011–3228.

Geology: Complex. In 1798 it was recorded that 'Ila has mines of lead mixed with copper: . . . iron called Bog Ore, veins of emery, and some of quicksilver'. Lead and silver were being mined in the 19th century near Port Askaig, with copper and manganese also present.

The northern part of the Rinns is calcareous Torridonian sandstone with good loamy agricultural soil, whilst the southern part is Archaean gneiss with patches of hornblende; rough, rocky and treeless. The far north of the island is Cambrian quartzite with Dalradian limestone belts running through it. A strip of mica schist with limestone cuts right across the island from Port Askaig to the Mull of Oa. South-east of this is a continuation of the geology of Jura with a similar landscape, and in the extreme south-east coast between Port Ellen and Ardtalla there is mica schist and hornblende creating a beautifully shattered coastline backed by woodland and scrub.

History: The island was formerly the 'capital' of the Western Isles. Written records go back further in time for Islay than for any other Hebridean isle. The Irish settled here in the 3rd century and for some three hundred years the island was part of the Scots kingdom of Dalriada. The Norse were in charge from about 850 to 1150, then Somerled, King of Argyll, defeated them in a sea-battle off Islay, took over the southern Hebrides, made the island his home and his headquarters and founded the immensely powerful Clan Donald. His main Macdonald stronghold, Dunyvaig Castle, overlooks Lagavulin Bay where his war-galleys would lie at anchor.

Islay, as the seat of government of the Lord of the Isles, thus became an autonomous principality powerful enough by the 14th century to have made its own treaties with England, France and Ireland, sometimes against the Scottish interest. New chiefs were proclaimed at the administrative headquarters at Loch Finlaggan near Port Askaig. This continued until 1493 when King James IV stripped John of the Isles of his titles and forced him to spend the rest of his days as a pensioner at the Stewart court.

In 1598 there was a vicious clan battle commemorated by a stone at the road junction south-west of the head of Loch Gruinart. James VI had granted land in Islay to the quarrelsome Sir Lachlan MacLean of Duart on Mull. The local Macdonalds understandably would not accept this so about four hundred MacLeans, with their chief, invaded the island. Nearly all of them, including Sir Lachlan, were slain. About thirty took sanctuary in the ancient church of Kilnave (G. – church of the saints) by Loch Gruinart but the Macdonalds set fire to the church and they were all burned to death.

In 1614 the Scots King granted Islay to Sir John Campbell of Cawdor but he had to fight for more than four years to gain possession from the Macdonalds. Sir John then gave Islay to his son as a wedding present, but his son was declared insane in 1639, and his grandson died young. All this strife and unrest devastated the island and impoverished the islanders. It was not until the early 18th century that the island was bought by

BOWMORE PARISH CHURCH

a Daniel Campbell and his family who did a great deal to restore it to its former glory and make it a 'leader and model of the other isles'. This testimonial was actually given by a Macdonald and with widespread agreement.

By 1847 the owner's philanthropy had bankrupted him. His son, John Francis Campbell (1822–85), spent his life recording Gaelic traditions, poetry and folklore for posterity and there is a monument to him overlooking the house at Bridgend on the island that he never inherited.

Wildlife: Otters can often be seen on the shores of Loch Gruinart. There are red deer in the south-east and wild goats in the Oa.

Islay has the richest birdlife in the Hebrides with over 180 recorded species, and over 100 breeding on the island including the rare and elusive chough. Although it is particularly noted for its geese – about 20,000 barnacle geese and 6000 Greenland white-fronted geese have been recorded – there is much more of interest. Some sites noted by the RSPB are:

Loch Gruinart: Geese, waders, and black and red grouse. Occasionally golden eagle, peregrine, hen harrier and merlin can be seen hunting.

Ardnave Loch: Oct–May. Mute swan, wigeon, teal, mallard, pochard and tufted duck.

Bowmore: Many sea-fowl including scaup, eider, common scoter and Slavonian grebe can be seen from the pier. Glaucous and Iceland gulls frequent the rubbish tip. Dabbling duck and waders are in the shoreline shallows.

Head of Loch Indaal. Shoveller in the small saltmarsh lagoons. Marvellous spectacle of barnacle geese at dusk coming in to roost. Pintail in the river channel.

Bruichladdich Pier. Rocks at distillery for purple sandpiper in winter and many divers and sea-duck.

Frenchman's Rocks. Sooty shearwater, gannet, storm petrel, Leach's petrel sometimes, arctic and great skua, kittiwake galore.

Saligo Bay-Sanaigmore coast: Sea-birds, buzzard, golden eagle, merlin, kestrel, hen harrier, peregrine, red grouse, stonechat, chough, raven, twite. Also whinchat and wheatear.

The Oa: Snow bunting in winter. Many breeding sea-birds on the cliffs.

Loch Ballygrant: for wildfowl and common woodland species.

Claggain Bay: for great northern divers Oct–May. Port Ellen for gulls and sea-fowl.

In 1993 Duich Moss – Eilean na Muice Duibhe – was made a National Nature Reserve by Scottish Natural Heritage.

* * *

ISLAY is probably better known for its whisky than for its birdlife. There are extensive peat deposits which are used as fuel and whose dark waters are used for the preparation of malt whisky. Working distilleries, famous for their distinctive flavours, are Ardbeg, Bunnahabhain, Bruichladdich, Bowmore, Lagavulin, Caol Ila, Laphroaig, and Port Ellen which only produces maltings for the others. And recently opened distilleries – Kilchoman (2005) and Port Charlotte (2007). About 180 years ago many of the illicit stills were legalised but no duty was payable on local whisky. As a result there was such widespread drunkenness that the parish ministers demanded government action. Today Islay produces about four million proof gallons of whisky each year, most of which is exported

Kildalton High Cross, Islay.
Jun '93

THE HIGH CROSS IN KILDALTON CHURCHYARD

overseas. Even so, the duty collected by the Government from sales on the home market alone is the equivalent of a generous income for every man, woman and child on the island.

The climate is relatively mild but it is difficult to avoid the Atlantic winds which constantly funnel through Loch Indaal. The landscape is generally undulating except where the line of Jura mountains cross the Sound of Islay and peter out in the south-east corner. The island has quite an extensive farming industry and there is rich machair grassland on the west coast.

Historically Islay was once the most important of all the Scottish islands and it has much of archaeological interest. The elegant, 2.4m high Celtic cross at Kilchoman on the Rinns south of **Loch Gorm** was erected by John, first Lord of the Isles in the 14th century in memory of his second wife, Margaret. The wishing stone beneath it in a worn stone basin has to be turned by any mother who wishes to have a son. The legendary pipers, the MacCrimmons of Skye, are thought to have originated from near here.

On the west coast peat-bog of the Rinns (G. *rinn* – promontory. 'Rhinns' is the incorrect spelling) between Loch Gorm and **Saligo Bay** is an area where thousands of barnacle, greylag and Greenland white-fronted geese winter every year. The birds cause considerable damage to surrounding farms and peat-cutting is essential for the whisky industry so there was a rousing disagreement between islanders and conservationists in 1985. The area, **Duich Moss**, or Eilean na Muice Duibhe, was eventually made a National Nature Reserve in 1993 after agreement was reached with the distillers to use peat from an alternative site. This has safeguarded a rich variety of wildlife associated with peatland and is a boon to the budding tourist industry. United Distillers actively assisted Scottish Natural Heritage in measures such as damming drainage ditches to allow the water table to rise to its normal level.

At the head of Loch Gruinart, which separates the Rinns from the rest of Islay, a bloody battle between the MacLeans of Duart and the MacDonalds of Islay in 1598 was won, according to the MacDonalds, thanks to the magical intervention of the black elf, *Du-sith*.

The north-east part of the island has sporting estates well stocked with deer, pheasants and trout streams and very few roads. This is hill-walking country. **Sgarbh Breac** (364m) is a good climb reached by way of Beinn Thrasda's summit (260m) with a stunning view down the Sound of Islay and over to West Loch Tarbert on Jura.

Port Askaig is a tiny indentation which just avoids the fierce tides in the Sound of Islay – tides which can be harnessed for future electricity generation. Its hotel dates from the 16th century. Ferries call here from Kennacraig on the mainland and Feolin on Jura. To the south is a wild and trackless mountain region with sport for the climber and hill-walker and wonderful views for the artist or photographer from the mountain slopes.

A main road cuts across the island from Port Askaig to Bridgend on Loch Indaal. Each of several lochs near Ballygrant has its own crannog. **Loch Finlaggan**, north of the village, was the Lord of the Isles' headquarters and is one of Scotland's most important archaeological sites, although little attention was paid to it before 1989. There are two islands (crannogs) in the loch, Eilean Mór (G. – big island) and Eilean na Comhairle [co**a**-oorloo] (G. – council island), both covered with ruins [NR389681]. In among the profuse wildflowers are the remains of at least 28 buildings of this ancient centre of Scottish Gaelic culture and administration including the Great Hall of the Lords, the chapel, scattered carved gravestones, buildings which held the 'parliament' of ecclesiastics and chiefs, living quarters, and many other crumbling ruins still to be identified. Excavation continues and the Finlaggan Trust now has a visitor centre on the site.

Bridgend is the home village of the former laird's mansion – Islay House, which is carefully screened from view by trees [NR334628]. The farm buildings have been beautifully renovated as craft workshops and together with the nearby Woollen Mill (1883) are worth visiting. The road on the north pebbled shore of **Loch Indaal** runs round to Bruichladdich with its distillery and on to the charming little fishing village of Port Charlotte, known as the **Queen of the Rinns**. This was built at the turn of the 18th century by a local minister, Rev Maclaurin. Every house is of identical plan and measures 9m x 7m. In the old Free Kirk is the Museum of Islay Life with a lot of interesting exhibits.

At **Nerabus**, two ancient burial grounds contain some of the finest medieval grave-slabs to be found in Scotland and 3km further on there are exotic wildfowl ponds at the Rodney Dawson

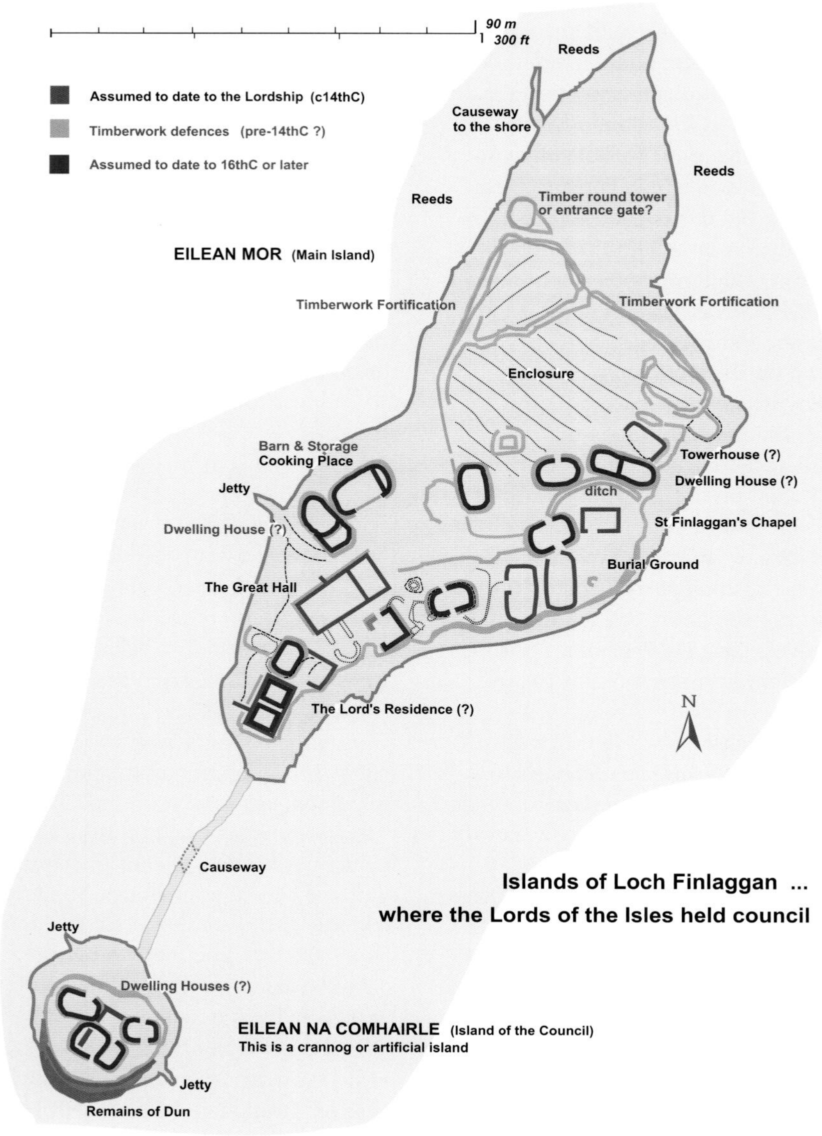

Assumed to date to the Lordship (c14thC)

Timberwork defences (pre-14thC ?)

Assumed to date to 16thC or later

90 m
300 ft

Reeds

Causeway
to the shore

Reeds

Timber round tower
or entrance gate?

Reeds

EILEAN MOR (Main Island)

Timberwork Fortification

Timberwork Fortification

Enclosure

Barn & Storage
Cooking Place

Towerhouse (?)

Jetty

Dwelling House (?)

ditch

St Finlaggan's Chapel

Dwelling House (?)

The Great Hall

Burial Ground

The Lord's Residence (?)

N

Causeway

Islands of Loch Finlaggan ...
where the Lords of the Isles held council

Jetty

Dwelling Houses (?)

EILEAN NA COMHAIRLE (Island of the Council)
This is a crannog or artificial island

Jetty

Remains of Dun

Memorial collection of birds. The main road ends at **Portnahaven,** an old fishing village, which faces the islands of **Mhic Coinnich** and **Orsay** with its ancient chapel and Stevenson lighthouse. This is now the site of the world's first commercial wave-energy electricity generator, a remarkable example of Scottish innovation. About 9km north of Portnahaven on a very rural road **Kilchiaran** (G. – cell of St Ciaran) was founded by St Columba in honour of his Irish tutor who had died in 548. **Eilean Liath** forms a reef beside the bay.

Turning south from Bridgend brings one to **Bowmore**, the present-day 'capital' of Islay, with a population of about 900. It was founded

by the laird, Daniel Campbell, in 1767. The rounded church of Kilarrow here [NR312596] was designed 'so the devil could find no corners to lurk in'.

Between Bowmore and Port Ellen a 10km shell-sand beach borders **Laggan Bay** with the airfield and a golf course on the machair at its southern end.

Port Ellen is the largest centre of population. The port construction was started in the 1820s by Walter Campbell, 4th of Islay, who named it Port Elinor after his wife. To the east of the town is the vestigial ruin of a chapel dedicated to St Lasar, an obscure 6th-century Irish nun, marked by two curious upright stones with holes cut through them. A pub near the harbour has several walls covered with excellent murals of island scenes and depicting local people. These were painted by an Irish artist, each character being placed in the composition in return for a dram – or two – or maybe three. I understand the poor chap died of drink – but he has left a fascinating memorial.

To the west of Port Ellen is **The Oa** – pronounced 'oh' – and on the Mull of Oa is an American Memorial [NR270415] commemorating US servicemen lost when the *Tuscania* was torpedoed in February 1918 and the *Otranto* was wrecked in a gale the following October. Many bodies were washed ashore beneath these cliffs. This is a storm-lashed area which overlooks the grey Atlantic but mountaineers appreciate the cliffs. A clean granite arête from sea-level to the cairn of Beinn Mhor provides an exciting 150m climb. Other good ridges are nearby to the east and also beyond the Memorial.

The southern road from Port Ellen to **Ardbeg** runs through one of the most archaeologically interesting parts of the island. It passes the Laphroaig distillery overlooking the island of Texa (No.2.1). Further east, by Lagavulin, are the ruins of 14th-century **Dunyvaig Castle** (G. – fort of the little ships) [NR406455], built either by Donald I or John of Islay, Lord of the Isles. This castle has a long and bloody history very similar to another Macdonald stronghold, Dunaverty Castle, on the Mull of Kintyre overlooking Sanda island (No.1.2). Further on, **Kildalton House** in a woodland setting is beside magic Loch a' Chnuic. This estate was owned by John Ramsay MP, who deported all his tenants to America in the 19th century. He was cursed by an old woman as she was dragged away and before long both he and his wife died and the estate fell into financial ruin.

Three kilometres further, the renowned **Kildalton High Cross** stands by a ruined chapel (G. *cille daltan* – the church of the disciple) [NR458508]. Carved in c.800 out of bluestone by a sculptor from Iona, it is considered by many to be the finest Celtic cross in the whole of Scotland. Beside it are some magnificent carved grave-slabs of the 15th century. The road dwindles to a track by Trudernish Point near a vitrified dun and standing stones.

Apart from the beautiful scenery, beaches, birdlife, and prehistoric and medieval remains, Islay also offers the visitor golf, riding, hill-

walking, sea angling, freshwater fishing, diving, and any amount of subject matter for the artist. And although the island attracts many visitors in the summer months it never appears crowded.

* * *

Access: Car ferry: Kennacraig on West Loch Tarbert (Kintyre)/ Port Ellen or Port Askaig. Crossing 2¼ hours. Several services daily, 08000-66-5000. Regular air service from Glasgow, 0870-850-9850. There are regular island bus services, 01496-840273. Tourist Information, Bowmore, 08707-200617 or 0845-2255-121.

Anchorages:
Note: The tidal range here is less than 2m and sometimes only 60cm – less than anywhere else in the British Isles. The movement at neaps is barely distinguishable.
1. Port Ellen. Hazards at entrance and west of harbour pier. 22-berth self-service charity operated pontoon in harbour in 3m dredged area; shelter good. Visitors' moorings NW of pier, but poor shelter in all S'lies. Kilnaughton bay W of harbour has better shelter from southerly swell or W winds and holding moderately good. Anchor N of Carraig Fhada lighthouse in 6–9m. This is a busy harbour so keep the approaches clear.
2. Lagavulin. Tricky approach and entrance. Two visitors' moorings at distillery or anchor in 3m in middle of pool, mud. Very restricted area and subject to swell.
3. Loch an t'Sailen. Approach to Lagavulin then follow a course 2c off the coast and leave the Ardbeg islet to port. Anchor NNE of Sgeir Dubh in 3m, rock and sand, good holding. Well sheltered.
4. Loch a' Chnuic (Kildalton Bay). Only suitable if no chance of winds from E to S, and in any case subject to heavy swell. Hazards on approach. Anchor near above-water rock in 3m, hard sand.
5. Ardmore Islands. A fascinating hideaway teeming with wildlife. Anchor SW of Eilean Craobhach or, with care, in the rocky but snug Plod Sgeirean behind a submerged reef.
6. Port Mór. Avoid N side and give S entrance point a wide berth. Head is shoal. Anchor in SW where depth suitable, sand. (*Best for visit to Kildalton Church and Cross.*)
7. Glas Uig. Between Port Mór and Aros Bay. Attractive but a number of dangers inside the anchorage and very restricted. Exposed to E and subject to swell. Anchor N of centre, 3m, sand and weed.
8. Aros Bay. A wide sandy bay with no off-lying dangers. Exposed N and E. Anchor in 3m in centre. (*Useful for visit to historic Kildalton Church and Cross but longer walk than No.6 above*).
9. Port Askaig. Strong tide and limited space. Alongside

ferry pier sometimes possible.

10. Caol Ila distillery. Better holding than Port Askaig but avoid obstructing pier.

11. Bunnahabhain Bay. Temporary anchorage in 4m ½c N of pier.

12. Tràigh Baile Aonghais bay near Gortantaoid point. Exposed. Occasional anchorage in suitable weather.

13. Nave Island. Anchor SE of island opposite church ruin, sand, good holding but limited shelter. Occasional anchorage in suitable winds.

14. Portnahaven (Orsay). Well-sheltered channel. North entrance foul with rocks. Approach from S but beware strong tides across the entrance. Anchor NW of Portnahaven quay, sand.

15. Port Charlotte, Loch Indaal. Temporary anchorage.

16. Temp. anchorage off pier at Bruichladdich, Loch Indaal, in suitable weather. Pier has 3m depth at head.

17. Bowmore, Loch Indaal. The loch head dries out about 7½c and shores are shoal. Indifferent shelter. Anchor well offshore N of the N'most of the two beacons.

2.5 Nave

(G. naoimh – island of the saint) According to Watson it is Nein's Island and named after one of the four saints of that name.

O S Maps: 1:50000 Sheet 60 1:25000 Sheet 353
Admiralty Charts: 1:75000 2168 or 2169 1:25000 2481

Area: 40ha (100 acres)
Height: 34m (111ft)

Population: no census records and uninhabited.

Geology: Mainly calcareous Torridonian sandstone.

History: This was possibly one of Islay's three monastic islands, – Texa, Orsay and Nave – although this is highly speculative. The island was part of the property of Iona Abbey until the Reformation. First mentioned by Dean Munro in 1549, the ruined church probably dates from the 13th century but its ovoid enclosure may be older still and date from Early Christian times, comparable with the similar enclosure on Eileach an Naoimh (No.2-13). The discovery on the island of a fragment of the arm of a cross which appears to be from the 5th century reinforces this supposition. Carved from local green schist this is now in the Museum of Islay Life at Port

Charlotte. By 1785 the church was ruinous but some years later the island was settled by a group of kelp-burners. They converted the church for kelp-burning by building a furnace and chimney in its north-east corner, carrying out various masonry alterations and constructing, it seems, a slated roof. There are no gravestones or carved effigies in the burial ground and these, if they ever existed, were probably stolen as is said to have happened on Eileach an Naoimh (No.2-13). No gravestones were used by the kelp-burners to construct the furnace and the chimney was built of poor quality bricks.

Wildlife: Nave Island is part of the Loch Gruinart and Ardnave Nature Reserve. Among the prolific birdlife the occasional rare chough can be seen rooting for insects in the grass. Nave is also a breeding ground for seals.

*   *   *

Low lying NAVE ISLAND has a convenient anchorage and landing place close to the ruined chapel and the shingle beach at **Port na h-Eaglaise** (G – port of the church). The church is south-west of a deep gulley about 6m wide which completely divides the island. It is called **Sloc na Maoile** (G – the deep gulley on the brow of the hill), and is thought to have been formed by the erosion of a geological dyke. North of the chapel is a large field of about 2ha area contained by a turf dyke and the 'sloc'. The ground shows signs of rig-cultivation probably dating back to the pre-18th century period when the island was intensively farmed.

The small church (7m x 4m approx.) is sheltered from the prevailing west winds by the rising ground. It was well-built of basalt rubble which was probably quarried on the site. The most notable remaining original features are the two arched windows in the south-east with their splayed ingoes, and a recess with a thin slab shelf or aumbry above it on the east gable. The most notable non-original feature is the oven and chimney in the north-east corner used for kelp-burning in the 19th century.

To the north of the church can be seen the remains of a number of buildings most of which were probably built during the agricultural period. According to local tradition there was a monastery on the island and signs of this could have been obscured by the subsequent agricultural work and buildings. Across the

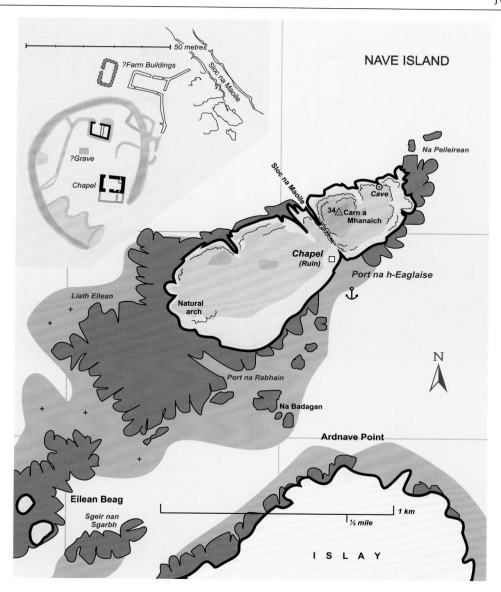

gulley to the north is a rocky knoll called **Carn a Mhanaich** (G – cairn of the monk). This name lends credance to the monastic suggestion.

Nave Island is part of a rocky ridge comprising Balach Rocks in the north-east, then Nave Island, the islets of Eilean Beag (part of the Nave estate) and the Boghachan Mór (G - bow-shaped reef) in the south-west.

* * *

Access: No regular access. Islay Sea Safari at Port Ellen, 01496-840510, may be able to help or by arrangement with Farsain Cruises, Craobh Haven, 01852-500664.

Anchorages:

If approaching from the N beware the Balach Rocks about 6 cables NE of Na Peileirean.

1. Port na h-Eaglaise, the small bay beneath the chapel ruin. Anchor off the small sandy beach as depth permits. Bottom sand and shingle. Reasonable shelter except from the east.

2.6 Jura

(ON jur-øy – udder island or the island of breasts) – to a Viking sailor the Paps of Jura would be the obvious identification. All expert sources, however, primly give the derivation as (ON dyr-øy – deer island) and one 7th-century document refers to the island as 'Doiradeilinn'.

THE PASSAGE TO INNER LOCH TARBERT

O S Maps: 1:50000 Sheet 61 1:25000 Sheet 355
Admiralty Charts: 1:75000 Nos.2168 and 2169 Sounds of
Islay and Jura 1:25000 Nos.2481, 2396 and 2397 Gulf of
Corryvreckan 1:25000 No.2343

Area: 36,692ha (90,666 acres)
Height: 785m (2575ft)

Owner: Multiple ownership. By 1938 the island
had been sold to separate purchasers and there
are now seven estates, plus a relatively small area
owned by the Forestry Commission. **Barnhill** in
the extreme north is owned by Jamie Fletcher and
a family member, Andrew Fletcher, owns and is
resident at **Ardlussa**. The area north of Loch
Tarbert, **Ruantallain**, was bought in 1984 by
Lindsay Bury, a businessman. Between the Corran
River and Loch Tarbert is the **Tarbert** estate
owned by (Ginge Manor Estates Ltd., Nassau,
Bahamas) assumed to have some connection
with Viscount Astor, the Prime Minister's wife's
stepfather. Lord Vestey, chairman of Vestey Group
Ltd., owns **Jura Forest**, the area east of the Paps
and Sir William J. Lithgow's family own **Inver**,
the western side centred on Feolin. In 2010
the southern estate of **Ardfin** was sold to Greg
Coffey, an Australian hedge-fund manager, which
included Jura House. Sadly he has closed the
beautiful walled gardens which used to be open to
the public.

Population: 1755–1097. 1794–929. 1831–
1312. 1881–773. 1891–619. 1931–364.
1961–249. 1971–210. 1981–228. 1991–196.
2001–188. 2011 – 196.

Geology: This is the largest area of metamorphic
quartzite in the Highlands producing poor soil
and a lot of peat. A narrow strip of schist runs
along the east coast and no other coast has so
many arches, caves and raised beaches as the
west side of Jura. The rocks are mainly white and
red granite with fine blue slate and micaceous
sandstone in the north. Iron ore is plentiful and
the good silica sand deposits on the west coast
were once used for glass-making. There are
about fifty very large caves – some were used as
mortuaries for the dead before the bodies were
shipped to Iona or Oronsay for burial.

History: About 678AD, in Dalriadic times, there
was a great battle fought on Jura between the
native Picts and the Scots from Ireland.

  During the time of the Lords of the Isles and
Macdonald power, Jura's importance was due to
its proximity to the headquarter territory of Islay.
This lasted until the Clan Donald sold Jura to the
Campbells of Argyll in 1607.

  In 1647 during the Wars of the Covenant the
Macleans of Jura were attacked by Campbell of

JURA

SCARBA

Gulf of Corrievreckan

Bàgh Gleann nam Muc
Uamh Breacain (cave)

Port an Tiobairt

Kinuachdrachd Harbour

Glengarrisdale Bay

Maclean's Skull Cave
Glengarrisdale

Barnhill

Glendebadel Bay

Ben Garrisdale

Caves

10 km

5 miles

N

Corpach Bay

Lealt

Beinn Bhreac

Fishing Loch

raised beaches

Shian Bay

Rainberg Mór

Ardlussa

Inverlussa

Lussa Bay

Loch Righ Mór

raised beaches

Nat. Arch

Inner Loch Tarbert

Chapel (ruin)

Sound of Jura

Ruantallain
Cruib Lodge
Rubh' an t-Sàilein
Caves

Eileanan Gleann Righ

Tarbert

Loch Tarbert

Tarbert Bay

raised beaches

Cumhann Mór

Cumhann Beag

woodland

Caves
Scrinadle

Beinn Bhreac

Lagg

Arch

Loch an Aircill
Beinn an Oir

Corra Bheinn

Achamore

Port Doir' a' Chrorain

Eilean Mór
(Chapel & Cross)

785
Beinn Shiantaidh

Paps of Jura

Beinn a' Chaolais

Loch a' Chnuic Bhric

Loch an t-Siob

An Dúnan

Gleann Astaile

Lowlandman's Bay

Glas Bheinn

Feolin
Loch na Mìle
Jetty

Burial Ground
Keils

Small Isles

Feolin Ferry

Dubh Bheinn

Craighouse

Eilean nan Gabhar

Distillery

Piers

Crackaig

Standing Stone

Jura House

wood

Castle
Am Fraoch Eilean

Brosdale Island

MAINLAND

Sound of Islay

ISLAY

Craignish and there was a fierce battle. 'MacLaine saved his lands with the loss of his reputation' according to Sir James Turner. General David Leslie arrived from Islay and Maclean promptly gave him his castle, his son, and 'fourteen prettie Irishmen who had been all along faithful to him' as hostages. Leslie had the fourteen hanged.

In 1767 fifty islanders sailed from Jura to settle in Canada and islanders continued to do so during the next seventy years. Walter Campbell of Jura inherited Islay in 1777 and sold his lands in Jura to concentrate his assets on Islay. About this time the island was divided into twenty-seven separate farms. In the 18th century and the early 19th century Jura was a centre for breeding Highland cattle. There was also a small number of hardy little sheep with a particularly fine wool, a lot of wild goats and some horses.

In 1812 experiments were conducted on Beinn An Oir to determine the boiling point of water in relation to altitude.

After 1840 there was widespread introduction of sheep and the crofters were cleared from the land. The grassy glens deteriorated in consequence and much of the ground is now only of use for deer stalking.

Wildlife: By the end of the 18th century the deer population had declined seriously but numbers have slowly increased again with encouragement from the hunting fraternity and today there are about 5000. There are also some wild goats.

It is dangerous to wander about after mid-August when the stag shooting season has begun and at any time it is sensible to request permission. (Enquire at the Isle of Jura Hotel at Craighouse.) There are many adders so wear sensible footwear. During a 3km walk on a hot summer day, I passed seven different rocks with adders sunbathing on them.

North along the beach from the ferry landing at Feolin is the largest heronry on the island and a favourite haunt for otters. At least 15 pairs of golden eagles are resident in the hills and hen harriers sweep over the lower ground. At the end of the 18th century it was reported that the 'many eagles... are very destructive to the lambs.' Loch Tarbert is a favourite haunt of mergansers and divers. Common seals frequent the skerries, mainly on the south shoreline.

The wild terrain is almost too coarse to encourage a great botanical variety but there are unexpected finds to be made. Many of the marshy pools are covered with water-lilies and an interesting variety of alpine plants thrive on the higher slopes. Palm tree look-alikes grow around Craighouse as a reminder of the mildness of the climate when sheltered from the wind.

JURA is the wildest island in the Inner Hebrides. It is a vast area of rock and blanket bog, most of it without roads or habitation of any kind and the haunt of deer and wild goats. Crossing this terrain of rough ankle-twisting rock and scree, or knee-high grass, heather, and bracken, is painfully slow. But this gives it added fascination. On Jura it is easy to believe that there is no such thing as the human race and that exploration of this remote environment is bound to yield some earth-shattering discovery. And scattered along the west coast of the ragged lonely landscape are spacious caves with dry floors and lofty vaulted roofs, great natural stone arches and pillars, and raised beaches which are almost artificial in their perfection.

Loch Tarbert nearly bisects the island. South of the first narrows, Cumhann Mór, there is a raised beach possibly ¾km in length and about 15m above sea-level with a lochan beside it. It is clean, with no weeds and the surface looks as though a gardener has just finished raking the smooth round pebbles. And yet it has been lying there for some 10,000 years!

Exploring Loch Tarbert by boat for the first time is an exciting experience. Negotiating the outer loch past the **Eileanan Gleann Righ** (G. – islands of the royal glen), through the narrow Cumhann Mór into the large middle loch with **Eilean Ard** to the north and finding, and passing through, the concealed entrance to the dog-leg passage leading to the inner sanctum. This entails slipping past rocks and tidal eddies, squeezing past little **Eilean an Easbuig**, and then, at last, the shallow inner loch opens up with its one deep patch in the centre.

Some of the many large caves include rudimentary altars which were built by the islanders when they stopped there while transporting their dead to Iona or Oronsay for burial, and there is one cave in **Bàgh Gleann Righ Mór** (G. – large bay of the valley of the king) in West Loch Tarbert which has a royal connection and an ancient history, but is the subject of conflicting scholarly argument [NR518824].

The **Paps of Jura** are almost as high as Goat Fell and almost as famous as the Cuillin. They were painted by McTaggart and many artists. There are, strangely, three paps: **Beinn an Oir** (a Corbett) at 785m (2575ft) (G. – the mountain of gold), **Beinn Shiantaidh** at 755m (2476ft) (G. – the holy mountain), and **Beinn a' Chaolais** at 734m (2408ft) (G. – the mountain of the kyle). North-west of Beinn an Oir is Sgriob na Caillich (G. – the witch's broom) – a large rock scar. A causeway was erected on Beinn an Oir by the Ordnance Survey in the mid-19th century.

For climbers who want to conquer all the Paps, there is a favourite steep scramble up Beinn Shiantaidh from the river outlet of Loch an t-Stob, down to the pass and lochans to the north-east

CRAIGHOUSE HAS LIFE'S BARE NECESSITIES. . .

and then a steep ascent of Corra Bheinn (575m) and a 5km round trip back to Shiantaidh: down the west ridge and across the 450m col and up to Beinn An Oir. Then descending the south spur, avoiding the steep ground overlooking Na Garbh-lochanan corrie to the col at 370m, and on up to Beinn a' Chaolais, the lowest of the Paps: after this a descent to Feolin on the west coast via Cnocbreac or to Keills near Craighouse via the shoulder above the head of Glen Astaile, under the east slope of Glas Beinn. Finish by passing the St Earnadail graveyard – if you are still able.

The west coast has always been underpopulated. It is now deserted but there used to be a small settlement at **Glengarrisdale** and another at **Ruantallain** at the entrance to West Loch Tarbert which was only abandoned about 1947. At Glengarrisdale Bay, in the far north-west, **Maclean's Skull Cave** contained a human skull and bones mounted on a cairn [NR647970] but about twenty years ago it was removed. This gruesome relic was alleged to be the remains of a Maclean who was slain when Jura was attacked by Campbell of Craignish in 1647 during the Wars of the Covenant.

Nowadays all the inhabitants of Jura live on the east coast, mostly in the vicinity of **Craighouse**. The distillery was built in 1963 and bottled its first malt in 1974. It replaced one built by the Campbells in the mid-19th century. Craighouse also has a post-office, shop, hotel, school and doctor. One of the two piers was built in 1814 by Thomas Telford. A string of islets known as the Small Isles form a breakwater to the bay. They are **Eilean nan Gabhar** (G. – island of the goats), **Eilean Diomhain** (G. – idle island), **Eilean nan Coinean** (G. – island of the rabbits), **Pladda** and **Eilean Bhride** (G – Bridget's isle).

At the south end of Jura, by the road running round from the ferry on the Sound of Islay, Jura

House stands in a woodland estate with its beautiful walled gardens just a short walk from the boathouse opposite Heather Island. Offshore is the small island of **Am Fraoch Eilean** (G. – the heather isle) on which are the ruins of Claig Castle [NR471627], a Norman-style square tower with 3m-thick walls built in 1154 by Somerled to defend the Sound of Islay and also used by his descendants as a prison. The Macdonald clan slogan is still 'Fraoch Eilean'. Jura House is a short walk from the boathouse opposite Heather Island and has beautiful walled gardens (open to the public). To the east of Am Fraoch Eilean by the Sound of Jura is **Brosdale Island** and to the west, in the Sound of Islay, are the sharp rocks of **Glas Eilean**.

In this area and up the east coast standing stones prove that early man also favoured the east of the island.

Jura's one and only public road continues north from Craighouse and passes the crofting hamlet of Keills with its **Chapel of St Earnadail** [NR524687] who was a little-known early Celtic missionary from Iona. Although he lived on Islay he insisted that he should be buried on Jura, and that a ball of mist would guide his mourners to a suitable burial place. A gravestone in the churchyard commemorates Gillouir MacCrain who died in 1645. Another MacCrain, Mary, died aged 128 in 1856 and is buried at Inverlussa. The tombstone inscription says that she was a 'Descendant of Gillouir MacCrain who kept One Hundred and Eighty Christmasses in his own house. And died in the reign of Charles I.' There is a wry sense of humour here! Until the 20th century Jura chose to recognise both the old and the new calendar (see Foula, No.11.6) so two Hogmanays and two Christmases could be celebrated each year.

The road continues up the east coast passing a wide stretch of beach at the head of **Loch na Mile**. Then it climbs and crosses a stretch of moorland before entering an area of attractive woodland at **Lagg**. Tarbert Bay, at the narrow low-lying neck of land adjoining West Loch Tarbert, has a small enclosed beach, standing stones and a ruined chapel and, a further 6km on, the road runs out at **Inverlussa**. Ardlussa estate, of about 6900ha, was once the only independent property on Jura. The present house was built by Lord Colonsay about 1840 and a small hydroelectric scheme provides power. A track continues up the coast from here to the north of the island passing Barnhill [NR705970] where George Orwell stayed when he wrote his famous novel *1984*.

From the most northern point of the vehicle track there is a fairly undemanding 3km hill-walk to a point above the clifftops overlooking the notorious **Corryvreckan** (G. *coire bhreacain* – the speckled cauldron). This is a marvellous vantage point to watch the swirl of the waters 100m or more below. The most dramatic sight is when a spring tide is in flood (i.e. running westwards at a speed of up to 10 knots) against a strong west wind. There have been many shipwrecks and disasters and Orwell recorded how he also nearly lost his life here in 1949 when trying to circumnavigate Jura.

It is often said that the tidal race was named after Breacan, a Norse Prince, who foundered with his entire fleet of fifty ships. But from Adomnan's *Life of St Columba* it would appear that this calamity occurred in the tidal race between Rathlin Island and Antrim. Nevertheless, Breacan is reputed to be buried in the 55m-deep cave [NM685005] on the south side of Bagh nam Muc (G. – bay of the swine), at the north-western tip of Jura and guarded by **Eilean Mór** and **Eilean Beag**. Martin Martin reported in 1695 that 'Breacan's stone', a tomb and an altar were in the cave.

*   *   *

Access: Car ferry Kennacraig/ Port Ellen or Port Askaig, Islay, 2hrs 20mins., 08000-66-5000. Scheduled air service: Glasgow/Islay, 0870-850-9850.
Bus service, Port Ellen/Port Askaig, Islay, 01496-840273. Car ferry, Port Askaig/Feolin, Jura, 5mins. 01496-840681. (Petrol is not available on Jura). Passenger Ferry Service Craighouse, Tayvallich. Advance booking required, 07768 450000.

Anchorages:
1. Craighouse. Avoid Goat Rock, E of Eilean nan Gabhar, and enter bay centrally between beacon and perch. Dinghy pontoon at pier. Visitors' moorings, (pay, 01496-820161) or anchor in 3m off old stone pier. Alternatively, in E'lies anchor as close as depth permits to the centre of the W side of Eilean nan Gabhar. Sand and kelp in both cases, holding poor.
2. Loch na Mile, N end. Sand and kelp, but cleaner than Craighouse. Subject to swell.
3. Drum an Dùnan bay. Small bay at S side of entrance to Lowlandman's Bay. Good anchorage in SW winds. Anchor in centre when the small islet off its point closes with the point, hard sand.
4. Lowlandman's Bay. Good shelter in W winds, but exposed to S and N winds which bring fierce squalls and a swell. Head dries out 1c and shoals a considerable distance. Best near E side, off stone jetty, thick kelp.
5. Lagg Bay is a shallow bight 3¾M NNE of Lowlandman's Bay. Temp. anchorage. Avoid central cable and anchor either side of it. Kelp and subject to swell.
6. Tarbert Bay, 1½M NNE of Lagg Bay is small inlet with central reef. Enter close to Liath Eilean on W side of inlet and anchor just N of it in 2–3m, sand. Everywhere else is dense kelp. Can be subject to swell.
7. Lussa bay, temp. anchorage with good shelter from N. Avoid reefs about ¾c from W shore. Anchor in centre, 2–4m, sand. Subject to swell.
8. Ardlussa bay, 1M NNE of Lussa bay, temp. anchorage midway between En Traigh and Ru an Fhaing, kelp.
9. Kinuachdrach harbour in NE of Jura. Temp. anchorage, close off N shore, in depths of 4–7m, cabbage kelp. Subject to swell.
10. Port an Tiobairt, at NE extremity, good occasional anchorage except for NE winds. Anchor centrally in 2–5m, sand and kelp. Subject to swell.
11. Bàgh Gleann nam Muc, in NW next Gulf of Corryvreckan, pleasant and safe, but with rocky shoals off both entrance points. Anchor at head of the larger bay off the small headland to port, firm sand. No swell except during NW wind at slack water.
12. Glentrosdale bay, the next bay SW of Bàgh Gleann nam Muc and 9½c NNE of Bàgh uamh nan Giall. Temp. anchorage, open NW.
13. Bàgh uamh nan Giall, about 8½c NE of E entrance point of Glengarrisdale Bay, is free from dangers, 4–6m.
14. Glendebadel bay and Glengarrisdale bay, 6¼M and 8¼M respec. NE of Shian Bay are small but easily accessible. Temp. anchorages when wind suitable.
15. Shian Bay, 3½M NNE of Loch Tarbert. Small, shallow, several rocks, exposed, and usually a heavy swell, but possible in fine weather.
16. Brein Phort, N of Ruantallain. Temp. anchorage in light E'lies in 6m inside the reef.
17. Rubh' an t-Sàilein, rocky headland at N entrance point of Loch Tarbert has small rocky cove on E side and bight close E again which are good landing points but poor anchorage.

18. Bàgh Gleann Righ Mór is an indentation E of Eileanan Gleann Righ, N side of outer Loch Tarbert. Easy access and good holding in 3–4m off W side of bay. Bay shoals. Heavy swell with W'lies but reasonable in N'lies.

19. Bàgh Gleann Righ Beag, a bight immediately ESE of Bàgh Gleann Righ Mór and NE of Aird Reamhar, gives occasional anchorage except in W'lies.

20. Cuan Mór Bay in outer West Loch Tarbert immediately NW of the Cumhann Mór (the narrows). Approach using leading lines. Anchor in centre avoiding reef on E side, mud, holding and shelter good.

21. Cairidh Mhor, S shore of Inner Loch. Most of bay dries. Good holding in mud and reasonable shelter in most conditions..

22. Cruib Lodge (bothy). Anchor well off-shore on N shore of the centre loch, S of lone cottage and drying rocks in the bay, mud.

23. Eilean an Easbuig pool (Halfway Anchorage). Fairly hazardous entry through the Cumhann Beag using several leading marks but good anchorage slightly N of centre of the pool in 4m.

24. Inner Loch Tarbert. Further passage to remote top pool. Anchoring in 'The Hole' is not advised as depth changes suddenly and bottom probably foul. (*1½ km track from boathouse to the east coast of Jura*).

25. Glenbatrick bay between Sgeir Agleann and Rubh' a' Bhaillein on S shore of Outer Loch Tarbert. Anchor in suitable depth, near Sgeir Agleann, sand. Sheltered SW. Mouth of river shoals 2c.

26. Whitefarland Bay. Opposite Caol Isla distillery in Sound of Islay. Clean, open bay out of main tidal stream. Anchor N of anchor-painted boulder in 3m. The boulder has a mooring ring.

27. Am Fraoch Eilean. Approach carefully as many foul and shallow areas. Occasional anchorage NNW of Am Fraoch Eilean and W of nearby boathouse and pier on Jura in 3–4m, sand and weed. (*2km walk to Jura House*).

2.7 Colonsay

(*ON – Columba's island*).

Oronsay

(*ON – Oran's island*). *Normally this is the Gaelic name for a tidal island (which this is) but here the name derives from St Oran who founded the island monastery in 563AD.*

O S Maps: 1:50000 Sheet 61 1:25000 Sheet 354
Admiralty Charts: 1:75000 No.2169 Scalasaig Harbour
1:12500 No.2474

Area: 4617ha (11,409 acres)
Height: 143m (469 ft)

Owner: Colonsay, with the exception of the church and the ferry pier, has been in the family of the one-time Minister of Defence, Lord Strathcona and Mount Royal, since 1905. Oronsay, except for the Priory, was also owned by the Strathconas but was sold to Adam Bergius, an American, for about £100,000 in the 1970s and another American, Ike Colburn, bought it in the 1980s. Mrs Francis Colburn of Massachusetts leased it to the RSPB.

Population: Approximate figures for Colonsay and Oronsay combined: 1792–718 (134 families). 1841–987.

	1881	1931	1961	1981	1991	2001	2011
Colonsay	387	232	164	133	98	108	124
Oronsay	10	6	2	3	8	5	8
	397	238	166	136	106	113	132

Geology: Lower mudstone strata with Torridonian sandstone containing lime, which breaks down into good soil. There are some basalt dykes, white limestone at the north end of Bheinn Bhreac, and a particularly fine raised beach north of Kiloran Bay which is worth a visit.

History: The Macphees or MacDuffies, archivists to the Lords of the Isles, were the islands' owners from at least the 15th century but they were dispossessed by the MacDonalds soon after 1615. The Campbells of Argyll then ousted the MacDonalds. Malcolm MacNeil of Knapdale acquired the islands (i.e. both Colonsay and Oronsay) from the Campbells in 1700 for an agreed exchange of land. This was one of the few Hebridean islands which was fortunate enough to escape the 19th-century clearances as the laird at the time, John MacNeil, had a liberal approach. Even so, many families had already emigrated to America in the summer of 1791 and the *Statistical Account* lamented, 'Pity it is that such numbers should bid farewell to their native country, when there is so great a demand for useful citizens.' By 1905 mounting debt forced the MacNeil family to hand over the island to Lord Strathcona (Donald Smith, a Canadian Scot) in lieu of £44,000 which they owed him.

Wildlife: There are many seals, particularly among the skerries of the grassy Ardskenish peninsula on the west coast, and also on

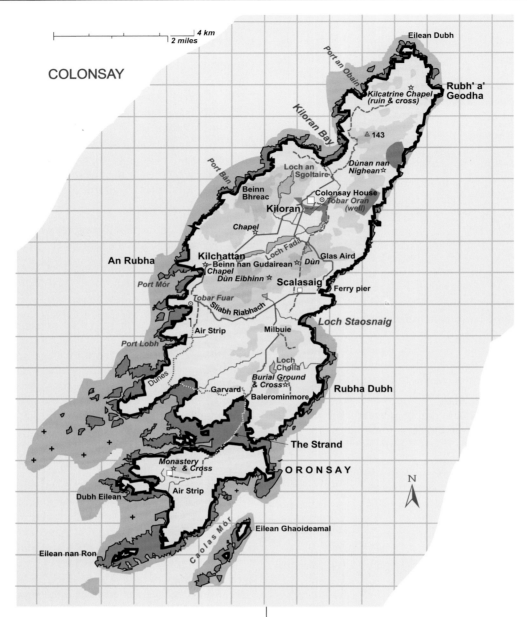

4 km
2 miles

COLONSAY

Eilean Dubh

Port an Obain

Kiloran Bay

Kilcatrine Chapel
(ruin & cross)

Rubh' a'
Geodha

△ 143

Port Bàn

Dùnan nan
Nighean ☆

Loch an
Sgoltaire

Beinn
Bhreac

Colonsay House
Tobar Oran
(well)

Kiloran

Chapel

An Rubha

Kilchattan
☆ Beinn nan Gudairean ☆ Dùn
Chapel
Dùn Eibhinn ☆

Loch Fada

Glas Aird

Scalasaig

Port Mór

Ferry pier

Tobar Fuar
Sliabh Riabhach

Loch Staosnaig

Air Strip

Milbuie

Port Lobh

Loch
Cholla

Dunes

Burial Ground
& Cross ☆

Garvard

Rubha Dubh

Balerominmore

The Strand

Monastery
& Cross ☆

ORONSAY

N

Air Strip

Dubh Eilean

Caolas Mór

Eilean Ghaoideamal

Eilean nan Ron

Eilean nan Ron (G. – seal island), which is a nature reserve. Rabbits were introduced 200 years ago to provide fresh meat and as there are no foxes, weasels or stoats they thrive enthusiastically. A few wild goats exist in the more remote areas and Hebridean sheep were introduced to Oronsay by the RSPB in 1999.

When Lord Strathcona bought Colonsay he was able to take advantage of the woodland planted in Kiloran valley by the MacNeils. He cultivated many rhododendrons, magnolia and azalea, and extended the tree cover with acacia, maple, poplar, sea-buckthorn, and eucalyptus. The woods include sycamore, beech, elm, ash, spruce, aspen, hazel, willow, larch, silver birch and pine. The sheltered valley is almost sub-tropical.

In late summer at Garvard by the Strand field gentians bloom and rock samphire hide in the clefts. Colonsay has, possibly, the greatest variety of flora in the Hebrides – some five hundred species.

Loch Fada and the lesser lochs in the centre of the island have a great variety of birds and also provide good fishing (permits from the hotel). Around the coast eider are so common that they are known locally as 'Colonsay duck'. Kittiwakes, guillemots and razorbills breed on the west coast and Oronsay is a wintering ground for barnacle geese. There is also – rare sight! – a small number of resident choughs.

*   *   *

COLONSAY and ORONSAY are separated by a wide expanse of shell sand called The Strand which can be walked across when the tide is out, following a defined route. Halfway across is the sanctuary cross: any Colonsay fugitive who reached it was immune from punishment provided he stayed on Oronsay for a year and a day.

These islands have been inhabited for 8,700 years. On the south side of **Kiloran Bay**, in Uamh Uir (G. – the cave of the grave-dust) the bones of domestic animals and Neolithic flint tools have been excavated. There are many pre-Christian and early Christian relics. A Viking warrior who had been given a ship burial in 855 with his weapons, horse and coins, was uncovered in the sand dunes here in 1882. Although it was a pagan burial two crosses incised on stone slabs were included as an additional safeguard.

Both islands have deeply indented coasts with numerous rocks and reefs and the west coast backed by machair. Colonsay is generally of good soil although the higher ground is moorland and scrub. Raised beaches on the west coast and sea beach debris in the interior mark a time when the land was lower in the sea and these were four separate islands. The economy depends on crofting, farming, a little fishing and tourism. Visitors may wander freely throughout the island, although cars are restricted in some parts.

In the extreme north, in a low valley of sand-dunes running down to a fine beach, the remains of **Kilcatrine** (G. – Catherine's chapel) are marked by a standing stone and cross [NR421999]. This may have been the site of a 13th-century convent.

According to legend the MacNeils first came to the island with their cattle in an open boat. MacNeil's wife gave birth during the voyage and to keep her and the baby warm they slaughtered a cow so that mother and child could shelter inside the carcass.

Palm trees and bamboo now grow in the mild and sheltered Kiloran valley where Malcolm MacNeil built Colonsay House in 1722. He is said to have salvaged stones from an old church or abbey which was nearby. The gardens were once considered equal to Inverewe, Crarae, and Achamore on Gigha (No.2.3), and are still beautiful, but Colonsay House is now partly converted to holiday flats and eighteen gardeners have been replaced by one man.

The inevitable Piper's Cave where a piper and his dog went to hunt for hell is on the coast at Port Bàn. Only the dog reappeared but from a cave four miles south with his hair burned off. (One wonders why this legend occurs on so many of the Scottish islands, see Barra, Gigha, etc.)

THE AUGUSTINIAN PRIORY ON ORONSAY

The ferry pier was built at **Scalasaig** (ON – shieling bay) in 1965. This is the main village and two other centres of population are Kilchattan and Kiloran. The island has a junior school, a minister of the church and, usually, a resident doctor, but no policeman. There is a hotel, some summer cottages, bed-and-breakfast accommodation and a brewery. The hotel at Scalasaig provides all the local tourist information. By the road between the hotel and the harbour is the Well of the South Wind where fishermen used to pray for a south wind and overlooking the village is an Iron Age fort, the most important of many on the island, called **Dun Eibhinn** [NR382944]. There is another one just to the north-east on Beinn nan Gudairean and this is also possibly the best viewpoint on the island [NR388950].

On the west coast opposite Scalasaig between **Tobar Fuar** (G. – cold well) and **Port Lobh** (G. – the port that smells of seaweed) is an 18-hole golf course. This stretch of Colonsay coastline has many skerries and off-shore islets – **Eilean nam Ban** (G. – women's isle), **Eilean Dubh**, **Eilean a' Chladaich** (G. – shore isle), **Eilean na Bilearach** (G. – sea-grass isle), **Eilean Leathan** (G. – broad island) and the inevitable **Glas Eilean** (G. – pale grey-green isle). This is in contrast to the east coast which boasts only one islet – **Eilean Olmsa**.

Across the sea from the old burial ground at **Balerominmore** [NR384914] in the south-east of Colonsay, which has a cross and carved slab, the Paps of Jura glow in the summer evening sun. Nearby at Garvard, overlooking the Strand, are the foundations of a cell or chapel, with a dun, and a standing stone.

* * *

ORONSAY has a very fine ruin, possibly second only to Iona in importance, of an Augustinian **Priory** built in c.1380 which is probably on the same site as St Oran's original monastery of 563 [NR350890]. This is a fascinating group of buildings in a reasonable state of preservation although, unfortunately, part of the stonework was removed by the MacNeils to build the adjacent farmhouse. Some human bones from the neighbouring graveyard are kept by the high altar in the chapel and beautifully sculpted medieval tombstones are protected in the Prior's House beside the delightfully-proportioned miniature cloisters. Outside there are two notable Celtic crosses, one of 3.7m height featuring a relief of the Crucifixion in commemoration of Prior Colin, who died in 1510. Oronsay is suffused with a feeling of tranquillity and it is easy to understand why St Oran chose it for a retreat (Columba is said to have rejected it because it was within sight of Ireland.)

Archaeological excavations on Oronsay have shown evidence of a Middle Stone Age settlement and there are a number of Mesolithic shell mounds. The grass airstrip by the monastery fights a losing battle with the rabbits.

A reef of islets, **Eilean Ghaoideamal** (G. – the blemished isle), **Eilean an Eoin** (G. – bird isle), and some skerries, lies parallel to the east coast of Oronsay creating a channel, Caolas Mór, which is the only partially sheltered anchorage in the area. A small sandy beach called Tràigh Uamha Seilbhe (G. – beach of the caves used as stock-pens) faces the kyle.

On **Eilean nan Ron** (G. – seal island) at the most southern tip, beyond the sheep and ponies grazing on the landing strip, is the ruin of an old kelp-gatherer's cottage. The huge expanse of skerries round this islet is a favourite breeding ground for the grey Atlantic seal. A thousand or more converge here in the autumn each year and the roar of battling bulls can be heard for miles.

* * *

Access: Vehicle ferry from Oban six times a week, 01631-566688; and from Kennacraig/Port Askaig on Wednesdays and Saturdays, 01880-730253. Caravans allowed only with permission, 01951-200308. Scheduled flights from Oban by Highland Airways, 0845-4502245. Boat excursions, Farsain Cruises, Craobh Haven, 01852-500664. There is an island post-bus and bicycles can be hired at the hotel.

Anchorages: There are no good anchorages.
1. Caolas Mór, Oronsay. Occasional anchorage in the bay opposite Eilean Ghaoideamal on a line between N extremity of En Ghaoideamal and boathouse on Oronsay. Beware reef Leac nan Geadh to the N which covers. (1¼km easy walk to Priory). Better shelter sometimes in the bight N of En Ghaoideamal behind the reef extending S from Eilean Treadhrach which is sometimes favoured. 4–6m in both cases, bottom sand, but swell from S and E.
2. Eilean Treadhrach. Occasional anchorage in N bay, sheltered from SW but negotiate with care, preferably at LW.

3. Loch Staosnaig. Anchor near head of bay towards S side, sand. Avoid line of submarine cable. Subject to swell but more room than Scalasaig.

4. Scalasaig harbour, tie alongside N side of pier at the wave screen, if there is room. Or anchor N of pier, but space very limited, sand. Open to E and subject to swell.

5. Balnahard Bay at NE tip of Colonsay. Occasional anchorage on S side in 6–10m sand and shingle.

6. Kiloran Bay. Occasional anchorage off sandy beach but can be subject to severe swell at times and dangerous in W'lies.

7. Port Mór, a bay central on W coast. Keep at least 5c clear of coast until line of the road passing the cemetery is completely open, then approach carefully on this line. The head shoals about 2c. Good shelter from E but subject to heavy S'ly swell.

2.8 Eilean Macaskin

(G. – Macaskin's Island)

OS Maps: 1:50000 Sheet 55 1:25000 Sheet 358
Admiralty Chart: 1:25000 No.2326

Area: 64ha (158 acres)
Height: 65m (213ft)

Owner: Was bought in 1934, together with Eilean Righ (see No.2.8) and Eilean nan Gabhar, by Sir Reginald Johnston for £1200. Now owned by Mr David P G Sillar of Winscombe, Somerset.

Population: 1841–no separate Census figures. 1881–6. 1891–0. No permanent habitation since.

Geology:
Metamorphic epidiorite with some Dalradian quartzite at the south end.

Wildlife: Many wildflowers although not as prolific as on Eilean Righ (No.2.9).

EILEAN MACASKIN lies at the entrance to Loch Craignish and has a narrow rock-strewn but easily navigable channel up the east side. The island consists of a long ridge running parallel with the loch, 65m high at its highest point, steep on the west side but with a strip of relatively level ground on the east. It is comparatively well wooded and comfortably sheltered except for the southern end which can catch the blast of the prevailing wind rushing up the Sound of Jura. A reef of skerries extends further south towards an islet called **Eilean nan Coinean** (G. – isle of the rabbits).

Eilean nan Gabhar (G. – island of the goats) lies between Eilean Righ (No.2.9) and Eilean Macaskin giving shelter to a pleasant little anchorage. It is steep, with patches of scrub cover, and more suitable for goats than sheep although the latter seem to cope quite well. The landing place for Eilean Macaskin is on a rocky grey sand beach at the north extremity which fringes some swampy ground. Beyond, old wooden sheep pens stand in a bed of foxgloves. Well-built dry-stone dykes run along the ridges and the patches of woodland and scattered mature trees give the settled appearance of parkland.

To the south-west of Eilean Macaskin is the powerful tidal race of the Dorus Mór (G. – great door) which tumbles with force through the gateway between Craignish Point and the small island of **Garbh Rèisa** (G. – the rough one in the tidal race). At 43m height this could almost be considered a doorpost. Adjoining Garbh Rèisa is **Eilean na Cille** (G. – chapel island). West of Craignish Point is **Rèisa an t-Sruith** (G. – the tidal-race island in the current) and north of it is

THE ANCHORAGE BY GOATS ISLAND

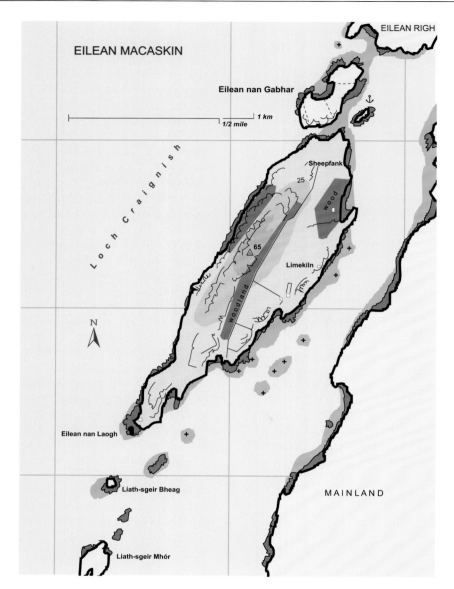

Rèisa Mhic Phaidean (G. – McFadyen's island in the tidal race). These little islands are all fairly insignificant rocks but they are worthy of respect when the tide is in full flood.

* * *

Access: Farsain Cruises, Craobh Haven, 01852-500664 or enquire at Ardfern.

Anchorages:

1. Eilean nan Gabhar (G. – goat island), N of En Macaskin. Anchor in limited space between the N end of the skerry and the reef which lies alongside the E side of Goat Island, 3–4m, firm mud and clay.
2. Temp. anchorage in small bay at NE corner but restricted swinging space and bottom falls away rapidly.

2.9 Eilean Righ

[elan ree] (G. – royal island) May have been named after the Danish sea-king Olaf who is reputed to have died in this region, or one of the early Scottish kings crowned in mid-Argyll.

OS Maps: 1:50000 Sheet 55   1:25000 Sheet 358
Admiralty Chart: 1:25000 2326

Area: 86ha (213 acres)
Height: 55m (180ft)

Owner: Bought in 1992 by Viscount Chewton for about £250,000. But on inheriting the Waldegrave earldom he sold it in 1998 for about £400,000 to Mr Siva-Jothy, former partner in

Goldman Sachs. Mr Siva-Jothy carried out further major works to the property including installing a helicopter pad and hangar. Up for sale in 2012 for £3 million.

Population: 1841–no separate Census figures. 1881–0. 1891–5 (2 houses). 1931–7. No Census records since but occasional occupation.

Geology: Mainly epidiorite and allied metamorphosed igneous rocks.

History: Once belonged to Sir Reginald Fleming Johnston, son of an Edinburgh solicitor and ex-tutor of Pu Yi, the last emperor of China. He was the author of *Twilight in the Forbidden City* and he was portrayed by Peter O'Toole in the film, *The Last Emperor.*

Wildlife: A fairly large area of mature woodland

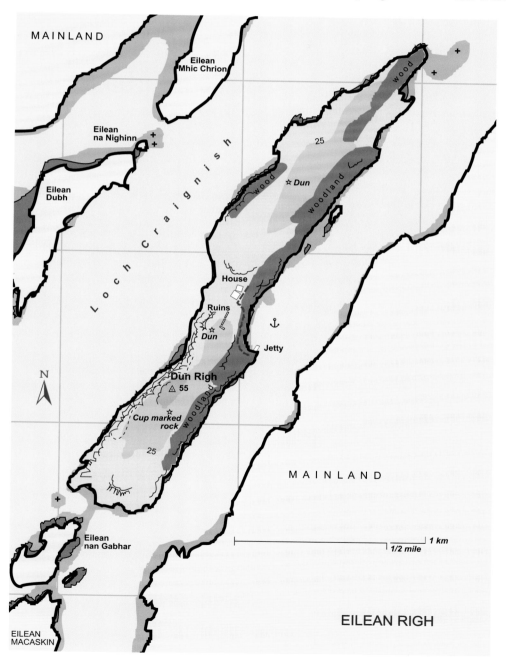

with oak, ash, rowan, alder and hawthorn spreads along the east shore, attracting many birds. There is a small herd of wild goats and rich pasture for sheep, scattered with buttercups, ragged-robin, yellow flag, ubiquitous bracken and very little heather. Wintering divers and wildfowl can be seen here from October to March.

There are wild mussel beds by the shoreline.

* * *

EILEAN RIGH is snugly situated in Loch Craignish between Eilean Macaskin (No.2.7) to the south-west and the tidal **Eilean Mhic-Chrion** (G. – MacNiven's Island) to the north across the loch.

Although it is a fairly small island it was evidently of some importance in ancient times for it has the remnants of two Iron Age duns and a name with royal connections. It is not known if the forts were contemporaneous or not but there is a further fort on the tiny Eilean na Nighinn which is part of **Eilean Dubh** on the north side of the loch. These would have controlled access to the head of the loch.

On Eilean Righ, the most northerly dun is 650m NNE of the house, set on the grassy summit of the ridge. It is oval-shaped and a number of minor artefacts were uncovered during excavation in 1982 [NM804022]. The second dun is south-west of the house at the summit of a flat-topped ridge. It is rectangular in plan with an oval structure in the south corner [NM800014].

The south side of the highest point, Dun Righ, has an interesting example of a large cup-mark on the lichen-covered rock [NM798010].

The former owner, Sir Reginald Johnston, with his female companion, modernised the island's two houses in 1934 with the addition of a Buddhist temple and lantern. The pleasant buildings, set round a courtyard with a central flagpole, have now been extensively and attractively renovated with a new helipad and hangar concealed to the south. The road from the rebuilt jetty has been widened where it climbs through a dense belt of mixed woodland, stippled with primroses amid a tangle of brambles.

It is said that when Sir Reginald died in 1938 (aged 65) valuable porcelain and china were thrown into the loch, but I have been unable to establish whether the story is true or not. However, it has been recorded that his last lover, Elizabeth Sparshott, on hearing of his death destroyed many of his documents and artefacts.

* * *

Access: Farsain Cruises, Craobh Haven, 01852-500664, or enquire at Ardfern.

Anchorage:
1. Good anchorage centre of E coast of the island, south of the farmhouse, 5m. Anchor at S end of the bay, NNE of the jetty, as N end is foul with weed. Shoal runs out for 50m in line with 2-storey gable of house.

2.10 Scarba

(ON skarpoe – sharp, stony, hilly terrain). Alternatively, but less likely, (G. sgarbh, or ON skarf – cormorant, ON -øy – island).

OS Maps: 1:50000 Sheet 55 1:25000 Sheet 355
Admiralty Charts: 1:25000 Nos.2326 or 2343

Area: 1474ha (3642 acres)
Height: 449m (1473ft)

Owner: Lord Richard Sandys, Worcestershire (the family of Lord Duncan Sandys, a former Minister of State). Previously owned by the late Mrs Yvonne Studd-Trench-Gascoigne of Leeds.

Population: 1794–50 (14 families). 1881–19. 1891–9. 1931–5. 1961–5. No permanent habitation since the 1960s.

Geology: Schist and slate in the east and quartzite in the west. A conglomerate of quartzite, limestone, and shale lies between, known as 'Scarba Conglomerate'.

History: This was the site of an early Christian settlement. At the end of the 18th century the island was divided into two farms.

Wildlife: There are many red and fallow deer, some wild goats, and otters among the rockfalls below the coastline cliffs. Sheep and the famous breed of Luing cattle are grazed here. Although drainage channels have been cut and new fencing erected to improve the grazing the ground is still very rough with heather, bracken and tufts of boggy grass and sphagnum moss. Ragged-robin, cotton grass, and at least two different varieties of orchid give vivid splashes of colour among the tussocks.

Natural oak woodland and scrub are scattered

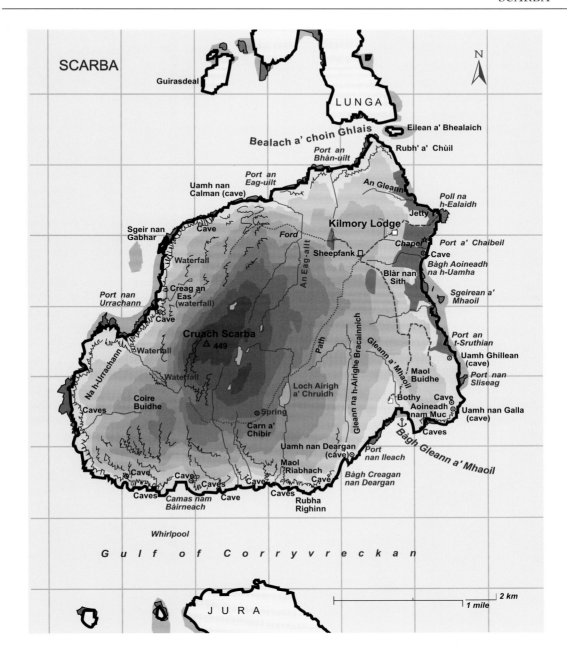

over parts of the east coast below the 50m contour. Together with some patches of planted conifers at a higher level, these attract a variety of birdlife.

*   *   *

SCARBA is a single mountain top which rises straight out of the sea to a height of 449m. It is set between two notoriously dangerous tidal races, the Corryvreckan to the south and the Grey Dogs to the north. Its coasts are bleak and rugged

with many great caves. The west flank is the most precipitous, the heather slopes tumbling steeply to the shore rocks with many unstable boulders covered by vegetation. Cut into this face is an exceptionally high raised beach – over 30m above sea level.

Above **Port nan Urrachann**, a bay on the west coast, the faint remains of Iron Age dwellings have been reported at the top of an ancient path which zig-zags up the steep slope.

The east side is gentler, with a small patch

of land fit for cultivation, and some scattered woodland. **Kilmory Lodge**, the main house or hunting lodge, is situated here and it is occasionally occupied by members and friends of the owner's family. Below the Lodge and by the eastern shore, south-west of Port a' Chaibeil, is an ancient chapel ruin, **Cille Mhoire an Caibel** (G. – the Virgin Mary's Church of the family graveyard) [NM718057]. The walls are still 1½m high but the only recognisable feature is the doorway. This was almost certainly the 'chapel of the Blessed Virgin, where many miracles occur' – mentioned by John Fordun in 1380 or thereabouts. There are still gravestones in the burial ground which was abandoned in the mid-19th century. I have been unable to confirm reports of nearby remnants of rudimentary beehive cells. If true, then – who knows? – Scarba may have rivalled Eileach an Naoimh (No.2.13) as a favourite retreat for the monks of Iona. Just south of the chapel is a cave [NM718055], which had associations with the early Christian community and beyond it and above the coastline trees is **Blàr nan Sìth**, which could be freely translated from the Gaelic as the Elysian Field!

Beside the road which leads from the pier to the Lodge there is an empty cist with a dislodged capstone. The islanders' village settlement was north of the Lodge.

Like so many of the Hebridean islands, Scarba had a reputation for healthy living and longevity – Martin Martin reported in the 17th century that an old woman had just died on Scarba aged 140, still having possession of all her faculties – but it also has its share of myths. The ghosts of evil sailors walk Scarba's cliffs as a penance. Others are chased by the Grey Dog which was drowned between Scarba and Lunga and which had belonged to Prince Breacan of Lochlann. To escape the dog's drooling fangs the phantoms must confess their crimes and these cries can be heard after dark on moonless nights.

There is a small cottage above the anchorage in **Bàgh Gleann a' Mhaoil** (G. – bay in the cleft of the mull), which was used for a time by an adventure school for children. The bay has a beach of large, multi-coloured pebbles. There is an interesting trudge up the ridge beside the bothy, then the next ridge and the next again. The going is rough: tufts of ankle-twisting grass, heather, and bracken with boggy patches between. Behind the ridges there is a small loch – **Loch Airigh**

THE BOTHY IN GLEANN A' MHAOIL

a' Chruidh (G. – loch in the horseshoe-shaped pasture) beside a vestigial path. Only a narrow earth barrier stops this loch emptying itself nearly 300m down the mountain-side. Following the path round the contours until it disappears brings you to the head of a steep gully which falls dramatically down to Camas nam Bàirneach (G. – limpet creek) and a deep-set cave. Beyond the creek is the main Corryvreckan whirlpool – a thrilling viewpoint! Deer spy on you from every rocky height.

The footpath, which encircles part of the mountain, starts from the sheep fank above Kilmory Lodge. The easiest climb to the peak, **Cruach Scarba** (G. *cruach* – stack or heap), and the low spine of rock at the top is from this path where it traverses the east side of the mountain. From the sheep fank it is also possible to reach the rough vehicle track which leads to Bàgh Gleann a' Mhaoil.

The tides run though the **Corryvreckan** (G. *coire bhreacain* – the speckled cauldron), west on the flood and east on the ebb, at speeds of up to ten knots. Beneath this channel is the rock-strewn record of some great primaeval cataclysm. There is a ridge running out from Camas nan Bàirneach on Scarba with a solitary rock stack on the end of it which rears up 44m and comes within 29m of the surface of the sea. When a westerly blows against the flood during a spring tide the noise of the violent overfalls can be heard many miles away. Local fishermen used to call the whirlpool which forms at these times over this submarine rock pinnacle, the Cailleach (G. – the old woman). According to legend a hag controls the maelstrom and decides which ships will sink and which survive. There are also enormous breakers and violent eddies elsewhere. Another submerged rock stack is in the centre of the Gulf and beside it a great narrow pit like a gateway to hell which descends 100m below the surrounding seabed to an overall depth of 219m.

The early writers' descriptions are interesting. Martin Martin declared: 'The sea begins to boil and ferment with the tide of flood, and resembles the boiling of a pot; and then increases gradually, until it appears in many whirlpools which form themselves in sort of pyramids and immediately after spout up as high as the mast of a little vessel and at the same time make a loud report.' And John MacCulloch said: 'Impossible to be engaged in this place without anxiety... danger is always

impending. The error of a few minutes might have been the price of as many lives... .'

There is a short period at slack water when it is safe to sail through the Corryvreckan but the timing has to be accurate. Even then, the turgid eddies, sudden movements and whorls sucking at the surface as the water spills over the irregular rock formations deep below create a palpable sense of menace.

*   *   *

Access: Farsain Cruises, Craobh, 01852-500664. Gemini Cruises, Crinan, 01546-830208.

Anchorages:
1. Bàgh Gleann a' Mhaoil, at the SE corner of Scarba. Occasional anchorage out of the tidal currents in 9m, sand with some weed. Exposed to S and SE and can be subject to swell. Avoid approach when tide is running strongly or conditions adverse.
2. Port a' Chaibeil. Temp. anchorage due W of Kilmory Lodge in 8–10m.
3. Poll na h-Ealaidh and jetty. A very restricted little landing-place on N side of promontory by Kilmory Lodge.
4. An Gleann. Temp. anchorage in quiet conditions off centre of inlet. (*Interesting walk to see the 'Grey Dogs'.*)
5. Port nan Urrachann, on W side. Approach from N using chart to avoid rocks and shallows, and anchor in 10–12m, sand. Exposed SW-N-NE, out of the tide but can be subject to swell.

2.11 Shuna

Possibly (G. sidhean – fairy, ON -øy – island), but probably of Norse origin.

OS Maps: 1:50000 Sheet 55 1:25000 Sheet 359
Admiralty Charts: 1:25000 Nos.2326 or 2343

Area: 451ha (1114 acres)
Height: 90m (295ft)

Owner: Owned by the Gulley family since 1946. Edward Gully, the 5th Viscount Selby was co-owner with his uncle but, aged 33, he was killed in a car accident in January 2001. He has a son and Shuna is still owned by the Gully and Selby families.

Population: 1841–69 (10 houses). 1881–14. 1891–11. 1931–12. 1961–3. 1971–3. 1981–7. 1991–1. 2001–1. 2011–3.

Geology: Shuna was one of the small group of islands cut off from the mainland by the

Firth of Lorn glacier in the last Ice Age. Unlike neighbouring Luing, there is no workable slate on Shuna – the rock is mainly phyllite and mica-schist – but on the west side a band of attractive blue crystalline limestone used to be worked.

History: A small rectangular enclosure just north of Shuna farmhouse holds a tombstone commemorating John McLean of Shuna and his wife Mary Campbell. This was probably the

John McLean who died in 1787 and whose son, Alexander, was the last of the McLeans to own the island. The McLeans' original life-rent was granted by Lord Neil Campbell in 1679.

When the owner, James Yates, died in 1829 he bequeathed Shuna to the City of Glasgow with the stipulation that the income should be 'devoted to benevolent purposes'. The Corporation preferred the capital value and sold the island.

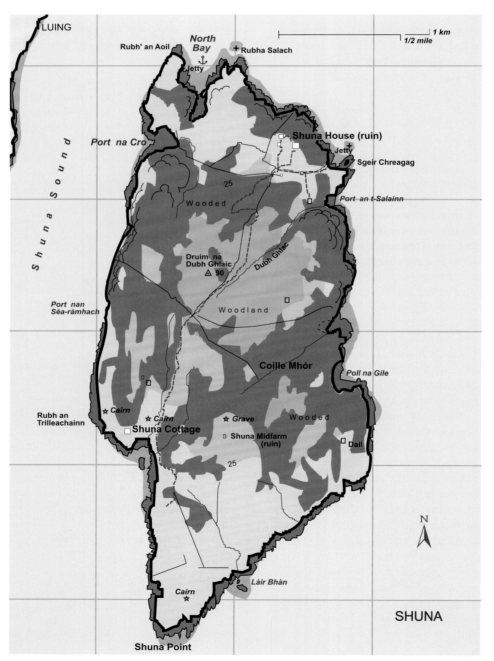

Wildlife: The very thick growth of alder, birch, hazel and scrub oak hides red, roe and fallow deer and attracts a variety of birds and woodland plants.

*   *   *

SHUNA lies between Luing and Craobh Haven. Shuna House, a ruined castellated mansion stands at the north-east corner of the island. It was built in 1911 and it is said that its local architect, having completed the commission, went down with the Titanic in 1912. The house fell into disrepair in the 1980s.

The island, much of which is wild scrub woodland is actively farmed and grazed by sheep. Some of the estate cottages, widely scattered, have been renovated and are let for holiday use, each with a boat and outboard motor. There is a fish farm at the north end.

In the north bay there is an old stone quay on the west side at **Rubh' an Aoil** (G. – lime-plaster headland), no doubt named when limestone was being quarried on the island. The east side has a concealed reef and is called **Rubha Salach** (G. – foul headland). At the head of the bay, which floods at high water, the wreck of an old wooden ferry *The Maid of Luing*, with a turntable and a livestock hold, lies on the rocks. It is a difficult walk round the shoreline which requires scrambling over hard vertical slabs of grey aerated rock like petrified Dunlopillo. Striking inland is no easier as sheep tracks mysteriously disappear and the tangled growth of alder, birch and undergrowth in the mossy humps and ravines is almost impenetrable.

Round the corner, on the west coast, is **Port na Cro** (G. – the sheep-pen port) which is too small and shallow for anything but a dinghy.

Roofless Shuna House is more distinguished and substantial when seen from a distance. Its scale is misleading. An estate road runs diagonally across the island connecting it with **Shuna Cottage** (which is actually a solid two-storeyed house rather than a cottage) in the south-west. Roughly in the centre of the island it passes **Druim na Dubh Ghlaic** (G. – the ridge by the black hollow), which is the highest point at 90m. A burn runs down the 'black hollow' to Port an t-Salainn (G. – the salt port) on the east side. South of this is further dense woodland in the Coille Mhór (G. – the big wood) and Poll na Gile (G. – clear pool), a little cove on the east coast.

The southern extremity, called Shuna Point, is marked by a prehistoric cairn, and there are two more cairns at **Rubh an Trilleachainn** (G. – oystercatcher point) behind Shuna Cottage [NM759075]. One of these is a chambered cairn which has been extensively robbed in the past.

A remarkable hoard of three bronze swords, possibly dating from the 8th century BC, was discovered on Shuna sticking point-down in the peat. They may have been placed in this way as a votive offering.

There are several islets near Shuna – **Eilean Gamhna** (G. – farrow cow island) and **Eilean Creagach** (G. – craggy island) to the north west; **Eilean Buidhe** (G. – yellow island) and Eilean an Dùin (G. – island of the fort) to the west now form part of the Craobh Haven marina breakwater. Together with **Eilean Arsa** (G. – ancient island), they used to be known as the Craobh islands. The old fort on Eilean an Dùin was, regrettably, virtually demolished when the breakwater was built. Craobh, incidentally, means a tree in Gaelic but it can also refer to bubbles in a glass of whisky – a much more poetic interpretation.

*   *   *

Access: No regular access. Boat trips by arrangement, Farsain Cruises, Craobh Haven, 01852-500664.

Anchorage:
1. Bay at N of Shuna with remnants of a stone quay on its west side. Anchor no further in than abreast the quay, 3m, mud and sand. There is a drying reef on SW side and a large part of the bay is shoal. Note submerged rock about ¾c N of the E point of the bay.

2.12 Lunga

(N langr-øy – isle of the longships) or (G. long – ship, N -øy – island)

OS Maps: 1:50000 Sheet 55   1:25000 Sheet 359
Admiralty Charts: 1:25000 2326 or 2386

Area: 254ha (628 acres)
Height: 98m (321ft)

Owner: Torquil Johnson-Ferguson. Previously owned by the Cadzow family of Luing until about 1964.

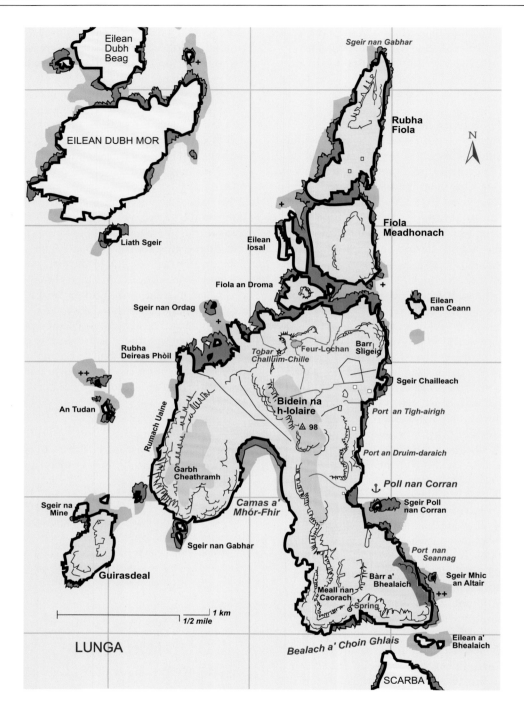

LUNGA

Population: 1794–29. 1881–17. 1891–15 (3 families in 1 house). 1931–5. 1961–0. 1971–0. 1981–3. 1991–2. 2001–7. 2011–0.

Geology: Schist and mica-schist run northwards towards the small 'slate' island of Belnahua, but the west, and part of the 'drying islands' to the north, are of 'Scarba conglomerate' (see No.2.10).

Wildlife: Grazed by domestic sheep and Luing cattle. Golden eagles have been reported over Bidein na h-Iolaire but buzzards are more common. This is part of a National Scenic Area and the Firth of Lorn marine Special Area of Conservation.

*   *   *

LUNGA is an untidy island, all humps and bumps, rocks and bogs, and a misshapen coastline which disintegrates into smaller tidal islands in the north – **Rubha Fiola** (G. – tidal island headland), **Fiola Meadhonach** (G. – middle tidal island) – these are sometimes called North and South Fullah, **Eilean Iosal** (G. – humble island) and **Fiola an Droma** (G. – drum-shaped tidal island). It is fortunate to have a reasonable anchorage sheltered from the prevailing wind just north of the skerry in Poll nan Corran (G. – the sickle-shaped pool) where there is a pebble beach. Birds of prey circle slowly above the dominant hill, Bidein na h-Iolaire (G. – pinnacle of the eagle) and seem to be acting a part – keen to prove that this really is eagle territory.

Walking on the island is not easy but the Luing cattle which graze there have trampled a number of muddy trails through the scrub. There are rock formations which could be mistaken for standing stones from a distance and many wildflowers in the crevices.

Tobar a Challuim-Chille (G. – the well of St Columba's church), a fresh-water spring bubbling into a mossy rectangular trough of ancient flagstones, is beyond the central ridge in the north-west [NM705091]. This has never run dry and in times of drought was used by the slate quarry workers from Belnahua. There are three houses on the main island, all in very poor condition and only one of which may still be habitable.

One of the tidal islands, Rubha Fiola, is run as an adventure centre by the owner and his family. It has a timber chalet for accommodation built beside the remains of an old blackhouse. Young people aged 9 to 16 are given training in survival techniques such as abseiling, cave-dwelling, canoeing, fishing, climbing and beach-combing, and the experience of living on an uninhabited island unaccompanied by adults (see No.2.15). This must be every adventurous youngster's dream come true!

The graves of some of the past inhabitants of Lunga are to be found in the burial ground of Kilchattan on Luing (No.2.14).

The channel between Lunga and Scarba is the famous **Bealach a' Choin Ghlais** (G. – the pass of the Grey Dogs). This can be almost as dangerous as the Corryvreckan as a sly tide pounds through at over 8 knots. The channel is narrow and divided by **Eilean a' Bhealaich**.

When the tide is at full flood the water south of the island is at two distinct levels with a spectacular downhill torrent. There is another dangerous overfall at the narrowest point, after which the race rushes westwards for another two miles passing the rocky islet of **Guirasdeal** (32m high).

Ormsa islet, also owned by the Johnson-Fergusons, lies directly north of Lunga and beyond it is the slate island of **Belnahua**. Belnahua, which belongs to the Carling family, has a very extensive drying reef to the north-west. In 1936 a Latvian vessel, *Helena Faulbaums*, struck this reef and sank with the loss of 16 lives. The visible duncan of the island is tiny and yet it supported a major slate industry. Now all that remains is the shattered quarry cutting deep into the heart of the island and the grey, deserted slate-workers' cottages. Beside Belnahua is the islet of **Fladda** (owned by the Platt family). Its lighthouse is a well-known sea-mark in the Sound of Luing.

* * *

Access: No regular access. By arrangement: Farsain Cruises, Craobh Haven, 01852-500664. Sea Fari Adventures, Oban, 01852 300003.

Anchorages:
1. Poll nan Corran (Puill a' Charrain). A bay on the E side. Approach from NE and anchor N of the Sgeir, off centre of pebble beach, 8–9m, mud. Exposed to NE, otherwise reasonably sheltered.
2. Camas a' Mhór-Fhir (G–bay of the giant). S-facing bay on W side of Lunga, outside Grey Dogs. Anchor near head of bay according to depth, 4–10m. Exposed S to W.

2.13 Eileach an Naoimh

*[el-uchĕn **noe**:v] (G. – rocky place of the saint). According to Watson the correct name is na h-Eileacha Naomha (G. – the Holy Rocks).*

OS Maps: 1:50000 Sheet 55 1:25000 Sheet 359
Admiralty Charts: 1:75000 2169 1:25000 2386

Area: 56ha (138 acres)
Height: 80m (262ft)

Owner: Lord Richard Sandys, Worcestershire (the family of Lord Duncan Sandys, a former Minister of State). All the monuments are in the care of Historic Scotland.

Population: Uninhabited and no census records.

Geology: The strata, mainly of limestone and Dalradian calcareous slate but with some sandstone, are severely tilted up to the north-west, where they are exposed as steep cliffs falling directly to a continuous rock-platform at sea-level. The south-east slopes are sheltered and fertile.

History: A monastery was founded here by St Brendan of Clonfert (Brendan the Navigator) in 542AD, twenty-one years before St Columba founded Iona. Although continuing to enjoy some significance as a religious shrine, the island appears to have remained unpopulated after the monastery was destroyed by the Vikings, possibly in the early 10th century. At a later stage for a limited time it was occupied by crofters who may have altered some of the original buildings or even added new features such as, possibly, the corn-drying kiln.

This is generally agreed to be **Hinba [een**-ba] the island mentioned by Adomnan: 'Inba' in early Gaelic means 'Isle of the Sea' and 'Hinba' is the plural. (Watson, in *Celtic Place Names of Scotland*, considered Hinba was Jura whereas Campbell thought Canna had a better claim). However, John of Fordun in 1380 mentions 'Helant-Leneou' as a

sanctuary and Latin texts of the early Irish Church say St Brendan established a church on 'Ailech'.

Responsibility for the site, arguably the oldest ecclesiastical building site in Britain, was taken over by the Office of Works in 1926 and is now protected by Historic Scotland.

Wildlife: The soil bedded on limestone gives an ideal growing medium and the verdant hillsides all face south. Provided no sheep have been grazing on the island, the grassy slopes and rocky crevices are covered with scarlet pimpernel, primrose, blue pansy, spotted orchids, spring cinque-foil, yellow iris, meadow-sweet, honeysuckle and many other species.

*   *   *

If the wind is light, and the portents good, one can risk an overnight stop although a West Highland friend once claimed: 'Only a very brave man would spend the night on **EILEACH AN NAOIMH**, it is so peopled by ghosts.' In spite of such ominous warnings *Jandara* spent a peaceful night there at anchor, although I must admit we did not venture ashore after dark.

The original Celtic monks searched for communion with God in the lonely deserts of the ocean, emulating the devotion of St John the Baptist. It was in the spirit of this search

. . . SEMI-DETACHED BEEHIVE CELLS

for solitude that St Brendan established his monastery here. Later it is supposed to have become the favourite retreat of his nephew, St Columba, who loved it as much as Iona and who came here for peace and contemplation. His mother, Eithne, Princess of Leinster, is also supposed to be buried here. A small upright slate slab roughly incised with a cross marks the spot near the top of a hillock south of the monastery ruins [NM639096].

The landing place is inside a lagoon formed by a line of skerries. **Sgeiran Dubha**. **Port Chaluim Chille** (G. – black skerries at the port for Columba's church) is a tiny creek with a shingle beach, and a fresh-water spring in a stone basin overgrown with watercress. This is at the foot of a gully which leads up to a shallow amphitheatre below the spinal ridge leading to **Dun Bhreanain**, the highest point. This space shelters the low, broken walls of the **Monastery** and **Church** [NM640097]. These are thought to date from the 9th century as St Brendan's earlier

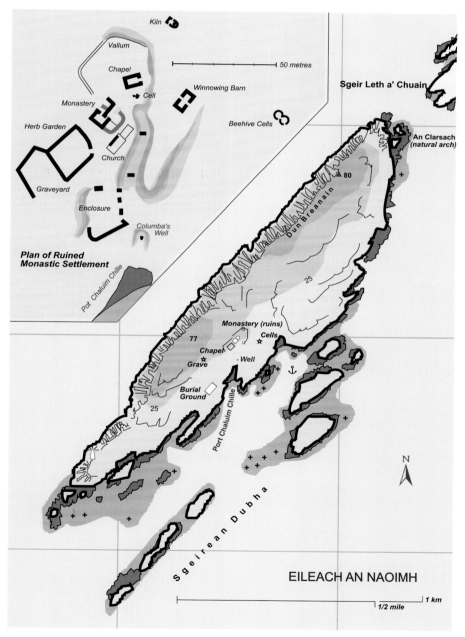

Plan of Ruined Monastic Settlement

EILEACH AN NAOIMH

structures would almost certainly have been of wood. Bones and a skull were found when a monastery wall was rebuilt to form a sheepfold in 1859. Just north of these ruins is a small cell structure and beyond it the **Chapel** standing in an open space contained by a low vallum or earth rampart. The chapel walls are nearly 1m thick and the inside measures about 6.7m by 3.7m with walls up to about head-height. A shelf or aumbry on the east wall is similar to that in the chapel on Nave (No.2.5). One indecipherable carved slab is inside the chapel.

Among other artefacts in the area are the remains of a stone oven or kiln with a fireplace and flue in which the monks may have baked bread, or dried corn, although this could have been built by the farmers in the late 18th century. The kiln is north of the chapel and to the east of it is a structure that may have been a winnowing barn.

A natural rock 'pulpit' stands by the landing place near the shore and on the slope above it (about 90m east of the chapel) there are two partly reconstructed 'semi-d' beehive cells [NM641097]. These are the finest Scottish examples of the ancient structures and only some cells on a cliff ledge of Skellig Michael Rock off Southern Ireland are better preserved. One of the cells of the **Clochain** – as this double cell is called – could have been an oratory with an underground cell beside it, like a Pictish souterrain, which may have been a wine cellar.

West of the landing place are two enclosures, the further being a herb garden. The burial ground beside it has a number of upended slabs, one of which bears a cross. It was reported in 1824, when the ruins were first publicised, that there were many carved tombs, ornamented stones and crosses but through the years these must have been stolen.

The north end of the island sports a splendid natural sandstone arch, **An Chlàrsach** (G. – the harp), gouged out at the time when the raised beaches were being formed. This can be reached fairly easily by an interesting walk (approximately following the 25m contour). Beyond the skerry of **Sgeir Leth a' Chuain** is the islet of **A' Chuli** (G. – the retreat), on which there was once a chapel. On old maps this is called culbrandon (G. – Brandon's retreat). St Brendan is reputed to be buried here. A bracing walk back to the landing

place on the springy turf along the top of the ridge is rewarding. On one side – larks singing above the lush grass; on the other – the sea frothing at the foot of the cliffs.

Access: No regular access. Boat trips by arrangement with Farsain Cruises, Craobh Haven, 01852-500664 or Sea Fari Adventures, Easdale, 01852-300003.

Anchorage:
1. Occasional anchorage on SE side between island and line of skerries and islets. Approach from E through SW side of main gap in the skerries, or from SW keeping parallel to, and fairly close to, the line of skerries. Anchor off the old landing place, or E of drying/submerged rocks in NE pool. Not recommended for overnight stay except in settled conditions.

2.14 Luing

[ling] (G. long – ship) or (ON lyng – heather).

O S Maps: 1:50000 Sheet 55 1:25000 Sheet 359
Admiralty Charts: 1:75000 No.2169 1:25000 No.2326

Area: 1543ha (3813 acres)
Height: 94m (308ft)

Owner: Multiple ownership but most of the agricultural land has been owned by the Cadzow family of Duncrahill, East Lothian, since 1947.

Population: 1841–no separate Census figures. 1881–527. 1891–632. 1931–312. 1961–192. 1981–157. 1991–182. 2001–212. 2011–195. These figures include the tidal island of Torsa which has one house.

Geology: Predominantly graphitic schists and slate. The north end has large partially quarried slate deposits but the north part of the central ridge is of hornblende-schist.

Wildlife: There are no rabbits but there are stoats. The birdlife is similar to the adjacent mainland and pipistrelle bats can be seen at Ardinamir on summer evenings. Wild boar were once common on the Scottish mainland but Luing is one of the few islands on which remains have actually been found.

*   *   *

LUING is an easy island to reach from the

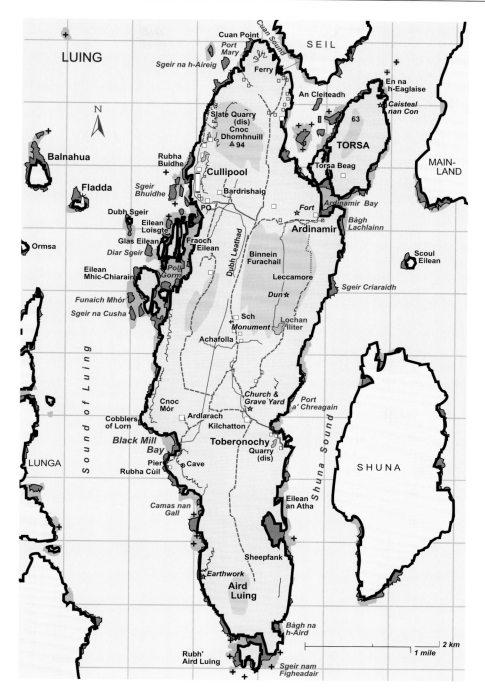

mainland as there is a fast and regular vehicle ferry service across the 200m wide Cuan Sound which separates it from the island of Seil (Seil in turn is linked to the mainland by the famous Clachan Bridge.) The spring tides rush through the Cuan Sound at nine miles per hour creating a 'step' in the water as the flood builds up a difference of level.

Slate was the principal industry on Luing and was still being quarried here beside the main village of Cullipool until 1965. One hundred and fifty skilled men were employed and 700,000 slates were produced each year. Iona Cathedral is roofed with Luing slates. Now livestock farming is the principal activity, in particular the famous and unique herd of prize beef cattle bred by the island's main farm since 1947.

Luing's other claim to fame is as a lobster-fishing centre. The lobster pond between **Eilean Loisgte** and **Fraoch Eilean** (G. – heather island) is one of the largest in Scotland.

Cullipool (G. – boat pool) is a pretty village of whitewashed cottages. These were the original slateworkers' houses but a number are now holiday homes or have been purchased by retired couples. In the evening the old slate workings to the north have a sculptural quality with subtle colours in the strata and to the west, across the many tiny islets in the Sound of Luing with Lunga and the Isles of the Sea beyond, there are the most magnificent Atlantic sunsets.

The secure little anchorage of **Ardinamir** (G. – headland by the bed of the river) is very popular but the entrance has to be negotiated with great care. Until 1991 its popularity owed much to Irene McLachlin who lived alone in her croft beside it – with her cat, McElvie. She kept the leading mark freshly painted and should a yachtsman hit a rock she would offer friendly advice in a voice which could be heard on the mainland. As an honorary member of the Clyde Cruising Club she had a register of every visiting yacht since the 1940s and prided herself on never forgetting a name. Irene spent many happy hours sitting at the open window admiring the West Coast Drizzle. McElvie, a very big cat with pink eyes, always occupied the single armchair.

On the hill above Ardinamir, just north of Irene's house, is a large Iron Age fort, **Dun Ballycastle** [NM752121], and further south on the next hill is another one, **Dun Leccamore**, which has the remains of a stairway and several rooms [NM751108].

Above the attractive village of **Toberonochy** beside the bay and overlooking Shuna (No.2.11) stands the bleak well-tended ruin of Kilchatton chapel which was abandoned after 1685 [NM745091]. It is surrounded by slate gravestones including the grave of Covenanter Alex Campbell who 'digged my grave before I died'. On his tombstone he advises against '... women that wear Babylonish garments... men that have whiskers... Quakers, Tabernacle folk, Haldians, Independents, Anabaptists...' and

IRENE'S HOME AT ARDINAMIR

so on.

At the centre of the island, near the ruined water mill, is the Fairy Knoll where visitors (who can spare one) are expected to place a hair on top to please the sprites.

The island's second highest point, **Binnein Furachail** (G. – the outlook pinnacle) is 87m (285ft). It lies on the central axis midway between Ardinamir and Poll Gorm (G. – the azure pool).

Luing has a number of satellite islands linked to each other or Luing itself when the tide is out. **Eilean Mhic Chiarain** and **Glas Eilean** in the west, **Rubh' Aird Luing** in the south, and, in the north-east, **Torsa** (ON – Thor's island) and **Torsa Beag** which are permanently joined by a narrow strip of land. The sole habitation on Torsa is a farmhouse on the south side by Ardinamir which was occupied until the 1960s and is now once again inhabited. On the north side the ruined 16th-century fortress of **Caisteal nan Con** (G. – castle of the dogs) [NM766136] was the site of a hunting lodge for the Lords of the Isles and may also have given the Cuan Sound its name, although (G. *cumhainn* – narrows) is more probable.

*   *   *

Access: By passenger and ro-ro ferry from Seil, across the Cuan Sound. Frequent, daily service, 01631-569160. Five minutes crossing time.

Anchorages:
1. Kilchatton Bay (Toberonochy) on E side about 2M N of Rubh' Aird Luing, good anchorage in 5.5m to 11m; sheltered except from SSW winds. Bay shoals rapidly all round and head dries out about ¾c. Avoid disturbing scientific research buoys.
2. Ardinamir bay, between NE side of Luing and SW bend of Torsa. Popular small shallow cove. Very narrow entrance channel between a rock drying 0.3m and an extensive rock ledge and shoal off Torsa shore with similar rock drying 1.5m opposite on Luing shore. Holding poor due to weed.
3. Cuan Sound. More secure than Ardinamir in S winds. Anchor off boat house slipway on Luing, SW of the Cleit Rock, 5m, sand and rock, but avoid drying reef just N of boathouse and foul ground near the islet.
4. Port Mary, a small creek on the W side, about 2¾c SW of Cuan point. Fairly shallow and exposed but useful temp. anchorage between the shore and the closer of two off-lying islets.
5. Cullipool. An interesting anchorage provided sailing directions are followed carefully. Least depth in narrow

N channel is 3.3m. There are leading marks for the W approach.
6. Glas Ford and Back o' the Pond, S of Cullipool. Needs careful negotiation at the right state of the tide. Secure anchorage but follow directions carefully.
7. Black Mill bay on W side, about 2M NNW of Rubh' Aird Luing. The head of the bay shoals ½c. Pier on S side of bay. Exposed to W.
8. Bàgh na h-Aird (Ard Bay) at SE corner. Temp. anchorage 1c off-shore but very exposed.

2.15 Eilean Dubh Mór

(G. – big black island) and **Eilean Dubh Beag** *[bek] (G. – little black island).*

OS Maps: 1:50000 Sheet 55 1:25000 Sheet 359
Admiralty Charts: 1:75000 2169 1:25000 2386

Area: 65ha (161 acres)
Height: 53m (174ft)

Population: No Census records and uninhabited.

Geology: Graphite schist with some quartzite interspersed with 'Scarba conglomerate'.

Wildlife: Droppings and bones indicate that deer occasionally swim over from Lunga. There are many nesting herring gulls with black-backed gulls waiting to pirate their nests and fledglings.

Among the numerous wildflowers are large patches of the low-growing Burnet rose *(Rosa pimpinellifolia)*.

*   *   *

There are a few rocks in the sea to the north-east of the anchorage between **EILEAN DUBH MOR** and Eilean Dubh Beag which must be avoided so boats normally approach from due north or round the top of Eilean Dubh Beag. The amount of swinging room is misleading. I have been told that the Highland Yacht Club sometimes uses this location for musters and that on one occasion forty boats anchored here!

Eilean Dubh Mór is composed of a single mound-shaped hill, 53m high connected by a saddle to a promontory on the north-east side which also has a small hill on it. The terrain is heather, rocks, peaty bog-land and bracken. There is a very small raised beach in the central saddle, just a patch of pebbles which is bare of heather. On the south-west side of the saddle is a

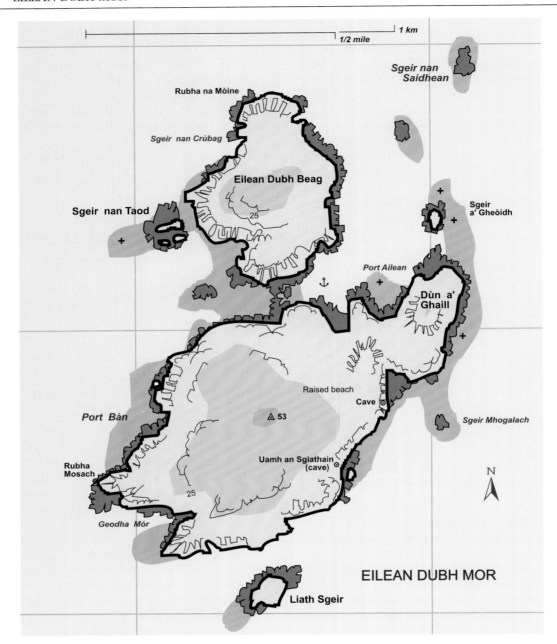

Rubha na Mòine

Sgeir nan
Saidhean

Sgeir nan Crùbag

Eilean Dubh Beag

Sgeir nan Taod

Sgeir
a' Gheòidh

Port Ailean

Dùn a'
Ghaill

Raised beach

Port Bàn

Cave

Sgeir Mhogalach

Rubha
Mosach

△ 53

Uamh an Sgiathain
(cave)

N

Geodha Mór

EILEAN DUBH MOR

Liath Sgeir

cove with cliffs round it and a cave. Further south another cave has a raised platform within it and a large quantity of dry bracken on the platform shows that it sometimes serves as a bed. This was unexpected on an uninhabited island until I learned the reason for it. The shoreline is rocky with small cliffs and indentations summed up by the name of the headland on the west side, Rubha Mosach (G. – the mean and nasty headland).

Eilean Dubh Beag (15ha) is almost a miniature replica of its big brother (or sister?) but it lacks the extra appendage. It is just a simple hump, 40m high, surrounded by lichen and seaweed covered rocks. The narrow channel between the two islands could almost be a man-made canal and is said only to dry out at the very lowest of tides.

Eilean Dubh Mór is sometimes used by the adventure centre on neighbouring Lunga (No.2.12). Youngsters are given the chance to test their survival techniques on an uninhabited island free of any direct adult supervision. They sleep and shelter in the caves with bracken for bedding. Whatever the rigours there are, no doubt, compensations and it is surprising how

VIEW FROM THE LANDING PLACE, GARBH EILEACH

often in these beautiful surroundings one will awaken to a clear still morning with air like sparkling wine. What promise of excitement and adventure!

There is, by the way, a pole set on the top of the hill. Its purpose, in case you wonder, is that the castaways can tie something to it should they be in need of assistance...

*   *   *

Access: No regular access. Boat trips by arrangement with Farsain Cruises, Craobh Haven, 01852-500664 or Sea Fari Adventures, Easdale, 01852-300003.

Anchorage:
1. E end of the channel between the islands. Approach from N keeping ½c off En Dubh Beag. Anchor as near the channel as convenient, off E side of Dubh Beag, or N of the promontory between the two foul bays on Dubh Mór, 4–10m, good holding when the weed can be avoided. Exposed N to E and occasional swell.

2.16 Garbh Eileach

*[ga:rv **el**uch]* (G. – rough rocky mound).

OS Maps: 1:50000 Sheet 55   1:25000 Sheet 359
Admiralty Charts: 1:75000 2169   1:25000 2386

Area: 142ha (351 acres)
Height: 110m (361ft)

Owner: Lord Richard Sandys, Worcestershire (the family of Lord Duncan Sandys, a former Minister of State).

Population: No Census records. Uninhabited.

Geology: This archipelago includes two members of the Dalriadan sequence, a white or pale limestone and a group which is largely quartzite and could be called the Boulder Beds. The strata are in a succession of sharp folds with white limestone at the core.

History: Signs of the past which prove that Garbh Eileach had its small place in history alongside its better-known neighbour are the remains of an ancient fort near the landing place and the historic indication of a small burial ground, Cladh Dhuban (G. – Duban's graveyard).

Wildlife: A small herd of red deer is resident and the scattered patches of birch woodland attract a variety of birds.

*   *   *

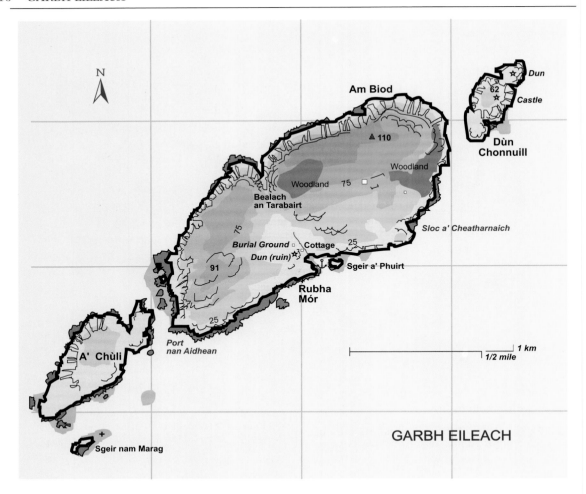

The largest of the Isles of the Sea, **GARBH EILEACH** has not the same historical interest as Eileach an Naoimh (No.2.13) but is still worth exploring. Just north-east of it, separated by a navigable channel, there is the small island of **Dùn Chonnuill** (G. – Conal's castle). Conal Cearnach was a minor 1st-century Ulster king. The present ruined castle was probably built by MacLean of Duart when he was given the island by Robert III about 1400. Sir Charles, son of the late, renowned, Sir Fitzroy Maclean, is 'Hereditary Keeper'.

The Isles of the Sea form a small archipelago of violently tilted rock-strata. As with the others, Garbh Eileach's north-western side is steep cliff whilst its south-eastern side has a grassy slope. The island is split almost centrally by a deep cleft, **Bealach an Tarabairt** (G. – the pass at the isthmus), where there is a small burn of clear water which has filtered through the limestone.

On the south side by the landing place, a stone

bothy is still maintained in reasonable condition for occasional use as living quarters. Sheep (and, formerly, cattle ferried over from Luing) graze on the lush green grass, but apart from such times as the cottage is occupied the island is only inhabited by memories.

There are magnificent and extensive views from the summit of the ridge. The highest point is difficult to locate, but is at the most northern extremity with almost vertical cliffs tumbling down to the sea below. For rock-climbers the limestone ledges are like the Dolomites in miniature.

Access: By arrangement: Farsain Cruises, Craobh Haven, 01852-500664 or Sea Fari Adventures, Easdale, 01852-300003.

Anchorage:

1. Temporary anchorage in small bay in middle of SE side. There is a drying rock approx ¼c directly S of the islet, Sgeir a' Phuirt, on E side of the bay. Anchor E of concrete

slip, thick weed over sand. There are mooring points on the islet, N of the islet and on the slipway.

2–Appendix Seil

Probably, (G. – sealg [sha:lg] – the hunting island) but maybe derived from the Indo-European root sal- meaning stream, flowing water, current (eg R. Shiel, Loch Moidart).

O S Maps: 1:50000 Sheet 55 (and 49) 1:25000 Sheet 359 (and 343)
Admiralty Charts: 1:75000 No.2169 1:25000 No.2386

Area: 1329ha (3285 acres)
Height: 146m (479ft)

Owner: Multiple ownership.

Population: 1881–661. 1891–548 (122 houses). 1931–367. 1961–303. 1971–326. 1981–424. 1991–506. 2001–560. 2010–560. 2011–551.

Geology: Large deposits of slate at the southern end of Seil were quarried extensively until 1965. Most of the island is a slatey schist with a patch of hornblende-schist in the south and basaltic tuff bordering the Sound of Insh.

Wildlife: The joints of the mossy old masonry of the Clachan Bridge support a rare and tiny fairy foxglove, *Erinus alpinus*, a native of the mountains of central Europe.

* * *

SEIL is proud of its insularity but it has been very much a part of the mainland ever since 'the Bridge over the Atlantic' was built. The **Clachan Bridge**, as it is correctly called, was designed by Robert Mylne and built in 1792/93 at a cost of £450. It spans the narrow, shallow and tidal Clachan Sound which can only be navigated at high water by shallow-draught craft. Whales fail to appreciate this fact. In 1835 a whale of 78 feet in length was stranded in the sound and two years later a school of 192 pilot whales was also trapped.

At the north end of the Clachan Sound there are some islets which form the popular anchorage of Puilladobhrain (G. – pool of the otter). Unfortunately, the 'yachters' have frightened away the otters. At the end of a line of drying islets, **Eilean nam Beathach** (G. – isle of the brutes or beasts), **Eilean nam Freumha** (G. – isle of the roots) and **Eilean Buidhe** (G. – yellow or pleasant island) – which give good shelter from the west, is **Eilean Dùin** (G. – fort island) which has a central rock outcrop like a small fort.

A well-trodden footpath leads over the hill from Puilladobhrain to the famous pub, Tigh na Truish (G. – the house of the trousers), by the Clachan Bridge. When Highland dress was banned by law after the Jacobite Rebellion, shore-going islanders swapped their kilts here for a pair of breeks (or so it is said, but it may merely mark the site of a tailor's house).

Seil is noted for its slate which has been quarried for nearly three centuries. The fourth Earl of Breadalbane, who was the landowner, built picturesque villages for the workers. The main quarry on the south side went deeper and deeper into the ground as the men chiselled out the slate. Gunpowder was then used for blasting and by 1880 the pit was 75m deep (nearly 250 feet below sea-level) with only narrow walls of slate keeping out the sea. In November 1881 the inevitable happened. There was a violent storm and the sea broke through. Luckily it was night and the pit was unmanned but 240 families lost their only means of support and severe poverty ensued. The place where the sea breached the wall can still be clearly seen.

The walls of Easdale harbour are of beautiful masonry work but with its disintegrating pier it is now a rather desolate place. In the 19th century this was a major port of call for ships collecting slate for transport through the Crinan Canal. 526 ships, including 245 steamers, used the harbour in 1825 alone.

The delightful village of trim white slate-workers' cottages was featured in the film *Ring of Bright Water* and now supports a thriving artists' colony. It is generally called Easdale although its correct name is **Ellenabeich** (G. – island of the birches) as it was an island separated from Seil by a narrow channel which was eventually filled in with quarry waste. On the slope above the east end of the village is **An Cala** (G. – haven or refuge) – a five-acre garden started in 1930 by Lord Elibank and his wife, the actress Faith Celli. Sweeping terraces provide dramatic views, and shelter belts of trees with an undercover of escallonia protect the garden from the prevailing sou'-westerlies. A burn tumbles over rocks and a high wall draped with clematis gives further shelter. The present owners, the Downies, open the garden to the public from April to September.

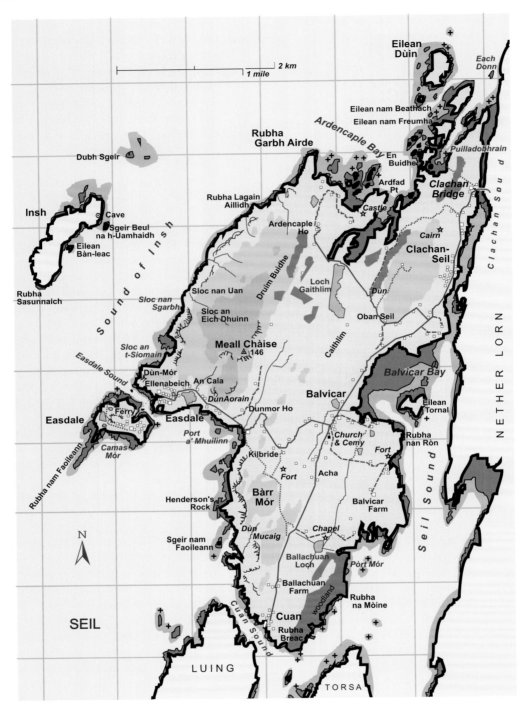

Seil's particular saint was St Brendan of Clonfert in Galway, who died in 577 (see No. 2.13). The Kilbrandon Parish Church, with an interesting graveyard of ancient carved slabs, is south of **Balvicar** on Seil Sound. **Eilean Tornal** (sold for £100,000 in 2005) is the islet in Balvicar Bay.

The broken-off outlier, **Easdale** (G. *eas* – waterfall, ON *dal* – valley) is largely owned by Jonathan Feigenbaum, whose father, Clive Feigenbaum, bought it for £16,500. He was a former chairman of Stanley Gibbons and introduced Easdale's own postage stamps. The population of this crowded piece of slate with its whitewashed slate-workers' cottages was 78 in 1931, only 16 in the 1961 Census, but had risen again to 59 by 2011 making it Scotland's most densely populated island. Easdale has a regular ferry service across the harbour, an interesting folk museum which is worth visiting and each year, the World Stone Skimming Championship.

Rocky **Insh** (G. *innis* – island), also known as Sheep Island, lies west of Seil and separated from it by the Sound of Insh. It was reputed to be owned by a Londoner who occasionally occupied the cave.

*   *   *

Access: Follow the B844 over the Clachan Bridge. Tourist Information, 01631-563122. Ferry to Easdale island, 01631-562125.

Anchorages:

1. Balvicar Bay. Perfect shelter but restricted by moorings where it does not dry out. Approach by mid-channel S of Eilean Tornal.

2. Easdale Sound. Anchor off the slate wharf which is N of the ruined pier. Navigation in the Sound requires care and close adherence to the sailing instructions. Reasonable shelter in moderate winds.

3. Ardencaple Bay. Occasional anchorage off Ardfad Point in settled weather. No difficulties if approached carefully from due N. Exposed N. Mud and weed.

4. Puilladobhrain. Very popular anchorage and often crowded. Careful identification of all hazards and beacons is required on approach.

CLACHAN BRIDGE – THE 'BRIDGE OVER THE ATLANTIC'

Mull and the Surrounding Islands

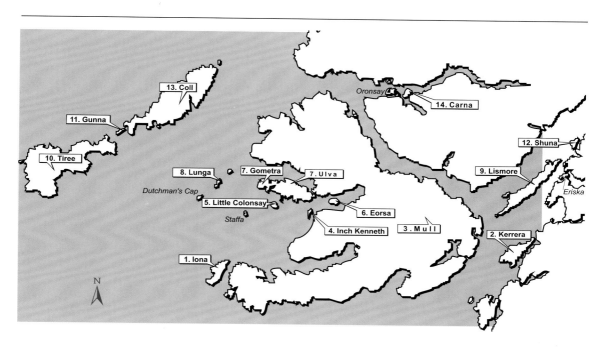

SECTION 3, Table 1: Arranged according to geographic position

No.	Name	Latitude	Longitude	Table 2* No.	Table 3** No.	Area in Acres	Area in Hectares	
3.1	Iona	56° 20N	06° 25W	44	70	2167		877
3.2	Kerrera	56° 24N	05° 33W	38	37	3000		1214
3.3	Mull	56° 27N	06° 00W	3	1	216299	87535	
	Erraid	56° 18N	06° 22W			462	187	
	Calve Island	56° 37N	06° 02W			178	72	87794
3.4	Inch Kenneth	56° 27N	06° 09W	144	122	136		55
3.5	Little Colonsay	56° 27N	06° 15W	115	104	217		88
3.6	Eorsa	56° 28N	06° 05W	106	72	301		122
3.7	Ulva	56° 29N	06° 13W	29	21	4917	1990	
	Gometra	56° 29N	06° 17W			1050	425	2415
3.8	Lunga	56° 29N	06° 26W	120	65	200		81
3.9	Lismore	56° 30N	05° 30W	30	50	5809		2351
3.10	Tiree	56° 30N	06° 52W	14	46	19358		7834
3.11	Gunna	56° 34N	06° 43W	131	141	170		69
3.12	Shuna	56° 35N	05° 23W	92	91	383		155
3.13	Coll	56° 37N	06° 34W	15	64	18990		7685
3.14	Carna	56° 40N	05° 53W	82	41	526		213
3.A	*Staffa*	56° 26N	06° 21W			82		33

*Table 2: The islands arranged in order of magnitude
**Table 3: The islands arranged in order of height

Introduction

With Mull in the geographical centre, most of the classified islands in this section are easily accessible and well known. Mull itself has such good communication with the mainland that it would be easy to forget that it is an island while its next-door neighbour Iona attracts tourists and pilgrims from all over the world.

There are a few tiny islets in the mainland firths which have not been mentioned elsewhere. **Eilean an Ruisg** (G. – bare island) in Loch Feochan, and **Eileanan Mór** and **Beag** at the entrance to lovely Loch Etive beside the castle, chapel and marina at Dunstafnage. On the loch itself are the **Abbot's Isles**, which are little more than scattered rocks with hardly a grassy foothold. **Eilean Choinneich** and **Eilean Munde** in Loch Leven are not much bigger but the latter islet, at the foot of Glencoe, is the traditional burial ground of the Macdonalds of Glencoe and close to it lies Eilean a' Chòmhraidh (G.- the meeting-place island).

Eriska (G. *ùruisg* – water-nymph island) is a flat tidal island at the entrance to Loch Creran with a bridge over the drying channel linking it to the mainland road network. It has a hotel and pleasant wooded grounds.

Staffa with its world-famous Fingal's Cave is well below the size limit of forty hectares which I have set for classification but it is much too remarkable to be ignored and is therefore included as an appendix to the section. The name of the legendary Irish hero, Fionn McCool, was given to the cave by Sir Joseph Banks because, so it was reported twelve years later, the local name for the cave was *An Uamh Bhinn* (G. – the melodious cave) and his interpreter mistook this for the Gaelic genitive form of Fingal – *Finn*. A plausible story, but not entirely convincing.

The traditional Gaelic term for a Norseman who had settled in the Hebrides was, and still is, *Fionnghall*, meaning a fair-haired stranger. (This is in contrast to *Dubhghall*, a dark stranger, for a Teuton or a Dane). Most Gaelic place names tend to be practical rather than poetic, so is it possible that the cave was simply known locally as the Norseman's cave?

3.1 Iona

In very early times called I [ee], IO, HII, HIA or IOUA – possibly from the Norse Hiöe [ee-ĕ] meaning island of the den of the brown bear. Later named ICOLMKILL (G. I Chaluim cille – island of Calum's monastery). Columba is a Latinised version of calaman (G. – dove), but the saint's given name was Calum. IOUA became corrupted to IONA in the 18th century through a typographical error.

O S Maps: 1:50000 Sheet 48 1:25000 Sheet 373
Admiralty Charts: 1:25000 No.2617

Area: 877ha (2167 acres)
Height: 100m (328 ft)

Owner: The sacred buildings and sites were presented to the Church of Scotland's Iona Cathedral Trust in 1899 by the 8th Duke of Argyll. The island as a whole was purchased from the Duke of Argyll by Sir Hugh Fraser in 1979 and given to the National Trust for Scotland.

Population: 1841–496. 1881–243. 1891–247. 1931–141. 1961–130. 1981–122. 1991–130. 2001–125. 2011–177.

Geology: Although Iona lies close to Mull it has a different geological composition. Much of it is Lewisian gneiss but on the east side there are clayey Torridonian beds, minor igneous dykes and glacial erratics from the Ross of Mull; raised beach deposits of late-glacial and post-glacial periods make up the western machair. On the south-east coast [NM268217] is the quarry for the original 'Iona marble' – actually a Lewisian gneiss with a large limestone content. The communion table in the abbey is made of it. The 'Iona marble' which is now sold on the island, and elsewhere, comes from Connemara in Ireland.

History: Iona was inhabited at least as far back as 1000BC and it may have been a religious centre long before St Columba. It has been called Innis nan Druinich (G. – the Isle of Druidic Hermits) but any association is speculative.

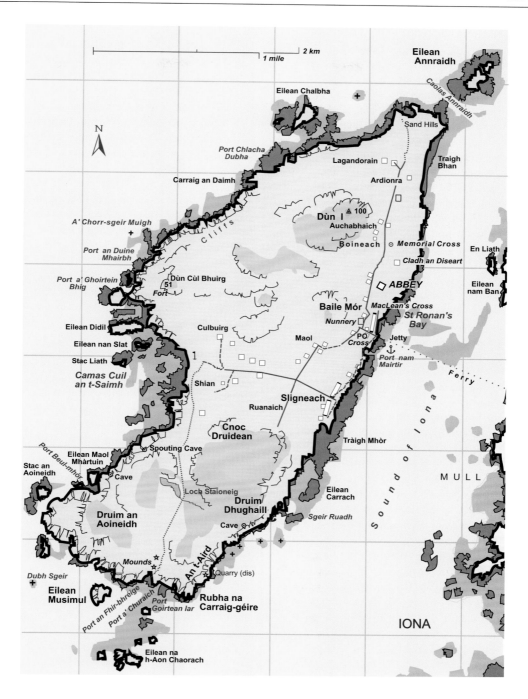

However, the Druid symbol of Bel – a circle – was later incorporated with the Christian Cross to become the well-known Celtic Cross.

Columba, an Irish prince accompanied by twelve companions, arrived in the year 563, when he was forty-two years old. He probably made his approach up the west coast of Islay in a large currach with a lug-sail. During the next thirty-four years he founded a monastery and turned Iona into a place of pilgrimage and Christian learning which was renowned throughout Europe. He died on the island in 597, having achieved his goal of conversion of the Picts to Christianity at a time when St Augustine had only started conversion of the English.

St Columba was not the earliest Irish missionary

to reach Scotland and may not even have been the greatest but he was a strong man with the confidence of a royal upbringing. When the king of Dalriada died Columba consecrated one of his relatives, Aiden, on the throne. With such powerful connections his fame grew and after his death it became established for posterity by the publication of no less than three biographies.

In 795 the first Norse raid on Iona took place with widespread destruction and pillaging. There was no defence. The monastery, which was built of mud, wood, wattle and thatch with an earthwork vallum and ditch to keep livestock out of the sanctuary area, was razed to the ground. It was rebuilt but the Norse struck again in 798 and 802, each time burning and levelling the buildings. Once more it was rebuilt. In 806 the Vikings again returned, destroyed the monastery, and murdered sixty-eight monks at Martyrs' Bay (200m south of the ferry jetty). In 849 after a further Norse raid in 825, the few remaining treasures were divided between Dunkeld in Scotland and Kells in Ireland including, it is thought, at least part of the beautifully illustrated *Book of Kells*, now in Dublin, and the Breccbennoch, a reliquary, now in Edinburgh. St Columba's remains were also moved after which they apparently disappeared, although it is possible that they were later returned to Iona and reburied in St Columba's Shrine next to the cathedral. Kells proved to be no safer than Iona and was ravaged seven times by the Vikings. Another murderous raid on Iona occurred in 986, when the abbot and fifteen monks were killed at the White Strand in the north of the island. It is little wonder that so few relics of this ancient seat of European culture have survived.

Queen Margaret is said to have rebuilt the monastery in stone and St Oran's Chapel in 1074 but whether this is true or not in 1203 Reginald or Ragnald of Islay, son of Somerled, founded a new monastery and abbey for the Benedictines on the site of the earlier monastery and also an Augustinian convent or nunnery whose fine pink granite ruins still remain. His sister became the first Abbess of Icolmkill. The greater part of the present abbey was built in the 1500s on the foundations of Reginald's Benedictine abbey.

From the 14th century the Mackinnons of Mull were the hereditary Abbots of Iona. In 1499 the Benedictine church on Iona, which was the seat of the Bishopric of the Isles, was given cathedral status until the dissolution after 1570. The island was seized by the MacLeans of Duart in 1574 but it was taken over by the Earl of Argyll in 1688. It has been said that during the Reformation 360 stone crosses were smashed and thrown into the sea but this could be a myth. In 1609 the Hebridean chiefs swore loyalty to the Stuart kings in the church on Iona (documented as the Statutes of Icolmkill) and agreed to measures which curbed their powers but which were designed to improve island life. Unfortunately, later statutes were repressive and led to severe restrictions on Gaelic culture. In 1617 the church on Iona was annexed to the Protestant Bishopric of the Isles.

The roofless old abbey church was restored by the Church of Scotland in 1902–10. The general restoration and maintenance of all the monastic buildings was in the hands of the Iona Community, a body founded by a Govan minister, the Rev George Macleod (later, Lord Macleod of Fiunary). It is now the responsibility of the Iona Cathedral Trust.

Wildlife: Corncrake can often be heard on Iona these days, although rarely seen. Fulmar, shag and kittiwake breed here and also rock dove and jackdaw. Linnet, twite and yellowhammer can be seen and both the common and Arctic terns.

* * *

'That man is little to be envied,' said Dr Johnson, 'whose patriotism would not gain force upon the plain of Marathon, or whose piety would not grow warmer among the ruins of IONA!' He was referring to the island cradle of Scottish Christianity and learning, a place of pilgrimage with religious associations stretching far back into antiquity. Sir Walter Scott may have found it 'desolate and miserable' but it inspired Wordsworth in 1835 to compose three sonnets.

The island is austere and windswept yet remarkably fertile. The coastline has a magic and mysticism which, to me, rivals or even surpasses that of the acknowledged religious sites. The shell-sands are clean and white, the rocks have subtle colours tinged with rose and the sea ranges from deep violet to translucent emerald green. There is a sparkle and clarity in the air which is unique to this island and which has proved a challenge and delight to many artists.

The lone and distinctive hill in the north standing above the cathedral has the pre-

IONA ABBEY

Columban name of Dùn I [**doon**-ee]. In this case the 'dùn' probably refers to the mound-like shape rather than to a fort. It is an easy ten-minute climb to the top of this mountain in miniature which has its own 'north face' and rock chimney. From the top, at 100m (328ft), there is a marvellous view of coastline and islands stretching from Islay to Skye.

To the north is machair and the notorious but beautiful White Strand of the Monks with **Eilean Chalba** and **Eilean Annraidh** and, beyond, the islands of Staffa and the Treshnish Group.

The east coast, facing peacefully across the narrow Sound to the pink granite rocks of Mull, has a violent past. **Martyr's Bay**, near the ferry jetty, is where sixty-eight monks were massacred. The cathedral-church, solid and square, sits below the hill like a great supporting boulder. Further down the sound beyond Sligneach the white sands of Tràigh Mhór (G. – big beach) reach out to **Eilean Mór** and **Eilean Carrach**.

The south coast has cliffs and bays and green serpentine pebbles on the beaches. **Port a' Churaich** (G. – port of the coracle), or St Columba's Bay, was the saint's traditional landing place when he arrived from Ireland and it lies beside Port an Fhir-bhrèige (G. – port of the manlike prehistoric mound). Entrance to the port leads past **Soa** (ON – sheep island) and between **Eilean Musimul** and **Eilean na h-Aon Chaorach**.

On the west, facing the Atlantic, there are fine farms and crofts on the machair while, out to sea, **Stac Mhic Mhurchaidh** stands proudly beside little **Réidh Eilean** (G. – levelled island). This is where tourists rarely go although there is a golf course overlooking Camas Cùil an t-Saimh (G. – ? the bay of twin recesses). South of this is Spouting Cave, beside an overhanging cliff. The bays here have semi-precious stones among the shingle.

The village, **Baile Mór** (G. – big town), facing the Sound of Mull sees half a million tourists a year tripping through it and like many tourist traps it is nothing to 'write home about'. However all the sacred sites are within easy walking distance of the ferry jetty.

Close to the jetty the first site to be reached, and the most beautiful, is the **Nunnery of St Mary** [NM284241]. It is of lovely mellow pink granite and the ruins, which are quite well preserved, include the church and choir, the Lady Chapel, cloister court, chapter house and refectory. Beside it the Romanesque **Church of St Ronan** (12th/13th century) serves as a museum.

Carrying on towards the cathedral you pass the 3m high MacLean's Cross dating from the 15th century [NM285242]. **Reilig Odhrain** (G. – graveyard of Oran) is on the right-hand side. A ridge in this simple cemetery is considered the burial place of many early Scottish kings up to the time of Duncan and Macbeth in the 11th century and some West Highland chieftains of the Middle Ages but in 2010 a ground-radar survey looking for Columba's original monastery site discovered a larger cemetery in a field by the abbey.

The little Norman-style **St Oran's Chapel** [NM285244], which was probably built as a family mortuary by the Lords of the Isles in the 12th century, has been restored.

Crossing the meadow in front of the cathedral and beneath Dùn I is the **Street of the Dead** – a 13th-century pavement of red granite along which kings were borne for burial.

The 10th-century **St Martin's Cross**, 4.3m high, is opposite the west facade and to the left of it is a concrete replica of the 9th-century **St John's Cross**. Near the well is the broken shaft of **St Mathew's Cross**. St Columba's remains may be within **St Columba's Shrine** at the north-west corner of the nave or they may be in **Tor Abb**, the mound just west of the cathedral.

The **Abbey** or **Cathedral** [NM286245] is built of a rosy granite quarried from Tormore on Mull. It has a heavy square tower 21m high centred over arches on a cruciform plan. Much of the building dates from the late 15th century, when Reginald's abbey of 1203 was rebuilt but there have been many additions and alterations since then. In the north the Sacristy doorway of golden sandstone from Carsaig on Mull dates from 1500. The **Cloister**, entered through Norman arches in the north transept, contains two medieval pillars. Several of the monastic buildings have been restored such as the **Chapter House** (1955) with Norman doorway, the **Refectory** and the **Undercroft** (1949), the **Reredorter** (1944) and the **Caretaker's House** (1950) which has a gable of the old Abbot's House. **Michael Chapel** (rebuilt 1960) and the **Infirmary** are built on the original Celtic foundations.

The **Abbey Museum**, behind the Abbey, shelters many of the notable grave-stones. It is also the specially constructed site of the original **St John's Cross**. The **Iona Heritage Centre** (the former Telford Manse) has local and natural history displays in the summer.

Ferry access is not cheap and is occasionally disrupted by the weather causing inevitable stress on the population. This uncertainty has led to talk of the possible construction of a causeway or low-level bridge.

Access: Frequent passenger ferry from Fionnphort on Mull (10 mins.), 01680-812343. Summer only or by request. No cars. Vehicle ferry Oban/Craignure on Mull, 08000-66-5000. Bus service Craignure / Fionnphort, 01546-604360. There is a taxi on Iona and bicycles can be hired.

Anchorages:
1. Martyrs' Bay, S of pier. Temporary anchorage in suitable weather, 3m, sand. Avoid cables and moorings and note that there can be strong tidal currents.
2. Port na Fraing (Traigh Bhan) N of abbey. Possibly better temporary anchorage, at least ½c offshore. Avoid power cable. Good holding when clear of weed.
3. Bull Hole, between Eilean nam Ban and Ross of Mull N of Fionnphort. Good, sheltered, but restricted anchorage in depths of 3–4m. Approach from S. Anchor near Limpet Rock if there is room or off ruined pier in entrance channel. 1M distance to Martyrs' Bay.

3.2 Kerrera

(ON Kjarbar-øy – Kjarbar's island) or (ON ciarr-øy – brushwood island).

O S Maps: 1:50000 Sheet 49 1:25000 Sheet 359
Admiralty Charts: 1:25000 No.2387 1:10000 No.1790

Area: 1214ha (3000 acres)
Height: 189m (620 ft)

Owner: Principal landowner, Mrs C H E MacDougall of MacDougall. 270 acres at north end were put up for sale by Lord Lovat in 1994.

Population: 1841–187. 1861–105. 1881–103. 1891–92. 1931–79. 1961–42. 1971–27. 1981–38. 1991–39. 2001–42. 2011–34.

Geology: The island is of secondary basalt, graphitic schists and red sandstone.

History: Kerrera has belonged to the MacDougalls since Somerled founded the clan in the 12th century. Alexander II and his fleet of ships anchored in Horse Shoe bay in 1249 to enforce suzerainty on Ewen of Lorn who was paying homage to King Haakon of Norway. Alexander died on the island before achieving his object. A few years later, in 1263, King Haakon's fleet also mustered in the bay on its way to the Battle of Largs. The remnants of his shattered fleet again gathered here after the battle before returning home to Norway by way of Orkney (where King Haakon died).

In 1647 during the Covenanting Wars General Leslie's army destroyed Gylen Castle, the MacDougall stronghold at the south end of the island. The Protestant minister, John Neave, persuaded the troops to slaughter every MacDougall defender – there were no survivors.

Wildlife: Wild thyme, wild roses, meadow-sweet and honeysuckle festoon the hill tracks.

Mute swan, eider duck, black guillemot and white-winged gulls inhabit Oban Bay all the year round. Buzzards are fairly common and rare red kites have been seen circling low over the island.

KERRERA is compact, rural, generally unremarkable, and forms a natural breakwater for the important harbour of Oban. Although it is so close to this bustling tourist centre it is a world apart, with lovely views, and many quiet and gentle walks. An easy climb up Càrn Breugach (G. – the false rocky hill) through shrub woodland is rewarding for its magnificent view of the Lorn coast. The island's main function for many years was as a stepping-stone for transporting cattle from Mull to the mainland.

The ferry channel leads between **Maiden Island** and the north end of Kerrera. Here there is a prominent memorial commemorating David Hutcheson, who was one of the founders of the ubiquitous Caledonian MacBrayne ferry service. Maiden Island, by the way, is one of many such

islands around Scotland which were so-named because they were used by chieftains as refuges for their womenfolk in time of war.

In **Ardantrive Bay** there are moorings, a boatyard, jetty and old slipway. The hillock south of the bay is called Mount Pleasant and **Heather Island** lies close by in the Sound of Kerrera. Across the island, on the north-west coast, is Oitir Mhór (G. – big shoal) – a large bay facing Lismore with several small islets on its west side. The largest of these is **Eilean nan Gamhna** (G. – island of the stirks). (A stirk is a year-old calf.)

The two-pupil school closed in 1997. Both it and the church were built in 1872 and the post-office was established in 1879. There is a lobster packing factory beside **Horse Shoe Bay** where lobsters from the storage pond at Cullipool on Luing (No.2.13) are packed for market. The ferry jetty is just north of the bay.

When Alexander II's fleet anchored in Horse Shoe Bay in July 1249 Alexander slept aboard ship. In the morning he mentioned that he had dreamed that St Columba had come aboard and told him to return home immediately. Alexander's nobles felt he should heed the warning but Alexander scoffed at the idea and went ashore. As soon as he landed he stumbled and before he could be carried back on board he died. The land behind the bay is still called Dalrigh (G. – the field of the King).

A road or track, which at times is little more than a footpath, runs from Horse Shoe Bay in a loop encompassing most of the southern half of the island. There is a proposal for a new improved road to include the north half of the island. Càrn Breugach, the highest point, sits above **Little Horse Shoe Bay** and there is a pleasant walk past the hill to the wild rocky site on the south coast with the fairytale turreted ruins of **Gylen Castle** (G. *caisteal nan geimhlean* – castle of the springs) [NM805265]. It was built in 1587 by Duncan MacDougall of Dunollie, the 16th Chief, on the site of an earlier fortification. The natural springs beneath the castle provided ample fresh water for the inhabitants. The building was besieged and burned in 1647 by General Leslie during the Covenanting Wars. The castle, which can look formidable on a gloomy day poised above the steep and rocky coastline, has an interesting passage underneath it. Carved heads can still be seen on the walls and an inscription which may have read – 'Trust in God and sin no more'.

GYLEN CASTLE – SCENE OF A MASSACRE

Gylen Castle was the repository for the MacDougalls' famous Brooch of Lorn. This is an 11cm (4½in) disc of Celtic silver with filigree ornament and a central dome concealing a cavity for sacred relics and supporting a large rock-crystal circled by eight jewelled obelisks. It is said to have belonged to Bruce.

When all the castle's defenders had been massacred, the Brooch was looted by one of Leslie's officers, Campbell of Inverawe. The castle was then burned down and for two centuries the MacDougalls believed their famous Brooch had been destroyed in the fire; that is, until 1825, when General Sir Duncan Campbell of Lochnell, who had inherited it, chose to present it to his neighbour, MacDougall of Dunollie, at a public ceremony.

The peninsula lying west of Gylen Castle which runs down to Rubha Seanach (G. – the venerable headland) has a number of caves in it and to the west is Ardmore Bay and the tiny tidal **Eilean Orasaig**. Lying off the western extremity and well into the Firth of Lorn is **Bach Island** (G. – windward island).

Another road and track leads directly across the centre of the island past Slatrach Bay on the west coast. Further south is Barr-nam-boc Bay (G. – billy-goat bay) and on the steep headland between these bays are two interesting caves – Uamh

Fhliuch (G. – wet cave) and Uamh nan Calman (G. – the doves' cave) [NM802294].
Access: Frequent daily passenger ferry from Gallanach 3km S of Oban. Crossing 5 minutes, 01631-563665.

Anchorages:

1. Little Horse Shoe Bay about 4¾c NNE of Sgeirean Dubha light-beacon, 2.7–5.5m, good holding. Avoid shoal area marked by buoy and drying reef off S point. (*Best anchorage for walk to Gylen Castle*).
2. Horse Shoe Bay, 4c NE of Little Horse Shoe Bay, sheltered with good holding. Anchor between central covering rock spit and cable beacon on S point.
3. Heather Island. Possible anchorage off the bight on Kerrera and N of Heather Island. Use trip line.
4. Ardantrive bay, opposite Oban Bay. Visitors' moorings and pontoon berths (pay, 01631-565333). Well-sheltered with good holding but many moorings. Beware drying reef at S point with wreck which covers.
5. Oitir Mhór bay, on N coast, affords reasonable shelter in moderate weather. Straightforward approach from NW. SW side of bay dries 1c. Charlotte Bay to N is more exposed.
6. There are no other suitable anchorages on the W coast and the S coast is very exposed. Temp. anchorage in suitable weather S of Gylen Castle in centre of cove, 4–6m, sand and shingle. (*Useful for a short visit to Gylen Castle*).

3.3 Mull

(*?G. meall – a lump or a rounded hill*) *This might refer to the rounded shape of Ben More. Alternatively, (?G. maol – bald). But the name is very ancient. 2000 years ago Ptolemy referred to Malaeos.*

O S Maps: 1:50000 Sheets 47, 48 and 49 1:25000 Sheets 373, 374 and 375
Admiralty Charts: 1:75000 Nos.2169 and 2171 1:25000 Nos.2386, 2387, 2390, 2392, 2617, 2652 and 2771 1:10000 No.2474 Tobermory Harbour

Area: 87,794ha (216,939 acres)
Height: 966m (3168 ft)

Owner: Multiple ownership but with sizeable areas controlled by the Government (mainly the Forestry Commission). In the early decades of the 18th century the Kilninian and Kilmore parishes were controlled by the house of Argyll, and the Duke of Argyll still has considerable land-holdings in these parishes.

Population: 1755–5287. 1794–8016. Overpopulation by 1821–10,600 inhabitants led to some voluntary emigration before the Clearances. 1841–8316. 1881–5229. 1891–4691. 1931–2903. 1961–2154. 1981–2197. 1991–2708. 2001–2675. 2011–2806.

Geology: Most of Mull is Tertiary basalt (trap) on top of Moine schist. In the mountain areas the basalt – volcanic lava flows of fifty million years ago – is weathered into terraces. These giant stepped formations are clearly seen round Loch Scridain and Loch na Keal. Ben More is the highest example of Tertiary basalt in Britain stepping down to a final 370m drop into the sea – the cliff at Wilderness on the Ardmeanach peninsula. Basalt cliffs at Ardtun have Tertiary leaf-beds petrified by liquid mud from the ancient volcano. Recognizable varieties are oak, hazel, plane, Ginkgo or maiden-hair tree, and various conifers – mainly Mediterranean varieties. The collapsed vent cores of volcanic eruptions centred on Beinn Chàisgidle and Loch Bà formed circular granite dykes 100m thick and some five miles in diameter. Columnar basalt is to be found near Tavool on Ardmeanach and also at Bunessan and Carsaig in the south. A sill of sapphires can be seen near the famous Carsaig arches. In this area the basalt sits on a chalk layer beneath which is an expanse of lias washed by lime-laden water.

North Mull is a basalt plateau with a volcanic plug at 'S Airde Beinn. On the headland overlooking the Treshnish Isles there is a fertile pre-glacial raised beach and raised beaches are also to be found on the east coast of Mull.

Between the masses of basalt there is a thin spread of Cretaceous and other sediments. This, and the friable rock, has given Mull well-drained and fertile soil.

Glen More, which has many glacial features and a terminal moraine, defines the southern part of Mull. Loch Spelve and Loch Buie in the south-east are at the end of the Great Glen fault.

The butt of the Ross of Mull is pink granite, with the largest mass of the mountain gabbro extruded in screes, or small outcrops and crags. The gabbro on Mull does not form the spectacular shapes it has on Rum and Skye and some of it contains olivine which gives it a sombre colour. Ben Buie has extrusions of breccias and ryolites (volcanic granite). The south crags of Creach Ceinn are granophyres (almost granite but interwoven with quartz and felspar).

History: As with so many of the islands, Mull

is rich in prehistoric remains – standing stones, cairns and many large crannogs of both stone and timber construction in the fresh-water lochs. The island was known to the classical Greeks and Ptolemy referred to it in the 2nd century AD as Maleus. In the same century the Irish Celts appeared on the scene. One can infer from the visible remains of forts and duns (about thirty-five of them) that there were many battles and skirmishes. For a time Loch Spelve, Glen More and Loch Scridain are said to have formed the boundary between the kingdom of the Picts and Dalriada, kingdom of the Scots. Christianity was introduced after St Columba's arrival on Iona in 563.

The Norwegians exercised tenuous control from about the 8th century but, even so, King Magnus plundered the island in 1100. The Lord of the Isles gained suzerainty in 1266. In the following century the Macdougalls, the senior clan descended from Somerled, supported Balliol instead of Bruce and this misjudgement led King Robert to transfer control to the Macdonalds, the junior branch which had given him support at Bannockburn. Thus the Macdonalds became Lords of the Isles and the most influential clan, and it was not until 1543, after an abortive revolt, that the Campbells gained ascendancy. The Mackinnons of Mull and the MacLeans of Duart, although party to the uprising and allied to the Macdonalds, managed by various subterfuges to maintain status with the Campbells.

James VI (James I of England) was determined to destroy Gaelic culture which he thoroughly detested. In 1608 he sent Lord Ochiltree and the Bishop of the Isles to Aros Castle on Mull. All the Hebridean chiefs were summoned to meet there for a conference. An inaugural service was conducted by the Bishop on board a ship in Salen Bay whereupon the chiefs were all imprisoned in the ship and then sent to Edinburgh.

In Charles I's reign the Protestant Earl of Argyll chose to lead the Army of the Covenant. There were religious stresses throughout Mull as, for instance, the Maclaines of Lochbuie were Catholic while the MacLeans of Duart were Protestant. MacLean however refused to join Argyll only to find that Argyll bought up all his debts compelling him to sign away his castles of Duart and Aros. To enforce this, Argyll invaded Mull with 2000 men in 1674 and occupied the castles amid

reports of needless barbarity. The Campbells rampaged through Mull and destroyed most of the priceless Gaelic library held by the Beatons of Pennycross.

Thomas Pennant observed in 1772 that although a Campbell lived in Aros Castle and government troops occupied Duart Castle, the MacLeans still retained about half the island. About this time the talented 5th Duke of Argyll, a very different man from some of his predecessors, was looking to the improvement of his estates. He instituted a system of nineteen-year leases for his tenants with fair rents related to means and as Governor of the British Fisheries Society he established the enchanting little port of Tobermory.

Wildlife: There is not much heather on the island due to the good soil but flag and meadowsweet and luxuriant fuchsia abound. The remaining patches of natural woodland are mainly oak, ash, birch and hazel. Carsaig is one of only two places in the western Highlands where watercress grows in the chalky streams, as it does in southern England.

Heavyweight stags can be seen in the mountain corries but red deer stalking in September and October restricts safe access to the hills. At least one family of otters feed on the brown trout in Loch Poit na h'I on the Ross of Mull. A growing population of about 30 rare pine marten are starting to pose a threat to the ground-nesting birds.

Mull and Ulva are the last refuges of the beautiful red and black Scotch burnet moth which is now extinct elsewhere.

Ptarmigan nest on Ben Buie's slopes at under 700m – a lower altitude than they require in the Central Highlands and the white-tailed sea eagle can be regularly seen here. There is year-round interest for ornithologists with a wide variety of bird habitats and many interesting species. Sites worth visiting are:

Loch Frisa forest track. Sea eagle viewing hide.

Glen More, (01680-812556). There are a number of resident pairs. Upland species: hen harrier, short-eared owl, golden eagle, kestrel, raven, buzzard. Also breeding curlew, cuckoo, whinchat. stonechat, and wheatear. Snow bunting in winter.

Mishnish Lochs near Tobermory: Little grebe, heron, goosander and red-throated diver. Hen

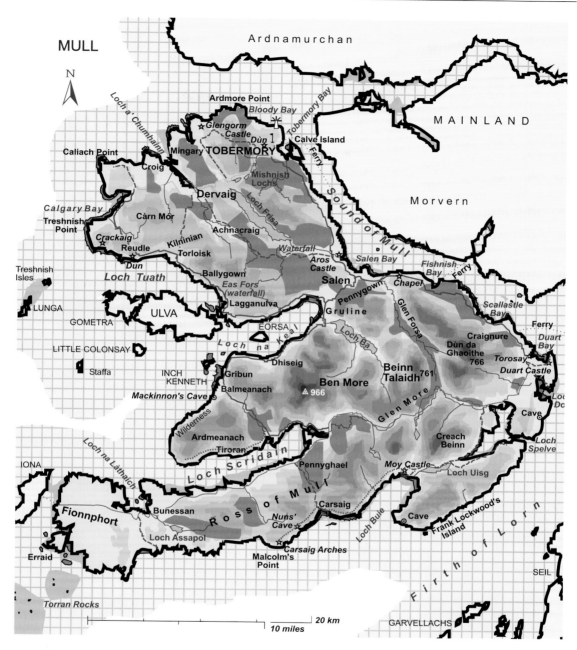

harrier, buzzard, short-eared owl and golden eagle hunt in the vicinity. Whooper swan and goldeneye in the winter.

Loch Don has resident heron, mute swan, eider, red-breasted merganser, redshank, buzzard and hen harrier. Common and Arctic tern in summer. Red-throated diver, little grebe, cormorant, greenshank, wigeon, teal, mallard, goldeneye and shelduck in winter. Passage waders such as grey plover, knot, sanderling, bar and black-tailed godwits and whimbrel. Pectoral

sandpiper, ruff, spotted redshank and green sandpiper have been seen.

Loch Na Keal: Excellent viewing of divers and the velvet scoter is sometimes seen. Also the Slavonian grebe.

Fionnphort and 1½km S at Fidden: Many migrant waders and passerines with Greenland white-fronted geese in winter. 1½km east at Loch Poit na h'I there are little grebe and, in winter, white-fronted geese, tufted duck and pochard.

Loch Scridain: In winter, red-throated, black-

DUART CASTLE – ANCESTRAL HOME OF THE MACLEANS

throated and great northern divers.

The main body of **MULL** is mountainous, rising to 966m at Ben More – the highest peak and the only Munro in all the Scottish islands excepting Skye. Ben More from the west and Beinn Talaidh from the north are very shapely mountains. The non-mountainous areas had good agricultural potential but much of this was lost when large-scale sheep farming was introduced in the 19th century. The island is so heavily indented with sea lochs that there is about 500km of coastline but, due to good drainage, inland lochs are comparatively few – even though Mull suffers the wettest weather in the Hebrides. (May is the driest month – usually.)

The vehicle ferry from Oban has its terminal at **Craignure** pier (built in 1964). On the way over it passes close by **Duart Castle** (G. *dubh aird* – black promontory), a much-photographed and perfect example of an island warlord's homestead [NM749353]. This has been the MacLeans' ancestral home since about 1250 although it

was burned by the Duke of Argyll in 1691, and confiscated after Culloden. The 26th Chief, Sir Fitzroy MacLean, bought it in 1911 and with Sir John Burnett as his architect, carefully restored it. It is presently occupied by the 27th Chief and is open to the public.

Eilean Rubha an Ridire (G. – island at the promontory of the knight) is across on the Morvern shore, where the **Glas Eileanan** (G. – grey-green islands) guard the entrance to the Sound of Mull. During a gale on the 19 October 1690 the Royal Naval frigate *Dartmouth* dragged her anchor in Duart Bay and was wrecked on this islet. The wreck, which is now protected, was discovered by divers in 1973. There have been many such accidents. Until quite recently the mast of the wrecked 'puffer' *Ballista* could be seen, but it has now disintegrated.

It was on **Lady's Rock** opposite Duart Castle, which is submerged at each high tide, that Lachlan Cattanach, the 11th MacLean chieftain, had his wife, Elizabeth, tied up and marooned because he considered that their marriage was a failure. The next morning, seeing that she had been washed away with the tide, he sadly reported her death to her brother, the Earl of Argyll. Argyll was sympathetic and invited Lachlan to visit him at Inveraray but when Lachlan duly arrived, and was shown into the dining hall, he was horrified to see his wife (who had been rescued by a passing fisherman) sitting at the top table next to her brother. Nothing was said, the meal proceeded pleasantly, and at the end Lachlan was allowed to leave unharmed. Through the years that followed the subtle torture continued but Lachlan married twice more and by his third wife, a son and heir was born. It was not until thirty more years had passed (in 1527) that he was found murdered in his bed in Edinburgh.

A relatively modern Scottish Baronial castle, **Torosay**, is also in the vicinity and open to the public [NM728353]. David Bryce was the architect in 1856 and the building has beautiful terraced gardens designed by Sir Robert Lorimer in 1899 with a walk bordered by nineteen life-sized Venetian statues. It can be reached from Craignure by the Mull & West Highland Railway, a 10.25 gauge miniature line.

North of Craignure, beyond **Scallastle Bay**, is the terminal for the small Lochaline-Fishnish vehicle ferry which crosses the Sound of Mull and connects Mull with Morvern. Approaching the foot of Glen Forsa at **Pennygown** there is the ruin of a medieval chapel with the shaft of a Celtic cross in it [NM604432]. This area was once the haunt of benevolent fairies who would complete small tasks for people. Then someone left a twig with instructions to turn it into a ship's mast and the fairies have been on strike ever since.

Nearby is the island's airstrip which was built in 1966 in only fifty-four days by the 38th Engineer Regiment as a military exercise. The road leads on to the small village of **Salen** which lies in the 'waist' of Mull, between Salen Bay and Loch na Keal. North of Salen Bay are the ruins of 13th-century **Aros Castle** built on the site of the first Norman-style castle to be completed by Somerled and last occupied in 1608 [NM563450]. One of the **Eileanan Glasa** (G. – grey-green islands) in the bay opposite Salen, called **Dearg Sgeir** (G. – red rock), was hit by the cargo ship *Rondo* in 1935. The collision wrecked the ship and the original lighthouse. Further along, in the beautiful woods at Baliscate, an ancient chapel has been the subject of recent archaeological work.

Tobermory (G. *tobar Mhoire* – Mary's well) is one of the loveliest and best-known small towns in Scotland. It was planned and built by The British Fisheries Society in 1788 and had burgh status from 1875 to 1975. The fine stone houses on the main street are brightly painted and form a cheerful backdrop to the beautiful harbour. Further up the hillside and among the trees is more recent housing. The town is well served with facilities. There are hotels, boarding-houses, a youth hostel, shops, bank, post-office, library, schools, museum and a tourist information office. The 1862 courthouse now serves as a police station and council offices. There is an attractive wooded public park and a nine-hole golf course. The eponymous St Mary's Well is at the top of the hill just west of the town beside a ruined medieval chapel. This was the original village in which Dr Johnson and Boswell stayed in 1773 in a 'tolerable inn'. As Boswell reported, 'Tobermorie is an excellent harbour. An island lies before it, and it is surrounded by a hilly theatre. The island is too low, otherwise this would be quite a secure port; but, the island not being sufficient protection, some storms blow very hard here. Not long ago, fifteen vessels were blown from their moorings'. Boswell's comments are correct but **Calve Island** (owned by the Cotton family who stay there during the summer), separated from Mull by a shallow tidal channel, is a fairly effective barrier nevertheless.

GLENGORM CASTLE

The famous wreck of a galleon or provision ship of the Spanish Armada, possibly *Almirante di Florencia*, is in the bay. Fleeing from the battle in 1588 she anchored here and took on provisions but when Donald MacLean went on board to ask for payment he was locked in the magazine and the Spaniards prepared to set sail. MacLean managed to escape but started a fire which blew up the ship. It was alleged that the ship carried thirty million ducats, and there have been many attempts to recover the treasure. These have probably been unsuccessful although there were rumours that part of the treasure was recovered and buried at Aros Castle. The wreck has now sunk deep in the mud and clay below the harbour.

Bloody Bay, between the lighthouse at Rubha nan Gall and Ardmore Point, was the setting for a sea battle between John, the last Lord of the Isles, and his son Angus. Ardmore Forest Walk, just north of the bay, is a popular cliff path with splendid views.

Dùn Urgadul, a vitrified fort, lies west of Tobermory [NM494553]. The minor road leading past it wanders through forests to **Glengorm Castle** [NM439572] in the north-west of the island looking across the sea to Ardnamurchan point. There was such an attractive haze in the air when the new owner arrived in the 19th century that he named it Glengorm (G. – the blue glen). He had not realised that the haze was caused by the smoke of burning crofts which were being 'cleared'. South-west of Tobermory the main road runs to Dervaig past the Mishnish lochs, well-stocked with trout, and on through open moorland.

Dervaig (G. *doire beag* – little grove) is a beautiful village built by the MacLeans of Coll in 1799. Kilmore Parish Church has an Irish style pencil-shaped steeple [NM431518]. Next door, the Mull Little Theatre, seating thirty-eight, was founded in this village. It is now at Druimfin, just outside Tobermory on the Salen Road (A848). In the summer there are often boat excursions from Dervaig to Staffa and the Treshnish Isles. The minor road (B8073) running south passes groups of standing stones and **Eas Corrach** (G. – steep waterfall) at the end of Glen Aros. Dervaig is at the head of Loch a' Chumhainn (G. – loch of the narrows), with a narrow passage connecting it to the sea. The anchorage of **Port Croig**, where cattle from the outer isles were landed on their way to market, is in a rocky inlet.

A basalt dyke on its north side gives **Calgary Bay** its name (G. *caladh garaidh* – the haven by the dyke). In 1883 Col J F MacLeod of the Royal North-West Mounted Police, after an enjoyable holiday at Calgary House, gave the Canadian city the same name. (The bay is also incidentally noted for a 12lb lobster caught here in the 1920s.) On the moor to the south stands the lonely ruin of Reudle schoolhouse and beyond the hills on the peninsula to the west – overlooking the Treshnish Isles (No.3.8) – is the extensive deserted village of Crackaig. Two hundred people were cleared from here in the 19th century and a villager hanged himself from the ash tree in the walled garden beside the burn. Still Cave, where the local whisky was made, is further down the burn. Ruined **Dùn Aisgain** which dates from 1BC stands on a headland to the east [NM377453] while **Dùn Bàn** is nearer the road [NM387453].

The road wends its way along the side of Loch Tuath (G. – north loch), the wide sea loch between Ulva and Mull through patches of natural woodland. In **Kilninian** burial ground [NM397457] there is a very fine medieval slab showing a kilted chieftain, and Torloisk (G. – burned hill) was the home of Alan of the Straws, a famous pirate. Many ancient artefacts are along the way and at Ballygown there is a broch, Dùn nan Gall, [NM433431] and an ancient fort [NM441431]. One kilometre further on is Mull's most spectacular waterfall, **Eas Fors** (G. *eas* – waterfall, ON *fors* – waterfall). At the head of Loch Tuath a group of tiny islets cluster in the narrow Sound of Ulva – **Eilean**

THE STURDY TOWER OF MOY CASTLE

NATURAL SCULPTURE – THE CARSAIG ARCHES

a' Bhuic (G. – buck island), Eilean Garbh (G. – rough island), and Eilean a' Chaolais (G. – kyle island) are the largest. The road passes the turn-off to Ulva Ferry and carries on round the sides of Loch na Keal (G. – loch of the cliff) to Gruline, where a mausoleum is maintained by the National Trust of Australia for Major General Lachlan Macquarrie (1761–1824) of Ulva, the first Governor of New South Wales and 'father of Australia'. **Ben More** dominates the southern side of Loch na Keal and the easiest point to scramble up it is by Abhainn na h-Uamha (G. – river of the cave), 1½km NE of Dhiseig [NM507368]. Beyond its slopes the road skirts the cliffs overlooking Inch Kenneth (No.3.4) and turns southwards through the giant rockfalls at Gribun. One of these huge boulders, lying beside a stone wall, fell and crushed the entire cottage in which a young couple were enjoying their wedding night.

Opposite **Eilean Dubh Cruinn** (G. – round black island) the road swings across country to Loch Scridain (G. – loch of the screes) cutting off the wild and trackless Ardmeanach peninsula. A 2km path from the turn-off to Balmeanach farm leads to the renowned **Mackinnon's Cave**, which was visited by Dr Johnson [NM440323].

Some 30m high and probably the largest cave in the Hebrides, it can only be entered at low tide. As usual there is the well-worn legend of a piper and his dog entering the cave. The variation on this occasion is that a witch living in the cave killed the piper and the entire party which he was guiding through the cave to the other side of the peninsula. Only the piper's dog, scorched and hairless, appeared on the southern shore.

The most remote part of **Ardmeanach**, which Americans would call the Badlands but is known locally as the Wilderness, can be reached on foot from Balmeanach (a long and very strenuous walk) or partly by rough vehicle track from Tioran above Loch Scridain followed by a 3km scramble with arrival timed for low water. The southern part belongs to the National Trust for Scotland and includes **MacCulloch's Tree**, a dramatic fifty-million-year-old fossil which is 12m high and a metre in diameter [NM402208]. Another lies toppled in a cave to the north. They can be located by two waterfalls on the cliff but ask for directions at Burg Farm. This area has a marvellous selection of wildlife and was given to the Trust in 1932 by A Campbell Blair of Dolgellau.

East of Tioran, at the head of the loch, the road

meets the main Craignure-Fionnphort road which is the route to Iona.

Mull has many attractions for the sportsman whether in hunting, fishing, shooting, pony trekking, riding, camping, exploring caves, wildlife expeditions or hill-walking. For the mountaineer, apart from the 'Munro' – Ben More (966m), and numerous sea-cliffs, there are also two 'Corbetts': Beinn Talaidh (G. – hill of Valhalla or allurement) (761m) and Dùn da Ghaoithe [doo:n da: goo-i] (G. – castle of the winds) (766m).

South of Craignure and Duart Castle a road runs down to the old ferry terminal at Grass Point by shallow **Loch Don**. This was the ancient pilgrims' way to Iona and also the drove road when island cattle were shipped from here to the mainland. On the coast between it and Loch Spelve is Port Donain, a small cove with a cave [NM741293] and chambered cairns above it.

Loch Spelve has two arms, a few skerries, and one islet, **Eilean Amalaig**. A minor road runs along the north side through mixed woodland and rhododendrons beneath the basalt heights of Creach Beinn and on past little Loch Uisg to Lochbuie. This valley is exceptionally fertile and used to be called the Garden of Mull. The sturdy tower of **Moy Castle** – near Mull's only example of a stone circle [NM618251] – overlooks the loch. The castle (now closed to the public) was built above a natural spring in the 14th century by the MacLaines of Lochbuie. It has a bottle-necked dungeon filled with water and a stone in the centre on which the prisoner sat in darkness.

The brother-in-law of the 21st MacLean of Duart was Solicitor General in 1894–5 and the tiny island east of the mouth of Loch Buie is named after him – **Frank Lockwood's Island**. Lord Lovat's bay at the entrance to Loch Buie has Lord Lovat's cave close north of it. On the east side of the loch is a medieval chapel reconstructed as a mausoleum for the MacLaines in 1864 [NM626236] and on the west side an 8km coastal path leads to Carsaig.

The main road runs beside the Lussa River in Glen More through a barren, glaciated landscape until one sees conifer forests on the way down to the head of Loch Scridain. At **Pennyghael** a cairn commemorates the Beatons, hereditary doctors to the Lords of the Isles. A minor road south meets the coast at the fertile farmland of **Carsaig**. This was a setting for the film *I Know Where I'm Going* which also featured the Corryvreckan whirlpool off Jura (No.2.6). Yachts find shelter behind the islet Gamhnach Mhór (G. – big cow) in Carsaig Bay. A long coastal walk to the west of Carsaig leads first to the **Nun's Cave** (G. – Uamh nan Cailleach) [NM524205], which has early Christian carvings and where nuns from Iona are reputed to have hidden during the Reformation. This is where sandstone was quarried in 1500 for dressing Iona Abbey and the masons' bankers with chips of stone beside them are still lying around. A further two hours walk beyond, at Malcolm's Point, are the spectacular rock formations of the Carsaig Arches [NM494185], one in the form of a very high pyramidal mass with arches in the middle and a solitary basaltic column on top. The arches are eroded sea-caves adjoining 220m-high cliffs lined with huge basalt columns.

The Ross of Mull is primeval moorland with scattered clumps of trees and a coast with many fine beaches and bays. **Bunessan** (G. – foot of the waterfall) on Loch na Làthaich provides a busy anchorage for fishing boats behind the shelter of **Eilean Bàn** (G. – pale island). The road finishes at **Fionnphort** [fina:foart] (G. – fair or holy port), the ferry terminal for Iona. Close by to the north, **Bull Hole** has a derelict stone jetty [NM301241] which was in use until the late 19th century, when the beautiful pink granite was quarried here for the construction of the Holburn Viaduct, Blackfriars Bridge, the Albert Memorial in London and several lighthouses.

Alongside the Sound of Iona, the tidal island of **Erraid** is accessible across the sands for two hours at low water. It featured in Robert Louis Stevenson's book, *Kidnapped*, which he is said to have written when staying on the island. This was the lighthouse shore station for **Dubh Artach** and **Skerryvore** until 1967 and the iron observatory at the summit of Crioc Mor {NM296203] was once used for signalling to the lighthouses. Erraid is surrounded by rocks and islets, including **Eilean Ghòmain**, **Eilean nam Muc**, **Eilean Chalmain**, **Eilean na Seamair** and, of course, the inevitable **Eilean Dubh** (two of them!).

South of Erraid lie the infamous **Torran Rocks** (G. *torrunn* – loud murmuring or thunder), which are scattered over a wide area like dragons' teeth. They lurk menacingly just beneath the surface, occasionally showing themselves in a froth of white spittle.

Access: Frequent vehicle ferries: 50 mins., Oban /Craignure: 20 mins., Lochaline /Fishnish: 35 mins., Kilchoan (Ardnamurchan) /Tobermory. All ferry information, 08000-66-5000. Direct flights, Glasgow/Tobermory, Loch Lomond Seaplanes, 01436-675030. Oban Tourist Information, 01631-563122. Tobermory Tourist Information, The Pier, 08452-255121. Island bus services, 01546-604360.

Anchorages:

1. Dòirlinn, Tobermory. Good anchorage in basin about 2c NW of the Narrows between Mull and Calve Island. Use anchor light.

2. Aros Bay, Tobermory. Far S corner of Tobermory harbour, by waterfall. Anchor between boathouse and fish farm in suitable depth.

3. Tobermory Bay. Busy, very popular marina/anchorage, convenient for access to the town. Pontoons for approx 50 boats and 25-ton visitors' moorings (charged per night), or free anchorage in the area provided near the landing stage. Bottom can be foul in deeper water (20m) beyond the moorings. Exposed NE; swell after N'ly gales; otherwise protected. Good facilities.

4. Ardmore bay. Temp. anchorage W of Ardmore point, affords shelter from S winds.

5. Loch Mingary. Temporary anchorage in quiet conditions. Tricky but worthwhile.

6. Loch a' Chumhainn (Loch Cuan), between Rubha an Aird and Quinish point. Head dries out 9½c and both sides rocky and foul. Good shelter but a trap in onshore winds. Approach with care.

7. Calgary Bay. Temp. anchorage only suitable in N and E winds and when no onshore swell. Less attractive than Lochs Cuan and Mingary. Head dries out 2c. Keep 5c off coast to the N when approaching the bay and when rounding Rubha nan Oirean.

8. Port Rainich (56 31N 06 12W), behind Eilean Rainich reef, half-way down N side of Loch Tuath, about 7c beyond Traigh na Cille, the sandy bay at Kilninian and almost SSE of Torloisk House. Limited room but useful in N'lies.

9. Sound of Ulva (56 28.5N 06 08W), S of the ferry, WNW of Sgeir Beul a' Chaolais, can be squally. Alternatively, in settled weather, E of this anchorage in the bay on the Mull shore beyond the drying reef.

10. Scarisdale, Loch na Keal. Useful anchorage but submerged rocks to negotiate. Subject to squalls.

11. Dhiseig. Shore of Loch na Keal, SE of Eorsa. Temp. anchorage 5c ENE of the Dhiseig burn (*direct access to Ben More*).

12. By Inch Kenneth. Approach with care. Temporary anchorage 4c SSW of Samalan Island in suitable depth. Exposed, subject to fierce squalls, holding poor.

13. Kilfinichen Bay, N side of Loch Scridain. Off burn at Tiroran House on W side of bay in 8–10m. Keep 2c clear of shore on approach.

14. Loch Beg at head of Loch Scridain is shallow but there is anchorage in 3.5m just within the entrance. Subject to swell and squalls.

15. Sgeir Alltach, S side of Loch Scridain. Good but restricted anchorage 1¾c SE of Sgeir Alltach, between Sgeir Chailleach and Sgeir na Rad. Careful attention to sailing directions required.

16. Bun an Leoib, on S shore of Loch Scridain entrance, E of Rubha Dubh. Anchor behind Sgeir Leathen and Sgeir Mor but not in N and NW winds as there is a heavy swell. Many drying rocks and reefs.

17. Loch na Làthaich (Bunessan). Well sheltered inlet on N side of Ross of Mull but busy with fishing boats and space restricted. Safest anchorage in this part of Mull but avoid fairway to main pier. Visitors' moorings (pay at boatyard).

18. Bull Hole, between Eilean nam Ban and Ross of Mull. Good but restricted anchorage. Approach from S. Anchor off ruined pier in entrance channel avoiding water pipeline and ferry passage to night mooring. Alternatively, anchor between En Liath and En nam Ban.

19. Fionnphort. Occasional anchorage in suitable conditions midway between ferry jetty and entrance to Bull Hole, sand. Avoid obstructing ferry.

20. Tinker's Hole. Popular restricted anchorage between Eilean Dubh and W side of Erraid in Sound of Iona. Well sheltered. Alternative is pool 2c N of Tinker's Hole or temp. anchorage in 'David Balfour's Bay' to the E.

21. Ardalanish (56 16N 06 17W). Small inlet on W side of Rubh' Ardalanish, S coast of Ross of Mull. Restricted but attractive in settled weather. S side is steep-to. Sometimes subject to swell.

22. Carsaig Bay. Occasional anchorage close N of Gamhnach Mhór, a reef of islets opposite the pier or at a suitable depth off the beach in the bay.

23. Loch Buie, exposed and not safe except in fine weather.

24. Loch Spelve, E coast of Mull. Croggan pier, depths of 2.7m at head. Best anchorage is in bight on W side of head of N arm of the loch S of the Lussa River. Gusty in W'lies particularly in S arm of the loch.

25. Loch Don, narrow and shallow, with many rocks and extensive shoals but there is a sheltered pool within. The sailing instructions must be followed very carefully. Anchorage off pier is exposed.

26. Duart Bay. Temporary anchorage NW of castle, 5–6m, or well offshore opposite jetty on N shore in 4–6m (*Visit to Castle or Torosay House*).

27. Craignure bay, exposed N to NE. Anchor NW of ferry

pier, or in S corner of bay in 4–5m. Avoid shoal water, moorings and ferry approach.

28. Scallastle Bay (56 29N 05 44W). Good anchorage in offshore winds but approach requires care.

29. Fishnish bay. Occasional anchorage near head of bay on 6m line. Head dries off 3c.

30. Salen (56 31N 05 57W). Approach with caution. Anchor SW of W'most ruined pier in 4m.

31. Aros Bay. Good anchorage if directions followed.

3.4 Inch Kenneth

Kenneth's island, named after Cainnech, follower of St Columba.

OS Maps: 1:50000 Sheet 47   1:25000 Sheet 375
Admiralty Charts: 1:25000 No.2652 or No.2771

Area: 55ha (136 acres)
Height: 49m (161 ft)

Owner: Owned in the 1930s by Sir Harold Boulton, composer of 'The Skye Boat Song'. Bought by Lord Redesdale (David Mitford) in 1938 for £900 and remained the property of various members of the Mitford family until 1966. Present owner is the family of Dr Andrew D Barlow of Kensington, London (descendants of Charles Darwin).

Population: 1841– no separate Census record. 1881–8. 1891–2. 1931–10. 1961–13. 1971–2. 1991–0. 2001–0. 2011–0.

Geology: Different from Mull as the rocks are sedimentary. Triassic conglomerates and limestone outcrops have been eroded and broken down into good soil.

History: Named after Kenneth, contemporary of St Columba, who is said to have saved the great man from drowning solely through the power of prayer. Kenneth became abbot of Achabo, in Ireland, and died in 600. The Prioress of Iona owned the island in 1569. It was considered second only to Iona in ecclesiastical importance.

Inch Kenneth achieved some fame, or notoriety, during the Second World War from its connection with the oddly dysfunctional Mitford family (related to the Churchills). It was purchased by David Mitford (Lord Redesdale) in 1938 when he, his wife Sydney and daughter Unity went to see it 'and loved it'. They had five other daughters and one son, Tom. Nancy, the author, and her sisters, Pamela, Jessica, and Deborah (Duchess of Devonshire) were bitingly witty but less concerned with politics. But their parents, Lord and Lady Redesdale, and siblings, Diana and Unity, and Tom for a time, were serious followers of the Fascist movement and great admirers of Hitler. Diana married Sir Oswald Mosley (the British Fascist leader and one-time Labour MP) in Germany in 1936. She was arrested and imprisoned in Holloway during the war.

Unity Valkyrie Mitford was a large and rather sulky girl, twice expelled from school – an exhibitionist with a coarse sense of humour. She idolised Hitler, followed him around and met him at last in 1935. Hitler was flattered by her attention and she spent many happy hours with him drawing up lists of Britons who would either cooperate or be shot. Hitler's entourage did not like her and called her 'Mitfahrt' (fellow traveller). When Britain eventually declared war

INCHKENNETH CHAPEL, WITH EORSA IN VIEW

on Germany Unity was so devastated that she shot herself in the head with a small silver pistol which Hitler had given her at the Nazi Nuremberg Rally. The bullet lodged in her brain and partially paralysed her. She returned to Britain, incontinent and brain-damaged. Inch Kenneth was listed as a wartime 'protected zone' requiring a special pass. David, who had repudiated Fascism at the outbreak of war, was given clearance and spent six months each year living there. Unity, on the other hand, was originally denied a pass due to her political activities. Later, however, in 1944 she spent some time on Inch Kenneth improvising religious services in the ruined chapel and planning her own funeral. She died in Oban Cottage Hospital in 1948 of meningitis.

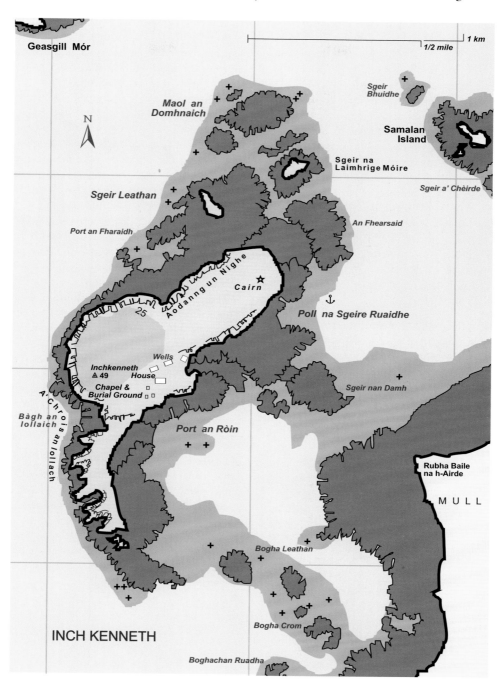

In 1945 David Mitford was in failing health so he made over the deeds of Inch Kenneth to Tom, his only son. Soon after this, Tom, who was serving in the Far East, was killed and David was astonished to find that under Scots Law, as he had died intestate, it was Tom's sisters who inherited the island. (Under English law his next of kin, i.e. parents, would have regained the title.) By this time, however, David had become a semi-recluse in Northumberland and had separated from Sydney and it was she who now spent more and more time on the island. 'The house is absolutely hideous,' she said, 'but comfortable inside. . . and the sea and rocks are so lovely.' She had a cook, housemaid, boatman, and three farm hands. She used no napkins (to economise) but ordered all her groceries from Harrods in London, sent them all her dirty washing to be laundered and dirty bank notes to be exchanged for crisp new ones.

Jessica, spitefully, tried to give her share of Inch Kenneth to the Communist Party – to 'compensate' for her family's Fascist leanings – but the Communist Party were not interested. Eventually, however she bought out her sister's shares so that their mother could live out her days on the island.

Sydney died in 1963 and Jessica sold Inch Kenneth in 1966.

Wildlife: The Statistical Account of 1845 reports that this was one of the main centres for kelp burning as the alkaline content of the ash was very high. The best seaweed was not the tangle, although this added bulk, but 'button wrack' which was prolific in the area.

In 1569 Dean Munro reported that rabbits were present in great numbers on Inch Kenneth so they have a long history here.

The island is popular with barnacle geese in winter. Shag, eider, red-breasted merganser, oystercatcher, curlew, redshank, razorbill and black guillemot are resident here all year round.

*   *   *

Like Tiree, **INCH KENNETH** is exceptionally fertile, and it once provided grain for the monks of Iona. There is a fine 19th-century three-storey mansion house and an attractive single-storey farmhouse.

Boswell and Johnson were entertained by Sir Alan Maclean, 22nd Chief of Duart, in the low-roofed stone building which is still standing but no longer occupied. Boswell considered Inch Kenneth 'a pretty little island'.

There is no trace now of the original monastery but there is an ancient ruined chapel of the First Pointed period, 12m x 6m (40' x 20'), with deeply splayed lancet windows [NM437354]. There are also the remains of a Celtic cross and many sculptured tombstones including that of Sir Alan Maclean who was Dr Johnson's host. It is the most elaborately carved slab in the Mull area and shows the Chief in armour with his dog at his feet. Many of the tombs are of Highland chiefs who were buried here when conditions were too wild to allow a crossing to Iona.

All the buildings are grouped centrally on the east side of the island.

Much of the island's economy is now provided by fish farming. Landing can be a problem unless the weather conditions are suitable as there is no ideal anchorage. The normal approach is close by the **Geasgill Islands**, avoiding **Maol an Domhnaich** (G. – Sunday rock, – but see No.7.5 Muldoanich derivation), and then between **Samalan Island** and **Sgeir na Laimhrige Móire** (G. – the rock of Mary's landing place). Inch Kenneth is encircled by wide areas of drying rocks, islets, reefs and skerries except for the west side where there is a 25m-high cliff above tumbled boulders. Just north of this is a low escarpment called **Aodann gun Nighe** (G. – the dirty face).

*   *   *

Access: No regular access. The owner's manager on Mull has private transport but try Turus Mara, Dervaig, Mull, 0800-085-8786.

Anchorages:
1. Red Skerry Pool (Poll na Sgeire Ruaidhe). E and N sides of the island are foul so approach with caution from N on given bearings. Anchor in bay on E side of island in 6–8m, holding poor. Subject to fierce squalls and landing can be tricky.
2. SE of Port an Ròin. Hazardous approach round the end of reef which extends SE of S extremity of island. Preferably only for shoal-draught vessels at mid-tide in quiet conditions.

3.5 Little Colonsay

(ON koln-øy – Columba's island) or (ON – Kolbein's island).

OS Maps: 1:50000 Sheet 47   1:25000 Sheet 374
Admiralty Chart: 1:25000 No.2652

Area: 88ha (217 acres)
Height: 61m (200 ft)
Owner: Michael Hare, 2nd Viscount of Blakenham. His daughter Cressida Cowell, author of children's books, has said that the island and its surroundings are the inspiration for many of her stories.

Population: 1841–16 (two households). 1881–0. 1891–2 (1 house). 1931–2. 1961–0. 1971–0. 1981–0. 1991–0. 2011–0.

Geology: Columnar basalt formations.

History: Between 1846 and 1851 Little Colonsay was cleared of its inhabitants by the owner F W Clark who also owned Ulva and Gometra

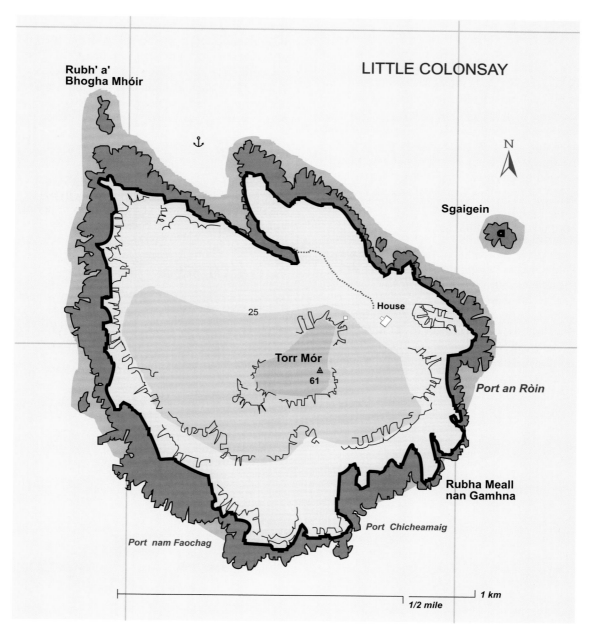

(No.3.7). In the early 20th century the island was farmed by John McColum (known as 'Johnny Colonsay'). He had occupied the Victorian house on it for most of his life but he and his family were forced to abandon it because of a plague of rats.

Wildlife: Countless primroses, wild violets and celandine – no doubt due to the absence of sheep. A few seabirds nest on the cliffs and outcrops. We saw no wild goats but they were reported in the 1930s.

The anchorage on the north side of **LITTLE COLONSAY** is approached from the east through the channel between Sgaigein and **Garbh Eilean**, a tidal island south of Ulva. **Sgaigein** is a large rock which only just shows at high water (0.6m high) and is about 1¾c north of the island. The householder keeps a lobster fishing boat on a private mooring. A path leads from the landing place through rocks covered with orange lichen. The lone house is surprisingly large and spacious with dormer windows and a slated roof. It is tucked into a hollow and protected from the prevailing sou'-westerlies by Torr Mór (G. – big hill), 61m high. It has been restored and an extensive water catchment system installed with storage tanks in a corrie on the hillside. Windbreaks of rowan tree saplings have also been planted but unfortunately many have not survived the gales.

This is a nice little island in a stunning setting with Ulva and Gometra close to the north, Inch Kenneth and the mountains of Mull to the east, **Erisgeir** islet and Iona to the south, and Staffa and the Treshnish Isles to the west. On a calm sunny day it is easy to be enthralled until you remember that the south-west is entirely exposed to the Atlantic with no sheltering land-mass between Little Colonsay and the shores of America.

The columnar basaltic rock formations of nearby Staffa are also to be found here, although in a considerably less dramatic form. The best examples are probably on the east side near **Rubha Meall nan Gamhna** (G. – humpy headland of the stirks). There are several small inlets called 'ports' in Gaelic, because it is possible to beach a small boat there. Two of them, **Port nam Faochag** (G. – port in the centre of the brow) directly south of Torr Mór, and **Port an Ròin** (G. – port of the seal) just north of Rubha Meall nam Gamhna may afford restricted anchorage in light northerlies but this has not been tested.

*   *   *

Access: Try Turus Mara, Dervaig, Mull, 0800-085-8786, or Ardnamurchan Charters, 01972-500208.

3.6 Eorsa

Derivation obscure. In the 18th century called Orsay. MacLean suggests (ON – Orri's island). Less likely, (ON Jorulf-øy – Jorulf's island) or a corruption of (G. àrsaidh – ancient).

OS Maps: 1:50000 Sheet 47   1:25000 Sheet 374 or 375
Admiralty Chart: 1:25000 No.2652

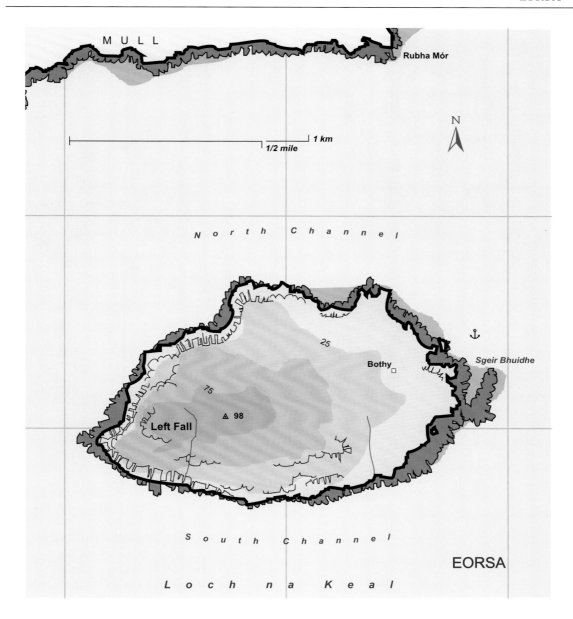

Area: 122ha (302 acres)
Height: 98m (321 ft)

Population: No Census returns and uninhabited.

Geology: Tertiary basalt bedrock.

History: Eorsa, together with Inch Kenneth, once belonged to the Priory of Iona.

Wildlife: The shores of Eorsa are sometimes the haunt of Great Northern, red-throated and black-throated divers. Very occasionally, velvet scoters may be seen and some Slavonian grebe can appear in early spring. The island is reported to have many adders, but this may not be correct.

EORSA is a compact island in the centre of Loch na Keal (G. *loch na caol* – loch of the kyle or narrows). It is part of the Loch na Keal Scenic Area. The west half of the island has a shoreline of high cliffs which were once frequented by wild goats but these moderate towards the east where a ruined bothy has a dramatic view of Ben More and the cliffs of Mull along the southern shore of the loch. There is the site of what may have been a hermit's monastic cell but there are no other features of note.

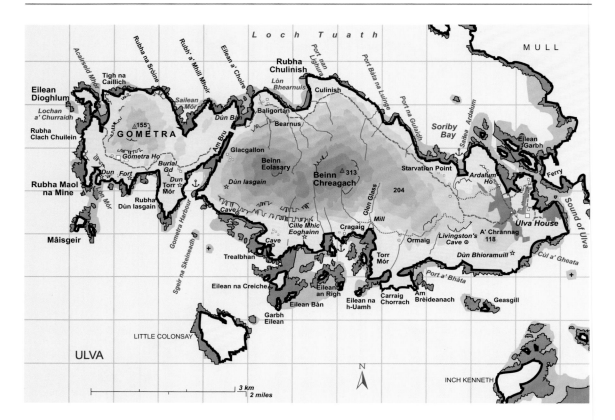

The island could provide reasonable grazing for sheep.

Eorsa served as a natural barrier across Loch na Keal during the First World War when the loch was used as a deep-water naval anchorage. During this period there were a number of visits by the Grand Fleet and it also provided a rendezvous for Atlantic convoys.

* * *

Access: Try Turus Mara, Dervaig, Mull, 0800-085-8786.

Anchorage:
1. Anchor ENE of the island on the 5m line. Loch na Keal is subject to squalls and W'lies cause a swell. Beware extensive reef S of anchorage.

3.7 Ulva

(ON ulv-øy – wolf island) or (ON – Ulfr's island).

Gometra

Derivation obscure.

O S Maps: 1:50000 Sheet 47 1:25000 Sheet 374
Admiralty Chart: 1:25000 No.2652

Area: 2,415ha (5,968 acres)
Height: 313m (1,027 ft)

Owner: Owned by the Clark family from 1835 until sold to Edith Lady Congleton in 1945. Her daughter, the Hon Mrs Jean Howard, now owns Ulva and her son, Jamie Howard, manages the estate. They also owned Gometra but sold it in 1983. Gometra had previously belonged to Mrs Boo Henderson of Sussex who bought it from her great-aunt Lady Mary Evelyn Compton Vyner in 1947. Gometra was again put on the market in August 1991 for offers in the region of £650,000 and bought by Mr Roc Sandford, a close relation of Mrs Boo Henderson.

Population: 1841 – 570 for Ulva and 78 (15 households) for Gometra but in 1848 the potato famines followed by clearances reduced the population to 150.

	1881	1931	1951	1961	1981	1991	2001	2011
Ulva	53	25	19	33	13	30	16	11
G'etra	30	37	10	15	4	0	5	2
	83	62	29	48	17	30	21	13

Geology: Basalt domes reminiscent of the early Egyptian pyramids and sea-cliffs of columnar basalt but generally a dark fine-grained igneous rock. The columnar formations on the south coast are particularly striking. There is no peat of any consequence.

History: Ulva belonged to the MacQuarries from the 10th century or earlier whereas Gometra belonged to the monastery of Iona before it came into the possession of the Duke of Argyll.

In 1543 Donald Dubh, aged sixty, recognised Chief of the Clan Donald and heir to the Lordship of the Isles, escaped from captivity in Edinburgh Castle after a total of fifty-five years' incarceration. This had been with the connivance of the First Earl of Argyll who was quick to exploit the situation after King James IV had decided to abolish the title of Lord of the Isles. It was the start of the Campbell takeover. The islanders rose to Donald's support – the Mackinnons of Mull, the MacLeans of Duart, the MacLeods from Lewis and Skye, the Macdonalds of Clanranald and the MacQuarries of Ulva. They held a Council at Finlaggan in Islay in 1545 in the traditional manner but Donald Dubh, weak from a lifetime in prison, died of a fever. He was duly buried with the honours of a Lord of the Isles and then the islesmen sadly returned home. 'It is no joy without Clan Donald, It is no strength to be without them...' said a Gaelic bard.

At one time the MacQuarries had a bright young piper called MacArthur who had been trained by the legendary MacCrimmons of Dunvegan in Skye. He founded his own piping college on Ulva which became renowned in its own right.

Lachlan McQuarrie had to sell Ulva to pay off his debts, just four years after he had entertained Dr Johnston and Boswell. It has been recorded that at this time every family on Ulva owned at least one boat and there was a surplus crop of potatoes for export, so the islanders themselves must at least have enjoyed, for a time, a reasonable standard of living. But with the increasing market value of kelp the islanders started neglecting their crofts and no longer used the seaweed for fertiliser.

In 1845 Ulva was again put up for sale and Gometra, which belonged to the MacDonalds of Staffa, was put up for sale simultaneously. Both islands were thus able to be purchased jointly by the notorious Mr Francis William Clark. It was also at this time that the kelp industry had foundered, followed by a severe potato blight on the impoverished land. Ulva was now seriously overpopulated with 604 starving crofters. In fairness, Clark tried various relief schemes before clearing the land and he did pay a proportion of the costs of emigration. But the heartless methods used by some of his employees, with or without his approval, are still remembered with disgust. In just four years – 1846 to 1851 – the new owner deported three-quarters of the total population. His factor and men turned some of the families out of their cottages without warning by setting fire to the thatch. They were not even given time to collect their few possessions and their livestock was forfeit.

Wildlife: A first impression of Ulva is of bracken galore and lots of rabbits but the island is in fact a feast of flora and fauna. There are plenty of mountain hares, red deer, seals, and an occasional otter, stoat and hedgehog. There are no foxes or adders. The island has a great variety of habitats for plant life and more than 500 recorded species.

Gometra has goats, a deer farm, and a small hardwood plantation on the east side.

The sea lettuce, a flat green seaweed found worldwide in different species, was given the genus name of Ulva by Linnaeus. When a large quantity of Ulva lactuca decomposes it gives off poisonous hydrogen sulphide gas which has caused several deaths in France.

Birdlife on both islands is varied, including buzzards, ravens, woodcock, snipe, occasional grouse and pheasant, common and Arctic tern, gannet, eider, oystercatcher, curlew, redshank and red-breasted merganser.

Ulva and Mull are the last refuges of the beautiful red and black Slender Scotch Burnet Moth, which is now extinct elsewhere, and Ulva also is home to the exceptionally rare blue dragonfly, *Orthetrum coesilesceus*.

* * *

Dr Johnson and Boswell visited **ULVA** in October 1773. In Boswell's own words:

'. . .a servant was sent forward to the ferry, to secure the boat for us: but the boat was gone to the Ulva side, and the wind was so high that the people could not hear him call; and the night so dark that they could not see a signal. We should have been in a very bad situation, had there not fortunately been lying in the little sound of Ulva an Irish vessel. . . (which) ferried us over.

'M'Quarrie's house was mean; but we were agreeably surprised with the appearance of the master whom we found to be intelligent, polite and much a man of the world. Though his clan is not numerous, he is a very ancient Chief . . . He told us his family had possessed Ulva for nine hundred years; but I was distressed to hear that it was soon to be sold for payment of his debts.

'M'Quarrie insisted that the Mercheta Mulierum . . . did really mean the privilege which a lord of a manor had to have the first night of all his vassal's wives. Dr Johnson said the belief . . . was also held in England . . . by which the eldest child does not inherit, from a doubt of his being the son of the tenant. M'Quarrie told us that still on the marriage of each of his tenants, a sheep is due to him. I suppose Ulva is the only place where this custom remains.

'Being informed that there was nothing worthy of observation in Ulva, we took boat and proceeded to Inch Kenneth . . .'

There is actually a great deal 'worthy of observation' on these islands although possibly not to Boswell's taste. The MacQuarrie's 'mean' house was later rebuilt by the new owner to an Adam design and it was visited and praised by Sir Walter Scott. The present Ulva House stands in pleasant woodland on the site of the Adam masterpiece which unfortunately was destroyed by fire. Virtually all the present dwellings on Ulva are grouped at the east end of the island in the neighbourhood of the ferry and there is also a small chapel designed by Thomas Telford and built in 1827–28.

A rough farm road leads up through the trees by **A' Chrannag** (G. – the pulpit), a hill lying west of Ulva House. On the south side of the hill is a 'sea-cave' – now well-above sea-level – called **Livingston's Cave** which was occupied by prehistoric man more than 7000 years ago. The name of the cave is a reminder that the father and grandfather of the famous explorer lived in the cave while building their croft house nearby. This road leads along the north side overlooking Loch Tuath (G. – north loch) all the way to the causeway crossing **Am Bru** (G. – the gut), a narrow tidal channel, between Ulva and Gometra. **Beinn Chreagach** (G. – rocky mountain), the summit of Ulva and almost in the middle of the

GOMETRA HOUSE

central ridge, is 313m (1027ft) high. Gometra's highest point which is in line with this ridge is 155m (508ft) high.

After the farm road has left the wooded area by Ulva House there is a track to the left which leads down to and along the south coast of Ulva. This passes a beautiful little ruined water mill with its lade connected to the burn tumbling down Glen Glass and the many sad ruins of the 'cleared' village of Cragaig. Some of the cottage doors still have their lintels in place. Beyond this point are standing stones beside the charming anchorage of Cragaig Bay, sheltered by tidal **Eilean Reilean** amid a peppering of skerries. A maze of sea-passages twist between the islets, **Eilean an Righ** (G. – royal island) and **Eilean na h-Uamha** (G. – cave island), and the many off-shore rocks. The track deteriorates further at this point but on the headland to the west are the remnants of **Cille Mhic Eoghainn**. A string of tidal islands, **Eilean na Creiche**, **Garbh Eilean**, and **Eilean Bàn**, form a natural breakwater for Cragaig Bay. In the west a dun on Ulva continues the chain of three duns stretching across Gometra.

General Lachlan MacQuarie (1761–1824), the 'father of Australia' was born on Ulva. He instituted liberal penal reforms in Australia while serving as governor of New South Wales. This made him so unpopular with the settlers that he was recalled. His mausoleum is at Gruline on Mull, by Loch na Keal.

Ulva was also the birthplace of some of the ancestors of the missionary and explorer, David Livingstone.

Thomas Campbell (1777–1844), in his famous poem 'Lord Ullin's Daughter', told the sad story of an eloping Chief of Ulva and his bride, who drowned when fleeing from her parents. They are reputed to be buried on the Mull shore in a grave between Oskamull Farm and Ulva Ferry. The channel at Ulva Ferry is very narrow and is even narrower where the islets **Eilean a' Chaolais** (G. – isle of the kyle) and **Eilean Garbh** restrict the passage, but it is navigable with care.

There is now a small tea room on Ulva – the Boathouse – which sells delicious fresh oysters from the home farm, and visitors are encouraged by an interpretive display to enjoy the island's many attractions with its beautiful walks and nature trails, 01688-500241.

* * *

GOMETRA was at one time, like Inch Kenneth, known as the granary of Iona. The land sheltering the tiny bay, Lòn Mór, in the south-west corner is still called Rhubha Maol na Mine (G. – flour-meal headland). The large low-lying skerry, **Màisgeir** (ON – seagull skerry), is almost a continuation of this headland. There are the remains of at least three duns and signs of old settlements. A Roman coin was found here in 1958. Gometra House, with its six bedrooms, had been unoccupied since 1983 but it was renovated and reoccupied in 1993. It has extensive outbuildings and a walled garden. The old schoolhouse still stands near the shore and the most easterly of the cottages near Gometra House is called Teacher's Cottage. It has occasionally been occupied by a resident caretaker and his wife and family. The four cottages beside Gometra harbour were formerly occupied by MacBrayne's Staffa boatmen, who used to row passengers out to the steamers which were unable to come alongside. Behind these cottages is an old graveyard.

Hugh Ruttledge, the Himalayan explorer, once had his home on Gometra.

A popular but shallow, confined, anchorage, Acairseid Mhór (G. – big anchorage) at the north-west corner has the never-failing attraction of a secret hideaway – a narrow passage past the rocks of tidal **Eilean Dioghlum** leads into an enclosed pool.

* * *

Access: Ulva Ferry (passenger) – on request during normal hours except Saturdays, 01688-500226 or signal at pier. Crossing time about five minutes.

Anchorages:
1. Sound of Ulva (56° 28.5'N 06° 08'W), S of the ferry, WNW of Sgeir Beul a' Chaolais, can be squally in S'lies, 3m, sand and mud. Alternatively, in settled weather, E of this anchorage in the bay on the Mull shore beyond the drying reef.
2. Cragaig Bay. Pleasant sheltered (except for strong S'lies) anchorage NE of Little Colonsay among rocks and islets on S coast of Ulva.
3. Gometra Harbour. Sheltered anchorage between Ulva and Gometra entered from S. Well protected except S'ly gales. Anchor off E shore, mud and weed.
4. Acairseid Mhór, N coast of Gometra. A snug but very

restricted anchorage behind Eilean Dioghalum. Anchor in 4m off E shore, sand and weed.

5. Soriby Bay (56° 29'N 06° 11'W), at SE of Loch Tuath. Good shelter except N'lies. Several hazards so follow sailing directions. Anchor at S end of W side of bay, or at inlet in SE corner.

3.8 Lunga

(ON langr-øy – longship island) or (G. long – ship, ON -øy – island). This is the largest of the Treshnish Isles, although Bac Mór, popularly known as the Dutchman's Cap, is much more prominent from a distance.

OS Maps: 1:50000 Sheet 46 or 48 1:25000 Sheet 374
1:10000 Sheet NM 24 SE
Admiralty Charts: 1:75000 No.2171 1:25000 No.2652

Area: 81ha (200 acres)
Height: 103m (338 ft)
Owner: The explorer and naturalist Col. Niall Rankin bought the Treshnish Isles in 1938. Put up for sale in 1994 for offers over £400,000. Sold in 2000 to the Hebridean Trust with assistance from Heritage Lottery Fund.

Population: 1800 – about 20. Year-round occupation ended in 1824 when Donald Campbell and his family left the island but regular summer occupation continued until 1857. Uninhabited since then.

Geology: All the Treshnish group are of volcanic origin with the distinctive hat shape of Bac Mór being an ancient volcano with a lava platform

BAC MÓR AND HARP ROCK FROM CORRAN LUNGA

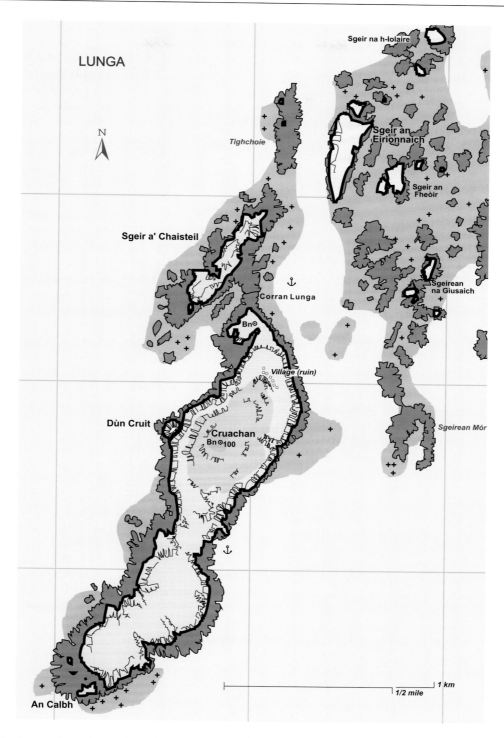

brim. On Lunga the volcanic flows have eroded to form a lava plateau.

History: When the Lord of the Isles acquired the Treshnish Isles in 1354 they were on the frontier between the Nordreys and Sudreys – the Northern and Southern Isles. There is more Treshnish history on Lunga's northern neighbours than on Lunga itself. Cairn na Burgh More has the remains of a castle on the site of an earlier Norse building. The castle is thought to have belonged to the Lord of Lorn, Chief of the Clan MacDougall. Beside the fort are the remains of a small chapel and the Well of the Half Gallon. It is claimed that during a clan feud Maclean of Lochbuie was imprisoned in the castle on Cairn na Burgh More with only the ugliest woman in Mull for company but Lochbuie rose to the occasion and gave her a son who eventually won back his heritage. At the Reformation of 1560 it is said that the monks of Iona buried their priceless library on Cairn na Burgh More for safety but it has never been recovered.

In 1680 after a prolonged attack by Argyll against the Macleans of Mull they retreated to the Treshnish Isles and held out for a long time but eventually had to surrender when Argyll obtained the King's support for his cause.

The ruins of a smaller castle or fort used during the 1715 Jacobite rising are on the smaller island of Cairn na Burgh Beg. But on Lunga itself, below Cruachan's north slope, there are only the well-preserved walls of a small village of black houses last occupied in 1857.

Wildlife: Primroses, violets, birdsfoot trefoil, buttercups, daisies, bluebells, orchids, sea campion, sea pinks, wild rose, honeysuckle, brambles, scotch thistles, cotton grass, yellow flags, tormentil, silverweed, dandelion, and the scarce oyster-plant are all to be found on this delightful island. It is a designated Site of Special Scientific Interest.

This is a popular and important breeding ground for grey seals but only three land mammals have been recorded – mice, rabbits and domestic sheep. The mice may be descendants of the house mice that lived in the village in the mid-18th century according to Fraser Darling, who stayed for three months on Lunga in 1937. The mice ate his notes.

A thousand or more barnacle geese fly in each winter and there are hundreds of thrushes, blackbirds and starlings in the summer. Guillemot, razorbill and puffin breed on Lunga in large numbers, also fulmar, shag, kittiwake and other gulls. From May to September one can see Manx shearwater, storm petrel, gannet and Arctic skua and occasionally, pomarine, great skua, and great and sooty shearwater.

LUNGA has been described as 'a green jewel in a peacock sea', which sounds an extravagant description until one lands and realises the truth

of it, for Lunga has a fresh and distinctive beauty all its own.

This is the largest island in the Treshnish group with a rounded hill called **Cruachan** (G. – conical hill) of 103m (338ft) and a magnificent view from its summit. To the south-west is the most conspicuous landmark of the Treshnish Isles, **Bac Mór** (G. – the big bank), or the Dutchman's Cap, which is an eroded volcanic cone encircled by a grassy rim of lava. It is only possible to land in the quietest of sea and weather and there is no safe anchorage either here or at nearby **Bac Beag**. This did not concern our ancestors for amid the wildflowers round the Dutchman's Cap can be found the remains of summer shielings.

Looking across the many rocks and skerries on Lunga's north-east side the smaller islands of **Fladda** (ON – flat island), **Cairn na Burgh Beag** and **Cairn na Burgh More** (G. *carn* – rock pile, ON *borv* – fort, – rock of the big fort) can be seen. Landing on both 'Carnburgs' is difficult and strong tidal streams don't help. It is easy to see how defensible they were. The larger Carnburg has its fortifications on the flat grassy top with a massive wall infilling a natural rock buttress on the perimeter. A further wall and stone gateway protects the castle and chapel.

On Lunga itself, **Dun Cruit** – Harp Rock – is a distinctive feature on the west side. It is a piece of sharply angled cliff, almost a stack, with a narrow chasm beside it into which the sea surges 30m (100') below. The shape is reminiscent of Boreray in the St Kilda group although the comparative scale is tiny and during the nesting season the rock disappears beneath a seething biomass of birds. The grassy summit and the edge of the surrounding cliffs are pitted with puffin burrows and the friendly, fearless, little birds will walk up to visitors, study them seriously, and pose for portraits.

In the past when sea-birds' eggs were an important item of diet, fishermen used to carry a mast up to Dun Cruit. They would lay this over the chasm and crawl across to collect the eggs and young birds. There is only one record of a man falling to his death.

North of Lunga at the end of a drying spit of tumbled boulders – Corran Lunga – is **Sgeir a' Chaisteil** (G. – castle rock), a castle-shaped rock. This is a popular area for nesting gulls and oyster catchers. The boulder beach is also the most direct landing place for a dinghy from a yacht in the anchorage. Overlooking Corran Lunga there is a plateau beneath Cruachan with the ruined village on it and what appears to have been a walled vegetable patch. A fresh-water spring in fairly close proximity is quite difficult to find as it is under the shelter of a secluded overhanging rock on the hillside south of the village.

A rudimentary path runs round the entire island from Corran Lunga in the north to **An Calbh** (G. – the headland) at the southern extremity. On the south-eastern side it skirts the edge of a vertigo-inducing drop to the sea and rocks below. Almost central there is a cave, or 'gloup' [NM276415] which leads from a hollow to the western seashore, with rough steps leading into it. There are ferns in this mysterious, silent cavern which is shaped like a circular pit with a narrow dark passage through to the sea. The ravine nearby is called the Dorlinn (G. – drying gravel beach). On the east side in the same area is a landing place for a dinghy.

Mountaineers may enjoy the fun of a climb on Harp Rock (provided it is not the breeding season for the seabirds). There is a possible line of ascent up a crack on the north side of the rock which is about 4m wide near the top, some 30m above the water.

Access: Frequent summer trips: Gordon Grant Marine, Fionnphort, Mull, 01681-700338: Turus Mara, Dervaig, Mull, 0800-085-8786: or Ardnamurchan Charters, 01972-500208.

Anchorages:
1. E of Corran Lunga. The approach is from N or S but both directions require great caution. Anchor SE of Sgeir a' Chaisteil off the boulder beach in about 4m, sand. Subject to swell.
2. Below cleft on E side and off small boulder beach. Occasional anchorage in light W'lies, 10–15m.

3.9 Lismore

(G. lios-mór – big garden). As well as 'garden' the Gaelic word lios can also mean a residence, palace, fortified place or enclosure.

O S Maps: 1:50000 Sheet 49 1:25000 Sheet 376
Admiralty Charts: 1:25000 No.2378

Area: 2351ha (5809 acres)
Height: 127m (417 ft)

Population: 1798–900. 1841–1399. 1881–621. 1891–561. 1931–280. 1961–155. 1981–129. 1991–140. 2001–146. 2011–192.

Owner: The Duke of Argyll is the main landowner.
Geology: Mainly Dalradian limestone. Until the Second World War this was quarried at An Sàilein, a cove on the west coast. Lismore soil is exceptionally fertile.

History: There are a number of duns, forts and cairns which testify to the long period of settlement on Lismore.

St Moluag was an Irish contemporary of St Columba. For many centuries after he founded his monastery here in 561–564 the island was an

TIREFORE BROCH GUARDS THE LYNN OF LORN

ecclesiastical centre. About the year 1200 John
the Englishman, Bishop of Dunkeld and Argyll,
appealed to the Pope to disjoin the Argyll see
because he was unable to learn to speak Gaelic.
The Pope complied and Lismore was chosen as the
seat of a separate diocese of Argyll and continued
so until 1507 when the centre moved to Saddell

in Kintyre. The bishops were called *Episcopi
Lismorenses*. A manuscript collection of Gaelic
and English poems which are of value as a guide
to the works of Ossian, the *Book of the Dean of
Lismore*, was compiled here in the 15th century.

Wildlife: There are many fine trees and shelter
belts, mainly sycamore, ash, lime and chestnut,

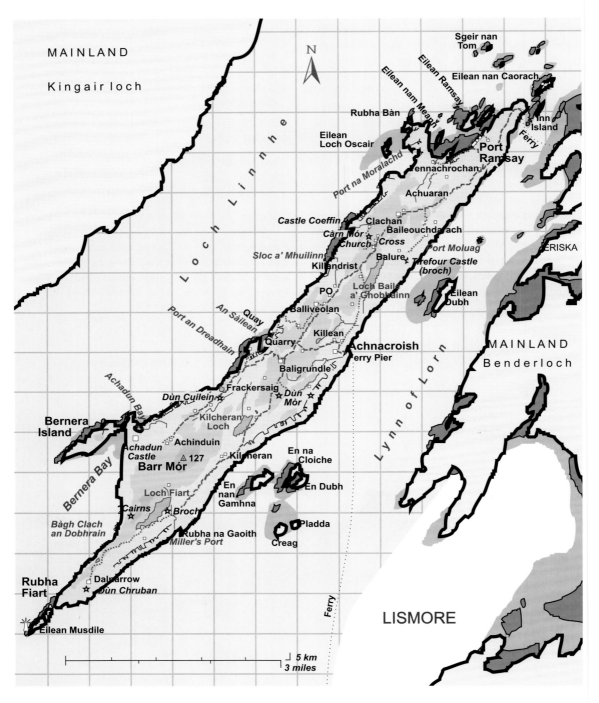

but little natural woodland although in 1596 the whole island was very thickly forested with oak. Thanks to the rich soil, wildflowers grow to larger than normal proportions; field gentians, rock rose (*Helianthemum*), mimulus, tutsan, ivy-leaved toadflax, wild orchids, yellow monkey-flower, cranesbill, brooklimes, water mints and speedwells are all to be found.

There are gulleries on the islets, Eilean nan Gamhna, and linked Eilean na Cloiche and Eilean Dubh in the Lynn of Lorn.

*　*　*

For delightful walking country **LISMORE** is supreme – a long narrow island with an undulating landscape of fertile soil in shallow longitudinal valleys. The highest hill is **Barr Mór** (G. – big tip), a modest 127m, but right in the centre of the southern area with a stunning panoramic view from its summit – north to the mountains of Ardgour, Lochaber with Ben Nevis to the north-east, Port Appin and Lochs Creran and Etive to the east, Oban, Kerrera and the Firth of Lorn to the south, Duart Castle and Mull to the south-west and the mountains of Morvern to the west. The walk along the ridge, over the summit of Barr Mór and down by the reed-fringed lochan to the south must be one of the finest walks in Scotland with views which are unequalled anywhere.

The lighthouse on **Eilean Musdile** at the southern extremity was built by Robert Stevenson in 1833. It was automated in 1965.

Lime was quarried on the west coast and lime kilns and quarrymen's cottages can still be seen on **Eilean nan Caorach** (G. – sheep island) among the skerries at the extreme north end opposite Port Appin and alongside **Inn Island** (G. ?*innis* – island). The boats carrying the lime operated out of Port Ramsay in the north. This sheltered anchorage between **Eilean Ramsay** and **Eilean nam Meann** (G. – kid island) is now used as an overnight stop by the occasional workboat from the giant quarry at Glensanda on the Morvern coast opposite Lismore. To the north is **Eilean Gainimh** (G. – island of fine sand) and **Eilean Glas** (G. – grey island). Port Ramsay is overlooked by a neat row of lime-burners' cottages most of which are now holiday homes.

The main road runs down the spine of the island with connections to the crofts and farms. In the 18th century the main crops were oats and

barley but nowadays cattle and sheep are more popular. Most of the dwellings are in the north. The ruin of a tall galleried broch called Tirefour Castle, about 4km from the north-east end of Lismore, lies on the summit of a 50m-high grassy knoll close to the east coast [NM867429].

Almost opposite Tirefour, on the north-west coast, **Coeffin Castle**, a ruined 13th-century structure, was probably built by the MacDougalls of Lorn on the site of a Viking fortress [NM853437]. The MacDougalls were defeated by Robert the Bruce. There is an ancient tidal fish trap on the shore below the castle and above it are the remains of the largest cairn in Argyll [NM859435].

The ferry pier is at **Achnacroish**, (G – field of the Cross), near the centre of the east coast where there is a general store and a junior school. Lismore has no mains water supply. All the water comes from wells and springs and these can run dry at times.

The disused lime quarry at An Sàilein (G. – the creek), across the island from Achnacroish, is sadly deserted today with its ivy-covered kilns and roofless cottages. Carthorses from far afield used to be landed at the old quay as the Lismore men were noted for their ability to break them in.

Much of the shoreline is low sea cliffs with a few pleasant shingle beaches. The cliffs in the south-east opposite Eilean na Cloiche are only some 25m high yet they can present a severe challenge for climbers. **Eilean na Cloiche** (G. – island of the stone) is a boldly shaped rock rising almost straight out of the sea for about 21m with **Eilean nan Gamhna** alongside and a dumbbell-shaped islet formed by linked **Pladda** and **Creag**. **Eilean Dubh**, further north in the centre of the Lynn of Lorn is worth a visit but not for climbing as it is very loose rubble.

The man who built the great folly on the hill above Oban, John Stuart McCaig, was born on Lismore. He was a banker, essayist and art critic.

Bernera on the west coast can be reached at low water and was once known as Bernera of the Noble Yew, an ancient tree under which St Columba was said to have preached. This giant yew was felled in 1850 to make a staircase in Lochnell Castle on the mainland and traces of the small chapel and well have almost disappeared [NM795392]. **Achadun Castle**, the so-called Bishop's Castle, overlooks Bernera [NM804393].

The bishop lived at some distance from the small cathedral which was founded at the start of the 13th century on the ancient monastic site known as **Kilmoluaig** (G. – St Moluag's cell or church). It is on the main road near Clachan [NM860434]. Unfortunately there are few remains of the cathedral which was burned during the Reformation but in 1749 the walls of the cathedral choir were reduced in height and roofed to create the present tiny parish church – one of the earliest parish churches still in use. There are some fine medieval tombstones in the graveyard which is also reputed to be the burial site of St Moluag (523-592). **Eilean Loch Oscair** is in the bay to the north.

The story goes that two competitive saints, Moluag and Mulhac, had a boat race across the Lynn of Lorn after agreeing that the first to touch Lismore would be entitled to found his monastery on the island. Moluag realised at the last minute that he would not reach the land first so he cut off his finger and threw it ashore. It landed on the beach just north of the broch at Tirefour. This gained him the title and he duly founded his monastery in 564AD. His pastoral staff, a thorn stick nearly one metre long, is still held by the Livingstones of Bachuil, hereditary keepers for the parish.

Access: Two ferries serve the island: Port Appin is passenger only, crossing time 10 minutes, 01631-569160: Oban, Mon–Sat, car ferry, crossing time 50 minutes, 08000-66-5000.

Anchorages:
1. Port Ramsay, close E of Eilean nam Meann at N end of Lismore, a well-sheltered anchorage, bottom sand and shells. Use the north approach.
2. Port na Moralachd, at NW corner, reasonable shelter except for winds SW-W which can cause a swell. Anchor close in at S side of the bay. Only approach is from SW
3. An Sàilein, middle of W coast. Shallow inlet. Moderate draught in neaps or small craft able to take the ground. Obstructed by fish farm.
4. Achadun Bay, occasional anchorage NE of Bernera in E'ly winds.
5. Bernera Bay, by the SE side of Bernera Island, occasional anchorage in N'ly winds. Keep near the E shore to avoid rocks 1c from SE side of Bernera.
6. Achnacroish is the Oban ferry terminal; a stone causeway and pier extend from the shore; least depth of 3m alongside the pier.

THE MEDIEVAL CHAPEL AT KIRKAPOL BESIDE THE LONG BEACH, TRÁIGH MHÓR

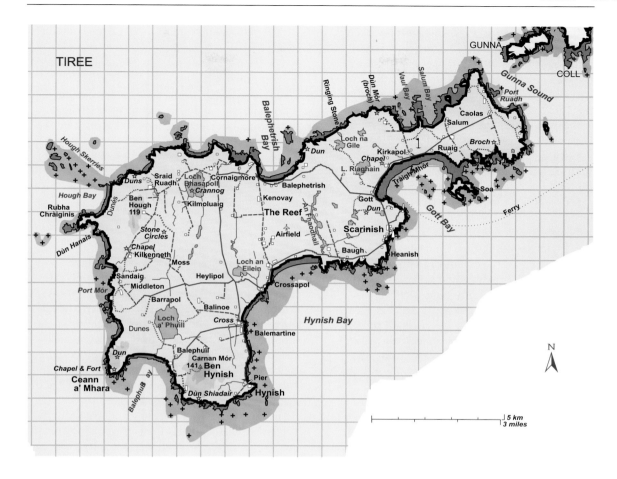

3.10 Tiree

[tY-ree or tseeree] (G. tir iodh – land of corn). Watson disputes this derivation and suggests the name may be pre-Celtic.

O S Maps: 1:50000 Sheet 46 1:25000 Sheet 372
Admiralty Charts: 1:100000 No.1778 Sound of Gunna
1:25000 No.2475

Area: 7834ha (19358 acres)
Height: 141m (462 ft)

Owner: The Duke of Argyll owns most of the island.

Population: 1755–2200. 1794–2555. 1830–4450. 1841–4391 (805 houses). 1881–2730. 1891–2449 (537 houses).1931–1448. 1961–993. 1991–768. 2001–770. 2011–653.

Geology: A flat fertile island with a bedrock of Archaean gneiss (a schist known as paragneiss). A limestone outcrop known as Tiree marble – pink flecked with green – was quarried at

Balephetrish from 1791 to 1794 and briefly again in 1910. (Stones now sold as Tiree marble come from Connemara in Ireland.) East of the quarry is Clach a' Choire (G. – ringing stone) – a glacial erratic which originated on Rum.

History: Pottery and tools of 800BC have been uncovered at Dùn Mór Vaul where there is a broch. St Columba sailed into Gott Bay on his way to visit the monastery founded by his cousin, Baitheine, at Sorobaidh. Apparently, on arrival, he struck a rock which nearly sank his boat, so he cursed it. Most sailors still follow this tradition.

St Comgall, a Pict and an associate of St Columba, also founded a monastery on Tiree.

In 672 the Vikings burned down the monastery, but some decided that they liked the island and settled. This however did not stop King Magnus of Norway – twenty-five years old and a born arsonist – plundering the island at the end of the 11th century and setting it alight. According to one of his skalds, Bjorn Cripplehand, 'The

happy wolf reddened tooth and claw with many
a mortal wound in Tiree...' Control passed to the
Kingdom of Man and then to Somerled, King of
the Isles, and his heirs in 1164. After the Battle of
Largs in 1263 Alexander III granted ownership to
the MacDougalls but they were indecisive owners
and there were continual disputes. By 1390
Lachlan MacLean was Bailie of Tiree and Coll,
which led to his descendants claiming ownership.
Eventually however, in the latter part of the 17th
century, the Duke of Argyll took control.

It was at this time that much of the arable
farming began to be replaced by cattle grazing,
although barley was still grown for whisky. Tiree
was exporting up to three thousand gallons of
whisky a year at the end of the 18th century.

The population which had been 4450 in 1830
had dropped to 2700 fifty years later due to
evictions and potato famines. In 1885 the Duke
of Argyll prevailed on the Government to send
fifty policemen and 250 marines on the *Ajax*
and *Assistance* to evict the crofters. The crofters
resisted and although the marines arrested and
held five crofters for a token period they were
generally sympathetic towards the islanders. The
matter was settled in 1886 with the passing of
the Crofters' Act which split the land into 270
crofts.

Wildlife: Tiree has hares, but no rabbits, foxes,
stoats or weasels.

The machair has a dense cover of meadow
flowers, particularly where there is restricted
access for sheep. There is very little actual grass,
the cover is mainly daisy, dandelion, red and
white clover, buttercup, blue speedwell, hop
and birdsfoot trefoil, eyebright, harebell, yellow
and blue pansy, silverweed, wild thyme, and the
common spotted orchid sub-species, *D. fuchsii
hebridensis.*

A mat of sea thrift rings the coastline with
marram grass tying down the dunes.

Tiree has great interest for birdwatchers all the
year round and in spring and summer wildfowl,
waders and seabirds breed there: skylark on
the machair, sedge warbler, corncrake and reed
bunting in denser vegetation. Exceptional sites are:

Loch a' Phuill: mute and whooper swans in
autumn and winter. Oct – April Greenland white-
fronted geese. Greylag geese all year. Wigeon, teal,
mallard, pintail, shoveller, pochard, tufted duck,
goldeneye, red-breasted merganser in winter.

Loch Bhasapol: Pochard, tufted duck and much
more.

The Reef: The centre of the island. Greenland
white-fronted geese.

Balephetrish Bay: ringed plover, sanderling,
dunlin, purple sandpiper and turnstone. Great
northern diver, eider and long-tailed duck in
winter.

Salum and Vaul Bays: good for feeding waders.

Ceann a' Mhara: Breeders: fulmar, shag,
kittiwake, guillemot and razorbill. Starlings nest in
the caves.

*   *   *

TIREE is sometimes referred to as *Tir-fo-Thuinn* –
the land beneath the waves. There are only two
high points, **Ben Hynish** in the south (141m)
with its 'golf-ball' radar station and **Ben Hough**
in the north-west (119m). Over two-thirds of the
island has been covered with wind-blown shell
sand which has created a fertile, plough-deep and
well-drained machair. It was this rich soil which
earned Tiree the title of the land of corn. Tiree is
virtually unique among Scottish isles in having
no peat-bog. The rainfall is low and from May to
September the climate is the sunniest in Britain,
but the wind that brought the rich soil blows
constantly and there is no natural shelter from it.
This is the windiest place in the United Kingdom
with an average annual wind speed of 17mph.
No wonder that every October it is the venue for
the world-renowned International Windsurfing
Championships.

This is still a thriving crofting community
(unlike its sister island Coll) maintaining a stable
and viable population, although the smallness of
the land-holdings make many of the crofts barely
economic. Cattle and sheep are grazed, the arable
farming being mainly for winter feed. The black
houses (G. – *tigh dubh*) with dry-stone walls up to
nine feet thick, rounded corners, a fire hearth in
the middle of the floor and thatched roofs within
the outer walls for wind protection are still here
but most have been 'modernised' and are now
white houses (G. – *tigh geal*), so called because
the original walls have been cemented and
whitewashed. Thatched roofs have been replaced
with felt or corrugated iron and the houses now
have fireplaces with chimneys.

In Gott Bay a fine sweep of sand (G. *Tràigh
Mhór* – long beach) leads round from the tidal

island of **Soa** (ON – sheep island) to the ferry terminal at **Scarinish** (ON – seagull headland). Here there is a post office, shops, hotel, and an old stone harbour (built 1771), now only frequented by the lobster boats, while on the beach lies the wreck of the *Mary Stewart*, one of the last sailing ships to trade in this area. West of Scarinish, in the flat centre of the island – called **The Reef** – is an airfield built by the RAF in 1941 for Squadrons 218 and 518 flying Warwicks and Halifax bombers. It is now used for commercial flights. The weather station here, which contributes to the shipping forecasts, was started by the Head Teacher of Consignor School who began keeping records in 1926.

At the southern tip, **Hynish** has granite houses and a small pier built for the workers on the **Skerryvore** lighthouse which is ten miles out to sea to the south-west. It was built by an uncle of R L Stevenson in 1838–43. It is 42m (138ft) high and sits on a rock only three metres above Mean High Water Springs. The 4000 tons of granite used in its construction came from the Bull Hole quarry on Mull. It was damaged by fire and has been unmanned since the 1960s. The granite tower at Hynish was used to send signals to the lighthouse, and is now a museum.

Tiree's largest loch, **Loch a' Phuill**, is near the west coast amid extensive areas of dunes which are grazed by sheep and cattle. The knuckle in the south-west corner, **Ceann a' Mhara** [kenë-va:rë] (G. – head of the sea) is littered with ancient relics while at the north-west corner numerous off-shore rocks and skerries surround the shell-sand bays.

Loch Bhasapoll is also in the north-west, with its two crannogs, marshy fringes, and wintering geese. A village called Baile nan Craganach (G. – place of the clumsy people) is said to have once stood on the loch's north shore, so called because the villagers all had six fingers on each hand. Further east, in the centre of the north coast, **Balephetrish Bay** (G. *baile pheadairich* – the place of the storm petrel) was the original source of Tiree marble.

Dun and broch remains (more than twenty of them), stone circles, standing stones, cairns and crannogs are scattered right across the island. **Dùn Mór Vaul** by Vaul Bay in the north-east is of particular interest [NM042492]. It was started as a timber structure in the 6th century BC and was later turned into a stone broch about the 1st

century BC. Galleries are still visible in the 4m thick walls. The brochs of Tiree and Lismore are the furthest south of all the island brochs.

The Ringing Stone, west of Vaul [NM027487], is covered with cup-marks and clangs eerily when struck. It should be treated with care as it is prophesied that if the stone is broken Tiree will sink forever beneath the waves.

Access: Vehicle ferry: Oban/ Coll/ Tiree, every day; via Barra, on Thurs. only, 08000-66-5000. Air services from Glasgow, 0870-850-9850 and Oban, 0870-242-1457. There is a bus service for most of the island, 0871–266333 or Ring'n'Ride, 01879–220419. Cars and bicycles can be hired locally.

Anchorages:
1. Scarinish. Both creek and drying harbour can occasionally be used if no swell is coming in. Near HW, or at neaps, temp. berth at old pier possible, or anchored in middle of creek.
2. Gott bay concrete pier has a depth of 3.4m (11') alongside. Landing slip on inner side. Foul ground extends 6c SE from pier.
3. Gott bay. Exposed but affords moderately good anchorage in settled weather or light W'lies in 4–5m, sand, N-NE of pier on SW side of bay. Several dangers both sides and in the fairway.
4. Clach Chuirr (Port Ruadh) off Gunna Sound affords some shelter from S and W. Anchor on either side of the power cable in 3m, sand.
5. Hynish pier. Some limited shelter from S in very settled conditions. Pier and dock dry out.

3.11 Gunna

(ON Gunni-øy – the island of Gunni the Dane) or, improbably, (G Eilean nan Gamhna – island of the yearling cattle).

OS Maps: 1:50000 Sheet 46 1:25000 Sheet 372
Admiralty Charts: 1:75000 No.2171 Sd of Gunna 1:25000 No.2475

Area: 69ha (168 acres)
Height: 35m (115 ft)

Owner: Marcus de Ferranti. The owner has built a summer residence overlooking the anchorage.

Population: No Census records.

Geology: Paragneiss schist with a light sandy soil. Metasediments in the west, undifferentiated gneiss

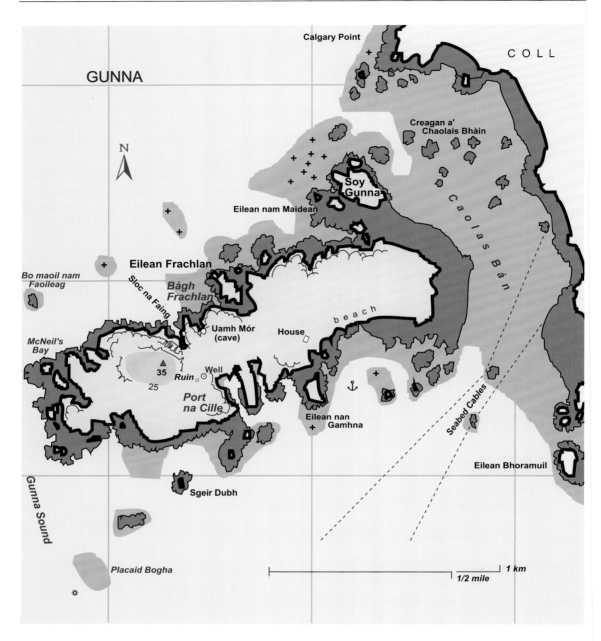

in the east.

Wildlife: The arctic tern, little tern, and possibly also sandwich tern plus three common species of large gull nest here but these ground-nesting birds suffer serious losses when brown rats, *Rattus norvegicus*, invade the island from Coll, which they do occasionally. Barnacle geese use the island for winter bed-and-breakfasting while large numbers of white-fronted and greylag geese sometimes appear. Shelduck are prolific in the spring.

This is a grey seal nursery, there are resident dolphins and the Sound is a gathering place for basking sharks.

* * *

Lying in the sound between Tiree and Coll, **GUNNA** was probably once inhabited by an anchorite. It is now only grazed by cattle and wild geese. It is separated from Coll by a shallow rock-strewn passage. Gunna is a narrow little wind-blown island, no more than 500m wide for most of its length, and with few prominent features. There is a spring at Port na Cille (G. – port of the chapel), with the ruin of a small cell or shieling beside it. There are also other signs of early habitation. A cave in the centre of the north coast may have served as a hermit's shelter [NM099514].

Gunna Sound, between Coll and Tiree is a relatively shallow stretch of water. The area near Gunna is peppered with rocks and there are more rocky patches off the Tiree shore. Islets near Tiree include **Creachasdal**, **Librig**, **Eilean Liath** and **Eilean Ghreasamuill**, while **Eilean Bhoramuil** lies off the southern extremity of Coll.

Access: No regular means of access. Try Skipinnish Sea Tours, Tiree, 01879-220009 or Coll Hotel, Coll, 01879-230334.

Anchorage: Occasional anchorage E of Eilean na Gamhna, 4–5m, sand, good holding. Exposed to S'lies.

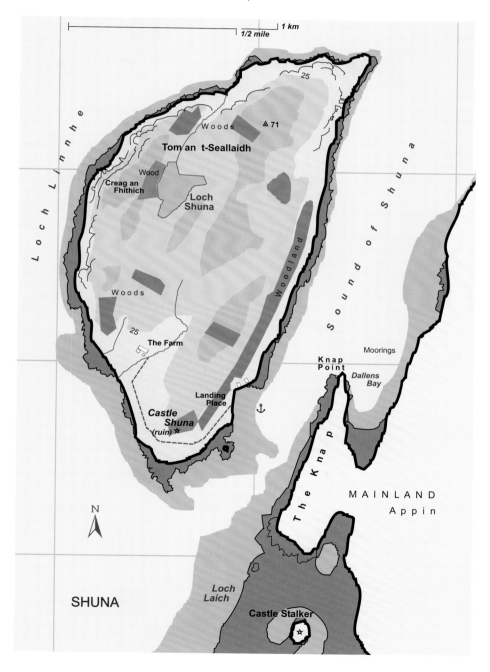

3.12 Shuna

Uncertain derivation, probably Norse or pre-Gaelic but possibly (G. sidhean – fairy hill, ON -øy – island).

O.S.Maps: 1:50000 Sheet 49 1:25000 Sheet 376 or 383
Admiralty Chart: 1:25000 No.2379

Area: 155ha (383 acres)
Height: 71m (233 ft)

Owner: Stephen P Newall DL LLD, a Deputy Lord Lieutenant of Dunbartonshire, and his wife, Gay S Newall, who bought it in the 1950s. Sold in 2012 to an overseas investor for a reported £1.85 million.

Population: 1881–8. 1891–6. 1931–4. 1961–1. 1971–0. 1981–0. 1991–0. 2011–0.

Geology: Mostly Dalradian limestone giving a good soil.

History: A document of 1577–1595 says that the island belonged to John Stewart, Laird of Appin. A further description in 1630 says that Shuna, property of the Laird of Appin is 'the most profitable and fertilest in all these Countries'.

SHUNA is sometimes rather needlessly called Shuna Island but this is probably to distinguish it from the other Shuna (No.2.10) which lies alongside Luing. It is a compact island separated from the mainland by the narrow Sound of Shuna and rising to a table-topped hill near the north-east end. In a hollow near the hill is a lochan with a stream running past some clumps of conifers. The view from here is dramatic, looking up Loch Linnhe to where the great flank of Ben Nevis can be seen beyond tiny **Eilean Balnagowan**.

Shuna (with 360 breeding ewes) has been farmed by the owner, and the pleasant white 7-bedroom farmhouse faces southwards towards Lismore (No.3.9) and Appin. There are several cottages also on the island. At the southernmost extremity are the substantial ruins of **Castle Shuna**, a small square building about 10m high [NM915483]. This is actually a domestic tower house rather than a castle. It was probably built near the end of the 16th century by John Stewart, who died in 1595, or his son, Duncan Stewart. The building was abandoned at the end of the 18th century.

Across the sound is another island fortress, **Castle Stalker** in Loch Laich. It was built about 1500, also by the Stewarts of Appin, and James IV used it as a hunting lodge. It was a ruin for many years but has now been restored.

In 1958 near Tom an t-Seallaidh (G. – the knoll of the vision) a rock-shelter on Shuna was excavated and deposits of limpet shells, stone-scrapers, deer horn and flints were found.

Unfortunately, on our first visit many years ago, both the anchorage in the Sound of Shuna and the beautiful setting were spoilt by the unpleasant odour from a mink farm on The Knap, a piece of ground projecting into the Sound. I am happy to report that nowadays this is no longer a problem and that the abandoned and derelict farm is an interesting relic to be seen on a short walk through the attractive landscape in the area of the Knapp.

Access: No regular access but enquire at Linnhe Marine (Paul Zvegintzov), 07721-503981.
Anchorages:
1. In Shuna Sound, SW of Knap Point (N of the narrows).
2. Linnhe Marine. Visitors moorings (pay) in sheltered Dallens Bay (Shuna Cove), E of Knap Point.

3.13 Coll

(G. coll – a hazel). Adomnan calls it 'insula Coloso' from which Watson infers a pre-Celtic origin.

O S Maps: 1:50000 Sheet 46 1:25000 Sheet 372
Admiralty Charts: 1:100000 No.1796 1:75000 No.2171
Sound of Gunna 1:25000 No.2475 Loch Eatharna (Arinagour) 1:10000 No.2474

Area: 7685ha (18989 acres)
Height: 104m (341 ft)

Owner: The Stewart family, owners of Coll since 1856, sold about two-thirds of the island estate to Coll Properties Ltd in 1964 (the Dutch businessman, Jan de Vries), but the Stewarts continued farming the rest until 1991 when they sold the remainder of the estate to Major N V MacLean Bristol of 'Project Venture' and Neil Smith of Ferndale Ltd. The de Vries estate was sold to the RSPB. Colin Kennedy owns the south end of the island. The Cairns of Coll were bought by the author Alexander McCall Smith in 2013 for £300,000.

Population: 1740– about 400. 1755–502.

1794–902. By 1841 it had reached 1442 (271 houses), which was greater than the island could support according to the laird, Maclean, and half the population emigrated to Australia or Canada. 1881–643. 1891–522 (111 houses). 1931–322. 1981–131. 1991–172. 2001–164. 2011–195.

Geology: Until comparatively recent times in geological terms, Coll and Tiree were one single island. Coll consists of low hummocks of a weathered rock called paragneiss, a schist metamorphosed from sedimentary rock, sticking through the grass and heather like currants in a bun, particularly in the eastern half. The south-western area around Gorton and Breachacha is of ancient sediments containing quartz and marble. High dunes and machair stretch along the west coast with raised beaches at Arnabost. Lead was once mined in the south of the island.

History: Coll and Tiree have a very similar early history. Angus Og of Islay, King of the Isles, was granted Coll by Bruce when MacDougall forfeited it around 1314. He was probably then responsible for building Breachacha Castle using the latest defensive techniques known to the Macdonalds.

The Maclean chieftains of Coll were an interesting and enlightened family. The 4th Chieftain, who died in 1560, was a bard who composed verse in both Gaelic and Latin. The 11th Chieftain, Lachlan Maclean, a renowned soldier, was drowned in an accident in 1687. His grandson, Hector, 13th of Coll, had a personal in-house harper at his new residence at Breachacha. He kept most of his clansmen from becoming embroiled in the 1745 rebellion and received a royal charter to his property so that he was not a vassal to the Campbells. He had two successive Campbell wives yet when the Duke of Argyll tried to lease two of his farms on Coll Maclean vowed that he would never let a Campbell move in. Neither of his Campbell wives gave him an heir, so his brother Hugh took over when he died in 1754.

Hugh maintained Neil Rankin, the last hereditary piper to the Macleans, in his household and constructed a mausoleum for his brother's remains. He subsidised a spinning school and the development of linen manufacture on the island. His son Donald, 'young Coll', embarrassed Boswell in 1773 by having to share his bed for the night when they met as guests on Inch Kenneth.

'He was a lively young man,' Boswell reported. 'We found he had been a good deal in England, studying farming, and was resolved to improve the value of his father's lands, without oppressing his tenants, or losing the ancient Highland fashions.' The young man tragically drowned the following year. His brother Alexander, who succeeded as 15th Chieftain in 1790, had many of the same ideals as his brother. He was Lieutenant Colonel of the Breadalbane Fencibles, a regiment which gave employment to many of his clansmen.

By 1841 the population had grown rapidly to over 1400 which was more than the island could support. The laird impoverished himself trying to feed the islanders during the potato famine and

paying the fares of those who wished to go to Australia and Canada, and finally had to sell the island to John Lorne Stewart in 1856. The new owner, despite the crofters' protests, raised the rents so in 1861 the 'great exodus' took place. Virtually all the tenants, overnight, left their crofts and moved from the arable south-east to the rock-bound north-west of the island. This area was under Campbell ownership and the promised rents were reasonable but the families had to improvise shelter while they built their new homes. Unfortunately overcrowding led to many families leaving the island in the ensuing years.

Towards the end of the 19th century the Stewarts decided that they now had to repopulate the land and offered crofts at attractive rents to Ayrshire dairy farmers. This resulted in the production of the famous Coll cheese – a favourite delicacy at the House of Lords up to the time that the market for dairy produce collapsed near the start of the First World War.

Wildlife: In 1939 botanists discovered the Irish Lady's Tresses orchid growing on Coll. It grows in Ireland but is actually native to North America. There are ten species of orchid in the Coll Nature Reserve and more than 200 species of flowering plant. Coll supports three endangered bee sub-species including the Great Yellow Bumble Bee and recently entomologists were astonished to discover a colony of flightless short-necked oil beetles on Coll not seen anywhere in the UK since 1940.

Due to intensive farming, most British corncrakes now only survive in the Outer Hebrides. The birds, which are more often heard than seen, like rough uncultivated conditions. There are about 120 pairs on Tiree and the RSPB has created a corncrake reserve for the twenty or so pairs on Coll.

Boswell gives an interesting account of the natural history (in 1773): 'There are no foxes; no serpents, toads, or frogs, nor any venomous creature. They have otters and mice here; but had no rats till lately that an American vessel brought them. There is a rabbit-warren on the north-east of the island, belonging to the Duke of Argyle. Young Coll (the laird) intends to get some hares, of which there are none at present. There are no black-cock, moor-fowl, nor partridges; but there are snipe, wild-duck, wild-geese, and swans, in winter; wild pigeons, plover, and great number of starlings; of which I shot some, and found them pretty good eating. Woodcocks come hither, though there is not a tree upon the island.' He also mentions the great variety of fish in the brooks and trout and eel in the lochs. Coll has no stoat or weasel and today the Duke of Argyll's rabbits have become a serious pest.

Little lochans scattered over the north end of the island, covered with white water-lilies in the summer months, are the home of red-throated divers and the heather conceals red grouse.

* * *

COLL, with its gnarled lumps of rock protruding through a thin skin of grass and heather, is wild and lovely by day and a star-gazers' paradise at night (it has 'dark night status'). And the trim whitewashed cottages of **Arinagour** (G. *airigh na gobhar* – shieling of the goats), lying beneath two churches on the hill, are welcoming. Built by Maclean, laird of Coll, in about 1800, they are now mainly holiday cottages with most of the 'Collachs' (the local inhabitants) occupying the council houses. Arinagour is alongside Loch **Eatharna** (G. – loch of the small fishing boats). There is an old stone pier and a ferry pier which

was built in 1969. The award-winning Isle of Coll Hotel is a pleasant building overlooking the loch. It has bicycles and mopeds for hire and is certainly the most useful information centre on the island.

Across the island from Arinagour is **Arnabost** where the ruined school was built over a medieval earth house with the entrance under the school porch [NM209600]. The islanders had used this as a hiding place during Viking raids and a gold brooch was found there in 1855.

East of Arnabost the land is virtually empty – low-lying, rocky, and peppered with lochans but the road runs up the northern coastal strip which was the most densely populated part of the island in the 19th century. The area was deserted by choice, not by forced clearance and the old township of **Bousd** is there to be seen. **Sorisdale**, at the northern tip, is a lovely crofting settlement of thatched buildings by a pleasant beach. Along this northern coast, the machair is so rich and fertile that there was an experiment to grow tulips in competition with the Dutch. The climate is mild, Coll is one of the sunniest spots in Britain, and the flowers were a great success but the cost and difficulty of transportation defeated the project. The road passes a cemetery and the remnants of a medieval chapel – **Cille Ionnaig** – where Young

BREACHACHA – WHERE MACLEAN FOUGHT MACLEAN

Coll, host to Dr Johnson and Boswell, lies buried [NM221618]. He was drowned the year following the visit when sailing from Inch Kenneth to Mull.

Off the northern extremity of Coll are some potentially dangerous rocks and islets although the space beside **Eilean Mór** known as Acairseid Mhór (G. – big anchorage) is a delightful haven. **Eag na Maoile** (G. – cleft bare rock) is north of Eilean Mór and **Sùil Gorm** (G. – blue eye) has a light tower on it.

Turning south-west at Arnabost the road passes **Grishipoll**. In the 15th century MacNeill of Barra set up a garrison at this farm when he chose to annex Coll. But Iain Garbh, his stepson and hereditary owner of the land, raised the Collachs, took the garrison and regained his inheritance. His descendants have owned part of Coll until the present time. The road turns into a track beside **Ben Hogh** (104m), Coll's highest hill. On it is a huge boulder balanced on three small ones which according to folklore was placed there by a giant. It is worth following Boswell's footsteps up this hill as it is an attractive viewpoint. (Dr Johnson chose instead to sit down and read a book).

From Arinagour a road leads to an airstrip on the sand dunes and **Breachacha** (G. – the field speckled with wild flowers). Here, on the shore of the loch, stands ancient Breachacha Castle, which dates back to the 15th century and probably earlier. It has been carefully restored by the Project Trust, a training scheme for young people to give voluntary service in underdeveloped countries. Near it is the attractive new castle, recently renamed Breachacha House, built in 1750 by Hector Maclean and visited in October 1773 by Boswell and Dr Johnson. The irascible Johnson 'relished it much at first, but soon remarked... that... it was a mere tradesman's box.' It was later enlarged and somewhat mutilated by a Victorian owner. It has been renovated recently and is now a private residence.

When the MacLeans of Duart invaded Coll in 1593 they were mown down by the Macleans of Coll and the burn that flows into Loch Breachacha was choked with the heads of the Duart clansmen. It has been called ever since Struthan nan Ceann (G. – the stream of the heads).

There are a number of prehistoric remains in this southern area – standing stones, cairns, traces of brochs and crannogs, and **Dùn an Achaidh**, an ancient fort beside the road from Arinagour [NM183546]. West of Loch Breachacha there are two large attractive bays, Crossapol Bay, with the off-shore islet of **Soa** almost linked to **Eilean Iomallach**, and Feall Bay, separated by marram dunes. The neglected shell of the 13th Maclean's Mausoleum is on the peninsula between the southerly bays [NM149524].

* * *

Access: Vehicle ferry: Oban/ Coll/ Tiree, every day; via Barra on Thurs. only, 08000-66-5000. Scheduled flights from Oban, 0870-242-1457. Bicycles for hire, Coll Hotel, 01879-230334. Tourist information, 01631-563122.

Anchorages: These anchorages are only suitable in favourable conditions and are all open to any directional swell.

1. Loch Eatharna (Arinagour). Popular but exposed to S'lies. Head dries out about ¾M. Divided into two parts by Eilean Eatharna 13.4m high. W part most used but open to S and only suitable for occasional anchorage in summer. Bottom sand. There are visitors' moorings (pay, 10 tons max). E anchorage very restricted with narrow entrance and many moorings but less swell.

2. Sorisdale Bay. Temp anchorage in 3m, sand, off concrete block and close to N side.

3. Acairseid Mhór, SSW of Eilean Mor. Claimed to be best anchorage on Coll. Approach from E until N of Glas Eileanan. Requires great care.

4. Hogh Bay on N coast. Occasional anchorage. Sheltered NE-E-S. Approach from N, head for break in sand-dunes. Anchor in 3m, firm sand.

5. Feall Bay on N coast. Occasional anchorage. Sheltered NE-E-S. Approach from N, slightly E of centre line, and anchor in 2–6m, sand and rock patches (usually visible).

6. Loch Breachacha. Many rocks. Head shoals gradually.

7. Loch Gorton. Narrow sandy cove 1M E of Breachacha. Anchor in 3m, sand.

3.14 Carna

(G. càrn – cairn, heap of stones, rocky mound, ON -øy – island).

O.S.Maps: 1:50000 Sheet 49 1:25000 Sheet 383
Admiralty Chart: 1:25000 No.2394

Area: 213ha (526 acres)

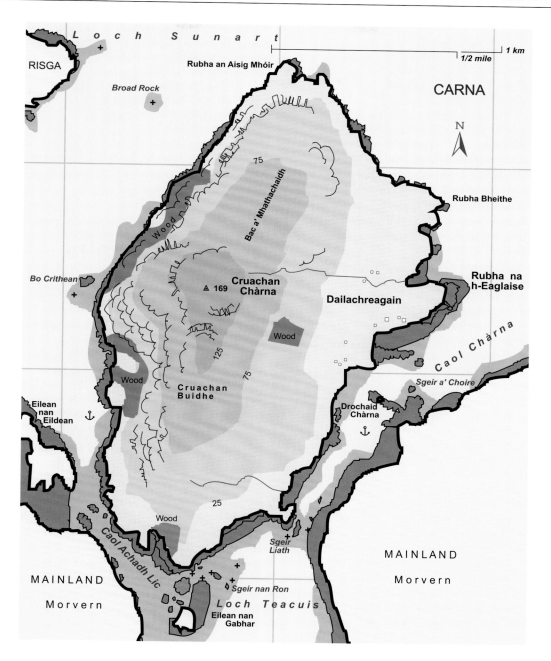

Height: 169m (554 ft)

Owners: Tim and Sue Milward and Mr Milward's sisters, Vanessa Towers and Frances Milward.

Population: 1881–7. 1891–10 (2 houses). 1931–3. 1961–2. 1971–3. 1981–0. 1991–4. 2001–0. 2011–0.

Geology: Mainly a Moine schist bedrock of quartz-felspar constitution, except for the west coastal strip which is mixed schists and mica-schist.

Wildlife: A well-managed herd of red deer and an interesting variety of habitat for, among others, willow warblers, redstarts, wheatears, whinchats, twites, ravens and kestrels. A rare protected coral-like serpulid reef in upper Loch Teacuis is to be found in only three other places in the world.

* * *

The dinosaur back of **CARNA** rears up behind the tidal island of Oronsay. It straddles the mouth of remote Loch Teacuis, one of the most interesting lochs on the West Coast, dividing the entrance into two narrow kyles. **Eilean nan Gabhar** (G. – goat island), usually covered with basking seals and not a goat in sight, is in the loch just south of Carna's southern headland.

For those approaching by land, Rahoy on Loch Teacuis is a beautiful spot in the heart of Morvern reached by a very minor road from Loch Aline. A walk up the east lochside towards Carna passes an excellent example of a vitrified fort set in oak woodland on a hill above the narrows [NM633564].

The west side of Carna is steep and unwelcoming. Wet, slippy and boggy with abrupt rocky slopes covered in a profusion of flag irises, tufts of sphagnum moss, bracken, grass and scrub birch.

There is a central peak, **Cruachan Chàrna** (G. – the conical hill of Carna), which is the highest part of the knobbly north-south ridge dividing the island. South of it is Cruachan Buidhe (G. – the yellow stack). The eastern slopes are sheltered from the prevailing winds and are much gentler than the west side. As on neighbouring **Oronsay**, the inevitable lonely little ruined cottages are scattered south of a stream which trickles down the mountain and into Caol Chàrna at Rubha na h-Eaglaise (G. – headland of the church). But at least Carna still has a token population with three or four intermittently occupied houses. There is not much in the way of level ground but there is a mellowness in the landscape with a stand of conifers and a small copse of deciduous woodland. A few rowan and birch trees are sprinkled over the higher ground. In 1845 Carna was considered to be more fertile and productive than the larger and less mountainous Oronsay, although there is a fish trap on Oronsay, which must have made a big contribution to its larder. Interestingly, the northern part of Carna is called **Bac à Mhathachaidh** (G. – the cultivated bank).

In the centre of Loch Sunart between Oronsay and Carna there is the steep little island of **Risga** with **Eilean a' Chuilinn** and **Garbh Eilean** further up the loch.

* * *

Access: Ardnamurchan Charters, Laga Bay, 01972-500208 run two holiday cottages on Carna and a passenger ferry from Tobermory on Mondays and Fridays.

Anchorages:
1. Temporary anchorage on W side, immediately N of narrow entrance to Loch Teacuis, off the bay opposite Eilean nan Eildean. 6–8m, sand with some mud and weed. Sheltered except NW-N.
2. E side, in the channel leading to Loch Teacuis in the pool immediately S of Drochaid Chàrna (G – Carna's bridge). Rather awkward entrance needing sailing directions but good shelter.

3–Appendix Staffa

(ON stafi-øy – stave or pillar island) The basalt columns resembled the vertical log staves used by the Norse for house construction.

The town of Stäfa on Lake Zurich in Switzerland was named after this little island by a monk from Iona.

O.S.Maps: 1:50000 Sheet 48   1:25000 Sheet 373
Admiralty Charts: 1:25000 No.2652 or No.2771

Area: 33ha (82 acres)
Height: 42m (138 ft)

Owner: Originally part of the Ulva Estate of the MacQuarries but sold in 1777. After a few years bought by Colin MacDonald of Loch Boisdale. Sold by Ranald MacDonald in 1816 to trustees. Bought in 1966 by a retired army padre, Gerald Newall who sold it to Alastair de Watteville, a direct descendant of the Boisdale MacDonalds. He sold it to the Langs in 1978 who held it until it was bought and donated to the National Trust for Scotland in 1986 by Mr Jock Elliott Jr of New York as a sixtieth birthday present for his wife Elly. She was appointed 'Steward of Staffa' by the Trust.

Population: 1772–1. 1784–16. Uninhabited since 1800.

Geology: Cliffs over 40m high are riddled with caves and the regularity of the basalt columns is such that it is sometimes difficult to realise that these are natural formations. At parts the columns have been twisted into dramatic and contorted shapes. This is a result of the same volcanic activity which created the Giant's Causeway in Ulster. The rock is an almost-black fine-grained Tertiary basalt surmounted by amorphous lava. Slow cooling caused the lava to split in a columnar pattern which then formed regular hexagons or, occasionally, pentagons after lateral compression. This is said to be the only sea-cave in the world formed entirely out of columnar basalt.

History: In the 3rd century Fionn MacCool, the Irish hero who was known to the Scots as Fingal (G. *fionn na ghal* – chief of valour) is said to have defended the Hebrides against early raids by the Vikings and to have died in battle in Ulster in 283. It is not known whether he ever visited Staffa but the beautiful cave on the island is now named in his honour.

On 13 August 1772, Sir Joseph Banks, President of the Royal Society, not long returned from the famous voyage with Captain James Cook and en route to Iceland, 'discovered' Fingal's Cave.

His ship had been driven by bad weather into the Sound of Mull. There he met an Englishman, a Mr Leach, who told him of this extraordinary island and he went to see it for himself. In spite of spending the night in the house of the island's sole inhabitants and becoming infested with lice as a result (his companions used a tent), Banks waxed lyrical about Staffa and following his report when back in London, tourists started to appear in droves. Among them in subsequent years were Sir Walter Scott, John Keats, Felix Mendelssohn, J M W Turner, William Wordsworth, Queen Victoria and Prince Albert, Jules Verne, Dr David Livingstone and Robert Louis Stevenson.

Staffa was made a Site of Special Scientific Interest in 1973.

Wildlife: In 1788 barley, oats, flax and potatoes were grown and in 1800 there were three red

FINGAL'S CAVE

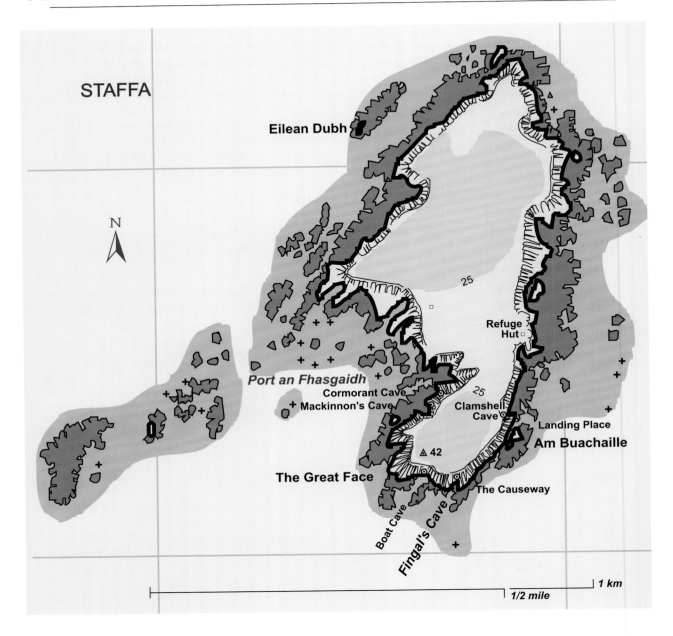

STAFFA

Eilean Dubh

N

25

Refuge
Hut

Port an Fhasgaidh

Cormorant Cave
Mackinnon's Cave

Clamshell
Cave

25

Landing Place

Am Buachaille

The Great Face

△ 42

The Causeway

Boat Cave

Fingal's Cave

1 km

1/2 mile

deer on the island. In 1801 one deer became dangerous and had to be shot and the other deer started following boats which left the island and on one occasion went too far and drowned. Goats replaced the deer and were followed by a small herd of black cattle which were resident for many years. These in turn gave way to sheep. Seabirds nest on the island but not in any great number.

We anchored off **STAFFA** very early on a morning in May. The sea lay like molten lead and it was warm in the sun. We were exceptionally lucky to have such favourable conditions and we had the island to ourselves. The landing place, which was constructed in 1991, is beside **Am Buachaille** (G. – the herdsman), a dramatic tidal islet composed of gracefully bent stone columns in a curious pyramid about 10m high [NM326351]. Nearby, across a narrow channel is **Clamshell Cave,** which has an entrance portico of twisted columns resembling a giant scallop. Shags give eery warnings from their nests in the shadows.

A path along the natural hexagonal paving,

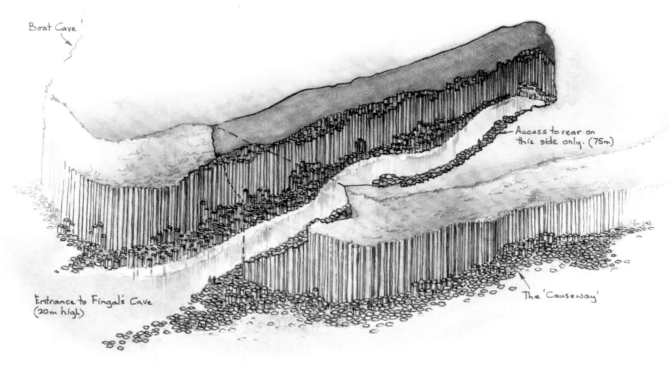

Boat Cave

Access to rear on
this side only. (75m)

Entrance to Fingal's Cave
(20m high)

The 'Causeway'

THE ANATOMY OF FINGAL'S CAVE

called The Causeway, leads along the beautiful colonnaded cliff-face and round the corner to **Fingal's Cave** which is spectacular and quite unique. It is lined with glossy black hexagonal columns which on the west side rise symmetrically 12m out of the sea: the roof, like a complicated Gothic vault, is 20m high and the cave is 75m long. A rough path runs over stumps of column to the back of the cave (a torch is needed) and below it is a 20m deep arm of seawater which sighs with the swell. This gives the cave its Gaelic name, An Uamh Bhin (G. – the melodious cave).

It is possible to reach the back of the cave (only lit by the sun on December 16th) by dinghy.

Mendelssohn visited the island in 1829 and was inspired to write his Hebrides Overture (Die Fingalshöhle). If conditions allow you to visit the island, and only if you can avoid disturbing other visitors, then for an experience that you will remember for the rest of your life play a recording

of the Overture inside the cave and afterwards sit in silence and listen to the music of the sea.

Crowds can destroy the magic so try to visit the island out of season. May and June are the best months. Wordsworth was disgusted at being accompanied by too large a crowd of fellow travellers in 1833:

We saw, but surely in the motley crowd
Not one of us has felt, the far-famed sight;
How could we feel it? Each the others blight,
Hurried and hurrying volatile and loud.

Round the southern end of the island and west of Fingal's Cave is the Colonnade, otherwise known as The Great Face, – a vast expanse of columns reaching up 17m towards the sky with **Boat Cave** below them. In May 1945 a vagrant mine exploded here and the marks can be seen on the cliff-face. Opposite this southern tip is a strange formation known as the Wishing Chair. Further round on the west side **Mackinnon's**

Cave (named after Abbot MacKinnon of
Iona, who died in 1500) is almost as grand as
Fingal's and has a tunnel connection through to
Cormorant Cave. These caves can be reached
at low water from the bay on the west side,
which is fully exposed to the wild Atlantic and
is called, strangely, Port an Fhasgaidh (G. – the
port to clean off vermin) though a slightly
different emphasis makes it the more probable,
Port of Refuge. Access is not easy.

Access: Frequent summer trips, often combined
with Lunga (weather permitting): Gordon Grant

Marine, Fionnphort, Mull, 01681-700338:
Turus Mara, Dervaig, Mull, 0800-085-8786: or
Ardnamurchan Charters, 01972-500208.

Anchorages:
No adequate anchorage and landing difficult except in
settled conditions.
1. At least 1c SE of the landing-place in 6–12m, bottom
mainly rock and weed. Use tripping line. Many unmarked
rocks so approach carefully from SE with the landing place
ahead and Erisgeir astern.
2. Small beach at NE end suitable for dinghy landing but no
anchorage.

The Small Isles

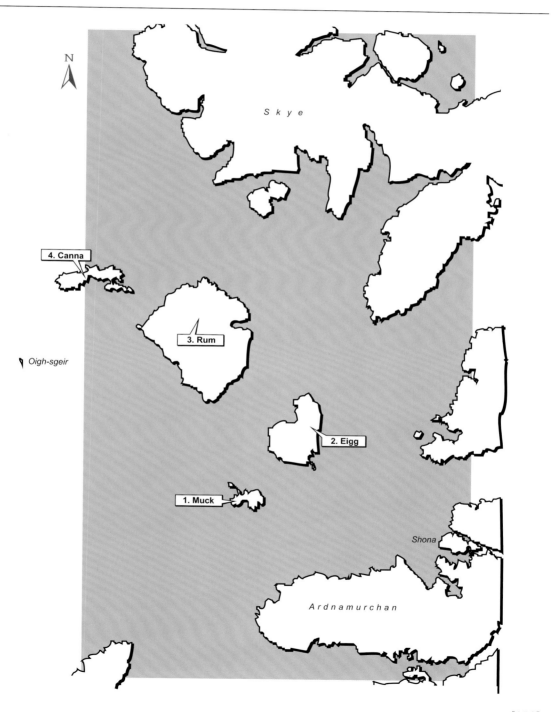

SECTION 4, Table 1: Arranged according to geographical position

No.	Name	Latitude	Longitude	Table 2* No.	Table 3** No.	Area in Acres		Area in Hectares
4.1	Muck	56° 50N	06° 15W	54	48	1381		559
4.2	Eigg	56° 54N	06° 10W	24	14	7534		3049
4.3	Rum	57° 00N	06° 20W	13	3	25854		10463
4.4	Canna	57° 04N	06° 33W	36	32	2792	1130	
	Sanday	57° 03N	06° 29W			455	184	1314

*Table 2: The islands arranged in order of magnitude
** Table 3: The islands arranged in order of height

Introduction

The four islands in this section are not particularly small but they are generally known as the Small Isles, or Sma' Isles, because that is the name of their parish. The total number of parishioners in 1755 was 943 and in 1794 it was 1339. Unfortunately these early statistics do not give separate figures for each island.

When sailing 'over the sea to Skye' from Ardnamurchan each island shows a very distinctive profile – the long stretch of Canna, the high cloud-wreathed mountains of Rum, the almost-primeval Sgurr of Eigg, and Muck creeping past like a grey-green submarine.

Some miles to the west, in an area renowned for its basking sharks, lies lonely **Oigh-Sgeir** (G. – maiden or virgin rock), maybe better known by its Norse name, **Hyskeir**. **Garbh Sgeir** (G. – rough rock) lies alongside with a neat little mooring in between. These rocks are only about four hectares (10 acres) in area, formed of hexagonal basalt columns – like Staffa, and rising to only 11m above sea-level. The lighthouse on Oigh-Sgeir was built in 1902–04 and, until it became automatic, the keepers grew vegetables and flowers in a walled garden and played golf on a miniature golf course. As ever there were many shipwrecks – the last on record was a Fleetwood trawler, the *Wyre Victory*, which sank about 4½ miles south-east of Oigh-Sgeir in 1976.

I am indebted to Malcolm MacGregor for the map information. He is the great-grandson of Robert Thom, one-time owner of both Canna (see No. 4.4) and Oigh-Sgeir. In the 19th and early 20th centuries sheep from Canna were regularly taken to Oigh-Sgeir to graze on the lush grass. The main islet is in three parts linked by a footpath. The largest part on the east is called Cnoc na h-Airigh (G. – knoll of the summer pasture) and the western part with the lighthouse and quay is called Cnoc nan Uibhean (G. – the lumpy knoll). In settled weather it is possible to lie alongside the quay.

On the north side, Camas na Cloiche Ruaidhe (G. – bay of the rose-coloured stone) almost looks like part of the rim of a submerged volcanic crater – and maybe it is, while the area to the south of the lighthouse has many dangerous rocks and reefs including Sgeir nan Cuag (G. – the twisted skerry) and, more ominously, A' Ghruagach (G. – the brownie).

Tucked away in the corner of the Ardnamurchan peninsula, Loch Moidart is split in two by tidal **Eilean Shona** which was leased by J M Barrie in the 1920s as a peaceful place to write the screenplay for *Peter Pan*. This lovely island of 525ha (population 2, in 2011) was sold in 1995 by Richard and Anna Stead to Robert Devereux of London for a price believed to be about £1.3m. It has high and precipitous hills, natural woodland, exotic trees and a large house and grounds. The house overlooks South Loch Moidart with a densely wooded islet called **Riska**, and romantic Castle Tioram [chee-rum] (G. *tioram* – dry, or fair) on its own drying islet, the home of Ranald, son of Somerled, Lord of the Isles.

Shona's old schoolhouse, now occasionally occupied as a holiday home, is on the opposite side of the island from the main house. It is reached by walking nearly two miles along a well-constructed track which follows the beautiful shore of North Loch Moidart. In the last century, I was told, the lady of the house ordered the school to be built as far from the house as possible so that she would not be disturbed by the children! The schoolmaster's house, renovated by a professor from the USA, has a stunning view over the Small Isles with sunsets that have the sort of magic no photograph can ever capture. Otters frequent this lonely place, herons pose on the shores of the loch, golden eagles nest in the heights, and civilisation is light-years away.

The entrance to North Loch Moidart from the sea is fairly straightforward once the skerries beside **An Glas Eilean** (G. – the grey island) and **Eilean Coille** (G. – wooded isle) have been located. **Eilean a' Choire** (G. – corrie isle) lies below the mountain slopes of Shona. The South Loch Moidart entrance is more devious and entails crawling past **Eilean Raonuill** (G. – Ranald's island) and then slipping round a rock pimple called **Eilean Corra** (G. – peaked island) with a few skerries in between providing interesting diversions.

North of Moidart the Sound of Arisaig is divided into Loch Ailort and Loch nan Uamh (G. – loch of the caves). **Eilean nan Gobhar** (G. – goat island) and **Eilean a' Chaolais** (G. – channel island) are at the entrance to Loch Ailort. Halfway along the loch are **Eilean nam Bairneach** (G. – isle of the limpets), **Eilean Buidhe** (G. – yellow isle) and **Eilean Allasaigh** (G. – tilted isle) and at the head of the loch are some very tiny islets –

the Black Islands or **Eileanan Dubha**.

On the north shore of Loch nan Uamh the **Borrodale Islands**, a string of skerries, give partial shelter for a yacht to anchor in attractive surroundings. The best spot is north of **Eilean nan Cabar** (G. – island of the rafters or poles). **Eileanan Sgurra** (G. – rocky isles), **Am Fraoch Eilean** (G. – the heather isle) and **An Glas Eilean** are to the south-west surrounded by rocks. At the head of the loch there is another anchorage to the east of **Eilean Gobhlach** (G. – forked island), an islet with a cleft between two hillocks.

At the entrance to the Sound of Arisaig a treacherous group of skerries, **Eilean an t-Snidhe**, can be a hazard in poor visibility. By the coast to the north **Eilean a' Ghaill** (G. – stranger's isle) has the remains of a fort on it.

Virtually all the off-shore hazards here are tidal,

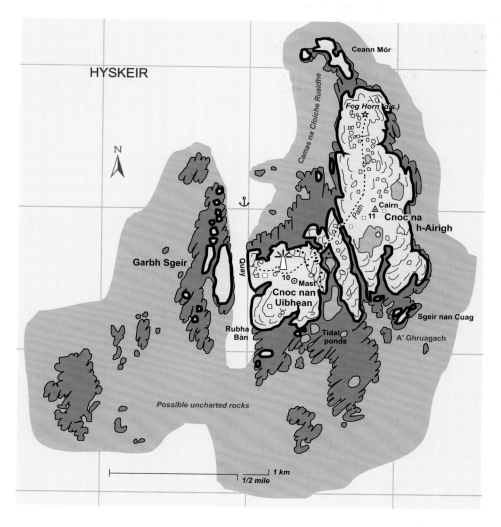

with **Luinga Mhór** and **Eilean Ighe** being the largest. Loch nan Ceall, which is the harbour for Arisaig, is guarded by a minefield of rocks, islets and skerries. There are perches to mark the passage through these but yachtsmen used to claim that the perches often swam about or the rocks did. This is no longer true as all the perches have now been renewed and painted and the passage is fairly easy. If nothing else, a visit by sea to Arisaig is a pleasant experience and there is the benefit of a large selection of buoys provided for visiting craft.

A rather shabby little islet, **Eilean na h-Acairseid** (G. – harbour island), lies off Mallaig near the entrance to the harbour.

4.1 Muck

(G. eilean nam muc – isle of pigs.) Fordun called it Helantmok – isle of swine. (G. muc-mhara – whale) is a kind but improbable option. In 1582 Buchanan referred to it as insula porcorum. When Dr Samuel Johnson met the Laird of Muck he was told that 'Muck' (i.e. Lord Muck) was the incorrect title. With a touch of wishful thinking the Laird asked to be called 'Monk' as he claimed that his property's original owner was a hermit from Iona.

OS Maps: 1:50000 Sheet 39   1:25000 Sheets 390 or 397
Admiralty Charts: 1:100000 No.1796   1:50000 No.2207

Area: 559ha (1381 acres)
Height: 137m (449 ft)

Owner: Purchased by the MacEwens in 1896. Lawrence and Ewen MacEwen are the principal owners.

Population: Early 1800s–280. 1841–68. 1861–58. 1881–51. 1891–48. 1931–48. 1961–29. 1971–24. 1991–24. 2001 – 30. 2001–30. 2011–27. The MacEwens advertise at intervals for young families to settle on the island as it is essential to maintain a viable primary school.

Geology: Mostly Tertiary sheet basalt with typical terraced cliffs, grassy ledges and flattened crowns. Dolerite dykes run NW to SE. Very fertile soil composed of glacial drift and sea-blown shell-sand which produces appetising potatoes as early as May.

History: In 1588 when a Spanish galleon was wrecked in Tobermory Bay, Sir Lachlan Maclean of Mull, encouraged by the Campbells, employed the surviving Spanish sailors as mercenaries and let them loose on several islands belonging to the MacDonalds. Consequently Muck was burned, plundered and left in a desolate state.

By 1773 when Boswell and Dr Johnson were passing by the island it was again reasonably prosperous, thanks to a considerate laird and the production of kelp (which was used to make potash). Boswell reported that the Laird had 'seven score of souls' on Muck. 'Last year he had eighty persons inoculated, mostly children, but some of them eighteen years of age. He agreed with the surgeon to come and do it, at half a crown a head. – It is very fertile in corn, of which they export some; and its coasts abound in fish. A taylor comes there six times in a year.' Almost Utopian, but some fifty years later, in 1828, the kelp market collapsed and 150 islanders were shipped off to Nova Scotia. Then in 1854 Muck was purchased by Captain Thomas Swinburne RN, who started a fishing industry but also rented the land for sheep farming, causing further depopulation. Only today is the island recovering once again – or at least surviving – thanks to the enlightened and benevolent policy of the owners.

Wildlife: Some alpine plants grow here 600m below their usual altitude – dwarf juniper, crowberry, club moss, rose root sedum, mountain cats-paw and pyramidal bugle. In early summer the fields are covered with the flowers of marigold, iris, cornflower and bluebell. The only heather

PORT MÓR

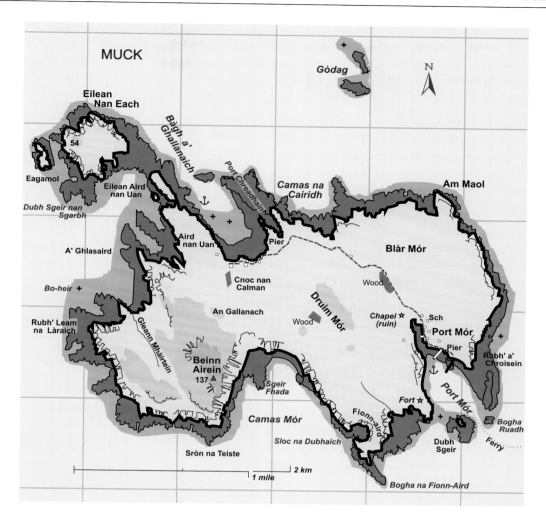

is in Glen Martin. There are a few acres of woodland mostly planted in 1922 but there are plans to plant more trees.

Some Rum ponies are bred on the island and as there used to be no stallion the mares were occasionally ferried over to Rum. Otters can be seen in Gallanach Bay and there are a number of small rodents but, luckily, no rabbits.

Gallanach Bay is also a popular playground for porpoises, which may have been a factor in the naming of the island as they are called 'sea-pigs' in Gaelic.

Over eighty species of birds nest here with the sea-birds favouring isolated Eilean nan Each. There are also many visiting species.

MUCK is a peaceful, low-lying island with attractive beaches but exposed to the Atlantic gales. This brings in the shell sand which keeps

the basalt soil fertile. Most of the coast is rocky and near the west end are cliffs 15m to 18m high. There are some springs of good water.

This is the most fertile of the Small Isles and Lawrence MacEwen, the laird, runs the main farm at **Gallanach** (G. – full of young trees), with his wife Jenny and some additional help. It is a mixed farm with cattle, sheep, a small dairy herd, and crops of potatoes, oats and root crops. There are also two small tenant farms and the island is self-sufficient in milk, eggs and vegetables with the islanders having a communal vagetable patch for their own use. Cars are of limited use as there are only two kilometres of road and the farm tractor is still an important means of powered transport. There is no peat so all fuel, apart from driftwood, has to be imported. Electricity is provided by two wind-powered generators installed in 2000.

Jenny's father was in the colonial service in

Africa and bought a croft in Soay (See No.5.1) which he saw advertised in *The Times*. He never reached it but his twenty-year-old daughter took up the challenge and it was there that she met Lawrence MacEwen when he sailed over to help ship the island cattle to market.

The island children were taught in a corrugated iron shed with an outside lavatory until 1992 when Highland Regional Council approved the building of a new school costing over quarter of a million pounds with an indoor lavatory and its own wind-powered electricity generator.

Port Mor in the south-east corner is the main harbour with a small settlement of houses and the ro-ro ferry pier which was constructed in 2001. Camping is allowed with permission and there is visitor accommodation in the form of a self-service holiday house, a guest house, and a bunkhouse. A craft shop and licensed tea room provides delicious freshly baked produce.

A graveyard and ruined chapel [NM421795] are on the hill above Port Mor and on the south side of the harbour entrance a few remnants of Dùn Ban (G. – white fort), an old Bronze Age fortification, are still visible [NM422787]. The ferry pier was completed in 2001.

In the north-west two drying islands form a peninsula, **Eilean nan Each** (G. – horse island) and **Eilean Aird nan Uan** (G. – island of the headland of the lambs). In **Gallanach Bay**, to the east of the peninsula, sea-beans from the West Indies are sometimes washed in by the Gulf Stream onto the beautiful stretch of shell-sand beach. They are looked on as lucky charms. Two long reefs form the east side of Gallanach Bay and between them is tiny **Port Chreadhain** with a small jetty. Beyond that is another small bay called **Camus na Cairidh** (G. – bay of the weir), possibly used for trapping fish in the past.

From the top of **Ben Airean**, which is an easy climb from Gallanach, the whole island reveals itself – with the Sgurr of Eigg and Rum as a backdrop. For a climber it may be more of a challenge to ascend the steep cliff on the west side of Camas Mór (G. – the big bay), but Muck is not really for such strenuous pursuits. It is much better just to ramble about and explore, and to revel in the ever-changing aspect of sea and sky.

* * *

Access: Calmac ro-ro ferry from Mallaig, everyday except Mon. and Wed. in summer, 01687-462403/011. 1½-hour stopover on Tues. (Vehicle permit required, 01397-709000). Arisaig Marine from Arisaig, most days in summer, 01687-450224. Accommodation 01687-462362 or hotel 01687-462365.

Anchorages:
1. Port Mór, on the SE side lies between two partly-submerged reefs. Entrance well marked but care needed. Anchor abeam or beyond the pier dolphin clear of ferry access. Exposed to S'lies.
2. Bàgh a Ghallanaich, on the N side of Muck, 4c SE of the E extremity of Eilean nan Each. Entrance requires great care. Exposed to N'lies. Anchor 1c SSE of Bo Haund in 4m, sand.

4.2 Eigg

[eg] (G. eag – a notch) – from Rum the silhouette shows a deep groove framed by the two humps of An Sgurr and Bein Bhuidhe. Until the 16th century called **Eilean Nimban More** *(G. – island of the powerful women) – note 'Loch nam Ban Móra' beside the Sgurr.*

O S Maps: 1:50000 Sheet 39 1:25000 Sheet 397
Admiralty Chart: 1:50000 No.2207

Area: 3049ha (7534 acres)
Height: 393m (1289 ft)

Owner: Keith Schellenberg, a Yorkshire farmer and sportsman, and his wife, bought Eigg jointly in 1975 for £265,000. Following divorce there was a prolonged court case over the joint ownership which Mr Schellenberg lost in 1992. The island was put up for sale and Schellenberg rebought it for just under £1 million but as, by then, his relationship with the islanders had seriously deteriorated, he sold Eigg in 1995 for about £1.5m to an elusive German artist who called himself 'Maruma'.

After extravagant, unfulfilled promises by the new owner, and further acrimony on the island, the residents launched a public appeal for funds to purchase Eigg for themselves. Their aim was achieved on 12 June 1997 when Eigg was bought for £1.5m from the true owner, a Hong Kong businessman, Hans Renier Erdhart, by the Isle of Eigg Heritage Trust (a partnership of Highland Council, the Scottish Wildlife Trust, and the islanders' own appeal fund).

Population: 1798– about 500. 1841–546 (peak). 1871–290. 1881–291. 1891–233. 1931–138. 1951–115. 1961–74. 1971–69.

1981–64. 1991–69. 1997–47 adults and 21 children – the highest proportion of children of all the Scottish islands. 2001–67. 2011–83.

Geology: An Sgurr (G. *sgùrr* – conical hill) or (G. *sgòrr* – sharp point, buck tooth) – the huge sugarloaf crag which dominates the island – is the largest residual mass of columnar pitchstone lava in Britain. It rests on an old river-bed in which there are driftwood fossils. The southern moor and north plateau are basalt which has weathered to a good soil. Eilean Chathastail in the south-east is of columnar basalt. The northern cliffs

are sandstone which has eroded into fascinating shapes at Camus Sgiotaig where the beach is renowned for its Singing Sands – when dry the grains of white quartz drone eerily underfoot and when damp they squeak like blackboard chalk. Sometimes when the wind blows the sand can sound like an Aeolian harp. Also north of the Bay of Laig are limestone nodules trapped in rock cages and rattled by the waves. At the north extremity fossilised fish and reptiles are to be found in shale at Eilean Tuilm just above the low-water mark. In 1840 the fossilised remains of a Plesiosaur, a swimming dinosaur with

paddle-shaped legs and a long neck and tail, were found on Eigg. In 1992 a similar fossil was found on Skye.

History: St Donan or Donnan, who had been trained at Whithorn and may have stayed for a time at Loch Alsh (Eilean Donan), eventually set up a sizeable monastery on Eigg but was murdered together with fifty-two of his monks in 617 according to the Irish annals.

The island was part of the Norse empire but was seized by the MacDonalds, Lords of the Isles. Robert the Bruce granted official title to MacDonald of Clanranald in 1309.

The earliest recorded meeting of island chiefs seems to suggest that it took place on Eigg – although Islay may be the correct interpretation: '...at Kildonnan in Eigg, where the staff of Lordship of Clanranald was given to one who was nominated Macdonnall and Donald of Isla...'

One story runs that in the winter of 1577 some MacLeods from Skye were sent home castrated after being caught raping MacDonald girls on Eigg. When the MacLeods, led by Alasdair Crotach (Hunchback Alasdair) from Rodel on Harris (see No.8.14), retaliated in force, 395 MacDonald islanders hid in Uamh Fhraing (G. – St Francis Cave) but were eventually discovered by the MacLeods who tried to smoke them out by lighting a brushwood fire in the entrance. Every MacDonald is said to have suffocated in the smoke and the cave is still known as 'Massacre Cave'. Some bones were removed from the cave for burial in the 19th century.

The population seems to have recovered quickly for eleven years after this incident Sir Lachlan Maclean and his Spanish mercenaries burnt and plundered the island.

The Reformation had left the islanders uncertain which religion it was safe to follow. At that time they were part of the Protestant parish of Sleat in Skye but their minister, Reverend Mackinnon, never visited them. A missionary priest, Father Ward, landed in 1625 and soon renewed their Catholic faith. Mackinnon was furious and sent soldiers to seize the priest but the people refused to yield. Mackinnon retreated and was looking for additional support when MacDonald of Clanranald (a Catholic) offered to pay Mackinnon one-third of the island's tithes if he left the islanders in peace. Mackinnon readily accepted.

The MacDonalds of Eigg supported the Catholic Jacobites in the 1745 rebellion so Captain John Ferguson of the King's ship, *Furnace*, was sent to arrest the leader John MacDonald. He surrendered and handed over all arms on the promise that there would be no reprisals against his clansmen but as soon as he was in custody Ferguson sacked the island and deported the young men.

In 1829 the MacDonalds sold Eigg to Dr Hugh MacPherson, Professor of Greek at Aberdeen University, for £15,000 and several minor clearances followed. The next owner, Robert Thompson, a wealthy shipbuilder, bought the island in 1893 and spent a lot of money on improvements including the construction of a large house which he called the White Lodge. It was a time of comparative prosperity for the crofters. Thompson died in 1913 and his grave is on Eilean Chathastail. A Danish shipping magnate, Sir William Petersen, was the next owner. When he was in residence his flag flew at the Lodge and his luxury yacht, *White Eagle*, would anchor near the pier but in 1924 a fire destroyed the White Lodge and a year later Petersen died in debt.

One of his creditors, Lord Walter Runciman, a shipowner, and his brother James, a writer, then took over the island. They built the present lodge, created the home farm, planted a semi-tropical garden of palms, bamboo and lush woodland and ploughed back profits. Relative prosperity was regained until a Shropshire farmer, Robert Evans, bought the island in 1966 for £82,000 and resold it for £120,000 in 1971 to a Christian charity, the Anglyn Trust, which had dreams of using the island for the treatment of mentally handicapped children.

This came to nothing and it was something of a relief for the islanders when the Schellenbergs took over in 1975.

Wildlife: Campion, golden rod, a variety of heathers, thyme, willow, remnant hazel scrub, and even some imported eucalyptus trees grow in the mild, damp climate which also encourages a wealth of saxifrages. A number of wild goats frequent the heights and there are some rare species of butterfly.

The island is managed as a wildlife reserve supervised by the Scottish Wildlife Trust, which is a member of the Isle of Eigg Heritage Trust.

A fairly large and noisy colony of Manx

GALMISDALE, CROUCHED BENEATH AN SGURR

house – a white Italian-style (15-room) residence once set in a garden of crazy-paving, catmint and carnations. It was in very serious disrepair but a couple of ecologists with a young family bought it in 2004 and were gradually restoring it and running courses on sustainable technologies. Meanwhile in 2008 a £1.5m development of hydroelectric, wind and solar electricity fed through 7 miles of underground cables has provided 'green' power for all.

At **Kildonnan**, (G. – Donan's cell) an ancient Celtic cross-slab is set near the ruins of a 14th-century church which was built on the site of a monastery founded by St Donan in the 7th century [NM489854]. The saint and his fifty-two monks were massacred in 617, some say by pirates, others by a band of Pictish warrior women who lived on a crannog in **Loch nam Ban Móra** (G. – loch of the mighty women) [NM455852]. The loch is in a sheltered hollow high in the hills behind the Sgurr. The women apparently disliked missionaries but it was Norsemen who had destroyed the monastery buildings, which archaeologists recently excavated.

Macdonald's Cave and **St Francis Cave**, both of them worth a visit, lie half a mile southwest of the old pier. Walk up the road towards An Sgurr and climb the first stile on the left. Follow the path to the cottage, then a sheep track to the cliff fence. Follow the fence to a zig-zag track leading down to the shore beside a small burn. Turn left to Massacre Cave (St Francis Cave) [NM476834] and right to Cathedral Cave (Macdonald's Cave). Cathedral Cave has been used for Catholic services, a custom dating from the persecution following the 1745 rebellion. A stone wall in the cave may have been an altar.

A strip at the extreme north end of the island is low-lying but ½km in from the shore steep cliffs rise to about 250m clearly marking, there and on the east coast, the change in sea-level since the Ice Age. Cliffs nearly encircle the island with the dramatic hump of the **Sgurr of Eigg** rising a further sheer 150m above the plateau. When the clouds are low, there is a touch of mystery; when the sky is blue, throw in some

shearwater burrows into the soil on An Sgurr, and there are some colonies of puffins on the sea-cliffs. Until about 1900 white-tailed sea-eagles had eyries on the cliffs of Eigg before disappearing from the list of native British birds.

*   *   *

For an island the size of **EIGG** it is unfortunate to have no harbour, and no bays or inlets which give satisfactory shelter, but a new ro-ro ferry pier was completed in 2004 at a cost of £7.8 million and passengers and goods no longer have to disembark from the ferry by flit-boat. Although most of the population lives at **Cleadale** in the north-west the ferry has always called at **Galmisdale** in the south-east, where rocky **Eilean Chathastail** (G. – castle island) gives some protection from the ocean swell. Although cars can reach Eigg without difficulty only islanders' cars are allowed to land – to maintain 'the peace and tranquility of the island'. However Eigg is a fairly large island and other forms of transport have been provided as it is a long walk to Cleadale and back.

Above Galmisdale is 'The Lodge' – the laird's

imaginary palm trees (there are real ones at the Lodge) and it could be Tahiti.

Kenneth MacLeod, composer of many beautiful songs including the 'Road to the Isles' was born on Eigg in 1872.

There are many enjoyable exploits for experienced climbers. On The Sgurr there is Collie's Cleft in the South Wall rated as severe; Eagle Chimney – hard severe; The Flue – very severe and Botterill's Crack – severe. The latter has a fossilised coniferous tree trunk at the foot. On the cliffs overlooking Cleadale, called the Cleadale Face, there is Laig Buttress – severe, and the Pod – very severe.

Less dangerous, but equally thrilling, is the fine hillwalk from An Cruachan (G. – the rounded hill) to Bein Bhuidhe (G. – pleasant mountain) with the sight of Rum's dark mountains, Ainshval and Askival, towering into the clouds beyond the windswept sound. JRR Tolkien holidayed here and this view is said to have been the inspiration for his mystical *Lord of the Rings*. He lived in Howlin croft house.

*   *   *

Access: Ro-ro ferry from Mallaig, every day except Wed. in summer, 01687-462403. 5-hour stopover on Mon. (Vehicle permit required, 01397-709000). Arisaig Marine, most days in summer, 01687-450224. Tourist Information, East Bay, Mallaig, 01687-462170.

Anchorages: There are no sheltered anchorages.
1. South of Galmisdale Point. Approach from SSW well clear of En Chathastail. Anchor in the NW part at least 1c off-shore and out of the tidal channel in 3–6m, sand. Exposed to SW and swell.
2. E of N extremity of En Chathastail. Beware 1½c reef just S of this. Anchor ¾c off the island. Exposed to E'lies and can be uncomfortable.
3. NE of Galmisdale Point. Approach through the narrows or from NE between the perches – with care. Very restricted anchorage in moderate weather NE of the end of the old pier avoiding moorings, reef and ferry. Bottom foul. Subject to swell. Shoal-draught boats may snug-in N of old pier.
4. Poll nam Partan, tidal pool within Rubha na Crannaig. Avoid S access. Approach from SE on leading line (2.3m depth at LW). Anchor in sand with weed patches.
5. N of Rubha na Crannaig, off Kildonnan. Depths shallow enough for anchorage up to 2c from shore of Eigg but very exposed. Useful in perfect conditions or in emergencies.
6. Bay of Laig. Occasional anchorage in quiet weather or

E'lies. Keep about 2c off S shore on approach.

4.3 Rum

[room, or rum] Probably pre-Celtic but possibly (ON rŏm-øy – wide island) or maybe (G. i-dhruim – isle of the ridge).

(Note: Sir George Bullough changed the spelling to Rhum to avoid the alcoholic association. 'Rh' is not a Gaelic form and in 1991 the Nature Conservancy Council of Scotland after consultation with the School of Scottish Studies at Edinburgh University asked for the spelling to be corrected.)

O S Maps: 1:50000 Sheet 39 1:25000 Sheet 397
Admiralty Charts: 1:100000 No.1796 1:50000 Nos.2207 and 2208

Area: 10463ha (25854 acres)
Height: 812m (2663 ft)

Owner: A Lancashire family, Bullough, were owners from 1888 to 1957. The Government purchased the island from Sir George Bullough's widow, Monica Lady Bullough, in 1957 for £26,000. The castle contents were donated to the nation by Lady Bullough. Later, control was transferred to Scottish Natural Heritage (SNH). In 2009 ownership of the small settlement at Kinloch Castle was transferred to the residents, and some new crofts were created with the aim of encouraging newcomers to settle.

Population: 1794– over 400. 1831–134. 1841–124. 1881–89. 1891–53. 1931–32. 1961–40. 1981–17. 1991–26. 2001–22. 2011–22. The population until 2009 was mostly made up of employees and families of SNH and a schoolteacher.

Geology: A platform of purple-red Torridonian sandstone fringed with sea-cliffs, some 150m to 300m high, with geologically unique formations. The range south of the Kinloch-Harris divide is called the Cuillin and includes the peaks, **Askival** (812m) (ON – mountain of the ash trees), **Hallival** (723m) and **Trollaval** (702m) (ON – mountain of the trolls) composed of rock allied to gabbro but with fewer basalt dykes than usual. Hallival has escarpments of allivalite, its own pale gabbro and the slopes between are of peridotite, a dark orange-brown variety. Small platinum deposits were reported in 1999. **Ainshval** (781m) (ON – hill of the strongholds) and **Sgurr nan Gillean** (764m) are capped by quartz-felsite overlying Torridonian sandstone. On the south

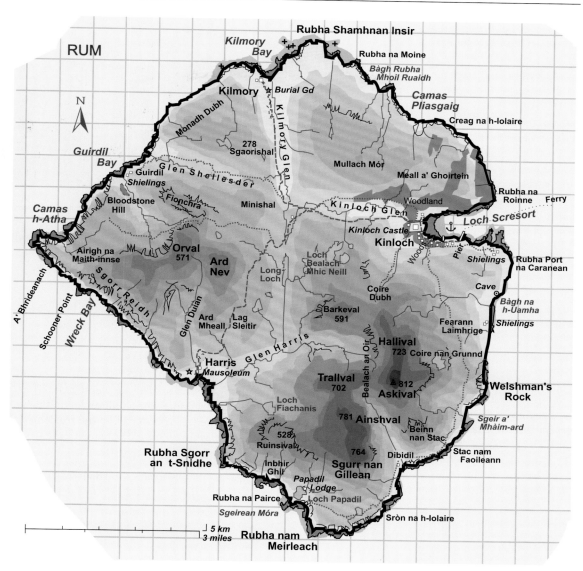

RUM

Rubha Shamhnan Insir

Kilmory Bay

Rubha na Moine

Bàgh Rubha Mhoil Ruaidh

Kilmory

Burial Gd

Camas Pliasgaig

Creag na h-Iolaire

Monadh Dubh

Kilmory Glen

278 Sgaorishal

Mullach Mór

Meall a' Ghoirtein

Guirdil Bay

Glen Shellesder

Guirdil Shielings

Minishal

Kinloch Glen

Woodland

Rubha na Roinne   Ferry

Fionchra

Bloodstone Hill

Camas h-Atha

Kinloch Castle

Loch Scresort

Kinloch

Airigh na Maith-innse

Orval 571

Ard Nev

Long Loch

Loch Bealach Mhic Neill

Shielings

Rubha Port na Caranean

A' Bhrideanach

Sgorr Reidh

Schooner Point

Wreck Bay

Glen Duian

Ard Mheall

Lag Sleitir

Coire Dubh

Barkeval 591

Cave

Bàgh na h-Uamha

Shielings

Fearann Laimhrige

Hallival 723

Coire nan Grunnd

Harris Mausoleum

Glen Harris

Trallval 702

Bealach an Oir

Askival 812

Welshman's Rock

781 Ainshval

Beinn nan Stac

Sgeir a' Mhàim-ard

528 Ruinsival

764

Sgurr nan Gillean

Dibidil

Stac nam Faoileann

Rubha Sgorr an t-Snidhe

Inbhir Ghil

Papadil Lodge

Loch Fiachanis

Rubha na Pairce

Loch Papadil

Sgeirean Móra

Sròn na h-Iolaire

5 km
3 miles

Rubha nam Meirleach

and western cliffs there is granite. The strongest gravitational pull in the British Isles has been recorded below Ard Mheall.

Rum was a centre of violent volcanic activity some sixty million years ago. During the last ice age it had its own independent glaciers, one of which carved out Kinloch Glen. There is a raised beach at Harris and long raised terraces cut by the sea into the spectacular western precipice which is now being carved by the Atlantic breakers at a lower level.

Only a few patches of arable land exist – at Harris, Kilmory and Kinloch.

History: In spite of its somewhat inhospitable climate today, Rum was one of the earliest places of human settlement in Scotland although little

is known of its early prehistory. Its interest for Mesolithic man was probably the availability of rare bloodstone from Bloodstone Hill – an attractive substitute for flint.

Various topological features have Norse names but there is little conclusive evidence of Norse settlement except for a carved narwhal ivory gaming piece found at Bàgh na h-Uamha in the 1940s.

Rum passed from the Norwegian to the Scottish Crown in 1266 and early records show that Rum was chartered to John of Islay in 1346. It was attacked and plundered by Sir Lachlan MacLean and his mercenaries in 1588, and in 1695 became part of the lands of the Macleans of Coll. The main industry – fishing – was damaged by the Salt Tax, and yet in spite of the difficult conditions the population steadily increased. By the beginning of the 19th century there was overcrowding and extreme poverty. A clearance was arranged and over 300 islanders were 'persuaded' to emigrate to Canada and the United States, leaving less than fifty inhabitants behind. Maclean leased the island for sheep-farming and 8000 sheep were introduced and some shepherds. They were joined by some families of crofters who emigrated from Skye and settled at Port nan Caranean in 1827. By 1831 the population had risen to 134 but eventually stabilised at about ninety. In 1845 Maclean sold the island to the Marquis of Salisbury as the sheep-farming was unprofitable. The Marquis converted Rum to a sporting estate by stocking the burns with trout and bringing in red deer before he too sold out.

There was a further unsuccessful attempt at sheep-farming by the Campbells of Oronsay and then in 1888 a Lancastrian MP, John Bullough of Oswaldtwistle, stepped in. He had made a fortune from the design and production of milling machinery. Rum became his holiday retreat and sporting estate and according to his widow he wrote poetry when out shooting while enjoying his after-luncheon cigar 'by some bonnie burn'.

His wealthy and eccentric son, George Bullough, aged twenty-one, took over in 1891. After sailing round the world he built Kinloch Castle in 1900–02. He imported London architects (Leeming & Leeming), red Arran sandstone, and Lancashire stonemasons to build a home on the island fit for a laird. The workmen were paid extra to wear kilts and tuppence a day for tobacco (midge money). Even the garden soil was imported from Ayrshire. This was a prime example of extravagant Edwardian opulence – live turtles and alligators in heated tanks; birds of paradise and humming-birds in the conservatory; a large mechanical 'orchestrian' with brass, woodwinds and drums for military marches and operettas; central heating, double-glazed stained glass, a baronial hall, a billiard room with air-conditioning (to remove the cigar smoke), and a Victorian 'jacuzzi' bath. Guests were brought to Mallaig by a private train, taken by steam yacht to Sresort and met by Albion motor cars which

KINLOCH CASTLE

were kept on the island. Grapes, figs, peaches and nectarines were grown in the glasshouses.

Sir George was married on Rum and stayed there for three weeks every year.

Wildlife: In 1957 Rum was declared a National Nature Reserve and has since been declared a National Scenic Area, a Special Site of Scientific Interest, a Biosphere Reserve, and a Specially Protected Area.

The entire ecology is being managed by Scottish Natural Heritage (SNH) to conserve the natural and cultural history of the island. The existing mixed woodland at Loch Scresort was mainly planted by the Bulloughs about 1900. Over one million native trees and shrubs have now been planted as part of an extensive woodland regeneration project and open heathland preserved for study and conservation of the natural flora and fauna in a unique environment. An excellent SNH booklet is on sale at the post-office.

Plant life is prolific and some is undisturbed since the last ice age. Rare arctic sandwort and penny-cress can be found, the spotted orchids, *Dactylorhiza maculata*, are of a sub-species unique to Rum, and there are three unique micro-species of eyebright. The moors are studded with blue heath milkwort, sundew, tormentil, butterwort, black bog-rush and bog asphodel, and thrift, roseroot and Scots lovage grow on the cliffs. Nineteen species of butterfly have been recorded.

Rum ponies are sometimes claimed to be descended from ponies saved from a wrecked Spanish galleon, or the offspring of Eriskay ponies. The current herd originate from a cross between an Arab sire and a West Highland mare but stand only 14 hands high (1.4m). Sir George introduced a pure white Arab stallion to improve the bloodstock.

Highland cattle are kept to maintain, by controlled feeding, the herb-rich pastures of Glen Harris and a small herd of feral goats favour the south-western cliffs. The biology and habits of the red deer are closely studied. One surprising discovery was that they are occasionally carnivorous – eating live young seabird nestlings, presumably to compensate for mineral deficiencies. (See Foula No.11.6 for carnivorous sheep). Rum ponies are used to bring the deer carcasses in during the annual cull by professional stalkers.

The peak season for ornithologists is April to October, with many varieties of upland species. In all, over 150 species of bird have been recorded. Corncrakes breed on the farm at Kinloch and there are sea-bird colonies on the south and north-east coasts – mainly kittiwake, puffin, razorbill and guillemot. About 61,000 pairs of Manx shearwater breed in mountain top burrows. Their ghostly sounds in the night probably gave Trollaval its name (a midnight ascent in May is unforgettable). Golden eagles are to be seen over the glens. One of Rum's great success stories has been the reintroduction of the white-tailed sea eagle during the 1970s and 80s using chicks taken from Norwegian nests. The last native Scottish bird was seen on Skye in 1916.

RUM is by far the largest island in the Small Isles group but because it is so mountainous and its climate is less mild it has never been able to support a population relative to its size. The average annual rainfall at Kinloch is 240cm but in the mountains above it is over 300cm. Before the 15th century most of the island was cloaked in native woodland but slashing and burning by man destroyed it all except for a few stray trees on rocky cliffs. The present bleak moorland slopes are a direct result of this, followed by overgrazing of sheep and deer.

A roadway connects the three 'settlements' of Kinloch, Harris and Kilmory and there is also a rough track running south from Kinloch to Dibidil and on to Papadil.

Kinloch on Loch Scresort is the main settlement centred round **Kinloch Castle**, which is filled with remarkable 'objets d'art' collected by Sir George in the Far East. Sadly, this unique and irreplaceable monument, with a running cost of £70,000 a year, is fast deteriorating, and despite many appeals, including one from Prince Charles with a large offer from his Regeneration Trust, there has been little progress. The **Post Office** is the oldest inhabited building on Rum. It used to be the kitchen for the original laird's house, Kinloch House, which was near the site of the present Castle. The beech and sycamore trees behind the Post Office were planted about 1830 when Kinloch House was being built.

Until the ferry pier was completed in 2001 everything was normally trans-shipped ashore to the old stone pier at **Loch Scresort** which is only accessible at high water. Electricity is provided by a small hydro-electric turbine but coal was formerly delivered only once a year and stored by the jetty.

A prehistoric site at Kinloch was discovered during ploughing in the summer of 1983. Excavations were carried out between 1984 and 1986 which revealed extensive Mesolithic and

THE BULLOUGH MAUSOLEUM – A GREEK TEMPLE IN REMOTE GLEN HARRIS

later activity dating from 7000BC providing the best evidence to date of the early settlement of Scotland. A vast number of artefacts were recovered, mainly stone tools made of Rum bloodstone and flint.

On the south side of Loch Scresort is the schoolhouse, built in 1962 in front of the previous schoolhouse, and further east on the headland are the remains of an old village, **Port na Caranean**. It lies across Gleann Carn nan Dobhran (G. – glen of the cairn of the otters) and otters can still be seen here in the early morning. The village population was twenty-seven in 1841 but by 1861 it was abandoned.

Harris in the south-west has the lowest rainfall on Rum (140cm). The main feature there is the Bullough mausoleum – as eccentric as everything else – built in the style of a Greek temple [NM336957]. It contains the tombs of John, George and Monica. John (Sir George's father) was first laid to rest in a tiled burial vault but a friend was overheard saying it looked like a public lavatory for London Underground so Sir George built a new mausoleum and blew up the vault with dynamite.

The track from Kinloch to **Dibidil** (ON *djup-dalr* – deep valley) on the south-east coastline passes Creag a' Wealishech (G. – Welshman's rock). Some Welsh slate quarriers widened a precipitous path near here. The track leads on round the southern extremity to **Papadil** (ON *papa-dalr* – valley of the hermit), romantically lonely and attractive with a loch backed by a small wood of mixed trees. The Lodge was built by Sir George but Lady Bullough disliked it and let it fall into ruin [NM366922]. There is a climbers' bothy there now.

At the opposite extreme in the far north **Kilmory** has a very fine beach, the remains of quite a large village settlement, an old burial ground [NG361036], one inhabited cottage and the original Kinloch Castle laundry. The area is sometimes closed to the public (for deer research).

For the mountaineering fraternity, both Askival and Ainshval are classed as 'Corbetts' but climbers and hill-walkers on Rum should always remember that there are no facilities for rescue. Furthermore, the estate staff can take no responsibility for rescue. Many interesting climbs have been listed – easy, moderate, difficult and severe. Allivalite is similar to the black gabbro of the Cuillin on Skye, rough, but firm. A traverse of

the main ridge involves little actual climbing yet is a classic expedition, and walking the ridges of Hallival, Trollaval and Sgurr nan Gillean, down Glen Dibidil, and back along the coast to Loch Scresort is a memorable experience.

There is also spectacular hill-walking (first contact the Reserve Office). For one long and strenuous walk, take the Dibidil track starting close to the pier at Loch Scresort, 8½km over a 230m ridge (easier than crossing the tussocky moor) to Dibidil then an indistinct 4km to Papadil. From Papadil and across Glen Harris, 6km, keeping roughly to the 200m contour to avoid the sea-cliffs.

The west coast may be reached from the road junction point. From there a stalker's path goes to the 370m bealach at the top of Glen Guirdil, then under the basalt summit cliff on Orval, across to 388m Bloodstone Hill and the fine sea-cliffs of Sgòrr Mhór. An alternative track leads down Glen Shellesder past waterfalls to the shielings at Guirdil. Both these walks are 6km there (and 6km back) and only the man-eating midges can spoil one's pleasure; but remember also that this is a big rough island, hard-going at places and distances are misleading.

Fishing may be purchased at the Reserve Office but there are no boats and all catches must be reported. Deer stalking can also be arranged (for a price). The only vehicles normally permitted are SNH's own jeeps.

*   *   *

Access: Ro-ro ferry from Mallaig, Mon., Wed., Fri., Sat. Sun., calls twice a day on Mon., Wed., Sat., giving stopover time, 01687-462403. (Vehicles not encouraged and permit required, 01687-462026). Arisaig Marine, Arisaig, every day in summer, 01687-450224. Accommodation at Kinloch Castle Hostel, 01687-462037. For use of campsite and cabins contact 01687-462404. AquaXplore, Elgol, Skye, full day trips by RIB., 0800-731-3089. Tourist Information, East Bay, Mallaig, 01687-462170.

Anchorages:
Generally, the bottom is rock off S and W sides, mud off E side with irregular depths, and sand off N side. There are no landing restrictions.
1. Loch Scresort affords good anchorage but subject to squalls in W'lies and swell from E'lies. It is shallow, and the head dries out about 2c. S shore moderately steep-to, except

for reef extending 2c N from Rubha Port na Caranean. Old pier dries and concrete slip has a least depth of 0.6m at outer end. Anchor well off the slip or NE of the old pier in sufficient depth, stiff mud and thick kelp.

2. Bay W of Rubha na Moine near N extremity of the island. Temp. anchorage in suitable conditions.

3. Kilmory Bay, near N extremity, has possible spots to anchor in depths of 2.5–5.5m, sand, but requires great care and suitable weather. Several rocks on both sides of bay.

4. Camas na h Atha, on NE side of A' Bhrideanach, the W extremity, is a small sandy bay with a rock off each entrance point. Temp. anchorage only when conditions ideal.

4.4 Canna

(EI cana – wolf-whelp) island, or (ON kne-øy – knee-shaped island), or possibly (G. cana – little whale or porpoise) island.

Sanday

(ON sand-øy – island with a conspicuous sandy beach)

O S Maps: 1:50000 Sheet 39 1:25000 Sheet 397
Admiralty Charts: 1:100000 Nos.1795 or 1796 1:50000 main anchorage and western part No.2208

Area: 1314ha (3247 acres)
Height: 210m (689 ft)
Owner: Ownership donated in 1981 to the National Trust for Scotland (NTS) by the late Dr John Lorne Campbell (1906–96) who had owned it since 1938.

Population:

	1841	1881	1891	1931	1961	1991	2001	2011
C'na		57	40	40	24	20	6	12
S'day		62	62	20	0	0	6	9
	255	119	102	60	24	20	12	21

(The Trust has advertised for more families to settle, with mixed success).

Geology: A lava platform of terraced Tertiary basaltic rock has formed a generally rich and fertile soil. The basalt columns on the south coast are up to 6m in height. Compass Hill (139m) at the north-eastern corner is undifferentiated tuff with a sufficiently high iron content to distort ships' compasses helped by a vein of iron ore which continues under the sea to the north.

History: Canna belonged to the Benedictine Monastery of Iona followed by Norwegian suzerainty although the monks continued to cultivate it until the Reformation. Piracy was such a problem however that the Abbot of Iona appealed to the Pope to threaten excommunication if the raids did not cease. Canna became part of the Kingdom of Scotland in 1266 under the nominal rule of the Lord

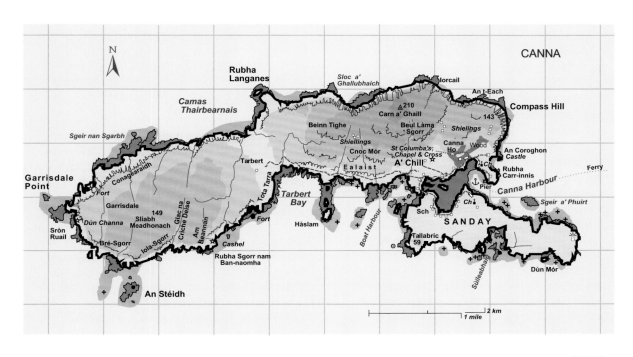

ESCARPMENT NEAR TARBERT BAY

of the Isles which passed to the Macdonalds of Clanranald. As with the other Small Isles, Canna was subjected to fire and plunder by Sir Lachlan Maclean's mercenaries in 1588.

Macdonald of Clanranald found himself short of income when the kelp boom collapsed so he sold Canna in 1827 to Donald MacNeil.

Severe clearance followed the death of MacNeil in 1848. His natural son, Donald, was still a minor at the time and therefore not responsible. In 1881 he sold the island to Robert Thom, a Glasgow shipowner, for £23,000. Thom brought in a much more benevolent regime which continued until 1938 when his family took the trouble to look privately for the right sort of understanding purchaser. This they found in the Gaelic scholar, Dr John Lorne Campbell, historian, folklorist, farmer and 'bonny fechter', who was sold Canna for just £9000 and took up residence on the island with his American wife. Campbell had founded the 'Sea League' with Sir Compton Mackenzie when they both lived on Barra in the 1930s – a pressure group to try to protect the West Coast fishing industry from external incursions. He worked for most of his life on the preservation and encouragement of Gaelic culture

and collected in Canna House the world's biggest library of Celtic language and literature. He also fought to keep Canna as a viable community although, 'I'm not a laird,' he said, 'I'm an owner-occupying farmer.' In 1981, when he gave Canna to the National Trust for Scotland, he also gave them his large and invaluable library and collections of Gaelic songs for safe-keeping. Campbell's hope was that the Trust would continue to support this small community and not allow it to become a mere tourist attraction.

Wildlife: Woodland of natural rowan and hazel interspersed with introduced sycamore, ash, elm, oak, birch, willow, elder, beech and some Sitka spruce, Corsican pine, Austrian pine and Japanese larch on the hillsides above the harbour with bluebells and wild garlic for ground cover. There are waxcap fungi in the undisturbed grassland. Hedgehogs were introduced by the Campbells – for better or for worse – and thistles are encouraged to support several species of butterfly and moth.

This is a superb bird sanctuary. It was being invaded by rats but these were (hopefully) eradicated in 2006 and Manx shearwater and puffins are returning. Occasionally white-tailed sea-eagles fly over from Rum – they were once indigenous here.

*   *   *

Viewed from due north or south, each end of **CANNA** appears to terminate in a bluff with the middle sinking to a low neck or saddle. Compass Hill is at the eastern extremity and the highest point **Carn a' Ghaill**, (G. – rocky hill of the storm) about 1km west of it, is 210m high.

SANDAY, close south, joined by a footbridge and a drying reef, rises to 44m height at its east end where there are several detached rocks in the sea. Two of these lie close to the cliff – a small one like a steeple and the other like a large tower (31m). They are Dun Mor and Dun Beag and they are known as the puffin stacks.

The space between Canna and Sanday forms a very well protected harbour with a ferry pier which was upgraded in 1992. The harbour is entered by rounding a graffiti-covered rockface – originally the names of fishing boats and early traders from the Baltic States, but now also those of day-trippers seeking immortality. There is a small restaurant which was granted a licence in 2003.

The principal house on this idyllic island is **Canna House** [NG273056], surrounded by thick woodland and overlooking the harbour. It was built about 1865 and was the home of the late Dr Campbell (1906–1996) and his wife, the American scholar, Margaret Fay Shaw (1903–2004). Above Canna House and partly concealed by the trees is **Tighard**, the house built in 1905 by Robert Thom. Close by is the main farm – The Square. With no high mountains to south or west, the clouds usually slip past Canna and the climate is pleasant and sunny. The fertile soil gives a rich and unusually early yield with particularly delicious early potatoes. Fields lying fallow are cropped by pedigree Highland cattle and Cheviot sheep.

The islanders are Catholic but there is a carefully maintained and charming little **Protestant Church**, built like early Celtic churches with a conical bell tower, on the east

The Scots Kirk, Canna. June 92

IN THE SCOTS KIRK

side of the harbour [NG277054]. This was constructed in 1914 as a memorial to Robert Thom. On Sanday and facing it is the much more ornate Catholic Church designed by William Frame and built by Lady Bute in memory of her father [NG275048]. This has now been tastefully converted to a Gaelic Study Centre – the **St Edward's Centre** – where scholars have the benefit of access to Dr Campbell's extensive library. The islanders now worship in a less elaborate building near the main farm. The proud title of **Post Office** is given to a tiny creosoted wooden shed with an adjacent telephone box – painted blue when I first saw it. It is beside Canna's oldest inhabited house, the Changehouse, which usually has resident collies. Canna is permitted to issue its own postage stamps.

A' Chill (G. – the cell or chapel), north-west of the harbour and above the main farm, was the site of the original township, cleared by MacNeil in 1851. Here there is a broken but beautifully carved Celtic cross [NG270055] but no sign of the remnants of the early 7th-century St Columba's Chapel. An adjacent standing stone probably proves that this is another case of the Early Christian policy of building on important pagan sites, although a small hole at head height in which an offender's thumb was supposed to be jammed has led to this being called Clach a' Pheannais – the pillory stone.

An Coroghon, on the coast east of the harbour [NG280055], is a medieval prison tower on top of an isolated stack built by John MacLeod of Dunvegan in 1666. Some say he used it to imprison his daughter, Mor MacLeod, but others say that an 18th-century laird imprisoned his beautiful daughter there to keep her from her lover, Iain Ban Og of Skye, but Iain rescued her and carried her off to his home. Sir Walter Scott wrote a sensible warning:

Seek not the giddy crag to climb
To view the turret scathed by time:
It is a task of doubt and fear
To aught but goat or mountain deer.

Tarbert Bay is almost central on the south coast, defined by the islet Hàslam like a punctuation mark. A ruined fort is on the bay's western shore and the remains of a very ancient nunnery or 'cashel' are on a grassy terrace beyond the bay, 4km along the road from the harbour [NG230043]. The site overlooks **Sgòrr nam Bannaomha** (G. – sharp rock of the holy women) and, 5km away to the south-west, the isolated basalt rock of **Humla.**

A very well-preserved Viking ship burial was uncovered near Rubha Langanes (ON – the long ness) in **Camas Thairbearnais** on the north side of the central neck. Signs of reputed Viking graves can still be seen and a rectangular outline of boulders is known as **Uaigh Righ Lochlainn** (G. – the grave of the King of Norway). On adjoining Sanday signs of Norse burials have also been discovered but unfortunately the graves had been rifled in the distant past.

A fairly long, but interesting, hill-walk to Garrisdale Point at the western extremity brings you to Dùn Channa (G. – Canna's fort). Garrisdale farm was abandoned in 1881 and there is another Pillory Stone at the deserted Conagearaidh farmstead. This distant end of Canna was fortified by a wall and there is another fort about ½km to the north-east.

*   *   *

Access: Ro-ro ferry from Mallaig every day except Tues. and Thurs. in summer, 01687-462403 and Thurs. in summer. 8-hour stopover on Sat. (Vehicle permit required, 01397-709000). For cottage accommodation or permission to camp contact NTS., 01463-232034. Arisaig Marine, Arisaig, trips from Arisaig daily in summer, 01687-450224. AquaXplore, Elgol, Skye, full day trips by RIB, 0800-731-3089.

Anchorages:
1. Canna harbour. One of the best and most popular anchorages on the west coast. Beware reef N of Sanday on the approach and rocks alongside pier. Visitors' moorings (pay). Bottom is prolific kelp on thick mud – good holding, but only if anchor is well bedded-in.
2. Tarbert bay. W of Sanday and SE of the central dip on Canna. Approach W side of bay keeping well clear of the islet called Hàslam then anchor in NE side 2c off-shore, 4.6m. Worthwhile in fair weather. Exposed S and subject to swell.
3. Boat harbour. Temp. anchorage between S side of Canna and W end of Sanday in settled weather. Many rocks to be avoided. Anchor in 4m N of Sgeirean Dubha with landing on sandy beach in SE corner.

SECTION 5

Islands Surrounding Skye

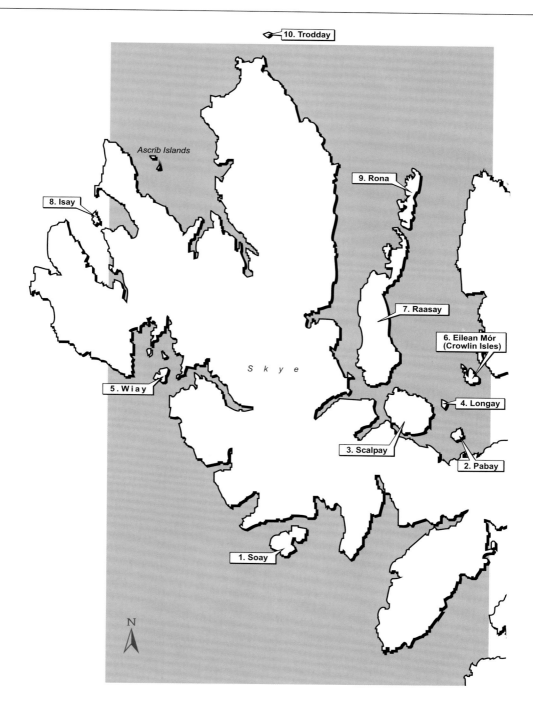

SECTION 5, Table 1: Arranged according to geographic location

No.	Name	Latitude	Longitude	Table 2* No.	Table 3** No.	Area in Acres		Area in Hectares
5.1	Soay	57° 09N	06° 13W	41	47	2560		1036
5.2	Pabay	57° 16N	05° 52W	104	158	301		122
5.3	Scalpay	57° 18N	05° 58W	28	15	6135		2483
5.4	Longay	57° 19N	05° 53W	147	96	124		50
5.5	Wiay	57° 20N	06° 30W	94	105	366		148
5.6	Eilean Mór (Crowlin I)	57° 20N	05° 50W	72	59	477	193	
	Eilean Meadhonach	57° 21N	05° 51W			190	77	270
5.7	Raasay	57° 25N	06° 03W	17	11	15397	6231	
	Eilean Fladday	57° 29N	06° 02W			297	120	
	Eilean Tigh	57° 31N	06° 00W			133	54	6405
5.8	Isay	57° 31N	06° 39W	138	156	148		60
5.9	Rona	57° 33N	05° 59W	42	51	2298		930
5.10	Eilean Trodday	57° 43N	06° 18W	164	126	105		42
5.A	Skye	57° 22N	06° 11W			409259		165625

*Table 2: The islands arranged in order of magnitute. **Table 3: The islands arranged in order of height

Introduction

I must admit to having misgivings about omitting Skye from a comprehensive book on the Scottish islands. But rules are rules and, having decided that a bridge destroys insularity, there was no other option. So, by my definition, Skye, which has always been the very essence of a Scottish island, no longer qualifies for inclusion. With the construction of a bridge it has now joined the mainland. Just as Seil took the same step many years ago.

To fend off criticism, however, I have compromised and included Skye as an appendix to this section. As with all the large islands, the description is necessarily brief. There are, after all, many excellent guides and books about Skye already available and my interest here is to pay more attention to the somewhat smaller islands which are given inadequate coverage elsewhere.

Apart from the ten classified islands in the vicinity of Skye, each of which has its own unique story and its collection of satellite islets, there are the other tiny islands hugging the mainland coast which at least deserve a mention.

North of Mallaig, at the entrance to sombre Loch Nevis, **Glas Eilean** (G. – green island) and **Eilean Dearg** (G. – red island) add an imaginative touch of colour and, further north, **Airor Island** shelters the small bay by the village of Airor in Knoydart.

Loch Hourn is a lovely loch to explore, stretching deep into mountain wilderness. **Eilean Ràrsaidh** with adjoining **Eilean a' Chuilinn**, just within the entrance of the loch and by the north bank, provide a delightful anchorage under the wooded crags of Beinn Mhialairigh. There is another anchorage south of **Eilean a' Phìobaire** (G. – the piper's island), on the south-west bank where there is a navigable channel between the island and the shore. At the first narrows a wide shoal and several tidal islets are beyond **Corr Eileanan** at Barrisdale Bay and beyond the second narrows – Caolas Mór – a central islet, **Eilean Mhogh-sgeir**, supports some twisted pines.

Eilean Chlamail is just north of the entrance to Loch Hourn, and projecting into the Sound of Sleat are the **Sandaig Islands**. These are all tidal with the exception of the largest, Eilean Mór, which has a light beacon on it.

Sailing through Kyle Rhea at mid-tide is like having a jet-engine attached to the hull. In the middle of Loch Alsh (which is a millpond compared to Kyle Rhea) **Glas Eilean** is little more than a permanent shoal covered with grass – a large flat expanse of grazing land. **Eilean Tioram** (G. – drying island) is tied to the land by a muddy tidal isthmus and beyond it another tidal island, **Eilean Donan**, linked by a bridge to the mainland, is the site of one of Scotland's most photographed castles. Loch Alsh also conceals possibily the world's largest colony of rare flame shells – some 75 hectares of brilliant molluscs.

The entrance to Loch Alsh is named after King Haakon, Kyle Akin. Some islets off Kyle of Lochalsh, **Eileanan Dubha**, lie in the navigable channel. Beyond is the site of the graceful Skye Bridge which makes use of Eilean Bàn (G. – white or unused island), a National Trust for Scotland property, for support. **Eilean Bàn** is a double islet with a drying channel between and there are lighthouse-keepers' houses beside the lighthouse on the western half. It was one of these houses that Gavin Maxwell occupied after writing his best-selling novel, *Ring of Bright Water*. Otters are resident on many of the islets in this area, most of which belong to the National Trust for Scotland. The larger of these islands are **Eilean a' Mhal**, **Black Islands** and round the corner by Duirinish – still all Trust property – **Eilean Dubh Dhurinish**, **A' Ghlas-leac**, **Eilean na Bà Mór** (G. – isle of the big cow) and **Eilean Dubh**.

Eilean a' Chait (G. – cat island) has a disused light beacon on it at the entrance to Loch Carron. The largest of the Strome Islands in the loch is **Eilean an-t-Sratha**. Plockton – that little gem of a Highland village – snuggles into a corner of the bay on the southern shore wrapped in its own private Mediterranean climate. **Ulluva** is the name of the little island which appears in every photograph of Plockton – a few lone pines standing to attention on warm-grey rocks covered with orange and yellow lichen. A similar island near the shore, **Eilean na Creig Duibhe**, is tidal.

Off the peninsula dividing Loch Carron from Loch Kishorn are a number of rocks and skerries dominated by **Kishorn Island** and **An Garbh-eilean**.

Very much further north, there is a tiny islet of no particular significance, **Eilean Chuaig** (G. – twisted island), where the mainland turns away to make room for Loch Torridon.

On the south side of Outer Loch Torridon, **Eilean Mór** shields a deep pool which is a pleasant but limited anchorage as the bottom drops away fairly steeply. Loch Torridon divides into three distinct parts but the middle section has a change of name – Loch Shieldaig. There are two little islets in this part, **Eilean an Inbhire Bhain** and **Eilean Dùghaill**, and one distinctive larger island of about thirteen hectares, **Shieldaig Island**, which sits in tree-covered splendour opposite the sleepy whitewashed village of Shieldaig. Shieldaig Island was bought by the National Trust for Scotland in 1970 as it represents a small surviving sample of the ancient Caledonian Forest which used to spread over this entire region. The Scots pine regenerate because there

are no sheep or deer to destroy them and they provide a refuge for many species of bird. There is a heronry at the north end of the island. In 1974 the cost to the NTS was reimbursed in full by Mr and Mrs Armistead Peter III of Washington DC who 'adopted' the island.

5.1 Soay

[so-ay or soy] (ON so-øy – sheep island)

O S Maps: 1:50000 Sheet 32 1:25000 Sheet 411
Admiralty Chart: 1:50000 No.2208

Area: 1036ha (2560 acres)
Height: 141m (462 ft)

Owner: The author, Gavin Maxwell, bought Soay in 1944 from Dame Flora MacLeod of MacLeod for £900. In 1946 he set up a shark-fishing venture with his wartime comrade, Joseph 'Tex' Geddes, as his harpooner. Maxwell eventually abandoned the project but Geddes continued it for a time and acquired crofting rights on the island. A Kent doctor, Nicholas Martin, bought the island for £100 in 1980 but he thought this included the crofting rights and there were long and expensive Land Court hearings. Dr Martin had a home on Soay. In 1993 'Tex' Geddes at last bought the island from him for an undisclosed sum but, sadly, died in 1997. His son Duncan is also known as 'Tex'. The island was put up for sale in 2003 for £280,000.

Population: 1821– one family. 1841–113. 1851–158 (the peak). 1861–129. 1881–102. 1891–78. 1931–64. 1953– most of the

MAXWELL'S DELELICT SHARK–OIL FACTORY

population moved voluntarily to Mull. 1961–11. 1981–8. 1991–14. 2001–7. 2003–2. 2011–1.

Geology: Mainly Torridonian sandstone alternating with greywacke traversed by a fine-grained igneous rock.

History: Soay was the property of the MacLeods of Dunvegan from the 13th century. They sold it to Gavin Maxwell in 1944. The island was very lightly populated until the Clearances on Skye in the mid-1800s when more than one hundred of the dispossessed crofters chose to settle on this infertile little island rather than go to America.

After the Second World War, the islanders petitioned the government for evacuation, mainly because communications were so poor. So on 20 June 1953, with a great deal of publicity and a lone piper playing a lament the *SS Hebrides* evacuated the 27 islanders and took them to Mull, where land had been purchased for them by the government at Java Lodge, Craignure. Only one family refused to leave – that of Mr Geddes who had bought some of the island's crofting rights from Maxwell in 1951 and the rest from the departing crofters. The affair had some overtones of the sad evacuation of St Kilda (No.9.1) in 1930. The purchase bankrupted Geddes and he had to sell the island on to Dr Michael Gilbertson in 1963 for £2500 but the doctor kindly gave a farm to the Geddeses with secure tenure and eventually they regained possession of the island. Recently the population has seriously dwindled.

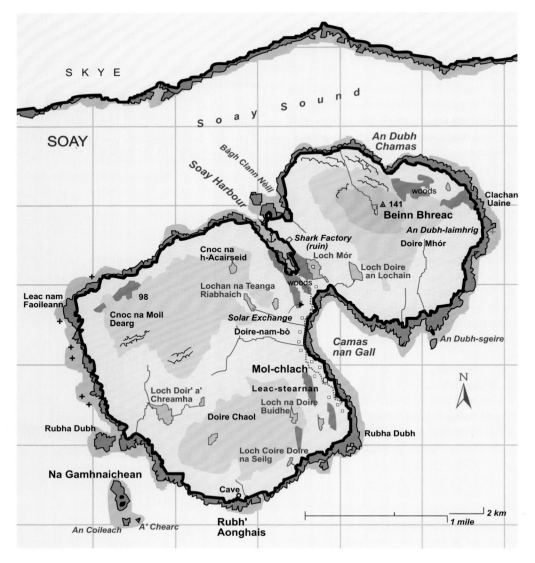

Mail and stores are received from Elgol on Skye and, when required, library books from Portree are transported in boxes with flotation buoys.

Wildlife: Not very fertile land but there is a profusion of deciduous bushes and trees such as birch, oak and rowan in the low saddle near the centre with a consequent variety of birdlife. Herons nest near the harbour and ravens cross the sound from Skye.

Unfortunately, in spite of his espousal of the cause of conservation, Maxwell's shark-oil venture on Soay contributed to a serious reduction in the numbers of basking sharks in West Coast waters. These inoffensive and harmless creatures may have been saved by the drop in value of shark oil in 1949 but, even so, they have taken half a century to recover from the onslaught. Maxwell wrote a book about his experiences – *Harpoon at a Venture*.

* * *

A dumbbell-shaped island with a narrow isthmus almost cutting it in half, **SOAY** is dwarfed by the Cuillin mountains which tower over it. **Acarsaid Soa** (G. – Soay harbour) is the northern part of the central gut.

When Maxwell bought Soay at the end of the Second World War he founded the Island of Soay Shark Fisheries Ltd and built a 'factory' for processing shark oil beside the harbour. But the venture only ran for three years and the harbour today has a deserted aspect. One or two fishing boats are moored or beached but there are abandoned fish cages and the old shark-oil factory buildings now form an attractive group of derelict structures [NG451151]. Blackbirds nest in the broken boiler stoke-hole, the generator base is covered in rust and the original two-storey house (built about 1849) has only a small part of its slated roof remaining. It was first constructed to help the fishing industry with curing facilities at ground floor level and accommodation for visiting fishermen upstairs. At least some of Maxwell's corrugated-asbestos-roofed buildings are still in use as stores for fishing gear. A dry 'mill lade' runs from a brick and concrete tank to an 'oven' by the house. The area was littered with the brass cases of rifle cartridges when I first saw it, presumably used to scare the herring gulls away.

A well-constructed cobbled pathway, constructed in the early 1900s with government funding, runs through birch, rowan and alder woodland in the central cleft and on past the solar 'telephone exchange' [NG453144]. This was the first in the world of its kind and powers nine telephones. The path leads on down to a settlement of pleasant, well-maintained houses, **Mol-chlach** (G. – village by the pebble beach), on the west shore of **Camas nan Gall** (G. – bay of the strangers, or Norsemen), a deep indentation on the southern side of the central isthmus. When the islanders were evacuated to Mull in 1953 only Tex Geddes, Maxwell's harpooner, and his family stayed on. The settlement grew again to a tiny community which has remained ever since on the verge of viability.

Two bright, fresh-faced and well-spoken boys (eleven or twelve years old when we met them) were the only pupils at the island school. They had a full-time schoolmaster who was, they said, 'really quite good'. But they soon left to attend high school and sadly, but inevitably, with no further intakes the teacher has gone and the school has been 'mothballed'.

The north-eastern part of the island is smaller and higher than the south-western area. It contains **Beinn Bhreac** (G. – speckled hill), almost central, 141m high and with wooded patches on its eastern slopes. It was more thickly wooded in the past and the area on its south side is still known as Doire Mhór (G. – the big oak wood). Two small lochs nestle directly north of Camas nan Gall – Loch Doire an Lochain, and Loch Mór which contains a small islet.

In October 1868 a schooner, *Woodman of Berwick on Tweed*, with a cargo of slate from Easdale (No.2A), foundered on the east coast of Soay. Her skipper, Thomas Weatherhead, and his wife were drowned but the crew of two men and a boy were swept ashore and rescued by the islanders. The off-lying rocks have always been a hazard in this area, particularly off the south-west side of the island.

South of Mol-Chlach is rough hilly ground with a number of lochans. Once again the names recall ancient woodland – Loch na Doire Buidhe (G. – loch of the pleasant copse), Loch Coire Doire na Seilg (G. – corrie loch of the hunting thicket) and the whole area is called Doire Chaol (G. – thin woodland).

Access: By arrangement with Bella Jane Boat Trips, Elgol, Skye, 0800-731-3089.

Anchorages: The tidal stream in Soay Sound appears to run continuously W.

1. An Dubh Chamas (G. – the black bay), a small bay on the N side of Soay, about 8c ENE of Soay harbour. Good shelter in S'lies. Anchor in centre, 4–8m, good holding.

2. Soay Harbour is a narrow creek with a shingle bar drying 0.6m at the entrance. Access after half flood along inconspicuous leading line. Anchor W of pier, 3–4m, black mud, good holding and good shelter.

3. Harbour entrance, temp. anchorage in light S'lies, outside the entrance, 8–10m, but beware drying reef.

4. Camas nan Gall on S coast. Exposed S-SE. Poor holding on shingle.

5.2 Pabay

(N pap-øy – hermit or priest island).

OS Maps: 1:50000 Sheet 32   1:25000 Sheet 412
Admiralty Charts: 1:50000 No.2209   1:25000 Nos.2498 or 2534

Area: 122ha (301 acres)
Height: 28m (92 feet)

Owner: Sir Donald Currie was the owner in the early 1900s. 1926–1933 Sir Henry Bell. 1934–1951 Captain Muntz. 1955–1971 C L & A L Whatley. 1972–1981 Mrs Ann Lillian Gerrard.

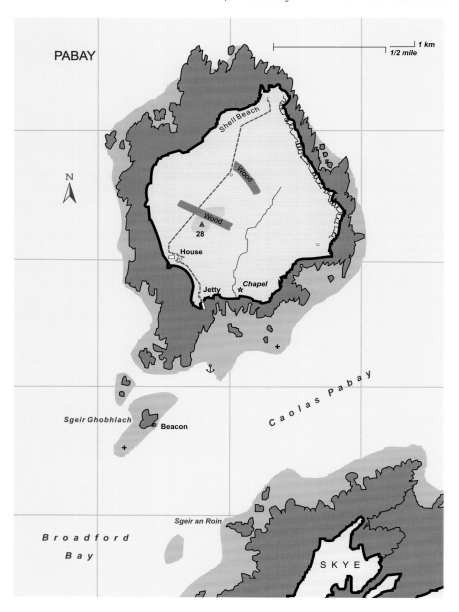

1985–1996 Alasdair K J Philip. For sale 1996 for £395,000. David Harris, the son of Jeff Harris of Somerset, is the present owner.

Population: 1841–21. 1881–10. 1891–7. 1931–3. 1961–7. 1971–5. 1981–3. 1991–0. 2001–0. 2011–0.

Geology: Pabay was formed at the bottom of a muddy sea about 190 million years ago. This has resulted in the island's Jurassic sedimentary rock being studded with fossils. It is interspersed with shales (Pabay Shales) and intersected by dark fine-grained igneous dykes formed by lava intrusions in the fractures. These have weathered less than the sedimentary rock and form substantial walls running across the island.

History: Possibly the holy man who originally occupied this island was never canonised because his name is not on record. But in the early days of Christianity Pabay obviously had some significance.

However, in the 16th century, pirates and so-called 'broken men' were using Pabay, which was then well wooded, as a base for their nefarious activities. Dean Monro in 1549 described it as 'full of woods, good for fishing, and a main shelter for thieves and cutthroats'.

A century and a half later much of the woodland must have been cleared because Martin Martin wrote; 'It excells in Pasturage, the Cows in it afford near double the Milk that they yield in Skie. In the Dog-Days there's a big Fly in this isle, which infests the cows, makes them run up and down, and discomposes them exceedingly.'

Wildlife: 75 acres of deciduous and coniferous woodland have been planted with seventeen different species. 32 breeding bird species have been recorded and there are resident otters, seals, shrews and rabbits galore.

The island plateau of **PABAY** with its lush pasture and woodland draped over it like a brightly coloured tablecloth lies almost straight ahead as one sails through the Kyle of Lochalsh. As the tide ebbs the island grows before your eyes as extensive drying reefs appear from beneath the surface of the sea.

The east and west coasts rise steeply to about 12m and there is then a very gradual slope to the highest point (28m) near the west coast. A road runs across the island from the concrete and stone jetty in the south west to Shell Beach in the north. A newly-constructed owner's home, the main farmhouse, a modern building with its own power supply, and several original farm buildings are not far from the jetty and look south across Caolas Pabay to Broadford Bay on Skye. The ancient (13th-century) ruined chapel and burial ground are east of the jetty [NG674265].

In the early 1990s the owner planted quite a large area of mixed native deciduous woodland and also extended some of the small existing stands of timber. The island is not now actively farmed and the livestock have been removed which is allowing the original native vegetation to regenerate.

Pabay is one of the few islands which is licensed to issue its own attractive postage stamps (stampenquiries@pabay.org). This is because it is uneconomic for the post-office to provide a service. Deliveries are left at Broadford for collection.

* * *

Access: No regular access. The owners have requested that they are advised before any landings, 07787-565401.

Anchorages: There are extensive drying rocks 2½c on W side, 3c on NW side, 1½c on E side and 2c from S side and foul ground extends 6½c to the SSW so it is important to study the charts very carefully.
1. The landing place is a concrete and stone jetty at the SW extremity of the island, the outer end of which is marked by an iron perch. Depth insufficient except near high water. Anchor at least 2½c S of the perch, sand and shingle with weedy patches, 4–6m.

5.3 Scalpay

(ON skalpr-øy – scallop island) for its shape?

O S Maps: 1:50000 Sheet 32 1:25000 Sheet 409
Admiralty Charts: 1:50000 No.2209 or 1:25000 No.2498

Area: 2483ha (6135 acres)
Height: 392m (1286 ft)

Owner: The island is owned by a merchant banker and farmed by his sons.

Population: 1841–90. 1881–37. 1891–49. 1931–27. 1961–2. 1971–5. 1981–6. 1991–7. 2001–10. 2011–4.

Geology: Almost entirely of Torridonian rocks –
red and grey sandstones, conglomerates, siltstones
and shales which were deposited about 800
million years ago. Part of the west coast is granite
but the ground by Scalpay House is on a patch of
fertile lias of the same type as Pabay.

History: Dr Johnson, in 1773, wanted to buy
the island and to 'found a good school, and an
episcopal church, ... and have a printing-press,
where he would print all the Erse that could be
found' but thought better of it after discovering

that ownership carried an obligation to spend at
least three months every year on the island.

In the 19th century Sir Donald Currie
constructed the first roads and planted trees.

Wildlife: The hill slopes are covered with heather,
mainly *Calluna vulgaris*, *Erica carnea* and *Erica
tetralix*.

The island's herd of red deer is carefully
managed and there are good trout in the
mountain lochs.

*   *   *

RUINED CROFT AT CAMAS NA GEADAIG

SCALPAY rises abruptly from its south and west coasts to **Mullach na Càrn** (G. – cairn hill), its highest peak of slightly more than 392m. It is rough and hilly, other main peaks being **Beinn Loch a' Mhuilinn** (G. – mountain of the mill loch), 291m, and **Beinn Reireag Bheag**, 225m. Mullach na Càrn stretches in a ridge across the centre of the island with a lochan-studded plateau and two mini-mountains, An Ailldunn (G. – the castle rock) and Sithean Glac an Ime (G. – the fairy hill in the butter bowl). Below lie the Mill Loch, the Black Loch, and the much-larger **Loch an Leòid**. The north-east coast is rocky and fringed by a reef but the mountain slopes here are more gradual.

Scalpay is separated from Skye by the narrow and shallow Caolas Scalpay. **Scalpay House** in the south-east corner of the island looks over a small tidal harbour with, beyond it, **Guillamon Island**, 24m-high, rocky and speckled with sea-birds. To the west of Scalpay House are the remains of a chapel, **Teampuill fraing** (G. – St Francis' Chapel), built on the site of an ancient Celtic cell [NG628281]. The area around Scalpay House is well cultivated and there are pleasant patches of woodland and several scattered holiday cottages.

A road runs from the harbour along the west coast, through extensive conifer plantations to a holiday cottage at **Corran a Chinn Uachdaraich** (G. – the upper projection), facing Skye. The track leads on from there up towards the summit of Beinn Reireag Bheag.

Some 1600ha is fenced off in this north-east area for red-deer farming which was developed with the support of the Highlands and Islands Development Board (now Highlands and Islands Enterprise). Venison was successfully exported to Germany where it is a very popular meat, but, unfortunately, with access to Eastern European venison this is no longer such a profitable enterprise.

A recently ruined croft in the north of the island is beside the aptly named **Camas na Geadaig** (G. – bay at the patch of lazybeds) because the lazybeds beside it can still be clearly seen beneath a layer of buttercups.

The heathery hillsides provide reasonably pleasant walking as, being sheltered by Skye from the wettest winds, the ground is not too boggy, but from whatever direction you approach you can still expect rough going to reach the bouldered summit of Mullach na Carn. However, the views from the top make the exercise worthwhile, and be sure to rest for a while by Loch Dubh where you can see the waterfall tumbling down the hill behind Loch an Leòid and listen to the skylarks.

Scalpay offers good camping and fishing subject, of course, to obtaining permission from Scalpay House.

*   *   *

Access: No regular access but try Peter Urquhart, Portree, 01478-613718 or Dan Corrigall, Portree, 01478-612333.

Anchorages:

1. Camas na Geadaig, at NW extremity. The head of the bay dries out about 1¼c. Beware reefs both sides of entrance. Occasional anchorage in the centre, 5–7m, sand. Sheltered from S'lies but squally in strong winds.

2. Loch na Cairidh (G. – weir loch). NW of the narrows. Anchor anywhere in suitable depth.

3. Caolas Scalpay. E of narrows, midway between narrows and Sgeir Stapaig. Can be squally.

5.4 Longay

(ON long-øy – longship island). Note also (G. long spùinnidh – pirate ship).

O S Maps: 1:50000 Sheet 32 1:25000 Sheet 409
Admiralty Charts: 1:50000 No.2209 1:25000 No.2498
Area: 50ha (124 acres)
Height: 67m (220 ft)

Population: Uninhabited and no Census records.

Geology: Longay is the southern end of a reef, Sgeirean Tarsuinn (G. – the traverse or oblique reef), running parallel with the east side of Scalpay. It is formed of large slabs of volcanic rock but with a considerable area of red sandstone.

History: Longay is one of the group of islands in this area which was frequented by pirates in the 16th century. It would have been covered with Caledonian Forest trees at that time giving added cover. The thieves and cut-throats, with no clan or territorial attachments, must have concentrated their attacks only on 'foreign' ships – Dutch, Lowland Scottish, Flemish and English commercial and fishing craft which ventured into the Inner Minch; otherwise the local clan chiefs would certainly have suppressed them. They had

ample power to do so. The pirates probably paid insurance to MacLeod of Raasay in the form of a proportion of the plunder but in any case their depredations helped to protect the local fishing grounds.

Wildlife: Sheep are occasionally pastured here. A fair number of nesting sea-birds take advantage of the lack of human disturbance.

There is little of note to report about the compact little island of **LONGAY**. It could be considered a good example of a desert island, but not an ideal one on which to be marooned.

We found no adequate anchorage. The chart shows a possible area of suitable depth on the east coast but we were unable to find less than a dubious 15m of possibly boulder-strewn bottom so we landed by dinghy while *Jandara* stood off. The island is covered with rough scrub making walking uncomfortable. It rises to a single central ridge with its peak 67m above sea-level. Crossing the ridge, the west slope has scattered patches of rowan and alder but the terrain is mainly heather, bracken and coarse boggy turf. In the extreme south-west corner a patch of beach made up of red sandstone pebbles lies above tongues of semi-submerged rock. Further north there is the impression of a wide cleft or cove with a copse above a narrow gravel beach. This may be a suitable spot for temporary anchorage but I have had no opportunity to test it.

At our landing place on the east coast directly below the crest of the hill there was a narrow rocky beach of tumbled volcanic slabs and a small cave [NG660313] with fresh water trickling down the back of it – a useful pirates' den.

Access: No regular access but try Dan Corrigall, Portree, 01478-612333 or Calum, Plockton, 01599-544306.

Anchorage: There is no recommended anchorage but temp. anchorage may be possible in depths of 12–15m clear of the reef on the S or E sides, or in less depth off the small beached 'cove' on the W side near the S corner. Be sure to use a tripping line.

5.5 Wiay

(G. bhuidhe – yellow or pleasant, ON -øy – island). Sometimes written in the past as 'Vuiay', or 'Buia' (Martin Martin).

OS Maps: 1:50000 Sheet 32 1:25000 Sheet 410
Admiralty Chart: 1:100000 No.1795

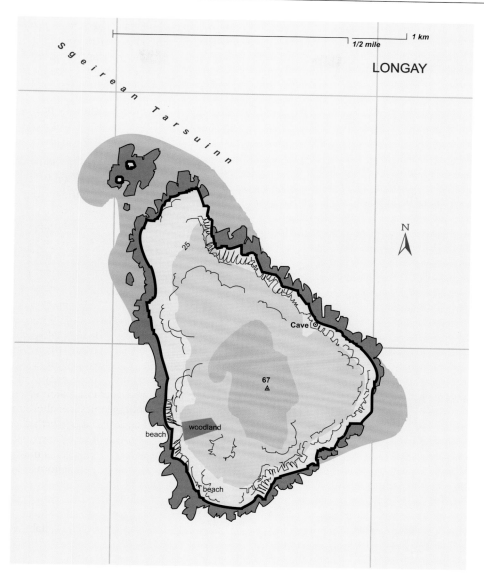

Area: 148ha (366 acres)
Height: 60m (197 ft)

Owner: MacLeod Estates.

Population: 1841–6. 1881–4. 1891–0. Uninhabited since 1890.

Geology: Basaltic lava.

History: One might assume that Boswell and Johnson visited the island of Wiay since Boswell reported:

'In the afternoon, Ullinish carried us in his boat to an island possessed by him, where we saw an immense cave... It is one hundred and eighty feet long, about thirty feet broad, and at least thirty feet high. This cave we were told had a remarkable echo; but we found none. They said it was owing to the great rains having made it damp. Such are the excuses by which the exaggeration of Highland narratives is palliated.'

Wildlife: There are large nesting colonies of shag, fulmar and black guillemot on the cliffs and herring gulls near the lochans above Geodha nan Faochag. There is at least one otter breeding holt near the shallow water in Camas na Cille.

* * *

WIAY is the largest island in Loch Bracadale. Most of the coastline consists of vertical cliffs

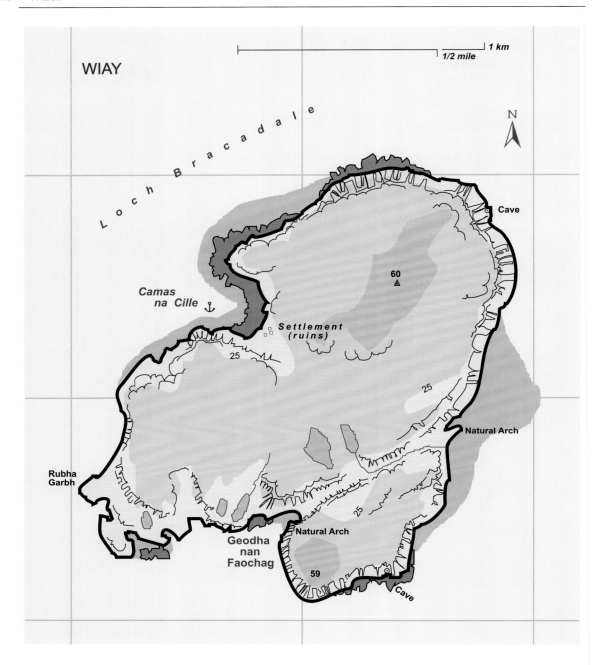

and the southern bluff is a striking overhanging cliff 59m high and covered with yellow lichens and sea-bird droppings. There is a large sea-cave [NG296356] at its base which amplifies the sound of the surf breaking in it and another large cave on the north-east side of the island [NG301370] and several smaller caves. I have been unable to establish if either of these caves was the one referred to by Boswell but it seems probable as there are no other prominent island caves close

to Ullinish where they were staying. Johnson's account was written from memory in London. He too mentions visiting a sea-cave by boat at low water but he could be describing a cave on Idrigill Point.

The beach in **Camas na Cille** (G. – church bay) is composed of round pebbles many of which are so large that they are better described as boulders. A pleasant green valley stippled with yellow irises, reeds and patches of bracken leads up from the bay to a plateau area of rough bog and coarse grazing for sheep. The derelict remains of at least three dwellings are near the beach, one of which was a black house [NG292366]. There was also a church in this area in bygone times although we saw no obvious trace of it. Flax was once grown here, and Seton Gordon mentions that Donald MacLeod of Ose had a tablecloth spun of Wiay flax, but the arable land has long since disappeared. The central summit (60m) is almost at the geometric centre of Loch Bracadale and the view is all-encompassing. To the east is the dramatic 'castle' of tidal **Oronsay**, great cliffs rising abruptly from the sea like a fortress. To the north are the lesser cliffs of **Tarner Island** and **Harlosh Island**, but **Macleod's Maidens** – three large rock stacks realistically sculpted by the sea – can only be seen from the southern part of the island as they are concealed by Idrigill Point.

In this area there are several tiny lochans and the entire south-western portion is almost isolated by a very deep cleft forming the **Geodha nan Faochag** (G. – narrow creek of the periwinkles). The cliffs here are the steepest and most cave-riddled on the island and the area is popular for diving.

* * *

Access: No regular access. Enquire at Portnalong, Loch Harport.

Anchorage: Admiralty Pilot says landing only possible in two places, one being the small bay on NW side. Shores clean to within 1½c.
1. Camas na Cille. Occasional anchorage. Rocks on NE side but clear in middle and towards SW side of bay. Approach centrally and anchor off the pebble beach in a suitable depth, shingle.

5.6 Crowlin Islands

[**kroa**-lin] *Probably (G. crò linne – eye-of-a-needle channel).*

Eilean Mór

(G. – big island).

Eilean Meadhonach

[meeoo-unuch] (G. – middle island).

Eilean Beag

(G. – little island)

ANCHORED IN THE EYE OF THE NEEDLE

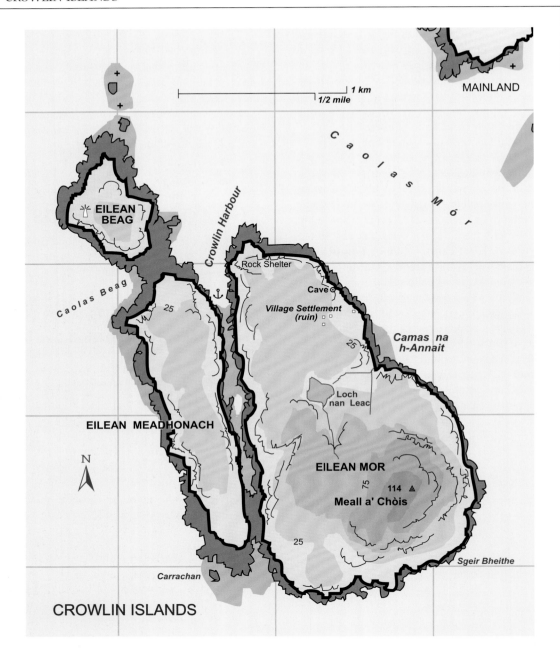

MAINLAND

1 km
1/2 mile

C a o l a s   M ó r

EILEAN BEAG

Crowlin Harbour

Rock Shelter

Cave

Village Settlement (ruin)

Camas na h-Annait

Caolas Beag

25

25

Loch nan Leac

EILEAN MEADHONACH

N

EILEAN MOR

75   114 ▲
Meall a' Chòis

25

Sgeir Bheithe

Carrachan

CROWLIN ISLANDS

OS Maps: 1:50000 Sheet 24 or 32   1:25000 Sheet 428
Admiralty Charts: 1:50000 No.2209   1:25000 No.2498

Area: 270ha (567 acres)
Height: 114m (374 ft)

Population: From about 1810 to 1820 some families cleared from Applecross on the mainland were reluctant to emigrate and settled here at Camus na h-Annait. They eventually returned to Applecross. 1841–40. 1881–9. 1891–9. 1931–0. Uninhabited since then.

Geology: This is a group of three eroded chunks of Torridonian sandstone with volcanic rock intrusions.

Wildlife: Common seals seem to be particularly fond of Eilean Beag

*   *   *

The largest island in this tight-knit group is **EILEAN MOR**. It is 170ha in area and rises to a height of 114m. There are some ruined cottages in the north-east corner near **Camas na h-Annait** (G. – bay of the church-land). In the north-west corner by the anchorage a rock shelter has provided storage for visiting fishermen [NG690353] and on the east coast there is an interesting cave [NG695352]. The islands have been denuded of trees and grazing sheep prevent regeneration. A small loch, Loch nan Leac (G. – tombstone loch), in the undulating central plateau of Eilean Mór overflows into a small burn leading down to Camas na h-Annait. On the south side a shallow cave was excavated recently and found to have evidence of human settlement from 8000 years ago.

Eilean Mór is separated from Eilean Meadhonach (50ha) by a narrow cleft which is only about 50m wide. Boats can enter from the north at a suitable state of the tide, and there is a pool in the centre which forms a snug little harbour, but reaching it can be a bit like threading a needle. A reef fringes the south coasts of both Eilean Mór and Eilean Meadhonach.

When approaching or leaving the anchorage at high water it is important not to cut the corners. To the west is a submerged reef and on the east a narrow rocky beach which covers, as one poor man discovered when he grounded his hired yacht on it. We arrived at low water to find him high and dry but unhurt. His blushes shone like a beacon in the driving rain.

The smallest island, Eilean Beag (3ha) has a light beacon on its summit and there are many small caves on the rocky shoreline. A reef extends northwards from this islet.

North of the Crowlin Islands is the grassy expanse of **Eilean na Bà** (G. – island of the cow) and, north again, sheltering the anchorage of Poll Creadha is **Eilean nan Naomh** (G. – island of the saints), which has a lot of seaweed-covered rock, but hardly enough dry land to support a single saint.

* * *

Access: No regular access but try Calum, Plockton, 01599-544306 or Dan Corrigall, Portree, 01478-612333.

Anchorages: Give S coast a wide berth and, similarly, N coast of Eilean Beag.
1. North entrance to harbour. Occasional anchorage just within the mouth of the gut between the two larger islands, 6–8m.

2. Harbour. Access above half flood through narrows for 1.5m max. draft. Safe anchorage in N of first pool. Reef projects from W shore at centre of pool.

5.7 Raasay

Possibly (ON raa-s -øy – roe-deer island) or (ON ross-øy – horse island)

OS Maps: 1:50000 Sheet 24 1:25000 Sheet 409
Admiralty Charts: 1:50000 Nos.2209 and 2210

Area: 6,405ha (15,827 acres)
Height: 443m (1453 ft)

Owner: The entire island was purchased by the Government in 1922. Raasay House and some other key properties on the island were sold for a low price in the 1960s to Dr John Green – a Sussex pathologist – who visited the island once and never returned. After considerable pressure over many years and the payment of a high price he was eventually 'persuaded' to sell out to the Highland and Islands Development Board in 1979. Highlands and Islands Enterprise (the successor to HIDB) still owns farmland, a hotel and other property on the island which is rented out at commercial rates. Some years ago the Government offered to transfer all the crofts it owns to a local trust but the crofters did not favour change.

Population: Figures include the tidal island of Eilean Fladday. 1780– over 400. 1803– over 900. 1841–676. 1881–532. 1891–489. 1931–377. 1961–223. 1976– ferry service introduced. 1981–152. 1991–163. Raasay has the lowest proportion of children of all the populated Scottish islands (10.4%). 2001–192. 2011–161.

Geology: The south is mainly Torridonian sandstone and shale but with two large areas of granite and an area of limestone in the south-east. Iron ore was mined here by Baird & Co using the labour of German prisoners-of-war during the First World War, but it became uneconomic and was closed in 1919. Some of the Torridonian shales on Raasay contain the oldest fossilised plant remains yet found. Unique loam at Glàm in the centre of the island at the 200–300m level is evidence that this part of Raasay probably escaped glaciation and therefore still has its rare and ancient living flora. The extreme north of the island is Archaean gneiss.

History: The first MacLeod on Raasay was Calum Garbh, younger son of Calum, the 9th Chief of Lewis. In 1518 he was granted title to Raasay, Rona and some estates on Skye and he had a lucrative line in piracy which he master-minded from Brochel Castle. He founded the cadet branch of Mac Gille Chaluim which survived mainly by avoiding involvement with his relatives, the Macleods of Lewis and Dunvegan. In fact the MacLeods of Raasay often preferred to support the MacDonalds of Sleat. Calum son of Gille Chaluim was a poet who was awarded a further charter

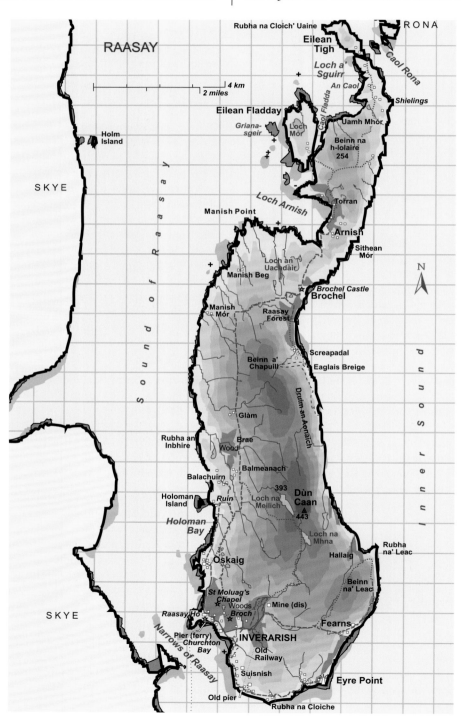

RAASAY HOUSE (WHERE DR JOHNSON STAYED)

to his estates by James VI. The next Calum, the 4th Chief, accepted the feudal superiority of Mackenzie of Kintail after Mackenzie had wrested Lewis from the Macleod Clan but there was family tragedy when his son, the much-loved Iain Garbh, met his death by drowning (see Trodday, No. 5.10).

Although the MacLeods were Protestants and the Skye Macleods supported the Government, the MacLeods of Raasay, in their usual contrary way, chose to support the Catholic Jacobites, possibly for purely chivalrous reasons. The islanders followed their Chief wholeheartedly and thus tiny Raasay provided one hundred men and twenty-six pipers at Culloden. Later, when Skye was being searched, they secretly rowed the Young Pretender over from Portree at dead of night. Government troops had already burned down the Laird's house and almost every dwelling on the island in reprisal for their Jacobite sympathies but Prince Charles was nevertheless hidden in a shepherd's hut and fed oat-bread and whisky. He was then smuggled over to Loch Broom where he

hoped to be rescued by a French ship.

Raasay's support of the Stuarts proved catastrophic. Homes and boats were destroyed, men murdered, women raped, and 'there was not left in the whole island a four-footed beast, a hen or a chicken.'

The MacLeods spent their family fortune on reconstruction and consequently within thirty years the island appeared to have made a remarkable recovery.

By the early 1800s, however, the population was increasing rapidly and poverty became widespread. Emigration began and the Laird, John MacLeod, did what he could to help but by 1843 he was so deeply in debt that he had to sell the island before he too emigrated (to Australia). George Rainy of Edinburgh bought Raasay for 35,000 guineas and genuinely tried to improve conditions on the island for a time, but having failed he turned to sheep-farming which resulted in the inevitable eviction of over one hundred families. Raasay's world-renowned Gaelic poet,

THE STABLES WHERE THE CLOCK STOPPED. . .

Sorley MacLean, has immortalised in haunting verse this sad period in Raasay's history.

After Rainy's twenty-seven-year-old son and heir died in 1872 there was a succession of unsympathetic owners until a commercial mining company, Baird & Co, bought the island in 1912 to extract iron ore. This brought jobs and housing until mining ceased in 1919. The Government eventually bought the island in 1922 for £37,000 after the episode of the Rona Raiders (See Rona, No.5.9).

Raasay is the traditional home of the Clan MacSween. It is also famous for its pipers, the finest being John MacKay (b.1767) who was sent as a child to Skye to study. He and his son Angus – first piper to Queen Victoria – are remembered for their exceptional talent and for recording and preserving much pipe music which would otherwise have been lost.

But the sound of music died in 1893 when Raasay became the centre for a strict and repressive sect of the Free Church introduced by a Mr Macfarlane. All pleasure was frowned upon and music, dancing and poetry were banned. Although there has been some adjustment of attitudes with the passing years, religious observance on the island, and particularly on the Sabbath, is still very strict. Raasay folk are friendly but they expect their beliefs to be respected.

Wildlife: Since Raasay partially escaped glaciation, extensive rare and ancient flora can be found on the steep grassy slopes of the east coast, particularly below the long Druim an Aonich (G. – steep sloping ridge) escarpment. There are many varieties of alpines, saxifrages, orchids, ferns and mosses. Sea aster and bog asphodel flourish beneath Dùn Caan. It is worth going to Hallaig in the south or Screapadal in the north to see the variety of the wildflowers and the island also has several areas of pleasant mixed woodland and some remarkable tree species.

Animal life includes red deer, alpine hare, otter, water shrew and a unique sub-species of bank vole, darker and twice the weight of the mainland vole; this may not in fact be a sub-species, but an ancient survivor of an original Scandinavian species. Raasay is the only Hebridean island on which the pine marten still survives.

Rabbits were introduced by a thoughtless proprietor, Herbert Wood, in the 19th century and they almost destroyed the agricultural economy.

Birdlife is more varied than usual and golden eagles can be seen circling over the rocky landscape in the north.

* * *

The long stretch of **RAASAY** is separated from Skye by a narrow sound and sheltered by it from the prevailing winds. Its east coast is steep with **Dùn Caan** near the centre, 443m high and very conspicuous – like a truncated Fujiyama – with the same appearance from all sides except the north-east. The view from the top is one of the most inspiring in the Western Isles. The southern half of the island is mountainous, with gentle gradients to the west and cliffs to the east while the northern portion is comparatively low except for **Beinn na h-Iolaire** (G. – hill of the eagle) about 3km from the northern extremity.

The main village is **Inverarish**, 2km north of the ferry terminal at Suisnish where the remains of Baird & Co's ore trans-shipment station are still to be seen. Inverarish was also partly built by the mining company. A roadway leads from it to the east coast bypassing the disused mine [NG567367], then on past a 3½km track leading to a waterfall by the shore at Hallaig, before reaching **Fearns** where the Rona Raiders seized land in 1919. Inverarish is set in pleasant woodland which is best experienced by taking a forest walk up the Inverarish Burn.

Dùn Borodale is an ancient broch with part of the walls and galleries remaining, in woodland just north of the village [NG555363].

Churchton Bay, overlooked by Inverarish, is named after the 13th-century chapel [NG548367] dedicated to St Moluag (who founded the monastery on Lismore. See No.3.9). **St Moluag's Chapel** ruins stand in an ancient wooded burial ground north-east of Raasay House, together with two other buildings, the smaller of which may be 11th century. Boswell considered there was 'something comfortable in the thought of being so near a piece of consecrated ground', when he and Dr Johnson were guests at Raasay House. A Celtic cross to commemorate the saint's landing place is in a small gated woodland enclosure off the lane behind Raasay House and overlooking the bay is **The Battery** [NG545363], a cannon emplacement on a knoll, built in 1807 and guarded by two busty stone mermaids. A shallow tidal harbour behind the knoll is not obvious from the sea.

Raasay House standing above the Battery and looking towards the mountains of Skye is on the site of the family home of the MacLeods. The original house was burned down by Government troops in reprisal for the help given to the Young Pretender during the Jacobite Rebellion. All the cottages on the island were also destroyed. Raasay House was rebuilt a few years later by the MacLeods but the Regency frontage was added in the early 1800s by John MacLeod and there have been subsequent additions since Dr Johnson stayed there. Raasay House was run as a hotel between 1937 and 1960 when it was bought by Dr Green. He allowed both it and the land to fall into serious disrepair but refused to sell, even when vandals wrecked the house and stole the contents including the library books. In 1979 after years of acrimony and inaction the HIDB spent all its available funds buying the property. It converted Borodale House into the Isle of Raasay Hotel and for 23 years run-down Raasay House was used for a hostel for outdoor activities. Then in 2007 the Raasay community, with public help, bought it and had almost completed a £4.5 million upgrade when it was destroyed by fire in 2009. Undaunted, the work to reinstate this beautiful house restarted within a year. The wooded grounds are still fairly derelict but with delightful surprises – mossy pieces of sculpture and a overgrown fountain. In 2010 the council at last completed work on a new ferry terminal in Churchton Bay, and in 2013 Raasay House was finally completed. It now has excellent accommodation (22 bedrooms), a good restaurant, bar and café and is once again a centre for outdoor activities.

The road passes beneath the clocktower of the **Raasay House Stables**. In 1914 the thirty-six able-bodied men of Raasay assembled here to go to war and only fourteen returned. The day they left the clock stopped and it has never been satisfactorily repaired. Beyond lies **Temptation Hill** with an incised Pictish Ogam-stone, possibly dating from the 7th century. Temptation Hill is supposed to have been named by the MacLeod who was first tempted by the magnificent outlook to become the island's owner.

Another Pictish stone in front of Raasay House has a cross of unique design incised on it and these stones may have been part of a number historically marking an area of sanctuary.

To the south of the flat summit of Dùn Caan,

on which James Boswell danced a reel 'in sheer exuberance', is **Loch na Mhna** (G. – the loch of the woman). A water-horse which haunted this loch devoured the daughter of a local smithy according to legend. The father trapped and killed the monster and found to his surprise that it was made of jelly. **Loch Storab** to the west is named after a Norwegian prince whose grave is beside it.

The tarmac road overlooks **Holoman Island** in Holoman Bay on the west coast – it is tidal and connected to the shore by a pebble strand. The road ends in the north at **Brochel Castle**, built by the MacSwans in the 15th century and which later became the pirate stronghold of the MacLeods of Lewis. Iain Garbh who died in 1671 was the last inhabitant. The fantastic fairy-tale ruin sits on a pinnacle of sheer rock – a volcanic plug – and originally stood three storeys high. A track runs 2km south through east coast woodland to the shielings of Screapadal, scene of the George Rainy clearances. This area has been immortalised in the poems of Sorley McLean (1911–1996), a Raasay man and one of Gaeldom's greatest poets.

The road running 2½km north from Brochel to **Arnish** was built by Calum MacLeod, a postman. His entire Arnish community of eight families was proposing to leave because there was no road access but the council refused to help. So in 1966, armed with a four-shilling book on roadbuilding, Calum constructed the road himself with a pick, shovel and wheelbarrow. He was awarded the BEM when he eventually completed the work but by then he and his wife were the last remaining inhabitants and he died soon after in 1988. Calum's Road is a most enjoyable walk through magnificent scenery.

A track leads on round the shore of Loch Arnish through Torran, where the school was closed in 1960, and branches off to the tidal island of **Eilean Fladday** which used to accommodate four families with their own school. The houses there are now holiday homes. Continuing to the northern tip of Raasay, remote **Eilean Tigh** (G. – home island) can be reached by crossing a rock ledge which is exposed at low water.

* * *

Access: Vehicle ferry from Sconser, Skye to Churchton Bay, Raasay, 08000-66-5000. Several crossings daily and two on Sunday. 25 minutes

crossing time. Note that there is no petrol for sale on Raasay. Boat excursions from Portree, 07769-701911.

Anchorages:
1. Churchton bay. Anchor south of ferry pier, holding good. Head dries off one cable and SE of bay is foul. 4 visitors' moorings available.
2. Oskaig Point. Some shelter during E winds, S of point.
3. Fladday harbour, on E side of S end of Eilean Fladday, is a narrow inlet. Secure anchorage in 5–10m but bottom foul. Approach from SW between Ard an Torrain and Fraoch Eilean following sailing directions carefully.
4. Caol Fladday, on E side of Eilean Fladday with easy approach from N avoiding Bo na Faochag. Holding can be poor due to kelp.

5.8 Isay

[**ee**shĕ] (ON ise-øy – porpoise island)

OS Maps: 1:50000 Sheet 23   1:25000 Sheet 407
Admiralty Charts: 1:100000 No.1795   1:25000 No.2533

Area: 60ha (148 acres)
Height: 28m (92 ft)

Owner: The three islands of this small group were owned for a time by Donovan, the folk singer, but sold in the early 1980s. In 2002 the present owner, Moneyedge, an English company, started selling one-square-foot 'unspecific' plots of the smallest island, Clett, through the Internet (Clett.com) for £22.50 each. Many Americans and Canadians, and a few Britons, are reported to have already bought plots giving them the right to an 'undivided' share of the 7½-acre island – i.e. the freedom to visit and explore.

Population: 1841–90. There was a final clearance of the last twelve crofter families in 1860. 1881–0. Uninhabited since.

Geology: Basaltic lava with shale and quartzite covered with a reasonably fertile soil.
History: Olave the Black, a Norwegian warlord, is understood to have been the earliest recorded owner of Isay, Mingay and Clett.

In the early 16th century Roderick MacLeod of Lewis, whose daughter had married twice, decided to eliminate two entire families so that his own grandson should inherit the island of Raasay (No.5.7) and the lands of Gairloch. He invited the families to a banquet on Isay promising that

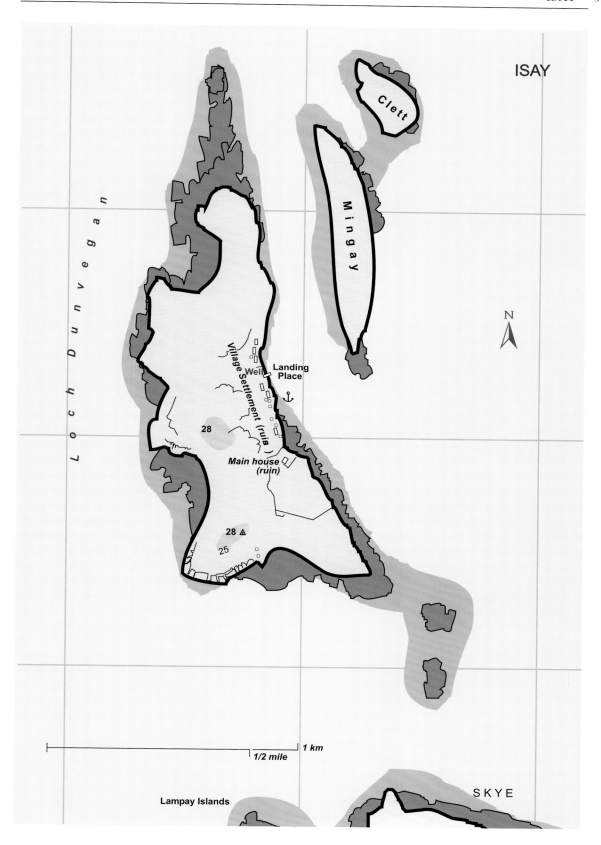

ISAY

Clett

Mingay

Loch Dunvegan

N

Village Settlement (ruin)

Well

Landing
Place

28

Main house
(ruin)

28

25

1 km

1/2 mile

Lampay Islands

SKYE

they would hear something to their advantage. They all turned up and during the meal Roderick said he wanted the private and personal views of everyone present on a matter of great importance. He left the room and each guest was summoned in turn to a room where Roderick had them stabbed to death.

Wildlife: On a June visit there were dozens of pairs of nesting wrens around the ruins and near the headland south-west of the laird's house a large colony of gulls were nesting on the grass. Eider and shelduck paddled along the shores with their young. Wildflowers were in bloom everywhere – marsh marigold, campion, thrift, common spotted orchids, and forget-me-not to name a few – but the many grazing sheep have obviously taken their toll.

*   *   *

Grass-covered **ISAY** with its two lesser companions, **Mingay** and **Clett**, lies peacefully in Loch Dunvegan. The south-western headland forms a vertical bluff over 20m high but the rest of the coast is generally low.

'. . .There is a beautiful little island in the Loch of Dunvegan, called Isa,' recalled Boswell in 1773. 'M'Leod said he would give it to Dr Johnson, on condition of his residing on it three months in the year; nay one month. Dr Johnson was highly amused with the fancy. I have seen him please himself with little things, even with mere ideas like the present. He talked a great deal of this island; – how he would build a house there, – how he would fortify it, – how he would have cannon, – how he would plant, – how he would sally out and take the isle of Muck; – and then he laughed with uncommon glee, and could hardly leave off... M'Leod encouraged the fancy of Dr Johnson's becoming owner of an island; told him that it was the practice in this country to name every man by his lands; and begged leave to drink to him in that mode: "Island Isa, your health!"'

At that time Isay was a populous and industrious island and by the early 1800s it was a big fishing station with its own general store. The evidence of human activity is still there but the people have long since gone.

A 'street' of more than eighteen cottages and black house ruins lines the east shore where there are also the remnants of a crude stone jetty. At the south end of this village is the main house [NG220567]. Its west gable has a large 'arched' opening like the west gable of a church. This is evidently where the fireplace for the main hall on the first floor used to be. The main entrance to this hall is from the higher ground level on the south side by way of a fine stone staircase with splayed stone balusters. The ground floor appears to have been divided into three rooms and there is an outhouse on the east gable – possibly the kitchen. One of these ground-floor rooms was presumably the site of the notorious 16th-century murders.

The soil is fertile but the land is now only used for grazing sheep.

South of Isay at the head of Loch Dunvegan the famous MacLeod castle is sheltered by **Gairbh Eilean**. **Eilean Grianal** and **Garay Island** are two tiny reefs or skerries alongside a double island, **Eilean Dubh** and **Eilean Mór**, linked by a drying channel.

On the other side of the Waternish Peninsula in Loch Snizort are the basalt **Ascrib Islands**, – **Eilean Iosal**, **Eilean Creagach**, **Eilean Garave** and **South Ascrib**. These were purchased in 1985 by Peter Palumbo, property developer and past Chairman of the Arts Council, as a site to build a subterranean residence for himself. 'There are already traces of underground 18th-century monks' cells and being below ground will cause the least disturbance to a beautiful environment,' he said at the time. However his family was not so enthusiastic and the islands, including a newly built traditional house, were up for sale in 1996 for offers over £200,000.

*   *   *

Access: Summer excursions from Dunvegan Castle slip, 01470-531500.

Anchorages:
1. Anywhere in the S part of the narrow channel between Isay and Mingay island. Well sheltered from all winds, but winds from the E and SE can sometimes raise an unpleasant sea. Best anchorage possibly in 6m opposite the village ruins S of the S extremity of Mingay Island but well-N of the chapel-like ruin of the main house, weed and mud. Bottom shelves steeply.
2. About the centre of the E side of Isay there is an iron stepladder giving access to a landing platform.

5.9 Rona

Probably (ON hraun-øy – rough island), but possibly (G. ròn – seal, ON -øy – island)

O S Maps: 1:50000 Sheet 24 1:25000 Sheet 409
Admiralty Chart: 1:500000 No.2210

Area: 930ha (2298 acres)
Height: 125m (410 ft)

Owner: Owned by the Department of Agriculture and Fisheries until 1992 then sold on the open market to Mrs Dorte Mette Jensen of Denmark for a price of, possibly, £250,000.

She also has right of pre-emption over 142 acres at the north extremity owned by the Ministry of Defence.

Population: (In 1763 the Laird of Raasay kept a cowman and 160 head of cattle on the island.) 1841–165. 1851–115. 1861–147. 1881–176. 1891–181. 1922–14. 1931–16. 1971–3. 1981–3: these were all Royal Navy personnel at the NATO station at the north end. 1991–0. 2001–2. 2011–3. A caretaker is now resident at the Lodge throughout most of the year.

Geology: The rocks, some of the oldest in Scotland (and western Europe), are of glaciated Archaean gneiss which is loosely described as Lewisian gneiss. This is a complex group containing dark masses of amphibolite and crystalline veins of pink pegmatite. The earliest metamorphosis – the Scourian – took place about 2500 million years ago.

History: In 1518 the first MacLeod to have taken up residence in Brochel on Raasay, Calum Garbh (Lusty Malcolm), younger son of Calum, the 9th Chief of Lewis, established the line of Mac Gille Chaluim, with the lands of Raasay, Rona and parts of Trotternish, Vaternish and Assynt. He came to an arrangement with the pirates and so-called 'broken men' hiding on the islands and raiding ships as they passed through the Sound of Raasay and the Inner Sound. Rona's perfectly concealed natural harbour of Acairseid Mhór (G. – big anchorage) was known at that time as Port nan Robaireann (G. – the robbers' port) because it was the centre for piracy in the area. So, like that other island chieftain, MacNeil of Barra, who carried out piracy on a much bigger scale, MacLeod and his descendants prospered. But in 1745 they made a grave misjudgement by backing the Jacobites and for this they paid dearly.

Although MacLeod entertained Boswell and Johnson royally, he was deeply in debt. So when the Duke of Argyll, Governor of the new British Fisheries Society which was planning the construction of a number of fishing stations (see Nos.6.4 and 6.8), sent a questionnaire to him in 1787, MacLeod speedily replied:

'There is a part of my property (an island called Rona) which is allowed by the best judges to be one of the most advantageous places on this coast for a fishing station. It is surrounded with numbers of banks which are daily discovered by the country people who come to fish from the mainland, which makes me think there is an inexhaustible fund of them about the island. It is likewise supplied with the best harbours at every creek, both for large vessels and small boats.'

But finance was not forthcoming and in the end the imposition by Whitehall of a salt tax stopped the enterprise and crippled the Hebridean fishing industry. Salt was needed to preserve the fish on the way to market.

By 1843 the MacLeod debts were so great that Raasay and Rona had to be sold. They were bought by George Rainy who was something of a philanthropist and in 1850 he did his best to negate the effects of the potato famine. But the population of Raasay had been rising and instead of turning to fishing the people tended to spread on to the more unproductive land such as on Rona. Rainy then started the inevitable sheep-farming and evicted over one hundred families. Some of these also settled on Rona – an island already much less able to support them than Raasay. Rainy died in 1863 and his eighteen-year-old son and heir took over. He did his best for the islanders but died only ten years later. The next owner George Mackay was a ruthless Gael who forced up the rents and within three years sold the two islands for a handsome profit to an Englishman, William Armitage. He in turn sold them on after eighteen months to another Englishman, Herbert Wood, whose only interest was sport. He imported deer, pheasants and rabbits and cleared the best agricultural land on Raasay which put even more pressure on Rona.

Throughout the Western Isles islanders were at last provoked into retaliation and there was the episode of the 'battle of Braes' on Skye in 1882, just across the water from Raasay House. Parliament responded with the Crofter Act, which was passed in 1886, and which protected the

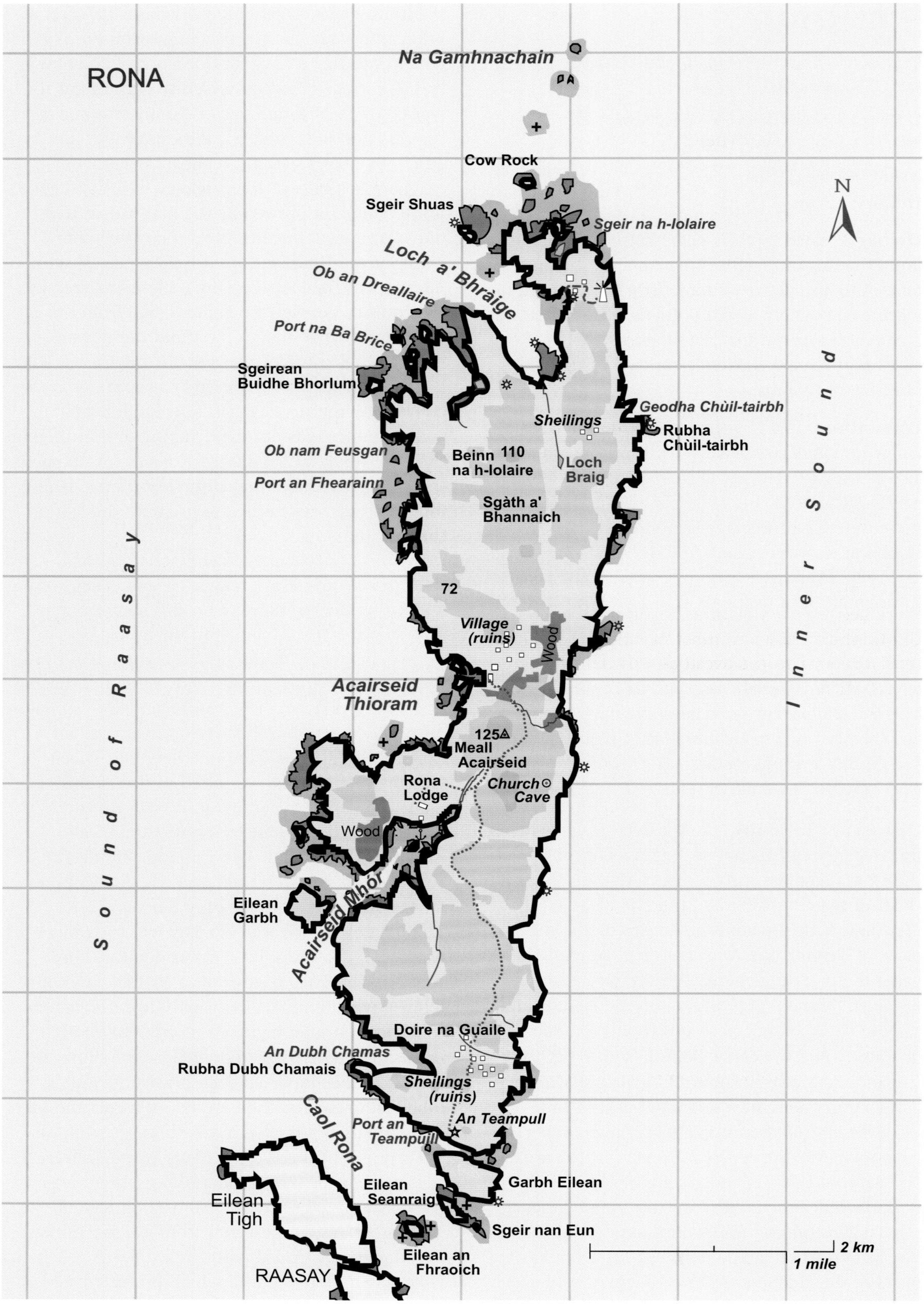

RONA

Na Gamhnachain

Cow Rock

Sgeir Shuas

Sgeir na h-Iolaire

N

Loch a' Bhràige

Ob an Dreallaire

Port na Ba Brice

Sgeirean
Buidhe Bhorlum

Geodha Chùil-tairbh

Sheilings

Rubha
Chùil-tairbh

Ob nam Feusgan

Beinn 110
na h-Iolaire

*Loch
Braig*

Port an Fhearainn

Sgàth a'
Bhannaich

72

*Village
(ruins)*

Wood

*Acairseid
Thioram*

125△
Meall
Acairseid

Rona
Lodge

*Church ☉
Cave*

Wood

Acairseid Mhór

Eilean
Garbh

S o u n d   o f   R a a s a y

I n n e r   S o u n d

Doire na Guaile

An Dubh Chamas

Rubha Dubh Chamais

*Sheilings
(ruins)*

Caol Rona

An Teampull

*Port an
Teampuill*

Eilean
Tigh

Eilean
Seamraig

Garbh Eilean

Sgeir nan Eun

RAASAY

Eilean an
Fhraoich

2 km
1 mile

crofters' existing holdings although it failed to return their dispossessed land.

Meanwhile the struggle for survival continued among dwindling numbers on rocky Rona. The small settlement in the north at Braig was abandoned in 1889. Then the Great War gave the chance to travel and see new horizons. In May 1921 seven of Rona's demobilised ex-servicemen and their families staked a claim to their own ancestral land at Fearns on Raasay. They built homes and had prepared ground for planting when they were arrested and given prison sentences. This created a public outcry which resulted in Raasay and Rona being purchased by the Government (Scottish Board of Agriculture) in 1922.

At this time there were fourteen tenants and their families still remaining on Rona at Doire na Guaile, Acairseid Mhór, and Acairseid Thioram, but by 1930 the numbers had dwindled to only two tenant families. The last of these, the Macrae family, left the island in 1943.

The Department of Agriculture stocked the island with fifty-five Highland cows and 150 Blackface ewes and let it as a grazing farm in 1946. There were a number of different tenants until 1987 when the livestock was removed and the island was put up for sale in 1992. The owner, Mrs Jensen, must be given great credit for sensibly renovating the house by the big harbour, converting the 'mission house' at Acairseid Thioram into two holiday homes, planting native trees, introducing a small herd of Highland cattle, improving the main track/road and installing a water supply without, thankfully, destroying Rona's wonderful ambience. As a result of this work (and the lack of sheep for many years) the native woodland is steadily regenerating and wildflowers are recolonising the area. Rental of the holiday homes helps to bring in a small income to contribute to the island's maintenance.

Wildlife: At one time there were some wild goats on Rona but these have been absent for many years. There are no rabbits. A small herd of pedigree Highland cattle (from the Ardbhan Fold of North Uist) was introduced in 1996 and these roamed freely over the island improving the soil and allowing native trees to regenerate. In 2002 six red deer hinds were brought in – much to the delight of a stag on neighbouring Raasay – and these have now formed an indigenous herd of about 75 animals fought over and willingly serviced by stags which swim over from Raasay. The rut is a popular sight for visitors. The Highland cattle have completed their work of conservation and have gone and a limited number of sheep have been reintroduced within a fenced area around the Lodge to help the island economy.

The mature patches of mixed woodland with some fine Scots pines provide cover for a variety of bird species. Please remember that with ground-nesting birds, calving deer hinds, etc., dogs must be kept on a lead at all times.

* * *

RONA, which is sometimes called South Rona to distinguish it from its namesake which lies well north of Cape Wrath (No.9.4), has a bare, rugged appearance from the sea. There are several hills of 60–90m in height which form a broken ridge and most of the eastern side of the island falls steeply to the sea. The highest hill, **Meall Acairseid** (G. – harbour hill), is 125m high and roughly central.

Rona has been part of the Raasay Estate (See No.5.7) for over 600 years. Martin Martin described it as '..the most unequal rocky piece of ground to be seen anywhere'. and the description in the Gazetteer of 1844 is also graphic as it shows the changing perception of beauty:

'...To an ordinary observer its aspect is quite repulsive; presenting no picturesque features and but little verdure to chequer its grey and sterile surface... Nearly all its arable ground lies round a scattered village which is situated at the head of a bay and contains most of the population.'

Unlike so many of the islands there is a small area of mature native woodland on Rona but at one time it was entirely covered with trees and was used as a source of timber for neighbouring islands. One remaining patch of about two or three hectares, which is on the north side of **Acairseid Mhór** (G. – big harbour), is mainly oak, birch, and hazel but interspersed with some fine Scots pine. Another patch to the north is mainly alder.

A stony road runs from the renovated house known as Rona Lodge at Acairseid Mhór, round Meall Acairseid which has a triangulation beacon on it, to the settlement at **Acairseid Thioram** (G. – drying anchorage). A track carries on to the lighthouse in the extreme north passing between Sgath a' Bhannaich (110m) and the long rib of gneiss to the east of it and then meandering by little Loch Braig. A track also runs south from Acairseid Mhór to the remains of the southernmost village, **Doire na Guaile**, and the ruins of An Teampull at the southern tip.

In the days when the lighthouse was manned, Callum MacLeod BEM, of Arnish on Raasay (See No.5.7), was for a time the Rona postman (this was before he built his famous road from Brochel to Arnish). He used to collect the mail at Arnish twice a week, walk to Eilean Tigh, row across Caol Rona, and then walk the entire length of Rona to the lighthouse, deliver the mail and retrace his steps, a total distance of 30km! Only when you have tried to follow in his footsteps for a few tortuous kilometres can you start to appreciate his dedication.

The lighthouse is now automatic but 142 acres next **Loch a' Bhràige** at the north tip of the island are used as a deep-sea listening post by the Ministry of Defence. To the west of it is **Ob an Dreallaire** (G. – the loiterer's creek) and a tidal pond which was probably used as a fish trap.

The three settlements on Rona boasted two schools and a church. The largest settlement was at **Acairseid Thioram** [cheerum]. The old schoolhouse ruin [NG622580] is still there near the renovated (2002) and sub-divided single-storey Mission House. Islanders worshipped there after it was built in 1878. It is now two holiday cottages. To the north are over 40 ruined cottages which reveal the island settlement as it once was. Some of the crofters evicted from Raasay in the 19th century settled at **Doire na Guaile** in the south-east of the island by Caol Rona. This is fairly close to the ecclesiastical site known as **An Teampull** (G. – the temple) [NG617544], which is thought to have been an early Christian monk's cell. A stone wall surrounds the ruin of a small chapel and there is one gravestone for a man called Graham. He is reputed to be the only person actually buried in Rona's hard and stony ground, everyone else being buried on Raasay.

Caol Rona is a relatively narrow stretch of water dividing Rona from Raasay and the tide runs briskly past **Eilean an Fraoich** (G. – heather island) in the centre of the kyle. **Eilean Seamraig** (G. – shamrock island) is a narrow islet on the north side of the kyle beside tidal **Garbh Eilean**.

On the east coast almost directly across the island from Acairseid Mhór is Giant's Cave [NG626571] now known as **Church Cave**. The islanders worshipped in this cavern until 1878 when the mission house was built and the tradition continued of having babies baptised in the cave. The entrance is like a large Gothic arch and there is a large rock which was used as a pulpit. Beside it is a depression in some stones fed by drips of water from the cave roof and this served as a font. Rows of stones were used as

THE OLD SCHOOLHOUSE AND THE MISSION HOUSE (NOW RENOVATED) AT ACAIRSEID THIORAM

pews by the congregation. A service was held in 1970 attended by thirty members from the Portree Parish Church and another service at Easter 2003 with sixty-four worshippers, and a young couple were married there in 2010.

This cave is well worth a visit but it is not marked on the Ordnance Survey maps. Take the road from Acairseid Mhór, follow it north from the junction with the south-going path and at the head of the rise there is a signpost. The track has been posted and partly bridged across some boggy patches. There is a ridge with a small cairn on its rocky top – cross it and carry on down the hill (approx. SE direction). Where a narrow cleft runs down towards the sea, turn right (approx. S) over a slight rise with old peat cuttings. This leads down and round the side of a cliff in which the cave is located. A rope rail has been kindly provided by Portree RNLI at the steepest parts. Wear stout shoes. Tough going, but even grannies used to do it!

In 1840 the tiny cottage by the slipway (now renovated with four bunk beds for visitors) was occupied by the Mackenzie family, the only residents of Big Harbour at the time. That summer Kenneth Mackenzie was lost at sea but his widow, Janet, would not believe it so she kept a light burning in the cottage window to guide his boat back into harbour. This was of such great assistance to other vessels that after some years the Navy gave her a £20 award and the Commissioners of Northern Lights also gave her a small annual sum to purchase lamp-oil. She kept the light burning for twelve long years but her husband never appeared and in 1852 she gave up and emigrated to Australia.

*   *   *

Access: Visitors welcome but should make a courtesy call at the lodge first; Bill Cowie, 07831-293963. There is a very small landing charge. Dogs must be kept on a lead at all times. Hot showers, bunkhouse, Rona whisky, venison, seafood, postcards and Rona stamps available. Regular Sat. ferry and day trips by arrangement from Portree, Kevin Simmister 01478-612435 and 07769–701911.

Anchorages:
1. Acairseid Mhór. Popular sheltered anchorage. Entrance concealed by Eilean Garbh and care needed in the approach. Shingle or mud, holding varies. Pontoon for dinghy access only. One mooring near visitor's pontoon (pay at Lodge – can be booked in advance).
2. Loch a' Bhraige. Anchorage used by MOD. Well lit, good shelter but unattractive and entry discouraged.

5.10 Eilean Trodday

(ON trod-øy – pastoral or cattle-pen island) or (ON – island of the trolls).

OS Maps: 1:50000 Sheet 23   1:25000 Sheet 408
Admiralty Charts: 1:50000 No.2210   1:100000 Nos.1794 or 1795.

Area: 42ha (105 acres)
Height: 45m (220 ft)

Owner: Has possibly been part of Duntulm (Skye) Common Grazings since 1911.

Population: Uninhabited and no census records but was certainly inhabited in the past. It is possible that by the mid-19th century habitation may have been limited to summer shielings: there is a ruined one at NG439790.

Geology: Trodday with its columnar dolerite is part of the Little Minch Sill Complex in common with many of the small islands north of Skye. Unlike the Lewisian gneiss which is extremely ancient, this rock was formed a mere 55 million years ago making it some of the youngest rock in Scotland. There is a slender dolerite rock stack on the north side of the island which reaches a height of over 30 metres and a lesser one on the west side.

History: According to the Chronicles of Mann, written in 1261, there was an island massacre in 1223 carried out by followers of Amlaib Dubh who was the heir to the kingdom of Man. Some escaped to a church and were spared. But Godred Don, who was the son of Ragnald, king of the Isle of Man, and who had tried to lay claim to the kingdom, failed to reach the sanctuary of the church and was caught by Paul Balkasson who castrated and blinded him.

The account seems to infer that the incident took place on Trodday but it is now considered that this was improbable and that the actual island concerned was in a loch (which has now been drained) on the Trotternish peninsula of Skye. Apart from a comment by Martin Martin mentioning a church in the past tense there is

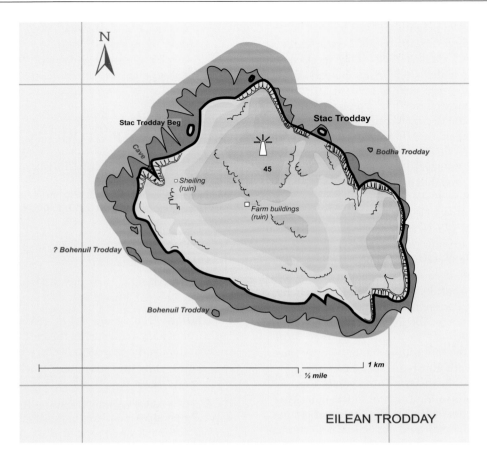

EILEAN TRODDAY

certainly no other record of a church on Trodday, and no trace has been found by the Royal Commission for Ancient and Historic Monuments in Scotland. It is possible that it was the story in the Chronicles which led Martin Martin to report that 'the isle of Troda . . . is two miles in circumference, fruitful in corn and grass, and had a chapel dedicated to St Columba.'

In 1671 the popular Iain Garbh, son of Calum, the 4th Laird of Raasay (see Raasay, No.5.7), was visiting his foster-mother who was a milk-maid on Trodday. When it was time to leave he and sixteen of his clansmen went aboard their birlinn and cast off. A few minutes later the birlinn capsized and sank and all were lost. Many accounts ascribe the disaster to witchcraft but it is more likely that it was bad weather, poor seamanship or too much drink to blame.

Wildlife: Trodday has a thriving seal colony with the birth of about 50 pups a year.

Seabirds include great skua (bonxies), lesser and greater black-backed gulls, herring gulls, and oystercatchers. Breeding passerines include wheatear and rock pipit and because the ground-nesters are thriving it is assumed that the island is rat free. Greenland barnacle geese are regular visitors.

* * *

TRODDAY, lying a mile north of Rubha na h-Aiseig in Skye's Aird, is a small island with few distinctive features except for the striking columnar stack off its north coast. The ground slopes upwards from the south to steep cliffs in the north. The whole island is covered with tufty grass which provides good grazing and there are the remains of extensive lazybeds. A light beacon, on the highest ground at 45 metres is now solar-powered but has been automatic since 1908. About half-way up the slope there are the remains of some farm buildings [NG441788] and records confirm that this was once an active dairy farm, certainly up to the late 18th century.

Whether Trodday was an island of the trolls or not it certainly had its own brownie. She was called The Gruagach [groo-uguch] and the farmworkers treated her with great respect.

She had a switch and immediately used it on anyone who failed to give her a fair share of the farm produce. Bad language also particularly aroused her fury. It was reported that in 1770 the dairymaids always poured a quantity of milk into a hollow stone every day for the gruagach and if they forgot they were severely beaten.

As the Gaelic term 'gruagach' is also used for a lovely head of hair she may have been a beautiful, bad-tempered brownie.

There are some treacherous rocks at Trodday. Bogha Trodday lies underwater near the cliffs on the north face and is believed to have sunk the cargo ship 'Nordhuk'; and one or other of the two submerged Bohenuil Trodday rocks on the south side are said to have sunk the 'Alexanders', a Dutch fishing vessel still visible at low water in 1974.

* * *

Access: SkyeXplorer, Uig, 01470- 542 243 or, try Dan Corrigall, Portree, 01478-612333

Anchorages:
Foul ground is reported around Trodday so best to give the coasts a reasonable berth. There is no recommended anchorage.

5–Appendix Skye

[sky] Probably (Early Celtic skitis, or G. sgiath – winged) isle. Interpreted by Norse as ?(ON skuy – misty) isle.

OS maps: 1:50000 Sheets 23, 32 and 33 1:25000 sheets 407, 408, 410, 411 and 412.
Admiralty Charts: 1:100000 No.1795 1:50000 Nos.2208, 2209 and 2210.

Area: 165,625ha (409259 acres)
Height: 993m (3257 ft)

Owner: Multiple ownership but the Scottish Government has sizeable holdings.

Population: 1755–11252. 1794–14470. 1821–20827. 1841–23082 (peak). 1881–16889. 1891–15705. 1931–9908. 1951–8537. 1961–7479. 1981–7276. 1991–8847. 2001–9232. 2011–10008.

Geology: The dramatic Cuillin mountains in the south were formed by volcanic activity some fifty million years ago. Narrow tilted strata of brittle rock run through the iron-hard gabbro,

which has been shaped by ice into great jagged and irregular teeth. The Red Cuillin on the other hand are of granite (gabbro which flowed out of the ground and cooled quickly) and this by comparison is soft enough to have eroded into more rounded shapes. The oldest rock on Skye, gneiss, is found south of Isle-ornsay on the Sleat [slayt] peninsula.

There is a wealth of geological variety on Skye. Marble is quarried near Torrin, there are coral beaches on Loch Dunvegan, and north of Trotternish there is a beach of green sand (due to the presence of olivine). Gold has also been found on the island.

History: St Columba visited Skye in 585AD. From the 8th century until 1266 – three years after King Haakon's defeat at the Battle of Largs – the Norse were in control. Later the land was divided between the MacDonalds, the Mackinnons and the MacLeods who were constantly feuding and fighting.

In 1745 twenty-four-year-old Flora MacDonald helped Bonnie Prince Charlie, with a price of £30,000 on his head, to escape capture. With the Prince disguised as a maid called Betty Burke, Edinburgh-educated Flora brought him by boat from Benbecula 'over the sea to Skye', landing at Kilbride Bay, where he hid in caves and cattle byres. Then he crossed to Raasay (See No.5.7) by night and arrived there just after the staunchly Jacobite island had been sacked by government troops from *HMS Furnace*. His French rescue ship failed to appear so he returned to Skye and then crossed over to Knoydart on the mainland. On the 19 September 1746 he was picked up from Loch nam Uamh by the French and escaped to France. He died in Rome in 1778. Flora was arrested and taken to London but she was freed in 1747 after the passing of the Indemnity Act by Parliament and became very popular with London society.

Many families were forced to leave Skye after the unsuccessful Jacobite Rising and between 1840 and 1880 a further 30,000 people were evicted from their crofts by landlords and forced to emigrate to the New World. Yet more left when bad harvests struck the island in 1881–85. The ruined houses and empty glens can still be seen as testimony of this misery.

Wildlife: Skye has a rich diversity of flora with a number of rare species. On the east side of the Trotternish ridge a relative of the sorrels which are native to Iceland was discovered in 1934. Mountain avens, guelder-rose and helleborine can be found in the birchwoods behind Broadford and rock whitebeam and red broomrape flourish on the cliffs and slopes above the sea.

'There are in Skye neither rats nor mice; but the weasel is so frequent that he is heard in houses rattling behind chests or beds as rats in England,' according to Dr Johnson, whose natural history was not always accurate.

The white-tailed sea-eagles nested on Skye until 1907, and the last sighting before their extinction was recorded in 1916.

*   *   *

The 'capital' of **SKYE** is **Portree**. It was called Kiltragleann (G. – the church of St Talarican in the glen) until the 16th century or thereabouts. It is said to have been renamed in honour of a visit in 1540 by King James V (G. *port-rìgh* – King's port) but some say the derivation is (G. *portrigheadh* – port on the hillside). The Royal Hotel is on the site of McNab's Inn where Bonnie Prince Charlie bade fond farewell to Flora MacDonald but there is little of historical interest. The building which used to be the courthouse and jail for the whole island now houses the tourist office. Highlighting Skye's recent insularity it is noteworthy that until 1949 the only electricity on the island was produced by a diesel generator in the Portree Hotel.

The road north to Trotternish passes by the **Storr** (G. – buck tooth) 719m high, with its conspicuous 50m-high rock-needle called **The Old Man of Storr** – first climbed in 1955. **Holm Island** lies off-shore to the south-east.

On the beach north of **Rigg** a church-shaped rock – **Eaglais Bhreagach** marks the place where the Clan MacQueen is said to have raised the devil using an ancient ritual which involved roasting live cats. A small carpark at **Lealt** is the start of an interesting climb down a ravine with a view of several spectacular waterfalls and further on, at **Lonfearn**, are the remains of early Christian beehive cells [NG526626]. These are known as druids' houses in Gaelic. High on the ridge above, near the summit of Beinn Edra (611m), a Flying Fortress bomber crashed in 1945.

Beyond Kilt Rock [NG507665], a piece of natural black basalt with folded strata, is **Staffin**, scene of the alleged wreck of a galleon of the Spanish Armada. This is where the small but intriguing **Staffin Museum** holds a collection of the dinosaur fossils and footprints from the mid-Jurassic period which have been discovered on the Trotternish Peninsula. Off-shore are **Staffin Island** and **Eilean Flodigarry**, where according to local tradition the owner once had his corn harvested for him in two nights by 150 fairies. Above Staffin is the **Quiraing**, a fantastic group of awesome rock formations. A short walk north-east from the highest point of the Staffin-to-Uig road [NG443682] leads to The Table, The Prison, and the 36m-high Needle.

As the road turns west at the head of the peninsula there is a striking viewpoint at **Bàgh nan Gunnaichean** (G. – bay of the cannons). To the north is **Eilean Trodday** (see No. 5.10) which once supported a settlement and a chapel. At the extreme north-west of Trotternish the ruin of 15th-century **Duntulm Castle** [NG410743], last occupied in 1732, overlooks **Tulm Island**. Further out to sea are a group of slab-shaped basalt islands owned by Torquil Johnson-Ferguson since 1983 (see Nos. 2.12 and 11.18), – **Lord Macdonald's Table** (G – *Am Bord*), **Gearran Island**, **Gaeilavore Island**, **The Cleats**, and **Fladda-chùain** with a ruined chapel in which, it is said, Sir Donald MacDonald of the Isles hid his title deeds before the 1715 Rising. The cell was founded in Columba's time by a giant of a monk called O'Gorgon and, strangely, the last man to live on the island was also of huge stature and known as Muileach Mór (G. – the big man from Mull).

About 2km south is a **Cottage Museum** in a reconstructed black house, and the burial place of Flora MacDonald. The original MacDonald mausoleum was slowly dismantled by souvenir-hunting tourists and the present memorial replaced it [NG400719]. West of **Balgown** a marshy loch with beehive dwellings and a nunnery on its islands was drained in 1824 [NG377689] (See No. 5.10).

The ferry terminal of **Uig** (ON *vik* – a bay), with services to Harris and North Uist, is in a large cove sheltered by basaltic cliffs.

Travelling south to Loch Snizort Beag, ruined **Caisteal Uisdean** (G. – Hugh's castle) overlooks **Eileanan Mór** and **Beag**. It was built about 1580 by Hugh MacDonald of Sleat with stone quarried from the Ascrib Islands (See No.5.8). Hugh's clan chief found that he had been plotting

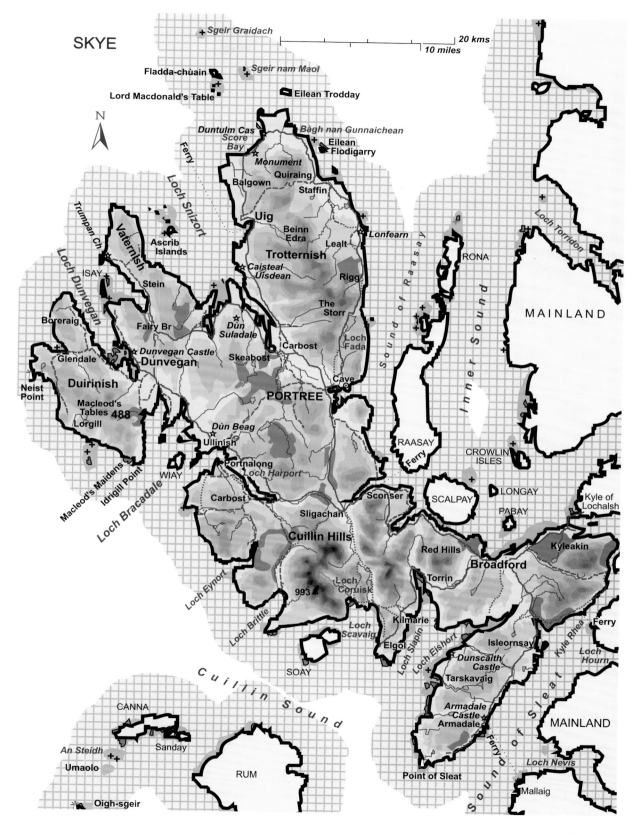

SKYE

PORTREE

against him so he entombed him alive in Duntulm
Castle with a piece of salt beef and an empty
water jug [NG381583].

A broad valley runs from Portree to Loch
Snizort containing the village of **Skeabost**. A
tiny island in the river below the Skeabost bridge
has associations with St Columba [NG418485]
and it was in this village that the poet Mairi Mhor
Nan Oran (Mary MacPherson) was born. West of
Clachamish are the remains of **Dùn Suladale**
[NG374526], one of the best-preserved brochs on
Skye.

The village of **Stein** on the Vaternish peninsula
nestles on the side of Loch Bay overlooking the
islands of Isay (No.5.8), Mingay and Clett. Further
on, at the end of the road, the windswept ruin of
Trumpan Church [NG225612] above Ardmore
Bay was the scene of one of the bloodiest episodes
in Scottish history. In 1578, while the MacLeods
were at worship, the MacDonalds of Uist decided
to avenge the massacre of Eigg (See No.4.2) so
they barred the door and set fire to the church.
One young girl escaped, although she severed one
of her breasts while struggling through a small
window, but all the rest were burned to death. The
girl raised the alarm and the MacLeods quickly
gathered a force together. Carrying their famous
Fairy Flag they rushed down on the MacDonalds
as they were leaving in their galleys. Every

MacDonald was slaughtered and the bodies were
buried in a dyke. The battle has been remembered
ever since as the 'spoiling of the dyke'.

The grave of Lady Grant is in the churchyard.
She was exiled to St Kilda (No.9.1) for eight years
by her husband and died in 1742, three years
after returning to Skye.

By the **Fairy Bridge** [NG278513] on Bay
River the road travels south to **Dunvegan Castle**
[NG247491], seat of the Clan MacLeod since
1200. This is the longest continuous occupation
of any Scottish castle although much of the
present castle was built in the 19th century.
On Skye, by the way, the *sìthiche* [shee-huch],
the fairies or little people, have often played a
prominent part in clan history. They were said to
live in the rounded grassy mounds called *sìthean*
[shee-hen] and enjoy many mischievous pranks.

Duirinish, the area west of Dunvegan, is
dominated by twin peaks called **Macleod's
Tables**, **Healabhal Bheag** which is the highest
(488m) and **Healabhal More**, larger but lower
(469m). Much of this area is wild moorland,
but there are several villages in the north
including **Boreraig**, home of the hereditary
pipers to the MacLeod chiefs, the world-renowned
MacCrimmons. The Piper's Cave is in the cliffs
below the reputed site of their piping college.
The MacArthurs founded the first piping school

on Skye but they moved to Islay (No.2.4) as hereditary pipers to the Lords of the Isles.

Through the valley to the west is **Glendale** with its restored 200-year-old dry-stone grain mill. Further west still there is a well-made path running out to the lighthouse on Neist Point where the view is panoramic. For memorable scenery try the bumpy road to Ramasaig, followed by a walk down the track to **Lorgill**. On 4 August 1830 every crofter in Lorgill was ordered to board the *Midlothian* in Loch Snizort or go to prison. (Those over the age of seventy were sent to the poorhouse instead). Experienced hill-walkers could take the cliff-top route from here to Idrigill Point but a safer bet is to drive to Loch Bharcasaig at Orbost and take the 6km track from there. Idrigill Point overlooks Loch Bracadale and **Macleod's Maidens**, three dramatic stacks like Victorian statues standing in the sea. They were named to commemorate the drowning of the wife and two daughters of a MacLeod chief.

Loch Bracadale is an interesting loch with many inlets and small islands. Dr Johnson stayed at Ullinish and visited **Dùn Beag**, an interesting ruined broch beside the road at Struan [NG339386]. At the entrance to Loch Harport, which opens off the southern end of Bracadale there is the small fishing village of **Portnalong** which was founded by crofters from Lewis and Harris in 1921, and the famous Talisker Whisky distillery is further south at **Carbost**. A narrow road connects Carbost to **Loch Brittle** in the south-west of Skye with its sandy beach, a campsite for climbers, and the cruel but beautiful spiked ridges of the Cuillin Hills towering above the glen. A 3.5 mile track leads down the south-east side of Loch Brittle to the point, Rubh' an Dùnain, where tiny *Loch na h-Airde* has been found to conceal an important Viking boatyard complete with a stone-lined canal connecting it to the Sound of Soay.

The road south from Portree meets the junction at **Sligachan**. There is a track from here [NG487298] which climbs over the mountains to **Loch Coruisk** (G. *coire uisge* – cauldron of water). The approach to Loch Coruisk by sea is from Loch Scavaig into Loch Cuilce (G. – reedy loch). The anchorage behind **Eilean Glas** and beneath a high cliff with a waterfall is one of the most dramatic on the West Coast. There is not much swinging room but there is an alternative spot by **Eilean Reamhar** (G. – fat island). Loch

Coruisk – fresh water, only 10m above sea level, and one of the most awe-inspiring places on earth – is only a short walk away. The deep dark loch, 30m deeper than sea-loch Scavaig, is set in a giant amphitheatre of lonely, primaeval mist-shrouded mountains. It was painted by Turner and visited by Sir Walter Scott.

Sgurr Alasdair, on the west side of Loch Coruisk, is Skye's highest peak at 993m (3257ft), while one of the longest rock climbs in Britain is the ascent of Sgurr a' Ghreadaidh (G. – peak of torment) from the head of Loch Coruisk.

The road from Sligachan runs through **Sconser**, ferry terminal for Raasay (No. 5.7), round Loch Ainort with a folk museum at Luib and on to Broadford Bay. **Broadford** lies under Beinn na Caillich (732m) and its eastward continuation is called Waterloo because many of the veterans of the 1815 battle made their homes here. The road to Elgol, a little settlement which overlooks Soay (No.5.1) by Loch Scavaig, runs through a broad valley south of Beinn na Caillich. On the way it passes close to **Coire-chatachan** [NG621227] where Mackinnon entertained Dr Johnson and Boswell during their tour of the Hebrides in 1773. Just beyond are the ruins of Cille Chrìosd (G. – Christ's church) and further on, past the **Torrin** marble quarry by Loch Slapin, the village of **Kilmarie** was once the home of the Mackinnon chiefs. A track from here leads over the hills to Loch Coruisk via 'Bad Step' while the view to the east is up lovely Loch Eishort with **Eilean Gaineamhach Boreraig** and **Eilean Dubh** dotted on either side of the narrows like the Morse code.

Sitting on the headland at **Suidhe Biorach** (G. – pointed seat) south of Elgol is reputed to make childless women fertile. There is a marvellous walk along the rocky shore at **Elgol** with its strange honeycomb cliffs facing gloomy Loch Scavaig. The east side of the Strathaird promontory has equally fine views of Sleat and, at Glasnakille, Spar Cave with its stalactites is worth a visit [NG538128].

The **Sleat** [slayt] peninsula between Loch Eishort and the Sound of Sleat is served by a road from Broadford. Opposite dour Loch Hourn on the mainland, lies the pretty little village and anchorage of Isleornsay. Unfortunately, the bottom is thick with weed and anchors easily drag. On the tidal island **Ornsay** (ON *örfiris-øy* – ebb island) there is a ruined chapel and an automatic lighthouse beside Eilean an Eòin (G. – isle of birds).

Further south the pier at **Armadale** for the Mallaig ferry shelters the Skye Yacht Club's anchorage. Above the road stands Armadale Castle [NG640047], which was built in 1815–19 for the second Lord MacDonald. It is surrounded by tree specimens from all over the world and is now the **Clan Donald Centre**. There are estimated to be three million MacDonalds in the world.

The southernmost tip of Sleat – the lighthouse at Point of Sleat with **Eilean Sgorach** (G. – scollop isle) beneath it – can be reached on foot by a track. On the west side of the peninsula ruined **Dunscaith Castle** [NG595120] is between the villages of Tokavaig and Tarskavaig. According to legend this was the home of the Queen of Skye who taught the art of war to Cuchulainn, an Irish hero. It was last occupied in 1570. **Eilean Ruaridh** (G. – Rory's island) is off-shore.

Kyle Rhea, north of the Sound of Sleat, with its privately-operated ferry from Glenelg is the traditional ferry crossing to Skye, although until 1906 cattle bound for market were tied nose to tail and made to swim across the narrows. The modern ferry terminal was at Kyleakin (King Haakon's kyle, commemorating his visit in 1263) until it was replaced by the bridge. Four miles west is the Skye airstrip and at the end of the runway a row of graves contain the dead from the cruiser *HMS Curaçao*, which was cut in two by the *Queen Mary* when she was her escort in 1942.

Access: Road access (A87) by bridge at Kyle of Lochalsh linking Skye and the mainland. Frequent (everyday in summer) vehicle ferry service, 1) Glenelg to Kylerhea, crossing 5 minutes, 01599-522273, and 2) Mallaig to Armadale, crossing 30 minutes, 08000-66-5000.

Anchorages:

1. Camas Daraich, at Point of Sleat. Keep in centre. Occasional anchorage more than 1c off-shore in 6–10m. Exposed S and subject to swell.
2. Port na Long, Sound of Sleat. Temp. anchorage well off-shore.
3. Port a' Chuil, Sound of Sleat. Temp. anchorage well off-shore.
4. Armadale Ardvasar. Beware rocks S of Armadale. Restricted space but good holding in sand. Exposed N and E. Subject to swell from S. All moorings managed by Skye

Yachts, 01471-844 216.
5. Knock Bay, Sound of Sleat. Anchor 1½c SE of castle ruin. Protected from NE swell but holding poor. W side of bay is foul. Beware sudden change of depth.
6. Loch Camas Croise. Temp anchorage, N side and not too far in, clay.
7. Isleornsay harbour. Easy access, good shelter except NE, but head dries out a long way and holding poor due to weed. Best holding due W of N beacon on Isleornsay.
8. Camas nam Mult, opposite Duisdale Hotel. Better holding than Isleornsay, and nearer shore. Visitors' moorings maintained by hotel, 01471-833 202
9. Loch na Dal. Head dries nearly 5c. Open SE but better than Isleornsay in N'lies.
10. Bagh Dunan Ruadh, S of Kyle Rhea. Occasional anchorage 2c S of river mouth, 2c off shore, good holding. Squally in NW'lies. Beware 2c drying bank at river mouth.
11. Sgeir na Caillich, N of Kyle Rhea. Anchor 2c WNW of the beacon, or closer to shore if using large-scale chart.
12. Loch na Béiste. Foul with old moorings, wreckage, fish farm, deep and weedy. Suitable small area near burn at head in 3–6m. Exposed E.
13. Ob na Partan. Probably foul with cables but sheltered anchorage ½c from W side in 7m. Use tripping line.
14. Kyleakin. 60m length of pontoon on N side of sheltered inlet (pay). Depths 3m outside, 2.5m inside.
15. North of Kyleakin village, off King's Arms Hotel. Beware cables E of hotel. Occasional anchorage, blue clay. Subject to swell from traffic and N'lies. Visitors' moorings available.
16. Corry Pier, Broadford. Anchor off pier on W side of bay clear of moorings and drying rock SE of pier or temp. alongside pier. Exposed N.
17. Caolas Scalpay, E of narrows. Anchor where convenient. Can be squally. Beware Sgeir Stapaig off Scalpay.
18. Loch na Cairidh, W of narrows. Anchor where convenient. Can be squally.
19. Loch Ainort. Anchor off Luib or in either corner at head. Can be very squally.
20. Loch Sligachan. Narrow entrance with several hazards. Anchor off W side of ferry slip at Sconser or less than ½c W of ruined slip at Peinchorran or towards head of loch in not less than 5m. Can be very squally.
21. Balmeanach Bay, S of Raasay narrows. Anchor clear of cables. Holding good.
22. Camas a' Mhór-bheòil, N of Raasay narrows. Beware drying rock in middle of bay. Uncomfortable in N'lies.
23. Tianavaig Bay. Sheltered SW to NNE. Anchor in 5–10m sand. Can be squally.
24. Portree. Restricted by moorings. Anchor NE of pier in 7–10m, soft mud, doubtful holding. Visitors' buoys available (pay) but uncomfortable in S'lies. Temp stay

alongside pier when tide and space suitable, but be ready to move off. Alternative anchorage at Camas Bàn, but subject to 'whirlies' in S'lies.

25. Staffin Bay. Enter from NE. Bay is clean but exposed NE and squally in W'lies. Anchor on W side of Staffin Island or SW corner of bay.

26. Kilmaluag Bay. Beware drying reef at entrance and submerged rock off N shore. Fierce squalls in strong W'lies. Exposed E. Anchor in 5–10m, sand and pebbles, good holding.

27. Duntulm Bay. Approach mid-channel by S entrance. Anchor close to NE side of Tulm Island but N of mid-point, or under cliffs at NE of bay. Some swell at turn of tide, but sheltered.

28. Uig Bay. Restricted space behind pier but bottom foul and most of the bay dries. Temp lie alongside pier may be possible in daylight. Camas Beag on S side of bay suitable in S'lies but deep until close to shore.

29. Poll na h'-Ealaidh (Port na Ella). Beware drying rocks N of entrance. Anchor close E of Dùn Maraig islet on S side. Sheltered except W'lies.

30. Loch Snizort Beag. Keep mid-channel on approach up the loch. Anchor just within the middle arm, SW of Skerinish Quay, 4m, mud, good holding and good shelter.

31. Loch Treaslane on W side of Loch Snizort Beag. Keep mid-channel. Head dries off for 4c. Good shelter.

32. Clachamish Bay, first bay on W side of Loch Snizort Beag. Suitable anchorage.

33. Loch Greshornish. Approach and enter loch on course midway between Eilean Mór and Greshornish Point and keep mid-channel up loch. Anchor SW of Borve. Excellent shelter.

34. Loch Diubaig. Head dries off 3c. Occasional anchorage. Exposed N.

35. Aros Bay. Clean and open. Occasional anchorage.

36. Ardmore Bay. W side shoal. Shelter from N'lies but holding doubtful.

37. Stein. Visitors' moorings but usually occupied by local fishing boats. Uncomfortable in S and W winds.

38. Dunvegan Castle. Anchor between Gairbh Eilean and castle, clear of rocks or anchor beyond pier as depths allow. (*Visit Dunvegan Castle*).

39. Loch Erghallan. Follow approach directions with care. Anchor ¾c from S of Eilean Mor.

40. Loch Mór. Follow approach directions and anchor in centre of basin or, for best shelter, ESE of Colbost slip.

41. Leinish Bay. Anchor in centre. Exposed N and E.

42. Loch Pooltiel. Occasional anchorage near head which dries off several cables, 3–5m, mud, good holding. Exposed NW but small boats might gain shelter between pier and Sgeir Mór, bottom stony.

43. Loch Bharcasaig, Loch Bracadale. Best anchorage in this area other than Loch Harport. Anchor in SW corner in 4m.

44. Loch Vatten. Anchor near bay in NW corner. Fair shelter but exposed to SW swell. Beware Harlosh Skerry on approach. Shallow-draught boats can enter Poll Roag at HW but not recommended.

45. Loch Caroy. Occasional anchorage exposed to S'ly swell with various hazards on approach. Anchor near jetty on E side.

46. Tarner Island. Approach from S and anchor close to NE side of island in 9m. Reasonable shelter.

47. Oronsay, bay on NW side. Clean and good holding in 4m, sand. Sheltered NE to SW, but some swell at HW.

48. Loch Beag, Loch Harport. Occasional anchorage but exposed SW. Holding poor, dries out halfway and obstructed by moorings.

49. Gesto Bay. Fair anchorage except in SW'-W'lies.

50. Carbost. Visitors' moorings or anchor near shore between pier and distillery. Beware extensive shoal at burn. Head of loch dries. Visitors' moorings. (*Visit Talisker distillery*).

51. Port na Long. Anchor off jetty, good holding and fair shelter except from E. Bay obstructed with moorings and fish cages.

52. Fiskavaig Bay. Temp anchorage off burn on W side, 7m.

53. Loch Eynort. Occasional anchorage. Exposed W but some shelter beyond bend. Holding uncertain. Head dries 8c. Subject to squalls.

54. Loch Brittle. Temp anchorage if no swell.

55. Loch Scavaig, Eilean Reamhar. Care needed on approach. Anchor NW of Eilean Reamhar, 10m, mud and weed. Reasonable shelter but subject to squalls.

56. Loch na Cuilce, Eilean Glas. Follow sailing directions carefully for approach to anchorage on NW side of Eilean Glas. Good holding in mud and sand but subject to violent squalls. (Access to Loch Coruisk).

57. Loch Slapin. Follow directions for the approach. Best anchorage near W shore beyond the narrows, 4–6m, mud. Head dries off 5c. Fish cages and occasional swell.

58. Loch Eishort, Heast Island. Follow sailing directions carefully for difficult approach. Anchor E of island, clear of moorings and N of fish cages, mud, good holding.

59. Bagh an Dubh Ard, SW of Loch Eishort narrows. Follow directions for approach. Occasional anchorage in suitable weather. Bottom shelves steeply.

60. Tokavaig (Ob Gauscavaig). Temp. anchorage in clean sand. (*Visit Dun Scaich*).

61. Tarskavaig. Occasional anchorage in settled weather, clean sand.

62. Acairseid an Rubha, on W side of Point of Sleat has a jetty for servicing the lighthouse. Not recommended.

Gairloch and the North Coast

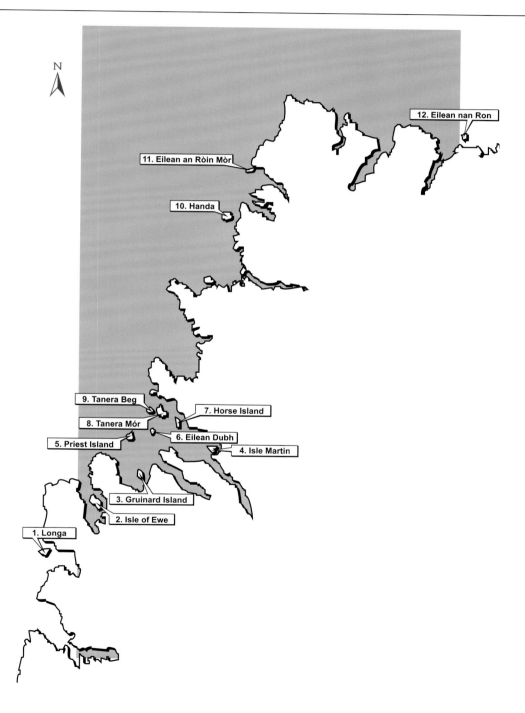

12. Eilean nan Ron

11. Eilean an Ròin Mòr

10. Handa

9. Tanera Beg

7. Horse Island

8. Tanera Mór

6. Eilean Dubh

5. Priest Island

4. Isle Martin

3. Gruinard Island

2. Isle of Ewe

1. Longa

SECTION 6, Table 1: Arranged according to geographic position

No.	Name	Latitute	Longitude	Table 2* No.	Tab 3** No.	Area in Acres	Area in Hectares
6.1	Longa	57° 44N	05° 48W	100	92	311	126
6.2	Isle of Ewe	57° 50N	05° 37W	68	90	764	309
6.3	Gruinard Island	57° 53N	05° 28W	86	63	484	196
6.4	Isle Martin	57° 57N	05° 13W	91	56	388	157
6.5	Priest Island	57° 58N	05° 30W	105	86	301	122
6.6	Eilean Dubh	57° 58N	05° 26W	161	80	108	43
6.7	Horse Island	57° 59N	05° 20W	145	107	131	53
6.8	Tanera Mór	58° 01N	05° 24W	66	55	766	310
6.9	Tanera Beg	58° 01N	05° 27W	133	81	163	66
6.10	Handa	58° 23N	05° 12W	67	52	764	309
6.11	Eilean an Ròin Mòr	58° 28N	05° 07W	155	102	112	45
6.12	Eilean nan Ron	58° 34N	04° 20W	98	88	341	138

*Table 2: The islands arranged in order of magnitude   **Table 3: The islands arranged in order of height

Introduction

There are no large islands off the north-west coast of Scotland from Skye to Cape Wrath but there is a surfeit of little ones.

What is the collective noun which best represents a collection of small islands? A cluster, a scatter, an accumulation, an agglomeration? How about a swarm or an assembly? A clutter or a hotchpotch? Anyway, some such term is badly needed for the medley of assorted islets scattered in patches along this coastline.

In the vast primeval landscape of the northwest, with its reedy pools, patches of heather, big skies and expanses of smooth pink rock, the islets are almost indistinguishable in the random mix of land and water. The land dominates. The sea is a mere intrusion.

But that is the view from the land, as always, the view from the sea is very different. Now the islets create a patchwork of mysterious channels, each one different, each turn revealing new vistas and tempting further exploration. The scale is more human and immediate, each discovery more exciting, possibly because speed is limited and distances are restricted by a sea-level viewpoint. The sea is in control and there are no hill-top views of distant horizons to give a foretaste of things to come.

This region prospered during the herring boom of the late 18th century. **Isle Ristol**, a tidal island near the **Summer Isles**, was the site of a fishing station founded in the later 18th century by Morison and Mackenzie. Close beside it is **Eilean Mullagrach** while **Eilean Ghlais** gives its name to a bay to the north. The Summer Isles, by the way, were so named because they were, and still

are, used for summer grazing.

The huge Inverpolly Nature Reserve abuts Enard Bay with the islets of **Eilean Mór**, **Eilean Mòineseach** (G. – shy isle), **Fraochlan** (G. – heather island) and **Green Island** immediately off-shore. There are anchorages in Lochan Sàl and Loch an Eisg-brachaidh east of these islets. The busy fishing harbour of Lochinver is a few miles to the north with **Soyea** (ON – sheep island) marking its entrance and **A' Chleit** (G. – the reef) nearby.

In the next huge bay to the north, Eddrachillis Bay, there are many islets. **Oldany Island** is larger than Isle Ristol but is also linked to the mainland by a drying channel. **Eilean Chrona** (G. – faulty island) is to the west of it and **Eilean nan Uan** (G. – lamb island), **Eilean an Achaidh** (G. – field island), and **Cùl Eilean** (G. – island at the back) are the larger of the tight group of islets to the east.

The islets in the centre of Eddrachillis Bay, **Meall Mór** (G. – big lump) and **Meall Beag** are almost a continuation of the line of a proto-peninsula formed by Calbha Mór which is part of the mainland, and **Calbha Beag** (G. – little headland), an independent island in spite of its name. They are at the entrance to Loch a' Chàirn Bhàin which is spanned by the beautiful Kylesku Bridge. **Eilean a' Ghamhna** (G. – isle of the stirks) is west of the bridge and **Eilean na Rainich** below the bridge on the east side. The bridge itself is built on the tidal islet of Garbh Eilean.

There is another **Eilean na Rainich** (G. – isle of the ferns) in the **Badcall Islands**. If any group of islets needs a suitable collective noun, this is it.

A 'school' is too orderly, a 'gaggle' sounds better. The larger islets are **Eilean a' Bhreitheimh, Ceannamhór** (G. – bighead), **Ox Rock, Eilean na Bearachd** (G. – island with the pointed snout) – the largest of the gaggle, **Glas Leac, Eilean Riabhach** (G. – grizzled island), and **Eilean Garbh** (G. – rough island).

Lochs Laxford and Dùghaill, between Handa Island and Kinlochbervie also have their share of 'wee ones.' **Eilean Ard** (G. – high island) is the largest. And there are also **Eilean a' Mhadaidh** (G. – isle of the dog), the inevitable **Eileanan Dubha, Eilean an Sithein** (G. – isle of the fairy mound), Eilean Meall a' Chaorainn (G. – island hillock of the rowan tree) and **Eilean Port a' Choit** (G. – isle of the small boat harbour) beside Weaver's Bay.

Loch a' Chadh-Fin which opens off Loch Laxford, and which is the magnificent setting for John Ridgeway's adventure school, has **Eilean an Eireannaich** at the entrance and **Eilean a' Chadh-fi** in the centre.

At Loch Clash by Kinlochbervie, barren **Eilean a' Chonnaidh** (G. – island of the faggot of firewood) has a thought-provoking name. Could this have referred to driftwood or was there a shipwreck there in some bygone age?

Once past the tiny group of rocks a mile off beautiful Sandwood Beach, the biggest rock descriptively named **Am Balg** (G. – the belly), the coast is devoid of islands all the way to wild Cape Wrath (ON *hvarf* – turning point).

Cape Wrath itself is a Ministry of Defence base which is full of activity in the summer months. Apart from firing practice and testing of explosives, tourists at Durness take great interest in the air-launched missiles and bombing runs which use tiny **Garvie Island** (G *An Garbh-eilean* – the rough island) midway between Cape Wrath and Faraid Head as the target.

6.1 Longa

(G. long, ON -øy – ship island).

O S Maps: 1:50000 Sheet 19 1:25000 Sheet 434
Admiralty Charts: 1:50000 No.2210 1:15000 No.2528

PRIEST ISLAND FROM TANERA BEG

Area: 126ha (311 acres)
Height: 70m (230 ft)

Owner: William and Moira Cameron of Big Sands.

Population: 1841–35 (6 houses) 1881–0. Uninhabited since then.

Geology: Mainly sandstone.

Wildlife: Preferably at dawn or dusk, this is one of the best places to see otters at work and play.

LONGA guards the entrance to Loch Gairloch (G – short loch). The island is covered with grass and heather and attains a height of 70m at **Druim an Eilein** (G. – the island ridge). The west side,

which has its own mini-peak called Carr Mór (G. – the big pap) and inlet, Camas nam Faochag (G. – bay of the whirlpools), is almost divided from the rest by a low neck of land between two bays. The north bay, **Camas na Rainich** (G. – bracken bay), has a small sandy beach backed by a bracken-covered slope. It is the favourite place to anchor provided the wind is not in the north. The south bay, which is rockier, is called **Eag Mhór** (G. – the big notch). Longa is separated from the beach and village of Big Sand on the mainland by Caolas Beag (G. – little channel).

There is one tiny lochan almost in the centre of the island and directly south of it a rocky promontory with a hooked silhouette descriptively

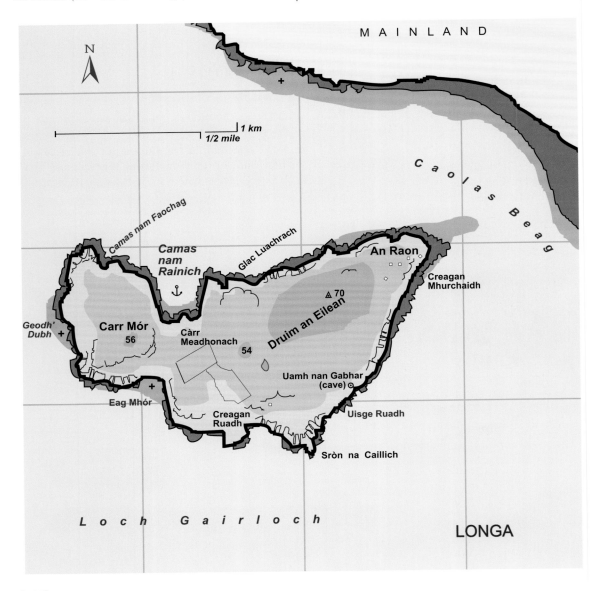

called **Sròn na Caillich** (G. – the old woman's nose). Further along the coast is Uamh nan Gabhar (G. – cave of the nanny-goats).

On the south side of Loch Gairloch and opposite Longa the small and crowded harbour of Badachro is sheltered by **Eilean Horrisdale**. Although unkempt with wild irises and bracken, the centrally-situated owner's house creates the impression from a distance that the island is an informal private garden. This tiny islet, less than one-third the area of Longa, supported twenty-seven people in four houses in 1841 and the population had risen to thirty-one islanders in five houses by the end of the 19th century. This was surely overcrowding, but they would be fishing folk so the area of land would be of little consequence.

Glas Eilean is a useful sea-mark when sailing up the loch to the pier by Charlestown and **Fraoch-eilean** (G. – heather isle) marks the entrance to Gairloch's Loch Shieldaig, which is a pleasant anchorage when you want to avoid being crushed by fishing boats at the pier.

* * *

Access: Try Gairloch Cruises, 01445-712636 or Hebridean Whale Cruises, Gairloch, 01445-712458.

Anchorages: The W coast of the island is foul for about ¾c off-shore and a reef fringes the island. Note that the mainland shore dries for 2c at Caolas Beag and there is a fairly shallow spit NE of the island.
1. Occasional anchorage in centre of bay on N coast. 5–8m, sand.

6.2 Isle of Ewe

Island of Loch Ewe. (El eo – yew tree) but Watson thinks (G. eubh – echo) from place-name on adjoining mainland.

O S Maps: 1:50000 Sheet 19 1:25000 Sheet 434
Admiralty Charts: 1:100000 No.1794 1:12500 No.3146

Area: 309ha (764 acres)
Height: 72m (236 ft)

Owner: J I H Macdonald-Buchanan and leased to the Grants. The Grant family have lived on the Isle of Ewe since the middle of the 19th century.

Population: 1841–34. 1881–43. 1891–39. 1931–37. 1961–10. 1981–11. 1991–12. 2001–12. 2011–7.

Geology: Torridonian sandstone with acidic soil in the north and a more fertile soil on New Red Sandstone (Permian or Triassic) in the south.

History: Loch Ewe was an important naval anchorage during the Second World War and it is occasionally still a scene of NATO activity. 19 of the Arctic convoys to Russia left from here with arms for the eastern front. In 2013 forty of the few remaining survivors returned to Loch Ewe to receive their Arctic Star medals in a very belated recognition of their courage. There are plans for a £2.5 million museum to be built on the site of the HMS Helicon, the wartime naval HQ, north of Mellon Charles near the entrance to the Loch.

Wildlife: Dean Munro recorded in 1549 that the island was wooded. Nowadays, most of the island is a working farm with the type of flora and fauna to be expected in such an environment but a visit to Loch Ewe provides the added bonus of access to the world-famous Inverewe Gardens – more than 2000 acres of magnificent landscaping and plant life now under the care of the National Trust for Scotland. Loch Ewe may be remote and at the same latitude as Hudson Bay or Siberia but these Gardens are visited every year by more than 100,000 people who revel in their subtropical splendour.

* * *

The **ISLE OF EWE** looks steep and rocky when approaching by sea from the north but from Aultbea (G. – the birch-lined stream), the nearby village on the mainland, it can be seen that much of the island is gently undulating farmland. The highest point (72m) is in the north-west above a cliff, **Creag Streap** (G. – climbing cliff), which has a large rock, Sgeir a' Bhuich (G. – rock of the roe-buck), in the sea below. North of it is Uamhag nan Gobhar (G. – rock shelters of the goats) which was used to anchor the anti-submarine boom-nets in World War II. The high ground (68m) on the north-east peninsula is called **Sitheanan Dubha** (G. – the black fairy hillocks) and the soil here is peaty with a thick cover of coarse grass, heather and sphagnum moss.

The anchorage at **Camas Angus** is echoed by a bay on the opposite side of the island, **Camas Beithe** (G. – birch-tree bay). A hummock between the bays called **Cnoc na Gaoithe** (G. – windy knoll) shelters the anchorage from the

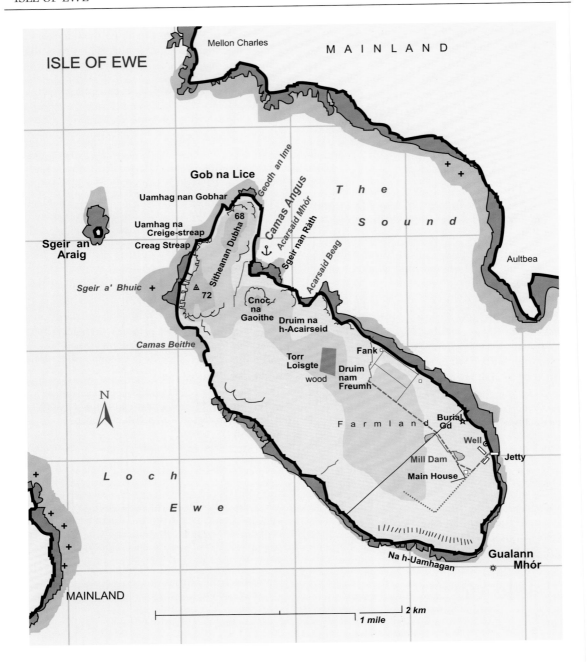

prevailing wind.

A small copse of trees on **Druim nam Freumh** (G. – ridge of roots) defines the northern limit of the arable land.

There are two families living on the island. Roddy Grant is a fisherman. He was born on the island and his family has lived here since the middle of the 19th century. He is married to Marion and their life revolves round work, family and church. Their two children enjoyed a carefree childhood. Neil, the elder, was born in 1987.

Roddy's cousin Willie is married to Jane, a Somerset girl who met him when she was a ship's engineer in the Merchant Navy. For ten years they sailed the world together but now Willie farms the island croft. Jane built a landing stage, helped Willie build their house, and cared for their children when they were young – but she would probably have preferred to strip diesels instead. She takes readings once a week at the nearby sampling site for Marine Scotland Science (MSS), – water temperature and chemistry salinity, phyto- and zooplankton – a detailed record of the health of the ocean, and she dives for scallops as recreation.

There were more families living on the island in the past but they left during the Second World War.

There is a direct telephone link to the island. Its installation was agreed by British Telecom before the company realised that the connection had to cross the sea and would cost a fortune! (That, of course, was long before the advent of mobile phones.)

Access: Enquire at Aultbea or try Creag Ard Charters, Ullapool, 01854-633380, or Gairloch Cruises, 01445-712 636. Ullapool Tourist Information, 08452-255121.

Anchorages:
1. Camas Angus (Acarsaid Mhór), in NE, 3c S of N extremity. Beware unlit buoys, and partly submerged reef to SE. Good shelter in W'lies.
2. The Sound. Off the island's SE jetty in 7m or more, good holding but exposed.
3. Acarsaid Beag, 2c SE of Acarsaid Mhór. Poor holding on kelp.

6.3 Gruinard Island

(ON groenn fjordr – green firth) island.

O S Maps: 1:50000 Sheet 19 1:25000 Sheet 435
Admiralty Charts: 1:100000 No.1794 1:25000 Nos.2500 or 2509

Area: 196ha (484 acres)
Height: 106m (348 ft)

Owner: Requisitioned by the Government from the Eilean Darach estate in 1942. When the owners asked for it back after the war they were paid £500 and told that it would be returned on payment of £500 but only when it had been decontaminated. This was not done until 1990.

Population: 1881–6. 1891–0. Uninhabited since the 1920s.

Geology: Mainly Torridonian sandstone with laminated shales and micaceous sandstone in the north-east.
History: Gruinard Island has a notorious recent history.

In 1942, during the Second World War, some scientists from Porton Down decided to use this uninhabited Scottish island as a test ground for biological warfare and bombed eighty penned sheep with highly virulent anthrax spores. The sheep duly died and their bodies were buried in a cave on the island under tons of rock or incinerated. Even so, one of the carcasses floated over to the mainland and infected some livestock but, as there was a war on, the affair was quickly hushed up and the owners compensated.

As there was no satisfactory antidote known at the time, anthrax was rather a foolhardy choice, but it was suspected that the Germans were carrying out similar experiments. Anthrax is a particularly deadly and indestructible bacillus. Even forty years after it was sprayed over Gruinard, up to 385 viable spores per gram of soil were found when the Chemical Defence Establishment carried out one of its periodic tests. In 1986, after many protests from environmentalists, the Ministry of Defence decided to disinfect the island by soaking the entire surface area in formaldehyde and sea-water. Sheep and rabbits were then introduced to test whether the result was satisfactory. They survived.

In April 1990 Gruinard Island was declared free of anthrax. It was opened to the press and public and returned to its pre-war owners with a 150 year Government indemnity. However Dr Brian Moffat, an archaeologist involved in the investigation of a medieval hospital at Soutra, claimed in a radio broadcast that anthrax spores had survived for 500 years on that particular site. Vegetation he claimed brings them up to the surface of the soil and certainly nothing on earth would persuade him to risk landing on Gruinard! The Ministry of Defence replied that this was an unfair comparison. Soil samples had shown that the island was clear of danger although no one could say there may not still be a few spores around; the sheep were fit and healthy and so were the wild rabbits.

Wildlife: In 1549 Dean Munro recorded that the island was wooded. The peak sea-bird season in Gruinard Bay is October to May. This is a prime area to see the great northern diver.

*   *   *

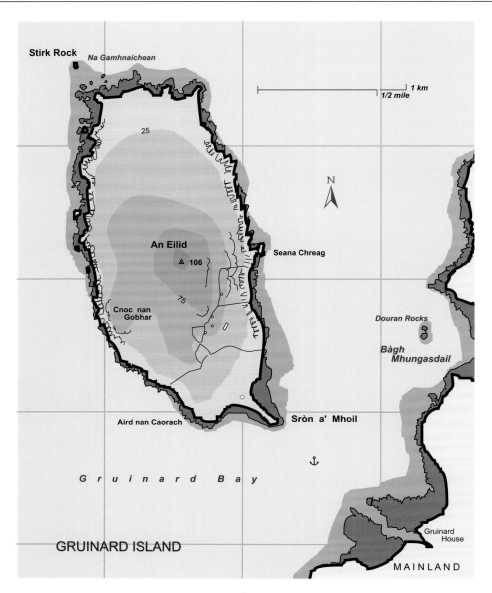

GRUINARD ISLAND rises gently to a rough rounded summit (106m) which is called simply **An Eilid** (G. – the hind). The island is covered with rough grazing – grass, heather and bracken and fringed by a rocky shore and occasional pebbly beach.

One good result of the Microbiological Research Establishment's unfortunate experiment on Gruinard was the development of an effective vaccine against anthrax for both animals and humans. But it is a pity that animals had to be introduced so quickly after the clean-up, as it would have been an excellent opportunity for botanists (wearing suitable clothing, of course!) to study the effect of forty-five years of sheep- and rabbit-free existence on the vegetation.

For the committed visitor keeping below the high-water mark should present no danger. Going above it is a matter of personal choice!

It is probable that historically the island has always provided useful pasturage, the flocks and herds being swum across the narrow kyle to a point near Gruinard House on the mainland. Certainly the headland beside the long spit at the southern extremity is called **Aird nan Caorach** (G. – sheep or livestock point).

Access: Try Creag Ard Charters, Ullapool, 01854-633380 or Hebridean Whale Cruises, Gairloch, 01445-712 458.

Anchorages: Reefs extend up to 1c off the island at places and the bottom is generally rocky. There are no regular anchorages but there are moderate depths SE and E of the island with some mud and sand.

6.4 Isle Martin

Named after Saint Martin to whom the island chapel was dedicated.

OS Maps: 1:50000 Sheet 19 1:25000 Sheet 439
Admiralty Charts: 1:100000 No.1794 1:25000 No.2500

Area: 157ha (388 acres)
Height: 120m (394 ft)

Owner: In 1965 Mrs Monica Goldsmith bought Isle Martin. She presented it to the RSPB in 1981, having carefully renovated four houses. In May 1999 the RSPB, in turn, gave it in trust to the communities of Lochbroom and Coigach (after, unfortunately, letting the houses fall into disrepair).

Population: 1841–45. 1881–42. 1891–47 (8 houses). In 1901–33. 1931–3. 1961–0. 1971–0.

ISLE MARTIN

1981–1. 1991–1. 2001–0. Occasional summer occupation of one house.

Geology: The island is a rounded hill of Torridonian sandstone.

History: In 1775 the British Fisheries Society built a curing station which prospered until the industry collapsed in 1813. In the 1930s, as the last islanders had left, the owner, Commander C G Vyner created employment by converting the ruined building into a flour mill and a school hut was built. Several families returned. But by 1949 the mill was losing money, the islanders moved elsewhere and the school closed. Vyner decided to build a causeway to the mainland to encourage repopulation of the island but planning permission was refused and, as he was being charged rates for the empty mill, he dynamited it in 1952.

Wildlife: Bird sanctuary.

Peak viewing November to May for wintering divers and gulls, especially Glaucous and Iceland. Otherwise, of particular interest are the red-breasted merganser, oystercatcher, ringed plover, heron, tern and eider. Corncrakes can be heard in June.

Two ecology graduates from Edinburgh University ran a tree nursery at Scourie (near Handa. No.6.10) and between 1982 and 1998, under the auspices of the RSPB, they reintroduced native trees to Isle Martin – willow, oak, ash, hazel, rowan and pine. This has already created a young forest which has its own micro-climate and is a larder for native wildlife. They have, in fact, turned the clock back to the island's traditional landscape before it was denuded of trees many centuries ago.

* * *

Close to, but separate from, the Summer Isles group, **ISLE MARTIN** lies beside the entrance to Loch Broom. From the sea it often merges with the background hills. It consists of a single rounded hill 120m high with rocky cliffs on the west and north coasts. The slope is gentle on the sheltered east side where there is a small bay. It is here that the restored houses and the remains of the old fish-curing station [NH096990] can be found but the scant remains of St Martin's chapel are further west. A fairly large settlement of ruined houses lies among the trees and beautifully constructed dry-stane dykes cross the hillside above the bay. The small valley on the west coast is called **Bad an Ling** (G. & ON – tuft of heather).

The British Fisheries Society, with ample funds from the south, built the port of Ullapool in 1788, and several curing stations on key island sites such as Isle Martin. This was to take advantage of the vast herring shoals for which Loch Broom was renowned. These swept into the loch between the months of May and September every year. For hundreds of years the local boats had enjoyed a bonanza as the shoals were so dense that it was possible to scoop the fish out of the sea by hand. The Society curtailed the activities of the local boats, and netted fish for themselves in vast quantities. The boom lasted for fifty years and then this depredation took effect. By 1830 the shoals had thinned and by 1880 they had disappeared. They have never recovered. The curing stations were abandoned and the local fishermen were left to search for alternative catches.

Isle Martin has its local legend. According to this a cooper once worked for the fish curing station and was ordered to cut brooms one evening. The little people took pity on him and miraculously transported him to the woodland on South Rona (No.5.9). In the morning he was back at work with all the brooms that were required.

Access: Landing is permitted by the Isle Martin Trust (01854-612937) but voluntary donations would be appreciated. For the Trust's island ferry contact Ullapool Tourist Information, 01854-612135.

Anchorage:

1. Good anchorage E of island in Loch Kanaird. Anchor N side of bight, bottom gravel and stones, or use the Trust pontoon (pay), 2.7m depth at MLWS.

6.5 Priest Island

(G. Eilean a' Chléirich – island of the Priest)

O S Maps: 1:50000 Sheet 15 1:25000 Sheet 439
Admiralty Charts: 1:100000 No.1794 1:25000 No. 2500, 2501 or 2509,

Area: 122ha (301 acres)
Height: 78m (256 ft)

Owner: Royal Society for the Protection of Birds.

Population: No Census records and uninhabited.

Geology: The island consists of two main masses of Torridonian sandstone cut by a glen running from south-west to north-east. The southern mass is a ridge in which the strata have tilted to form rugged cliffs of fluted columns facing the glen to the north. The southern slope is less steep. The sandstone is smoother and redder than that on the mainland.

History: Rudimentary stone circles are proof of early human interest and the name shows that this was a retreat or hermitage in the early Christian era, possibly associated with the monastery on Isle Martin (No.6.4). In the 18th century an outlaw banished from the mainland settled here and founded three generations of crofters but his descendants abandoned the island in the 1850s.

Dr Frank Fraser Darling stayed here during the late 1930s and wrote about it in his book, *Island Years*.

Wildlife: Heather is dominant south of the glen, but in the north and west apart from some erica and calluna there are plantain and thrift, bog asphodel, bog cotton, crowberry, sheep's fescue and buckthorn.

Aspen, poplar, royal fern, honeysuckle, willow and the inevitable flag irises are widespread around Lochan Fada.

As with all the Summer Isles there are many birds. Shelduck, fulmar, heron, snipe and eider are common and merganser breed along the banks. Twenty-nine species of bird are known to breed here, the most notable being greylag geese and a large number of storm petrel, but according to Fraser Darling, forty-three species of bird which breed on Tanera Mór (No.6.8) do not breed on Priest Island – probably due to the wind.

Grey seal, pigmy shrew (to be found near the caves in the south according to Fraser Darling) and otter can all be seen. In particular the two lochans in the main glen are much frequented by otters. All the eight lochans are reputed to have excellent fishing.

*   *   *

The most westerly of the Summer Isles, 4 miles or 7km south-west of Tanera Mór, **PRIEST ISLAND** has no proper landing place and with its exposed position and a persistent heavy swell getting ashore at its one and only 'anchorage', a bay in the centre of the east coast, can be difficult. Getting off again can be harder still! The alternative landing places depend on wind direction but none is comfortable or easy.

Approaching from due south the island appears to be smooth-topped with two summits near its east end, but from elsewhere its outline is rugged. As there are several small lochs providing a plentiful water supply this could account for the fact that in spite of its inaccessibility it has been

LOCH FADA ON EILEAN A' CHLÉIRICH

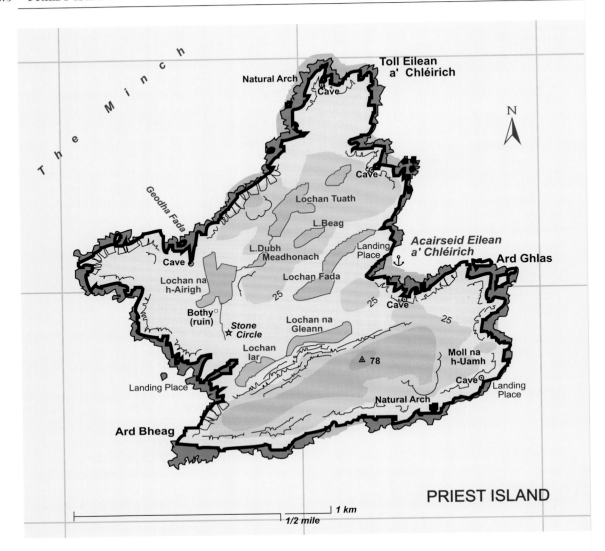

PRIEST ISLAND

1 km
1/2 mile

inhabited off and on since pre-history.

The highest point (78m) is south of the anchorage at **Moll na h-Uamh** (G. – cave point). This particular cave [NB930017] is on the south-east coast below the ridge and is the one in which Fraser Darling dug up bones of pig, ox, deer, guillemot, fulmar and petrel. Further interesting and fairly deep caves are to the north of the anchorage. One, at a little boulder beach, has signs of human habitation and was probably used by smugglers [NB927026]. Part of a whisky still was found near **Lochan na h-Airigh** (G. – shieling loch). The sea booms eerily as it enters **Toll Eilean a' Chléirich** (G. – Priest's Hole) in the north-east corner – a sea-cave with a fallen roof [NB927029].

The main glen runs right across the island from the anchorage to the west coast and contains two lochans. To the north of the glen there is a tumbled landscape with more lochans, several pools and patches of bog ending abruptly at the steep cliffs and fissures of the north-west coast.

Evidence of an ancient chapel has been uncovered on level ground on the south side of Lochan na h-Airigh [NB920021] which is also the site of the 19th-century ruined bothy. The ground here has been cultivated in the past. A prehistoric stone circle is beside the burn which flows out of the loch. This was originally on the west side of the burn but the Victorian yachtsman and naturalist, Harvie-Brown, found after several visits that it had sunk into the boggy ground and disappeared so he dug it up and transferred it to the dry ground on the other side of the burn!

Between Priest Island and Tanera Beg is the small island (11ha) of **Glas-leac Beag** (G. – little green slab). It is, as described, narrow and flat-topped, about 29m high, and on a fine day its covering of grass, gloriously fertilised by a colony of black-backed gulls, makes it appear bright green.

Access: Landing is prohibited without prior permission from the RSPB, 0131-311 6500. Summer Isles Cruises, Achiltibuie, 01854-622200 or Creag Ard Charters, Dundonnell, 01854-633380. Achiltibuie Tourist Information, 01854-622200.

Anchorages: All are subject to considerable swell.
1. Acairseid Eilean a' Chléirich, bay on E side. Occasional anchorage in settled weather, clean but bottom mainly boulders. Landing best on or near 'pier rock' on NW side of bay.

2. Landing point at cleft in bay on W side of island. Temp. anchorage possible in settled weather ½c off-shore in 15–20m.

3. Landing point at cave on SE side of island. Temp. anchorage possible in settled weather in 15–18m.

6.6 Eilean Dubh

(G. – black or dark island)

O S Maps: 1:50000 Sheet 15 1:25000 Sheet 439
Admiralty Charts: 1:100000 No.1794 1:25000 No. 2500, 2501 or 2509

Area: 43ha (108 acres)
Height: 87m (284 ft)
Owner: Dr C Gordon Van Arman, PhD., and his wife, Dr Desiree Armstrong, of Pennsylvania, USA, bought Eilean Dubh in about 1978 and

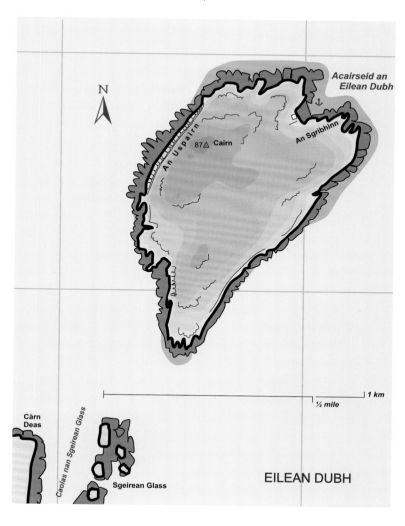

EILEAN DUBH

built a pleasant Finnish log house overlooking the bay. They also planted many trees. Having retired they spent a lot of time there, loved the area and enjoyed sailing among the islands. Dr Van Arman, who died in 2002 aged 84, was a noted scientist who pioneered work on magnetic resonance imaging (MRI). There are two sons, John and Thomas.

Population: 1841–1971 no records and presumed uninhabited. 1981–1987, during construction of the house? 1991–0. 2011–0.

Geology: Mainly fine medium-grained Torridonian sandstone.

Wildlife: This is a breeding site for the storm petrel.

*   *   *

EILEAN DUBH lying between Tanera Mor and Priest Island is a small compact island with a prominent hill and a single bay on the northeast side. The owner has built a substantial Finnish log house overlooking the bay.

If climbing to the summit there is a lot of rough vegetation covering the slopes which can make progress difficult.

Bottle Island (an evocative name! – said to be for its shape which is not, however, at all bottle-shaped. 'Bothy Island' is more likely) lies to the south-west of Eilean Dubh with a group of skerries between them – **Carn Iar** (G – the west cairn) uninhabited but apparently having permission to produce its own postage stamps, **Carn Deas** (G – the south cairn) and **Sgeirean Glass** (G – pale green skerries). West of Eilean Dubh there is another skerry, **Sgeir nam Mult** (G – skerry of

the wedder, a castrated male lamb). A small Motor Prawn Boat sank here in 1970. All these skerries form a marine eco-system which makes this a very popular diving area.

Access: Summer Isles Cruises, Achiltibuie, 01854-622 200 or Creag Ard Charters, Dundonnell, 01854-633 380. Achiltibuie Tourist Information, 01854-622 200.

Anchorages: On NE coast, approach on centre line and anchor in centre of bay off the beach at a suitable depth, sand.

6.7 Horse Island

O S Maps: 1:50000 Sheet 15   1:25000 Sheet 439
Admiralty Charts: 1:100000 No.1794   1:25000 No.2501

Area: 53ha (131 acres)
Height: 60m (197 ft)

Population: Uninhabited and without Census records but is reputed to have been inhabited in the 19th century.

Geology: Torridonian sandstone.

History: Treasure from a ship of the Spanish Armada is said to have been hidden here in 1588. The story is reinforced by a local record that a shepherd in the 19th century found a gold doubloon in his boot-top after stumbling in the heather. He rushed to the mainland and told his friends, who immediately organised a treasure hunt but when they were on the island they could find nothing. One piece of heather looks much like another and the shepherd then wondered if he had remembered the correct spot where he tripped. The dejected group

HORSE ISLAND FROM THE SOUTH WITH ACHILTIBUIE BEYOND

returned empty-handed. Unlike so many local legends, the unsatisfactory ending makes this story ring true!

Wildlife: Multi-coloured lichens, thrift, sea campion, lovage and scurvy grass grow on the ledges of the cliffs.

Only wild goats inhabit Horse Island nowadays but no one is sure how they came to be on the island. The first official record of their presence was in 1837. But there seem to have been resident goats in earlier times as the drying islet at the north end is called Meall nan Gabhar (G. – hillock of the she-goats).

*   *   *

HORSE ISLAND is separated from the mainland by a deep channel called Horse Sound. The highest point (60m) is **Sgùrr nan Uan** (G. – conical hill of the lambs) – near the south-east coast. **Meall nan**

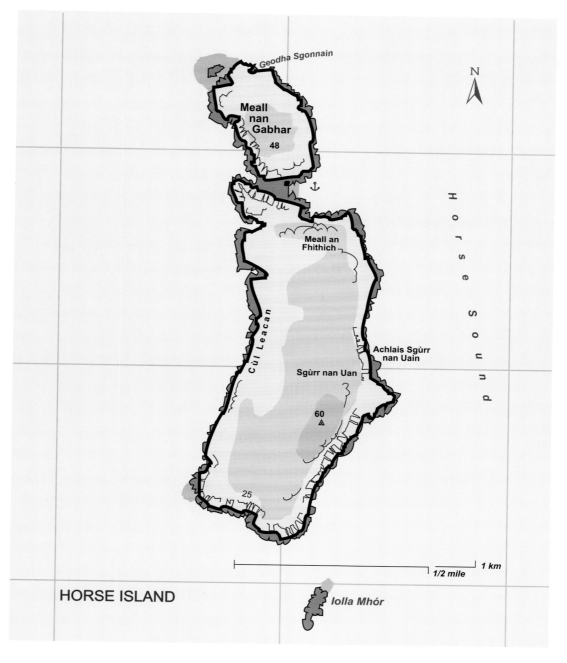

HORSE ISLAND

Gabhar (13ha) is at the northern extremity and connected to the main part by a reef which dries at low water. The opposite hill on the main island is **Meall an Fhithich** (G. – raven's hill). **Iolla Mór** (G. – big drying rock), lying off the south coast, is a flat rock which is extensive at low water.

Similar plants to those on Horse Island are to be found on **Carn nan Sgeir** – two small islands separated by a shingle spit which lie to the south but, unlike the rest of the Summer Isles which are of Torridonian sandstone, these islets are of Hebridean gneiss.

It is natural that in this animal-farm region of horses and goats another nearby islet should be called **Meall nan Caorach** (G. – sheep hump).

Access: Summer Isles Cruises, Achiltibuie, 01854-622200, or Creag Ard Charters, Dundonnell, 01854-633380. Achiltibuie Tourist Information, 01854-622200.

Anchorage:
1. Good anchorage in bight SE of Meall nan Gabhar but keep in N half as there is an uncharted reef in the S half, 3m, sand and some weed. Exposed to E.

6.8 Tanera Mór

(ON hawnar-øy – island of the haven, pasture, G. – large) or (ON taren-øy – the kelp island).

OS Maps: 1:50000 Sheet 15 1:25000 Sheet 439
Admiralty Charts: 1:100000 No.1794 1:25000 No.2501

Area: 310ha (766 acres)
Height: 122m (400 ft)

Owner: Sold by Summer Isles Estate in 1991. Bought in 1996 by the Wilders, a Wiltshire family, for about £700,000 and the island is managed by their daughter and son-in-law, Lizzie and Richard Williams. With a young family to be schooled they reluctantly put the island up for sale in 2013 at an asking price of £2.5 million.

Population: 1745–21 families. 1841–99. 1881–119. 1891–95 (19 houses). 1901–70. 1931–0. 1961–6. 1971–2. 1981–8. 1991–0. 2001–5. 2011–4.
Geology: Torridonian sandstone mostly covered with peat, pasture and heather.

History: In 1784 Murdoch Morrison of Stornoway was installed as manager of the newly founded fishing station at Tigh-an-Quay (between Ardnagoine and Garadheancal). As with the stations on Isle Martin (No.6.4) and Isle Ristol, this was built by the London-based British Fishery Society. It was a very prosperous enterprise while the herring stocks lasted. Up to 200 vessels at a time would anchor in the bay and salted herring was even exported to the West Indian colonies.

After the fishing spree was over in 1820, and the company was bankrupted, there followed a period of many changes of ownership and greedy tacksmen demanding high rents. So the resourceful islanders took up the distillation of illicit whisky. In 1900 another lucrative sideline was introduced when the island was acquired by Captain MacDonald, a local smuggler, There is a rumour that a cargo of rum was buried at Tigh-an-Quay and another story of buried treasure in the 'big park' between Tigh-an-Quay and Mol Mór.

Wildlife: The climate is mild and there are wild flowers everywhere – heather galore, common orchids, forget-me-not, foxgloves, dandelions, clover and burnet rose. Near An Lochanich there are flag irises, honeysuckle, willow and aspen poplars which grow to 3–4m in height. Bluebells and primroses are sheltered by rowan and birch which grow on the slopes. Unlike Priest Island (No.6.5) the lochs here are almost lifeless except for tadpoles.

Gulls and arctic terns are common but few other sea-birds are to be seen. There is, however, a wide variety of general birdlife including breeding heron, shelduck, buzzard and red grouse.

* * *

TANERA MOR is the largest of the Summer Isles, a small group of a dozen or so islands lying close to the mainland which were used for summer grazing. The highest hill, **Meall Mór**, (122m) has a flat summit when viewed from the south and below it is one of the best natural harbours in the north-west. It is known as **The Anchorage** and was a great favourite with the Vikings but they would not recognise it today as it is usually packed with fish-farming cages.

The last permanent inhabitants left in 1931 but from 1938 to 1944, Frank Fraser Darling, the naturalist, farmed on the island and wrote his book *Island Farm*. He believed the name meant 'island of fire' and that Meall Mòr has no peat on it because the Vikings used it as a beacon. There followed another period when the island was uninhabited and then in 1963 the new owners, Summer Isles Estate, restored and let many of the cottages and the schoolhouse as holiday accommodation and provided facilities for boating, sailing and fishing. (All the nine houses have drainage, water, and electricity, some are centrally heated and six are holiday-lets at present). There is now a Summer Isles Post Office – situated in a tea room open when a boatload of tourists arrive – which is officially permitted to issue its own postage stamps. These are most attractive and popular with collectors.

Rock shapes on the coasts of Tanera Mór and Tanera Beg can take on exquisite colours in the changing light. There are two tiny islands in The Anchorage – **Eilean Mór** and **Eilean Beag** – and a drying island, **Eilean na Saille** (G. – salt island), on the north-west coast sheltering **Acairseid Driseach** (G. – anchorage of thorns).

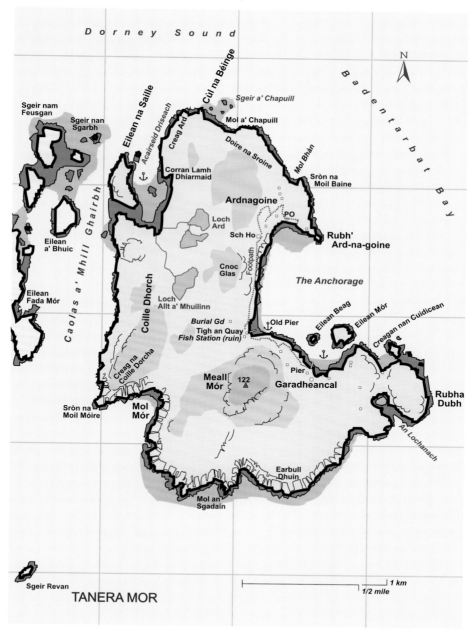

TANERA MOR

'THE CABBAGE PATCH' BEYOND THE ANCHORAGE

Burns feed into this anchorage from three small lochs. In the south-west there is another cove, Mol Mór (G. – the big pebble-beach) while the north extremity of the island is called Cùl na Béinge (G. – the back of the bed-board or bench)

Between the two settlements, **Ardnagoine** and **Garadheancal** (G. – the cabbage-patch or kail-yard), are the remains of the herring fishing station at **Tigh-an-Quay**. The old building is now partly used for fish-farm storage purposes and also houses an electricity generator beside a level area above the quay known as the 'Planestones'.

When Fraser Darling first purchased Tigh-an-Quay the ruin was much more extensive. The northern part of the stone structure was a three-storey building with an attic and slate roof – part of which was still intact. An alleyway had divided this building from the fish factory on the south side but an arcaded wall between the alley and the factory had collapsed in the 1870s leaving an enclosed unroofed area with two gables still standing. He called it the 'Walled Garden', removed much of the rubble, and demolished the top of the gables which were in a dangerous state. He also demolished the roof and upper floor of the residential buiding as the timbers were rotten

and the wind turned the slates into dangerous missiles. He rebuilt some of the lower walls and reconstructed the quay to its original design.

The walled field between Tigh-an-Quay and the hill to the north, **Cnoc Glas** (G. – green knoll), is called 'Little Irish Park' because much of the soil came from Ireland as ships' ballast. The large field west of Tigh-an-Quay is the 'Big Park' with a rocky hillock in it called Cnoc an-t-Sidhe (G. – fairy knoll). Using coral sand from Tanera Beag (lime), and seaweed and boiler slag (potash), Fraser Darling reinstated this field as productive arable land. Clover provided the nitrogen content.

*   *   *

Access: Summer Queen Cruises, Ullapool, 01854-612472. Summer Isle Cruises, Achiltibuie, 01854-622200. Ferry, Achiltibuie, 01854-622272 or Creag Ard Charters, Dundonell, 01854-633 380. Achiltibuie Tourist Information, 01854-622 200.

Anchorages:

1. The Cabbage Patch. Between, and S of, the two small islands on the S side of The Anchorage; best shelter and good holding but cluttered with moorings.

2. The Anchorage. Anchor between fish-cages and old pier in SW corner of bay, or between fish-cages and beach at N of bay.

3. Acairseid Driseach (at NW corner of Tanera Mór). Enter from N and anchor between Eilean na Saille and Tanera Mór, but not further S than mid-island, 4m sand.

6.9 Tanera Beg

(ON hawnar-øy – island of the haven, pasture, G. Beag – little) or (ON taren-øy – the kelp island).

OS Maps: 1:50000 Sheet 15 1:25000 Sheet 439
Admiralty Charts: 1:100000 No.1794 1:25000 No.2501

Area: 66ha (163 acres)
Height: 83m (272 ft)

Owner: (?) Summer Isles Estate.

Population: No Census records and uninhabited.

Geology: Torridonian sandstone, mostly covered with peat, pasture and heather. There is a bank of coral sand and on the shores unusual displays of

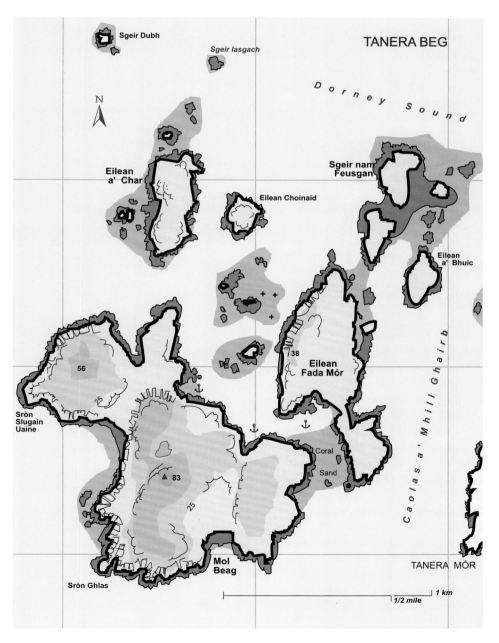

pink coral can be seen at low water. Nearby Eilean
Fada Mor which lies between Tanera Beg and
Tanera Mór has similar coral.

Wildlife: Honeysuckle, irises, dwarf willow and
aspen poplars flourish.

Merganser ducks breed along the water edge
and gulls nest among the pink thrift on the
shoreline rocks Wheatears and pipits frequent the
heathland and many other mainland varieties
thrive.

Seals breed here but not in any great number.

TANERA BEG, or more correctly Tanera Beag,
is separated from Tanera Mór (No.6.8) by a fairly
narrow but easily navigable channel, Caolas a'
Mhill Ghairbh (G. – channel of broken pieces).

Its coastline is very irregular with delightful
little pebble coves sheltered between low cliffs
overhung by green terraces. Beneath the summit
of the central hill (83m) is a tiny pool, the only
one on the island, and from there the heather-
clad slope runs down to a bluff above a shallow
valley with a large cave – Cathedral Cave – at sea
level.

Tanera Beg's main claim to fame must surely
be its bank of fine coral sand – something which
is quite uncommon in this part of the world. It
lies close to the best anchorages in the corner
of the 'lagoon' but it is only visible at low water
[NB972074]. Luckily it was not entirely destroyed
by Fraser Darling (see No.6.8) in his search for
fertiliser.

The anchorages to the north are protected by
several islets and many rocks and skerries. **Eilean
Fada Mór** (G. – big long island) hides little
Eilean a' Bhuic (G. – buck island) behind it and
the larger **Sgeir nam Feusgan** (G. – skerry of the
mussels). And directly north is **Eilean a' Chàr**
(G. – island of seal-flesh) and **Eilean Choinaid**
(G. – rabbit island). **Glas-leac Mór** (G. – big
green slab), a fair-sized islet to the north-west
with heather slopes and a small lochan, is almost
part of the same group.

Tanera Beg is a wonderful island to explore.
Small, but with a twisted coastline which hides
surprises round every corner. Together with the
mass of small islets scattered mainly to the north
it forms an intricate maze with some lovely spots
to anchor in peace and solitude. On our last visit
we sipped sundowners while we watched an otter
family playing and splashing on the shoreline

near us.

* * *

Access: Summer Isles Cruises, Achiltibuie,
01854-622200, or Creag Ard Charters,
Dundonnell, 01854-633380. Achiltibuie Tourist
Information, 01854-622200.

Anchorages:
1. S side of Eilean Fada Mor. Good anchorage in bight,
north of shoal, 4m, sand. Strong tide at springs.
2. Pool SW of Eilean Fada Mor. Anchor in 10m, sand.
3. Inlet in centre of NE side of Tanera Beg, 3m, sand.
Beware reef of drying rocks N of the inlet.

6.10 Handa

(ON hund-øy – dog island) or (ON sand-øy – sand isle).

OS Maps: 1:50000 Sheet 9 1:25000 Sheet 445
Admiralty Charts: 1:100000 No.1785 1:25000 No.2503

Area: 309ha (764 acres)
Height: 123m (403 ft)
Owner: Major and Dr Jean Balfour of Scourie
Estate, the owners, gave the RSPB a twenty-five-
year lease in 1961 to run the island as a nature
reserve. They extended the lease in 1986 for five
years. However in 1991 Dr Balfour did not renew
the lease as she felt that it was appropriate that a
solely Scottish conservation body should run the
island. The Scottish Wildlife Trust now manage
the island, a body which did not exist when the
original lease was signed. Dr Balfour is a founding
member of the Trust and she is also a former
chairman of the Countryside Commission for
Scotland.
Handa is a Site of Special Scientific Interest.

Population: 1841–65 (11 houses). 1851–
onwards, uninhabited. 1991– no permanent
inhabitants but about 5000 visitors each summer.

Geology: An outcrop of Torridonian sandstone
separated by the Sound of Handa from the
mainland of Lewisian gneiss.

History: In early times the island was used as a
burial ground by people on the mainland so that
wolves would be unable to scavenge the corpses.
Later, seven families settled and started cultivating
the rough pastureland. They were self-sufficient,
living on a staple diet of oats, potatoes, fish and
sea-birds. The population grew, they had their

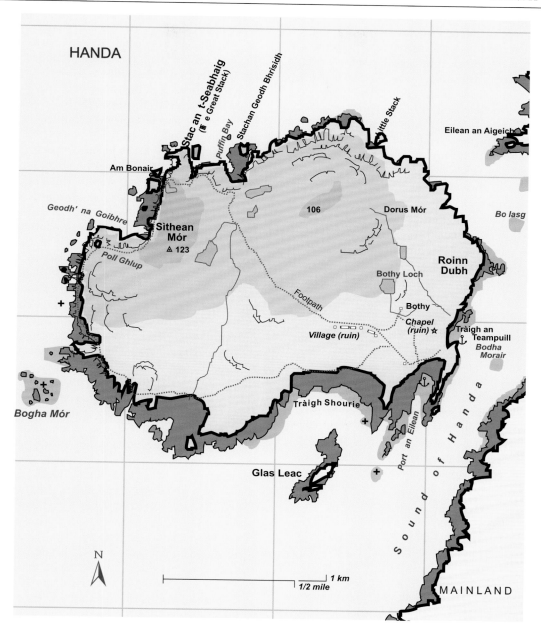

HANDA

Stac an *t-*Seabhaig
(The e Great Stack)
Puffin Bay
Stachan Geodh Bhrisidh
Little Stack
Eilean an Aigeich

Am Bonair

Geodh' na Goibhre

106
Dorus Mór
Bo Iasg

Sìthean
Mór
△ 123

Poll Ghlup

Roinn
Dubh

Bothy Loch

Footpath
Bothy

Chapel
(ruin) ☆
Tràigh an
Teampuill
Bodha
Morair

Village (ruin)

Tràigh Shourie

Port an Eilean

Sound of Handa

Bogha Mór

Glas Leac

N

1 km
1/2 mile

MAINLAND

own 'queen' – the oldest widow – and the men held a daily parliament to decide the allocation of work. It was, in fact, a very similar form of society to that on St Kilda (See No.9.1).

But then in 1848 the potato famine struck and the islanders emigrated to Nova Scotia. Handa has been uninhabited since that time but the old cottages and lazy-beds can still be seen.

Wildlife: Handa is renowned for its birdlife.

Best bird-watching is from early-May to mid-July, by August the cliffs are deserted. Over 170 species have been recorded, with thirty regular breeders. Twelve species of nesting seabirds include large populations of guillemot (120,000 pairs – the largest colony in Britain), razorbill, fulmar and kittiwake. There are also four other gull species, shag, puffin, black guillemot and small numbers of Arctic and great skua.

No raptors breed here at present, but golden eagle, buzzard, peregrine falcon, sparrowhawk and merlin may be seen. White-tailed sea-eagles last nested here in 1864.

Other interesting species include great northern

diver, red- and black-throated diver, eider and shelduck, oystercatcher, ringed plover, common and Arctic tern and rock dove. Inland breeders include snipe, wheatear, stonechat and sometimes, red grouse, golden plover and reed bunting. Migrants include pink-footed and greylag geese, dunlin, greenshank, turnstone, sanderling, whimbrel, Pomarine skua and Manx and sooty shearwater. A few barnacle geese turn up in winter.

Rats had become a serious problem, particularly to the puffin and Manx shearwater populations, but they were eliminated in 1997 by the same method as that used on Ailsa Craig (No.1.1).

216 species of plants have been recorded and more than 100 species of mosses. The only trees are small plantations of lodgepole pine and alder. The island is home to thousands of rabbits.

Whales are fairly frequent visitors in this area and sometimes swim through the Sound.

HANDA is mostly heather, peat-bog and rough pasture on top of a large tilted block of Torridonian sandstone which rears sharply out of the sea to a height of over 100m on the precipitous north and west sides. Here the cliffs are dark-red and brown with horizontal strata sharply outlined in white by sea-bird droppings. In the north-west and close to the cliffs is the higher of the two hills, Sithean Mór [shee-hen moar] (G. – the big fairy-hill). From the top the view stretches almost to Cape Wrath with the tall thin figure of the Old Man of Stoer on the far point of Eddrachillis Bay. Directly north of Sithean Mór the cliffs form an amphitheatre, Am Bonair, with a natural arch [NC130488]. On the east side of this bluff in an inlet or 'geo' and separated by a gap only 24m wide, stands the **Great Stack**, a gigantic rock 115m high and balanced on three legs [NC132488].

The first recorded crossing from the cliff-top on Handa to the flat top of the Stack was in 1876 by Donald MacDonald of Lewis swinging hand-over-hand from a rope. This terrifying narrow chasm has a sheer drop of over 100m down the wet sandstone face to turbulent ocean surf pounding the rocks far below.

In 1967 the original crossing was re-enacted by Dr Tom Patey of Ullapool except that on this occasion the traverse was made by a 180m nylon rope stretched from one side of the geo to the other and lying over the Stack. 'A thought-provoking experience,' he said afterwards.

For a different experience details of the route up the 'very severe' north face can be obtained from the Scottish Mountaineering Club.

Close to the east of the Great Stack is another stack, **Stachan Geodh Bhrisidh** (G. – stack of the broken chasm) in a cove which is usually referred to as Puffin Bay.

The Trust's hut is between **Bothy Loch,** one of Handa's six lochs all of which provide ample water but contain no fish, and the ruined chapel [NC147477] beside **Traigh am Teampull** (G. – temple beach) with its view south over the distant **Badcall Islands** and **Eilean a' Bhuic** off Scourie Bay.

From the landing place by the south-east promontory and **Port an Eilean** (G. – island port) a path runs along the south coast beaches, climbs slowly to the top of the high cliffs, chasms, stacks and natural arches of the west coast, and then turns south-eastwards across the centre of the island, sloping gradually down towards the Sound of Handa – the ocean channel separating Handa from the mainland. The path is partly paved with duckboarding to try to protect the fragile machair from the effect of thousands of pairs of tramping feet each year. A few shells of the old cottages are alongside the pathway before it reaches the burial ground. This has no walled boundary as on St Kilda or Tanera Mór but merely some rough weathered headstones in the grass. This clockwise walk (6km), on an island that combines startling topography with a deep sense of history and an astonishing variety of birdlife, is a 'must'. And a fitting climax is to circumnavigate the island by boat and see the drama on the cliffs from sea-level. Dorus Mór – the big door – is on the north-east side facing the narrow horse-back ridge of **Eilean an Aigeich** (G. – stallion island).

* * *

Access: There is a small charge for visiting. Information or permission to camp from Scottish Wildlife Trust, 01463-714746, or from the warden (resident April–August). Overnight accommodation in a bothy occasionally available. A private ferry operates from Tarbert (unclassified road off A894 2M N of Scourie), S MacLeod, Scouriemore, 01971-502347.

Anchorages:
1. Port an Eilean. Approach from S. Avoid reef of drying

rocks on west side. Good holding in sand, but some swell from S.

2. Traigh an Teampull. Beware Bo Morair in centre of Sound. Anchor off ruined chapel in 3m weed. Beware dragging in strong current.

6.11 Eilean an Roin Mor

(G. – the big part of the island)

Eilean an Roin Beag

(G. – the little part of the island)

OS Maps: 1:50000 Sheet 9 1:25000 Sheet 446
Admiralty Charts: 1:100000 No.1758 1:25000 No. 2503

Area: 45ha (112 acres)
Height: 63m (206 ft)

Owner: This is part of the Sandwood Estate owned by the John Muir Trust.

Population: No census records and uninhabited.

Geology: Undifferentiated Permian or Triassic sandstone.

* * *

EILEAN AN ROIN MOR and **BEAG** (G. – large and small part of the island) are linked together by a narrow gulley and only a very shallow, rocky and narrow channel separates them from the mainland. From the sea they look like a peninsula and as with so many of the islets in this part of the world, they have little vegetation and the rock faces protrude through the surface vegetation in large smooth sensuous shapes, as though sculpted by Henry Moore.

In 1874, the wooden schooner Mercy with a cargo of salt struck the north side of the island and sank and only four years later the wooden schooner Gem, also with a cargo of salt, struck the north side and repeated the disaster.

* * *

Access: Enquire in Kinlochbervie for transport to and from the island.

Anchorages:
The N side is generally foul and the SW corner should

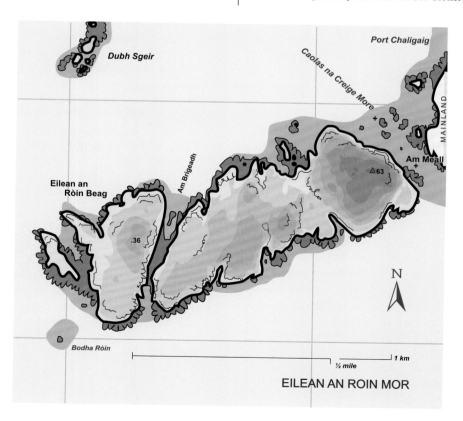

EILEAN AN ROIN MOR

be given a reasonably wide berth. The southern side is cleaner but the bottom falls away steeply. For a longer stay Kinlochbervie has a visitors' pontoon.

1.Temp. anchorage should be possible in quiet weather conditions at the south end of the kyle, Caolas na Creige More, in line with the southern face of the island in 6–7m, sand.

2. It is reported that the south entrance to the cleft between En Mor and En Beag is suitable for a small craft to anchor but the space is very restricted.

6.12 Eilean nan Ron

(G. – island of the seals)

OS Maps: 1:50000 Sheet 10   1:25000 Sheet 447 or 448
Admiralty Charts: 1:200000 No.1954

Area: 138ha (341 acres)
Height: 76m (244 ft)

Owner: Sutherland Estates. (Countess of Sutherland.)

Population:1841 42 (7 houses). 1881–73. 1891–63 (8 houses). 1931–30. Last three families evacuated in December 1938. Uninhabited since.

Geology: Undifferentiated Permian or Triassic sandstone.

Wildlife: This is a Site of Special Scientific Interest (SSSI). Hundreds of grey seals gather here in the autumn to pup and about 350 calves are born annually. It is also a popular wintering ground for barnacle geese.

EILEAN NAN RON was well populated for much of its history but, like so many of the Scottish islands, is now only populated with ghosts. The main island has an abrupt rocky shoreline, an irregular grassy surface and two similar hills in the northern part of almost identical height, **Cnoc an Loisgein** (76m) (G – flaming knoll) and **Cnoc na Caillich** (75m). (G. – hag's knoll). There are steep cliffs on the east side, north of a natural arch at **Leathad Ballach** (G.– spotted slope) and these continue round to the north coast. Here many broken inlets, another rock arch and a cave have been carved out by the sea. **Eilean Iosal** (G. – low or humble island) is a drying islet connected at a narrow channel

on the north-west side. It is steep – just over 50m in height – with a cave, **Uamh nan Ròn** (G. – the seals' cave) on its south side. Beyond lies a smaller islet called Meall Thailm (G. – sling shot) according to the Ordnance Survey, or Meall Holm according to the Admiralty (G. and ON – blob of an islet).

The settlement of houses and ruins is in the waist of the island. The islanders were noted for their self-sufficiency – they even grew their own tobacco. To the west is **Mol Mór** (G. – big pebble beach) and a rock-strewn bay. **Port na h-Innse** (G. – island port) is adjacent with a cave on either side – Night Cave to the north and Day Cave to the south.

The **Rabbit Islands** in Tongue Bay can be seen from here. They are aptly named and worth a visit. A partly sheltered anchorage is off the beach on the south side of the larger island.

Port na h-Uaille (G. – false port), well-named – with a gravel beach and many hidden rocks, and **Mol na Coinnle** (G. – oily-surfaced pebble beach) are east of the old settlement.

The island is separated from the mainland by Caol Raineach. East of it, lying just off the coastline, is **Neave Island** (G. *naomha* – sacred), also known as **Coomb Island**.

West of the Kyle of Tongue **Eilean Hoan** (G. & ON – haven island) and **Eilean Clùimhrig** lie at the mouth of Loch Eriboll. Deep within the loch, **Eilean Choraidh**, otherwise known as Horse Island, was taken to represent the German battleship *Tirpitz* when it was used for target practice by wartime Mosquito bombers. The Census of 1931 recorded a population of one lonely male on Eilean Choraidh and one hopes left before the war began.

*   *   *

Access: No regular access but local boatmen usually arrange visits in the summer months.

Anchorage: Beware below-water rock off NE extremity of island and W coast is foul. E and S sides clean to within ½c. 1. Mol na Coinnle. The most southerly small bight on SE side. Shelter from W and NW winds. Anchor opposite corrugated-iron roofed hut near shore. Beware unchartered rocks on approach. Steps up the steep cliff have disintegrated.

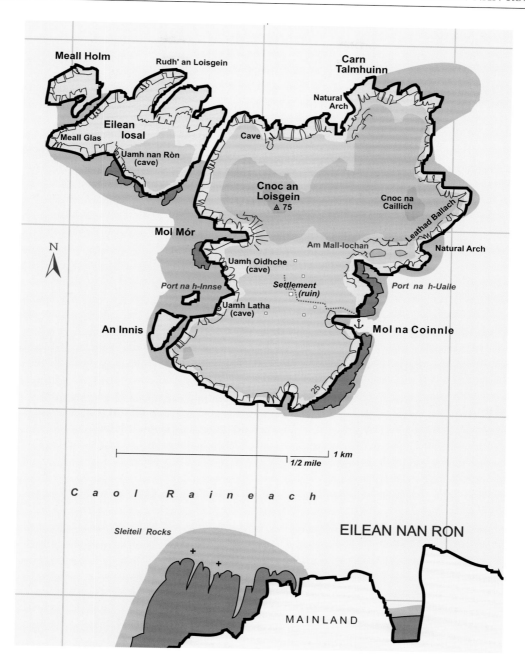

Meall Holm

Rudh' an Loisgein

Carn
Talmhuinn

Natural
Arch

Eilean
Iosal

Cave

Meall Glas

Uamh nan Ròn
(cave)

Cnoc an
Loisgein
△ 75

Cnoc na
Caillich

Leathad Ballach

Mol Mór

Am Mall-lochan

Natural Arch

N

Uamh Oidhche
(cave)

Port na h-Innse

Settlement
(ruin)

Port na h-Uaile

Uamh Latha
(cave)

An Innis

Mol na Coinnle

25

1 km

1/2 mile

C a o l   R a i n e a c h

Sleiteil Rocks

EILEAN NAN RON

MAINLAND

The Outer Hebrides – South of the Sound of Harris

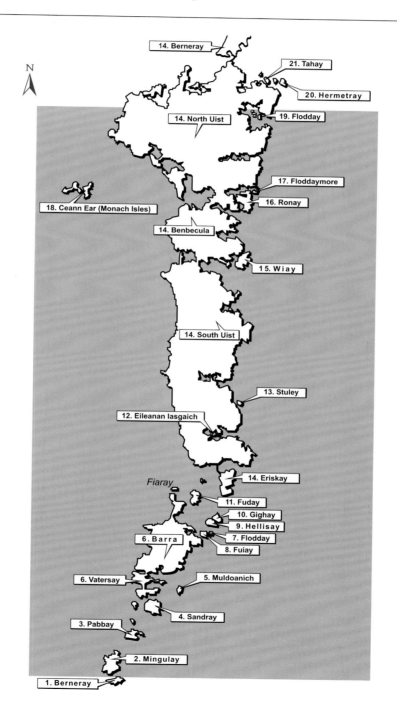

SECTION 7, Table 1: Arranged according to geographic position

No.	Name	Latitude	Longitude	Table 2* No.	Table 3** No.	Area in Acres		Area in Hectares
7.1	Berneray	56° 47N	07° 38W	84	36	504		204
7.2	Mingulay	56° 49N	07° 38W	52	25	1581		640
7.3	Pabbay	56° 51N	07° 35W	76	39	618		250
7.4	Sandray	56° 54N	07° 31W	57	33	951		385
7.5	Muldoanich	56° 55N	07° 26W	122	44	193		78
7.6	Barra	56° 59N	07° 28W	16	17	14517	5875	
	Vatersay	56° 56N	07° 32W			2372	960	6835
7.7	Flodday (E Barra)	56° 60N	07° 21W	167	131	99		40
7.8	Fuiay	56° 60N	07° 22W	119	62	208		84
7.9	Hellisay	57° 01N	07° 21W	96	85	351		142
7.10	Gighay	57° 01N	07° 20W	113	74	237		96
7.11	Fuday	57° 03N	07° 23W	79	78	573		232
7.12	Eileanan Iasgaich	57° 09N	07° 19W	148	162	124		50
7.13	Stuley	57° 12N	07° 15W	158	135	111		45
7.14	South Uist	57° 17N	07° 20W	4	6	79136	32026	
	North Uist	57° 36N	07° 19W			74884	30305	
	Benbecula	57° 27N	07° 19W			20270	8203	
	Berneray	57° 43N	07° 11W			2496	1010	
	Baleshare	57° 32N	07° 23W			2249	910	
	Grimsay	57° 29N	07° 14W			2058	833	
	Eriskay	57° 05N	07° 17W			1737	703	
	Vallay	57° 40N	07° 25W			642	260	
	Kirkibost Island	57° 33N	07° 25W			507	205	
	Oronsay	57° 40N	07° 18W			210	85	74540
7.15	Wiay	57° 24N	07° 12W	58	66	927		375
7.16	Ronay	57° 29N	07° 11W	53	58	1391		563
7.17	Floddaymore	57° 30N	07° 09W	141	157	143		58
7.18	Ceann Ear (Monach Isles)	57° 31N	07° 37W	61	165	502	203	
	Ceann Iar	57° 31N	07° 39W			381	154	357
7.19	Floddy (Loch Maddy)	57° 36N	07° 07W	166	161	104	42	
7.20	Hermetray	57° 39N	07° 03W	129	143	178		72
7.21	Tahay	57° 40N	07° 06W	146	99	131		53
7.A	Fiaray	57° 04N	07° 26W	–	–	96		39

*Table 2: The islands arranged in order of magnitude   ** Table 3: The islands arranged in order of height

Introduction

Like Australia's Great Barrier Reef the chain of Outer Hebridean islands parallels and protects the mainland coast from ocean storms. The side facing the Atlantic is an almost continuous strand of sand-dunes and machair while the east coast is savagely indented and irregular with sea-lochs which disintegrate into a maze of inlets between reefs and tidal islets. For the yachtsman, all these lochs and sounds are a wonderland and there are anchorages to suit most conditions.

The beautiful but shallow Sound of Barra is a Special Area of Conservation (SAC) because of its fragile marine habitats.

Loch Eynort, near the centre of South Uist, presents a navigational challenge where the wide outer loch suddenly channels through the dog-leg of Sruthan Beag (G. – little tidal streamlet). The tide tumbles through at seven knots with eddies and overfalls but with care it is possible to sneak through at slack water. Once through, the islet **Risgay** and a rocky patch are straight ahead, and to left and right there are many bays and secret inlets in which to anchor (some free of fish cages!).

Although few fish-farms are locally owned there is no doubt that fish-farming has brought limited, but welcome, employment to Scottish islands. Yachtsmen are aware of this and have accepted that some of the finest and safest anchorages are now filled with fish-cages. Their only plea is that when fish-farming ceases the cages should be removed completely. Some cages are being abandoned and left to disintegrate on the sea bottom, thus creating a hazard and effectively denying use of that anchorage for a century or more.

At the north end of South Uist where it meets Benbecula the land shatters into fragments. **Corr-eileanan, Eilean an Fhraoich Mia, Glas-eileanan, Eilean a' Bhogha, Glas-eilean na Creige, Eilean a' Mhadaidh** (G. – dog isle) and **Gasay** (G. – swept isle) are only some of the many islets and skerries in the area.

The east shore of Benbecula continues this broken landscape. North of the island of Wiay (No.7.15). **Greanamul Deas** (G. – south Greanamul) and **Greanamul** (ON – green hump) itself act as eastern markers. **Maaey Riabhach** (ON & G. – grizzled seagull island), **Maragay Mór** (G. – big pudding isle) and **Maragay Beag** stand guard at each side of Loch Uiskevagh. **Bearran** islet is in the centre of the loch.

In the channel between Benbecula and Grimsay two islets **Calavay** and **Eilean Leathan** are linked by a long tidal strand.

Loch Eport, in North Uist, is another lengthy sea-loch. Shallow Loch Langass which connects with it near the head can be explored for miles by dinghy or kayak and is an alternative route to see the chambered cairn on Ben Langass. Most of the islets in Loch Eport are tidal except possibly **Treanay** at Bay Sponish and **Eilean nam Mult** (G. – island of the castrated rams) in the centre of the loch.

7.1 Berneray

(ON – Bjorn's island.) As the southernmost island of the Outer Hebrides Berneray is often referred to as Barra Head.

OS Maps: 1:50000 Sheet 31 1:25000 Sheet 452
Admiralty Charts: 1:100000 No.1796 1:30000 No.2769

Area: 204ha (504 acres)
Height: 193m (633ft)

Owner: National Trust for Scotland. Acquired in April 2000 from the Barrahead Isles Sheep Stock Co., a syndicate of Barra crofters and owners since 1955. The price for archipeligo was said to be just under £500,000.

Population: In the 18th century the population was over fifty. 1841–30. 1881–56. 1891–36 (9 houses). From 1910 the three lighthouse-keepers and their wives were the only occupants of the island until the lighthouse was automated in the late 1970s.

Geology: The granite to build the island's own (Barra Head) lighthouse in 1833 was quarried on the island. Most of Berneray consists of gneiss.

History: In 1992, sponsored by Historic Scotland, Berneray was surveyed by archaeologists from Sheffield University and Prague and eighty-three sites and monuments were noted and recorded. Less than forty were thought to be of post-medieval date.

Wildlife: Designated a Site of Special Scientific Interest in 1993 and a special bird protection area, in early May the hillside is a riot of colour with primroses, celandine, wild violets and yellow flag iris.

Grey seals frequent the cove by the landing place and the island supports 15 species of sea-bird including large numbers of kittiwake, guillemot, auk and some puffins.

Martin Martin (1695) recorded that Berneray 'excels other islands of the same extent for cultivation and fishing. The natives never go a-fishing while Macneil or his steward is in the island, lest seeing their plenty of fish, perhaps they might take occasion to raise their rents.'

In 2009 the National Trust decided to have the remaining Cheviot-cross-Blackface sheep on the island removed as their maintenance was too difficult. They were taken to Canna (No. 4.4).

* * *

BARRA HEAD LIGHTHOUSE – OVER 200M ABOVE THE SEA

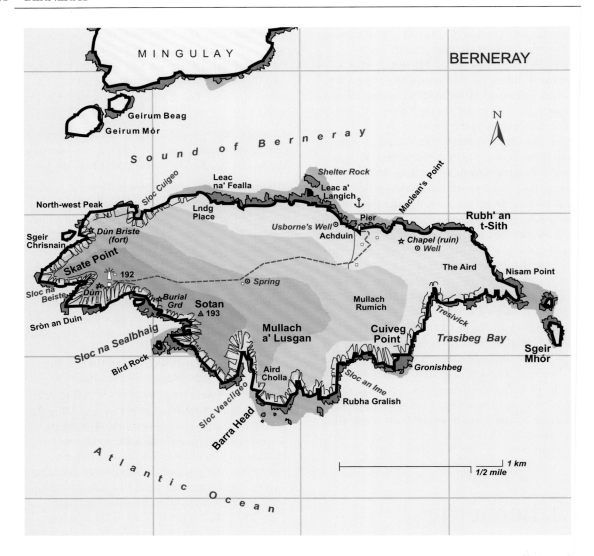

BERNERAY has a wedge-shaped appearance when approaching from the north-east or south-west. The south coast consists of rugged cliffs which have a least height of about 40m at the east end. Barra Head lighthouse is a white stone tower on top of **Sròn an Dùin** (G. – fortress promontory) above the western cliffs.

This is the most southerly point of the Outer Hebrides. The magnificent cliffs of 190m height (623ft) on the west side at Skate Point take the full force of gigantic seas because there is no shallow water to impede them. Small fish are often found in the grass at the top of the high cliffs after severe gales. Even if one might suspect that sea gulls dropped them the lighthouse-keepers said that this was not so and as proof of the ferocity of the gales it was reliably reported in

1836 that a forty-two ton rock was moved almost two metres during a violent storm (five feet).

A vehicle track climbs up the hill from the landing place to the lighthouse at the summit. A 'chalybeate spring' (water with traces of iron in it) is about halfway up, at the side of the track, with a pumphouse to provide water for the lighthouse. A helicopter pad near the top allows maintenance teams to service the lighthouse now that it is automatic.

Two duns or fortified mounds are situated near the summit of the island. One is called **Dùn Briste** (G. – the broken fort) [NL549805]. Unfortunately, the other one, a galleried dun of the Iron Age, was largely destroyed when the lighthouse was constructed. This will be the fort that Martin noted – 'having a vacuity round the walls, divided in little apartments'. A gateway now leads through the ancient wall from the lighthouse yard onto a cliff-top area completely surrounded by a natural parapet of stone slabs and boulders. From here the cliff drops vertically to the surging waves 200m below. Alongside, there is a great chasm – **Sloc na Beiste** (G. – ravine of the monster) – 100m long by 200m deep leading to a cave, but exploration would require considerable expertise in mountaineering. The roar of the sea breaking into the chasm far below forms a bass chorus to the cries of thousands of sea-birds wheeling past the cliffs.

Apart from the site of a chapel (near the landing place) [NL567803], Berneray has five cists, five suspected burial cairns and four megalithic chamber tombs so the island appears to have been well occupied in the Neolithic/ Bronze Age, possibly less intensively settled in the Iron Age but followed by renewed activity in the Christian and medieval period.

Fresh water can be scarce, and in dry summers the islanders had to ship water over from Mingulay.

* * *

Access: Barra Fishing Charters, 01871-890384. Island Adventures, Castlebay, 01871-810284. Tourist Information, Castlebay, Barra, 01871-810336.

Anchorage: Landing on the slippery jetty from an inflatable dinghy can be difficult and potentially dangerous due to the swell.
1. On N side, except in heavy seas, anchor off the concrete jetty and storehouse, 7–8m, good firm sand. This is out of the tidal stream and sheltered from S through W to NW. Very heavy squalls sometimes during S and SW gales and very exposed to the E.

7.2 Mingulay

(ON mikil-øy – big island).

O S Maps: 1:50000 Sheet 31 1:25000 Sheet 452
Admiralty Charts: 1:100000 No.1796 1:30000 No.2769

Area: 640ha (1581 acres)
Height: 273m (895 ft)

Owner: National Trust for Scotland. Acquired in April 2000 from the Barrahead Isles Sheep Stock

Club, a syndicate of Barra crofters and owners since 1955.
Population: 1841–113 (18 houses). 1881–150. 1891–142 (29 houses). 1901–135. In 1908 many of the islanders claimed land on neighbouring islands, some becoming known as the Vatersay Raiders (See No.7.6) and after this the remaining population dwindled rapidly. The last inhabitants left in 1912.

Geology: Almost entirely of gneiss but with some granite.

History: Mingulay must have been first settled long ago as the island has several potential archaeological sites. Crois an t-Suidheachain (G. – cross of the sitting-place), was a structure on a level area of ground above the road at Aneir. Nothing remains but it has been variously described as a standing stone, a stone circle, or a group of three 'cells or chests'. There may be some Viking graves but the record of Viking influence is in the topographical names such as Hecla, Skipisdale and, for that matter, Mingulay.

When the MacNeils of Barra owned Mingulay they took a paternal interest in their tenants, arranging new husbands and wives for widows and widowers, helping to feed the children, or making good the loss of a milking cow. The community thrived. The laird's annual rent was mainly *fachaich* – shearwater chicks collected from the precipices. As on St Kilda, life here depended on the sea-birds, although fishing also played its part. The famous 'Mingulay Boat Song' was never sung on Mingulay. It is a West Highland air with words written in 1938 by Hugh Roberton for his famous Glasgow Orpheus Choir to sing.

Wildlife: Sorrel and wild celery grow on the hillsides and nettles frame the village ruins. This is a place of annual pilgrimage for ornithologists as it is a principal breeding station for guillemot and kittiwake. A boat trip around the awe-inspiring western cliffs, virtually inaccessible and covered with sea-birds, is an unforgettable experience. A really close approach is difficult except on the rare days of calm water. In the breeding season the granite stacks and very high cliffs are festooned with nesting kittiwakes, razorbills and guillemots and there are also large colonies of puffins and black-backed gulls.

Mingulay was designated a Site of Special

Scientific Interest in 1993 and a European bird protection area.

* * *

The islands south of Barra and Vatersay used to be known as the Bishop's Isles and **MINGULAY** is the largest of the group. It is almost an in-shore Hirta (No.9.1) with its St Kilda-like stacks, its towering cliffs and even its village bay. It shows several rounded summits when viewed from the sea, **Carnan** the highest at 273m, **Hecla** (219m) (ON – hooded shroud) close south-west of it and **Macphee's Hill** (224m) in the north. Between them is **Tom a' Mhaide** (G. – hillock of the stick), a smaller peak of over 150m. The west coast has precipitous cliffs but the south and east coasts slope gradually down to a rugged foreshore.

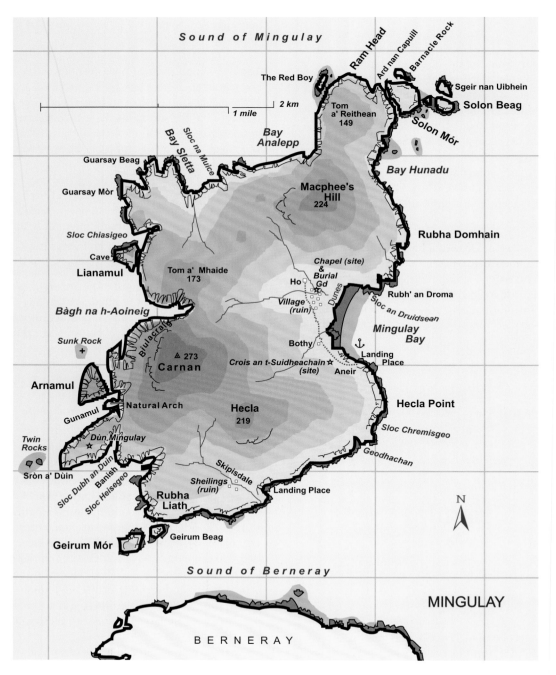

THE CHAPEL HOUSE AND MACPHEE'S HILL

Mingulay Bay (or Village Bay) is centrally situated on the east coast with a half kilometre of sandy beach and the extensive remains of the deserted village above it.

The **Schoolhouse** [NL568825], at the south end by the track to the landing place, was built in 1881 for the sum of £494. It replaced the traditional thatched structure established by the Free Church Ladies' Association in 1859. The building was used as a bothy and sheep-fank since sheep-farming took over in 1912 and was reroofed with corrugated iron in 1986 to allow the shepherds to use it on their annual visits. The Catholic priest's house, at the north end beyond the ruined village, was built in 1898. With a chapel on the upper floor [NL564834] it was known as the **Chapel House** but it collapsed in late 1996.

One island story relates how, in the time of MacNeil of Barra's ownership, a rent collector, Macphee, was landed on the island and found everyone dead. He rushed back to the boat and called to the men to take him off quickly as there was 'plague' on the island. On hearing this the men rowed away and left him to his fate. For a whole year he had only the corpses for company. Every day he would climb the hill to the north of the village and signal frantically to passing

ships but they would wave back and pass on. He survived and eventually MacNeil decided it was safe to have the island resettled. He made a special grant of land to Macphee by way of compensation and since then the hill has always been known as Macphee's Hill.

This north part of the island has an additional promontory with a small hill on it called **Tom a' Reithean** (G. – hillock of the ram). It has a number of large detached rocks and islets clustered round it including the remarkable stack, **Red Boy**, on the north-west side and on the opposite side, **Solon Mór** (G. – big gannet) which is almost detached by a deep cleft. The Big Gannet has a fledgling called **Solon Beag**.

The sea-cliffs on the west side towering up to 215m in height are among the most dramatic in the British Isles and have many fantastic rock formations. The greatest sheer drop is at **Biulacraig**, below Carnan. ('Biulacraig' is the MacNeils of Barra' war-cry). There are large colonies of seabirds on the treacherous cliffs and the islanders used to scale them to collect the eggs and young birds.

Normally these great rock-faces can only be seen clearly from the sea but an interesting and not too demanding walk westwards up the valley from the derelict village arrives at a point above **Bàgh na h-Aoineig** (G. – bay of the steep promontory), a gigantic cleft cutting deep into the island. From here it is possible to look across the cleft towards Carnan and see the utterly breath-taking height of the precipice rising straight out of the sea and soaring towards the sky. Near the top it leans further and further out in a great rock cornice which looks as though it might overbalance at any moment. Every little horizontal crack, ledge and crevice is stippled white – each insignificant dot another nesting bird.

Sheep were grazed on the grassy tops of the two famous stacks, **Arnamul** (ON – erne mound) and **Lianamul** (ON – flax mound), which stand close to the cliffs on either side of Bàgh na h-Aoineig. For many years Lianamul, which has a sea-cave, was reached by a rope bridge spanning the chasm but this had disappeared by 1871. Before the bridge was constructed the *Statistical Account* of 1794 described how the people would climb to the top of Lianamul 'at the risk of their lives, and by means of a rope carry up their wedders to fatten'.

A huge natural arch at **Gunamul** is on the southern side of Arnamul where the cliffs are over 150m in height [NL547824]. It is possible to sail a small boat through it on the rare occasions when conditions are suitable. South again there is an island-like promontory called **Dùn Mingulay** [NL545821], which was the site of an Iron Age fort.

Two rocky islets, **Geirum Mór** and **Geirum Beag** break into the Sound of Berneray and further east a burn runs down the south side of Hecla through **Skipisdale** (ON – ship valley) and discharges into the sound. This is sometimes the best spot to land from a dinghy and it was so used by the people of nearby Berneray when collecting water in times of drought.

*   *   *

Access: Barra Fishing Charters, 01871-890384. Island Adventures, Castlebay, 01871-810284. Tourist Information, Castlebay, Barra, 01871-810336.

Anchorages:

1. Mingulay Bay. Occasional anchorage off middle of beach, sheltered from W and NW winds. There is usually a considerable swell which can make landing – and leaving! – difficult. Usually easier to land at rocks at Aneir – S end of beach.
2. Skipisdale. Occasional landing place but no anchorage.

7.3 Pabbay

(ON papa-øy – priest or hermit island)

OS Maps: 1:50000 Sheet 31 1:25000 Sheet 452
Admiralty Charts: 1:100000 No.1796 1:30000 No.2769

Area: 250ha (618 acres)
Height: 171m (561 ft)

Owner: National Trust for Scotland. Acquired in April 2000 from the Barrahead Isles Sheep Stock Club, a syndicate of Barra crofters and owners since 1955.

Population: 1764–16. 1794– three farming families, about 20 people altogether. 1841–25 (3 houses). 1881–16. 1891–13 (3 houses). 1901–11. 1911–5. Uninhabited since.

Geology: The shell-sand is extremely rich in lime and frequent rains have broken this down to produce beds of impure limestone. Otherwise the island mainly consists of gneiss.

History: In early Christian times Pabbay, as its name would infer, had a hermitage or cell located on it and there is an ancient symbol stone and cross slabs on the slope above Bàgh Bàn.

Martin Martin wrote in the early 18th century: 'the natives observe that if six sheep are put a-grazing in the little island of Pabbay, five of them still appear fat, but the sixth a poor skeleton, but any number in this island not exceeding five are always very fat.' This possibly refers to Lingay (N of Pabbay). Martin's map shows Pabbay and Mingulay interchanged. Today, Pabbay supports about 100 breeding ewes.

On 1 May 1897 every able-bodied man was lost in a fierce storm at sea while out fishing. The Mingulay boat survived the same storm. The island never fully recovered from this disaster and the population dwindled. Within fifteen years no one remained.

Wildlife: Heather is scarce, possibly due to the areas of alkaline soil but the rough grazing is full of daisies and celandine, and sundew and flag irises grow in the damper areas.

There are many rabbits and ground-nesting seabirds. Cliff-nesters are almost absent.

*   *   *

PABBAY is another member of the Bishop's Isles (recently called the 'Barrahead Isles') and another 'Priest's Isle'.

The summit, **The Hoe**, rises to a height of 171m at the south-west extremity where there are steep sea-cliffs and a massive arched overhang. The settlement which reached a peak population of twenty-six in 1881 was on the eastern side above the blinding-white shell-sand beach in **Bàgh Bàn** (G. – white bay). A cottage still stands on the small central promontory of Sumula. Between Bàgh Bàn and the ruined settlement is an artificial-looking mound about 5m high. The mound may be a burial ground as human bones have been uncovered by the drifting sands. Three cross-marked stones may be gravestones and a fourth marked with a crescent, a cross and a lily is probably Pictish as it is of a design quite different in style to the interlacing Celtic patterns usually found in the Outer Hebrides [NL607874]. Visible traces of an ancient

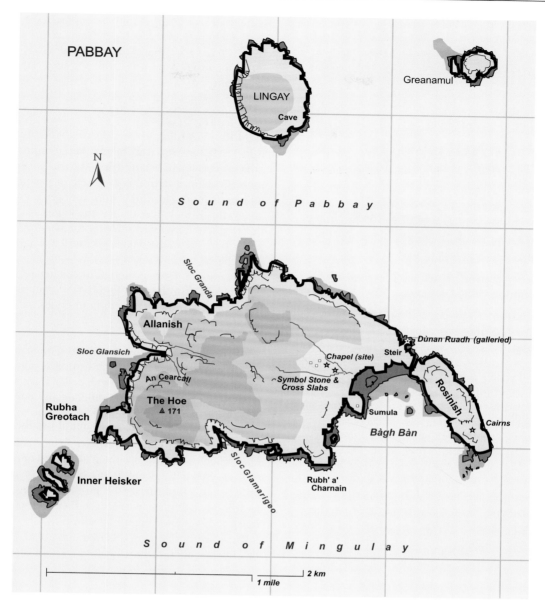

chapel were reported in 1915 beside the nearby rivulet.

Sloc Glansich, said to be named after an Irishman called Glancy, is a steep cleft which concealed the local centre for illicit whisky distillation.

The **Rosinish** peninsula, really a drying island, forms the east side of Bàgh Bàn and rises to 43m where it juts into the waters of the Minch. Near the junction – a narrow cleft – is **Dùnan Ruadh** (G. – the red fort) [NL613876], a ruined galleried broch which looks across the Sound of Pabbay to its opposite number on Sandray (No.7.4).

Dark, narrow vertical fissures intersect the cliffs on the south-west coast by The Hoe where they tower over the islets of Inner and Outer Heisker. These lie in the Sound of Mingulay. To the north is the Sound of Pabbay with the small hump of **Greanamul** (ON – green mound) in it and the larger island of **Lingay** (ON – heather isle). Lingay is steep but is occasionally used for grazing sheep. It has a cave in its south-east side.

Access: Barra Fishing Charters, 01871-890384. Island Adventures, Castlebay, 01871-810284. Tourist Information, Castlebay, Barra, 01871-810336.

Anchorage: There is no recommended anchorage.
1. Bàgh Bàn is mainly rocky but there is a 4.1m charted sounding off the small headland called Sumula which is sand and affords temp. anchorage in calm conditions. Approach with caution.

7.4 Sandray

(ON sandr-øy – sand island). Old charts have it as Soundray, Sanderay or Sandera.

O S Maps: 1:50000 Sheet 31 1:25000 Sheet 452
Admiralty Charts: 1:100000 No.1769 1:30000 No.2769

Area: 385ha (951 acres)
Height: 207m (679 ft)

Owner: Government owned (Department of Agriculture).

Population: 1835–population cleared for sheep. 1841–14 (2 houses occupied by shepherds' families). 1861–9. 1881–10. 1891–4. 1901–3 shepherds. Temporary influx of evicted people from Mingulay in 1908. 1911–0. Uninhabited since.

Geology: Mainly gneiss bedrock.

History: Neolithic settlements and tombs were identified by Sheffield University archaeologists in 1991. The Iron Age dun which is still some 2m in height is prominent above a steep ridge on the west side of Cairn Galtar [NL638913] facing Dùnan Ruadh on Pabbay. The ruin of another dun was reported on the east coast, and various Iron Age dwellings.

Faint traces of the old chapel site, Cille Bhride (G. – Bride's or Bridget's cell) were reported in 1915 to be partly covered by a sheep dip [NL650918]. The chapel served the nine crofts into which the island was divided in the early 18th century.

The *SS Fair Branch* from Sunderland was wrecked on Sandray in 1882.

Wildlife: According to Dean Monro, who visited it in 1549, Sandray was 'inhabit and manurit, guid for corne and fishing', and Martin Martin in 1695 claimed that 'it is designed for pasturage and cultivation... fruitful in corn and grass'. Today, this is no longer true as the landscape is deserted and fairly barren but in the windbeaten grass there are many wildflowers and a profusion of orchids.

There are no trees, although hazels have been recorded in the past, and the commonest mammals on Sandray are, without doubt, rabbits.

* * *

SANDRAY is a fairly circular island with a central peak, **Cairn Galtar** (207m). A lesser hill to the east of Cairn Galtar is called Carnach (179m) (G. – heap of stones) and, again, to the east of Carnach there is a huge sand-dune 52m high. This has always been a well-known sea-mark as it clearly identifies Sandray's east coast. MacCulloch said: 'At a distance the island appears as if covered with a coating of snow.' My own impression is that the sand is possibly no longer as striking as it once was. Maybe there is more marram grass covering it nowadays.

The grazing rights on this island are held by an association of Barra crofters. There is a

SANDRAY FROM THE SOUTH-EAST

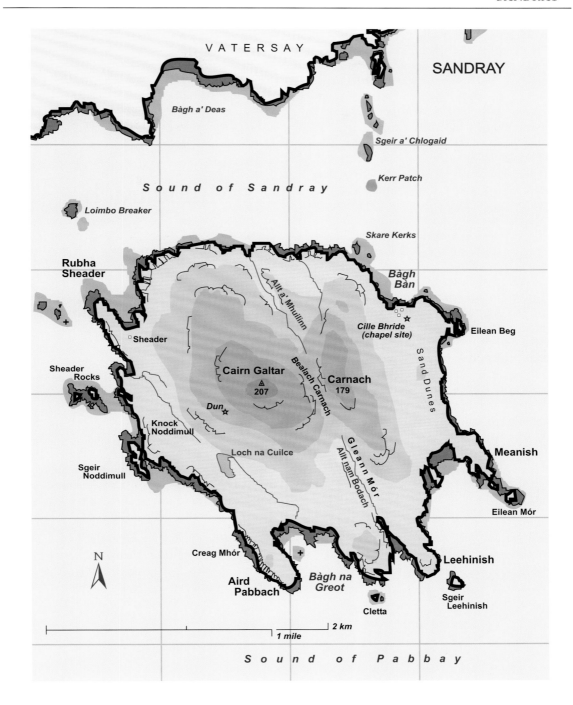

reasonable supply of fresh water from two good streams, one in the big glen, Gleann-Mór, and one flowing from a small loch, **Loch na Cuilce** (G. – loch of the reeds). Large, relatively flat rock plates make walking on parts of this island a pleasure.

A Gaelic tale recorded in Barra in 1859 told how the wife of a herdsman on Sandray had her kettle borrowed every day by a woman of peace (a fairy). Before she would let go the kettle the wife would say: 'A smith is able to make cold iron hot with coal. The due of a kettle is bones, so bring it back again whole.' The kettle was returned every day with fresh meat and soup bones in it.

One day, as the wife was leaving by boat to visit Castlebay on Barra, she warned her husband to say the same words when the fairy came to borrow the kettle. But when the woman of peace came to the door the husband took fright and refused to open it. Then the kettle started jumping and it jumped right through the smoke hole in the roof. When the housewife returned the husband confessed that he had lost the kettle.

So the housewife went to the fairy hill and found her kettle there with flesh and bones in it. She had just picked it up when two vicious fairy dogs started chasing her. She held them at bay by throwing them the contents of the kettle and managed to reach her home unharmed. But the fairy never returned to borrow the kettle.

This story is a fairly typical fireside tale. According to tradition fairies always feared iron and it is of course particularly mentioned in the wife's rhyme. Some scholars suppose that these fairy stories originated in the time when the new Iron Age immigrants met the wild and shy Neolithic settlers.

About one nautical mile west of Sandray the interesting little island of **Flodday** is 43m high, with black cliffs on its west coast and a natural rock arch in the centre. This is a small, but popular, grey seal nursery. There is no shelter whatsoever and the island is constantly windswept by Atlantic gales yet, remarkably, Flodday has its own unique subspecies of butterfly – a tiny pale-coloured form of the dark green fritillary *Argynnis aglaia scotica*.

* * *

Access: Barra Fishing Charters, 01871-890384. Island Adventures, Castlebay, 01871-810284. Tourist Information, Castlebay, Barra, 01871-810336.

Anchorages: There are no recommended anchorages but, proceeding cautiously, temp. anchorage in suitable conditions is possible at the following locations:
1. Small bay directly SW of Meanish. Occasional anchorage off centre of sandy beach in 4–5m, sand. Subject to swell.
2. Wide bay in E between Meanish and Eilean Beg. Temp. anchorage in 7–8m, sand. Avoid N end of bay. Subject to swell.

7.5 Muldoanich

(G. – Duncan's mound) or (G. maol Domhnach – Sunday mound.) Dean Munro in 1549 seems to refer to it as Scarp and it is Scarpa on Blaeu's 1654 map (ON scarfr – cormorant) – island, or (ON – sharp, stony, hilly terrain) but in 1695 Martin Martin called it 'Muldonish'.

O S Maps: 1:50000 Sheet 31 1:25000 Sheet 452
Admiralty Charts: 1:100000 No.1796 1:30000 No.2769

Area: 78ha (193 acres)
Height: 153m (502 ft)

Owners: Donald and Archibald MacLean of Castle bay.

Population: No Census records and has possibly never been inhabited but, nevertheless, there are several structures on the island.

Geology: Lewisian gneiss with an amphibole block of softer Scourian gneiss in the north east. A navigable sea tunnel of about 300 metres in length crosses the island under the E-W fault line.

History: The island was part of the domain of the MacNeils of Barra. Dean Monro claimed in 1549 that 'Scarp' once had a chapel on it and that it was 'full of pastures and very guid for fishing'.

Haswell-Smith

MULDOANICH FROM THE SOUTH-EAST

Wildlife: Botanists have found the rare pyramidal bulge growing on Muldoanich and there are wildflowers such as Foula eyebright, red campion and honeysuckle. In 1695 Martin Martin said that, 'Muldoanich is high in the middle, covered over with heath and grass, and is the only forest here for maintaining the deer, being commonly about seventy or eighty in number'. (A deer forest, of course, does not require trees.) I presume in Dean Munro's time it was cattle that were pastured on the island but that MacNeil of Barra had stocked it with deer to provide his family with a regular source of venison. The deer were there for about 150 years and Muldoanich was often, consequently, called Deer Island.

This was a nesting place for the sea-eagle before it was exterminated in the early 20th century.

* * *

This distinctive dark hump of an island lies two miles east of Vatersay and clearly marks the entrance to Castlebay on Barra.

It was MacCulloch who suggested that the name **MULDOANICH** came from St Duncan. The chapel, if it ever existed, may have been dedicated to this important saint but MacCulloch's idea is generally considered to be incorrect.

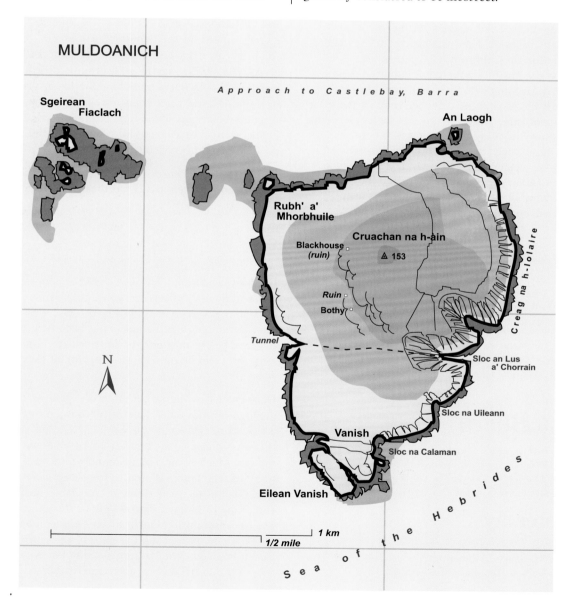

MULDOANICH

Sgeirean
Fiaclach

Approach to Castlebay, Barra

An Laogh

Rubh' a'
Mhorbhuile

Blackhouse
(ruin)

Cruachan na h-àin

△ 153

Creag na h-Iolaire

Ruin

Bothy

Tunnel

Sloc an Lus
a' Chorrain

Sloc na Uileann

Vanish

Sloc na Calaman

N

Eilean Vanish

Sea of the Hebrides

1 km

1/2 mile

Muldoanich has no level ground and rises fairly steeply on all sides to a central rounded summit of 153m – **Cruachan na h-àin** (G. – midday hill). A small blackhouse ruin is, improbably, reputed to have been a jail [NL687940]. There is a ruined structure to the south with a rounded corbelled wall of uncertain purpose [NL687938] and to the south-east of this is a two-roomed bothy. The east side, near the summit of the island, has the highest cliffs with two deep clefts defining **Creag na h-Iolaire** (G. – eagle crag). This probably referred to the once-common white-tailed sea-eagle. The rudimentary inlets on this coast are **Sloc an Lus a' Chorrain** (G. – spleenwort hole), **Sloc na Uilean** [oylun] (G. – honeysuckle hole) where a tunnel, navigable by dinghy or kayak, leads right through the island, and **Sloc na Calaman** (G. – pigeon hole).

On the north side there is a detached rock called **An Laogh** (G. – the calf) and on the north-west is another detached rock off **Rubh' a' Mhorbhuile.** This is assumed to be a misspelling of Miorbhuil (G. – miracle point).

The southern headland is called **Vanish** [vay-neesh] (ON – headland of the sacred place). The Old Norse 've' may be related to the Socts word 'rey'. Taransay (No. 8.9) has similarly named, but much larger promontory.

* * *

Access: Barra Fishing Charters, 01871-890384. Island Adventures, Castlebay, 01871-810284. Tourist Information, Castlebay, Barra, 01871-810336.

Anchorage: No recommended anchorages.
1. Temp. anchorage is possible in suitable conditions NE of Rubh' a' Mhorbhuile but beware foul ground north and west of this headland.

7.6 Barra

(ON Barr-øy – Barr's island). Barr was a 6th-century saint (G. Finbar – St Barr). He was an Irish missionary and disciple of St Columba who is reputed to have been sent to Barra because his predecessor had been eaten by the inhabitants.

Vatersay

Probably (ON – fathers' island), priest island. (ON vottr-øy – glove island), from the finger-shaped peninsulas? or (ON vatr-øy – wavy island), have also been suggested.

O S Maps: 1:50000 Sheet 31 1:25000 Sheet 452
Admiralty Charts: 1:100000 No.1796 1:30000 Nos 2769 and 2770

Area: 6,835ha (16,889 acres)
Height: 383m (1,256 ft)

Owner: About 9000 acres of Barra were owned by the 46th Chief of Clan MacNeil and the 26th MacNeil of Barra – Ian MacNeil, a renowned American law professor of Northwestern University, Chicago. In 2003 he gifted nearly all the land, including fishing and mineral rights and Kisimul Castle, to the Scottish Government for an annual rent of £1 and a bottle of Talisker malt whisky to be managed until the community wished to take over. The Scottish Government already owned the crofts in the north of the island so this made a total holding of some 440 crofts. The MacNeil family will continue their long association with Barra and Clan MacNeil by visits to Kisimul Castle, their home at Garrygall, and meeting their many friends and acquaintances.

The Scottish Office owns Vatersay which the Scottish Board of Agriculture bought in 1909 for £6250.

Population: Barra only: 1755–1150. 1794–1604.

	1841	1891	1931	1961	1991	2001	2011
Barra	1977	2131	2001	1369	1244	1078	1174
V'say	84	32	240	95	72	94	90
	2061	2163	2241	1464	1316	1172	1264

Geology: The island, of heavily glaciated gneiss, has a rocky and broken east coast and fine, sandy bays on the west coast backed by machair. East of the central fault line the gneiss has been sheared to give a belt of mylonite, or flinty crush. A mile–long coral reef lies at a depth of 100m off Barra's coast.

History: Following the centuries of Norse domination Alexander, Lord of the Isles, granted a charter to Gilleonan MacNeil in 1427, and this was confirmed by James IV in 1495. Some say that MacNeil ownership actually goes back to 1030. The family is reputed to be descended from Niall of the Nine Hostages, the 4th-century High King of Ireland. By the 16th century the MacNeils were using Castlebay on the island as a pirate base for raids on the ships of the English Queen Elizabeth. MacNeil explained to James VI (James I) that his actions were merely because

BARRA

Sound of Fiaray

Scurrival
Point

Sound of Fuday

FUDAY

Dùn Scurrival

Eoligarry

Jetty

Cille-bharra

Oitir
Mhór

Dunes

Orosay

Greanamul

Dùn Chlif

Tràigh Mhór

Airfield

Ferry

Atlantic Ocean

N

Greian
Head

Cleat

Grean

Ben
Erival

Pier

North
Bay

Fuiay

Dùn Cuier

Loch
an Dùin

Bayherivagh

Ben Verrisey

Loch Obe

Borve Point

Beinn
Mhártainn

Tigh Talamhanta

Dùn Bharpa
(Ch Cairn)

Bruernish

Sch

Borve

Ch Cairn

Ben
Gunnary

Halaman Bay

Hotel

Dùn Bàn

Tangasdale

Hartaval

Earsary

Heaval

Loch St Clair

Tower

383 △   Statue

Sch

Leanish

Ben
Tangaval
333

Jetty

CASTLEBAY

Sch

Beinn nan
Carnan

Brevig Bay

Rubha Mór

Sound of Vatersay

Kisimul Castle

Castle
Bay

Orosay

Rubha Chàrnain

Bo Vich
Chuan

Heishival Mór
△ 190

Uidh

Uinessan

Ferry

Biruaslum

Sch

Snuasimul

Bàgh Siar

Vatersay Bay

Sea of the Hebrides

Dun

VATERSAY

Bàgh
a' Deas

Sound of Sandray

MULDOANICH

Flodday   SANDRAY

┤ 5 km
  3 miles

The Croig

'that woman' had killed James' mother (Mary Queen of Scots). The comment saved his life. The MacNeils were keen sailors and it is said by some that an invitation from Noah to a MacNeil of Barra to sail with him on his ark was turned down by MacNeil because he had a boat of his own.

Martin Martin in the 18th century said that when the islanders were too old to work the MacNeil chief would take them into his household and provide for them. Boswell recounts the Earl of Argyll's comment on receiving a letter from MacNeil of Barra – 'His style of letter runs as if he were of another kingdom.'

PUFFER IN CASTLEBAY

By 1838 the 21st chief General Roderick MacNeil was so heavily in debt that he had to sell the island. It went for £38,050 to Colonel Gordon of Cluny who had also bought Benbecula, South Uist and Eriskay. Without any consideration for the islanders the colonel offered Barra to the Government for use as a penal settlement – an offer which was not accepted. Then in 1851 on the grounds of receiving insufficient rent he imported policemen to clear both Barra and Vatersay of their crofters, confiscate their stock and belongings, and send them penniless to the New World. These were some of the most cruel and shameful cases of inhumanity ever seen on the West Coast. In 1858 when the colonel died he was said to be the 'richest commoner' in Scotland. The estate and its few survivors then passed to Lady Gordon Cathcart and her husband, who, in their dealings with both Barra and Vatersay, followed in the unlamented colonel's footsteps.

Most of Barra was bought back in 1937 from the Cathcart estate by Robert Lister MacNeil, an American who had been recognised by the Lyon King of Arms as the Clan's 45th chieftain. In 1979 MacNeil offered to transfer the freehold of all the crofting land to the crofters for only £30,000 but the crofters for various reasons preferred to keep to the traditional arrangement.

Wildlife: Over 150 bird species and 400 plant species have been recorded. This is comparable with the rest of the Outer Hebrides but the island is particularly noted for the profuseness of both its wildflowers and its butterflies.

*   *   *

There are spectacular views from both of the highest hills on **BARRA**, **Heaval** (383m) and **Ben Tangaval** (333m). Little idea of the island's size can be gained at Castlebay but from the top of Heaval one can see great rolling hills to the north and the wide sweep of the Borve Valley dropping down to the sandy west coast. But take care when walking in these hills for the mists and sudden climatic changes have given rise to many ghost stories and mysterious disappearances. There are enjoyable walks from Garrygall to Brevig, Ben Tangaval to Tangasdale and Glen Dorcha to Northbay. **Northbay** is a second harbour for the island. It is beyond the **Black Islands**, which are south of **Lamalum** islet, and in a sheltered corner but it is a rather rocky, bleak, and uninspiring area.

A pleasantly energetic 18km hill-walk from Castlebay can include climbing the five highest summits (1040m or 3400ft of total ascent). Heaval – 396m ascent, Hartaval – 60m, Greanan and Corrabheinn – 76m, then west by **Dùn Bharpa** chambered cairn [NF672019] to Beinn Mhártainn – 122m, down to sea-level and 4km along the coast road before climbing Ben Tangaval, over the top, and back down to Castlebay.

Another interesting walk is from Cleat past Ardmhor with its seals and bird life to **Vaslane Sands**. There is reputed to be an underground passage running from Cleat to **Uaimh an Oir** (G. – cave of gold) on the east coast. Two hairless mad dogs which emerged from Uaimh an Oir were reported to have entered the Cleat cave with their masters several days before but the men were never seen again. (This is another example of the standard Hebridean cave tale.)

In the late 19th century, **Castlebay**, the principal town, was a very active and prosperous herring port with a fleet of over 400 boats using the harbour. This was started by James Methuen in 1869 with associated curing and packing industries to take advantage of the herring boom. Castlebay has shops, a post-office, tourist office, schools, hotels, a bank and a cottage hospital and its residents are cheerful and good-natured. In fact, Barra is full of friendly people.

The medieval fortress of **Kisimul Castle** (?ON – tax or tribute mound) which includes a keep, hall and castle is built below the town on a rocky island outcrop in the bay. The first fortifications were built in the 11th century but the present building dates from the 15th century. Beneath the castle there is a very convenient geological pipe which provides a supply of fresh water to a well. A herald used to proclaim from the Great Tower: 'Hear ye people and listen ye nations. The great MacNeil of Barra having finished his meal, the princes of the earth may dine.' The castle was burned down in 1795. The MacNeils had to sell Barra in 1838 due to debt but the 45th Chief of the Clan MacNeil, Robert Lister MacNeil, an American architect, bought back the ancestral

home in 1937 together with almost half of Barra. He restored the castle which had been uninhabited for more than 200 years and turned it into a place of pilgrimage for MacNeils from all over the world. He died in 1970 and is buried in the castle chapel. His late son ensured that the castle would remain a centre for the MacNeil clan and a visitor attraction.

Cars can be hired in Castlebay but it is possible to have a strenuous walk round the island in an afternoon. One of the world's most exciting airfields, a great sweep of beach in the north of the island called **Tràigh Mhór** or the Cockle Strand is covered at every tide. In the 18th century as many as 200 cartloads of live cockles were collected from this famous beach every day during times of famine. There is talk of building a hard airstrip here as few aircraft are now suitable for beach landings, but opinions are, naturally, divided on the consequences. Worse still, there has been the threat of closure of this vital lifeline and tourist attraction.

The 1745 Jacobite rebellion led to the chief of the Clan MacNeil (a Catholic) being imprisoned for implication in the revolt although he had taken no active part. Two years later the clan moved its headquarters from Castlebay to **Eoligarry** in the extreme north of the island. A small cemetery

CASTLEBAY

here, **Cille-bharraidh** [NF705074], is the burial ground of the MacNeils. The only Hebridean example of a Norse sculpted stone (which is now in the National Museum of Antiquities in Edinburgh) was found here among the three ancient chapels and interesting tombstones dating back to the 14th century. Sir Compton Mackenzie, the famous novelist who made Barra his home, is also buried here in sight of Eriskay (See No.7.14) – the setting for his novel *Whisky Galore*. It was at *Suidheachan*, his home by Tràigh Mhór, that Sir Compton and John Lorne Campbell (See No. 4.4) formed the Sea League in the 1930s to try to persuade the Government to protect local fishermen.

A prehistoric galleried fort, **Dùn Scurrival** [NF695080], is beside a cave near Eoligarry.

A hotel set in striking scenery with an outlook over the wild Atlantic at **Halaman Bay** on the west coast was used as a hideout by the children of the Shah in the lead-up to the Iranian Revolution. Their nurse came from Barra. Across the sand dunes from it is fresh-water **Loch St Clair**, stocked with trout and with Castle Sinclair perched on an islet [NL648996]. Nearby is Barra's perfumery where visitors are welcome.

The island is predominantly Catholic and on the slopes of **Heaval** is a white Carrara marble statue of the Madonna and Child [NL679992].

The remains of a fine chambered cairn [NF677012] are further north on the west slope of Grianan, and there are a pair of standing stones [NF653015], said to mark the grave of a Norse warrior killed by a local champion, on the way to Borve Point. An old burial ground and black houses are nearby.

* * *

VATERSAY, whose economy is based on sheep – and cattle – farming, and fishing, is linked to Barra by a long-awaited causeway which was completed in 1990 at a cost of £3.8m. To send the cattle to market they traditionally swam across the Sound of Vatersay to Barra to meet the ferry but when a prize bull, Bernie, drowned in 1986 the resulting publicity at last helped to persuade the Government to build the causeway.

In 1853 off the west coast of Vatersay the *Annie Jane* ran aground and capsized. The bodies of 450 emigrants bound for the New World were washed ashore.

Lady Gordon Cathcart owned Vatersay for a period of fifty-four years but only visited it once. Her tenant ran the island as a single sheep farm. At the turn of the century the demand for land by the people of Barra was so great that pressure was put on her to sell land for crofting. She refused, so, in 1906, several men from Barra including descendants of the original inhabitants landed on Vatersay and laid claim to some land which included their original family crofts. These men became known as the **Vatersay Raiders**. They were brought to trial and imprisoned but due to a public outcry they were released after six weeks and in 1909 a Government Board bought the island and divided it into fifty-eight crofts.

The highest hill on Vatersay is **Heishival Mór** at 190m. Entering the Sound of Vatersay by sea from the east you pass a small tidal island called **Uinessan** with the remains of a church on it [NL665956]. This is known as the Chapel of Mary of the Heads. (Apparently Mary was a short-tempered islander who beheaded anyone who upset her.) **Snuasimul** islet east of Uinessan marks a narrow but navigable shortcut between Vatersay Bay and Castle Bay. Avoid all other shortcuts.

* * *

Access: Vehicle ferry (summer): Oban to Castlebay, every day; return every day except Sat.: Lochboisdale to Castlebay, Mon., Tues., and Thur.; return, Wed., Fri., Sun., 08000-66-5000. Vehicle ferry: Eriskay/ Barra, frequent daily service, 08000-66-5000. Island post bus circuit includes airport and ferry terminals, 01871-810312. Scheduled air service: Glasgow/ Barra, and Benbecula/ Barra daily except Sun., 0870-850-9850. Hotel accommodation. Bicycle hire. Fishing permits from Post Office. Tourist Information, 01871-810336.

Anchorages:
1. Bagh Beag, Castlebay. Good shelter but tricky narrow channel with only 1.3m at half-tide and inadequate information on chart. Risky.
2. Castle Bay, NW of castle. 12 visitors' moorings, or anchor in 6m, mud, holding poor unless well bedded-in. Avoid obstructing ferry pier. Reasonable shelter except S'lies.
3. Castle Bay, NE of castle. Good shelter but very limited space between drying rocks and moored craft, 3.5–5m or close W of the castle in 7m mud.
4. North Bay on E coast affords good shelter. Anchor in

Bruernish Bay, in inlet W of the Black Isles or continue into N side of Bagh Hirivagh and anchor 2c W of the jetty if there is room. Not the most attractive anchorage. There are other options among the islets NW of Fuiay.

5. Oitir Mór in the Sound of Barra. Best approach N of Gighay and pass 5c N of Greanamul midway between the beacons. Anchor SE of freshwater stream on Fuday in clay and sand, with some weed. Unpleasant in E'lies. Beware rock in bay.

6. Eoligarry Jetty, about 6¼c NNW of N side of Orosay is a tidal harbour with pier where small craft might find shelter.

7. Sound of Fiaray is a possible anchorage but the approach is difficult and potentially dangerous.

8. W coast of Barra has no anchorages but the Admiralty Pilot records one landing place amongst the rocks 1M S of Greian Head.

9. Sound of Vatersay. Some useful shelter may be found in the the Sound where it is blocked by the causeway. Beware rocks at entrance.

10. W coast of Vatersay has no anchorages. Bagh Siar has moderate depth and sandy bottom but no shelter.

11. Vatersay Bay – good anchorage. Enter passing 2–3c S of Muldoanich and then steer centrally for the bay. Anchor W of Sgeir Vichalea in suitable depth, sand.

12. Cornaig Bay, S of causeway and Orosay. Pipeline, cable and rocks to be avoided but well sheltered from SW.

13. Causeway bay, between causeway and Orosay is a useful anchorage but pipeline and cable must be avoided.

7.7 Flodday

(ON floti – a raft or flat island) This island is east of Barra. There is another smaller Flodday south-west of Barra which does not appear to have ever been inhabited.

O S Maps: 1:50000 Sheet 31 1:25000 Sheet 452
Admiralty Charts: 1:100000 No.1796 1:30000 No.2770

Area: 40ha (99 acres)
Height: 42m (138 ft)

Population: 1841–7 (1 house). The island was cleared in the mid-19th century and has been uninhabited since then.

Geology: The bulk of the island is made up of gneiss with a sufficient covering of soil to provide good grazing.

Wildlife: The low-lying nature of the island gives encouragement to only a few seabirds but rock-pipit and twite can be seen and may even be resident.

FLODDAY rises gradually to a height of 42m and is covered with grass and heather, but Rubh' a' Chaolais (G. – the kyle headland) in the south-west is bare and rocky. Opposite it in the south-east is the equally barren Grey Rock. It is an easy island to explore but has few features of any particular interest.

The 1991 Census quotes Flodday as having a population of eight but this refers in fact to the tidal island which is part of Benbecula in the Civil Parish of South Uist and should not be confused with this Flodday. The name was very popular and applied freely to any flat island.

Flodday never appears to have supported more than one family and it was cleared for sheep by Colonel Gordon of Cluny in 1851. It has no reliable source of fresh water so water would have had to be brought in by boat when there were long dry spells.

A small, drying islet off the north extremity called **Snagaras** lies at the end of a reef.

* * *

Access: Barra Fishing Charters, 01871-890384. Island Adventures, Castlebay, 01871-810284. Tourist Information, Castlebay, Barra, 01871-810336.

Anchorage:
1. The only recommended occasional anchorage is NE of Irishman Rock, W of the N extremity of Flodday, in 13–14m, mud. It may be possible to find a shallower spot (5–6m) in the channel S of Irishman Rock but the bottom is uncertain.

7.8 Fuiay

Probably (G. bhuidhe, ON -øy – yellow or pleasant island).

O S Maps: 1:50000 Sheet 31 1:25000 Sheet 452
Admiralty Charts: 1:100000 No.1796 1:30000 No.2770

Area: 84ha (208 acres)
Height: 107m (351 ft)

Population: The island was populated with at least six households during the 19th century, possibly until about 1850, but I have found no Census records. Uninhabited since.

Geology: Gneiss generally, but large dark slabs of volcanic rock with pronounced cleavage planes.

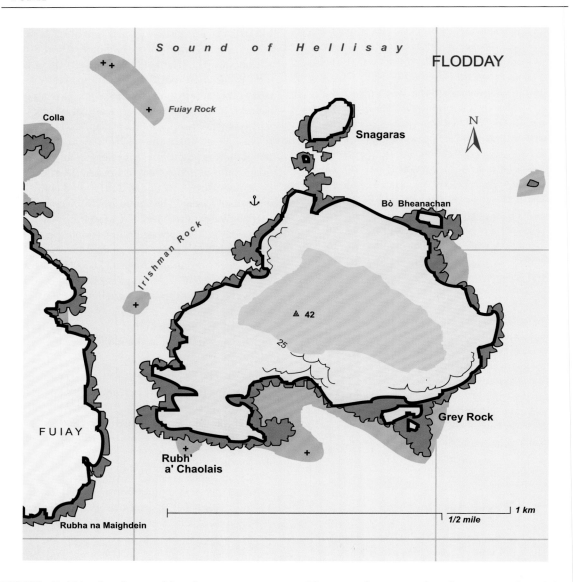

Wildlife: Rabbits, bracken and heather.

FUIAY is a bit of a puzzle.

Firstly, I have found no record of any
population. And yet, **Rubh' an Aiseig** [ash-ug]
(G. – ferry headland), has the ruins of a neat
village 'street' [NF737027] laid out along the
side of the tidal inlet. There were at least six
cottages and by comparison with similar ruins
elsewhere they were probably occupied until the
mid-19th century and possibly later. Of course,
the ten-yearly census only started in 1831, and
it was fairly sketchy to begin with, so the odds
are that Fuiay's inhabitants were either forgotten
or included somewhere but not specifically
mentioned.

The second mystery, if such it is, is at the tidal
inlet. We visited the island at high water and the
sea was flowing downhill *into* the inlet. A stony
shelf or bar crosses the entrance opposite the
ruined cottages and there was about 300mm, or
one foot, difference between the two water-levels.
The inlet is like a miniature sea-loch when full
but is shallow and dries out at low water. Our
conclusion was that when the tide ebbs and the
outside sea-level falls below the 'floor-level' of the
inlet the water in the inlet drains out through
the rock strata, but when the tide rises the water
cannot seep in fast enough to fill the inlet: the
sea therefore floods over the 'bar' when it reaches
the required level. This would seem to create a
natural fish trap at the spring tides which the

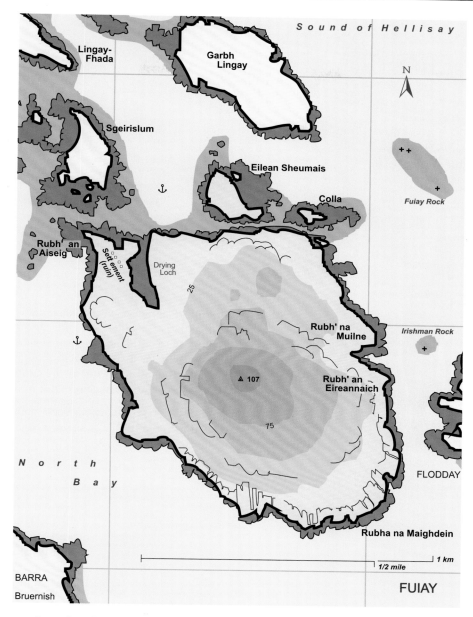

islanders must have found very convenient.

Fuiay has a prominent peak (107m) which is almost at the exact centre of the oval-shaped island. The headland in the south-east is called **Rubha na Maighdein** [myjun] (G. – maiden's headland) – a name which begs another intriguing question.

The sea to the north and north-west of Fuiay is littered with islets, skerries, and rocks. The nearest islets are **Eilean Sheumais**, **Colla** (G. – hazel island), and **Sgeirislum**. Beyond these lie **Garbh Lingay** and **Lingay-fhada** (G. – rough heather-isle and long heather-isle).

To the south there are more rocks off Barra's Bruernish peninsula gathered around an islet called **Heilem**. The large lone rock, **Curachan**, is prominent in the south-west with patches of sea-grass on it.

Access: Barra Fishing Charters, 01871-890384. Island Adventures, Castlebay, 01871-810284. Tourist Information, Castlebay, Barra, 01871-810336.

Anchorages: There is a tricky navigable channel through the reefs between Sgeirislum and Fuiay, except possibly at LW.
1. Off N coast. Anchor midway between Sgeirislum and

Eilean Sheumais, 5m mud. Good
anchorage but partly obstructed
by fish-cages. If approaching from
E keep close S of Garbh Lingay to
avoid rocks N of En Sheumais.
2. W of Rubh' an Aiseig.
Occasional anchorage about ½c
off-shore and about 3c S of the N
extremity of the headland opposite
some rocks which form a natural
'jetty', 5–6m mud.

7.9 Hellisay

*(ON – island of caves) but Blaeu's
map of 1654 uses 'Hildesay' (ON –
Hilda's island), which may be more
acceptable as the number of caves is
not excessive.*

OS Maps: 1:50000 Sheet 31 1:25000 Sheet 452
Admiralty Charts: 1:100000 No.1796 1:30000 No.2770

Area: 142ha (351 acres)
Height: 79m (259 ft)

Population: 1764–56. 1841–108. 1851–7.
1861–20. 1881–9. Uninhabited since 1890.

Geology: Mainly gneiss with occasional quartz
veins.

RUINED HOUSES BY THE TIDAL LOCH, FUIAY

History: Clearances on the adjoining islands led
to an influx of population in the early 1800s.
Then in the 1840s the people of Hellisay were
themselves evicted and by 1851 there were only
seven inhabitants left. Most of the families cleared
from Hellisay found refuge on Eriskay.

Wildlife: Every pocket in the rocks above sea-level
is filled with sea-thrift. There are many grey seals
and apart from sea-birds we saw falcon and a pair
of golden eagles.

*   *   *

THE SECRET ANCHORAGE BETWEEN GIGHAY AND HELLISAY

There are two distinct
peaks on **HELLISAY**,
Meall Meadhonach
(G. – middle mound),
in the south-east
(79m) and **Beinn a'
Charnain** (G. – cairn
hill), in the north-
west (73m). Meall
Meadhonach has a
vertical face over 60m
high on its west side
with distinctive orange
lichen near the top.
It is on a peninsula
which finishes steeply
at **Rubha na h-Uamh**
(G. – cave headland).
Meall Mór (G. – big

mound) is on this peninsula and is virtually an extension of Meall Meadhonach [meeoo-unuch]. At 75m it is not as high, but its position is more prominent.

The most westerly part of the island is **Rubh' an t-Seana Bhalla** (G. – headland of the ancient wall). Most of the island is rocky and uneven and it is difficult to see how it could have supported over 100 inhabitants at one time, even with the advantage of good fishing in the Sound of Barra. The main settlement was on the lower ground at **Bualavore** [NF754046].

The easiest landing place by dinghy in Hintish Bay is in the south-east corner. On the outside of the neck of land the sea surges into a narrow rock cleft with a noise like severe indigestion. From here there is a pleasant scramble up Meall Mór and Meadhonach with extensive views from the top.

Hellisay is an island rich in fairy tales and myths. The stories of Alasdair Alpin MacGregor tell of a magic land of strange happenings remembered by the old folk on winter nights by the peat fire.

Access: Barra Fishing Charters, 01871-890384.

Lady Anne boat trips, Kallin Harbour, (Nick
Ingleden), 01870-602403. Island Adventures,
Castlebay, 01871-810284. Tourist Information,
Castlebay, Barra, 01871-810336.

Anchorages: The anchorages are in the sound between the
two islands. Entrance to the sound is tricky and there may
be uncharted rocks.
1. Hintish Bay. In the SE part of the sound, anchor NW of
Charish. Excellent shelter, good holding, sand and mud.
2. Pool in W part of the sound, ENE of Beinn a' Charnain.
Many submerged rocks.

7.10 Gighay

*(ON – Gydha's island) Gydha was a woman's name in Old
Norse.*

O S Maps: 1:50000 Sheet 31   1:25000 Sheet 452
Admiralty Charts: 1:100000 No.1796   1:30000 No.2770

Area: 96ha (237 acres)
Height: 95m (312 ft)

Population: Dean Monro recorded that Gighay
was inhabited in 1549, but there is no other
information. The island was known to be
inhabited at the end of the 18th century but it
has been deserted for a long time and there are no
Census records.

Geology: Mainly gneiss. The Hebridean Fault Line
runs approximately NE–SW at Eilean a' Ceud and
Hintish Bay.

History: It is probable that the increase in
population recorded for Hellisay during the
Clearances in the mid-19th century overflowed on
to neighbouring Gighay.

Wildlife: Heather is fairly widespread – mainly
calluna with very little erica. Banks of nettles
surround the areas of former human habitation.
The wet areas have marsh marigolds and yellow
flag among the reeds and there are daisies and
wild violets on the slopes.

Rats frequent the area near the sheep-dip.

When we visited Gighay it was the month of
May. Oystercatchers were busy on the shore,
skylarks larking in the sky, and an eagle was
being mobbed by falcons above Mullach a'
Charnain's cliffs.

* * *

Like its sister island, Hellisay, **GIGHAY** is
another magical place, no doubt given additional
charm by the fairly difficult entry into its secret
anchorage. Because *Jandara*, having achieved
entry, was trapped until the tide rose again the
feeling of isolation was exaggerated. We were
marooned.

The easiest landing place was in the bay behind
Eilean a' Ceud [ked] (G. – hundred island).
Only the sheep and sheep pens beneath the bluff
destroyed the impression that man had not set
foot on the island for many years.

This is the area that was once inhabited
because among the reeds, nettles and bracken
there are still signs of the old habitations. Over a
dozen are easily discovered – small, rude, stone
dwellings giving an impression of desperate
poverty; and on the opposite slope of the bay, to
the northwest, there are the regular striations of
old lazybeds.

A short visit here is delightful, particularly in
fine spring weather but the islanders' existence
must have been finely balanced. Gighay is barren
enough in late spring – what must it be like
during the long winter months? Only the inland
sea, the Sound of Gighay, sheltered between
the islands, could tip the scales by providing
all-weather fishing with nothing but seals for
competition.

The highest peak **Mullach a' Charnain** (G. –
cairn summit), 95m high, has a steep cliff on its
south-west side above the anchorage. There is also
a high flat point in the extreme north-east ending
in a hummock called **Meall an Laoigh** (G. – calf
hill). The calf itself, **An Laogh**, is a miniature
stack at the end of this promontory. Round the
corner, on the exposed north-west coast there is
an indentation with enough space to draw small
boats ashore called **Ruadh-phort** (G. – red port).

Although the anchorage beside Eilean a' Ceud
is excellent, if the wind is in the north or north-
west squally gusts can come tumbling over the
cliff. In that case it is better to cross the sound to
the Hellisay side, but remember that at high water
a large reef crossing most of Hintish Bay is not
visible.

* * *

Outer Oitir Mhór

An Laogh

Fionnphort

Meall an
Laoig

Ruadh-phort

Creag an Caora

Bualaveg

△ 95
Mullach a'
Charnain

Eilean a' Ghamhna

Càrnach

Clach Eagach

Settlement
(ruin)

Eilean a' Ceud

Rubha na
Muireart

Colla

Creag an Teirm

HELLISAY

Sound of Hellisay

Fuiay Rock

Snagaras

N

GIGHAY

FUIAY

FLODDAY

Access: Barra Fishing Charters, 01871-890384.
Island Adventures, Castlebay, 01871-810284.
Lady Anne boat trips, Kallin Harbour, (Nick
Ingleden), 01870-602403. Tourist Information,
Castlebay, Barra, 01871-810336.

Anchorages: The anchorages are in the sound between
Gighay and Hellisay. Entrance to the sound can be tricky,
depends on the state of the sea and the tide, and there may
be uncharted rocks.

1. In the small bay NW of Eilean a' Ceud, thick mud.
2. Pool in W part of the sound just S of the line between
Mullach a' Charnain on Gighay and Beinn a' Charnain on
Hellisay. Many submerged rocks.

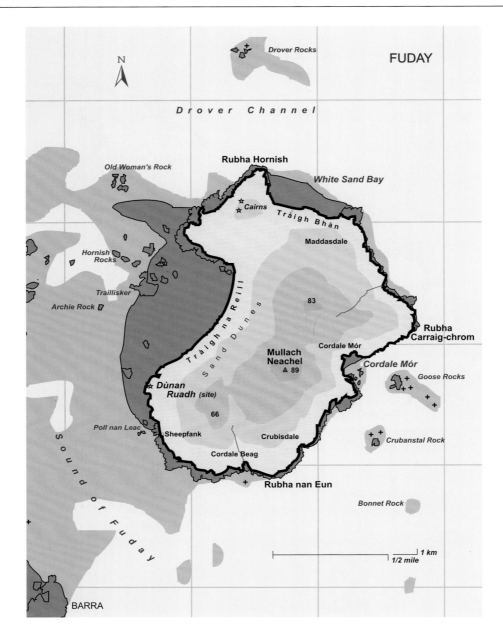

7.11 Fuday

Possibly (ON fut-øy – bailiwick or bailiff's island) or (ON ut-øy – outside isle).

O S Maps: 1:50000 Sheet 31 1:25000 Sheet 452
Admiralty Charts: 1:100000 No.1796 1:30000 No.2770

Area: 232ha (573 acres)
Height: 89m (292 ft)

Population: Walker's list for 1764 gives a population of 56 for 'Fuda' but doesn't mention the island of Hellisay (No.7.9). Yet in 1841 Hellisay had 108 and Fuday only 5. Francis Thompson says that Hellisay was sometimes known in Gaelic as 'An t-eilean Fuideach' which may be the cause of confusion. 1841–5 (1 house). 1861–7. 1881–6. 1891–7 (1 house). 1901–4. Uninhabited since.

Geology: The island is covered with grass on a core of Archaean gneiss and with a wide sand-based shelf on the west side.

History: Fuday is supposed to have been the

WHITE-TAILED SEA EAGLE

last retreat of those Norsemen, a small section of King Haakon's defeated forces, who remained in the Hebrides after the Battle of Largs in 1263. According to tradition, an illegitimate son of MacNeil of Barra wished to ingratiate himself with his family. He managed to attract the attention of one of the Norse maidens and courted her assiduously. She fell in love with him and through her he gained detailed information about the Norse defences. He then led a raid on the island and wiped out the entire population.

Wildlife: Seabirds nest on the southern headland, Rubha nan Eun (G. – headland of the birds) and among the sand dunes on the west coast. Otters have also been seen here.

Tradition says that **FUDAY** was a Norse burial ground. Certainly graves can still be seen in the sand, built of rounded stones. The Norse liked to have a quiet island for the dead to rest in peace although, if the MacNeil massacre actually took place, it is uncertain who buried the dead. At the north end of the island, **Ru Hornish**, there are two cairns which are evidence that the Norse were not the first inhabitants.

The Sound of Fuday which separates the island from the Eoligarry peninsula of Barra is full of rocks and shifting sandbanks and at low water it is sometimes only a few centimetres deep but it can be navigated with care at the right state of the tide.

The island rises to three rather flat hills. The central hill, **Mullach Neachel** (G. – lone summit) is 89m high with a slightly lower hill to the north. The westward slope runs down to a wide expanse of high sand-dunes and a great stretch of beach, **Tràigh na Reill**, exposed by the low tide. South-west of Mullach Neachel and joined to it is a small hill called **Dùnan Ruadh** (G. – the red heap). A crystal clear burn runs from the saddle of this hill down to Cordale Beag on the south coast where it discharges into the sea. On the east side a rock-strewn sandy cove, **Cordale Mór** (G. and ON – the big tapering valley) is sheltered from the north by Rubha Carraig-chrom (G. – cliff-ridge point) and on the north coast there is a wide attractive beach, **Tràigh Bhàn**, or White Sand – a white chalk-mark on a blue ground when seen from across the Sound of Barra.

Greanamul is an islet which provides a useful point of reference when approaching Fuday from the south because navigating in this area of skerries and shifting sand-banks requires care.

* * *

Access: Barra Fishing Charters, 01871-890384. Island Adventures, Castlebay, 01871-810284. Lady Anne boat trips, Kallin Harbour, (Nick Ingleden), 01870-602403. Tourist Information, Castlebay, Barra, 01871-810336.

Anchorages: No recommended anchorages.
1. Cordale Beag. Best approach N of Gighay and pass 5c N of Greanamul midway between the beacons. Anchor SE of freshwater stream by Rubha nan Eun. Clay and sand, with some weed. Unpleasant in E'lies. Beware rock in bay.
2. Cordale Mór. Temporary anchorage NW Goose Rocks, outside the bay, 4–6m, sand. Very careful navigation required. Goose Rocks cover so best to approach near LW.

7.12 Eileanan Iasgaich

(G. – the fish, or fishing, islands).

O S Maps: 1:50000 Sheet 31 1:25000 Sheet 453
Admiralty Charts: 1:100000 No.1795 1:12500 No.2770

Area: 50ha (124 acres)
Height: 23m (75 ft)

Population: No Census records and uninhabited.

Geology: Gneiss bedrock with scanty areas of soil.
Wildlife: The many pockets and cracks in the rocks provide a home for prawns and lobsters and shelter for fish.

* * *

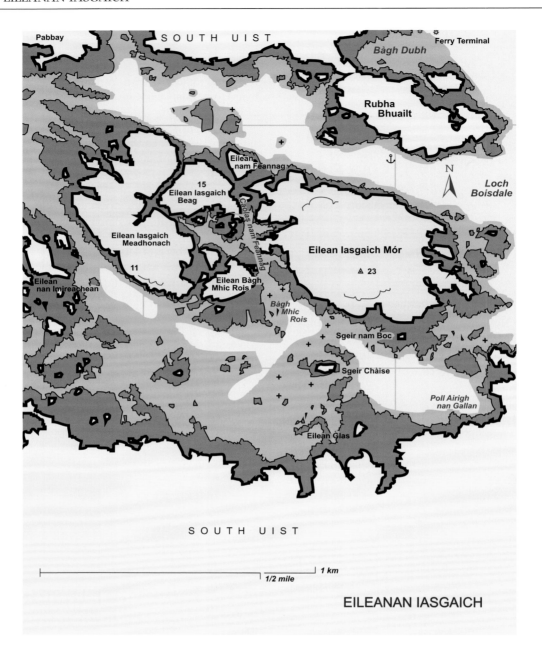

EILEANAN IASGAICH

EILEANAN IASGAICH is an ill-defined group
of low-lying islands in Loch Boisdale linked by
reefs and skerries at low water. The largest of the
group, **Eilean Iasgaich Mór**, is the most easterly
and it rises to a central hummock which is just
23m high. Vegetation is sparse due to the lack of
soil and the high salt content. There is a channel
in the centre of the group which has a sufficiently
narrow entrance to form a natural tidal fish-trap
and it is possibly that this gave the islands their
name.

Loch Boisdale is generally shallow and studded
with tidal islands and rocks. The most conspicuous
islets, both of which are in the entrance to
the loch, are **Calvay** and **Gasay**. Calvay has a
ruined castle on it which guarded the entrance in
medieval times and the ubiquitous Prince Charles
Edward Stuart spent a night in hiding there. To
the west of Eileanan Iasgaich are **Eilean nan
Imireachean** (G. – island of the processions),
tiny at high water but extensive when the tide is
out, **Eilean Mór** (G. – big island), and **Pabbay**

to the north-west. These are all tidal islands. It is out of character for a Pabbay, or priest island, to be tidal as it would allow the hermit to interrupt his isolation and walk ashore to meet his friends whenever the tide went out. This was obviously the abode of an extrovert anchorite.

* * *

Access: No regular access. Enquire at

Lochboisdale. Landing can be difficult due to seaweed-covered reefs.

Anchorages:

1. Rubha Bhuailt. In channel N of Eileanan Iasgaich. Fish cages block much of the anchorage. Holding reported to be poor.

2. Rubha Arinangallan. Anchor 1c NW of the ruined pier on S shore of Loch Boisdale. Beware drying rock and shoal patch NW of the pier and Hut Shoal N of the pier.

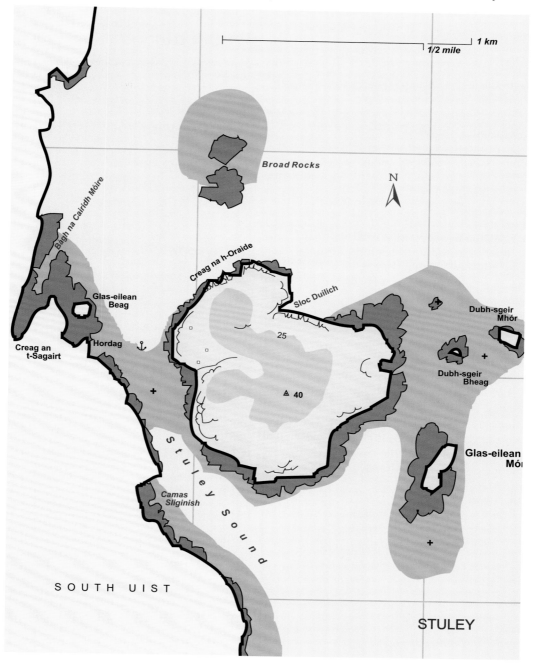

7.13 Stuley

(ON – Stula's island) The peak on South Uist overlooking Stuley is Stulaval (ON – Stula's hill).

O S Maps: 1:50000 Sheet 22 1:25000 Sheet 453
Admiralty Charts: 1:100000 No.1795

Area: 45ha (111 acres)
Height: 40m (131 ft)

Population: No Census records and uninhabited.

Geology: Intermediate and basic Lewisian rock with a distinctly greenish colour.

STULEY is made up of three low grass-covered hills with the highest point (40m) near the centre. Both the island and its grazing sheep have a leisurely unassuming appearance.

We approached the island from the north-east and then rounded the coastline between Stuley and Broad Rocks to enter the Sound. According to both the chart and the Pilot there is a shoal area at the north end of the sound fairly close to **Creag an t-Sagairt** (G. – priest's rock) but we failed to find it. The echo-sounder gave a steady reading of 20m right up to the point where the sound narrows in width although the depth certainly decreases south of this point. The original soundings, of course, were by leadline and date back to 1852. It is not a bad little anchorage, given suitable conditions, and landing is easy on the green, slatelike, slabs of rock.

Although I have found no written record of permanent human habitation the green ridges of old lazybeds and a few scattered shieling ruins show that Stuley was probably yet another place where people who were considered of less importance than sheep fought to survive. The cleft in the north is called **Sloc Duilich** (G. – awkward gulley) and the cliffs facing the Priest's Rock are – according to one old map – aptly named **Creag na h-Oraíde** (G. – sermon crag).

Glas-eilean Mór (G. – big green island), south-east of Stuley, is, as its name suggests, covered with a sward of bright green grass.

Access: Lady Anne boat trips, Kallin Harbour, (Nick Ingleden), 01870-602403, Uist Outdoor Centre, Lochmaddy, 01876-500480, or try a Lochboisdale boat-owner.

Anchorage:
1. Stuley Sound between South Uist and Stuley. According

to the Admiralty Pilot 'small vessels pass through or use it as an anchorage'. It is about ½c wide at its narrowest and a submerged rock is charted about midway but the channel appears to be clean if a course nearer to Stuley is maintained.

7.14 Uist

[yoo-ist] (ON – west)

Benbecula

(G. beinn bheag a' bh-faodhla – little mountain of the fords) referring to the only means of access before the causeways were built.

Berneray *or* Bernera

(ON bjarnar-øy – bear island) or possibly (ON – Bjorn's island).

Baleshare
(G. baile ear – east town)

Grimsay
(ON – Grim's island)

Eriskay

(G. ùruisg, ON -øy – goblin or water-nymph island). 'Eric's island' is sometimes given as the derivation but this is probably incorrect.

Vallay

(ON – hill island)

Kirkibost Island

(ON – church farm)

Oronsay

(G. – drying or tidal island)

O S Maps: 1:50000 Sheets 18, 22 and 31. 1:25000 Sheets 453 and 454.
Admiralty Charts: 1:200000 No.2722. Complete E coast 1:100000 No.1795. Sd of Barra & Loch Boisdale 1:30000 No.2770. E coast, L Skiport to L Eport 1:25000 No.2904. Berneray (part) 1:20000 No.2642. Lochs on E coast 1:15000 No.2825.

Area: 74,540ha (184,189 acres)
Height: 620m (2034 ft)

Owner: The MacDonalds of Clanranald held South Uist and Benbecula until 1838. In 1838 Colonel Gordon of Cluny bought Benbecula and his family were owners until 1942. Since 1961 Eriskay and almost all of South Uist and Benbecula were owned by South Uist Estates, the rest is owned by the Scottish Government and the Ministry of Defence. In 2006 the whole of South Uist Estates passed into community ownership for £4.6 million (HIE and the Lottery each contributed £2 million).

The MacDonalds of Sleat owned North Uist. The greater part of it (including Grimsay and Baleshare) is now owned by Lord Granville's family as the North Uist Estate Trust 1990. The RSPB also has a sizeable holding. Berneray was part of the Bays of Harris estate. It was bought in the 1920s for £500 (without crofting rights). The current laird is Rodney Hitchcock, an English businessman.

Population: Approximate pre-Census totals excluding Berneray and Eriskay: 1755–4118. 1794–6668. 1821–11009.

A HERRING DRIFTER IN THE 1930S

	1841	1891	1931	1961	1991	2001	2011
N.U't	3870	3250	2349	1622	1404	1271	1254
Be'a	2160	1787	1006	1390	1803	1249	1330
Be'y	713	501	331	201	141	136	138
S.U't	5093	3708	2810	2376	2106	1818	1754
Ba'e	157	318	136	59	55	49	58
Gr'y	269	281	259	239	215	201	169
Er'y	80	454	420	231	179	133	143
Va'y	59	34	19	0	0	0	0
Ki't	25	6	6	0	0	0	0
Or'y	102	0	0	0	0	0	0
	12528	10339	7336	6118	5903	4857	4846

*Be'a includes Grimsay (South) and Flodda

Geology: North Uist, Berneray, Benbecula and the northern half of South Uist is a 2.5-million-years-old gneiss but the southern half of South Uist and Eriskay is younger gneiss – about 1.5 million years old. On Berneray there are no workable peat deposits. In 1607 a tidal wave removed the sand-bank which at that time almost connected Berneray to Pabbay. During the last ice ages there were minor glaciers on Hecla (whose rocks are mildly magnetic), Beinn Mhór in South Uist and on Eaval in North Uist with the result that the rocks in the bealachs (mountain passes) are ice worn but the summits are not. There was never a heavy all-enveloping ice-sheet as on the mainland. The 'long island' was in fact one long island at this time and it was only in the post-glacial era that the sea-lochs broke through. Ancient peat and the stumps of forest trees can be found below mean sea-level at Borve on Benbecula, at Loch Eynort, Lochboisdale, on the west coast of South Uist and off the Prince's Strand at Eriskay.

History: In 1098 King Magnus III of Norway pillaged the Hebrides, 'gained much gold', and set the Uists on fire.
On 23 July, 1745 on the beach of Coilleag a' Phrionnsa (G. – the Prince's cockle-shell strand) on the west coast of **Eriskay** Prince Charles Edward Stuart was put ashore from the French ship *Du Teillay*. This was the first time he had set foot on Scottish soil. The MacNeils of Barra owned Eriskay at the time and this continued until 1758 when the island passed to the MacDonalds of Clanranald.

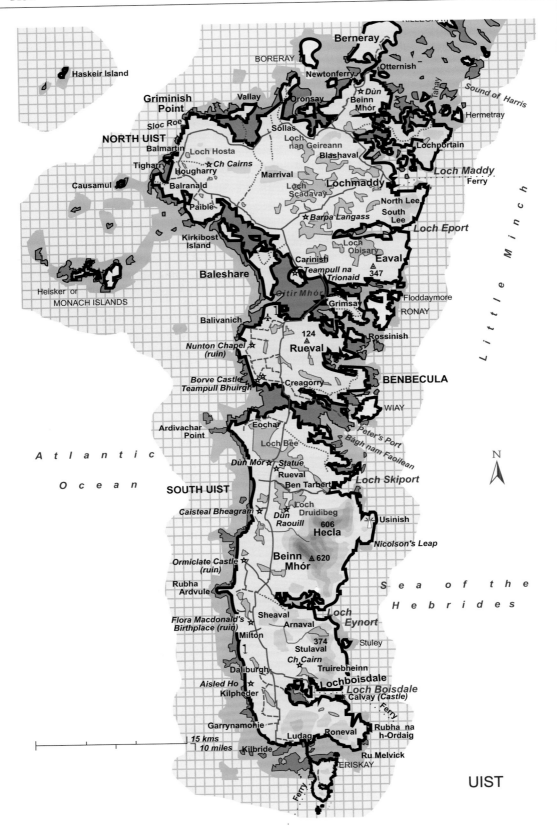

Haskeir Island

Berneray
BORERAY
Newtonferry
Otternish
Griminish Point
Vallay
Oronsay
☆ Dùn Beinn Mhór
Tahay
Sound of Harris
Hermetray
Sloc Roe
Sollas
Loch nan Geireann
NORTH UIST
Balmartin
Loch Hosta
Blashaval
Lochportain
Tigharry
☆ Ch Cairns
Marrival
Lochmaddy
Loch Maddy
Houghharry
Ferry
Causamul
Balranald
Loch Scadavay
North Lee
Paible
South Lee
Loch Eport
Kirkibost Island
Carinish ☆
Barpa Langass
Loch Obisary
Eaval
Baleshare
☆ Teampull na Trionaid
347
Oitir Mhór
Grimsay
Floddaymore
Heisker or MONACH ISLANDS
RONAY
Balivanich
124
Rossinish
△
Nunton Chapel (ruin) ☆
Rueval
BENBECULA
Borve Castle ☆
Creagorry
Teampull Bhuirgh
WIAY
Ardivachar Point
Eochar
Peter's Port
Loch Bee
Bàgh nam Faoilean
A t l a n t i c
Dùn Mór ☆ ☆ Statue
Rueval
Ben Tarbert
Loch Skiport
O c e a n
SOUTH UIST
Loch Druidibeg
Caisteal Bheagram ☆
Dùn Raouill ☆
Usinish ☆
606
Hecla
Nicolson's Leap
Ormiclate Castle (ruin) ☆
Beinn Mhór
△ 620
Rubha Ardvule
S e a   o f   t h e
H e b r i d e s
Sheaval
Loch Eynort
Flora Macdonald's Birthplace (ruin) ☆
Arnaval
Milton
Stuley
374
1
Stulaval
☆ Ch Cairn
Truirebheinn
Daliburgh
Lochboisdale
Aisled Ho ☆
Loch Boisdale
Kilpheder
Calvay (Castle)
Ferry
Garrynamohie
Rubha na h-Ordaig
15 kms
Ludag
Roneval
10 miles
Kilbride
Ru Melvick
ERISKAY
Ferry
UIST
N

Little Minch

South Uist, which had been ruled by the Clanranald chiefs since the Norse occupation, has also many associations with Bonnie Prince Charlie following the collapse of his venture. The Prince landed in Corodale Bay, directly beneath Beinn Mhór, on 14 May 1746 and hid in a forester's hut. From Prince's Cave he watched the Royal Navy patrolling the Minch in the search for him. Neil MacEachain MacDonald who was helping him, introduced him to the twenty-three-year-old Flora MacDonald who had arrived from Skye on a visit to her brother, and it was he who suggested that when Flora returned to Skye she should take the Prince with her disguised as her servant girl. The island at the mouth of Loch Boisdale, Calvay, has the ruins of a 13th-century castle on it where the Prince took refuge on 15 June 1746.

During the clearances which followed the purchase of Eriskay, South Uist and **Benbecula** by Colonel Gordon of Cluny in 1838 some crofters were chased into the hills by the police and more than 1000 destitute islanders were shipped from Lochboisdale to America on *The Admiral*. Cluny turned a blind eye when some of the crofters whom he had evicted from Uist settled on Eriskay as he considered the land to be too poor even for sheep to survive. But many crofters preferred destitution in Scotland to forced emigration and they built raised lazybeds of peat and seaweed on the rocky ground and grew meagre crops of barley, oats and potatoes for sustenance.

The MacRuairidhs ruled **North Uist** after the Norse occupation until the MacDonalds of Sleat were given official title by James IV in 1495.

About 1850 Lord Macdonald of Sleat brought police there and ruthlessly evicted many families. This resulted in bloody fights, burned cottages and much misery but it was a pointless exercise as only five years later Macdonald sold the island to Sir John Powlett Ord.

In 1614, when Tormod (G. – Norman), third son of Ruaridh Mór chief of the Clan MacLeod, was five years old he was settled with **Berneray** by his father. The remains of the home that he later built are still to be seen. He received a knighthood after the Restoration for his services to the exiled Charles II. Sir Norman, who died in 1705, was an ardent supporter of Gaelic art and literature and he gave a house on Berneray to Mary MacLeod, the famous Gaelic poet.

At this time the MacLeod Chiefs were reasonably good proprietors and keen to ensure satisfactory communication between the islands. In 1705 a boat was purchased by MacLeod of Harris for use as a ferry. Lauchlan MacLean as ferryman was instructed to maintain a regular service between Harris and Skye and also the islands of Berneray, Ensay, Killegray and Pabbay.

Wildlife: White and yellow water-lilies dapple the surface of the many fresh-water lochs. These are now scarce on the mainland due to disturbance and plundering by plant collectors. The small islands in these lochs have dense thickets of the native willow, aspen, birch, hazel and rowan growing on them because they are beyond the reach of hungry sheep. Originally these trees were the elements of widespread island afforestation. Martin Martin wrote of Berneray in 1695: 'The west end of this island which looks to St Kilda, is called the wooden harbour, because the sands at low water discover several trees that have formerly grown there. Sir Norman MacLeod told me that he had seen a tree cut there, which was afterwards made into a harrow.' A patch of trees still clings to a heathery rock-wall on Beinn Mhór on South Uist, and a few other sheltered corries in the hills north of Loch Eynort. Here too are several varieties of fern, including the royal fern, *Osmunda regalis*, and many alpine species.

But for sheer profusion and floral display nothing can compare with the machair in the spring and summer months spreading down the entire west coast. About 200 different species of wildflowers have been identified which bloom in sequence giving rolling waves of colour throughout spring and summer. On Berneray there is very little heather and with no peat bogs there are few midges. The soil structure is rich in shell-sand and, fortunately, with no rabbits the machair is particularly beautiful.

It has been claimed that the pink sea-convolvulus (*Calystegia soldanella*) growing above the beach on Eriskay came from seeds dropped by Bonnie Prince Charlie when he stepped ashore. It is however also found at several other places in the Hebrides including Vatersay (No.7-6). It blooms in June with a small heart-shaped leaf and large trumpet.

Nests of the very rare northern *colletes* mining bee have been found in the sand dunes of North Uist.

Mute swans are sometimes seen on South Uist's

shallow Loch Bee. The Uists have the highest density of breeding waders in Britain and many rare bird species although these could be seriously threatened by hedgehogs which were thoughtlessly introduced in 1974 and mink which have swum over from Harris. Culling of the hedgehogs and mink has gone ahead despite some controversy. Some of the more interesting

SHORT-LIVED ORMICLATE CASTLE

birds to be seen throughout the year are: corn bunting, reed bunting, twite, raven, wheatear, stonechat, black guillemot, rock dove, short-eared owl, a rare snowy-owl, rock pipit, greenshank, redshank, snipe, golden plover, hen harrier, buzzard, golden eagle, merlin, peregrine, red grouse, red-breasted merganser, eider, shoveller, teal, gadwall, little grebe and heron. Red-necked phalarope arrive from Peru in mid-May. Also pink-footed goose, pintail, knot and bar-tailed godwit. In summer quail, knot, sanderling and ruff. Later, little stint, curlew sandpiper, dunlin and whimbrel. In winter, turnstone, purple sandpiper, scaup, water rail, jack snipe and woodcock, and many more.

The Loch Druidibeg National Nature Reserve on South Uist, lying astride the main road, is the most important breeding ground of the native British greylag goose; and the Balranald RSPB Nature Reserve in North Uist is an equally outstanding site.

Corncrakes, which can be heard from mid-April, benefit from this being an Environmentally Sensitive Area (ESA), allowing crofters to be paid to manage their land in ways which benefit corncrakes and conservation.

Eriskay ponies stand only 12 to 13 hands high (just over 120cms) and are now proven to be a distinct, ancient Scottish breed, but one teetering on the brink of extinction. They have a pleasant temperament and were bred for croftwork such as carrying peat and seaweed.

For the local fishermen, the velvet crabs which

were once thrown away or used as bait now fetch good prices in southern Europe. The coastline is generally rich in sea-life – a fact appreciated by the numerous grey and common seals.

* * *

Off the southern tip of Eriskay lie the **Stack Islands**, where the ruin of Weaver's Castle can be seen on **Eilean Leathan**, the largest of the group. The castle was the base for a notorious MacNeil pirate and wreck-plunderer. The other islets in the group **Eileanan Dubha** and **Eilean a' Gheòidh** are linked together by drying reefs.

* * *

ERISKAY itself, which is joined to South Uist by a causeway completed in 2001, is possibly best-known for the lovely 'Eriskay Love Lilt' and several other beautiful Gaelic songs. In a way, the music is more beautiful than the land for this is a barren island, the only soil being rocky moorland. Even so there is a relatively large population.

The main township, **Haun** (ON *havn* – harbour), is on the north coast with some additional scattered houses close to small settlement beside the natural harbour. A number of the men are prawn and lobster fishermen and the women knit fishermen's jerseys and gossamer shawls in distinctive Eriskay patterns.

Almost all are Roman Catholics. A former priest who was born on South Uist, Father Allan McDonald, is remembered for his valuable collections of Gaelic folk-tales, his dictionary of Gaelic phrases and his poetry. In 1893 he

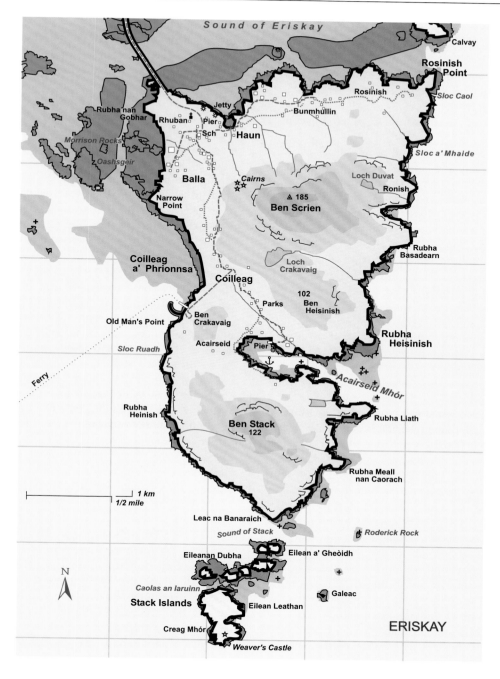

built a new church at Haun. He died in 1905 at the early age of forty-six, a simple man and a dedicated scholar. Unfortunately, much of his literary work was mutilated by Ada Goodrich-Freer, a German woman, who befriended him, persuaded him to hand over his manuscripts and then published much of the material, incorrectly edited, under her own name. Luckily, what was left of Father Allan's work was rescued by John Lorne Campbell of Canna (No. 4.4).

Others followed the lead of Father Allan. Hebridean songs and folklore were passed on orally so it was important that they should be recorded before they were lost. Unfortunately, some of these records are now the subject of controversy such as *The Songs of the Hebrides* (which included the famous 'Love Lilt') published by Marjory Kennedy Fraser. She, with the help of the Rev Dr Kenneth MacLeod of Skye, visited Eriskay in 1905 to record Hebridean songs.

The church built by Father Allan, **St Michael's Church**, has a bell which is the ship's bell from the German battle-cruiser *Derfflinger*, scuttled at Scapa Flow (see No.10.7), and the altar base is the bow of a lifeboat from the aircraft-carrier *Hermes*.

The 12,000-ton steamship *The Politician* sailing from Liverpool and bound for New York, avoided striking the lone islet of **Hartamul** east of Eriskay, but foundered in the Sound of Eriskay near the islet of **Calvay** and broke in two. This was on 5 February 1941, at the height of the Battle of the Atlantic when Hitler's U-boats were exacting a terrible toll on merchant shipping. The Harrison Line ship was unaccompanied and trying to avoid attention by sneaking through the Minch but she should not have ventured into the shallow Sound of Eriskay. Among her assorted cargo of plumbing fittings, motorcycle parts, art silks and Jamaican currency were 264,000 bottles of whisky. The story goes that as soon as the crew were safe the islanders naturally turned their attention to the precious cargo. Before long, nearly every living creature on the island, including the ponies, was blind drunk. During the ensuing weeks the cargo was steadily removed from the wreck. Then, to the islanders' surprise, Charles McColl and Ivan Gledhill of H M Customs & Excise appeared on the scene with some police and began searching the crofts. Most of the whisky miraculously disappeared into peat stacks, hot-water bottles and rabbit holes. The local police disliked the affair and withdrew but thirty-six islanders were sent to court by the excisemen, including a fourteen-year-old boy. Nineteen were found guilty of illegal possession and imprisoned at Inverness.

Some years later Sir Compton Mackenzie based his hilarious book *Whisky Galore!* on the incident (but naturally omitted the sad fact that islanders had been prosecuted). The film was made by Ealing Studios on the adjoining island of Barra (No.7.6) in 1948.

In 1989 a company was formed to try to salvage any whisky remaining in the wreck but the whole expensive operation only yielded a few bottles. The stern of the ship, which contained No 5 hold and the whisky cases, can still be seen at low tide where it has drifted some distance north-west of Calvay but much of it is now bedded deep in the sandy bottom.

Strangely enough, Eriskay had always been a 'dry' island until its first public house was opened in 1988. Naturally it was called *Am Politician* and the Eriskay islanders could be found there happily drinking a dram with their friends. I first visited it on a Thursday, mid-afternoon. It was crowded, and the sweet smell of spirit and soft Gaelic voices encouraged dreams of secret treasure troves of golden liquid. Some bottles still occasionally turn up in unlikely hidey-holes. The islanders call them 'polly-pottles' and I was told by John Alan MacNeil of Barra that genuine ones can be recognised because they are stamped – 'No resale without Federal approval.' They were of course originally destined for the United States.

The best anchorage for the island is unfortunately some distance from Haun. **Acairseid Mhór** (G. – big anchorage) is an inlet which cuts deep into the centre of the island between the two main peaks, **Ben Scrien** in the north (185m) and **Ben Stack** in the south (122m). Practically all the houses, brightly painted and with a distinctly Scandinavian flavour, are in the north at Haun clustered near the north anchorage. This is a shallow little bay, but it was the terminal for the vehicle ferry from South Uist, and the lifeline for the community, until the causeway was built. Besides the church there is a well-stocked village store, a post-office, and a primary school which was sadly closed in 2014.

*   *   *

SOUTH UIST has a spine of mountains along its eastern side the highest being **Beinn Mhór** at 620m (2034ft). Hecla is also conspicuous at 606m. The spine is broken by three sea lochs, Boisdale, Eynort, and Sheilavaig; and a fourth, Skiport, which slices right through the island by joining up with Loch Bee on the west coastal plain. The Atlantic coast, which is the populated side, is virtually a continuous stretch of white shell-sand backed by dunes and flower-filled machair. Between the machair and the barren and mountainous east coast is a maze of lochans interspersed with peat moorland and deserted black houses. These lochs are well stocked with trout but angling is strictly controlled.

South Uist is predominantly Catholic. **Lochboisdale** with a population of about 300 is the ferry port, and the only township on the east coast.

ILL-FATED NUNTON CHAPEL

A chambered cairn, 26m diameter and 6m high, can be found about 2½km north-west of Lochboisdale and due west near **Kilpheder** on the west coast there is a wheelhouse dating from about 200AD which was excavated in 1952 [NF734203]. It has a circular plan with the hearth at the hub. It was probably a farmhouse. Nearby at Garrynamonie School, as with most of the island schools in the early 1900s, the children were never allowed to speak in their native tongue – Gaelic.

At Cladh Hallan near **Daliburgh** in 2002 the 3000-year-old mummified remains of a family were found under a Bronze Age roundhouse. These are the first deliberately mummified prehistoric bodies to be found in Britain. And nearby at *Askernish* a golf-course designed in 1891 by the world-famous golfer, Old Tom Morris, was 'rediscovered' in 2005 under the machair sward and fully restored in 2008. Now hailed by experts as 'the most natural links course in the world'.

About 5½km north of Daliburgh and just north of **Milton** is the birthplace of Flora MacDonald. It was here, to the family home [NF741269], that she came to visit her brother when her chance meeting with the Young Pretender put her name in the history books. The house is now a ruin. At nearby **Loch Kildonnan** a Norse church and island settlement similar to that at Loch Finlaggan (See No.2–4) were recently investigated. A further 5½km brings one to the ruins of **Ormiclate Castle** built in 1701–8 by a French architect and burned down in 1715 during a boisterous Jacobite party. It was the short-lived residence of the Clanranald Chiefs [NF740318].

Off the south shore of Loch Druidibeg and about 1½km from the road is an islet with rectangular **Dùn Roauill** on it [NF778371]. This is perhaps the best dun on South Uist. **Caisteal Bheagram**, the ruin of a small 15th or 16th-century tower, is on the other side of the road on an islet in Loch an Eilean [NF761371].

A road crosses from the **Loch Druidibeg Nature Reserve**, a waterfowl paradise, to Loch Skiport's decayed pier which was built for steamers in 1879 [NF829387]. South of the Usinish peninsula on the east coast is **Nicolson's Leap**. The story goes that Nicolson was found in bed with the wife of the Clanranald Chief. As he escaped he snatched the Chief's baby son as hostage and to escape the clansmen he leapt the 5m chasm on to the rock stack [NF864332]. From there he tried to bargain with his pursuers but ultimately jumped to his death into the sea below with the boy in his arms.

The Royal Artillery Missile Range, which was built in 1961, is in the north-west corner of South Uist. The range is sandwiched between the main road and the Atlantic, and its missiles are tracked from Hirta (St Kilda, No.9.1) which is more than forty miles to the north-west. It is operated by Qinetiq for the Ministry of Defence. On the Hill of Miracles, Rueval, just east of the road, stands the great granite statue of **Our Lady of the Isles** sculpted by Hew Lorimer in 1957 [NF776408] and above the statue is 'space city' – the range control installation.

Just south of the causeway across Loch Bee there is a small loch to the west of the road with clear traces of a large dun – **Dùn Mór** [NF775415]. Loch Bee itself, a west coast loch, is like a Panama Canal cutting right through South Uist because it has a long arm with a flood gate which connects with an arm of Loch Skiport, an east coast sea-loch. Loch Skiport has a number of fascinating channels and anchorages just asking to be explored. By **Shillay More** and **Shillay Beag** there are two popular pools, joined by a shallow but navigable channel, known as Wizard Pool and Little Kettle Pool. **Ornish Island** marks the entrance to Loch Skiport with **Luirsay Dubh** and **Luirsay Glas** on the north headland.

South Uist provides some excellent hill-walking and climbing. Ben Tarbert, Hecla, Feaveallach, Beinn Mhor, Ben na Hoe, Sheeval, Arnaval, Stulaval, Triuirebheinn, Roneval and some of the lesser peaks are all recommended. On the south wall of Coire Hellisdale by Beinn Mhór are 260m high cliffs with deep gullies.

WIZARD POOL – LOCH SKIPORT

*   *   *

BENBECULA is the stepping stone between the Uists, not only physically but because it is here that the predominant religion changes from the Catholic south to the Protestant north. The island is mainly low and flat but has an almost-central solitary hill of 124m, also called **Rueval** like the adjacent peak on South Uist. There is a magnificent view from the top. The causeway which crosses the sands of South Ford and links South Uist to Benbecula was built in 1983. It replaces a wartime bridge built in 1943 to serve the airfield.

In 1896 a pier was built at **Peter's Port** [NF849457] in the narrows between Benbecula and the island of Wiay (No.7.15). This was a typical Governmental folly as there was no road access and a difficult approach by sea. A road and causeway were eventually built but the pier has never been of much practical use.

Beside the west coast road is the remnant of **Borve Castle** [NF773506]. This was probably the castle of 'Vynvawle' granted in a royal charter to Ranald, son of John of Islay, in 1372. Opposite it is the ruin of **Teampull Bhuirgh** [NF769503].

Surprisingly for the Atlantic, the water is very shallow for a long distance off-shore. Consequently shipwrecks here have had few fatalities as they would run aground and crews could almost wade ashore.

South-west of the airport is the island's main village, **Balivanich** with the army base built in 1970 to house the men servicing the rocket range on South Uist. This is a transient population which has been a great help to the economy of the island. Just south are the ruins of 14th-century **Nunton Chapel** – a nunnery which was wrecked during the Reformation and the nuns massacred [NF766537]. It was from Lady Clanranald at Nunton House that Bonnie Prince Charlie obtained the clothing with which he disguised himself as Betty Burke, maidservant to Flora MacDonald. Nunton House was built by the MacDonald chieftains after Ormiclate Castle on South Uist was burned down but it has had alterations since.

The east coast has many small coves and rocky islands and it was in April 1746 that the Prince's party landed on the peninsula of Rossinish where they took shelter in an empty boat. It was also from here that he sailed 'over the sea to Skye' with Flora MacDonald.

North Ford causeway over **Oitir Mór** (G. – the big shoal) was opened in 1960. The strand can be crossed on foot in fine weather when the tide is out but the crossing can be dangerous.

* * *

NORTH UIST is low-lying and so sprinkled with lochs that half the total area is under water. The lochs teem with trout and salmon (this is one of the earliest salmon runs in Scotland). Loch Scadavay alone has an area of 8 sq km and a shore line of 83km. The highest hill is **Eavel** (347m) but hills are few and far between and the Atlantic winds blow over the island virtually unchecked. The Rev Cruttwell wrote in 1798 – 'In the warm season of the year, no country in the highlands can exhibit a more delightful prospect but in bad weather when the wind blows the sea swells to a prodigious height and rolls with inexpressible violence against the shores, exhibiting a prospect awfully grand beyond description.'

Most of the crofts in North Uist are large enough to be just-about economically viable.

In the south east the drying island of **GRIMSAY** is linked to North Uist and Benbecula by a causeway which was completed in 1960. This is the centre for North Uist's fishing industry (mainly lobster) and there is an active processing plant. **Baymore** is an attractive spot for artists.

After crossing Oitir Mhór the road cuts straight through the middle of a stone circle with a chambered cairn to be seen to the north-east [NF837603]. Just beyond in the hamlet of Carinish is the Ditch of Blood – where a battle between the MacLeods of Harris and the MacDonalds of Uist took place in 1601. Nearby is a curious ruin, **Teampull na Trionaid** (G. – Trinity Temple) with twin churches founded by Somerled's daughter, Beathag, in about 1200 on an earlier Celtic site [NF816603]. The churches were later rebuilt with a unique vaulted roof and fine carved stonework by Robert II's daughter, the wife of John, first Lord of the Isles. This is said to have been a seat of learning similar to Iona and is one of the most important archaeological sites in the Western Isles. The college was attended by Duns Scotus (c1265–1308), who became a renowned teacher at the universities of Oxford, Paris, and Cologne. Because he argued that religion depended on faith and not on reason the establishment called anyone with similarly 'stupid' views a 'dunce'.

The last battle in Scotland fought without firearms was between the MacDonalds and the MacLeods at Carinish in 1601.

The main road circles the island. At Ben Langass there is a chambered cairn, **Barpa Langass** (NF837657), 5½m high and 22m wide which is entered through a tunnel. After crossing a desolate central stretch of loch-strewn moorland the road then reaches **Lochmaddy**, the main ferry terminal and administrative centre for North Uist. Here there is a court house and jail, a cottage hospital, a bank, a garage and a comfortable hotel which particularly caters for the needs of anglers and sailors. Loch Maddy or **Loch nam Madadh** (G. – loch of the dogs) is named after the two large rocks, **Madadh Beag** and **Madadh Mór,** standing guard on each side of the entrance to the loch with a further one to the south called **Madadh Gruamach** (G. – the surly dog). In the 16th century this was a favourite pirate rendezvous but a century later it was hosting a fleet of 400 fishing vessels and by the 18th century the port was frequented by many ships trading from Ireland, the west coasts of the English and Scottish mainlands, and as far afield as the Baltic. Sponish is the site of one of the local industries, a factory to process seaweed for alginates.

Loch Maddy is full of islands, many tidal or little more than skerries. It is worth mentioning **Glas Eilean Mór, Faihore, Ruigh Liath, An Glais-eilean Meadhonach, Hamersay, Ferramas, Cliasay More** and **Beg,** and **Keallasay More** and **Beg.**

North-west of Lochmaddy the road skirts the hill of **Blashaval.** On its western slope are three standing stones called Na Fir Bhreige (G. – the false men) [NF887717]. They are reputed to mark the graves of three traitors who were buried alive although another story claims that they are three men from Skye who were turned to stone for having deserted their wives.

Near here a minor road wanders eastwards through the broken land to the north of Loch Maddy. It passes through **Lochportain** with its small fishing pier and ends up at Cheese Bay in the furthest north-east corner.

After the main road has skirted Crogary Beag hill a secondary road runs north by **Newtonferry** to the jetty for a car ferry at **Otternish** which sails to Leverburgh (An t-Obbe) on Harris (No.8.14). Here also is the causeway (opened 1998) to Berneray. The latter ferry route passes close to **Torogay**, a large islet with extensive reefs which shelter the ferry jetty in **Loch nam Ban**. Near Newtonferry is a lochan with a causeway to the remains of a broch last occupied in 1602 by Hugh MacDonald of Sleat [NF897777]. There is also a white house where W. S. Morrison, later Lord Dunrossil, was brought up. He was a Speaker in the House of Commons who became Governor General of Australia. A scramble up **Beinn Mhór** (190m) is rewarded by a superb view of the Sound of Harris and the fragmented Uist landscape.

The main road crosses Loch nan Geireann where, on **Eilean-an-Tighe**, are the remains of the earliest Neolithic potter's workshop yet found in Western Europe. The drying island of **ORONSAY** lies to the north in Vallaquie Strand – uninhabited since the Clearances – and further west the road passes **Sollas**, forever remembered as the centre of one of the most inhumane Clearances. The culprit was Lord MacDonald of Sleat.

Evidence of a Norse settlement has been found on the low sandy peninsula to the north of here.

The road now skirts Vallay Strand. **VALLAY**, another drying island, is like a long breakwater so that the Strand is virtually an enclosed sea-loch when the tide is in. When it is out a track fords the huge expanse of sand and stone to reach ruined Vallay House which was built on the island by Erskine Beveridge, owner of linen mills in Fife. He wrote an authoritative book on the archaeology of the area. Vallay is crowded with antiquities – duns, standing stones, and chapel ruins. The family of the 5th Lord Granville, who was the benign landlord for much of North Uist and undertook valuable experiments in land improvement, stayed at Griminish overlooking Vallay. His son, the present Earl and his wife, Countess Granville, inherited the estate but bought a smokehouse at Clachan where they fillet, smoke and sell salmon and sea trout. 'We are determined to stay in North Uist and we're not quite as rich as some people assume,' he says.

Loch Olabhat is near the road. Its tiny island, **Eilean Domhnuill**, is a crannog built nearly 5000 years ago – predating Ireland's earliest-known crannogs by 2000 years [NF747753].

A 9m-high natural rock arch is at **Griminish Point** at the north-west corner of North Uist.

Sloc Roe (G. – the pit passage) is a cave with an entrance from both sides of the point and two holes opening to the surface. During gales, the water spouts through these to such a height that it can be seen from ten miles away at sea [NF727765].

Turning south through **Balmartin**, Loch Hosta is said to cover a drowned village, and across the road in the cliffs of Tigharry (G. – house on the rock) is another spouting cave, the Kettle Spout. A track leads east up South Clettraval where there are two chambered cairns and an impressive view of the loch-strewn landscape [NF749714]. The RSPB's **Balranald Nature Reserve** juts into the Atlantic at the next headland and includes the tiny off-shore islet of **Causamul**. An even smaller islet, **Deasker** (G. – south skerry), lies nearly three miles south. The churchyard of **Hougharry** holds the graves of many of the island's 'nobility' [NF708706].

Off the wide white sand beaches lie the drying islands of **KIRKIBOST** and **BALESHARE**. Kirkibost Island is now uninhabited whereas Baleshare (G. – east town), the first Hebridean island to gather kelp, has a small but thriving population. Baleshare's sister island, Baile-siar (G. – west town) and nearby Husabost township were swept away in the 1607 tsunami (see Monach Islands No.7.18).

North of the road at this point a prominent hill stands alone among the moorland lochans. A 2½-km cross-country trek leads to **Unival** chambered cairn or barrow – a large New Stone Age tomb [NF801669] – near a 3m-high standing stone on the barren hillside.

There are many interesting walks among the hundreds of lochs, and some of the best fishing in the Western Isles, but always take a good map and a compass.

* * *

The two hills on **BERNERAY** are both on the east side. The west is a wide stretch of low-lying machair, rough grazing and sand dunes and one of the loveliest stretches of white shell-sand beach in Britain – about 4km of perfection. **Beinn Shléibhe** (G. – mountainous hill), also known as Moor Hill, is 93m high and south of it is **Borve Hill** (ON – fort hill), 85m high. Between these two hills is a wide freshwater loch, **Loch Bhruist**, and a reef-ridden sea-loch, **Bays Loch**, forming a deep indentation on the south-east coast.

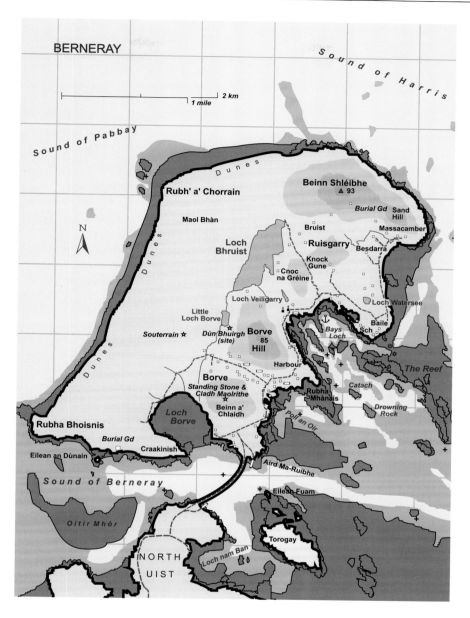

Although Berneray lies close to North Uist it was traditionally part of the parish of Harris. All the habitation is on the south-east side. The village of Borve lies south of Borve Hill but the road which runs almost the full length of the east coast links this settlement with its northerly neighbour, **Ruisgarry**. In between, on Bays Loch, is the post-office, the harbour, the shop, and the church and manse (a rare example of church and manse under one roof). At one time there were three churches on Berneray.

It is a good little harbour, well sheltered, built with EC funds in the late 1980s. Fuel and water

are available although the nearest water tap sometimes produces more peat than water.

The harbour is particularly appreciated by visiting sailors after successfully dodging the rocks in Bays Loch. For years there was no reliable guide to the position of these rocks which the locals navigate entirely by instinct. One old islander bringing a visitor across from Harris ran his boat on to the rocks. 'But I thought you knew all the rocks!' cried the visitor. 'Aye,' said the old man, 'I do. And that is one of them.'

Even when the kelp boom was over Berneray survived on its potatoes. The light sandy soil, still manured with kelp, grows a generous and tasty crop and for many years most of the potatoes eaten on Harris were imported from Berneray. Nowadays, sheep farming and fishing are the main industries although potatoes are still grown. The fishing is for prawns, lobsters and velvet crabs. Berneray is a good example of how years of decline have been replaced by hope and a belief in a viable future. Trim new suburban bungalows, however incongruous in such a beautiful setting, are appearing among the deserted black houses.

In the late 1980s the Prince of Wales wanted to 'get away from it all' and experience life among these gentle and friendly people. He arranged to spend some time on Berneray, lodging in a typical household. The home of 'Splash' McKillop and his wife was chosen. It says much for Hebridean loyalty and respect for privacy that both during his stay and thereafter not a single man, woman or child breathed a word about their famous guest to the media. It was the Prince himself who revealed the facts four years later.

While there the Prince went lobster fishing, helped gather potatoes and dip the sheep. He planted some trees, a few of which have survived the gales and, along with a few replacements, have become established. 'Splash' died in 2009.

There are few prehistoric remains here but part of a stone circle [NF912807] stands on a hillock, **Beinn a' Chlaidh** (G. – hill of the churchyard), beside Loch Borve – a large shallow and circular sea-loch. And there is a souterrain west of Borve Hill [NF907816] near Little Loch Borve – a freshwater lochan.

Berneray was the birthplace of the 'Cape Breton Giant' – one of the world's tallest and strongest men. Angus MacAskill (1825-1863) was a well-proportioned 2.36m (7ft 9ins) in height and weighed 425lbs. He died in Canada.

*   *   *

Access: For all ferry information, 08000-66-5000. South Uist ro-ro ferry: Lochboisdale/ Oban, Wed., Sat.; Oban/ Lochboisdale, Tue., Thu., Sat.; Ro-ro ferry: Eriskay/Barra and return, frequent daily service.

North Uist ro-ro ferry: Uig(Skye)/ Lochmaddy, daily both ways. Ro-ro ferry: Berneray, North Uist/ Leverburgh, Harris, several daily return sailings, 01876-500337.

Benbecula; scheduled daily return air service from Glasgow, Barra and Stornoway, 0870-8509850.

Post bus services cover most of the island including Benbecula airport; Lochmaddy, 01876-500337; Lochboisdale, 01878-700288. There are also a number of private bus services and hire cars. Hotel and bed & breakfast accommodation available. Western Isles Tourist information, 01851-703088 (Lochboisdale 01878-700286, Lochmaddy 01876-500321).

Anchorages:
1. Acairseid Mhór, Eriskay. Well sheltered. Follow sailing directions to avoid drying rocks at entrance. There are 2 visitors' moorings or anchor S of the pier. W of pier is foul with old moorings.
2. Bàgh Hartavagh. Some shelter not more than 2c within entrance except from NE.
3. South Loch Boisdale. Ruined pier on south shore. Beware drying rock and shoal patch NW of the pier and Hut Shoal N of pier. Anchor E of the ruined pier, SE of the fish cages.
4. South Loch Boisdale. 50-berth pontoon, 50m pier and a slipway on Gasay Island connected to Lochboisdale village by new causeway and road.
5. Loch Boisdale, in channel W of Ru Bhuailt. Fish cages block much of anchorage but quieter in SE gales.
6. Lochboisdale. 4 visitors' moorings NE of pier.
7. Stuley Sound, about ½c wide. Submerged rock is charted about midway, position uncertain.
8. Cearcdal Bay, Loch Eynort, SW corner of outer loch, NW of Eilean Eallan, sand. Clean and easy access but exposed E and SE swell. Or, occasional anchorage N side of loch due N of Eilean Eallan in 10m, mud. Holding good but open SE.
9. Poll Craigavaig, Loch Eynort, W of first narrows. Entrance difficult and subject to tides. Restricted by fish cages.
10. Upper Loch Eynort. Plenty of room for anchorage clear of rocks and fish cages, 2–10m, mud. Dramatic scenery, good shelter but seldom visited due to difficult entrance.
11. Mol a Tuath, bay on NW side of Usinish promontory, temp. anchorage with moderately good holding.
12. Loch Skiport, enter N of Ornish Island. Anchor S of Shillay Beag in Wizard Pool – squally in S'lies; or, in Caolas Mór (Little Kettle Pool); or Bagh Charmaig – not so good; or Poll na Cairidh – excellent shelter in S'lies; or Linne Arm – holding poor.
13. Caolas Luirsay just N of Loch Skiport entrance. Narrow, shallow, entrance behind Luirsay Dubh. Affected by swell in N'lies. Anchor in settled weather in 7–11m mud.
14. Loch Sheilavaig, N of Loch Skiport. Fish farms and featureless but rocky challenge. Anchor SW of Canmore Island, 4m rock. Inner loch obstructed by fish nets.
15. Loch Carnan, approach S of Steisay and along marked channel. Jetty for Uist power station and oil terminal is

55m long with 2.5m depth. One visitors' mooring, or anchor clear of fairway and moorings NW of quay, or 3c further NW beyond Direy. Beware rocks and shoals.

16. Peter's Port, 3¼c W of SW extremity of Wiay, approach round N side of Lingay. Slipway at SE extremity of Eilean na Cille has depth 2.4m, rocky bottom. Alongside it and only 15m away is a parallel reef. If anchoring, keep clear of approach to slip.

17. Loch a' Laip. Enter between Wiay and Bo Carrach keeping ½c off Wiay until Bàgh a Bhràoige opens, then cross to N side and follow right through into NW arm beyond Keiravagh Islands. Anchor E of 0.6m drying rock. Good shelter.

18. Loch Keiravagh. Enter with caution and anchor anywhere suitable.

19. Loch Meanervagh. Approach with caution. Good, but very restricted by fish farm.

20. Loch Uskavagh, between Maaey Riabhach and Greanamul. Intricate navigation required but well-protected anchorage. Anchor anywhere suitable. Neavag Bay is very soft mud. Scarilode Bay has many rocks.

21. Caolas Wiay Beag, W of Maragay Mór and Beag. Enter with caution. Anchor N of Ballagary or further in.

22. St Michael's Point, opposite Sugar Bay on W side of Ronay. Anchor 1½c W to NW of Ru na Monach in 4–7m, sand. In summer there is seldom any swell. Or, 2c NNW of Ru na Monach and ¾c from W side of Ronay. Or small craft can anchor in bay surrounded by drying reefs N of islet N of St Michael's Point. Pass 20m NE of islet.

23. Kallin Harbour, 2.5m depth inside but 1.7m at entrance, very restricted temp. space. Approach with care by Vallastrome W of Garbh Eilean Mór. Anchorage difficult as fairway narrow, rocks at the sides and strong tide. There is one visitors' mooring.

24. Acairseid Fhalaich in Flodday sound between Ronay and Floddaymore. Tight entrance to restricted anchorage. Metric chart of rocks considered incorrect (see Martin Lawrence's Pilot).

25. Upper Flodday Sound. Beware mid-channel rocks SE of Haunaray if near LW. Anchor in pool SE of E end of Haunaray, or W of Floddaybeg, or in W side of Poll nan Gall.

26. Moireaig Bay or Harbour. Concealed and awkward entrance about 3c N of Floddaybeg, but good, interesting anchorage. Follow directions carefully.

27. Loch Eport. Follow sailing directions carefully for entrance to loch then possible anchorage E shore of Acairseid Lee or either side of Deer Island. Holding poor due to weed and soft mud, and subject to squalls. Better anchorage in Bàgh a' Bhiorain but narrow entrance to bay between reefs. Other anchorages can be found from Chart 2825 or anchor at head of loch (tricky approach) E of pier,

2m mud, or N of Eilean a Cairidh, 4m mud.

28. Loch Maddy, Ardmaddy Bay, on S shore 6c WSW of Rubha nam Pleac. Anchor off SE shore, 3–5m, no swell. Squally in SW'lies. Exposed NE. 2 visitors' moorings.

29. Loch Maddy, Ferry Terminal. Visitors' moorings or anchor SW of pier and well clear of ferry approach.

30. Loch Maddy, south basin or Vallaquie, in SW corner of Loch. Anchor between old mooring buoy and wreck but beware reef and squalls can be heavy. Fish cages.

31. Loch Maddy, Charles Harbour, W of Hamersay, space confined, rocks, fish cages, and bottom soft mud or rock. Best E of Eilean Fear Vallay where there is 1 visitors' mooring or, if any space, in small pool by Oronsay.

32. Loch Maddy, Sponish Harbour, cleaner than Charles Harbour but poor holding. Anchor at head or in pool E of Ferramas.

33. Loch Portain (Partan), off Loch Maddy. Well-sheltered but holding uncertain in soft mud. All sides shoal. Careful approach required. Anchor where suitable but not more than 2c beyond islet.

34. Bàgh Chaise (Cheese Bay), W of Groatay. New 26-berth marina and moorings.

35. The Caddy, W of Orasay. Approach S of Righe nam Ban and beware Strome Rock. Anchor off concrete slip, WNW of Orasay or try tricky Calm Bay, E of Orasay.

36. Berneray causeway – east side. Good anchorage sheltered from the W by the causeway.

37. Berneray Harbour. Excellent shelter but very restricted. Follow buoyed ferry passage into Bays Loch. (See Martin Lawrence's pilot or CCC for instructions).

38. Berneray by Cope Passage (remember that navigation in these waters is not a science but an art). Temporary anchorage in settled weather off the sandy beach 2–3c N of the Reef beacons. Turn S from Buoy 12 and pass 1c off Massacamber.

39. Bays Loch. Pass through the narrow gap in the Reef keeping 5m E of both beacons, ease round to starboard and follow the deeper water about ½c off the shore. 3 Visitors' moorings W of school, or anchor in N corner of bay, 3–4m, mud. Sheltered except from SE. No swell.

40. Lingay, in large bay between Sound of Berneray and Caolas a' Mhòrain. Anchor close off the island's SW side in 5.5m, sand. Open to NW but very little swell. Note that Lingay strand connects E side of Lingay to the shore. Beware shoaling sandbanks in this area.

41. Vallay, a drying island midway between Griminish point and Aird a' Mhòrain. Anchorage in Vallay Sound is rock encumbered and difficult to enter. Depth inside 1.8m, sand, and protected from swell. Anchorage S of E side of Vallay has a bar to cross (0.6m depth at LW). Pool inside is 1.5–2.7m deep and sheltered from swell. Avoid shoals ¾c S of Vallay.

42. West coast of N Uist, Benbecula and S Uist has no shelter or safe landing places. Nor are there any sheltered anchorages on the S coast of S Uist.

7.15 Wiay

(G. buidhe – yellow or pleasant, ON -øy – island.) Sometimes written in the past as 'Vuiay', or 'Buia' (Martin Martin).

O S Maps: 1:50000 Sheet 22   1:25000 Sheet 453
Admiralty Charts: 1:100000 No.1795 or 1:25000 No.2904

Area: 375ha (927 acres)

Height: 102m (335 ft)

Owners: Previously part of the South Uist Estate. Leased to Malcolm McRae by Lady Gordon Cathcart in 1912. Bought by Sarah Chettle and her late husband Robert for £20,000 in 1980. Put on the market for £500,000 in 2013.

Population: 1861–6. 1881–5. 1891–10 (2 houses). 1901–4. Uninhabited since the mid 1940s.

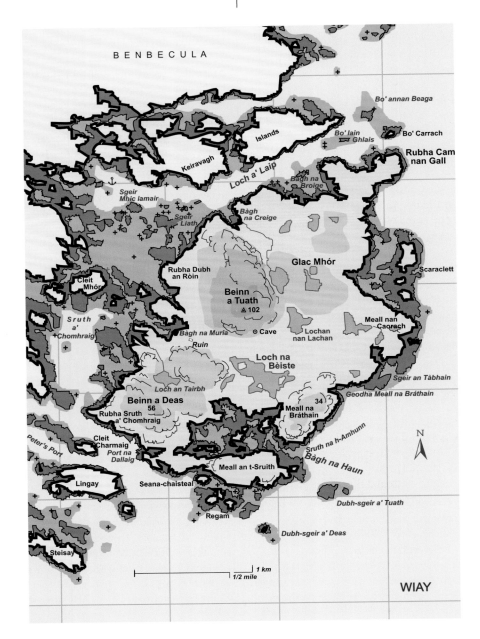

Geology: Lewisian gneiss, similar to the east side of Benbecula.

Wildlife: Wiay is home to a number of species of raptors together with a good selection of marsh and shoreline bird species. Occasional shooting rights are granted for red deer, woodcock, snipe and duck. There are brown trout in the loch. Tenants' rights were purchased in 2003 so there are no sheep.

* * *

WIAY is the largest of the many rocky islands lying to the east of Benbecula.

The rounded summit of **Beinn a Tuath** (G. – north peak) near the centre of the island is the highest point at 102m with **Beinn a Deas** (G. – south peak) considerably lower at 56m. The island is thickly covered with heather and pasturage on fairly gentle slopes and has only a few rocky outcrops but many lochans. The largest of these is **Loch na Bèiste** (G. – loch of the beast) which was once believed to shelter a monster. It has three small islands in it, one of which may be a crannog. North-west of it, in the valley between the two hills and overlooking Bàgh na Muria are the ruins of at least one croft house which is still capable of reconstruction. Although this is a relatively large island it never appears to have been densely populated.

In the south, **Meall an t-Sruith** (G. – the hillock by the tidal channel) shelters a shallow rock-strewn bay, **Bàgh na Haun** (ON *havn* – harbour) with a narrow channel through which the tides rush. The islets, **Lingay** and **Steisay** are to the south-west.

The north of Wiay is bounded by rocky Loch a' Laip (G. – spoon-shaped loch) with the tidal **Keiravagh Islands** to the north. The entrance to the loch is guarded by Rubha Cam nan Gall (G. – crooked headland of the strangers). On our first entrance into this loch, creeping tentatively between the reefs and islets we were hit by a violent squall which flattened the water and covered the rocks with spume. **Bàgh na Creige** was too restricted for shelter and **Bàgh na Bròige** cluttered with fish cages. The squall was so strong that we left on a reciprocal course but, needless to say, as soon as we reached the open sea the wind dropped, the rain stopped and the sun appeared.

Wiay is puddled with lochans with **Lochan nan Lachan** (G. – little loch of the wild duck) the most central. Near here, at the foot of **Beinn à Tuath**, is a well-concealed cave known as **Leabaidh à Phrionnsa** (Prince Charles' Rest) [NF87154608] since the Young Pretender hid there for several days in 1746 after Culloden. It has a tiny entrance but a good view out to sea to watch the Royal Navy vessels which were hunting for him. His guide throughout was Neil MacEachen, a native of Howbeg in South Uist, who was the boatman when Flora Macdonald crossed to Skye with her 'maid', Betty Burke.

Peter's Port on **Eilean na Cille** [NF849457] to the west of Wiay was completed in 1896 at a cost of £2000 in response to a demand for a new Hebridean port. Parliament wanted to be helpful, and the County Council gave assistance, but the result was a typical bureaucratic blunder. Not only was access by sea difficult but there was not even any access by land. Nevertheless the pier was built and extra expenditure of another £100 approved for the removal of a large rock which blocked access to the end of the pier. Although the sea approach was still considered hazardous, without a road the pier was, in any case, unusable.

At last a further grant of £1800 was obtained to construct a road which, if nothing else, helped communication between the local crofts and the pier is now used by the occasional small prawn boat. The 1931 edition of the *West Coast Pilot* dryly remarked '. . . the approach is so difficult, and there is so little room to turn, that it is not used by the local steamers. The port should not be entered without local knowledge . . .'

Wiay is the only Scottish island to have had a resident grizzly bear. In 1980 during filming for a Kleenex advertisement 'Hercules', a very large grizzly, decided that he rather liked the area. He eventually swam over to North Uist where the film crew found him 24 days later and persuaded him to leave.

Access: Try Uist Outdoor Centre, Lochmaddy, (Neil Johnson) 01876-500480 or Lady Anne boat trips, Kallin Harbour, (Nick Ingleden) 01870-602403.

Anchorages:

1. Bàgh na Bròige, Loch a' Laip. Enter Loch between Wiay and Bo Carrach keeping ½c off Wiay until Bàgh na Bròige opens. Formerly best anchorage behind drying rock, now probably no room due to fish cages.

2. Bàgh na Creige, Loch a' Laip. Cross over to N side of

Loch when Bàgh na Bròige opens, then SW course for Bàgh na Creige. Just enough room at bay entrance for smaller craft.

3. Loch a' Laip. Best anchorage is in far NW corner, N or S of 0.6m drying rock. Good shelter but ½M distance from Wiay.

4. Sruth a' Chomhraig, W side of Wiay, approached from S. Not now suitable as fish cages obstruct W side and too many rocks on E side. The traditional landing place was in Bàgh na Muna.

5. Peter's Port approach. Beware drying rocks SSW of Wiay. Approach round N side of Lingay and anchor in 4m, sand on rock, leaving clear approach to slipway. Awkward anchorage, about 4c from Wiay.

6. It may be possible to find a temp. anchorage in suitable conditions N or W of Cleit Charmaig in 6–8m but the bottom is mainly rock.

7.16 Ronay

(ON hraun-øy – rough island).

O S Maps: 1:50000 Sheet 22 1:25000 Sheet 453
Admiralty Charts: 1:100000 No.1795 1:25000 No.2904

Area: 563ha (1391 acres)
Height: 115m (377 ft)

Owner: Owned by the same family since 1968 or earlier.

Population: 1826–180 (Gaelic School Society *Moral Statistics Report*). Cleared for sheep in 1831, many settling on the neighbouring tidal island of Grimsay. 1841–9. 1861–4. 1881–6. 1891–6. 1931–6. Uninhabited since then.

Geology: Lewisian gneiss with some flinty crush and a peaty soil.

History: Ronay appears to have had a number of religious associations in its past. It has a priest's hill, a monk's headland, a Druid's hill, and it had a chapel according to Martin Martin. Archaeological investigation may prove interesting.

Wildlife: One of the few islands in the area which is home to the Atlantic grey seal – protected by a special Act of Parliament in 1921. There are red deer, grouse and woodcock with occasional shooting by special arrangement and the lochs are well-stocked with trout. The bird-life includes many raptors and the occasional sea-eagle.

* * *

RONAY is a fairly large rugged island with an extremely indented coastline. It has a series of hills which are bare to the north but heather clad to the south. The northern peninsula, Ronaybeg, is joined to the rest of the island by an isthmus and encloses a large and very shallow bay in the north-west called **Bàgh nan Uamh** (G. – bay of the caves). South of this bay are the two highest hills, Beinn an t-Sagairt (G. – the priest's hill) at 104m and **Beinn a' Charnain** (G. – the cairn hill) at 115m.

Ronay is divided from North Uist by a channel on the west side, which is an impenetrable morass of rocks and reefs although the island could be circumnavigated by a small craft like a dinghy in suitable weather and at the right state of the tide (distance almost nine miles). **Garbh Eilean Mór** (G. – big rough island) is in the middle of the channel with **Eilean a' Ghobha** (G. – island of the dipper) to the north.

Martin Martin noted that there was 'a little Chappel in the Island Rona, called the Low-landers Chappel, because Seamen who dye in time of Fishing, are buried in that place.' This apparently refers to a pre-Reformation chapel. Fishermen from Ronay may have been buried at St Michael's Chapel on Grimsay [NF882548]. The ruins are clearly visible only just across the water from **Rubha na Monach** (G. – headland of the monks), Ronay's south-western tip, and Martin may have confused the geography. On the other hand there is a small rocky knoll near the west side of Ronay known as Cnoc nan Gall which could be translated as (G. – knoll of the Lowlanders) so maybe there was a 'Lowlander's chapel' actually on Ronay.

The hill in the centre of Ronay is called **Beinn nan Druidhneach** [drooi-niach] (G. – hill of the sorcerers). There was a Gaelic tendency to attribute anything ancient, like a Neolithic ruin for instance, to Druids or sorcerers but the hill may well have been the site of pagan rites.

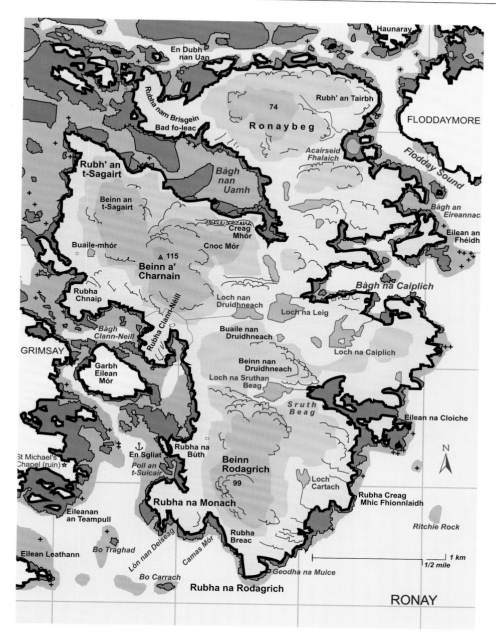

Access: Try Uist Outdoor Centre, Lochmaddy, 01876-500480, Lady Anne boat trips, Kallin Harbour, (Nick Ingleden) 01870-602403, or Sea Trek, Uig, Lewis, 01851-672464.

Anchorages:

1. Off St Michael's Point, on W side of Ronay. Anchor 1½c W to NW of Ru na Monach in 4–7m, sand. In summer there is seldom any swell. Or 2c NNW of Ru na Monach and ¾c from W side of Ronay.

2. Acairseid Fhalaich in Flodday Sound. Very tight entrance between two islets to restricted but snug anchorage. Metric chart of rocks may be incorrect (see Martin Lawrence's Pilot) as channel depth may be 4m.

3. Haunaray. Restricted temp. anchorage between Haunaray and Rubh' an Tairbh. Bottom mud but depth increases rapidly when clear of drying rocks.

7.17 Floddaymore

(ON floti, G. mór – big raft).

O S Maps: 1:50000 Sheet 22   1:25000 Sheet 453
Admiralty Charts: 1:100000 No.1795   1:25000 No.2904

Area: 58ha (143 acres)
Height: 28m (92 ft)

Population: No Census records and uninhabited.

Geology: A low-lying slab of Lewisian gneiss.

Wildlife: Barnacle and greylag geese stop off here in winter.

* * *

FLODDAYMORE, or Flodday Mór, lies close off the north-east side of Ronay. **Floddaybeg**, or Flodday Beag, lies to the north of it.

It is a low and fairly barren island but it is not short of fresh water as it contains one large central loch with its own islets and two other lochans connected to a stream in the south. The western headland, which is almost disconnected, is called **Rubha nan Caorach** (G. – the headland of the sheep or cattle). This may still be a landing place for stock. In the north continuous skerries join up a number of small islets and only a very narrow channel separates Floddaybeg from Floddaymore.

All these small islands such as Floddaymore offer rather poor-quality grazing but they are popular with sheep-farmers and crofters because no fencing is required. This largely compensates for the fewer sheep per acre and the difficulty of access.

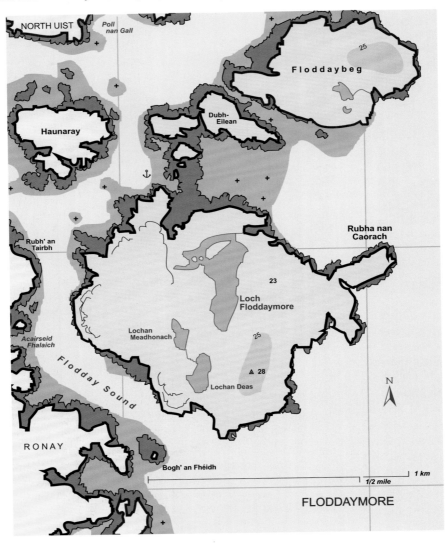

FLODDAYMORE

To the north-west the definitive hump of **Haunaray** divides the channel between Floddaymore and Ronay at a deep pool. Among the shallows beyond here is **Eilean nan Gearr** (G. – isle of the hares).

Our landing on Floddaymore was abrupt. *Jandara* was temporarily anchored south of Haunaray and near the Ronay shore. Two of us had no sooner cast off the dinghy than the outboard cut out. The gusty west wind immediately caught us and as we blew clear of Ronay's shelter we were thrown across the channel with almost hurricane force. Oars were useless and in a different situation there could have been nasty consequences. As it was we came to a comfortable stop at our intended destination cushioned on a heap of Floddaymore kelp.

Access: Try Uist Outdoor Centre, Lochmaddy, 01876-500480 or Lady Anne boat trips, Kallin Harbour, (Nick Ingleden) 01870-602403.

Anchorages:

1. Acairseid Fhalaich in Flodday Sound. Very tight entrance channel between two islets to a restricted but snug anchorage. Metric chart of rocks may be incorrect (see Martin Lawrence's Pilot) as channel depth may be 4m.
2. Haunaray. Restricted temporary anchorage between Haunaray and Ronay, N of Rubh' an Tairbh (G. – bull point). Bottom mud but depth increases rapidly when clear of drying rocks.
3. Upper Flodday Sound. Beware mid-channel rocks SE of Haunaray if near LW. Anchor in pool SE of E end of Haunaray (off N point of Floddaymore), or W of Floddaybeg.

7.18 Monach Islands

(G. and E. – monk islands) Also known as Heisker.

Ceann Ear

[er] (G. – east head)

Ceann Iar

[eeur] (G. – west head)

Shillay

(ON selr-øy – seal island)

O S Maps: 1:50000 Sheet 22 1:25000 Sheet 454
Admiralty Charts: 1:200000 No.2722

Area: 357ha (883 acres)
Height: 19m (62 ft)

Owner: North Uist Estate Trust 1990 (Lord Granville). Schoolhouse owned by Franklyn Perring the famous botanist who died in 2003 (leased to Scottish Natural Heritage).

Population: In 1595 the islands were said to be able to raise twenty men of military age suggesting a population of about one hundred. 1764–70. In 1810 the population left because of the failure of the soil due to overgrazing which had exposed large areas of sand. Before the ground could recover there was a great storm which tore up the remaining turf and covered the islands with sand. By 1841 39 people had returned (4 houses). Later, marram grass was planted to stabilise the soil and by 1861 the population had risen to 127. 1881–24. 1891–140 (17 houses). 1914–80. 1921–66. 1931–33. Everyone then moved to North Uist except the lighthouse-keepers who were there until 1942. One family returned 1943–1947. Since uninhabited.

Geology: Schistose and granite bedrock covered with fine shell-sand and uncultivated machair, but great changes in the surface take place from Atlantic storms acting upon such a light soil.

History: Human settlement goes back to before 1000AD. In about the 13th century a nunnery or convent having connections with Iona was established on Ceann Ear, and the now-deserted lighthouse on Shillay marks the site of a monastery in which part of the monks' duties was to maintain a light as a guide for mariners. The religious associations of the Monachs however failed to survive the Reformation although the islands continued to be well populated until the 20th century.

Lady Grange (see Hirta No.9.1) was held prisoner here for two years (1732–34) by MacDonald of Sleat before being transferred to St Kilda by MacLeod of Dunvegan. She had hidden behind a sofa and overheard a Jacobite plot at her house in Edinburgh. Stupidly, she threatened to denounce the conspirators so, with her husband's agreement, she was sent to the Western Isles while Edinburgh society attended her 'funeral' at Greyfriars Church.

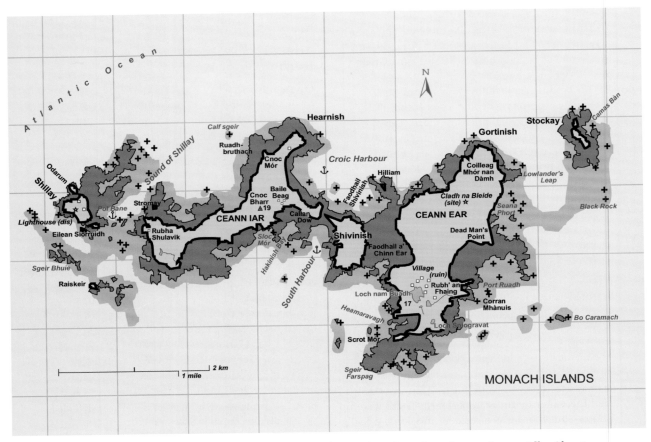

MONACH ISLANDS

Wildlife: The Monachs are a National Nature Reserve and permission to land is required from Scottish Natural Heritage, 0131-447 4784.

There are no trees but there is good machair consisting of very little grass but a great deal of buttercup, red and white clover, dandelion, eyebright, blue speedwell, daisy, harebell, hop and birdsfoot trefoil, pansy, silverweed and wild thyme; over 200 flowering species in all.

Fulmars which normally prefer high cliffs nest here in the sand dunes and herons nest in an empty house as there are no trees. A huge population of black guillemot also make this their home in the spring and it is a favoured wintering place for barnacle geese and frequented by common, Arctic and little terns. 31 breeding species have been counted and over 100 bird species.

The grey seal was one of the world's rarest seals with two-thirds of the total population of about 160,000 animals in the British Isles, and more than half that number in the Hebrides. However the Monarchs are thought to be the world's largest colony of grey seals and recently

numbers have been increasing rapidly. About 4000 pups a year come from the Monachs and the reefs of Stockay are a favoured breeding location in the last four months of each year. This is a comparatively recent phenomenon as the area was only colonised after the islanders had left. Grey seals are more cautious of man than the common seal. In the past, islanders found seals useful for food and clothing. They were easily killed when breeding, so depopulation of the islands has been of some benefit to the species.

* * *

Five small islands and several drying rocks form the **MONACH ISLANDS** group which lie about five miles west of North Uist and Benbecula. The group is also known by the old Norse name of **HEISKER** (bright skerry). The three central islands are all interconnected at low water. **Ceann Ear** is the largest of the group (231ha), connected to **Shivinish** (28ha) which, in turn, is almost a part of **Ceann Iar** (134ha). There are difficult waters round about but these low-lying islands – little more than sand-banks – have wide sandy beaches and high dunes which offer shelter from the worst of the westerlies. Several sandy hillocks near **Gortinish**, in the north-east of Ceann Ear, reach their highest point of 18m at **Coilleag Mhór nan Dàmh**. To the east there is an islet called **Stockay**, and to the west one called **Shillay**.

It is said that there was once a great five-mile stretch of sand which was exposed at low water and which linked the entire group to North Uist. But in 1607 an enormous tidal wave – the same titanic tsunami which formed the Sound of Pabbay (See No.8.4) – swept away the sand-banks. The Monach Islands and their inhabitants have been isolated ever since. History does not record how many of the islanders, if any, survived this disaster.

The remains of some patches of grazing and cultivated land can still be seen in the vicinity of the small village in the south-west of Ceann Ear. This village is visible from Croic harbour and lies between **Port Ruadh** (G. – red port) and **Loch nam Buadh** (G. – loch of virtues). The village had good amenities, a post-office and a school which was maintained by the Church until 1874 and thereafter by the School Board. There were no shops – but there was a resident missionary. Sadly, the deserted village is disintegrating although the old schoolhouse is still kept weatherfast for the accommodation of visiting lobster fishermen from time to time. The village houses were unusual for the Hebrides as they had grain-drying kilns built inside them instead of in out-houses. This arrangement is common to Shetland.

Port Ruadh is south of **Rubh' a' nam Marbh** (G. – dead man's point). To the north is the probable site of the old monastery and churchyard, **Cladh na Bleide** [NF644624].

As one of the duties of the ancient monastery and convent on Ceann Ear the monks were expected to maintain a fire on the small western island of **Shillay** to help ships avoid the many rocks in the area. Eventually a red brick lighthouse was built in 1864. This was abandoned in 1942 but there is now a solar-powered replacement. A dressed stone from the old lighthouse is now built in to the church wall at Paible. On it the lighthouse-keeper had carved – 'Eternity oh eternity.'

Although by the 1930s the last of the islanders had left the Monachs this was no St Kilda type of evacuation. It was merely that, as with so many

of these isolated settlements, the young people had travelled 'abroad' and failed to return and numbers steadily dwindled away.

Hebridean sailors believed, and maybe still do, that if they drown the sea will always carry their body home. A cairn on Ceann Iar marks the grave of Lieut Wm A McNeill RN, who drowned off Northern Ireland when his ship, *Laurentic*, struck a mine in 1917. His body was washed up on Ceann Iar which is part of the clan lands of the McNeills.

* * *

Access: By arrangement; try Kilda Cruises, Leverburgh, Harris, 01859-502060, Seatrek, Uig, Lewis, 01851-672464 or Lady Anne boat trips, Kallin Harbour, (Nick Ingleden) 01870-602403.

Anchorages: Navigation around the Monach Isles requires great care as there are many hazards.
1. Croic Harbour. Good shelter except from NE, but uncomfortable swell in W to N winds. Good holding in sand or clay, 6m. Anchor middle of W side of bay, or in SE corner, clear of drying rocks.
2. Port Ruadh, on E side of Ceann Ear was the boat harbour for the village but it almost dries and has many reefs. It is well protected by high rocks and has very little swell but is rather open to SE winds.
3. South Harbour. Good shelter in N'lies, but scend may be uncomfortable. Beware drying rocks.
4. Shillay. Only approach from N, with stone beacons on Eilean Sìorruidh [shioorooi] (G. – eternal island) in line. Anchor off lighthouse jetty, 5m. This is the best anchorage but ill-positioned for easy exploration of the islands.

7.19 Flodday

(ON floti-øy – flat island).

O S Maps: 1:50000 Sheet 18 1:25000 Sheet 454
Admiralty Charts: 1:100000 No.1795 1:12500 No.2825

Area: 42ha (104 acres)
Height: 25m (115 ft)

Population: No census records and uninhabited.

Geology: Archaean gneiss with a sandy soil.

Wildlife: A favourite staging-post for barnacle geese.

* * *

FLODDAY is a flat and featureless island which

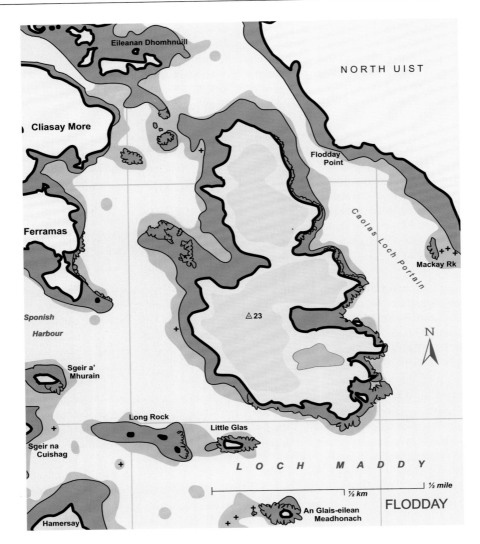

lies in the sheltered waters of Loch Maddy. There
is a narrow isthmus almost splitting the island into
two unequal portions. The larger southern section
has a loch of slightly brackish water.

There are several fish farms between Flodday's
west shore and the neigbouring islands of
Ferramas and Cliasay Mor, and the east is bounded
by Caolas Loch Portain which has a considerable
tidal current. South-west lies the small islet of
Hamersay.

Loch nam Madadh with its maze of islands and
channels is, in geophysical terms, considered the
most complex sea-loch (known as a fjard) in the
European Union.

* * *

Access: Try Uist Outdoor Centre, Lochmaddy,
01876-500480, Lady Anne boat trips, Kallin
Harbour, (Nick Ingleden) 01870-602403, or one
of the local boatowners

Anchorages: No recommended anchorages.
1. Occasional anchorage between Ferramas and Flooday in
suitable depth, sand. Approach with great care and keep a
close check on the chart.

7.20 Hermetray

(ON Hermundr-øy – Hermundr's isle). Hermundr was a man's
personal name.

O S Maps: 1:50000 Sheet 18 1:25000 Sheet 454
Admiralty Charts: 1:100000 No.1795 1:20000 No.2642

Area: 72ha (178 acres)
Height: 35m (115 ft)

Owner: Scottish Government.

Population: 1841–8 (1 house). Uninhabited since mid-19th century.

Geology: Lewisian gneiss.

History: In 1633 Charles I founded a 'Company of the General Fishery of Great Britain and Ireland' with its 'registered offices' in Lewis. (He already had proposals afoot for the purchase of Lewis by the Crown.) Lord Seaforth, who was owner of Lewis at the time, was invited to join the board so that his influence would 'keep the islanders in awe'. The corporation set up one of its fishing stations on Hermetray but the scheme collapsed in 1640 due to the start of the troubles which eventually led to the civil war. Charles II tried to revive it but it was seriously under-capitalised. In 1695 Martin Martin wrote that when he visited Hermetray he saw 'the foundation of a house built by the English in King Charles the First's time, for one of their magazines to lay up the cask, salt, etc, for carrying on the

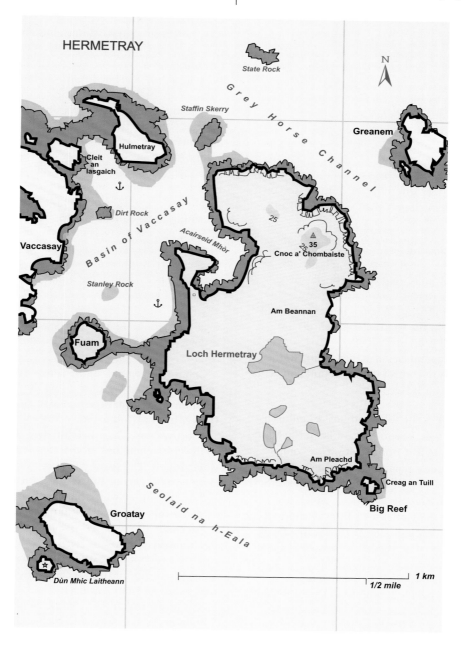

fishery, which was then begun in the Western Islands; but this design miscarried because of the civil wars which then broke out.'

In 1921, on the 16 March, following a savage storm, Alexander (Alex Beag) MacDonald was out checking his lobster pots when he saw two men waving on Compass Knoll, Hermetray. He found a ship broken apart on the rocks and three survivors in poor condition. Among the wreckage was a case of whisky so he first tried to persuade them to drink some but they refused. They were Norwegian and spoke neither English nor Gaelic. MacDonald had dry clothing aboard and after making them as comfortable as possible he took them home to Berneray where his wife and a neighbour fed them well and gave them a bed for the night. The following day, arrangements were made by the islanders for the men to travel to the mainland and thence to Scandinavia. Strangely, at no time did the men give any indication of gratitude or thanks to their rescuers and they were never heard of again. The name of the ship was the *Puritan* and to this day the islanders consider this must account for the men's inexplicable behaviour – their refusal to drink good whisky!

Wildlife: Some strange humps near the shores like large goose-pimples have been created by generations of gulls' nests. The rough grass, scattered with ragged robin and bog cotton, provides good grazing. Adder's tongue fern and flag iris grow in the wet turf and white clover where the soil is drier.

Buzzards sometimes make their home in the low cliffs and help to control the rat population. There are no fish in Loch Hermetray.

HERMETRAY is the southernmost island of a group which lies close to North Uist in the Sound of Harris. **Cnoc a' Chombaiste** (G. – compass knoll), the highest point, is only a mere 35m above sea-level. It is in the north-east opposite Acairseid Mór (G. – big harbour), which is a shallow and weedy inlet with a rocky shore. It is formed by a neck of land with a rectangle of dry-stone walls (now used as a sheep-fank) and some ruined shielings. The sheep fank is probably the remains of the single house mentioned in the 1841 census and it might in fact cover the site of the original fish station. The east coast is moderately steep but Loch Hermetray in the

centre of the island is low-lying. It contained fresh, clean and drinkable water when I tested it but it might occasionally pick up sea-spray when the wind is in the east.

The irrepressible Martin Martin reported that Hermetray had '...a moorish soil, covered all over almost with heath, except here and there a few piles of grass and the plant milkwort. Yet, notwithstanding this disadvantage, it is certainly the best spot of its extent for pasturage among these isles, and affords great plenty of milk in January and February beyond what can be seen in the other islands'. Hermetray still provides good all-year-round pasturage, but for sheep – not cattle, and peats were cut here until quite recently. The island is on the North Uist/Harris boundary and officially is part of Harris.

There are many small islands and skerries surrounding Hermetray, with **Greanem** (ON – green holm) to the north-east. Site Rock lies due north of State Rock and both cover at high water. About a century ago two Berneray men, with their guns and a dog were landed on Site Rock at low water to shoot sea-birds. A strong wind blew up and the boatman lost an oar when returning to take them off the rock. The wind and tide carried his boat away but, luckily, it blew him back to Berneray. He immediately roused a rescue party. By then it was blowing a gale and night had fallen but in pitch darkness the rescuers managed to navigate through the reefs and reach Site Rock. The tide was still rising and by the time they reached the rock the fowlers only had their shoulders above water with the dog on one man's back.

Groatay [groa-ay], to the south-west, has a small drying islet between it and the North Uist coast on which can be seen the ancient ruins of **Dùn Mhic Laitheann** (G. – MacLean's fort). The fort was used as a herring magazine in the 17th century and has an artesian well for its water supply. The seaway between Groatay and Hermetray is part of the **Seolaid na h-Eala** (G. – channel of the Swan), named after a famous 17th-century Skye-built birlinn called *White Swan*.

Vaccasay (ON *vagr-øy* – island with a bay) lies immediately west of Hermetray and with extensive reefs linking it to **Hulmetray** provides valuable shelter for the Vaccasay basin. Martin referred to an island 'in Loch Maddy' called 'Vacksay' on which there 'is still to be seen the foundation of a house, built by the English, for a magazine, etc., for carrying on a great fishery.' It would seem likely that he was referring to Vaccasay (and not Loch Maddy) as the Hermetray fishery project would have used the Vaccasay basin for its anchorage. The full name for the drying islet forming the south barrier to the basin is **Fuam an Aon Fhoid** (G. – far-out isle of the one peat). It has shallow soil which only allowed a cutting depth of one peat.

To the north of Vaccasay is the large, almost circular 'Cabbage Patch' group which contains the Grey Horse reef, **Opsay**, and two islets, **Sarstay** and **Narstay**, sounding like the ugly sisters in a pantomime.

* * *

Access: Try Uist Outdoor Centre, Lochmaddy, 01876-500480, Lady Anne boat trip, Kallin Harbour, (Nick Ingleden) 01870-602403, or Free Spirit, Leverburgh, 01859-520251.

Anchorages:

1. NE of Fuam in Vaccasay Basin. Beware fish-farm, Stanley Rock 1c NNE of Fuam, and drying reef between Fuam and Hermetray. Good anchorage NE of Fuam off pebble beach on Hermetray.

2. Acairseid Mór, narrow inlet on NW side of Hermetray. Except for the entrance only really suitable for shallow draught boats and very restricted space. Bottom mainly weed.

3. Between Vaccasay and Hulmetray, Vaccasay Basin. Beware Dirt Rock 1c E of Vaccasay. Anchor N of Dirt Rock. Distance to Hermetray 3–4c.

7.21 Tahay

(ON tagg-øy – island with a prominent hill).

O S Maps: 1:50000 Sheet 18 1:25000 Sheet 454
Admiralty Charts: 1:100000 No.1795 1:20000 No.2642

Area: 53ha (131 acres)
Height: 65m (213 ft)

Owner: Scottish Government.

Population: 1841–0. 1851–34 (6 households). Uninhabited since 1855. Although close to North Uist, Tahay is part of the administrative district of Harris.

Geology: Lewisian gneiss.

History: Six families (five MacLeods, one MacAskill) – evicted from Pabbay in 1846 tried to make a home for themselves on Tahay. Although there is virtually no arable land they hoped to survive by fishing. They constructed houses and a boat harbour; the ruins are still visible and one of the old houses has been converted to a sheep-fank. Several children were born on the island but conditions were appalling and in the mid-1850s the families gave up the struggle and emigrated to Australia with financial assistance from the Highlands and Islands Emigration Society.

Wildlife: A few small stunted rowan trees less than a metre in height support the only heronry in the Sound of Harris. A number of families of the birds like to group together for protection with their young of differing ages.

TAHAY is 65m high, easily the highest and most conspicuous island in the surrounding group. It has a regular – almost rectangular – shape and a central peak. There is a very narrow and shallow channel between tidal **Trollaman** and Tahay which is all that separates it from North Uist. Tahay has small inland cliffs and hilly tracts of heath and peat bog; peat has always been the main source of fuel for the Berneray islanders. The normal landing place for the peat boats was at **Rubha Mòr Nighean Tormaid** (G. – promontory of Morag, daughter of Norman).

To the north and north-west are **Sursay** and **Votersay**. The ruined shieling on the south side of Sursay is called Airigh na h-Aon Oidhche (G. – one-night shieling) because in the late 19th century a lone shepherd had to stay overnight on the island but was awakened by screeching seagulls and his terrified dog. He rushed outside and saw with horror what he described as an enormous cartwheel in the sky making a strange noise. As frightened as his dog, he ran to his boat, and beat all records to reach North Uist. He never returned to Sursay.

To the south of Tahay there is a group of three islets with the curious name of **Righe nam Ban**

(G. – ?shieling of the women) although they are better known locally as Eileanan na Yacht.

Access: Try Uist Outdoor Centre, Lochmaddy, 01876-500480, Lady Anne boat trips, Kallin Harbour, (Nick Ingleden) 01870-602403, or Free Spirit, Leverburgh, 01859-520251.

Anchorages: There are no recommended anchorages for Tahay.
1. Temp. anchorage is possible in suitable conditions due S of Tahay hill and ESE of Trollaman in 7m sand and shingle. Approach with care ½c N of Righe nam Ban.
2. The Caddy. Off concrete slip on N Uist, 5c S of Tahay and WNW of Orasay, 3–4m, subject to weed. Approach S of Righe nam Ban keeping closer to Orasay. Beware Strome

Rock and other rocks W of Righe nam Ban.
3. Bàgh Chaise (Cheese Bay) on North Uist is ¾M SE of Tahay but is the best available anchorage in the vicinity. Anchor SW of central islet but beware drying rocks.

7–Appendix Fiaray

(G. feur – grass or pasture, ON -øy – island).

O S Maps: 1:50000 Sheet 31   1:25000 Sheet 452
Admiralty Charts: 1:100000 No.1796   1:30000 No.2770

Area: 41ha (101 acres)
Height: 30m (98 ft)

Population: No Census records and uninhabited.

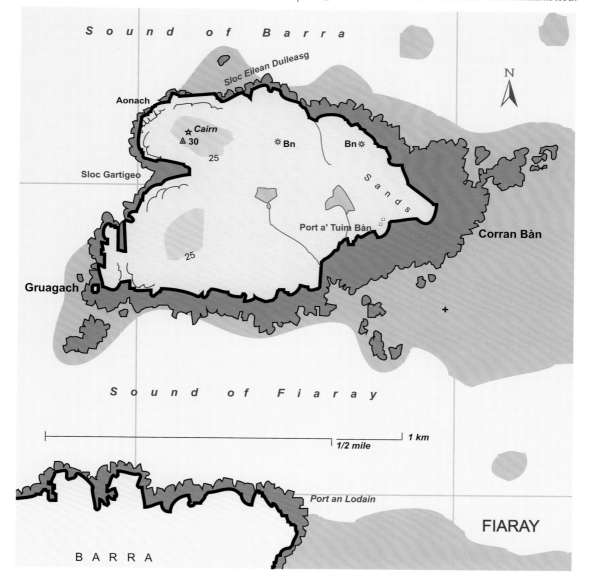

Geology: Archaean gneiss with a sandy soil.

Wildlife: A favourite staging-post for barnacle geese.

* * *

Except for two small hillocks on the west side, **FIARAY** is a flat and featureless island. The most northerly hill is the highest at 30m. There is a distinctive sandy promontory at the east side called **Corran Bàn** (G. – white sickle-shaped tapering point) and a seaweed-covered headland on the other side of the island facing the Atlantic called **Gruagach** (G. – beautiful head of hair). The original shielings were at **Port a' Tuim Bàn** (G. – port of the white knoll) near Corran Bàn.

Fiaray boasts, which is remarkable for such a tiny island, two little lochans and it is entirely surrounded by a drying reef. Some local fishermen would swear that this is the home of a fairy woman, often seen by passing boats.

In a collection of folk stories the Rev. Fr. Allan McDonald (d.1905) recorded that towards the end of 1890 people on the shore of South Uist heard dreadful cries coming from **Lingay** (ON – heather isle). Lingay is the little islet in the middle of the Sound of Barra, east of Fiaray. A rescue boat put out for the island as it was assumed that sailors were drowning. The screaming suddenly stopped when they were close to Lingay and although they searched the area they could find nothing to account for the cries. Almost exactly eight years later, in October 1898, a boat from Eriskay was wrecked on Lingay and the sailors cries brought help from South Uist. All were saved but the first incident was claimed by the islanders to have been a forewarning. (Nowadays it would be called, in science-fiction terms, a 'time-warp'.)

Access: Barra Fishing Charters, 01871-890384. Island Adventures, Castlebay, 01871-810284. Tourist Information, Castlebay, Barra, 01871-810336.

Anchorage: No recommended anchorage.
1. Temp anchorage in Sound of Fiaray in settled weather but carefully follow sailing directions.

The Outer Hebrides –
The Sound of Harris and North

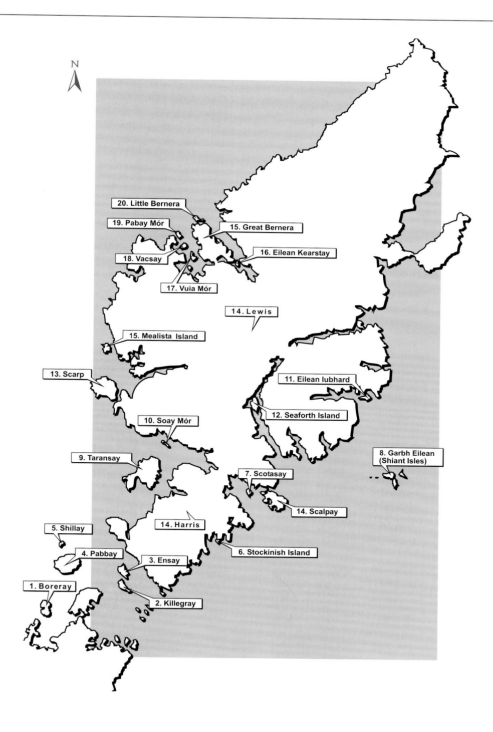

N

20. Little Bernera

19. Pabay Mór

15. Great Bernera

18. Vacsay

16. Eilean Kearstay

17. Vuia Mór

14. Lewis

15. Mealista Island

13. Scarp

11. Eilean Iubhard

12. Seaforth Island

10. Soay Mór

9. Taransay

8. Garbh Eilean (Shiant Isles)

7. Scotasay

14. Scalpay

5. Shillay

14. Harris

4. Pabbay

6. Stockinish Island

3. Ensay

1. Boreray

2. Killegray

SECTION 8, Table 1: Arranged according to Geographical Position

No.	Name	Latitude	Longitude	Table 2* No.	Table 3** No.	Area in Acres		Area in Hectares
8.1	Boreray	57° 43N	07° 18W	85	110	489		198
8.2	Killegray	57° 45N	07° 05W	90	125	435		176
8.3	Ensay	57° 46N	07° 05W	87	121	460		186
8.4	Pabbay	57° 46N	07° 14W	46	35	2026		820
8.5	Shillay	57° 48N	07° 15W	152	84	116		47
8.6	Stockinish Island	57° 49N	06° 49W	150	129	121		49
8.7	Scotasay	57° 53N	06° 45W	149	109	121		49
8.8	Garbh Eilean (Shiant I.)	57° 54N	06° 22W	95	42	217	88	
	Eilean an Tighe	57° 54N	06° 20W			136	55	143
8.9	Taransay	57° 54N	07° 02W	33	27	3645		1475
8.10	Soay Mór	57° 56N	06° 58W	153	139	111		45
8.11	Eilean Iubhard	58° 00N	06° 26W	102	89	309		125
8.12	Seaforth Island	58° 00N	06° 44W	71	31	675		273
8.13	Scarp	58° 01N	07° 08W	40	22	2582		1045
8.14	Lewis/Harris	58° 03N	06° 40W	1	4	5384126	217898	
	Great Bernera	58° 13N	06° 51W			5243	2122	
	Scalpay	57° 52N	06° 40W			1614	653	220673
8.15	Mealista Island	58° 05N	07° 07W	103	87	306		124
8.16	Eilean Kearstay	58° 12N	06° 46W	125	138	190		77
8.17	Vuia Mór	58° 13N	06° 53W	118	95	208		84
8.18	Vacsay	58° 14N	06° 55W	160	145	101		43
8.19	Pabay Mór	58° 14N	06° 56W	110	94	250		101
8.20	Little Bernera	58° 16N	06° 52W	99	134	341		138

*Table 2: The islands arranged in order of magnitude
**Table 3: The islands arranged in order of height

Introduction

The Hebrides are said to derive their name from the Norse word, *Havbrødøy* – meaning islands on the edge of the sea. On the other hand, long before the Norse era, Pliny called them the Hebudes – inhabited by the Ebudae tribe – and Ptolemy in the 2nd century wrote of the Eboudai islands above Ivernia (Ireland).

The great archipelago of the Outer Hebrides can look like a single island and is often spoken of as the 'Long Island'. Geologically it was, in fact, one long island in the distant past but, as the ground level changed in relation to the sea several shallow but distinctive interruptions were formed. The most significant of these is the Sound of Harris – the popular access to the Atlantic but a navigational challenge nevertheless. Lewis and Harris, north of the Sound of Harris, combine to form the largest off-shore island of mainland Britain and Ireland. For comparison, it is more than twice the area of the next largest island – mainland Shetland – and one-third larger in area than Skye. The Isle of Man is not much bigger than Harris alone and the Isle of Wight does not even enter the lists.

It is hard for the modern city-dweller to realise the importance of water transport in early ages. Without roads, or even satisfactory tracks, and with forests, bogs, rocky escarpments, wild animals, and possibly hostile tribes, the sea was the main thoroughfare. The smaller islands were every bit as important then as our townships are today and, by the standards of the time, island access was relatively simple.

From this viewpoint it is easy to see why Lewis and Harris were thought of as separate islands. They are divided by a forbidding mountain barrier and to get from one to the other required a long boat ride round an irregular coastline. Mankind has farmed this land for some 5000 years yet the sheer size of the land-mass meant that, for centuries, human settlements clung only to the coastline. Inland was a large area of forest wilderness and swamp. Peat was scarce as the climate was warmer so timber was the primary fuel. Steadily the forests were cleared both for fuel and to gain more land for subsistence farming. Such were the conditions 4000 years ago when the stones of Callanish on the west side of Lewis were erected on open meadowland. A thin layer of fine soil lay over the ashes and pollen grains of ancient forest.

Within a few more centuries only scattered patches of scrub birch, hazel and rowan remained and it was about this critical time that the climate turned colder. Tundra-type vegetation now took over the barren, treeless land. Heathers, sphagnum and other mosses, bog cotton and coarse grasses failed to decompose in the cold atmosphere and peat started to build up. When Callanish was excavated in 1856 the peat had reached a thickness of five feet (1½ metres) and in some areas it is as much as twenty feet deep (6 metres).

Magnus Barelegs, the Norse marauder, is usually blamed for burning down the forests in Lewis in 1098 but although he caused devastation virtually all the woodland had been destroyed by the islanders themselves long before Norsemen arrived in the area.

8.1 Boreray

[**baw**-rĕ-ray or **baw**-rĕ-rĕ] (ON borgarøy – fort of the island)

O S Maps: 1:50000 Sheet 18 1:25000 Sheet 454
Admiralty Charts: 1:200000 Nos.2721 or 2722

Area: 198ha (489 acres)
Height: 56m (184 ft)

Owner: Owned by the Scottish Government and leased to Borve Township on Berneray (except for an 87-acre croft in the north-east of the island owned and worked by Mr Jerry Cox).

Population: 1841–181. 1881–137. 1891–152 (37 houses). Evacuated by request in 1923 but one family stayed on with a land-holding of 87 acres. 1931–8. 1961–5. Uninhabited since late 1960s to 1999. Since then – 1.

Geology: Lewisian gneiss with a light sandy soil.

History: Boreray has been inhabited since prehistoric times and coins dating from the reign of James IV have been found in its sands.

Boreray was MacLean territory and the MacLeans of Boreray – up to the 13th laird who died in 1821 – are buried in the family graveyard on the east side of Aird a' Mhòrain, North Uist.

Wildlife: Eels breed in Loch Mór. Barnacle geese fly in each winter from Greenland to its shores and common seals collect round the coasts in high summer. Huge flocks of starlings can be seen and Boreray is at the southern limit of the range of the purple sandpiper.

* * *

BORERAY's highest point is **Mullach Mór** (G. – big top) which is 56m high and has a flattish summit. It is in the larger northern part of the island which is connected to the flat southern part by a strip of rocks and a low neck of land with sand dunes. The dunes continue on to the south-eastern shore while the north and west coasts are shelving cliffs.

The sand dunes curve round a wide bay bounded by **Tràigh na Lùibe** (G. – the bay beach). Ruins of an abandoned village are scattered on the flank of Mullach Mór and near a small burn which babbles down to the sea at Breivik (ON – broad bay). An archaeological site known as the **Nuns' Burial Chamber** lies north of the village [NF857816]. The old schoolhouse is now occupied by the sole island resident and the nearby crofthouse is holiday accommodation. South of the dunes there are more black-house ruins by the shore and below the chapel and churchyard site with its cup-marked stones [NF856805] a lone standing stone marks the edge of the rocks. **Cladh Manach** (G. – the monks' churchyard) was renowned in Martin Martin's time (1695) – 'for all the Monks that dyed in the Islands that lye Northward from Egg were buried in this little plot'.

In the centre of Boreray and almost cutting it in two is **Loch Mór**. The loch has its east side protected by the line of sand dunes but the Atlantic, when the mood takes it, breaks over the steep rocky reef closing the west side (there was also said to be a submarine passage in Martin's day) and consequently the water is brackish. The rocky point beside the reef is aptly called **Sròn Fhuar** (G. – cold nose). Just south of Loch Mór is Loch Beag – a mere puddle by comparison – but fresh water.

Late in the 19th century, in an attempt to increase the area of fertile land, Loch Mór was drained for a time. It was proudly recorded that this action created '47 Scotch acres of good alluvial soil at a cost of only £125'.

A large vessel of the Spanish Armada (over 30m length) is said to have sunk in the area between Berneray's Rubha Bhoisnis and Boreray during a severe Atlantic storm. A collection of small boats brought survivors ashore at Port nan Long on North Uist but the dead were buried near the south-east corner of Boreray.

* * *

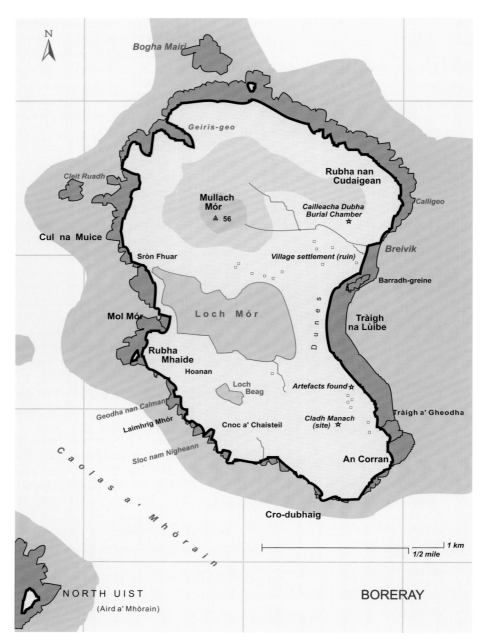

Access: Ask the sole resident, Mr Jerry Cox, 07733-065382; Sea Trek, Uig, Lewis, 01851-672464; or Uist Outdoor Centre, Lochmaddy, 01876-500480.

Anchorage: There is no safe anchorage near Boreray and no large-scale charts available (Imray's C66 is 1:150000, only slightly better than the Admiralty Chart). The deeper water has a rocky bottom and where there is sand it is either shoal or exposed to swell, but on a rising tide and in quiet weather it is possible to find temporary anchorage among the sand-banks to the east of Boreray.

8.2 Killegray

(ON kjallard-øy – graveyard island).

OS Maps: 1:50000 Sheet 18 1:25000 Sheet 455
Admiralty Charts: 1:50000 No.2841 1:20000 No.2642

Area: 176ha (435 acres)
Height: 45m (148 ft)

Owner: Bought by Sir Harry Wolfe in September 1985 from the Campbell brothers of Leverburgh.

Population: 1841–7 (2 houses). 1861–5. 1881–6. 1891–8 (1 house). 1911–3. 1921–3. 1931–5. 1951–0. 1961–0. 1971–2. 1981–0. House was being renovated in 1991. 1991–0. 2001–0.

Geology: As there is no suitable building stone in Leverburgh on Harris many of the black stone lintels used there have been brought over from Killegray.

History: This was one of the group of islands in the Sound of Harris served by ferryman Lauchlan MacLean in 1705 on the instructions of MacLeod of Harris.

The most expensive gravestone in the Rodel cemetery on Harris, apart from the MacLeod mausoleum, is in memory of John MacDonald, the MacLeod estate factor and former Army officer, who died on Killegray, his personal domain, after thirty-one years of service.

Wildlife: The shallow waters and many reefs in this area are a rich breeding ground for velvet crabs and lobsters.

*   *   *

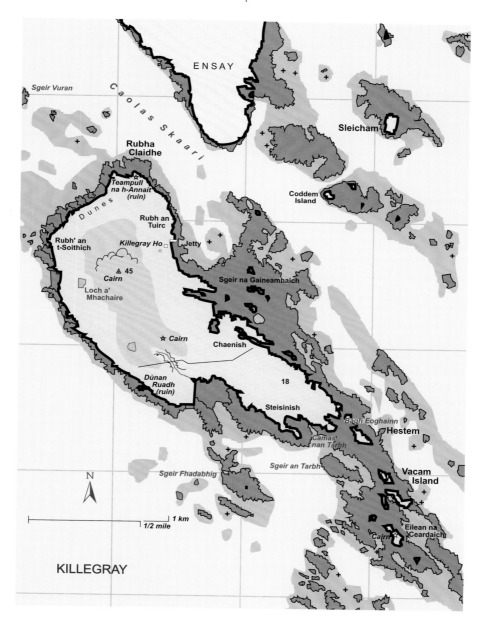

KILLEGRAY is the most southerly of the two larger islands which lie opposite Leverburgh (An t-Obbe) – the small ferry-port on the south coast of Harris. **Killegray House**, a fine late 18th century farmhouse renovated in 1991, overlooks a shallow reef-rimmed bay on the north-east side with a pleasant beach and a small stone jetty. Behind the house a grassy hill 45m high has a conspicuous cairn on its summit. In 1991 the house, which is the only one on the island, was being renovated.

The island provides rich grazing for sheep in the summer months. On the north coast there are sand dunes between **Rubh' an t-Soithich** (G. – ship headland) and **Rubha Claidhe** (G. – churchyard headland) – the site of a ruined chapel, **Teampull na h-Annait** [NF975846]. This could be the churchyard site that gave its name to the island. Two tiny lochans sparkle in the machair on the west coast guarded by a small ruined fort to the south [NF975831]. Here, a small burn runs through a cleft which divides off the southern peninsula. An old dyke spans the island at this point and the ground south of it is uncultivated deep moss and a good source of peat which was worked for a time. There is an attractive sandy cove near Steisinish on the south coast, but the south-eastern extremity deteriorates into a confused group of drying islands, **Hestem**, **Vacam**, and **Eilean na Ceardaich** (G. – the tinker's island), and weed-covered skerries.

Both Killegray and Ensay were visited occasionally by the Royal Family in the past when cruising in the royal yacht.

To the south-east a group of tiny green islands guard the northern side of the Sound of Harris, **Groay**, **Gousman**, **Gilsay**, **Lingay** and **Scaravay** with an even tinier group beside them – **Langay**, **Gumersam Mhór** and **Bheag**, and **Dùn-aarin**. To explore these islets it is possible to anchor on the east side of Groay (north-west of Lingay). This is a sheltered spot but can be uncomfortable sometimes due to the swell.

* * *

Access: Try Free Spirit, Leverburgh, 01859-520251 or Hamish Taylor Scenic Cruises, 01859-530310.

Anchorage: There are no recommended anchorages.

1. Caolas Skaari between Ensay and Killegray can be reached by a narrow channel extending to the Groay group

of islands. This requires considerable navigational care and is best attempted near low water when most dangers are visible. Occasional anchorage due NE of Killegray House but beware central shoal patch.

8.3 Ensay

(ON – Ewe island) or, possibly, (ON – John's island).

OS Maps: 1:50000 Sheet 18 1:25000 Sheet 455
Admiralty Charts: 1:100000 No.1795 1:50000 No.2841
1:20000 No.2642

Area: 186ha (460 acres)
Height: 49m (161 ft)

Owner: Archibald Stewart, Lord Dunmore's factor, bought Ensay in 1856 and rebuilt Ensay House. In 1931 the chapel (restored by the family in 1910) was bequeathed to the Episcopalian Church. Simon Mackenzie of Leverburgh bought the island from the Stewart family in 1933 and in 1957 the Mackenzies sold Ensay House to John David, a surgeon. The Mackenzies put Ensay on the market in 1999 for offers over £500,000 but the David family still own Ensay House.

Population: 1841–16 (2 houses). 1861–15. 1881–6. 1891–11 (1 house). 1931–8. 1951–2. 1961–2. 1971–2 (seasonal shepherds). 1981–0. 1991–0. 2001–0. 2011–0.

Geology: Gneiss bedrock.

History: A standing stone in the north proves that Ensay was of interest to prehistoric man. There are also two cup-marks on a small rock ridge lying parallel to the shore and about 100m north of the pier. The island, which is said to have been well wooded up to that time, was raided by Norsemen about one thousand years ago. They slew the inhabitants and slashed and burned the woodland. It never recovered. The islanders resorted to 'lazybeds' to make up for the deficient soil and the overgrown ridges are still clear to see but the fallow soil has now regained its fertility.

Ensay was linked by the ferry service paid for by MacLeod in 1705 with Berneray, Killegray, Pabbay and Obbe (Leverburgh) on Harris.

In 1779 MacLeod of Harris' factor, Donald Stewart, bought Ensay from him together with some other properties when the MacLeod was facing bankruptcy. Donald is said to have ruthlessly evicted the tenants and his son John

Stewart of Ensay followed in his father's footsteps. But it is also said that the Stewarts were good farmers who, for instance, introduced a horse-drawn precision seeder on Ensay when dibbers were still being used elsewhere. In due course the Stewarts sold Ensay and it changed hands several times before Archibald Stewart bought it in 1856. **Wildlife:** Stunted elder, fuchsia, and sycamore – almost laid flat by the wind – struggle with beaten

veronica bushes to survive by the main house.

In summer sheep are grazed on **ENSAY** which is very similar in appearance to neighbouring Killegray. The ground rises to a maximum height of 49m. A small stone jetty juts into a cove near the south-east end of the island, and **Ensay House** overlooks an attractive bay on the east side with a gateway and steps leading down to

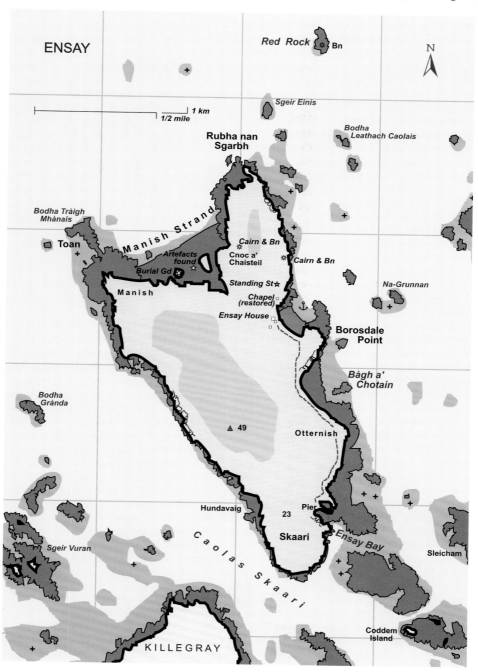

a crescent beach of white sand. The house was rebuilt in the mid-19th century on the site of the original late-18th century building. It has 14 rooms and was completed in the Edwardian era but with lack of occupation is deteriorating sadly. The late-medieval chapel [NF981866] near Ensay House was restored in 1910 as an Episcopalian chapel. It has a fine carved oak door and a stone piscina.

Toan, the north-west extremity and **Rubha nan Sgarbh** in the north are steep dark-coloured rocky points with a beautiful shell-sand beach, **Manish Strand**, between them. One of the tidal islands on the beach is the site of an old burial ground. A 12th-century chapel [NF975868] possibly buried by the great storm of 1697 or the earlier tsunami, has been partly excavated from three metres of sand. There may well be much earlier remains at a lower level. A Stewart grave has also been exposed and Viking relics have been found nearby. Martin recorded in 1695 – 'there is an old chapel here, for the use of the natives; and there was lately discovered a grave in the west end of the island in which was found a pair of scales made of brass, and a little hammer, both which were finely polished.'

It was from Ensay that Martin set off on his later voyage to St Kilda, on 'the 29th of May, at Six in the Afternoon, 1697, the wind at S.E...'

As with Killegray, Ensay is surrounded by rocks and skerries. The only ones which might justify the title of islets are **Stromay** in the north-east, **Saghay More**, **Saghay Beg**, and **Suem** to the east, and **Sleicham** and **Coddem Island** to the south-east. **Sùnam** is beside the entrance to An t-Obbe (Leverburgh) harbour but the **Carminish Islands** on the coast of Harris are all tidal.

The town of Ensay in Victoria, Australia was named by a nostalgic emigrant islander.

Access: Try Free Spirit, Leverburgh, 01859-520251 or Hamish Taylor Scenic Cruises, 01859-530310.
Anchorage:
1. In bay on NE side off Ensay House, sand. Approach with caution following sailing instructions carefully. Sheltered except for N'lies and E'lies. Note reef on SE of bay.

8.4 Pabbay

(ON pap-øy – hermit or priest island).

OS Maps: 1:50000 Sheet 18 1:25000 Sheet 455
Admiralty Charts: 1:200000 Nos.2721 or 2722 1:50000 No.2841 1:20000 No.2642

Area: 820ha (2026 acres)
Height: 196m (643 ft)

Owner: Bought from the Stewarts by the Campbells of Rodel (Harris) at a London auction in March 1934. Sold in 1974 to Mr David Plunkett – a Lloyd's broker. North Uist Estates Trust (Lord Granville's family) own the crofting rights.

Population: In the early 19th century there were twenty-six families (about 100 people) living in comparative comfort. 1841–338 (61 houses). The island was cleared for sheep in 1846. 1861–21. By 1868 only a single shepherd's family remained. 1871–8. 1881–2. 1891–3 (1 house). 1931–3. 1961–2. 1971–4. 1981–0. Uninhabited since.

Geology: Gneiss bedrock with a fertile sandy soil and very little peat.

History: It is not known which priest or hermit settled on Pabbay. Columba never crossed the Minch and although the small chapel was dedicated to St Moluag it is doubtful if he ever landed here.
In the early 15th century the MacLeods of Pabbay spotted a raiding party of MacDonalds approaching. All the islanders took cover so when

MARY'S CHURCH ON PABBAY

the MacDonalds landed they found the village deserted and set about looting and burning the houses. The MacLeods meanwhile set the MacDonald boats adrift and then rowed over to Berneray to summon help. A large party returned to Pabbay and found the MacDonalds now intent on dividing the spoils and rounding up the cattle. They hid by the shore and when the MacDonalds tried to escape to their boats they were trapped and slaughtered. The final battle probably took place between Seana-Chaisteil and the river, Abhainn Lingay, but the whole area has now been covered with sand dunes.

Pabbay was a favourite island of the MacLeod chiefs and some years after the Norsemen left they built a castle which, at the time, was equal in importance to Dunvegan in Skye. It was not until the 16th century that their interest concentrated on Dunvegan and the castle on Pabbay lapsed into disrepair. In 1467, Iain Borb, Chief of the MacLeods, died at the castle while fencing with his cousin. He apparently lost his temper and an old battle wound on his forehead could not be staunched when it started bleeding profusely.

It is recorded that in 1680 there were four 'townships' on Pabbay – Baile fo Thuath, Baile Meadhonach, Baile Lingay, and Baile na Cille – but in 1697 a violent storm destroyed Baile Meadhonach, stripped off the topsoil and buried the wrecked village in sand.

Pabbay once had a considerable population and most of the Stewards of St Kilda were Pabbay men. In 1705 a boat was purchased by MacLeod for use as a ferry to serve Pabbay, Berneray, Ensay, Killegray, Harris and Skye. Unlike the MacLeods of Berneray who had Jacobite sympathies, the MacLeods of Pabbay supported the Government in the 1745 rebellion.

There was a population of about one hundred at the start of the 19th century living in comparative comfort and producing, and even exporting, corn, barley and illicit whisky. Pabbay was then part of the 'quod sacra Parish of Bernera'. Numbers had risen to over 300 by 1841 before the island was cleared for sheep. It is known that there were still a few cattle because three of these won a prize for the heaviest Highland cattle at Smithfield – proof of the richness of the island machair. Some of the displaced population went to Canada and Australia, but many settled on Scalpay, Berneray and in the Bays area of Harris. But with the

island clearance in 1846 the value of centuries of careful husbandry was lost to coarse grazing.

The island is now run as a single sheep-farm.
Wildlife: Ancient birch tree trunks, roots and peat deposits are sometimes exposed by the wind and sea, particularly during abnormal spring tides, in the intertidal zone at the north end of the Quinish reef and on the shore opposite. Marram-grass on the dunes struggles to hold down the windblown sand. It is also found in patches by the ruined main homestead at Baile fo Thuath – probably originally seeded from the thatched roofs.

A small resident herd of red deer, introduced in 1880, graze on Beinn a' Charnain. Shag and fulmar nest on the low north-coast cliffs but gulls and eider prefer the tidal reef at Quinish. Barnacle geese winter on Pabbay in large numbers.

* * *

The island of **PABBAY** was once rich and green and known as 'the granary of Harris'. But since clearance in the mid-19th century, drift, sea spray and lack of care have destroyed much of its former fertility and sheep now graze on the wildflowers of the machair. Nevertheless, it is still one of the most beautiful islands in the Hebrides with its white sands, rich machair and aquamarine sea. **Beinn a' Charnain** (G. – cairn hill), a sharp-peaked hill in the north is the highest point at 196m.

A pointed sandy hillock between two beaches on the south-west coast still shows traces of the walls of **Seana-Chaisteal** (G. – ancient castle). This is the site of the old MacLeod castle or dun [NF902871]. The wide beaches below the castle are backed by sand dunes.

West of the castle site and beyond Abhainn Lingay (ON and G. – heather burn) is the landing place of Haltois below **Bailenacille** (G. – Kirktown). A small cottage which is used by visiting shepherds faces the sea with a burn behind it dividing it from the ruin of **Teampull Mhóire** (G. – Mary's Church) in its old kirkyard [NF890870]. One gable and part of the walls remain. The age of the building is uncertain but it may be early 16th century. Only four metres to the west are the remains of an earlier chapel which was probably dedicated to St Moluag and between these ruins and the Lingay Burn is an old corn-drying kiln.

The stone from many of the old houses has

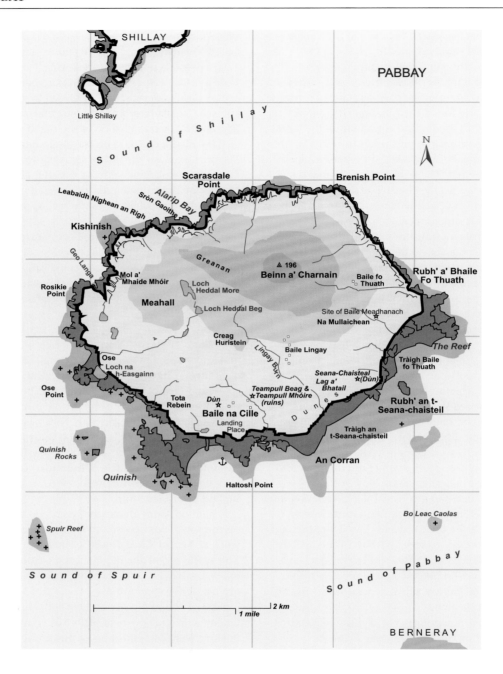

been used to build a wall enclosing a Pairc Mhor (G. – big park) for the sheep at lambing time and within this area is a ruined Iron Age dun.

The lost village of **Baile Meadhonach** (G. – Midtown) lay to the north of Seana-Chaisteal but the houses of **Baile Lingay** are clearly visible beside the Lingay Burn. These form two groups – the MacNeill farm buildings, and the workers' houses higher up the hillside and above the arable land. West of the workers' houses is Creag

Huristein – an odd collection of eroded erratic boulders likes pieces of imaginative modern sculpture.

Baile fo Thuath (G. – Northtown) is high on the western hillside with a T-shaped main farmhouse and a circular ruin behind it. Looking across the Sound of Harris from here the **Druim na Beisde** (G. – the ridge of the beast) can be seen as a pale shape across the water. This three-mile long sand-bank shifts its position frequently and sometimes cuts off the passage to Pabbay.

The north coast consists of rugged cliffs which stand against the tide that sweeps through the Sound of Shillay. In the cliff-face at **Sròn Gaoith** (G. – nose of the wind) is a cave known as Carn mhic an t-Sronaich after a notorious murderer who is said to have hidden there and the small plateau to the west of it is called, strangely, **Leabaidh Nighean an Righ** (G. – the king's daughter's bed).

The lochs in this remote western side of the island have a few peat deposits near them and were probably, therefore, the site of the old illicit whisky stills.

Although there are the ancient remains of sacred buildings on Pabbay, in recent centuries folk usually crossed the Sound (weather permitting) to attend church on Berneray. The sand spit from Berneray was once said to be so close to Pabbay that a wife could throw her washboard across the channel between them.

* * *

Access: Try Free Spirit, Leverburgh, 01859-520251 or Hamish Taylor Scenic Cruises, 01859-530310.

Anchorage: Avoid the N coast as local fishermen say there are uncharted in-shore rocks, the W coast is too exposed and the SW foul with skerries. On the E side the shoals and sand-banks move and must be navigated carefully.
1. Temp. anchorage on S coast near Haltois Point, E of drying reef in 4m, sand. Land, and re-embark, at or above half-tide, swell permitting.

8.5 Shillay

(ON selr-øy – seal island).

OS Maps: 1:50000 Sheet 18 1:25000 Sheet 455
Admiralty Charts: 1:50000 No.2841 1:20000 No.2642

Area: 47ha (116 acres)
Height: 79m (259 ft)

Owner: Scottish Office (Department of Agriculture). Borve Township, Berneray has the grazing rights.

Population: No Census records and no signs of past habitation.

Geology: Gneiss with a light sandy soil.
Wildlife: In 1695 Martin Martin said that he had found sheep on Shillay with the biggest horns he had ever seen.

Both storm and Leach's petrel breed among the boulders on Shillay and probably also the Arctic tern, *Sterna paradisaea*.

Hundreds of grey seals, once one of the world's rarer species, also breed here producing between 150 and 200 calves per year. They collect in huge numbers on the foreshore during the pupping season. When the weather is particularly bad seals which normally give birth on Haskeir join those on Shillay. The seals on Shillay were studied in detail when a special camp was set up in October 1961. Juveniles were branded to track their movements but as a consequence some of the seals moved over to Coppay to give birth.

The Sound of Shillay yields reasonable quantities of the edible crab, *Cancer pagarus* and some of the tastiest lobsters in the Hebrides. Donald MacKillop of Berneray records that in 1946 a lobster found under a rock on the North Uist shore was 35ins long, 15½ins in circumference, with 7½ins of cutting edge on the scissors claw and an empty shell weight of 10¾lbs.

* * *

The water lapped gently under our hulls as *Jandara* lay alongside *Berneray Isle* in the Sound of Shillay. We had stopped for a chat with Angus MacAskill and his nephew Roddy who were out lobster fishing. The sunlight glinted off the wet seaweed on the rocks of Shillay. *Berneray Isle* is the boat in which Prince Charles, Lord of the Isles and Duke of Rothesay, went lobster fishing with all the long experience of Angus to assist him (and it was Angus's wife, Mary, who cooked the Prince his favourite clootie dumpling).

SHILLAY has dark-coloured vertical cliffs at its northern end beneath a round-topped hill of 79m height. Vegetation is sparse but offers grazing for sheep. The southern part of the island slopes towards the **Sound of Shillay**, the channel between Pabbay and Shillay, and has a small bay with a sand and boulder beach on its south-east side where the grey seals gather in the autumn sheltered by **Aird an Laoigh** (G. – headland of the seal-calf). Although the gentle slopes make it easier for the seals to come ashore it also means greater infant mortality when there are storms and high seas. These sweep the young ones into the water before they can fend for themselves.

Little Shillay, lying south-west of Shillay, is a rocky outcrop that rises to a height of 30m. And

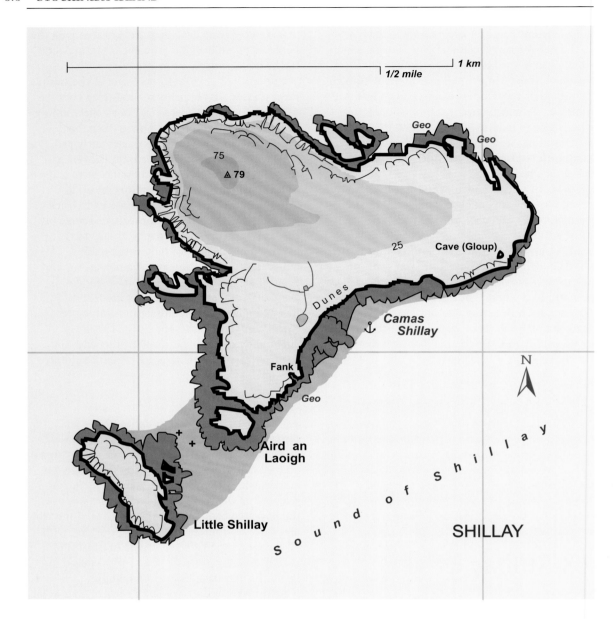

some distance away in the opposite direction, guarding the north-west entrance to the Sound of Harris is the steep little island of **Coppay** (ON – cup-shaped island).

*   *   *

Access: Try Free Spirit, Leverburgh, 01859-520251 or Hamish Taylor Scenic Cruises, 01859-530310, or ask on Berneray.

Anchorage: Temporary anchorage when winds between NW and NNE off the centre of the sandy beach on the SE side in suitable depth. Bottom chiefly sand with patches of rock and kelp which can normally be seen and avoided.

8.6 Stockinish Island

(ON stakkr – stack, ON nes – promontory.) Rock stacks guard the seaward approach.

OS Maps. 1:50000 Sheet 14 1:25000 Sheet 455
Admiralty Charts: 1:100000 No.1795 1:50000 No.2841

Area: 49ha (121 acres)
Height: 44m (144 ft)

Owner: Tenancy held by Donald MacLeod, Stockinish. Previously held by the Campbell brothers, Leverburgh.

Population: No Census records and uninhabited

Geology: Lewisian gneiss similar to the geology of neighbouring Harris with small pockets of poor peaty soil.

* * *

Loch Stockinish is another of the many firths penetrating the frayed eastern edge of Harris – dark brown, barren, and beautiful. Where the Golden Road skirts the loch there is a youth hostel and a few houses scattered in the hollows. **STOCKINISH ISLAND** at the entrance to the loch is separated from the 'mainland' by a long,

narrow, but navigable channel – **Caolas Beag** (G. – little channel). In fact, in spite of its narrowness (27m minimum), it is an easier route into the loch than **Caolas Mór** on the west side, which is wide but littered with rocks. A tiny islet, **Eilean Leasait**, snuggles by the west shore of Stockinish Island.

Stockinish has no habitation on it and matches the surrounding landscape – pink and grey glaciated rock with little pockets of dark-umber peat and a tangle of twisted heather. Its main feature is a large shallow central pool, Loch an t-Sàile (G. – saltwater loch), opening off an inlet from Caolas Beag which may once have served

as a fish-trap but which is now permanently dammed and used by the local fishermen as a lobster pond. The island's highest point (44m) is a steep hillock beside this inlet.

At the southern end of the island there is a deep skirt of drying islets, rocks, reefs and stacks.

Access: Try Free Spirit, Leverburgh, 01859-520251, Hamish Taylor Scenic Cruises, Tarbert, 01859-530310 or a boat-owner at Poll Scrot.

Anchorage: No recommended anchorage close to the island. 1. Loch Stockinish. Easiest access to loch is through Caolas Beag, E of Stockinish Island; best before half-tide. Very narrow (only 27m at one point) but clean if close in to Stockinish Island. After passing Stockinish Island keep just NE of mid-channel. Anchor in mouth of westerly arm at head of loch, completely sheltered, 9m sand. Beware rock off Ardvey Point & overhead cable to N (15m? clearance). Distance is slightly over 1M by dinghy to Stockinish Island.

8.7 Scotasay

Probably (ON – Skati's island) but possibly (ON Skot's-øy – Scot's island).

OS Maps: 1:50000 Sheet 14 1:25000 Sheet 455
Admiralty Charts: 1:100000 Nos.1794 or 1795 1:12500 No.2905

Area: 49ha (121 acres)
Height: 57m (187 ft)

Owner: Bought in 1962, together with Scalpay,

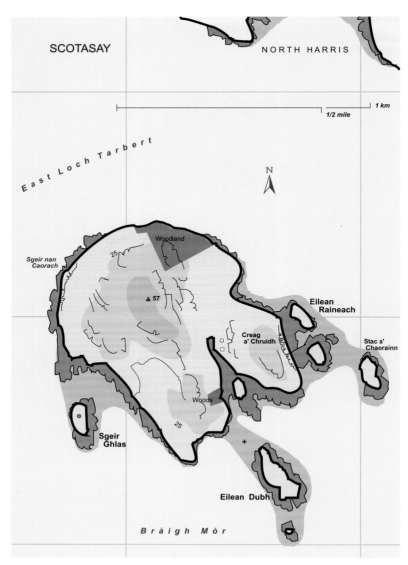

by Mr John Taylor, an English architect. Since 1987 his son, Mr Fred Taylor, has owned it through a family trust.

Population: 1861–14. 1881–0. 1891–18 (2 houses). 1901–15. 1911–20. 1921–19. Uninhabited since, except for summer visits by the owner.

Geology: Banded gneiss bedrock.

Wildlife: The owner planted 7000 lodgepole pines to encourage wildlife on the island but mink are a serious problem and many of these savage killers have been trapped. Mink have been seen swimming three miles from land so the ocean is no barrier.

*   *   *

Mainly covered with heather, rough grazing and peat bog, **SCOTASAY** also has a pleasant patch of woodland which was planted in the 1960s. The highest point of 57m is towards the north. The island is in a central position in East Loch Tarbert and together with Scalpay provides valuable shelter for the ferry terminal at Tarbert. Until now, when visiting, the owners have lived in the main croft house which is in the cleft running up from the cove on the south-east side. However the owner has recently had a modern timber house built on stilts beside the tidal lagoon and intends to spend more time on the island. The design by Dualchas, architects, uses a wind turbine with battery storage for electricity and rainwater collection from the roof for water supply. There is also a wood-burning stove.

The plan is to build some smaller units for visitors in due course.

There is a fish farm on the north-east side, near **Eilean Raineach**.

The rowan tree on **Stac a' Chaorainn** (G.

CORNCRAKE

– stack of the rowan tree) no longer grows there, and **Sgeir Ghlas** (G. – pale grey-green skerry) with its beacon is more of an islet than a skerry. **Eilean Dubh** is part of the underwater reef which extends south of Scotasay while the islets, **Eileanan a' Ghille-bheid** and **Eilean Arderanish**, continue the parallel line of the Gloraigs opposite Scalpay.

*   *   *

Access: Try Hamish Taylor, 01859-530310 or Kilda Cruises, 01859-502060 or enquire at Harris Hotel, Tarbert.

Anchorages: No recommended anchorages.
1. Occasional anchorage opposite the small bight on the NE side in 10m if not obstructed by fish-farm.
2. Tem. anchorage E of Sgeir Ghlas.

8.8 Shiant Isles

[sh-unt] (G. na h-eileanan seunta – of the enchanted islands).

Garbh Eilean

(G. – rough island)

Eilean an Tigh

(G. – house or home island). Pre-19th century this was called Eilean na Cille (G. – church island)

*The largest separate island is **Eilean Mhuire** (G. – Mary's island).*

The entire group of about a dozen islands and skerries is also known locally as Eileanan Mora.

OS map. 1:50000 Sheet 14 1:25000 Sheet 457
Admiralty Charts: 1:100000 Nos.1794 or 1795

Area: 143ha (353 acres)
Height: 160m (525 ft)

Owner: Sir Compton Mackenzie bought the group at a London auction for £500 in 1925. He renovated the shepherd's derelict cottage on Eilean an Tigh and stayed there very occasionally during the summer months when he wanted solitude for writing. He sold the islands in 1936 to a Colonel Macdonald from Skye who resold them to the publisher Nigel Nicolson in 1937 for £1300. The Nicolson family still own them. The grazing rights are let to a sheep farmer on Scalpay.

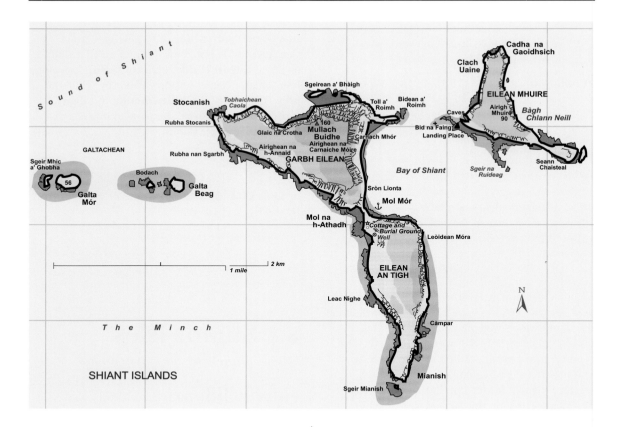

SHIANT ISLANDS

Population: There are scattered signs of early settlements on Garbh Eilean at Annat and Bagh, on the plateau of Eilean Mhuire (although these may have been summer shielings), and on two areas of Eilean an Tigh, and it seems that about forty people in five families were still living on Eilean an Tigh in the mid-18th century. By 1770 the Shiants were uninhabited but in the 1820s under the Stewart tenure a shepherd and his wife were again living on Eilean an Tigh. It was at this time that it started to be called 'home island' instead of 'church island' – Eilean na Cille. For twenty years after 1842 there were no inhabitants but in 1862 a shepherd, Donald Campbell, and his wife Catherine Morrison moved in. Their two strikingly beautiful – and accommodating – daughters, Mòr and Catriona, gained widespread renown. The Victorian yachtsman and naturalist, Harvie-Brown, said that Mòr would have graced any ballroom – 'one of the very loveliest women I ever beheld', and that they were both 'uncommonly handsome girls', A few years later both girls gave birth to children fathered by visiting fishermen, whom they brought up as part of the family. The Campbells left the island in 1901.

Nigel Nicolson met Mòr Campbell in 1946 on Harris when she was a forlorn 86 years old. The Census shows that in 1881 there were two males and four females in the Shiants. 1891–8 (3m,5f) 1901–1 family (4m,4f) Since then, uninhabited.

Geology: Geologically the Shiants are outliers of Skye, although they are closer to Lewis. The rock formations are similar to Staffa, the Giant's Causeway in Antrim and parts of Mull – columnar (tertiary) basalt, forming spectacular cliffs of over 120m in height. The columns are almost 2m in diameter on Garbh Eilean's north face. This is geologically young rock; not like the ancient weathered gneiss of the 'Long Island'. There are fine natural stone arches on Eilean Mhuire's south-west shore and also a natural arch on Eilean an Tigh. Basalt is not generally a suitable rock for climbing.

Martin Martin said there was a blue stone in the Shiants and that he had seen a set of 'table men' carved from it.

History: In the 1820s two brothers, Alexander and Archibald Stewart of Pairc (Park), Lewis, were notorious and sadistic tacksmen who severely punished any fisherman who landed on the Shiant Islands, even in an emergency. It was always assumed that they were sheep-stealing (and sometimes, no doubt, they were). Their tenure lasted until 1842.

Lord Leverhulme, the Lancashire soap magnate, bought Lewis (which included the Shiants) in 1917 and planned at one stage to breed silver foxes there.

Wildlife: The common seal breeds here and basking shark, dolphin, porpoise, blue shark, and Minke whale often frequent these waters.

There are no rabbits but the islands are rat-infested, probably from a shipwreck, and someone (Compton Mackenzie) imported cats to try to deal with them. The cats have died out (or been eaten by the rats, which are fearless!) and, as the rats live in the scree below the cliffs and steal the sea-birds' eggs and young, it was planned to eradicate them by the same method as that used on Ailsa Craig (See No.1.1). But it was then realised that these were not common Brown Rats, *Rattus novergicus*, but Black Rats, *Rattus rattus*, the 'plague rats' of old. As they are very rare in the British Isles (much rarer than puffins) it was decided in the interests of conservation that they should be declared – like puffins – a protected species. So we now have puffins and black rats sharing an island habitat and apparently co-existing.

Some 240,000 puffins nest here in the turf at the top of the sea-cliffs – about two per cent of the world population. There is a colony of herring gulls, and oystercatchers, nesting eider, shag, snipe, lark, pipit, wheatear, greater and lesser black-backed gulls, rock dove, turnstone, hooded crow, blackbird, and many other species have been seen.

Thousands of kittiwakes, guillemots, razorbills and fulmars nest among the huge fluted basalt columns on the northern cliffs.

*   *   *

According to legend the ghostly and menacing Blue Men of the Minch live in the Sound between the **SHIANT ISLANDS**. Some say they are storm kelpies who must be treated with great respect by sailors, and others that they are bad-tempered angels who fell into the sea when they were expelled from Heaven. The minister of Tiree from

1861 to 1891, the Rev John Campbell, claimed that one followed a fisherman's boat when he was sailing in the area – 'a blue-covered man, with a long, grey face, and floating from the waist out of the water'. The creature sometimes came so close that he could have touched him.

If you are accosted by a Blue Man it is important to have the Gaelic. One skipper had to answer a Blue Man's questions in rhyming couplets on the threat of being dragged to the bottom of the Minch if his replies were not poetic.

Even if you don't see any Blue Men, the columnar basalt rock formations are every bit as spectacular. This is the back-street Manhattan of the Western Isles. A vast skyscraper city of seabirds, noisy and rank-smelling. In *The Highlands and Isles of Scotland* MacCulloch (1773–1835) claimed that these '. . . form one of the most magnificent colonnades to be found among the Western Islands. But these islands are nowhere more striking than when viewed at a sufficient distance from the northward; the whole of this lofty range of pillars being distinctly seen rising like a long wall out of the sea; varied by the ruder forms of the others which tower above or project beyond them, and contrasted by the wild rocks which skirt the whole group'.

The well-known pillars of Fingal's Cave on Staffa are a mere 10m high, those on the Shiants are over 150m (500 ft). In comparing them MacCulloch said that they 'exceed them in simplicity, in grandeur, in depth of shadow, and in that repose which is essential to the great style in landscape'.

The Shiants are a group of two islands and several islets and outlying rocks. There is pasturage for sheep brought over from Scalpay (No.8.14) but there are no permanent inhabitants nowadays. **Eilean an Tigh** which is the southern part of the largest island of the group is connected with **Garbh Eilean**, the northern part, by a low narrow neck of polished pebbles. This isthmus covers at spring tides or during storms. Garbh Eilean is very steep; Eilean an Tigh is lower but has precipitous cliffs on its eastern side. Eilean Mhuire lies a short distance to the east of Garbh Eilean, so that the group almost forms a bay with a south-eastern exposure.

There is a cottage on the west side of Eilean an Tigh near the shingle link with Eilean Garbh [NG418976]. This is the cottage that was renovated by Sir Compton Mackenzie when he owned these islands. Behind it is the ruin of an older dwelling and on the north side there are the limited remains of a probable graveyard and a small church. This would account for the island's former name of Eilean na Cille (church island). A crystal clear spring of fresh water about one hundred yards from the cottage is hidden by lush green grass and wild flowers. The large scale Ordnance Survey map shows three wells or springs on Eilean an Tigh but only the one near the cottage is reliable.

In the early 19th century only a shepherd and his wife were living on the island. In order to collect seabirds and their eggs he would lower his wife down the cliff-face. When she had caught and killed each bird she would attach it to the rope round her waist to keep her hands free. One day the rope broke and she fell into the sea. She was unable to swim but the collection of dead birds kept her afloat. Her husband could not get down the cliff in time to save her and watched helplessly as, crying for help, the tide carried her away.

Eilean Mhuire, the Virgin Mary's island, has also been inhabited and it is in fact the most fertile island in the group. There are steep cliffs on all sides and access is up a rock 'stair' but the top is like the 'lost world' – a large plateau covered with arable land and ancient lazybeds, and the remains of turf dwellings marked by clumps of nettles – a certain sign of human occupation.

It has always been assumed that the chapel on these holy islands was on the Virgin Mary's island because Martin Martin had recorded that: 'Island-More hath a chapel in it dedicated to the Virgin Mary, and is fruitful in corn and grass; the island joining to it on the west is only for pasturage.'

But Adam Nicolson has suggested that Martin Martin's 'Island-More' was only referring to 'the main island' and not Eilean Mhuire. The island joining to it on the *north-west* would then be Garbh Eilean which is certainly only fit for pasturage while Home Island, or Church Island as it used to be known, was relatively fruitful in corn and grass. This seems to me to be a reasonable assumption. Churches and graveyards are usually linked and whereas there are the apparent signs of a graveyard on Eilean an Tigh, none has yet been found on Eilean Mhuire.

Martin Martin claimed that the cows on the 'Siant' were much fatter than any he saw on Lewis. It must have been a hard life but at least the islanders had the means to be self-sufficient. There would be seafood and seafowl, potatoes, cabbages, kale, milk, eggs, meat, seal-oil, driftwood and some peat, and fresh water: all the essentials for a healthy existence.

* * *

Access: Try Woody, Stornoway, 01851-703908; Kilda Cruises, Tarbert, 01859-502060; or Hebridean Whale Cruises, Gairloch (Mainland), 01445-712458. No visiting April/May during lambing.

Anchorages: Tidal currents are strong in the vicinity of these islands and there are overfalls both N and S. Landing can be hazardous.
1. Approach from N or S for occasional anchorage between the islands in settled weather. Avoid reefs extending 1½c W and 1½c S of Eilean Mhuire. Anchor E of neck of gravel between Garbh Eilean and Eilean an Tigh but the bottom slopes steeply and holding may be uncertain. Exposed NE to SE but sheltered S through W to N. With SW winds a heavy swell sets in. Better holding has been reported in the NW corner of the Bay of Shiant in 10m sand.
2. Temporary anchorage on W side of neck of gravel between Garbh Eilean and Eilean an Tigh. Sheltered N to E.

8.9 Taransay

(ON – Taran's island) or (ON taren-øy – the kelp island).

O S Maps: 1:50000 Sheet 18 1:25000 Sheet 455
Admiralty Charts: 1:200000 No.2721 1:50000 No.2841

Area: 1475ha (3645 acres)
Height: 267m (876 ft)

Owner: Owned by brothers Angus and Norman Mackay of Horgabost, Harris since 1967 and used for sheep farming. Sold in 2011 to Adam and Cathra Kelliher for a reputed £2m. The Kellihers own a plant on Lewis making health additives and Borve Lodge on Harris which overlooks Taransay.

Population: 1841–88 (16 houses). 1881–55. 1891–56 (12 houses). 1911–76. 1931–33. Last family left the island in 1942 but it was later reinhabited. 1961–5. 1971–5. 1974– again abandoned. This is Scotland's largest uninhabited island.

Geology: Grey gneiss traversed by veins of granite with a grassy top-soil. The isthmus is mainly sand.

History: Eponymous Taran is an uncertain figure in Celtic history. According to Adomnan he was the son of a noble Pictish family who requested St Columba's protection. Columba agreed and asked Feradach, a rich man on Islay (No.2.4), to accept him in his retinue and treat him as a friend but Feradach chose instead to have him murdered. Columba was naturally outraged and condemned Feradach with a divine judgement.

Some scholars however consider that Taran was the Irish Saint Ternan or Torannan who had great influence on the Pictish mainland. As one of the chapels on Taransay was dedicated to St Taran this may be a more likely candidate.

Prehistoric man was well-established on Taransay and the Vikings probably settled here judging by the wealth of Norse nomenclature.

In 1544 a raiding party of Morrisons from Ness, Lewis, was slain on the shore at Sgeir a' Bhuailt, smitten-rock, by the chief of Berneray

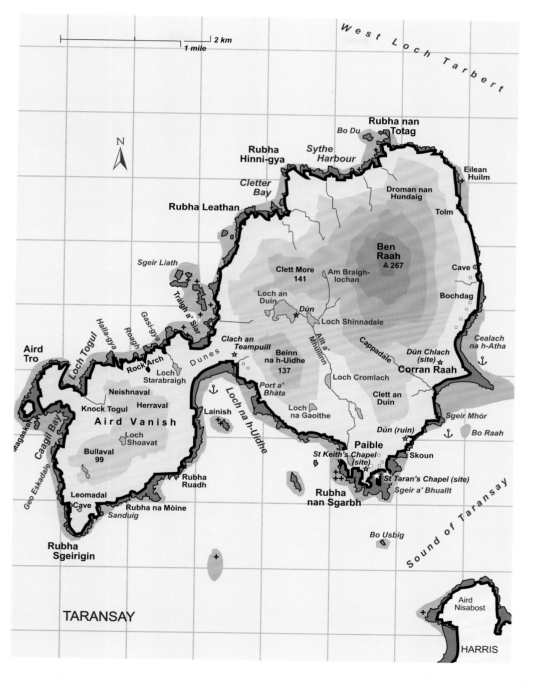

and his men but in 1549 Dean Munro described Taransay as a place with good barley, corn and fishing, where people delved with spades.

Taransay was chosen by the BBC in 1999 as the site for their 'Castaway 2000' series of programmes and again gained star status as the setting for the film story of Herr Zucher and his rocket mail experiment on Scarp (No.8.13).

Wildlife: The shoreline is magnificent in summer with brilliant white sands and the sea-thrift in bloom. There is a herd of about 200 red deer and the burns and lochans teem with brown trout.

Unfortunately, mink – which are strong swimmers – have established themselves on the island and are attacking ground-nesting birds, in particular the populations of puffin and shelduck. In 2003 Stirling University started co-ordinating a Taransay research project to radio-track the elusive predators with a view to finding a way of eradicating them.

*   *   *

TARANSAY is divided into two shapely hills by a low sandy neck of dunes. The village of **Paible** which is on the larger part of the island was the main settlement with a maximum population of seventy-six, but the school (next to the landing) closed in 1935 and numbers gradually dwindled until the last permanent residents left in 1942.

Then in 2002, after the BBC left, and after the island had been used for filming *The Rocket Post*, the schoolhouse and the Mackay farmhouse were renovated and let out for holiday accommodation.

Beinn Raah, 267m high, dominates the northern section with a ridge to the north and lesser peaks to the south-west where there are a number of small lochs. **Loch an Duinn** [NB022013] has a dun and probable crannog near its east shore. It is linked to Loch Shinnadale and then by Allt a' Mhuilinn (G. – the mill burn) to Loch Cromlach. The stream eventually reaches the sea beside Paible. North of Paible is the ruin of another Iron Age dun at **Corran Raah** [NB041005]. Little is known of the history of either of the two duns on Taransay.

The sites of two ancient chapels are at Paible, one dedicated to St Taran where only women were buried and the other to St Keith where only men were interred [NG030991]. This time-honoured method of segregation was upset, it is said, when a mixed burial took place in one of the graveyards. The following morning one of the bodies was found lying on the surface of the ground beside the grave.

Loch na h-Uidhe (G. – loch of the isthmus), the sea-loch which divides the island into two parts, is bounded by a magnificent stretch of shell-sand beach. **Aird Vanish** (ON *ve-nes* or *van-nes* – promontory of the sacred place or of Wane, the fertility god), the south-western part of the island, is a rough and lonely area, riddled with sea-caves. It has twin peaks, Herraval and Bullaval.

Taransay is separated from Harris by the Sound of Taransay. At no point is the sea here deeper than 12m. The sandy spit of Corran Raah projects into the Sound and the bay on its north side is called Cealach na h-Atha (G. – the fireplace of the kiln). This presumably refers to the shape and should not give visitors a misleading impression of the temperature.

*   *   *

Access: Day trips to Taransay from Horgabost beach, Mon. to Fri., weather permitting 01859-550260.

Anchorages:
1. South of Corran Raah and Bo Raah in Sound of Taransay. Close inshore, sand. Good shelter from NW but beware Bo Raah.
2. Cealach na h-Atha, on N side of Corran Raah. Anchor well in-shore, sand. Sheltered from SW winds by Corran Raah.
3. Loch na h-Uidhe. Beware Old Rocks and Langaraid on approach. Keep nearer E side of bay when entering to avoid rocks on W side. Reasonable shelter, except in S'lies.

8.10 Soay Mór

(ON so-øy – sheep island, G. mór – big).

OS Maps: 1:50000 Sheet 13   1:25000 Sheet 456
Admiralty Charts: 1:200000 No.2721   1:50000 No.2841

Area: 45ha (111 acres)
Height: 37m (121 ft)

Owner: Findlay Campbell (?). The islands are leased by a fish-farming company.

Population: 1841–no census record. 1881–0. 1891–15 (2 houses). No further record of any habitation.

Geology: Lewisian gneiss with some granite and quartz.

The two islands, **SOAY MOR** and its associate **Soay Beag**, reach the same height of 37m and have few features of note. Reefs extend from both sides of the southern extremity of Soay Mór and drying rocks fill the passage between Soay Mór and Soay Beag. The fish-farm is on the north-east side of Soay Mór facing Soay Sound.

West Loch Tarbert lies south-east of Soay Mór with small but steep **Isay island** (ON – porpoise isle) in its centre.

Access: No regular access. Boat excursions by Seatrek, Uig, Lewis, 01851-672464.

Anchorage:
1. Occasional anchorage near centre of bay at N end of Soay Mór, facing Soay Sound if fish cages permit. An approach from direction of Soay Beag is safest.

8.11 Eilean Iubhard

[elan **yoo**-*urt] (G. – yew-tree island).*

OS Maps. 1:50000 Sheet 14 1:25000 Sheet 456
Admiralty Charts: 1:100000 No.1794

Area: 125ha (309 acres)
Height: 76m (249 ft)

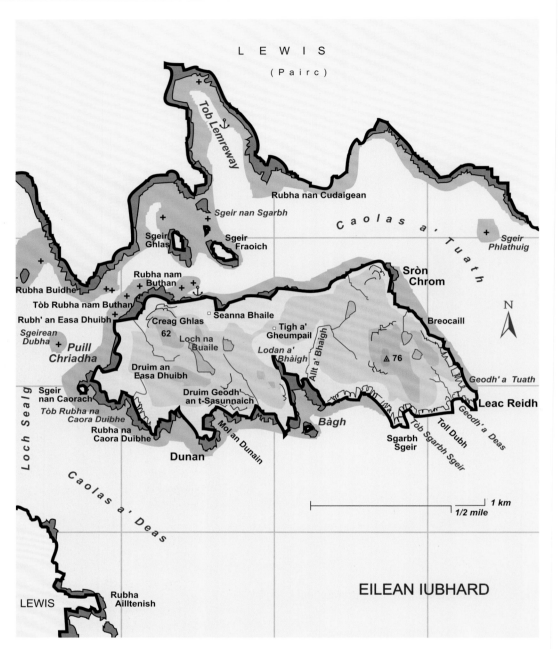

EILEAN IUBHARD

Owner: Part of the Parc Estate owned by Parc Crofters Ltd (Lomas family).

Population: No Census records, uninhabited today and apparently uninhabited in 1746 – see below – but five families lived here in the early 19th century at Seann Bhaile (G. – old town) and Tigh a' Gheumpail.

Geology: Gneiss bedrock with some basaltic intrusion.

History: On 4 May 1746 Prince Charles Edward Stuart with two companions and a guide landed near the head of Loch Seaforth at Aribruach. They set off across country to Stornoway where Donald Macleod had arranged for a ship to take the Prince to France. The party lost its way during the night among the bogs of Arnish moor and only reached the outskirts of Stornoway in the late morning very wet and tired. They were sheltering under a rock when Donald Macleod reported to them that news of the Prince's approach had reached Stornoway and the captain of the ship now refused to sail. Mrs Mackenzie, a farmer's wife, provided overnight shelter and food for the party and at 8am on the 6 May the Prince, O'Sullivan, O'Neill, Donald and Murdoch Macleod, Ned Burke and four boatmen set sail in Donald Campbell of Scalpay's boat. They intended to cross the Minch to Poolewe but the wind was against them and ships of the Royal Navy could be seen on patrol. So they chose instead to land the Prince in the bay on the south shore of Eilean Iubhard and, as the boatmen refused to leave, the boat was possibly concealed on the north side of the island.

It was raining heavily and the party stretched a sail over a 'low pitiful hut' and spent four days there. Local fishermen used the island for drying their catches so Ned and the Prince cooked some of these fish for sustenance.

Wildlife: Dean Munro (1549) reported: '. . .guid to pasture and schielling of store, with faire hunting of ottars out of their bouries.'

* * *

EILEAN UIBHARD lies at the entrance to Loch Shell – or Loch Sealg – on the east coast of Lewis. It shelters an inlet and the village of Lemreway but it lies close to the coast and on approaching from the sea it can be difficult to recognise it as an island at all. It looks much more like a part of Lewis.

There are two minor peaks at opposite ends of the island, the one in the west being 62m high and the other in the east 76m high. The ground is very rough and irregular and there are several lochans and a number of small burns. Most of the coastline drops abruptly into the sea but there is a shallow bay at the west end called **Puill Chriadha** (G. – clay pool) and a cove in the centre of the south coast called merely **Bàgh** (G. – bay).

The eastern half of Eilean Iubhard is separated from Lewis by **Caolas a' Tuath** (G. – north channel) but at the western end this kyle becomes shallow and is obstructed by a number of rocks and islets.

* * *

Access: Try Hamish Taylor Scenic Cruises, 01859-530310 or enquire at Lemreway or Scalpay.

Anchorage:
1. Occasional anchorage on narrow shelf close to N shore of Eilean Iubhard, S of Sgeir Fraoich, but mainly obstructed by fish cages. Sheltered in S'lies. If winds change, move N into Tob Lemreway.

8.12 Seaforth Island

(G. Mulag from ON Múlí – craggy ridge between fiords).

OS Maps: 1:50000 Sheet 13 1:25000 Sheet 456
Admiralty Charts: Only 1:100000 No.1794 covers Loch Seaforth but it is unsatisfactory.

Area: 273ha (675 acres)
Height: 217m (712 ft)

Owner: Heirs of A S Halford-MacLeod, CMG.,CVO. (Bought 1964)

Population: No Census records and uninhabited.

Geology: Lewisian gneiss bedrock covered with poor acid soil supporting rough grazing.

History: Seaforth Island belonged to the MacLeods until they were usurped by the Mackenzies in 1610. Francis Mackenzie, or Lord Seaforth, inherited the island in 1783.

* * *

Loch Seaforth is a long narrow loch wedged between high mountains and towering cliffs. The winds whisper through the peaks, build up their strength, meet in the corries, and then without warning sweep savagely down the mountain sides and flatten the waters of the loch with unpredictable ferocity. **SEAFORTH ISLAND** sits four-square in the centre of Loch Seaforth, six and a half miles from the entrance. It is a great heap of rough heather and bracken-covered slopes reaching up to a height of 217m above the loch with few signs of any human habitation or cultivation. When, in a strong sou'-westerly, the rain is whipped straight up the island's steep face like smoke the locals tell their youngsters that the fearsome witch who lives inside it is cooking a meal of naughty boys and girls.

A couple of miles down the loch on the western shore is Loch Maaruig – where naval craft sometimes anchor near little **Maaruig Island**. The loch here forms the boundary between Harris and Lewis: Harris to the west, Lewis on the precipitous east side.

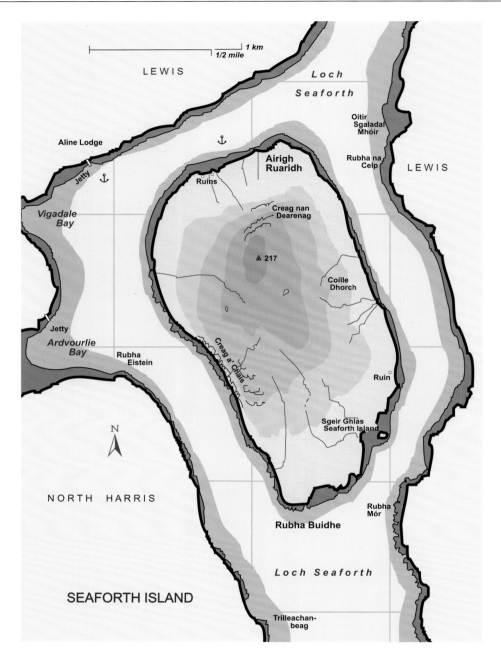

Seaforth Island (Mulag) lies on the county boundary. Shepherds from the Barvas area in Lewis (Ross & Cromarty county) used to regularly invade Harris (Inverness county) and occupy shielings as far south as the Vigadale river and sometimes beyond while Harris fishermen would often enter Lewis territory to cut kelp and collect shellfish. This led to many, occasionally violent, disputes. These were at last settled in 1851 when the boundary line was agreed with the unusual decision to allocate the entire, *undivided* island to both counties *equally*.

The loch entrance is guarded by **Rhenigidale Island** on the Harris side and three islets on the Lewis side, **Eilean Mór a' Bhàigh**, **Dubh a' Bhàigh** and **Beag a' Bhàigh** (G. – big, black and little island at the bay).

Access: It may be possible to arrange transport on one of the local boats at the jetties at Aline Lodge or Ardvourlie beside the A849.

Anchorages:

1. Anchor off the N coast of the island ½M NE of Aline Lodge jetty in 7m, or off Aline Lodge jetty itself which is NW of the island. Good shelter and holding but can be subject to violent squalls.

2. Temp. anchorage where suitable depth can be found in the navigable channels W and E of Seaforth Island but beware squalls.

8.13 Scarp

(ON skarpoe – sharp, stony, mountain terrain).

O S Maps: 1:50000 Sheet 13   1:25000 Sheet 456
Admiralty Charts: 1:200000 No.2721   1:50000 No.2841

Area: 1045ha (2582 acres)
Height: 308m (1010 ft)

Owner: Bought by a Panama company for £100 in 1978. In 1983 sold for £50,000 to LIbco Ltd who resold it to Orbitglen Ltd for £500,000. Both deals were by Nazmudin Virani, a director of BCCI – the bank which held the title. BCCI collapsed and the property was resold in 1995 to Mr Anderson Duke Bakewell of Oxfordshire for £155,055. The present owner is Mr Bert Bakewell.

Population: There were eight crofting tenancies in 1802. About 1823, thirteen villages in Harris between Loch Resort and Bunabhainneadar

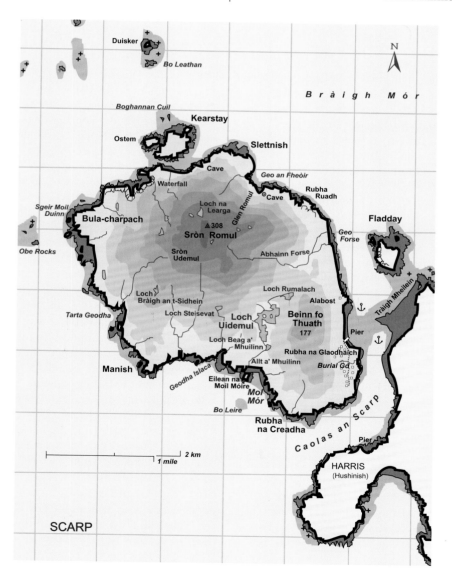

were cleared and some of the displaced villagers settled on Scarp. 1841–129 (23 houses). In 1850 the original eight crofts were subdivided into sixteen smaller units. 1861–151. 1881–213. 1891–143 (29 houses). 1931–95. 1951–74. 1961–46. 1971–12. The last two resident families, seven people in all, left Scarp in December 1971. 1981–0. 2001–0. Uninhabited since.

Geology: Chiefly gneiss and gneissose granite but containing some soft asbestos-bearing rock above Tarta Geodha (G. – the noisy creek) which is geologically unique in this region. The asbestos content was noted by geologists in the early 1930s.

History: On 14 January 1934, attended by an eighty-five-year-old midwife in her home on Scarp, Mrs Christina Maclennan gave birth to a child. On the following day her condition was poor and as there was no telephone on Scarp an islander crossed to Hushinish. But the telephone there was out of order so the postman's son was sent to Tarbert to call the doctor. The doctor decided that Mrs Maclennan must go to hospital. The sea was rough but she was taken to Hushinish tied to a stretcher laid across a bouncing open boat. There she was laid on the floor of the local bus for the seventeen miles of bumpy road to Tarbert. She was then taken by car to the hospital at Stornoway where the cause of her distress was discovered. She gave birth to a second healthy child, and felt much better for it! Thus the twins were born on different islands, in different counties and in different weeks.

This story, widely reported in the press at the time, came to the ears of a young German rocket-enthusiast who had dreams of future space travel. He had already built a number of large solid-fuel rockets and become a local celebrity. So on 28 July of the same year – which came to be known as 'Latha na Rocait' (G. – the day of the rocket) – twenty-six-year-old Gerhard Zucher chose to demonstrate his rocket-mail invention on Scarp. Special stamps were printed for the occasion and a letter was written to the King. The one-metre-long solid-fuel rocket weighed 14kg and could carry several thousand letters at 1000 mph but when Gerhard lit the fuse the rocket exploded scattering mail over a wide area. The local postmaster had the letters collected and

he stamped each cover with violet ink reading – 'Damaged by first explosion at Scarp – Harris'. A second experiment with the same mail fired from Harris back to Scarp was successful but the project was abandoned, although a few letters addressed to Orkney actually reached their destination having travelled by rocket, ferry, automobile, mail-steamer, railway, and Highland Airways.

When Herr Zucher, unaware that the Nazis were secretly experimenting with rockets, returned to Germany, he was accused by the Gestapo of selling rocket technology to the British, imprisoned for fifteen months, and at one stage transferred to an asylum. He was banned for life from conducting any further rocket experiments. During the war he served in the Luftwaffe but was invalided out in 1944. He died in 1985.

*   *   *

The population of **SCARP** – one of Britain's most westerly and isolated outposts – was well over one hundred at the start of the 20th century but it was dwindling steadily. The authorities were unconcerned and it was not until the 1950s that they chose to build a small jetty on the island (but much too late to stop the island depopulation). The Hydro-Electric Board would not provide an electricity supply and in 1966 the Church of Scotland refused to replace the lay preacher. The small island school closed in 1967 and the post-office in 1969 with the cessation of all mail deliveries. Then the single telephone cable was severed in a storm and the GPO refused to repair it. So in December 1971 the seven remaining islanders had little choice but to abandon their homes. Angus Macinnes and his wife Margaret were the last to leave with their son, Donald John, aged twenty-one. Donald John now lives in Dunbartonshire but his brother Murdo still crofts in Harris and visits Scarp frequently to tend the sheep.

The island is rocky and the north part is 308m in height (over 1000ft) with a steep drop to the sea. The village, mainly of well-built stone houses which are now in serious disrepair, is in the south-east corner and partly sheltered from the Atlantic winds by a low hill. The only land capable of cultivation is in this area. It is easy to see how the island could not support a large population and the lack of an all-weather anchorage was also a serious deficiency which must have contributed to the depopulation of the island. The local economy would have been very basic – potatoes, cabbages, oats, turnips, milk, fish; lobster fishing for the Billingsgate market; wool and Harris Tweed; and the sale of a few livestock. There was no electricity and oil lamps were the only means of illumination but there was some piped water. The village had one small shop and the telephone line was installed in 1947.

Scarp has a proud educational record and it is claimed that more professionally qualified people came from the island than from any other island community of similar size. As for its remote situation, the Hebridean writer, Francis Thompson, tells of the Londoner who was amazed at the sheer isolation of Scarp and asked a Scarpach how he ever got the news from London. 'Well,' was the puzzled rejoinder, 'how do you get the news from Scarp?'

Although the **Kyle of Scarp** is a short crossing, landing at the pier can be difficult when there is any swell. The sea here is very shallow.

The drying islet by Slettnish in the north, **Kearstay** (ON – an enclosed area for farm animals), is divided from Scarp by a narrow channel less than 1m deep called the Sound of Kearstay. To the north there is a reef marked by **Duisker** (G – *Dubh Sgeir*, black skerry). Another small island, **Fladday**, lies somewhat further off-shore on the east and there is **Liongam** near the Lewis coast to the north-east. Low-lying **Gasker**, marked by a navigation light, is some five miles south-west of Scarp. In spite of its small size and lack of height it has some fresh-water pools on it. The landing place in suitable conditions is in a cleft on the south side. Gasker is principally noted for its large well-established seal colony.

* * *

Access: No regular access but Seatrek, Uig, Lewis, 01851-672464, and Sea Harris, East Tarbert, 01859-502007, provide boat charters and excursions.

Anchorages:

1. Occasional anchorage in suitable weather just S of the bar in Caolas an Scarp, off Rubha na Glaodhaich.

2. Occasional anchorage in suitable weather in N entrance to Caolas an Scarp, N of the bar and SW of Fladday.

3. Sound of Kearstay. Temporary anchorage in E entrance of the sound in 9m, sand. Good shelter from SE and WNW.

8.14 Lewis

The derivation normally given is (G. leogach [loo-ach] – marshy). The entire area together with its off-shore islands, once MacLeod territory, is referred to as 'The Lews'. (G. Eilean Leodhais [loo-is] – Leod's island). Leod or 'Ljod' is Norse for 'clan'. The Norse occasionally referred to the whole island as (ON Ljodusherad – Lewis Province).

Harris

(ON hearri – hills) or (G. na h-àirdibh – the heights).

Great Bernera

(ON bjarnar-øy – bear island) or (ON – Bjorn's island).

Scalpay

(ON skalpr-øy – scallop island).

OS Maps: 1:50000 Sheets 8, 13, 14, and 18 1:25000 Sheets 456, 457, 458, 459 and 460
Admiralty Charts: 1:500000 No.2635 1:200000 No.2721 west coast 1:100000 Nos.1785, 1794 and 1795 east coast 1:50000 No.2841 south-west coast 1:20000 No.2642 Sound of Harris 1:12500 Nos. 3381 and 3422 Loch Roag 1:12500 No.2905 Loch Tarbert various scales No.2529 Loch Erisort and Stornoway

Area: 220673ha (5390983 acres) **Height:** 799m (2621 ft)

Owners: Multiple ownership. The largest landowners are several community trusts, the Stornoway Trust, Scottish Office, Richard Kershaw, Barvas Estates, Rodney Hitchcock, J N Oppenheim Partnership, Helen Panchaud, and the Lomas family. Jonathan Bulmer, the cider heir, bought North Harris with Amhuinnsuidhe Castle in 1994. But in 2003, under the Community Right to Buy Act, the Harris islanders (North Harris Trust) bought his 55,000 acre estate with the support of public funds and were joined by Mr Ian Scar-Hall who bought the castle and its 600 acre grounds for a total of £4.5 million. In 2005 the Harris Trust also bought the nearby 7,472 acre Loch Seaforth Estate. Then in 2007 the 53,000 acre Galson Estate in North Lewis was bought out by Lewis crofters under the same Government act.

In 2010 the West Harris Trust bought the state-owned 16,247 acre Borve, Luskentyre and Scaristavore estates for £59,000. In 2012 the residents of Scalpay (1,614 acres) were granted the island free of charge by the owner, Mr Fred Taylor. His father bought Scalpay in 1962 from the North Harris Estate. Most of the island is under crofting tenure.

Great Bernera was owned by a popular laird, Robin Mirrlees, Prince of Coronata, Comte de Lalanne, Freeman of London and Patrician of San Marino – and a close friend of Ian Fleming, of James Bond fame. He bought it in 1962 and had his home (and fish farm) there. He died in 2012 and is survived by his son Patrick de la Lanne whose mother was Margaret the Duchess of Wurttemberg.

Population: In 1755 Harris had a population of 1969 and Lewis (excluding Bernera) 6386. By 1801 the equivalent figures were 2996 and 9168. The Harris factor settled twenty crofting families on Scalpay about 1843 and five years later added another twenty families – some evicted from Pabbay (No.8.4) in the Sound of Harris.

	1841	1891	1931	1961	1981	1991	2001	2011
L'is	16988[1]	27045	24685	21614	22476[2]	21737[2]	19918[2]	21031[2]
H'is	3058	3681	3357	2493				
Ber'a		535	514	317	292	262		
Sca'y		517	636	470	461	382	322	291
Total	20046	31778	29192	24894	23229	22381	20240	21322

[1] includes Great Bernera, Pabay Mór (No.8.19) & Little Bernera (No.8.20)   [2] Lewis/Harris combined

Geology: Almost the entire island is gneiss, both orthogneiss and paragneiss, much of it overlaid with glacially deposited boulder clay; the orthogneiss is predominant. It has been metamorphosed from igneous as opposed to sedimentary rock and although it is complex and highly variable it is loosely known as Lewisian rock. It has a crystalline texture, is pink or grey in colour, and glitters with granules of mica or quartz. It is hard and is short of minerals required to make a good fertile soil.

Exceptions are scarce. Near Stornoway there are a few small areas of New Red Sandstone; in Uig scattered areas of granite (Britain's biggest sapphire was found here in 1995); a few linear basalt dykes; a steeply-angled bed of serpentine traversing a promontory at the eastern end of Scalpay; and, at Lingerbay in Harris and in two spots near the Butt of Lewis, anorthosite predominates. This is the only anorthosite in Scotland – a mineral valued as a road aggregate for its reflective and skid-free properties.

The hills of South Lewis and North Harris have been shaped by relatively lightweight glaciers emanating from a central ice-cap during the last Ice Age.

Central Lewis is a vast dark undulating plain of peat moorland which began to be laid down about 4000 years ago and continues to grow in thickness each year as the cold, wet, and acidic conditions delay decomposition of the previous year's layer of dead plants. In other words Lewis is reducing the 'greenhouse effect' by absorbing excess carbon dioxide! Peat is still an important fuel source for many of the islanders and the rate of growth exceeds the rate of consumption.

History: Marauding Vikings probably started settling in Lewis/Harris in the 9th century and the island appears to have been controlled until the 12th century by the Norwegian Nicolsons. They were wealthy farmers and became known as 'Clan MacNicol of the porridge and barley bannocks'. But Torquill Macleod 'did violently espouse' MacNicol's only daughter and gained possession of the whole of the Lews. The Nicolsons retreated to Skye.

After Norwegian rule had been broken, Bruce's son, David II, granted Angus Og's son, John Macdonald, King of the Isles, many of the Hebridean islands including Lewis and Harris. That was in 1335. Lewis became one of the four regional administrative centres for the island kingdom. Later, having demoted himself to 'Lord of the Isles' in deference to the Scottish king, Macdonald granted Lewis and Harris to the indigenous vassal clan Leod and thereafter the Macleods officially ruled the island.

Lewis/Harris was the last area of the western isles to adopt the Gaelic tongue and even today the spoken language of Lewis has many associations with Norse.

King James VI – the 'wisest fool in Christendom' – had no love of the Gaels. He promoted a company called the Fife Adventurers to plunder Lewis, if need be with 'slaughter, mutilation, fyre-raising, or utheris inconvenieties' and openly recommended genocide. Three raids on Stornoway were mounted – in 1598, 1605 and 1609 – but all were beaten off by Neil Macleod and his Lewismen and the Adventurers eventually went bankrupt. James spitefully withdrew the Macleods' charter and granted title to the Mackenzies of Kintail, who took over control of Lewis in 1610. The Mackenzies developed Stornoway and dominated the Macleod clansmen, but their Chiefs – the Earls of Seaforth – never took up residence in the old Macleod castle in Stornoway harbour. Their main interest in Lewis was deer hunting in Park, otherwise they chose to remain absentee landlords.

The Seaforths lost their title following support of the Jacobites in 1715 but they quickly regained it by supporting the Hanoverians in 1745. Even so, Bonnie Prince Charlie stopped off at Scalpay in Seaforth territory in 1746 and Donald Campbell, a local farmer, gave him refuge and the use of his boat. The Free Church manse now stands on the site of Campbell's house. Throughout this period, the Seaforths retained possession of Lewis and from their residence in London supported an oppressive regime. Tacksmen, such as the notorious George Gillanders in the late 18th century, were

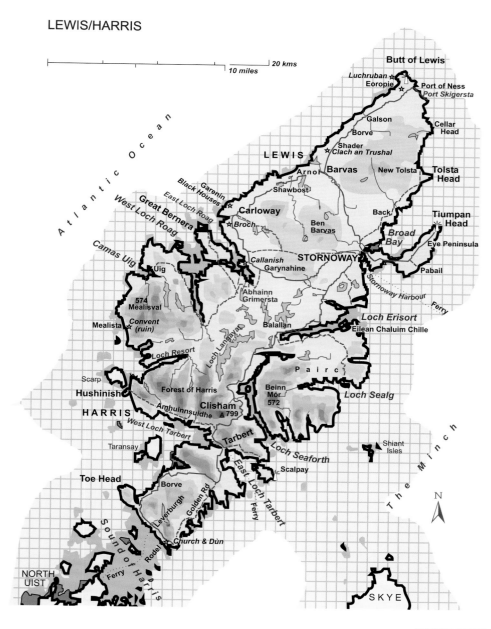

LEWIS/HARRIS

permitted to charge extortionate rents and run what amounted to 'protection' rackets.

In 1778 the Earl of Seaforth raised a regiment to fight in the American War of Independence – the Seaforth Highlanders – for which he was paid a handsome Government levy but his soldiers received no pay until they mutinied in Edinburgh.

In 1783 a younger son of the Mackenzies inherited Lewis, was created Lord Seaforth, and proved a much more understanding landlord but although he had four sons they all predeceased him.

By the early 1800s Stornoway's fishing industry was booming. Mrs Stewart Mackenzie – Lord Seaforth's daughter – sold Lewis in 1844 to Sir James Matheson for £190,000. He then spent nearly £½m – earned from trade with China – on improvements. He also paid the costs of 1,800 people who wished to emigrate to Canada, for more than half the population had signed on with the Destitution Fund as this was the time of the potato famines.

Matheson's tenure was benevolent and there were no evictions. Nevertheless in 1887 crofters desperate for more land killed 200 deer in the Park area, roasted the venison, and held a feast for journalists in order to attract public attention to their cause. This was one of the last 'uprisings'

in what became known as the Crofters' War. The leaders were later charged with mobbing and rioting and tried in court, but they were found not guilty.

In 1918 Lord Leverhulme, the soap magnate, bought the entire island, both Lewis and Harris, and spent nearly a million pounds trying to develop the fishing industry. In 1923 he gifted the 25,000-hectare parish of Stornoway to the people and offered crofts as free gifts although only forty-one tenants accepted. His plans were starting to bear fruit when he died in 1925 but his executors abandoned the project, split the island into several large estates and sold out. Poverty followed and more than 1000 young men emigrated to North America, although some returned during the years of the Depression.

The Macleods of Harris had controlled the southern part of the island until 1779 when it was sold to Captain Macleod of Berneray (No.7.14) who built the harbour at Rodel, constructed roads, restored Rodel church, planted many trees and developed the fishing industry. Unfortunately the Harris population was increasing rapidly and the demand on the land was excessive. As a consequence the islanders were unable to meet their rent obligations.

In 1834 Macleod sold Harris to the Earl of

THE EAST SIDE OF HARRIS

Dunmore, and unlike Sir James Matheson in Lewis the Earl evicted islanders from their west coast crofts in order to lease the land to sheep farmers. However, he did attempt to carry out the evictions in a reasonably humane manner by giving three years' notice to quit. And his wife is to be remembered as the person who first popularised Harris tweed and thus created a new industry. The Earl's heirs sold North Harris to Sir Edward Scott in 1868 and South Harris directly to Lord Leverhulme in 1919.

Much of the recent successful development of Lewis and Harris is thanks to the efforts of Highland and Islands Enterprise (HIE), and a number of projects funded by grants from the European Community.

Wildlife: Some 4000–5000 years ago Lewis and Harris were covered with stunted forests mainly of alder, oak, pine, ash and elm. But with settlement by man the island was steadily denuded of trees. A change of climatic conditions dealt the final blow.

Lewis has relatively little machair as the west coast has many rocks and cliffs, but the central plain is rich in peat with ling and bell-heather, cross-leaved heath, bog asphodel, sundew, cotton grass, bog-myrtle, blue moor grass, deer's hair grass and sphagnum moss.

Among the Harris mountains there is little heather but wild thyme, saxifrages and violets are everywhere. There are a few alpine willow and roseroot but no *Silene acaulis* and *Azales procumbens*, as these prefer granite. When ferrets were introduced rabbits were almost exterminated and the ferrets also preyed on ptarmigan. But the rabbits, as always, have survived – and multiplied.

Seton Gordon, when writing *A Highland Year*, found Clisham and its environment singularly devoid of animal and birdlife. He mentions grouse and meadow pipits but no golden plover, curlew, buzzards or eagle.

In Stornoway a colony of grey seals inhabit the harbour and the woodland surrounding Lews Castle has been colonised by many species of birds including a large rookery.

On the west coast there is a wildfowl refuge at Loch Mór Barvas and corncrakes nest in the undisturbed old burial grounds. And, surprisingly, in the treeless north at Ness there are breeding tree sparrows.

Escapees and releases from the mink farms of the 1950s are now unfortunately established predators threatening the endangered bird populations. They are virtually impossible to eradicate and as they are strong swimmers they are colonising adjoining islands and have spread south to the Uists.

* * *

Although **LEWIS** and **HARRIS** are parts of a single island there is a natural six-mile barrier of high mountains and forbidding moorland between the great sea-lochs of Seaforth and Resort. This so effectively separated the two communities throughout history that they were considered entirely separate islands. Even today, although now connected by road, they speak Gaelic with a distinctly different dialect.

* * *

HARRIS, the southern part of the island, is itself divided into two parts, North and South Harris, where sea-lochs nearly meet at Tarbert (G. *tairbeart* – a narrow isthmus). The west coast has dunes backed by machair which is so thick with wildflowers in early summer that milk from the grazing cattle is said to be perfumed. Here the white shell-sands are blown over the machair by the winds giving it a natural dressing of lime while the islanders spread seaweed as an organic fertiliser. The other traditional farming practice, lazybeds, is reserved for the barren east coast – strips of peat and seaweed built laboriously by hand on top of the rock strata and used for growing oats and potatoes.

At the time of the Clearances the population was larger than the land could support and the standard of living was low. Islanders were turned off their productive west coast crofts and many, loath to leave their homeland, tried to eke out a living on the desolate east coast where the landowners had no interest in such an uneconomic region. To make matters worse families evicted from the neighbouring islands in the Sound of Harris also settled here and lazybeds consequently stretched far up the hillsides amid terrible poverty. In the end depopulation by emigration seemed the only answer.

From the ferry terminal at **Tarbert** there are connections to Skye and North Uist but the town itself, although the largest settlement on Harris, is small, consisting of a few shops, a hotel, post-office, school, small tourist office, churches, and some stores and workshops for the fishermen.

The narrow, winding, road on the east coast south of Tarbert is called the **Golden Road** because it was so expensive to build. In this area, known as Bays, the bare gneiss is pockmarked with tiny lochs, the predominant colours are rich dark browns and greys, and the coastline is a broken conglomerate of inlets and islands. There are mere pockets of sodden charcoal-coloured peat and the ground is so rocky that the dead had to be taken to the west coast for burial. It is difficult to imagine a more desolate, yet awe-inspiring, landscape with human habitation limited to an intermittent smattering of neat little houses near the shoreline.

> The narrow bay
> Has a knuckle of houses and a nail of sand
> By which the sea hangs grimly to the land.
> *Norman MacCaig. 'Harris, East side'.*

The Golden Road serves the scattered settlements around the bays. Every turn brings a new picture-postcard scene of white houses in rocky coves, moored boats, lobster pots and nets. There are two islets in Loch Grosebay – **Càiream** and **Eilean Dubh** and at the next firth, Loch Stockinish, a youth hostel overlooks Stockinish Island (No.8.6). Two more islets in bays further to the west are much smaller than Stockinish – **Eilean Mhànais** outside Loch Gheocrab and **Eilean Quidnish** in Loch Finsbay. The road winds and twists past Lingara Bay and **Lingarabay Island**, about

which the pros and cons of a gigantic quarrying venture were argued about for years, and arrives at Rodel near Renish Point, the southern extremity of Harris. **Renish Island** is no more than a punctuation mark at the end of Renish Point.

The village of Rodel has an attractive little harbour which was built in the 18th century by Captain Macleod of Berneray. It was here that the Harris ferry would put passengers ashore by tender before the new terminal was built at Tarbert. Above the harbour stands **St Clement's Church** [NG0488832] which was built by Alasdair Crotach (Alasdair the Hunchback), the 8th Macleod in about 1500 using sandstone imported from Carsaig on Mull (No.3.3). Its solid rectangular tower is a distinctive landmark which is unique in the Western Isles, and Macleod's tomb within the church is beautifully carved and well worth a visit. The church was restored in 1787 and again in 1873. If locked, the key can usually be obtained from the nearby hotel.

Leaving Rodel and travelling parallel to the Sound of Harris one arrives at **Leverburgh**, now restored to its original name of **An t-Ob** (G. – the haven). It was named Leverburgh by Lord Leverhulme when he tried to make it a centre for the herring fishing industry after the First World War and spent a considerable sum on providing facilities. But the project languished and he sold out in 1923. The township never really recovered from its growth pains until 1996 when the popular direct vehicle-ferry link across the Sound of Harris to Berneray (and North Uist) breathed new life into the area.

Further to the north-west beyond **Northton** is the distinctive peninsula of **Toe Head**. Its dominant peak is Chaipaval (339m). From its summit on a clear day the St Kilda group (Nos. 9.1/9.2/9.3) can be seen to the west, and the Cuillin of Skye to the east. Between the road and Chaipaval is a vast stretch of perfect Hebridean beach, **Tràigh an Taoibh Thuath** (G. – beach on the north side), which continues on to **Tràigh Scarasta** (G. – beach, ON – the farm in the pass)

ST CLEMENT'S CHURCH, RODEL

AMHUINNSUIDHE CASTLE IN THE FOREST OF HARRIS

with its sand dunes below the machair. The golf course here was described by Nick Faldo as one of the world's most beautiful. The road winds along the Atlantic coast and the scenery is dramatically different from the desolation of the east; wide open meadows, pale pink or cream shell sands, turquoise sea and white surf. At **Borve** (ON – fort) there is a standing stone and an ancient dun and the hills to the south conceal a large loch – Loch Langavat (ON – long water). Borve Lodge, surrounded by woodland planted by the Earl of Dunmore, was Lord Leverhulme's home on Harris. Opposite Taransay (No.8.9) there is another wide stretch of sand – Tràigh Seilebost with a spit of sand dunes separating it from the estuarine sands of Tràigh Luskentyre. Here the road turns eastwards through a long valley before returning to Tarbert.

The bare mountains of the Forest of Harris are north of Tarbert; an area with large herds of red deer and lochs rich with salmon and trout. Beneath, on the shore of West Loch Tarbert, the remains of a whaling station built by Norwegians before the First World War and abandoned in 1930, are a reminder of another age. There are dramatic views from the coast road as it runs west round Loch Meavaig and beneath the windows of **Amhuinnsuidhe Castle** [a:vin-soo-ee] (G. –

river seat) beside Loch Leosavay [NB043084]. The castle was built by the Earl of Dunmore in 1868 beside stepped falls where the waters of Loch Leosaid tumble over smooth rock slabs and into the sea. Salmon jump these falls in June and July. It was here in 1912 that James Barrie, of *Peter Pan* fame, wrote the drama *Mary Rose*. He was inspired, it is said, by the islets in Loch Voshimid at the head of Glen Meavaig. North of the loch are two medieval beehive huts. A hydro-electric scheme hidden in the hills provides most of the electricity requirements for Harris.

The coast road comes to an end at beautiful **Hushinish Bay** with the island of Scarp (No.8.13) to the north and Taransay (No.8.9) to the south.

For anyone proposing to camp on Harris many sites are boggy and midgy, so be prepared. However, as compensation, there is rock-climbing for enthusiastic climbers on Clisham which is the highest peak in the Outer Hebrides at 799m (a Corbett), or Sgurr Scaladale, Cnoc a Chaisteil, Creag Mò, Glen Scaladale, Gillaval Glas, Sgaoth Ard, Toddun, Craig Stulaval, Oreval, Ullaval, Stron Utadall and Taran Mor. There are also many fascinating walks along the hill-tracks which are marked on the Ordnance Survey maps; for example, Vigadale Bay on Loch Seaforth to Loch

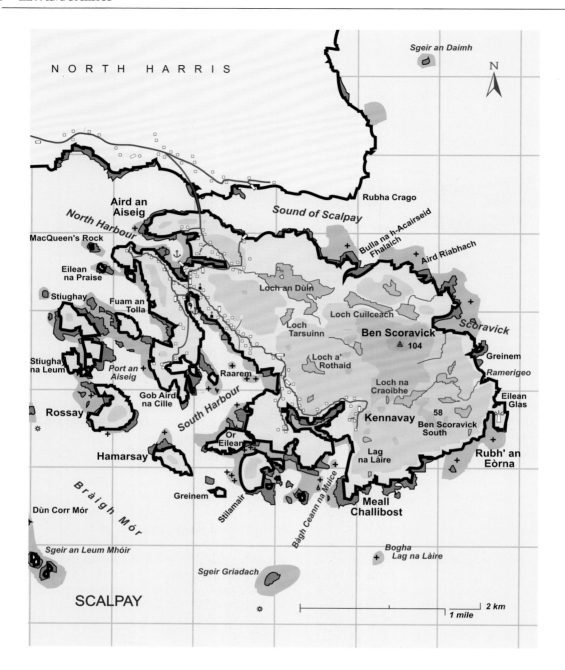

Voshimid, or Aline Lodge to Loch Langavat (a much larger loch than that of the same name in South Harris).

*   *   *

Travelling in the other direction, east from Tarbert, leads to the island of **SCALPAY**. The owner is well-liked by the local people because he 'leaves us alone', I was told by a Scalpay ferryman. That was before the ferry was replaced by a bridge in 1997. But although Scalpay thus lost its nominal independence as a separate island, it regained it to some extent in 2012 when the landlord, Mr Fred Taylor, gifted the ownership to the islanders themselves.

It is a thriving island with change being the penalty for success. The Scalpachs have always managed to maintain a vigorous community when many other islands have lost theirs. Although there is a reasonable agricultural base, which produces a good crop of oats from forty crofts, the land is poor and the traditional industry is fishing, principally for prawns. Many of the islanders own their own boats and there are also a number of trawlers.

All the settlements are on the south-western seaboard. In the past with a large population having less interest in fishing there was extensive lazybed cultivation. But there were too many mouths to feed and fishing became an essential occupation which eventually led to relative prosperity.

> The ferry wades across the kyle. I drive
> The car ashore
> On to a trim tarred road. A car on Scalpay?
> Yes, and a road where never was one before.
> The ferrymen's Gaelic wonders who I am
> (Not knowing I know it), this man back from the dead,
> Who takes the blue-black road (no traffic jam)
> From by Craig Lexie over to Bay Head.
>
> A man bows in the North wind, shaping up
> His lazybeds,
> And through the salt air vagrant peat smells waver
> From houses where no house should be. The sheds
> At the curing station have been newly tarred.
> Aunt Julia's house has vanished. The Red Well
> Has been bulldozed away. But sharp and hard
> The church still stands, barring the road to Hell.
> . . . from 'Return to Scalpay' by Norman MacCaig.

In recent years, such a large number of people on an island of this size has created an almost urban atmosphere and the excellent harbours, surrounded by crisp whitewashed houses, are usually busy.

Scalpay has a very irregular outline with deep indentations. On the east side is **Beinn Scoravich**, 104m high with Loch na Craoibhe (G. – loch of the tree) separating it from 58m-high Ben Scoravich South. The north-west is rough territory of rock and heather-covered slopes, pockets of peat bog, lochs running parallel to the coast – **Loch Cuilceach** (G. – loch of reeds), **Loch an Duin** (G. – loch of the fort) and **Loch Tarsuinn** (G. – the crosswise loch) at right-angles to the others.

Eilean Glas lighthouse, on the east coast, was erected in 1789 by the Commissioners of Northern Lights to the design of Thomas Smith. It was the first and for a long time the only lighthouse in the Western Isles and was placed strategically on the busy sea lane which existed at that time between Skye, Harris and the Baltic. A new higher tower was designed by Stevenson in 1824 with an oil-burning light and this was converted to incandescent in 1907. The lighthouse has been automatic since 1978 and the keepers' houses are now holiday homes. They were built of Aberdeen granite by Robert Louis Stevenson's grandfather.

The road ends by the peat diggings beyond Kennavay but there is an interesting walk around or over Ben Scoravick – down past the east-coast lochans to the lighthouse with its rented accommodation and small restaurant and then along an unmapped south-coast path for the return journey.

The west side of Scalpay shelters behind a line of small islands, **Eilean na Praise** (G. – pot island), **Stiughay**, **Fuam an Tolla**, **Stiughay na Leum**, **Rossay**, **Hamarsay** and **Greinem**: and across the deep channel called Braigh Mór (G. – big neck) is a great cluster of islets and rocks with the largest being **Gloraig a' Chaimbeulich**, **Eilean Mhic Fhionnlaidh**, **Eilean na Gearrabreac** (G. – guillemot isle) and **Eilean na Sgaite** (G. – skate isle).

Scalpachs are renowned throughout the islands for their excellent seamanship. This was proven when, in December 1962, the trawler *Boston Heron* was in difficulties in a full sou'-westerly gale and was driven on to the rocks of **Stilamair** off the south coast of Scalpay. Stilamair is a tidal island near Greinem islet. As there was no time to spare six Scalpay men set out immediately in a small open boat to try to give assistance. In spite of the ferocious seas they managed to rescue three of the trawlermen, one of whom was clinging exhausted to the rocks. They were unable to save the other seven but their heroism was rightfully recognised by the RNLI.

* * *

LEWIS has a mixed economy of weaving, fishing and crofting and occasional construction work for the oil industry. Although Harris tweed, known locally as *clò mór* (G. – big cloth), originated in Harris, the centre of production is now in Lewis, probably because the great majority of the population live there. Until quite recently the tweed was still produced on hand looms and the weavers resisted attempts to introduce power looms although spinning and dyeing were done in a factory. The 650 weavers on the island can produce about 4½ million yards of tweed each year. Unfortunately, with widespread central heating and a preference for light-weight clothing there was an inevitable decline in sales of this fine, warm, water-resistant, and almost indestructible material. But the fashion pendulum has swung back in its favour as lighter-weight cloths of broad width are now available.

CARLOWAY BROCH

The road connecting Harris and Lewis runs from Tarbert to Stornoway skirting the shores of Loch Seaforth and Loch Erisort. Loch Seaforth is twelve miles long and the area between it and Loch Erisort is called Park (G. *Pairc*), a 23,000-hectare estate of wild country with many herds of red deer. Much of this area is fairly inaccessible and the simplest method of reaching it is probably by boat from Loch Seaforth. This is a truly remote wilderness just waiting for exploration by hill-walkers although it should be avoided during the hunting season. It was on this sporting estate in 1887 that crofters killed 200 deer to draw attention to their desperate need for land.

At the head of Loch Erisort, another long sea-loch, by **Balallan** (G. – Allan's town) there are roads leading into the north-east of Park, the only area accessible by vehicle. At the loch entrance is a drying-island, **Eilean Chaluim Chille** (G. – island of Columba's church) having, as expected, an ancient ruined church dedicated to St Columba [NB386211] and a small burial ground next to what may have been a monastery. Macleod of Lewis kept an orchard on this island at one time and Murdo Mackenzie, 'Mac Mhic Mhurchaidh,' the first of Lord Seaforth's factors, lived here. **Eilean Cheois** is in the centre of the loch while **Eilean Thòraidh** and **Eilean Rosaidh** are east of the Cromore headland. The **Barkin Isles** are to the north at the entrance to Loch Leurbost; they comprise **Tabhaidh Mhór**, **Tabhaidh Bheag**, **Tannaraidh** and **Bhatarsaidh**.

North of Park is the parish of Lochs with its steep and rocky coastline cut deeply by sea-lochs. The dark peat moorland is spattered with lochans like pools of mercury gleaming under a cloudy sky.

STORNOWAY (ON *stjorna* – steering or anchor bay) is the only town of burgh status in the Hebrides and the administrative centre of Comhairle nan Eilean Siar, the Western Isles Council. It has a population of about 8100 and the town is centred on its fine natural harbour. Strangely, it was the Dutch who first recognised the fishing potential of Hebridean waters and during the 17th century their fishing fleets were often to be seen in Stornoway harbour. Although cod and ling were caught, it was herring that proved the great attraction. In 1798 Cruttwell's Gazetteer reported that '...the coast is annually visited by myriads of herrings. So immense are the shoals of dog-fish that pursue the herrings that their dorsal fins are sometimes seen like a thick bush of sedges above water as far as the eye can reach'. By the 19th century Stornoway had become a major fishing port and its architecture reflects the prosperity of this period. The local history is illustrated in the Stornoway Museum in Cromwell Street.

The oldest building still standing is possibly the 18th-century net-loft on **North Beach Quay** while **St Columba's Parish Church** on Lewis Street was erected in 1794. At the upper end of Francis Street is **St Peter's Episcopal Church**, built in 1839, which has an ancient sandstone font brought from the Hermit's Chapel on the remote Flannan Isles (See the appendix to Section 9). Its Tower Bell of 1631 once summoned the burghers of Stornoway to civic meetings and David Livingstone's 1608 Bible which he carried in Africa is kept in the vestry.

Arnish Point, at the entrance to Stornoway Harbour, is the site of a wind-turbine fabricator and a seaweed-processing plant. Nearby is a monument to Prince Charles Edward Stuart and on the opposite side at Holm Point is another monument to the 205 Lewis men who were drowned on New Year's Day, 1919 [NB445305]. They were returning home from service at the end of the First World War when their ship, the *Iolaire*, was wrecked on the Beasts of Holm, the rocks just north of the entrance to the harbour while their waiting families watched helpless from the pier.

Sir Alexander Mackenzie, the explorer who made the first overland crossing of Canada, was born in Stornoway and **Martins Memorial** (1885) stands on the site of the house where he was born. West of the town is Sir James Matheson's **Lews Castle** [NB420332], built in 1856–63, which served for a time as a technical college. It is surrounded by spacious grounds and the substantial area of mixed woodland is a unique sight in the Outer Hebrides.

Although Stornoway lies on the periphery of Europe it is a remarkably cosmopolitan place with an unexpected bustle of activity quite unlike the rest of the Outer Isles. Some of the shops are run by Asians who speak fluent Gaelic.

To the east of Stornoway, beyond the airport, is the comparatively densely populated **Eye Peninsula**, known as Point (G. *an rubha*). It is almost an island and on the north shore of the narrow isthmus is the 14th-century St Columba's church and graveyard where nineteen Macleod chiefs are buried [NB485322]. The church was last used in 1828.

West of Stornoway a road crosses the island to Loch Roag and another strikes north-west across the moors to Barvas. Much of Lewis is dark peat moorland with hundreds of shallow lochs and intricate patterns created by centuries of peat cutting. In early summer 'going to the peats' is an important social occasion and the peat is still cut for fuel in the traditional way. It has been estimated that there are eighty-five million tons of peat on the island. An average family uses about 15,000 blocks of peat each year, and this takes at least fifteen man-days to cut, dry and stack.

A road runs round **Loch Roag** crossing **Abhainn Grimersta** which is considered one of the best salmon rivers in Europe. The waters come from distant Loch Langavat through a tortuous succession of remote lochs before discharging into Loch Roag. A branch road leads to the large island of **GREAT BERNERA** (G. *Bearnaraidh Mór*) which lies in the centre of the loch. Its access bridge, the first pre-stressed concrete bridge to be built in Europe, was constructed in 1953 after the islanders threatened to dynamite the hillside to form a causeway. Many of the islanders are called MacDonald and are said to be descended from a watchman who was given the island by the MacAulays of Uig as a reward for his services. Great Bernera is a lobster-fishing centre; the processing plant at Kirkibost was built in 1972.

Loch Roag is a fascinating area and one could spend weeks exploring its many islands and inlets. The freshwater lochs which surround it provide excellent brown trout fishing. The beaches and coves near **Valtos** are of particular beauty.

Beyond Loch Roag is **Camas Uig** (G. *camas* – bay, ON *vik* – bay) and the magnificent Sands of Uig. The Uig sands frame one of the most beautiful views in Scotland – wide, clean, flat and virginal white with an indigo to viridian sea and purple heather-covered Mealisval and Tahaval behind. In the extreme southern

THE THRUSHAL STONE AT BALLANTRUSHAL

KIRKIBOST PIER, GREAT BERNERA

corner is the Abhainn Dearg (G. – red river) whisky distillery, launched in 2011; the first legal distillery on Lewis for 170 years.

The road carries on down the coast from here but it slowly loses importance and dwindles to a track at **Mealista** where there are the remains of an army camp adjoining the ruins of a Benedictine convent called Tigh nan Cailleachan Dubha (G. – house of the old women in black, i.e. nuns) and traces of a 'souterrain' [NA991241].

If spending time by the white sands of Uig or Mangersta Bay try to find the secret cliff-top bothy with its view of Eilean Molach to the north! There are exciting hill walks and many good climbs in this region – Mealisval 574m, Cracaval, Tarain, Tahaval, Teinnasval or Tamanaisval – to name a few.

Back at the head of East Loch Roag the main road from Stornoway reaches one of Britain's most famous landmarks – the ancient standing stones of **Callanish** [NB213330]. It was only in 1857, when the surrounding peat was excavated, that the true height of these stones was realised. This is the second greatest prehistoric stone circle in Britain, about 5000 years old – older than both Stonehenge and the Pyramids. The alignment of the stones may relate to observations of the moon, unlike Stonehenge which relates to the sun. The monoliths form an oblique cross, 123m from north to south and 43m east to west with a central circle and cairn in which the remains of a cremation were found. The tallest standing stone is 4½m – nearly 15 feet – high. Many other small stone circles in the vicinity of Callanish are probably related to it. (Calanais Visitor Centre. Mon.–Sat. 10am–7pm.)

Local legend claimed that the standing stones of Callanish were giants petrified by St Kieran for refusing to be christened.

About 8km north of Callanish is **Doune Carloway** one of the best-preserved brochs [NB190413]. It is 15m in diameter, parts of the galleries and staircase are still intact, and the quality of the dry-stone masonry is remarkable. The broch is on a height overlooking Loch Carloway. An islet, **Craigeam**, is concealed behind its northern headland.

Just north of the village of Carloway, **Gearrannan** village is the last remaining group of black houses on Lewis. These are clustered above a shingle beach in a sheltered cove [NB193442]. The last inhabitants left in 1973 but the houses have now been beautifully restored and re-occupied with some let as self-catering holiday homes. This is a far-sighted project to preserve the village in its original state.

Lewis' north-west Atlantic coastline is steeped in history. There is a folk museum at **Shawbost**, a 6m high whale-bone arch at **Bragar** with the harpoon which killed the whale suspended from it and a Black House Museum at **Arnol** [NB311493]. This *tigh dubh* was occupied as recently as 1964 and with a peat fire kept burning in the centre it is possible to see an authentic interior with the original straw-lined box beds. It makes one realise how well these houses were suited to the climate. Walls 2m thick and thatch and turf roofs weighted with stones created a warm, dry interior no matter what the state of the weather outside.

At **Barvas** a road cuts across the moors to Stornoway with the rare sight of a petrol station at the junction. There are many prehistoric sites near the coast on the route north. For instance, the tallest standing stone in Scotland (5.5m) is at **Ballantrushal** [NB376537]; a 15m burial cairn and large enclosure is at **Shader** [NB396541]; and there are many brochs, duns and temple ruins.

The main road ends at **Port of Ness**. From here Lewis men sail every August to Sula Sgeir, forty-one miles to the north, to bring back *guga* – young gannet, which is considered a great delicacy but is certainly an acquired taste. Port of Ness is a delightful little harbour although it offers only very limited shelter. Just north of it is **Dun Eistean**, a tiny piece of land broken from the coastline with the remains of an old fort on it. This was a place of refuge for the Clan Morrison when the MacAuley's chose to attack and an iron bridge was built over the gorge in 2002 to allow the Morrisons to hold Clan gatherings there.

Near **Eoropie** (ON *eyrar-boe* – beach village), the most northerly settlement, is a natural stone arch and 'pygmy's isle' – **Luchruban** or Eilean nan Daoine Beaga (G. – isle of the little people) [NB508661]. A pygmy race was believed to have lived here and Dean Munro said that they had their 'ane little kirk in it of ther awn handey wark.' The chambered building is on the steep summit of the island. In an excavation many small bones were found which were thought to be human but were later identified as animal bones.

Just north of Eoropie is the restored 12th-century **Teampull Mholuidh** (G. – Church of St Moluag) [NB519653]. The key for access is kept in the local store.

A little more than another kilometre to the north the Outer Hebrides come to a dramatic end at the **Butt of Lewis**. The brick lighthouse overlooks a mist-shrouded tumble of stacks and rocky precipices: the sea boils in the chasms between and the eery sound of the fog-horn sometimes echoed from the cliffs. Apart from Sula Sgeir and Rona there is nothing now but wild sea until one reaches the Faeroes 200 miles to the north.

* * *

Access: Ro-ro ferries daily, Stornoway, Lewis, 01851-702361/ Ullapool, (3hrs) 01854-612358; Tarbert, Harris, 01859-502444/ Uig, Skye, (1¾hrs) 01470-542219; Daily: Leverburgh, Harris/Berneray, North Uist, (70min) 01859-502444.

Stornoway Bus Station, 01851-704327. A good selection of Council and private bus services serves the whole island (and the Uists). Scheduled air services to Stornoway, from Glasgow, Inverness, Benbecula, Edinburgh, and Aberdeen. General enquiries, 01851-702256.

Tourist Information: Stornoway, 01851-703088; Tarbert, 01859-502011.

Anchorages:

1. An t-Obbe (Leverburgh). There is 4.3m depth alongside head of pier but anchor as convenient clear of pier, moorings and ferry. Sheltered and safe in channel 2½c SE of Rubh' an Losaid in 5.5m, very good holding, but very restricted and access difficult.

2. Carminish bay, has some shelter from NW–E in 5m but mostly too shallow.

3. Port Eisgein, Sound of Harris, 1M NW of Renish Point, small inlet noted in Admiralty Pilot. No other information.

4. Loch Rodel, Renish point. Exposed to S'lies but temp. anchorage off boulder beach on NE side, W of church (conspic.). Beware Duncan rock.

5. Poll an Tigh-Mhail, Rodel. Enter from Loch Rodel thro' Bay Channel (which dries 0.5m with large stones). When base of Pillar Rock perch is covered there is 3.4m depth. Pool is deep with perfect shelter. Three visitor's moorings on N side of Vallay. Harbour by hotel dries completely. Anchoring possible but holding poor.

6. Lingara Bay, by Lingarabay island. Good shelter but untenable in E'lies. Anchor just past S side of Eilean Collam in 5m. Go no further in.

7. Loch Finsbay. Little sea, good holding and perfect shelter in all winds. Beware rocks N of Finsbay Island, west of Eilean Quidnish and in loch at Ardvey. Anchor mid-channel N of Ardvey promontory in 4m, mud. Hard to recognise in misty weather but fairly easy entrance if directions followed carefully.

8. Loch Flodabay. Not recommended due to number of rocks but ¾c wide channel along NE shore is charted as clear.

9. Loch Gheocrab. Poor shelter except for pool at head of loch behind a drying reef but obstructed with fish cages.

10. Loch Beacravik, which is the W arm at the head of Loch Gheocrab is well-protected but has fish cages and E side is foul at entrance. Avoid rocky patches on bottom when anchoring.

11. Loch Stockinish. Access best through Caolas Beag, E of

Stockinish Island, before half-tide. Very narrow (only 27m at one point) but clean if close-in to Stockinish Island. After passing Stockinish keep just NE of mid-channel. Anchor in mouth of westerly arm at head of loch, completely sheltered, 9m sand. Beware rock off Ardvey point and to N. Poll Scrot off Caolas Beag has 3m depth alongside pontoon.

12. Loch Grosebay. Safe anchorage but poor shelter N of Sgeir a' Chais at head of loch in 9m mud. Several hazards on approach.

13. Loch Scadabay, on N side of entrance to Loch Grosebay. Passage W of Eilean an Duine is shallow and only 30m wide. Keep to E side to avoid drying rocks. Pool depth less than 2m but soft mud. Perfect shelter.

14. Plocrapool, East Loch Tarbert, 57 50.5N 06 45W. Snug but shallow. Approach carefully by sailing directions. Pass W of rock at entrance, steer 210°. and anchor in suitable depth.

15. Ob Meavag, Loch Ceann Dibig, East Loch Tarbert. Many rocks but sheltered. Dries 2c from head. Approach from NW as sailing instructions. Beware fish cages.

16. Bàgh Diraclett, Loch Ceann Dibig. Sheltered but beware drying rocks on approach. Good holding.

17. Eileanan Diraclett, 57 53N 06 47W. N of entrance to Loch Ceann Dibig. Sheltered anchorage but go no further than 1c into inlet on W side of islands.

18. East Loch Tarbert. Little space due to moorings and ferry access. Ferry needs space to turn on S side of pier. Anchor W of pier only if space permits.

19. North harbour, Scalpay. A fine natural harbour in a small bight at NW end, with depths of 1.8m to 5.5m but limited space. Beware MacQueens rock and a reef and wreck near the entrance.

20. South harbour, Scalpay. On SW side, enter between Hamarsay and Rossay. Keep midway between south-east shore and Raarem islet. When past Raarem turn north and keep ½c off E side of Raarem and continue close to W shore at the narrows. Anchor SE of islet in inner loch. Beware drying rock ½c SE of islet.

21. Loch Scoravick, Scalpay. Good holding on S side, 5m. Exposed to E'lies.

22. Loch Maaruig, 2½M into Loch Seaforth on W side. Anchor W of Goat Point, mud. Beware rock awash SW of Goat Point. Well sheltered. In places the shore is so steep that it is possible to moor to it and lie afloat.

23. Aline Lodge. Anchor off the jetty, or better, ½M farther NE in 7m. Sheltered but subject to squalls.

24. Loch Claidh. 1M into loch on E side, anchor NE of Eilean Thinngarstaigh (Hingarstay) in 8m, mud and sand. Space just over ½c width. Enter W and N of En Thinngarstaigh. Good holding and shelter and little swell.

25. Tob Smuasavig, inlet on NE side of Loch Claidh. Anchor at head of inlet, bottom stiff clay, shells and stones.

Uncomfortable in S winds.

26. Loch Bhalamuis (Valamus). Approach with care only when loch well open and keep W of centre when in the loch. About ½M into loch on E side anchor ½c N of Transit Point if sufficient depth found clear of drying rock and boat mooring.

27. Loch Bhrollum. Tob Bhrollum on NE side of Aird Dhubh is well sheltered but some swell sets in with S'lies. Skirt W and N sides of Aird Dhubh at a distance of 30m until Rubh' a' Bhaird is shut in by Aird Dhubh then anchor as convenient in 4–6m, good holding. This position is east of a sunken rock in the entrance.

28. Loch Bhrollum. Anchor at head of loch on E side of islet. Shallow but soft mud.

29. Loch Shell or Sealg. S side clean but there are rocks W of Eilean Iubhard. Anchor in Tòb na Gile Móire on S side, at head of loch, in Tòb Eishken (beware rock E of entrance) on N side, in Tòb Stiomrabhaigh (Stemervay) or Tòb Orinsay. All areas shoal or shallow, partly exposed and some may be foul with old moorings or obstructed with fish cages. Easy access, good shelter but squalls possible.

30. Tòb Lemrevay (Limervay), Caolas a' Tuath. Follow directions for approach. Anchor off E side of inlet with just enough room to clear shoreline rocks. Good holding but subject to N squalls.

31. Loch Odhairn (Ouirn). Anchor towards the head, opposite N shore jetty, on S shore behind promontory. Bottom good, no sea in any wind, but heavy squalls in SW gales. Loch free from dangers.

32. Loch Mharabhig (Mariveg), 58 05.4N 06 23.5W. Tortuous entrance by Caolas na h-Acarsaid, S of Eilean Rosaidh, or S of Eilean Thòraidh, and several rock obstructions in loch. Best anchorages SE of Sgeir a' Bhuic or in NW corner. Well sheltered.

33. Eilean Thòraidh (Torray), at entrance to Loch Mharabhig. Fairly tricky approach. Anchor between W side of Torray and mussel farm or in opposite bay off Aird Fhalasgair (beware drying rock off S point). Well sheltered.

34. Camas Thormaid (Witches' Bay), SW of Aird Fhalasgair Beware drying rocks at centre of approach. Approach on course 20m from S shore and anchor no further than SW of islet, clay. Well sheltered.

35. Orasaidh. Anchor in the basin, S or SW of Orasaidh.

36. Camas Orasaidh, inlet W of Orasaidh. Keep to W side on entering. Good holding, mud.

37. Tòb Cromore, on SE side of Peacam, near entrance to Loch Erisort. Snug anchorage in 2–4m, clay, shoal near head and foul ground near shores. Note rock off NW shore.

38. Peacam (Cromore) 58 06.5N 06 25W, E of Eilean Chaluim Chille. Anchor S of Sgeir Peacam.

39. Loch Thorasdaidh (Hurista), S of Eilean Chaluim Chille. Sailing directions must be followed with care. Anchor W of

Toa peninsula in soft smelly mud. Alternatively pass S and E of the central islets and anchor S of Toa. Some swell in W'lies.

40. Keose, 58 06N 06 29W, on N shore of Loch Erisort. Anchor SW of jetty in 3m mud or N of Garbh Eilean.

41. Loch Erisort. Several bays with good anchorages. Some drying rocks but no serious navigational difficulty.

42. Loch Leurbost on N side of approach to Loch Erisort. Approach S of the Barkin Isles; Tabhaidh Mhór and Bheag, and Bhatarsaidh and beware drying reef 1c SW of Tannaraidh. Anchor in basin W of Risay at S side of loch entrance, 2–3m, soft mud. Enter basin from N.

43. Loch Leurbost, head is shoal for 3c. Anchor off jetty at Aird Feiltanish: or off slip by the Free Church at Crossbost: or in Tòb Shuardail on S side of loch but note Jackal Shoal (1.8m depth) on approach: or near head of loch S of Orasaigh.

44. Loch Grimshader, 58 09N 06 23W. Well protected. Beware Sgeir a' Chaolais mid-channel. Anchor either side of Buaile Mhor at head. Good holding. SW part of loch is soft mud. Beware power cable over Loch Beag.

45. Glumaig harbour, bay SW of Stornoway Harbour, is best anchorage but far from town and in industrial area. Reefs marked with beacons on W side of entrance and 1c N of Arnish Point. Bottom foul, anchor should be buoyed.

46. Stornoway Harbour. Poll nam Portan opposite commercial quays. Note drying rocks. Crowded with moorings and exposed to S'ly swell. Avoid swinging into fairway if anchored. North Beach quay, N of No 1 pier in Stornoway Harbour has over 2.7m depth on its W side and over 1.8m on its N side but going alongside amid traffic can be hazardous. Pontoon berths (pay, 01851-702688).

47. Bàgh Phabail (Bayble Bay) on Eye Peninsula. Occasional anchorage. Protected from SW winds. Concrete pier at head with 3.7m at HW at outer end.

48. Broad Bay, N of Eye Peninsula. Some shelter from SW at head.

49. Port of Ness (Callicvol), 2M SE of lighthouse. Small open bay free of dangers but subject to swell. Bottom sand, depths moderate. Exposed E'lies. Boat harbour on N side dries; enter after half flood but not in stormy weather.

50. Eoropie bay. Extensive sandy beach can be approached carefully but avoid Aird Dell vicinity. Temp. anchorage in suitable conditions. (2km walk to Luchruban)

51. Loch Shawbost, small bay open N and subject to swell. Shoal with sandy bottom. Keep to centre. About 1c swinging room.

52. Loch Carloway. On approach avoid channel between N headland and Craigeam island. In the loch keep nearer N shore and note shoal patch 1 c WSW of Dunan Pier. Anchor SSW of pier, 3–5m, sand and mud. (Slip on S shore convenient for access to famous Carloway Broch). Good

holding but heavy swell in W'lies.

53. Port a' Chaoil, 58 14N 06 46.5W, on E shore of East Loch Roag. Sheltered. Several rocks to be noted. After entering mid-channel anchor close to E shore near head of bay.

54. Tòb Breasclete, E of Keava. Anchor S of old jetty which is E of new pier, mud, good holding and no swell.

55. Callanish, 58 11.5N 06 45W. Temp. anchorage in 2–3m NW of Bratanish islands which are drying islets E of Eilean Kearstay (No.8.18). (Callanish Standing Stones are close-by.) Submerged rock S of Bratanish Mór, and another off E shore of anchorage. If going further S, beware power cables over Loch Ceann Hulavig entrance (only 5.7m clearance).

56. Dubh Thob, East Loch Roag, 58 13N 06 48W, between Great Bernera and Vacasay. A secure little anchorage but a number of hazards on entry. N entry easiest.

57. Loch Beag Breaclete, W of Loch Risay, narrow inlet in Great Bernera with 2–9m depth. Rocks on both sides at entrance. Too open to N for good shelter.

58. Kyles of Little Bernera (Bernera Harbour), good anchorage. Keep N of mid-channel on entering, then S of Sgeir a' Chaolais (marked with beacon) and anchor off ruin in NW side of inlet or 1c SW of beacon. Beware submerged rock 1c WSW of beacon near fish cages.

59. West Loch Roag. A large selection of interesting anchorages can be found with the aid of Chart 3381. Examples are: Aird Torranish opposite S of Great Bernera; Loch Drovinish; Miavaig Bay between Floday and Carishader; or the bay by Eilean Teinish.

60. Loch Miavaig, snug, little harbour with free pontoons, or anchor in 3.7m to 9m, very soft mud. Shoal beyond power cable. Water at pier.

61. Shiaram Mór, an islet in Kyles Pabay near Valtos pier. Anchor at NW or SE end.

62. Camas Uig. Occasional anchorage in pool behind two small islets off Carnish, 3m sand. Dangerous to enter or leave in NW'lies.

63. Caolas an Eilean – temp. anchorage in settled weather or quiet W'lies off beach on E shore of Mealista Island (No.8.17), sand.

64. Loch Tamanavay (Hamnaway). Remote and scarcely inhabited. Keep close to east shore to avoid Bo Thorcuill in mid-entrance. Good, well-sheltered anchorage at head of loch but depths decrease sharply.

65. Loch Tealasavay. Occasional anchorage at S side of loch head.

66. Loch Resort, 4M length, good and safe anchorage at loch head or about half-way along at Diriscal on S side, black smelly mud.

67. Loch Cravadale. Occasional anchorage at head of bay.

68. Caolas an Scarp. Anchor in settled weather N or S of the sand-bar. Avoid passage between Fladday and Harris.

69. Husinish bay, temp. anchorage in settled weather in 6m, sand.

70. Govick bay, close E of Rubha Bogha Sgeir. Temp. anchorage in 9m.

71. Loch Leosavay (*by Amhuinnsuidhe*), drying rock off NE shore, at steps S of jetty. Keep towards W side of loch and anchor in bay off mansion, 4m, mud. Sheltered.

72. Loch Meavaig, 2¼M ESE of Glas sgeir, in 2m to 9m, soft mud and shells. Anchor half-way up the loch in 4–6m, beyond which shoals rapidly. Subject to swell.

73. Loch Bun Abhainn-eader (Bunaveneader), excellent shelter off whaling station. Anchor clear of fish cages to suit wind direction, mud. Landing can be difficult.

74. West Loch Tarbert. Anchor W of jetty on S side. (There is also a pier on the N side.) No heavy seas, but squalls in S'lies and swell in NW'lies.

75. Traigh Nisabost. Occasional anchorage in sandy bay E of Aird Nisabost in Sound of Taransay. Beach landing can be difficult due to swell.

76. Camas nam Borgh, a sandy bay 2M E of Toe Head. Drying reefs off W shore. Good shelter and holding in S'lies in SW corner of the bay, but beware windshifts to NW or N.

8.15 Mealista Island

(ON muli-staoir-øy – island by the promontory farm).
Also spelt – Mealasta.

OS Maps: 1:50000 Sheet 13   1:25000 Sheet 458
Admiralty Charts: 1:200000 No.2721   1:50000 No.2841

Area: 124ha (306 acres)
Height: 77m (253 ft)

Population: Mealista was inhabited until 1823 when it was cleared for sheep. In the 1861 Census, the crew of a fishing boat from Rosehearty near Aberdeen, including a female cook, was living in a tent on the island.

Geology: The bedrock is gneiss, some of which contains a reddish quartz.

History: The Celtic saint Catan, who is believed to have lived in the 6th–7th century and to have had a cell on the Eye Peninsula on the east side of Lewis, had a shrine dedicated to him at Mealista in Uig, just north-east of Mealista island. The extensive remains of a nunnery – the House of the Old Women in Black – is by the shrine. Knowing the love of isolation of the early Celtic saints, it would be surprising if the island did not feature at some time in the life of St Catan or one of his followers.

Wildlife: Much of the island is covered with grass and grazed by domestic sheep.

*   *   *

MEALISTA ISLAND is about half a mile off the west coast of Lewis, after the road from Brenish has passed the ancient convent ruins and then disappeared into the confused shoreline where the mountains approach the sea. A clean sandy beach faces on to **Caolas an Eilean** (G. – the island kyle). The island is uncultivated but offers good grazing. The west coast is rocky and unwelcoming.

MEALISTA ISLAND FROM THE LEWIS SHORE

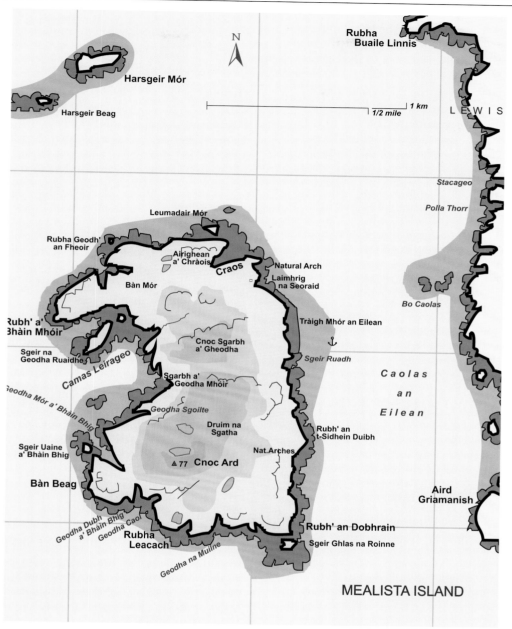

MEALISTA ISLAND

On the south coast **Sgeir Ghlas na Roinne** (G. – grey rock of the seals) is beside Rubh' an Dobhrain (G. – otter point). The west coast is dominated by a deep bay between rocky headlands called Camas Leirageo (G. – the bay with the obvious cleft). Cnoc Ard (G. – high knoll) is the highest point at 77m. At the northern extremity one can look north from Airighean a' Chràois (G. – shielings by the gaping inlet) to the skerries and scattered rocks near the Lewis coast and see the little island of **Greineim** – 19m high. Another islet, **Eilean Molach**, near the entrance to Uig Bay is hidden from sight by Aird Brenish.

There are some ruined houses on Mealista Island showing that it once supported a small community, but in 1823 the island was incorporated into a sheep farm and, although I have found no record, one must assume that the islanders were 'encouraged' to leave the island at about that time. Certainly there is no record of any population in the 1831 or 1841 census. The small Lewis township of Mèalista was itself cleared in 1838 with the majority of the inhabitants being sent to Canada.

Sheep are still grazed on the island and stock is ferried across at Leac na h-Aiseig (G. – ferry ledge) by Rubha Buaile Linnis on the Lewis mainland. This is where the south-going coastal track finally expires. The island collection point is **Laimhrig na Seoraid** (ON – loading rock G. landing place by the primroses).

There was always a desperate need for timber on the islands. Even driftwood was the property of the laird under the old laws and the tacksmen would sometimes ruthlessly enforce this by entering houses and removing driftwood used for roof supports. In 1795 a boat from Mealista was bringing timber back from the Scottish mainland when it ran aground at Bàgh Ciarach in Pairc on the west coast of Lewis. Her crew was murdered for the precious cargo.

It was said at one time that anyone born on Mealista Island would eventually end up as an idiot. Certainly there is a record of one unfortunate islander in the early 19th century called Wild Murdoch. His 'friends' apparently would try to restore his sanity by tying a rope around his body and towing him behind their boat, sometimes with a large stone attached. They claimed he couldn't drown and one day, to prove it, abandoned the poor man on Greineim islet nearly two miles away and surrounded by surging Atlantic tides. Yet he swam back to Mealista. In the end, however, Wild Murdoch could take no more. He murdered his sister, was arrested and died in an asylum or a prison.

* * *

Access: No regular access. Boat excursions offered by Seatrek, Uig, Lewis, 01851-672464.
Anchorage:
1. Caolas an Eilean. Temporary anchorage in settled weather, or quiet W'lies, off the central beach on E shore of Mealista, sand. Holding may be unreliable.

8.16 Eilean Kearstay *or* Chearstaidh

Probably (ON garthr-øy – an island with livestock enclosures). Munro called it 'Kertay'. There is another Kearstay north of Scarp.

OS Maps: 1:50000 Sheets 8 or 13 1:25000 Sheet 458
Admiralty Charts: 1:200000 No.2721 1:12500 No.3422
Area: 77ha (190 acres)
Height: 37m (121 ft)

Owner: Sold in 1990 by the laird of Great Bernera, Count Robin Mirrlees to two Australians, Rosemary Nicolson Samois (who has a Lewis family background) and Anne Inglis of Sydney, NSW. Price understood to be £20,000. Since resold to a purchaser who wished to build a cottage on the island but was refused Council permission in 1994.

Population: No Census records.

Geology: The Admiralty Pilot notes that there is a local magnetic anomaly in this area with the compass needle, unusually, being repelled from the centre of disturbance.

History: A party, attended by many notable Highlanders and Islanders, and the Australian Consul, was held in August 1990 to celebrate the new ownership of the island. An Australian gum tree was planted, supported by Gaelic prayers and classical pipe music. The new owners, who had a shop in Portree on Skye, said they planned to market a specially designed handwoven tweed of local wool which would be called 'Cearstaidh' but by 1993 they had sold the island.

* * *

The seaward approach to **EILEAN KEARSTAY** is southwards through lovely East Loch Roag, between **Vacasay** and **Grèinam** islet and then through Kyles Keava beside the fairly substantial island of **Keava** after which the view of Callanish opens up. There is a narrow channel on each side of Eilean Kearstay, the west one being formed by Rubha na Sidhean (G. – headland of the fairy knoll) projecting from Great Bernera, while the shallow east channel is bounded by the Callanish peninsula.

Eilean Kearstay has few distinctive geographical features but there would seem to be a reasonable chance, in view of its proximity to Callanish, for the discovery of prehistoric associations. The island is smooth and grassy and rises to a low central plateau with a conspicuous cairn at the north end. This is at virtually the same height as

Cnoc Gasamail (37m) in the south-west, which is the highest point and which overlooks **Eilean Scarista**, an islet tucked into a small bay on the Lewis coastline.

South-east of Eilean Kearstay, Loch Ceann Hulavig shelters **Eilean an Tighe** and **Eilean Trosdam**.

Access: No regular access. Boat excursions offered by Seatrek, Uig, Lewis, 01851-672464.

Anchorage: Temp. anchorage in suitable conditions can be found at several points around the island with the aid of the East Loch Roag chart (No. 3422), e.g. off Rubh' an Tairbh.

1. The nearest overnight anchorage is E of the Bratanish islands, S of Callanish. (*For a visit to Callanish*).

CALLANISH

8.17 Vuia Mór

(G bhuidhe, ON -øy, G. mhór – big fair and pleasant island).

OS Maps: 1:50000 Sheet 13 1:25000 Sheet 458
Admiralty Charts: 1:200000 No.2721 1:12500 No.3381

Area: 84ha (208 acres)
Height: 67m (220 ft)
Owner: Uig Crofters Ltd. Part of the Uig (Valtos) grazings.

Population: There were four families in 1807 and in 1841 there were seven houses on the island accommodating forty-six inhabitants. The island was then cleared and there has been no permanent habitation since.

Geology: Mainly Lewisian gneiss.

History: I was told that some of the local people are disinclined to discuss Vuia Mór because of the brutality of the Clearances and that some are even reluctant to land on the island. Others, however, claim that this is a ridiculous notion.

* * *

VUIA MOR is yet another example of an island that once supported a thriving community, was cleared for sheep in the 19th century, and now lies deserted and uncared for. It is almost L-shaped with the northern leg, **Rubha Rollanish**, divided by a shallow valley and rising to a low hill (45m). There are caves in the rocky east coast of this headland. The main part of the island rises to a central hill, **Mullach na Beinne** (G. – top of the hill), with a cairn on the summit (67m). The south-west side of this hill falls abruptly to the sea at **Creag na h-Iolaire** (G. – eagle cliff) and in the words of the Admiralty Pilot this steep cliff '... is very noticeable from the vicinity of **Old Hill** (a remarkable islet about 90m high identifying the entrances to East and West Loch Roag)'.

The south coast has three headlands, Rubha na Mòine (G. – mossy headland), Rubha Liath (G. – grey headland) and in the middle, Rubha Eadar Dhà Thòb (G. – the headland between two coves).

Some years ago Mr Norman Buchanan, a nonagenarian resident of Valtos, said he could still remember a neighbour, Mrs Kate Morrison, who was born on Vuia Mór. She died in Valtos in 1908 aged one hundred.

Mr Kenneth Smith, a crofter at Earshader, told me that during the clearances, 'one young married couple were evicted by the Bernera Ground Officer, and they went to Canada. The Ground Officer was later removed from office, and he went to Ontario, Canada, where he died as a tramp. One day he had gone to a certain door to beg for a piece of bread. The lady of the house recognised him at once, but he did not recognise her. She gave him a good piece of bread and never said a word until he had eaten it. She then asked if he was satisfied and he said he was and only then did she tell him that he had evicted her from Vuia Mór'.

There are many small islands in this corner of Loch Roag: **Eilean nam Feannag, Linngeam, Cliatasay, Garbh Eilean** in the entrance to

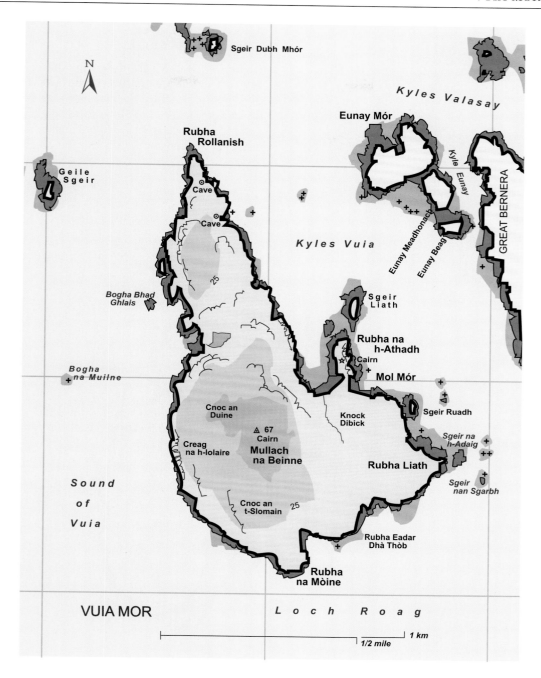

VUIA MOR

Little Loch Roag, **Vuia Beag** – little sister of Vuia Mór, **Gousam** and **Floday**. Both Vuia Beag and Floday were inhabited until 1827 when they were cleared for sheep and became part of Linshader Farm.

Access: No regular access. Boat excursions offered by Seatrek, Uig, Lewis, 01851-672464.

Anchorages: No recommended anchorage and beware

submerged rocks in Kyles Vuia. There is a rough stone jetty of uncertain depth.

1. Occasional anchorage in suitable conditions in N-exposed cove on E side, SSW of Eunay Mór. Anchor in centre of bay, W of the cairn on Rubha na h-Athadh, 4m sand.

2. Temp. anchorage in suitable weather conditions SE of Rubha Liath, the SE extremity, and W of Sgeir nan Sgarbh (dries 1.5m), in 6m.

8.18 Vacsay

(G. Bhacsaidh) (ON vagr-øy – bay island) or (ON bakki-øy – island with a hillock or peat-bank). The present owner tried to change the name to 'Robert Burns Island' although the poet had no historic association with Vacsay.

OS Maps: 1:50000 Sheet 13   1:25000 Sheet 458
Admiralty Charts: 1:200000 No.2721   1:12500 No.3381

Area: 41ha (101 acres)
Height: 34m (112 ft)

Owner: Previously part of the Uig (Valtos) Estate. Sold in 1983 for £9500 to a private buyer but the Uig Estate retained the grazing rights. Resold for £80,000 in 1993 to Sirdar Iqbal Singh, a retired Sikh property dealer from London, now living in Lesmahagow, Strathclyde. Mr Singh

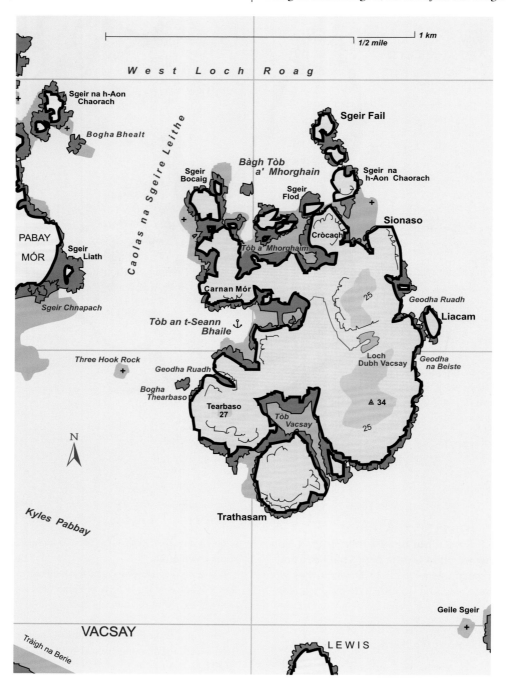

purchased the English title 'Lord of Butley Manor' in 1986.

Population: 1861–9. No permanent habitation since then.

Geology: Lewisian gneiss with peaty soil.

History: In 1827 Vacsay became part of Linshader Farm and was partly cleared for sheep.

* * *

VACSAY in West Loch Roag lies off the beautiful white beach of Tràigh na Berie – a popular camping and caravanning spot among the sand dunes.

The island has a very irregular coastline with a confusion of islets and skerries to the north; a small cove between Sionaso and **Liacam** – a drying islet – on the rocky east coast; a larger cove, **Tòb an t-Seann Bhaile** (G. – cove of the old settlement) on the west coast; and a sizeable drying island, **Trathasam**, on the south coast enclosing a shallow pool which forms a natural fish-trap. In between there are a number of irregular hillocks, the highest at 34m in the south-west.

Between Vacsay and the village of Kneep on Lewis is the conspicuous islet **Shiaram Mór** and across the loch to the north-east, beside Great Bernera, is another islet, **Grèinam**. Shiaram Mór was bought in 1983 for £11,000 by Mr Sati Gulhati, a London hotelier.

Access: No regular access. Boat excursions offered by Seatrek, Uig, Lewis, 01851-672464.

Anchorage:
1. Occasional anchorage in central bay on W side, 4m, sand. On approach from SW (vicinity of Shiaram Mór) beware Three Hook Rock (covered) and Bogha Thearbaso (dries 1.5m).

8.19 Pabay Mór

(ON pap-øy, G. mór – big island of the priest).

OS Maps: 1:50000 Sheet 13 1:25000 Sheet 458
Admiralty Charts: 1:200000 No.2721 1:12500 No 3381

Area: 101ha (250 acres)
Height: 68m (223 ft)

Owner: Bought for £19000 in 1983 by Mr John

Hobbs, a leading London vascular surgeon and phlebologist. He and his family visit Pabay Mór for a month each summer. Valtos crofters retain the right to graze sheep on the island as allowed for by the Crofting Act of 1886.

Population: Cleared for sheep in 1827. In 1861 there were two crews totalling fifteen fishermen and two female cooks, all from Banffshire, living in one of the caves. In 1881 nine Uig men were living in a tent on the island at the time of the Census. Uninhabited since then except for occasional visits by fishermen, shepherds and the owners.

Geology: Lewisian gneiss with a light soil.

History: Pabay was a MacLeod island and at one time Norman, brother of the last chief, Ruaridh ('Old Rory'), lived there when 'he wald be quyeit, or yet fearit'. But MacLeod power waned and about 1800 the island was given to Sergeant Evander MacIver in lieu of a pension on his retiral from the Seaforth Regiment. The MacIver family settled on the island, but in 1827 or thereabouts they were evicted to provide unimpeded grazing for the sheep of Linshader farm. The family moved to Kneep and their descendants still live in Valtos. Both Valtos and Kneep overlook Kyles Pabay and Pabay Mór. I was told that when the MacIvers were cleared from the island their youngest child was a little girl aged one. For the rest of her life she was known in Uig as 'Pabay-one-year-old' – 'in the Gaelic, of course'.

* * *

The Lewis coastline opposite **PABAY MOR** has superb shell-sand beaches backed by dunes. The tide runs briskly through the narrow stretch of sea, Kyles Pabay, and in bad weather the surface is broken and dangerous where the Kyle opens out into the Atlantic. But between Pabay Mór and its little brother, **Pabay Beag**, there is a wide and pleasant pool, well sheltered from the weather, which is reputed to have been the haunt of pirates in times long past.

After the First World War some locals claimed that boxes of provisions were found, proving that a German U-boat had visited the island secretly. An even more tenuous claim to fame is that the founder of the Cunard shipping line is thought to have been closely related to the MacIvers of Pabay.

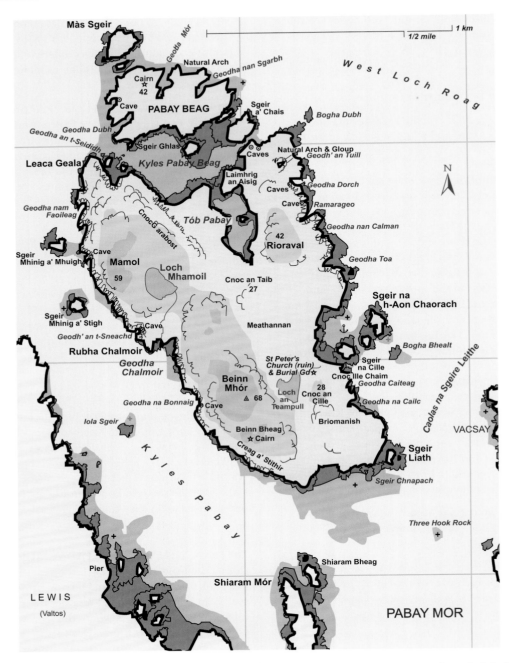

A cairn marks Pabay Beag's highest point (41m) and there is another one near the summit (68m) of **Beinn Mhór** (G. – big hill) on Pabay Mór. East of Beinn Mhór, in a shallow valley beside **Cnoc an Cille** (G. – church knoll), are the ruins of a church and burial ground [NB105377]. A burn runs past the ruin and across a white sandy beach into a sheltered cove. It comes from a heart-shaped lochan, **Loch an Teampull** (G. – temple loch), between Beinn Mhór

and Cnoc an Cille. There is another, slightly larger, loch to the north-west, **Loch Mhamoil** (G. – loch by the pap), with its stream discharging into Geodha Chalmoir on the steep-sided west coast.

There are many rocky caverns on Pabay and a natural stone arch in the north-east where the sea sucks and blows through a passage penetrating the hillside before it reaches an inland pool [NB104386]. This is the formation called a 'Gloup' in the Northern Isles.

North of the Pabays is the solitary rock, **Harsgeir**, and a dramatic group of islets and attendant rocky stacks guarding the entrance to Loch Roag, **Bearasay**, **Floday**, and **Old Hill** which rises 90m sheer above the sea like a giant loaf of bread.

* * *

Access: No regular access. Boat excursions offered by Seatrek, Uig, Lewis, 01851-672464.

Anchorages:
1. Tràigh na Cille (Church beach), inlet W of Sgeir na h-Aon Chaorach on E coast. Approach from NNE and keep slightly S of centre of the inlet, 2–3m, sand. *(Church ruins are above the beach)*.
2. The WC Pilot states that the channel between Pabay Mór and Pabay Beag forms an excellent little harbour with depths from 0.4m to 3.2m (the large scale chart shows less depth than this), sand, where boats with local knowledge can lie safely in any weather. Use W entrance after quarter flood owing to rocks that dry. If using the narrow E entrance beware Bogha Dubh.
3. Rubha Caol, S extremity of the island. Occasional anchorage off sandy beach, 3m. Beware Three Hook Rock 2c SE of SE corner and drying rock W of Sgeir Chnapach.
4. S of Tràigh na Cille (S of Sgeir na Cille) giving Bogha Bhealt a wide berth. Anchor off cave in 5m, sand. Some swell at HW.

8.20 Little Bernera

(ON bjarnar-øy – bear island) or possibly (ON – Bjorn's island).

OS Maps: 1:50000 Sheet 13 1:25000 Sheet 458
Admiralty Charts: 1:200000 No.2721 1:12500 No.3381

Area: 138ha (341 acres)
Height: 41m (134 ft)

Owner: Comte Robin de la Lanne Mirrlees owned the island from 1962 until his death in 2012. It was for sale from 1993–96 but was then withdrawn. He also owned Floday, Kealasay, Old Hill, and Bearasay. He is survived by his estranged son Patrick de la Lanne, Mayor of Delhemhort, and three grand-children.

Population: Two inhabitants were recorded in 1807– Neil and Donald Macdonald – (who may have had families) but they later moved to Great Bernera. However by 1831 numbers were sufficient for a school to be established by the Edinburgh Gaelic School Society and nineteen boys, twenty girls, and one adult were enrolled. But in 1832 or 1833 most of the islanders were cleared or 'resettled' at Dun Carloway on the Lewis 'mainland' (including two families called MacAuley) and the school was closed. The last record of any inhabitants was in the 1861 Census.

Geology: Lewisian gneiss with a light, very fertile soil and acidic pockets.

History: Two of the twenty five pre-Reformation churches listed by Martin Martin were located here. Most of the small islands had connections with one or other of the early Celtic saints but in Little Bernera's case it is two saints, St Donan and St Michael. St Donan may have been a Pict and he is noted for his monastic centre on Eigg.

Following the clearance of Little Bernera for sheep-farming, and dissatisfaction with the intolerable demands of Sir James Matheson's factor, crofters on Great Bernera revolted in 1874. It was a relatively minor incident, an altercation with a sheriff officer, but it became known as the Bernera Riot and aroused public sympathy.

Wildlife: Cattle of the Scaliscro estate on Lewis have grazed the island for twenty-five years. A rogue bullock took charge in 1992 and for two years the cattle refused to be rounded up and ran wild.

* * *

LITTLE BERNERA lies immediately north of Great Bernera in Loch Roag on the north-west coast of Lewis. According to that intrepid 16th-century traveller Dean Munro, it was full of rough little craigs with fertile earth between. That description still applies today except that after a century of rough grazing the earth is probably no longer quite as fertile or 'manurit' as it once was. When Bernera Beag was populated and productive, apart from good pasturage for sheep and black cattle, it had a yield of 200 bolls of barley a year, which is approximately forty-two tonnes. This is a ruggedly beautiful island and its seclusion made it a favourite picnic stop for the royal family when they sailed in Britannia. At one time the Count even talked of leaving the island to Prince Harry!

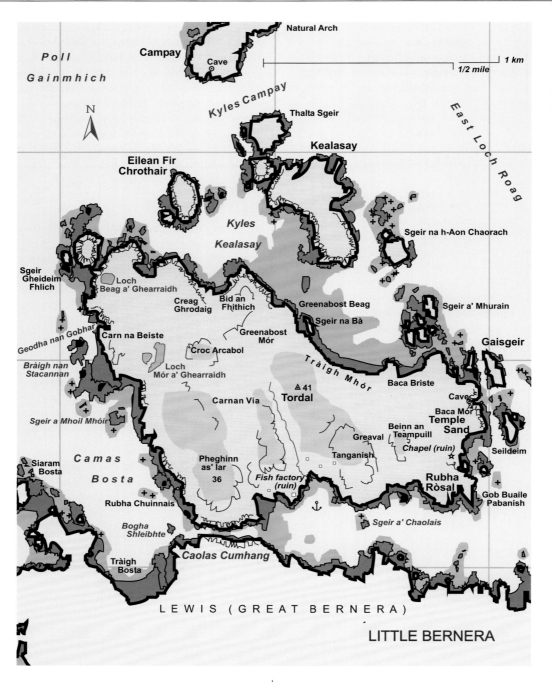

The ruins of an old fish-curing building, no longer clearly visible, overlook the Kyles of Little Bernera. At its west end the channel becomes very narrow at **Caolas Cumhang** (G. – constricted strait) before reaching the wide, rock-fringed Camas Bosta.

Tordal is Little Bernera's highest hill (41m) but only fractionally so as there are a number of such 'little craigs', all of nearly similar height.

Beneath Tordal on the north coast is the beautiful wide sweep of pale shell-pink sand, **Tràigh Mhór** (G. – big beach). This borders a lagoon, Kyles Kealasay, where the deep blue sea on a sunny day has a touch of South Sea magic, provided one avoids putting a foot in the water! Opposite are **Eilean Fir Crothair** (G. – isle of the shepherd) and **Kealasay**, both surrounded by low cliffs, and **Sgeir na h-Aon Chaorach** (G. – lone sheep rock). Further north and exposed to the full brunt of the Atlantic gales is **Campay**, another steep, rocky, islet with a natural stone arch at its north end and a large sea cave in the south. Màs Sgeir (G. – seagull skerry) is about a mile further north.

East of Tràigh Mhór, by a small bay among the St. Donan skerries off Little Bernera's east coast is the ruin of **St Donan's** chapel and the island graveyard.

Bearasay, the small rocky island to the north-west, was the retreat of Neil MacLeod, the great Lewis patriot, in the 16th century. He assisted in the defeat of the Fife Adventurers – the merchants who were offered Lewis by James VI and who tried to take over the herring fishing industry. James VI had a prejudice against the Gaels and wanted them to be exterminated and replaced by Lowlanders. In his words: 'As for the Highlanders, I shortly comprehend them all in two sorts of people: the one that dwelleth in our mainland that are barbarous, and yet mixed with some show of civility: the other that dwelleth in the Isles and are all utterly barbarous.'

Neil, and forty companions, stayed on Bearasay for three years and defied the attempts of the Mackenzies, who supported the King, to capture him. On one occasion he intercepted a pirate ship, the *Priam*, with a very valuable stolen cargo including silver and jewels and delivered both it and the skipper to the Crown in the hope of obtaining a pardon. He received a pardon but it was worthless for on leaving Bearasay he was captured by a fellow clansman and handed over to the authorities. He was put on trial, found guilty of piracy, and executed in 1613. He died, according to the official report sent to the King, 'verie Christianlie'.

* * *

Access: No regular access. Boat excursions offered by Seatrek, Uig, Lewis, 01851-672464.

Anchorage:

1. Bernera Harbour (Kyles of Little Bernera) between Little and Great Bernera. Approach from E with care following sailing instructions. Anchor WNW of Sgeir a' Chaolais where possible, 4m, mud. Safe anchorage, but may be obstructed by fish cages. Alternative E of Sgeir a' Chaolais in 5–8m, sand. Good holding, no swell.

SECTION 9

The Atlantic Outliers

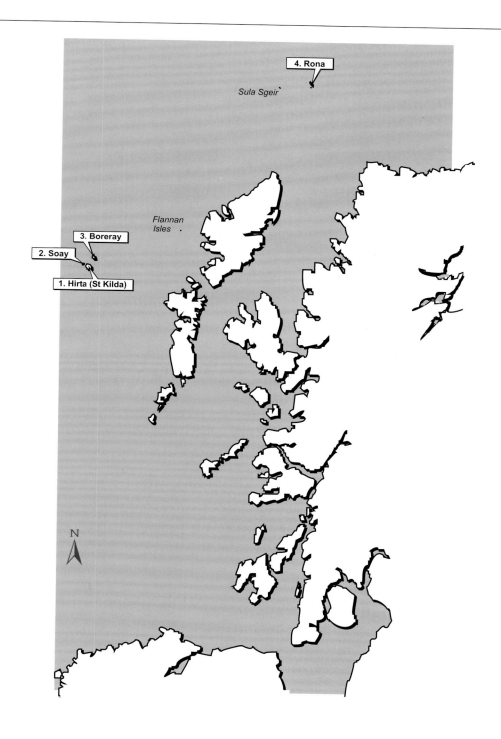

SECTION 9, Table 1: Arranged according to geographical position

No.	Name	Latitude	Longitude	Table 2* No.	Table 3** No.	Area in Acres	Area in Hectares
9.1	Hirta (St Kilda)	57° 49N	08° 35W	50	12	1656	670
9.2	Soay	57° 50N	08° 38W	112	18	245	99
9.3	Boreray	57° 52N	08° 29W	124	16	190	77
9.4	Rona (North Rona)	59° 07N	05° 50W	107	61	269	109
9.A	*Eilean Mór (Flannan Isles)*	*58° 17N*	*07° 35W*			43	17

*Table 2: The islands arranged in order of magnitude
**Table 3: The islands arranged in order of height

Introduction

In the desert wastes of the North Atlantic a rock stack or a mountain-top breaks the surface. These specks of land represent the outermost regions of the British Isles and at times they are virtually inaccessible. Modern navigational aids locate them with ease but the weather can be so atrocious that landing is often impossible. Yet long ago prehistoric man arrived in his flimsy craft, settled and maintained some sort of intermittent communication with the mainland.

The St Kilda archipelago is the largest island group in this section. It has a mystique all its own and I shall never forget our pleasure when *Jandara* first made landfall there.

The group was declared a National Nature Reserve on the 4 April 1957. It was also designated as both a National Scenic Area and an Ancient Monument by the Secretary of State for Scotland and it is, furthermore, recognised as a Reserve by UNESCO and listed by the International Union for the Conservation of Nature as a World Heritage Site. It deserves all these accolades and one hopes that no visitor will ever introduce a foreign species, whether a plant or an animal such as the domestic cat. This would wreak devastation in such a fragile environment.

The most outlying outlier of all is, of course, **Rockall.** Although well-known to the St Kildans it was only officially annexed by Britain on 18 September 1955 when the Benbecula rocket range was opened. A party from *HMS Vidal* landed by helicopter. The first recorded person to set foot on Rockall was Basil Hall, a lieutenant on the forty-gun frigate, *HMS Endymion* on Sunday 8 September 1811. Hall commented: 'The stone of which this curious peak is composed is a dark-coloured granite, but the top being covered with a coating as white as snow, from having been for ages the resting-place of myriads of sea-fowl, it is constantly mistaken for a vessel under sail'.

In 1831, after attaining the rank of Captain, Hall wrote a book called *Fragments of Voyages and Travels*, which is an illuminating record of life in the Navy at that time. Further landings took place, one possibly in 1887–8, and another in 1921. In 1955 it was merely incidental that geologists were talking of the possibility of oil reserves under the Atlantic but the addition of national fishing grounds was recognised. The Union Flag was hoisted on the rock and it was decreed that Rockall should be subject to the law of Scotland and form part of the district of Harris. A navigation beacon was added in 1972. Rockall and neighbouring Hasselwood Rock (57° 36N 13° 41W) are 230 miles west of Manish Point on North Uist so this action effectively made Scotland the same size as England!

The original Gaelic name for Rockall is Sgeir Rocail [rokawl] which could be translated as the sea-rock or skerry which roars hoarsely. No one else worried too much about ownership of this nasty little 21.4m-high obstruction until the possibility of discovering oil became more likely, whereupon the Irish Republic, Iceland and Denmark all laid claim to it. So in the 1980s John Ridgeway, British adventurer and Atlantic rower, volunteered to confirm British ownership by actually living on the rock. He did so by the remarkable feat of lying for forty days in a tiny shelter bolted down on a narrow ledge which is known as Hall's ledge in honour of the first man to land there.

Somewhat nearer home – eight miles west of the Sound of Harris (57° 42N 07° 42W) are two islets – **Great Haskeir** (Haisgeir Mhor), on which there is a lighthouse built in 1997 at the highest point (37.5m), and **Haskeir Eagach** (ON – wild or deep-sea skerry, G. *eagach* – notched) which is about half a mile to the south-west. Their bold geometric silhouettes have an almost classical quality when seen through a pale sunlit summer mist – as though Jason and the Argonauts had just passed by. The main island is studded with vertical rock formations, a high cliff (Castle Cliff) on the north side and several natural rock arches. There is no anchorage and, if attempting to land, it is difficult to find a purchase on the slippery slabs. The remains of a bothy may have originally been a shelter for fishermen built by the Monach islanders. There is edible scurvey grass and sorrel and a few sea-pinks, -campion, -plantain and orache where sheltered from the worst gales. The smaller islet, Haskeir Eagach, is a colonnade of five stumpy rock stacks like the silhouette of a crude Greek temple.

North (59° 06N 06° 08W), in the direction of the Faeroes, the cries of the birds on **Sula Sgeir** (ON – gannet skerry) are carried for long distances by the wind. The Butt of Lewis is forty-one miles south of here and the men of Lewis still traditionally collect their supplies of *guga*, or young gannet, from these rocks every year. It is said that St Ronan's sister, Brianuil, lived with him on Rona until one day Ronan admired her beautiful legs. 'It's time to leave,' she said. She went to Sula Sgeir and died there after several years of solitude.

Rona (No.9.4) with its ancient history lies due east of Sula Sgeir and far beyond Rona are **Sule Stack** (59° 02N 04° 30W), also known as Stack Skerry, a single rock column sticking unexpectedly out of the sea to a height of 37m, and **Sule Skerry** (59° 05N 04° 24W) which is four miles further on and thirty-seven miles from Mainland Orkney. Sule Skerry (ON – lone skerry) is identified by its lighthouse. Both Sule Stack and Sule Skerry are part of Orkney district.

9.1 Hirta

(G. Hiort) Possibly (EI hirt – dangerous, deathlike, ON -øy – island).

St Kilda

The name for the archipelago rather than the island – first appears on a Dutch map of 1666. There was no saint of that name but the derivation may be (ON sunt kelda – sweet wellwater) or that Dutch sailors assumed the popular watering hole above the village, Tobar Childa (G. tobar – well, ON kelda – well) followed the normal practice of dedication to a saint.

Dun

[doon] (G. – castle or fort).

OS Maps: 1:50000 Sheet 18 1:25000 Sheet 460
Admiralty Charts: 1:500000 No.2635 1:200000 No.2721
various scales No.2524 – the outliers

Area: 670ha (1656 acres)
Height: 430m (1410 ft)

Owner: Donated in 1956 to the National Trust for Scotland by the fifth Marquess of Bute. The Ministry of Defence, Scottish Natural Heritage and Historic Scotland all have an interest in this dual-status World Heritage Site. There are only twenty-five sites in the world with this status.

Population: Continuous habitation for at least 2000 years until evacuation in 1930. 1695 – about 180. 1834 – 93 (21 houses). Thirty-six islanders emigrated to Australia in 1852 with State aid. Men were also lost at sea and in accidents on the cliffs, and there was severe infant mortality due to *Tetanus infantus*. 1861–78. 1881–77. 1891–71 (18 houses). 1911–80 (18 houses). 1921–73. 1930–36. 1931–0. 1961–65 (military establishment) 1971–65. 1981–46. 1991–0.

Geology: Hirta is almost entirely composed of two igneous rocks, a light-coloured granite or granophyre and a darker gabbro. The east part of the island is chiefly granite but interspersed with some gabbro. Some of the rock is highly magnetic. The coastline is honeycombed with caves and the sharp jagged skylines are because the ice during the Ice Age failed to reach the St Kilda archipelago and the rocks are unworn.

When marine scientists conducted an underwater survey of the whole archipelago in 2000 they found that the separate islands were peaks of a single large mountain. About 18,000 years ago the sea level was approximately 120 metres lower than now and there is clear evidence of the ancient shoreline.

History: In a study of Hirta on behalf of the National Trust for Scotland an ancient stone building was discovered near the top of a high cliff. The structure, possibly a place of worship or a tomb, is thought to date from the Bronze Age. Archaeologists have still to make a detailed investigation but this may show that Hirta has been inhabited for about 3500 years.

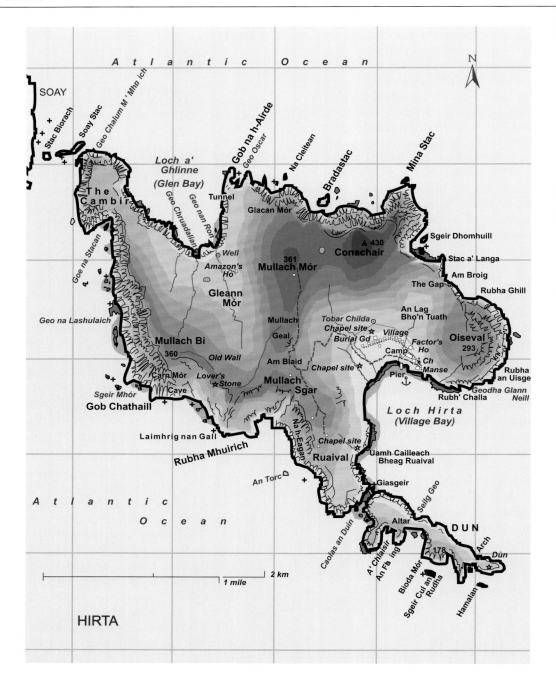

HIRTA

Glen Bay is the site of a pre-Viking settlement but it was not until Dean Monro visited Hirta in 1549 that the first written record appeared. He described a 'simple, poor people, scarce learnit in aney religion'.

Martin Martin, during his visit in 1697 estimated that 180 St Kildans ate about 22,600 birds annually. Stac Lee alone provided about 6000 gannets a year. Rye grass and barley were cut green and stored in the 'cleitean'. Martin found the population – 'happier than the generality of mankind, as being the almost only people in the world who feel the swetness of true liberty'.

One separate dwelling or cleit, south of the main 'street' is known as Lady Grange's house. She was exiled on the island for eight years to prevent her revealing her husband's Jacobite sympathies. She died in 1745, the year of the Rebellion, and is buried on Skye. (See Section 5–Appendix and No.7.18.)

In the early 18th century there were outbreaks of cholera and smallpox introduced by visiting ships and after 1750 the population possibly never exceeded 70. The islanders paid rent to the owners, the MacLeods of Harris and Dunvegan in Skye, who had been given the islands by a descendant of the Lord of the Isles. The rent was paid in the form of produce such as tweed, wool, feathers or oil from the sea-birds and once a year a steward called from Harris to collect the goods. At this time visitors reported a surprising level of general prosperity among the islanders although they held everything in common ownership and had no personal property. They also had no leadership structure. A 'Parliament' would meet each day to decide what work had to be done. This was by general agreement, but there were occasions when it could take all day to reach a decision!

The *Glenalbyn* was the first tourist ship to call at the island in 1834 and it marked the start of the loss of the islanders' independence and the end of St Kilda. They were almost completely naive and were cheated out of many of their essential possessions by the tourists. They came to rely on modern communications and a post-office was opened on the island in 1899 but this was really to satisfy tourists.

The other vital contribution to the eventual collapse of society on the island was the hell-fire and damnation of crusading Christian ministers. By far the most notorious was the Rev John Mackay who was resident from 1865 to 1889. By the end of his evil ministry the islanders had been browbeaten into so much church attendance every day of the week that there was insufficient time for growing and gathering food.

Apart from imported diseases the islanders were healthy except for 'eight-day sickness' which was 'God's will' and killed 80% of the babies born. In the 1890s it was discovered that the source of the disease was tetanus, now thought to come from the midwife's dirty hands when traditionally anointing the umbilicus with fulmar oil. The new minister, unlike his predecessor, studied midwifery in Glasgow in order to persuade the islanders that God disapproved of this practice.

Because the community was near starvation in 1912, a wireless transmitter was installed by the Government. During the First World War this resulted in a German submarine shelling

HIRTA'S 'HIGH STREET'

the island. The church was damaged and a store destroyed but no one was hurt and the submarine was later captured by an armed trawler. A gun was installed south-east of the army camp to stop a repetition of this incident but it has never been fired.

After the war, conditions continued to deteriorate. Many of the active young men emigrated leaving the aged and the very young. Eventually matters became so desperate that the thirty-six remaining St Kildans were more-or-less compelled to agree to evacuation. They were persuaded to do so by Nurse Williamina Barclay who, in 1927, had been sent to assist them.

The sad event took place on the 29th of August 1930. The St Kildans were given jobs and housing near Loch Aline, planting trees for the Forestry Commission, but they never really adjusted to life on the mainland. They were industrious and intelligent but they did not appreciate the use of money, the way of life, the type of diet, and they had never seen piped water, a staircase, or for that matter, a tree.

In 1957 Hirta was resettled with a military base and missile-tracking radar station on Mullach Mór which, since 1998, has been manned by civilians. National Trust volunteers are restoring the village houses and in 2008 a small desalination plant was installed to provide reliable drinnking water from the sea. But the native St Kildans are no more although, sadly, everything that they needed to provide a viable community is now available on the island.

Wildlife: There are no plants which grow above grass level, but even so there is a wealth of species. Scurvy grass, scentless mayweed, moss campion, plantago sward, and common sorrel are widespread. In the wet ground there are common cotton-grass, tormentil, lousewort, St John's wort, field gentian, bog pimpernel and bog asphodel to name a few. On the hillsides there are primrose, roseroot, heath-spotted orchid, calluna, crowberry, butterwort, heath milkwort, sundew, tiny willow, deer grass and ragged robin and a unique small hairy dandelion, *taxacum pankhurstianum*, only discovered in 2012. On Dùn can be found lesser celandine, wild angelica, sea campion, red fescue and thrift. In all, more than 130 flowering plants have been recorded and 194 varieties of lichen – including some that are very rare – and beneath the sea here lies one of the world's most colourful marine-life sites, a veritable wonderland.

Hirta is noted for some unique forms of wildlife: the St Kilda wren, a sub-species; the mouflon sheep recently introduced from neighbouring Soay; and a species of long-tailed fieldmouse which is twice as heavy as the mainland variety, with larger ears and a very long tail. There was also a St Kilda housemouse, *Mus muralis*, but this poor little creature died out when the islanders left.

On Dùn, the St Kilda wren, puffins, and Leach's petrels nest in large numbers, and the cliffs and peaty turf of Hirta are home to eighteen breeding species of seabirds including the oldest and largest colony of fulmar in Britain. Great skuas are a recent arrival.

The Scottish Seabird Centre in North Berwick near Edinburgh has a direct live video link giving the public a close-up view of the St Kilda wildlife.

* * *

HIRTA is the largest of the spectacular ST KILDA group of lonely Atlantic islands, owned by the National Trust of Scotland. This is a dream destination for any committed island explorer. All the members of the group are of granite and gabbro forming dramatic jagged stacks and towering cliffs. **Conachair**, the highest peak on Hirta is 430m high but there are four other high

THE ST KILDA FIELD-MOUSE AND THE ST KILDA WREN

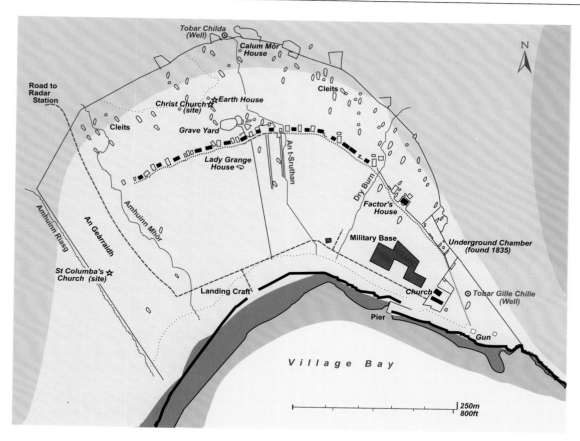

LAYOUT OF THE VILLAGE ON HIRTA

peaks and the awesome sea-cliffs are over 300m (1000ft) high.

Dean Monro in 1549 wrote that there are '... three grate hills, quhilk are ane pairt of Hirta, quhilk are seen affar off from the fore landis. In this fair ile is fair sheipe, falcon nests and wild fouls biggand, but the streams of the sea are stark, and are verey eivil...'

Village Bay in the south-east shelters the main settlement. Among the cottages and scattered up the mountain side are hundreds of small dry-stone structures with turf roofs called 'cleits' (G. – a stone beehive bothy, water-tight but cross-ventilated). These were mainly used as larders for storing the sea-birds which were the St Kildans' staple diet, but they were also used as general stores for fishing tackle, ropes, etc. Village Bay is an impressive example of a Stone Age culture. The area is covered with dry-stone structures which are the product of centuries of effort.

In 1830 much of the original village was demolished and new black houses were built but most of the present cottages, which are gradually being restored by the National Trust, were built in the 1860s to Victorian standards and using mortar joints. The Army camp is beside the pier and near the church, manse and schoolhouse. It is unsightly, but the island environment is so overpowering that it can be largely disregarded, and the military authorities have in fact been of benefit to the island in many ways. Through the camp and among the village ruins wander primitive Soay sheep, untidily shedding their umber-coloured fleeces in the summer months. The population fluctuations of these evil-eyed, goat-like creatures are being studied with interest by scientists. The native St Kildans only kept domestic sheep on Hirta. They left the Soay sheep on their home territory of Soay (No.9.2).

There are a number of archaeological sites in Village Bay. Less than 40m north-east of **Lady Grange House** [NF101993] stone coffins were discovered in 1835. In the same year an underground chamber was found by the path north of the church. The small stone-walled graveyard is just behind the line of houses

[NF100994]. It was too small for the number of burials so older corpses were removed in rotation to make way for new arrivals. Just north of it is the **Earth House**, a souterrain dating from the period 400BC–500AD. A number of artefacts have been found – Hebridean Iron Age pottery, two Christian crosses engraved in stone, Viking brooches and a Viking sword.

Above the village there are fox-holes in the west scree slope which are invisible from below. These were dug by the islanders in case they had to hide from pirates – the great fear of every islander.

Martin mentioned three churches and 'monkish cells' in the 17th century which have now disappeared. One of these, Christ Church, was beside the Earth House, and St Columba's Church was west of Amhuinn Mhór (G. – big river) which is west of the village [NF099991].

At the opposite end of the island is Loch a' Ghlinne and **Glen Bay**. Here there is a ruin called the **Amazon's House** [NA087001] and complexes of small chambers similar to Iron Age settlements. The bay is enclosed by a western peninsula, **The Cambir**, and high cliffs covered with nesting seabirds. On the east side at **Gob na h-Airde** (G. – nose of the point) the sea tumbles through a large deep tunnel which penetrates the rock and frames Boreray beyond [NA088008]. High above, **Mullach Mór** (G. – big top) (361m) broods over the bay with its twin peak **Mullach Bì** (G. – pitch-black top) (360m) on the other side of **Gleann Mór** (G. – big valley). Parts of a Sunderland flying-boat, ML858, were scattered down the glen where it crashed in June 1944. (The gullies below Conachair conceal another wartime wreck – a Beaufighter, LX798). Both crews were lost. The side of Mullach Bì facing the sea is like a cataclysmic land-slip with an abrupt drop from the summit to the sea. Close to the highest point is the **Lover's Stone** [NF085990] where there is a terrifying drop on to the rocks in the surf far below.

St Kilda men were agile climbers and would scale the awesome heights with homemade ropes to collect thousands of sea-birds and their eggs. Fulmars were the most important catch as the body of each bird provides a quarter litre of oil. This oil was used for lamps and also exported. Gannets and fulmars were eaten and puffins were caught for their feathers but nothing was wasted and the entrails were used for manure. Before marriage each suitor had to prove his climbing

ability by balancing on one heel right on the edge of the Lover's Stone while holding the other foot with his hands.

These cliffs are only surpassed by Conachair's cliffs on the north-east coast. They are the highest cliffs in the British Isles although Foula's (No.11.6) cliffs are considered more precipitous. Conachair is the highest point of a ridge which runs past Mullach Mór and then curls southwards and descends in two steps, **Mullach Geal** (G. – bright top) and **Mullach Sgar** (G. – the dividing summit). The ridge descends further to **Ruaival**, the south-western arm of Village Bay. **Oiseval** is the opposite arm of the bay.

DUN is almost joined to Hirta at Ruaival but there is a narrow separating channel, **Caolas an Duin**, which is thickly strewn with rocks and reputed to dry during exceptionally low tides. This channel does, however, obstruct invasion by the sheep which roam freely on Hirta with the result that vegetation on Dùn is much more lush. The island is nearly a mile long and looks, with its deeply serrated backbone, like a dragon hanging on to Hirta.

Old maps show the remains of a dun on the headland furthest from Hirta, Gob an Duin (G. – Dùn's beak), but there is little trace of it today [NF109972].

Almost two miles beyond Dùn, the rock ridge which runs through Mullach Sgar, Ruaival and Dùn, and then disappears into the sea, resurfaces at **Levenish**, a lone guano-spattered stack.

* * *

Access: Those wishing to land (or join a work-party) should contact the National Trust, 0131-243-9300. There are a number of cruises to Hirta but weather conditions must be right for landing. Try Kilda Cruises, Tarbert, Harris, 01859-502060; Hebridean Whale Cruises, Gairloch, 01445-712458; Seatrek, Uig, Lewis, 01851-672464; or, on a different scale, the NTS' own cruise ship, 0131-243-9334; or *Hebridean Princess*, 01756-704704.

Anchorages:

1. Village Bay is the only relatively safe anchorage but can be untenable in winds NE–S. There is usually a swell. Squalls during gales can be violent. Anchor anywhere off the beach but best in 5–6m off pier below the church. Holding good, firm sand. The concrete pier has steps and an iron ladder on its W side and a boat slip behind it. The

pier is usually accessible but landing can be difficult due to the swell. (In 1993 most of Village Bay beach and part of the landing craft slip was reported to have been swept away in a storm).

2. Loch a' Ghlinne. (G. – glen bay). Temp. anchorage in SE gales. A valley and stream runs SE between the hills at head of bay. Landing possible beside the stream. Bay sheltered except from N, but too deep to anchor except very close to shore. Swell uncomfortable and there are strong winds off the cliffs.

9.2 Soay

[soa-ay] or [soy] (ON so-øy – sheep island).

OS Maps: 1:50000 Sheet 18 1:25000 Sheet 460
Admiralty Charts: 1:500000 No.2635 1:200000 No.2721
various scales No.2524 – the outliers

Area: 99ha (245 acres)
Height: 378m (1240 ft)

Owner: Together with the rest of the St Kilda group, Soay is owned by the National Trust

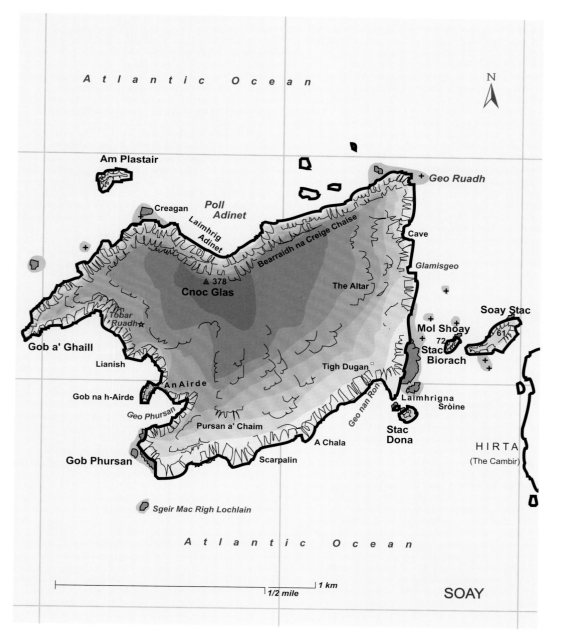

for Scotland and managed by Scottish Natural Heritage as a Nature Reserve.

Population: Uninhabited and has probably never been permanently inhabited.

Geology: Formed by a separate precipitous mountain peak rising straight from the same submarine mountain mass as Hirta it is composed mostly of a dark breccia of gabbros and dolerites, but with some granite. It has escaped any Ice Age erosion.

History: Although the St Kildans held everything in common ownership, the one exception was sheep. These could be personally owned, although there was communal interest in their well-being. Thus the Neolithic sheep on Soay belonged to a few St Kilda families. When these families emigrated to Australia in the 1850s the laird, MacLeod of MacLeod, paid them for their sheep to help defray their expenses.

After Hirta was evacuated in 1930 the Earl of Dumfries arranged for a balanced flock of 107 sheep to be collected from Soay by some St Kildans who had made a summer visit to their old home. The sheep were transported to, and released on, Hirta (No.9.1) and these form the basis of today's sheep population which is being studied by the Soay Sheep Research Team. All the islanders' domestic sheep were removed from Hirta at the time of the evacuation.

Wildlife: Soay is the home of the species of horned sheep, *Ovis aries*, which were first brought to the British Isles about 5000BC. They are like mountain goats in appearance, wild, but unconcerned with man so long as man is unconcerned with them. Until the 1930s the sheep were entirely confined to Soay and were not to be found anywhere else. When conditions permitted the St Kildans would climb the steep slopes of Soay to the lush grazing plateau and sometimes kill a beast for fresh meat. But mutton was considered a rare and special delicacy and the main interest was the wool. Soay sheep are never shorn. The fine soft wool is merely plucked when it is being shed naturally. The St Kildans used it to make tweed.

The soaring cliffs which surround Soay afford nest space for many thousands of gannet, fulmar, storm petrel, Manx shearwater, razorbill, great skua, and Leach's petrel although larger numbers of the latter bird nest on the Cambir on Hirta, opposite Soay Stac. Colonies of puffins inhabit the cliff-tops.

*   *   *

Ancient **SOAY** has no dinosaurs but it has primeval yellow-eyed sheep as compensation.

The inclined grassy, and boggy, plateau reaches a rounded summit, **Cnoc Glas**, (G. – grey eminence) 378m high where it falls away on the west coast in a nearly vertical black cliff, and it forms a very steep grassy incline to the east coast. The north and south have almost vertical cliffs but the cliff at the south-east end is less precipitous. The only objectional quality in this solid chunk of rock is that it overshadows the north end of Hirta at sunset.

The plateau is cut off abruptly at the Atlantic cliffs like a sliced piece of cheese at **Bearraidh na Creige Chaise** (G. – edge of the rocky precipice). On a level patch beneath a shallow escarpment on the west coast is **Tobar Ruadh** (G. – red well) [NA060015]. No doubt this provided water for the men from Hirta, when they spent some days on Soay wool-gathering. It is however quite a distance from the bothy site, **Tigh Dugan** (G. – Dugan's house), which is on the more sheltered south-eastern slope [NA068013]. To the north, below the **Altar** cliff lie the remains of a Wellington bomber which crashed in tyhe Second World War but was not investigated until 1978.

In the Sound of Soay at the end of rocky **Laimhrig na Sròine** (G. – nose of a landing place) stands a 15m-high rock called **Stac Dona**. There are two more rock stacks in the Sound, the awesome **Stac Biorach** [**peer**ich] and **Soay Stac**. Young St Kilda men were tested for their

THE NEOLITHIC SHEEP OF SOAY

climbing ability on Stac Biorach (G. – sharply pointed stack) which at 72m (236ft) is certainly not the highest stack in the St Kilda group but is regarded as the most difficult and dangerous to climb. It was nicknamed the 'Thumb Stack' because the only hold on the rock was no bigger than a thumb. An interesting description was written by Sir Robert Murray in 1698: '... after they landed, a man having room for but one of his feet, he must climb up 12 or 16 fathoms high. Then he comes to a place where having but room for his left foot and left hand, he must leap from thence to another place before him, which if hit right the rest of the ascent is easy, and with a small cord which he carries with him he hales up a rope where by all the rest come up. But if he misseth that footstep (as often times they do) he falls into the sea and the (boat's) company takes him in and he sits still until he is a little refreshed and then he tries it again, for everyone there is not able for that sport.' The first recorded outsider to climb both this stack and Stac Lee was Charles Barrington in 1883 (he also made the first ascent of the Eiger).

It is reckoned that only three days in a summer month on average are suitable for landing on Soay and there is always the danger that a rapid change in the weather may leave you marooned.

Sailing through the deep but narrow channel between Soay Stac (61m) and Hirta is possible in good weather.

*   *   *

Access: Try Kilda Cruises, Tarbert, Harris, 01859-502060 or Seatrek, Uig, Lewis, 01851-672464.

Anchorages: There are no anchorages. The usual landing place at Laimhrig na Sròine near the SE corner, or Mol Shoay, a boulder beach, can only be used in very settled weather due to the swell. The Poll Adinet landing place, Laimhrig Adinet, entails mountaineering. The NTS warden from Hirta should be present during any landing.

9.3 Boreray

[baw-rĕ-ray or -rĕ] (ON borgarøy– fort of the island or island like a castle).

OS Maps. 1:50000 Sheet 18 1:25000 Sheet 460
Admiralty Charts: 1:500000 No.2635 1:200000 No.2721 various scales No.2524 – the outliers

Area: 77ha (190 acres)
Height: 384m (1260 ft)

Owner: The National Trust for Scotland.

Population: No Census records and uninhabited.

Geology: Boreray is almost entirely gabbro and there has been no Ice Age erosion.

History: Inextricably linked with Hirta and used as another food source by the St Kildans. In 2011 an Iron Age stone building was discovered and partially excavated and, with evidence of crop terraces and settlement mounds, it seems that a community must have survived here in prehistoric times. This is quite remarkable given the conditions! However in later centuries the island became just another food source for the St Kildans and by the end of the 19th century they were only visiting Boreray three or four times a year for fowling and tending the sheep.

Wildlife: In spite of its remote position and barren, rocky appearance there are at least 130 types of flowering plant on Boreray including some alpines which probably relish the cool climate and absence of disturbance.

The St Kildans kept some crossed black-face/ Cheviot sheep on Boreray which had originally been introduced to Hirta from the mainland. Although the domestic sheep on Hirta were cleared in 1930 Boreray was fairly inaccessible and the sheep were abandoned when the islanders were evacuated. They have now reverted to a wild state.

A count in 1959 showed 45,000 pairs of gannets on Boreray and its two adjoining stacks, nearly half the British population and nearly 40% of the world population. On the relatively level top of Stac Lee alone there was a solid concentration of 6000 nests in 1971.

Many other seabirds also nest on Boreray in great numbers.

*   *   *

BORERAY is a quite remarkable, jagged heap of black volcanic rock rearing 386m (1260ft) above the sea. It is an unforgettable sight, particularly when the cloud swirls around its summit and the gannets plunge from breathtaking heights. It is an island of superlative emotions that change with the weather. In the words of the yachtsman, R A Smith, who sailed there in *Nyanza* in 1879:

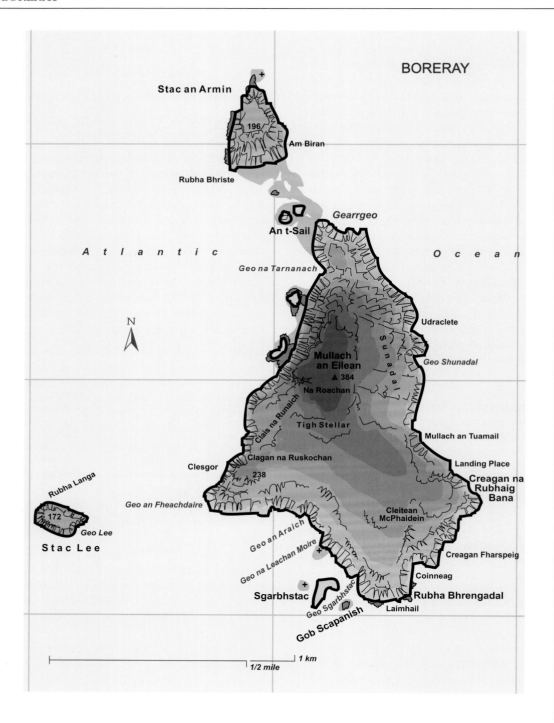

'Had it been a land of demons it could not have appeared more dreadful.' But he probably saw it on a wild, grey day. It lies about 3½ miles to the north-east of Hirta and it has two enormous stacks standing guard beside it, Stac an Armin, and Stac Lee. It is possible to sail between Boreray and Stac Lee – quite an experience – but the channel between Boreray and Stac an Armin is littered with rocks and should not be attempted.

Landing can be dangerous and considerable skill is required. The mountaineers, Williamson and Boyd, reported that a short distance above where they landed near **Sgarbhstac** (G. – cormorant stack) they came to a chasm in the

STAC AN ARMIN AND BORERAY

southern crags. It is nearly two metres wide at the narrowest point and they had to jump across with the sea surging 30m below them.

A party from the University of Durham succeeded in landing on the island in July 1980 with Army assistance. They stayed on the island for about a fortnight studying the ecology and wildlife. They were helped by the presence of an old bothy which was used by the St Kildans for shelter and which may date from the Iron Age. There may be other undiscovered archaeological remains.

In spite of its exposed situation the skewed summit of Boreray is covered in lush grass. There are still traces of lazybeds and one can only marvel at the thought of carrying loads of seaweed up these high cliffs to manure the potato beds. Understandably, by 1889, sheep had replaced the lazybed culture and the St Kildans only made occasional visits each year.

The most dangerous annual visit took place in September. The gannets, or guga (G. *guga* – a young solan goose, or a fat silly fellow), had to be killed at night when they were on their nests. Normally, about seven men would land, wearing woollen socks at this stage to avoid slipping on the slimy rock. The boat would then stand off with a crew of five and drift around all night.

Gannets always post a 'sentry' and this bird had to be killed silently first. Then the sleeping birds were quietly clubbed to death or strangled with fowling rods – which sounds easy until one remembers that the gannet is a big bird, ferocious when disturbed, and the rocky ledges are narrow and treacherous in the dark. Some birds would be gutted and left stored in the cleits on Boreray, but several hundred would be loaded aboard the Hirta boat at daybreak. Despite this annual massacre nature kept an equilibrium. Birds still survive on St Kilda, it is the human beings who have gone.

In April or May the St Kildans visited Boreray to collect eggs and count the sheep. In June they returned to collect the wool. These were not Soay sheep and had to be partly sheared but this was done with a penknife. Dogs were carried up the cliff to help gather the flock. After several days, the men would cut out an area of turf. This could be seen from Hirta and was the signal to send a boat – weather, of course, permitting. In earlier times women accompanied the men and while the men tended the sheep the women would catch and kill puffins.

Stac an Armin (G. or ON – stack of the warrior or steward) at 196m (643ft) is the highest monolith in the British Isles and yet it was regularly climbed by the St Kildans to collect eggs and birds. Sadly, it was on Stac an Armin that the last great auk seen in Britain was killed by two St Kildans who beat it to death in July 1840. They said they thought it was a witch.

Stac Lee (Martin called it Stac-Ly) is certainly not in the lee of Boreray so far as the prevailing wind direction is concerned so the name probably derives from the Norse (ON *ly* – shelter) in a more general sense; a small, ancient bothy or shelter sits on top of Stac Lee, dry inside, and able to accommodate two people. When it was climbed by mountaineers in 1969 the south-east corner was considered the best landing point but best is a relative term – even on a calm day the Atlantic swell will move a boat up or down by five metres or more. Apparently the St Kildans lassoed an iron peg when landing. As the boat reached the top of the swell they would jump, find slippery hand and footholds, and start to climb.

* * *

Access: Try Kilda Cruises, Leverburgh, Harris, 01859-502060.

Anchorage: There are no anchorages but there is one place at the south end, close to Sgarbhstac, a rock lying close off the SW side of Boreray, it is possible to land when conditions are unusually calm. Landing on the E side at Sunadal must not be attempted during April–August, the bird breeding season. The NTS warden from Hirta should be present during any landing.

9.4 Rona

Probably (ON hraun-øy – rough island) but, maybe, (G. ròn, N -øy – seal island), or named after St Ronan to whom the island chapel is dedicated.

OS Maps: 1:50000 Sheet 8 1:25000 Sheet 460
Admiralty Charts: 1:200000 No.1954 1:25000 No.2524

Area: 109ha (269 acres)
Height: 108m (354 ft)

Owner: Barvas Estates Ltd

Population: 1796– 1 family. 1841-3 (last inhabitant evacuated in 1844). Uninhabited since, apart from one brief interlude (see below).

Geology: Gneiss and hornblende schist with pegmatite intrusions.

History: Dean Monro comments: 'Towards the north northeist from Lewis, three score myles of

sea, lyes and little ile callit Roney, laiche maine land, inhabit and manurit be simple people, scant of ony religione.'

Monro found a people which had continuously inhabited North Rona for at least 700 years. The first inhabitant was supposed to have been St Ronan, who built a hermitage there during the 8th century, but the island may well have been occupied from earlier times. In 1680 Martin recorded the report of the Rev Donald Morison who had visited Rona that there were five families living in their own stone and thatched houses, each with a barn, storehouse, cattle-shed and 'a porch on each side to keep off the rain or snow'. He said they were simple and contented people who took their surname 'from the colour of the sky, rainbow and clouds'. Their only interest in the outside world was in the north part of Lewis which they very occasionally visited. They had no interest in money or wealth, using barter if necessary as they had enough food and raiment for all their needs. They restricted their population to 'thirty souls', by sending their 'supernumerary' people to Lewis.

Martin reported that soon after this came tragedy. Rats from a ship invaded the island and ate all the food. Then some seamen landed and killed the only bull. Within the space of a year 'all that ancient race of people' were dead.

The disaster was discovered by a party from St Kilda (100 miles away!) who were shipwrecked on Rona after being blown there by a storm. They lived for seven months on the island while they built a boat out of driftwood which they then sailed to Stornoway.

The minister of Barvas on Lewis had the island resettled. But by 1796 there was only one family left on Rona, that of a shepherd, as the rest had apparently drowned in a fishing accident. The island was rented by a Ness tacksman for £4 sterling per annum paid to the owner, MacLeod of MacLeod, and he in turn received produce from the islanders in the form of corn, butter, cheese, wild fowl and feathers, a few sheep and sometimes a cow.

When Dr MacCulloch landed on Rona in 1815, the shepherd, Kenneth MacCagie, with his wife, three children, and old deaf mother, ran away and hid. They had 'seen no face' for seven years and had taken MacCulloch's party for 'pirates or Americans'. MacCulloch managed to persuade them that he meant no harm. There was plenty of food and six or seven acres planted with potatoes and cereals. The shepherd was indentured for eight years at an annual wage of £2 worth of clothing. He had no boat in case he deserted but he caught fish without difficulty with a rod. His house was mostly underground. The MacCagies left Rona about 1820.

About this time, with the herring industry booming, it was seriously suggested that six fishermen from Great Bernera on Lewis should be settled on Rona to form a fishing 'station' at a rent of £30 per year but there were no volunteers. So in 1829 John MacDonald, known as Iain Buidhe, took over as shepherd on Rona accompanied by his wife Cirstina and daughter Catherine. Three more children were born on the

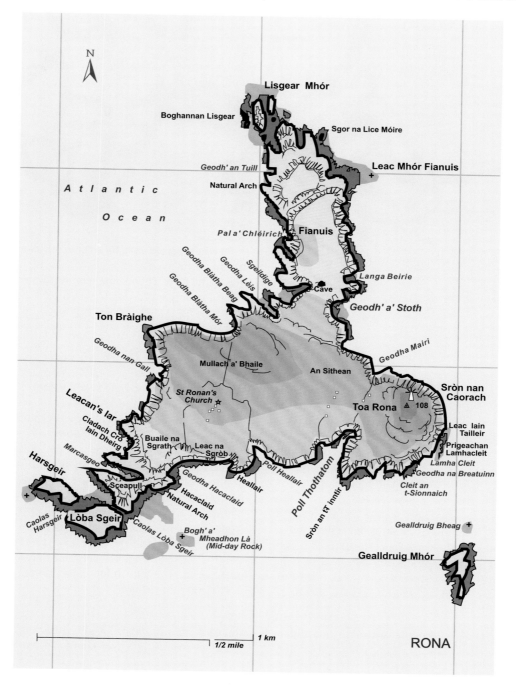

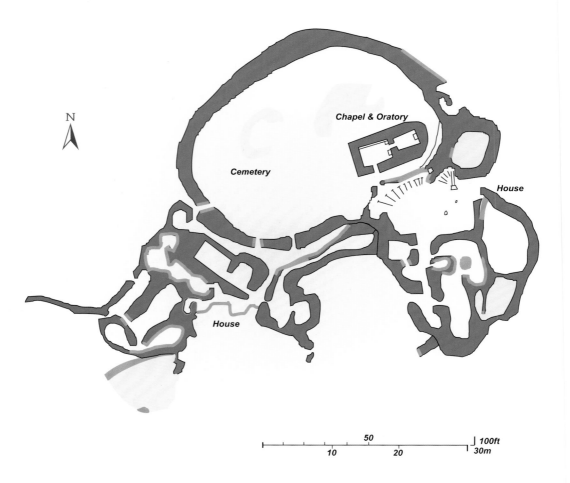

N

Cemetery

Chapel & Oratory

House

House

50   100ft
10   20   30m

PLAN OF ST RONAN'S CHAPEL AND CEMETERY

island. The family returned to Lewis about 1834 and their recorded experiences are a valuable record of life on the island.

In 1844 Rona's single inhabitant, Donald MacLeod, the 'King of Rona', was evacuated after spending a year there and in 1850 the island was offered free to the Government for use as a penal settlement. This was not accepted.

Rona lay deserted until 1884–5 when two men from Ness went there in a fit of pique after an argument with their minister. They vowed never to return to the parish. In February 1885 a relief boat called and found them both dead, one from natural causes, the other from 'exhaustion after nursing his friend.'

Wildlife: Harvie-Brown, a Victorian yachtsman and naturalist, reported seeing whimbrel on Rona in June 1885. He was excited by the extensive

bird life and also listed the island plants – about forty-three different species in all.

Rona (including Sula Sgeir) was declared a National Nature Reserve in 1956 because of its importance as a breeding ground for guillemot, puffin, kittiwake and fulmar. There are also large numbers of petrel, both Leach's and stormy, which breed in burrows.

Another reason for the importance of this wildlife station is that it is one of Britain's largest breeding grounds for the grey seal. More than 7500 of them breed here every autumn resulting in the birth of at least 2500 calves annually.

There are no rabbits.

*   *   *

RONA is an uninhabited island situated about ten miles east of Sula Sgeir and forty-four miles from the Butt of Lewis. It is roughly triangular in shape and covered with undulating turfy moorland but on the south-east corner there is a steep hill, **Toa Rona**, 108m high with a vertical cliff on its south side. Along the north-west coast the ocean storms have piled up an embankment of boulders over 20m (66ft) high. In spite of this protection sheets of seawater come splashing over the embankment during gales and the water has eroded deep channels in the turf which go right down to the bedrock.

During the many centuries of human habitation this remote little island was not only self-sufficient but even produced a surplus. Dean Monro said that there was an abundance of corn grown on the island and clover-grass for sheep. (The name of the hill, Toa Rona, may come from the Norse for a patch of grass.) A fine bere-meal (ground barley) was stuffed into the skins of sheep and sent with mutton and fowls to MacLeod each year as rent.

Nowadays the land supports only sheep which are shorn and tended by a party of Lewis shepherds on an annual visit.

St Ronan's Chapel is possibly the oldest relatively unaltered Christian building in Britain [HW809323]. Certainly the Royal Commission on Ancient Monuments lists it as one of the three oldest known structures of the Celtic Church but it is worth noting with some concern that Frank Fraser Darling claimed to have 'rebuilt' part of it. (*A Naturalist on Rona – Essays of a Biologist in Isolation. 1939*). The building has two chambers, the east cell is probably of the 7th or 8th century and the chapel probably of the 12th century. The ruin, which is near the remains of some prehistoric, partially underground houses, stand in pasture sloping down between the south-western and eastern promontories. The 'village' may have been occupied by Norse settlers in the 8th century.

In the burial ground beside the chapel there once stood a stone cross with three holes through it and the much-eroded figure of a naked man carved on it, possibly as a fertility symbol. This cross was removed in the 1930s and placed in Teampull Mholuaidh at Europie on Lewis (No.8.14). It is reputed to be 6th–7th century work and may have marked St Ronan's grave.

No one is very sure who St Ronan was. There were twelve saints of that name in Donegal, and two were recorded in Scotland. There are

dedications to St Ronan on both North Uist (No.7.14) and Islay (No.2.4). The St Ronan, who was Abbot of Kingarth and who died in 737 usually receives the honour, particulary as he is said to have arrived at Rona on the back of a whale.

THE RONA CROSS

Sula Sgeir, eleven miles south-west of Rona, is a narrow goose-neck shaped islet which is appropriately named gannet skerry (ON *sula skeri*). It is a small rocky island almost surrounded by cliffs and with a sea-cave running right through it. Although this is now a Nature Reserve the men of Ness in Lewis have special permission to harvest the young gannets (G. *guga*) once a year in September as this is an ancient tradition. The oily flesh of guga is considered a great delicacy but it is definitely an acquired taste.

The Lewismen used to row the forty-one miles to Sula Sgeir in an open six-oared boat without a compass and yet accidents were very rare. A ring is fixed to the rocks at the only landing place, Geodha a' Phuill Bhàin, as there is no anchorage or beach. Nor is there any soil or fresh water on the islet but there are five stone bothies which the guga-hunters live in for a few days during their annual expedition.

*   *   *

Access: Permission to land is required from Barvas Estates Ltd, North Lewis and from Scottish Natural Heritage, Inverness, 01463-239431. Ness (Lewis) shepherds generally visit during July or August. Try Kilda Cruises, Leverburgh, Harris, 01859-502060, or Beyond the Blue Horizon, Stornoway, 07920-067774.

Anchorages: Approach Rona carefully, especially from the SW.
1. There is no recommended anchorage but Geodh' a' Stoth is usually favoured. Landing is generally difficult, but the best places, depending on wind direction and sea state, are a) Geodh' a' Stoth, b) Poll Thothatom or Poll Heallair, c) Sgeildige (requiring a climb up a cliff), or d) W side of Sceapull.

9–Appendix Flannan Isles

Named after St Flannan, St Ronan's half-brother.

Eilean Mór

(G – big island)

OS Maps: 1:50000 Sheet 13. 1:25000 Sheet 460. 1:10000 NA7146
Admiralty Charts: 1:500000 No.2635. 1:200000 No.2721. 1:15000 No.2524.

Area: 17.5ha (43 acres)
Height: 88m (289ft)

Population: Uninhabited.

Geology: Dark breccia of gabbros and dolerites intruding through Archaean gneiss.

History: St Flannan was St Ronan's half-brother by repute (see Rona. No.9.4): and there was St Flannan, an Irish prince, who became Abbot of Killaloe in County Clare and died in 778; and there again there was Flann, the son of Maol-duine, Abbot of Iona, who died in 890. Take your choice.

Wildlife: A good selection of sea-birds.

* * *

The **FLANNAN ISLES** can be seen on a fine day twenty-one miles west of Lewis (58° 17N 07° 35W). This group of islets consists of three small clusters. The main group has two islands, **EILEAN MOR** (G. – big island) and **Eilean Tighe** (G. – house island), two small islets in between, and some rocks scattered about. Eilean Tighe still has a ruined stone 'house' on it although it is a very tiny construction near the edge of a cliff. East of Eilean Mór are two small outliers, **Gealtaire Mór** and **Gealtaire Beag** (G – the big and little cowards). The smaller southerly cluster consists of **Soray**, **Sgeir Toman** and **Sgeir Righinn** (G. – princess skerry). The most westerly cluster, one-and-a-half nautical miles away, is **Eilean a' Ghobha** (G. – isle of the blacksmith), **Roareim** with a natural rock arch, **Bròna Cleit** (G. – sad sunk rock) and a plethora of rocks in between. These tiny islands are sometimes called the Seven Hunters but Dean Munro in 1549 called them the Seven Haley (Holy) Isles. He said they were uninhabited but with 'infinit wyld sheipe' which 'cannot be eaten be honest men' but make good tallow. People living in Uig on Lewis made an annual pilgrimage to worship in

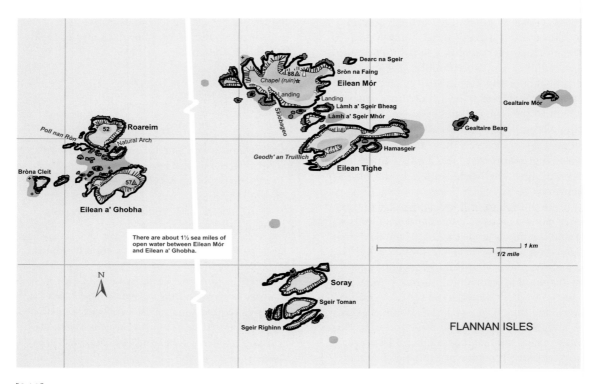

There are about 1½ sea miles of open water between Eilean Mór and Eilean a' Ghobha.

FLANNAN ISLES

St Flannan's Chapel but *at* St Flannan's Chapel would be more appropriate. The chapel is so small that the lighthouse-keepers used to refer to it as the 'dog kennel'.

In Martin Martin's time (1695), landing on Eilean Mór was subject to strict conventions and newcomers had to be accompanied by someone who knew the rules. For instance, it was forbidden to relieve oneself near the mooring-place, to kill a bird after evening prayers – or at any time with a stone, to eat anything in private, or to take sheep suet back home. On reaching the plateau of the island it was essential to take one's hat off and make a *deiseil* – a sunwise turn – giving thanks to God, and when twenty paces from the altar to strip off outer garments and place them on a stone. It was also important always to refer to the Flannans as 'the country', water as 'the burn' and rock as 'the hard'.

Grazing on the Flannans is of very high quality and sheep are still grazed there by the Bernera crofters. Landing can be a challenge as there is often a heavy swell. There is an expanse of slippery concrete reached by a rusty ladder and then a climb up a staircase of 195 steps partly cut from the cliff face with only the remains of a rusty guard-rail for protection.

The lighthouse, which was built by David Stevenson in 1899, is on the largest island in the group – Eilean Mór – where there are also the ruins of the tiny corbelled 6th(?) century St Flannan's Chapel and the Bothain Chlann 'ic Phail (G. – Macphail bothies) used by visiting shepherds. The light is 101m above sea-level and the stubby lighthouse which has been automatic since 1971 stands on high ground at the top of 88m (289ft) cliffs. This was the lighthouse which was the scene of a remarkable unsolved mystery.

On the night of 15 December 1900 it was noted in the log of a passing steamer that the light was not working. Before receiving this information at Oban, however, the lighthouse relief tender *Hesperus* had sailed for the Flannan Isles. She had to battle through an Atlantic gale and did not arrive until Boxing Day. The crew was surprised that there was no response to the ship's whistle and when the men landed they could find no trace of the keepers. The logbook was complete up to 13 December and notes for the log were recorded until 9am on the 15th. A meal of cold meat, pickles and potatoes was untouched on the kitchen table and, apart from one kitchen chair

being knocked over, there was nothing amiss. The island was searched from end to end but nothing was found to explain the disappearance. It was however noted that equipment normally stored 110 feet above the West Landing was scattered about, the iron railings round the crane were badly twisted, and a boulder weighing about one ton was lying on the access steps.

A report by Superintendent Muirhead of the Commissioners of Northern Lights after a detailed examination decided that the men had gone to the West landing 'and that a large body of water going up higher than where they were, and coming down upon them, had swept them away with resistless force.' But this explanation is not entirely convincing. For instance, only two sets of oilskins were missing. If the third man had to rush out in his shirt-sleeves to help, how did he know there was an emergency in the first place? The landings are too far away from the lighthouse to hear a cry for help. And if he was in such a hurry, why did he close the doors and the gate?

. . . Aye though we hunted high and low and
hunted everywhere,
Of the three men's fate we found no trace
Of any kind in any place.
But a door ajar and an untouched meal
And an overtopped chair . . .
Wilfred Wilson Gibson (1878–1962)

Walter Aldebert, who was a keeper of the Flannan light from 1953 to 1957, whiled away many hours trying to find a solution. The west landing is in a narrow inlet, Skiobageo, which ends in a cave. Aldebert photographed waves to show that occasionally a giant wave would thunder into the inlet causing air pressure in the cave to explode and throw tons of water across the cliffs. His conclusion was that such a wave washed one man into the sea. The second rushed back to the lighthouse for help then as the two reached the west landing a second wave carried them away. This is plausible but the records show that such explosive waves are very rare and for two to occur so close together would be an extraordinary coincidence.

Suffice it to say that when the news from Eilean Mór was first published the press had a heyday, with sea monsters, the ghost of St Flannan, and murder by the Secret Service all put forward as plausible explanations. The mystery has exercised lively imaginations ever since but, like the Marie Celeste, it is probably a better story left unsolved.

*　*　*

Access: Excursions by Kilda Cruises, Leverburgh, Harris, 01859-502060 or Seatrek, Uig, Lewis, 01851-672464.

Anchorage: There are two landing places, but these are no longer maintained and may be unsafe. Temporary anchorage is possible close to either landing place and there are rusty mooring rings, but the bottom is rock.

Stroma and the Orkney Islands

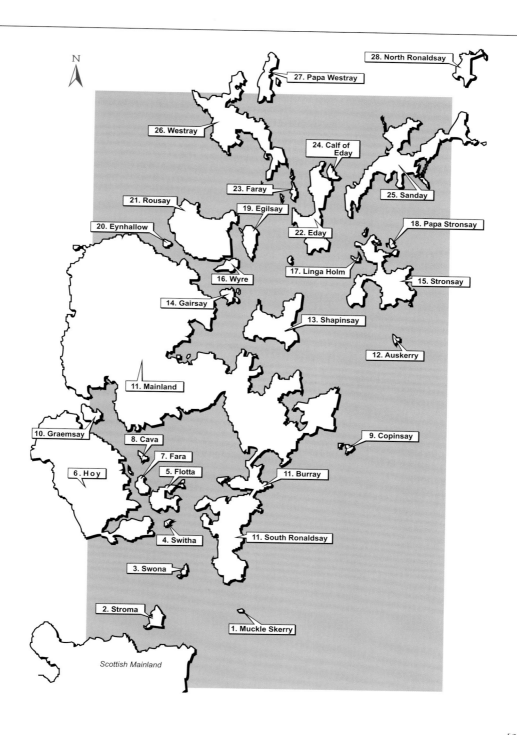

N

28. North Ronaldsay

27. Papa Westray

26. Westray

24. Calf of Eday

23. Faray

25. Sanday

21. Rousay

19. Egilsay

18. Papa Stronsay

20. Eynhallow

22. Eday

17. Linga Holm

16. Wyre

15. Stronsay

14. Gairsay

13. Shapinsay

12. Auskerry

11. Mainland

10. Graemsay

8. Cava

9. Copinsay

7. Fara

5. Flotta

11. Burray

6. Hoy

4. Switha

11. South Ronaldsay

3. Swona

2. Stroma

1. Muckle Skerry

Scottish Mainland

SECTION 10, Table 1: Arranged according to geographical position

No.	Name	Latitude	Longitude	Table 2* No.	Table 3** No.	Area in Acres		Area in Hectares
10.1	Muckle Skerry	58° 41N	02° 55W	162	164	103		42
10.2	Stroma	58° 41N	03° 07W	59	116	927		375
10.3	Swona	58° 45N	03° 03W	114	133	227		92
10.4	Switha	58° 48N	03° 06W	153	155	116		47
10.5	Flotta	58° 50N	03° 07W	45	108	2165		876
10.6	Hoy	58° 51N	03° 18W	10	8	35380		14318
10.7	Fara	58° 51N	03° 10W	69	130	729		295
10.8	Cava	58° 53N	03° 10W	109	140	264		107
10.9	Copinsay	58° 54N	02° 41W	128	100	180		73
10.10	Graemsay	58° 56N	03° 17W	56	103	1011		409
10.11	Mainland (Orkney)	59° 00N	03° 05W	6	26	129295	52325	
	South Ronaldsay	58° 47N	02° 57W			12306	4980	
	Burray	58° 51N	02° 54W			2231	903	
	Hunda	58° 51N	02° 59W			247	100	
	Glimps Holm	58° 53N	02° 55W			136	55	
	Lamb Holm	58 53N	02 53W			99	40	58308
10.12	Auskerry	59° 02N	02° 34W	117	166	210		85
10.13	Shapinsay	59° 02N	02° 52W	25	101	7285		2948
10.14	Gairsay	59° 05N	02° 58W	78	67	593		240
10.15	Stronsay	59° 07N	02° 36W	23	127	8093		3275
10.16	Wyre	59° 07N	02° 58W	65	148	768		311
10.17	Linga Holm	59° 08N	02° 40W	142	168	141		57
10.18	Papa Stronsay	59° 09N	02° 35W	127	167	183		74
10.19	Egilsay	59° 09N	02° 56W	51	142	1606		650
10.20	Eynhallow	59° 09N	03° 07W	126	152	185		75
10.21	Rousay	59° 10N	03° 02W	19	28	12009		4860
10.22	Eday	59° 12N	02° 46W	27	68	6783		2745
10.23	Faray	59° 13N	02° 49W	89	150	445		180
10.24	Calf of Eday	59° 14N	02° 44W	77	118	600		243
10.25	Sanday	59° 15N	02° 34W	18	97	12461		5043
10.26	Westray	59° 18N	02° 57W	20	40	11646		4713
10.27	Papa Westray	59° 21N	02° 53W	43	124	2268		918
10.28	North Ronaldsay	59° 22N	02 25W	49	163	1705		690

*Table 2: The islands arranged in order of magnitude
**Table 3: The islands arranged in order of size

Introduction

The islands to the north of Scotland are not easily confused with those of the west. Not only is the geology very different from that of, say, the Hebrides, but the entire social structure and language is distinctive. Both areas came under Norse influence in the first millennium but whereas within a few centuries Celtic civilisation had gained control in the west, the north remained a Norse dominion until comparatively recent times. Gaelic has never been a natural language in the north. When Norn (partly Old Norse, partly Icelandic) died out it was replaced by English or Lowland Scots.

Apart from a very few outliers, the islands in this region form two archipelagoes and just as the northern isles as a group are very different from the western isles so too does each archipelago

have its own distinctive characteristics. The Orkney archipelago is agriculturally rich thanks to its base of Old Red Sandstone, while the Shetland archipelago, 50 miles further north, has poorer soil and its economy therefore depends on the wealth of the sea. Hence the well-known saying that 'an Orcadian is a farmer with a boat while a Shetlander is a fisherman with a croft.' The richness of the Orkney soil has always made fishing a secondary occupation. The sea is all around, but it is primarily for transport or recreation rather than for sustenance, whereas in Shetland it is a life-giving force.

Between Duncansby Head (beside John o' Groats) on the Scottish mainland and Brough Ness at the southern tip of South Ronaldsay is only a matter of six miles, or a mere ten kilometres. But this narrow strip of water contains the treacherous Pentland Firth in parts of which the spring tides run faster than almost anywhere else in coastal Britain. The western end of the Firth has a notorious tidal race called the Merry Men of Mey which forms on the ebb and which is so turbulent that a small vessel can be put in severe danger.

The eastern end also has its troublesome areas, such as near the Pentland Skerries in mid-firth. There are heavy breaking seas in this area which are particularly lethal when the wind is against the tide.

It would be a pity to discuss Orkney without mentioning the strange story of Henry Sinclair.

When the wealthy Order of the Knights Templar was branded heretical by the Vatican in 1307 many Knights fled to Scotland and set up their headquarters in Midlothian on the lands of the St Clair family. The St Clairs, or Sinclairs, were descended from Vikings and held powerful earldoms in Caithness and Orkney. Their connection with the Templars brought enormous additional wealth.

Henry Sinclair was born in 1345. Tall and strong, he could speak fluent Latin, Norse and Lowland Scots, and he hunted, crusaded, fathered thirteen children, and dreamed of conquest. He became a Knight Templar – a defender of the Holy Grail – and he wanted a kingdom so much that he was nicknamed 'Prince'.

Prince Henry had heard all the Norse tales of a land far west of Greenland so he persuaded two of his Venetian friends, Nicolo and Antonio Zeno, who had made vast profits from ship-building, to come to Orkney and join his venture. Nicolo died after an initial exploratory voyage to Greenland, but Antonio carried on and described events in long detailed letters to his family in Venice. These became known as the Zeno Narratives when they were eventually published in 1558.

According to these letters the adventurers fitted out a small fleet and Antonio armed it with Pietro cannons which he brought from Venice. In 1398 Prince Henry, Antonio Zeno and 300 colonists set sail for the west in twelve ships. They eventually reached Newfoundland and spent their first winter in Nova Scotia.

The Mi'Kmaq Indians' tribal history tells of the arrival by sea centuries ago of a bird with a broken wing, and a prophet called 'Kluskap' and it was about this time that the Mi'Kmaqs

started fishing with European-style nets. A couple of hilltop castle ruins in Nova Scotia have been dated to this period by Canadian archaeologists and a ship's cannon dredged from Digby Harbour in Nova Scotia in 1849 has been identified as a 14thC Pietro cannon. Hardly conclusive evidence but interesting nevertheless.

The following spring (1399), the colonists sailed down the coast to look for land on which to settle. Once again there is circumstantial evidence. A recently discovered boulder at Lake Memphremagog on the Canadian/US border near Montreal has been carved with an outline of the Sinclair coat-of-arms next to a fairly accurate map of the North American coastline.

In Rhode Island an ancient round stone tower, called the Newport Tower, has a striking resemblance to Orkney Mainland's church at Ophir (No. 10.11) and rock carvings in Westford, Massachusetts, accurately depict a medieval Scottish knight in full regalia.

It is known that Prince Henry sailed back to Orkney in 1400, possibly to collect more prospective colonists or essential provisions, but according to the Narratives he was killed by the English. (Henry IV of England invaded Orkney at that time.)

No one knows what became of the settlement but genetic testing of native Americans might have a story to reveal.

Some years later – in 1446 – the Sinclair family built Rosslyn Chapel on their land near Edinburgh with its famous Apprentice Pillar and stone carvings of Indian maize and aloe cacti. (And later still, in 1537 the Dutch globe, Frisius-Mercator, shows the area west of Greenland as 'the land discovered by Britons'.)

So can one really be certain that it was Christopher Columbus who 'discovered' America in 1492?

10.1 Muckle Skerry

(S. – great, ON. - sea rock or reef)).

OS Maps: 1:50000 Sheet 7 1:25000 Sheet 461 or 462
Admiralty Charts: 1:50000 No.2162 1:26000 No.2581

Area: 42ha (103 acres)
Height: 20m (65 ft)

Population: 1841–11. 1841–17. The population

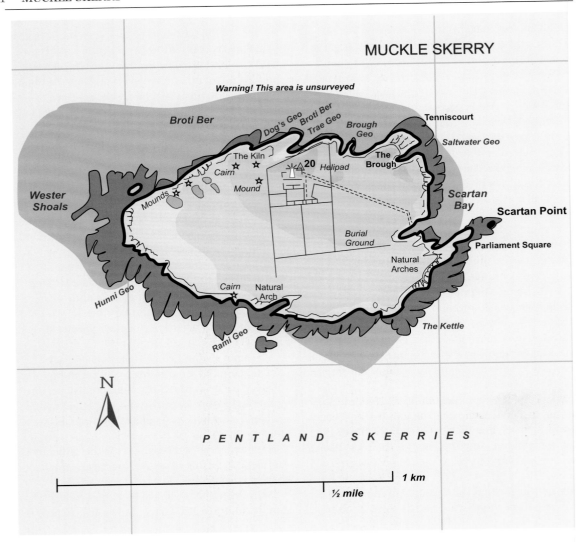

MUCKLE SKERRY

Warning! This area is unsurveyed

Broti Ber

Dog's Geo

Broti Ber

Trae Geo

Brough Geo

Tenniscourt

Saltwater Geo

The Kiln

Cairn

△20 Helipad

The Brough

Mound

Scartan Bay

Wester Shoals

Mounds

Scartan Point

Burial Ground

Parliament Square

Natural Arches

Cairn

Natural Arch

Hunni Geo

The Kettle

Rami Geo

N

PENTLAND   SKERRIES

1 km

½ mile

then declined until only the lighthouse keepers were resident. In 1994 they also left, when the lighthouse was automated.

Geology: Well-weathered Old Red Sandstone of the Middle period.

Wildlife: This is a site of Special Scientific Interest (SSI). There is an important breeding colony of Arctic tern and smaller numbers of many other seabirds. The grassland is rife with tormentil, tufted hair-grass and common cotton-grass except on the clifftops which are affected by the salt spray.

*   *   *

MUCKLE SKERRY is the largest of a small group of islets in the east end of the Pentland Firth, an

area better known as Hell's Mouth. Here there are fast tides and the island lies north of a dangerous reef consisting of Little Skerry, Louther Skerry, Clettack Skerry and numerous rocks, known overall as the Pentland Skerries. At high water these islets can almost disappear among the waves with only the Ben Barvas shipwreck on Little Skerry being visible. She was wrecked in 1964, fortunately without any loss of life, and the rusty hulk is usually quite conspicuous.

Except in fog Muckle Skerry is much more obvious as it is 20m high and has a 36m lighthouse on it (52m light elevation). There is a rough roadway leading to the lighthouse buildings from the landing point in Scartan Bay. In 1881 the island supported seventeen people living in four houses. These were probably the families of the lighthouse keepers but this policy was later abandoned and the lighthouse keepers themselves became the sole inhabitants. Then, in 1994 when the light was automated, they also left – completing 200 years or continuous service on the island.

The Pentland Skerries lighthouse on Muckle Skerry was the first lighthouse in which the famous Stevenson family was involved. Robert Stevenson (Robert Louis Stevenson's grandfather) was already an accomplished engineer in 1786 when he went into partnership with his stepfather, Thomas Smith, who was Engineer to the Board of Northern Lighthouses. They designed and built the two lighthouses on Muckle Skerry in 1794, of different heights and about 18m apart. Ships were taking the longer route round Orkney in order to avoid the dangers of the Pentland Firth and the Commissioners were keen to open the Firth to shipping. The two lights were rebuilt in 1821 and 1830.

In spite of the lighthouses, ships were still wrecked on the Skerries. For instance, the Vicksburg of Leith went aground in 1884 and the Kathe Neiderkirchner went aground and sank in 1965. The 50 passengers and crew were all saved thanks to the assistance of the lighthouse keepers. Divers say that the wreck is now attractively covered with red seaweed and peacock worms.

On the 22nd February 1941 the Germans machine-gunned the light-towers without causing any substantial damage.

* * *

Access: Enquire at Burwick on South Ronaldsay, Wick or Thurso.

Anchorages: Give a wide berth to the coasts of Muckle Skerry.
1. Temporary anchorage, if conditions are suitable, just within the entrance to Scartan Bay. 3-4m depth, shingle and weed.
2. In northerly winds there is a landing place at Hunni Geo west of Rami Geo.

10.2 Stroma

(ON straum-øy – island in the tidal stream).

OS Maps: 1:50000 Sheet 7 1:25000 Sheet 461
Admiralty Charts: 1:200000 Nos.1942 or 1954 1:50000 No.2162 1:26000 No.2581

Area: 375ha (927 acres)
Height: 53m (174 ft)

Owner: James Simpson, (now retired) and his son William. Mr Simpson has owned Stroma since 1960. He is a Stroma man by birth and a former haulage contractor.

Population: 1841–186 (42 houses). 1881–341. 1891–327 (66 houses). 1931–193. 1961–12. Uninhabited since 1950s except for lighthouse keepers and their families. 1971–8. 1981–0. 1991–0. 2001–0. 2011–0.

Geology: Weathered Middle Old Red Sandstone in flat layers known as Rousay flags. There is a fault line running north to south through the centre of the island – almost on the line of the road.

History: Earl Harold chased Svein Asleifsson to Stroma (see Gairsay No.10.14) during a feud, but the two men apparently settled their differences amicably after spending a night on Stroma sheltering from a gale according to the Orkneyinga Saga.

It is usually true to say that the survival of an island population in the present day depends on the availability of good education and good communications. Well, Stroma is the exception that proves the rule.

Although there was an active and viable population of eighty people living there in the early 1950s with a good primary school to serve the children (and even with their own issue of postage stamps), tide-wracked Stroma lacked adequate harbour facilities. So officialdom rose to the occasion and in 1955 a new harbour was constructed at great expense and the contractors were pleased to employ local people to carry out the work. Wages were so good that by the time the harbour was completed many of the islanders had made sufficient money to leave and establish themselves on the mainland. Too few were then left to maintain a viable population and within a few years the island was deserted except for the lighthouse-keepers; and they too left in 1996 when the lighthouse was automated.

Wildlife: Always a popular breeding ground for seals, the numbers have dramatically increased since the last residents left.

* * *

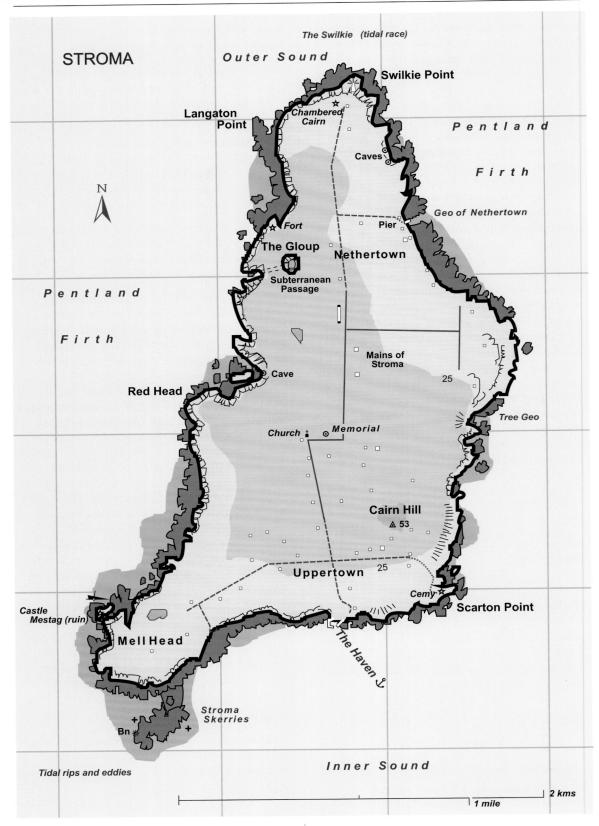

STROMA

The Swilkie   (tidal race)

Outer Sound

Swilkie Point

Langaton
Point

*Chambered
Cairn*

P e n t l a n d

Caves

F i r t h

Geo of Nethertown

N

Pier

☆ *Fort*

The Gloup

Nethertown

Subterranean
Passage

P e n t l a n d

F i r t h

Mains of
Stroma

25

Cave

Red Head

Tree Geo

Church   ⊙ *Memorial*

Cairn Hill

△ 53

Uppertown   25

Cemy ☆

*Castle
Mestag (ruin)*

Scarton Point

Mell Head

The Haven ♪

*Stroma
Skerries*

+

Bn ✳   +

Inner Sound

Tidal rips and eddies

|⊢——————————————————⊣ 2 kms
|⊢————————————⊣
 1 mile

STROMA is officially part of Caithness and not one of the Orkney isles. The powerful ocean tides, deflected by the British mainland, funnel into the Pentland Firth – the gap between Caithness and Orkney. Stroma obstructs their flow and turbulent seas are the result. Only a short distance west is the wide and dangerous tidal race known as the Merry Men of Mey and off Swilkie Point at Stroma's northern shore the sea can be equally violent.

The Picts are thought to have first settled in Orkney and the name of the Pentland Firth is a corruption of Pictland Firth. Stroma lies in the southern part of the Firth with the Inner Sound separating it from the mainland. The west side of the island is mainly cliffs but the east side is fairly low and flat. The Norse ruin of **Castle Mestag** [ND340764] caps Mell Head in the south-west and in the far north, beside the lighthouse which was automated in 1996, there is a chambered cairn [ND353791].

A roadway runs down the centre of the island from the lighthouse in the north to the harbour in the south connecting what were the two main settlements, **Nethertown** in the north and **Uppertown** in the south. The main island farmhouse, **Mains of Stroma**, is central. **Cairn Hill** (53m), the highest point, is in the south-east. The church and school, and the old croft houses, stand derelict. Only the sheep find shelter in them now.

A deep rocky pit in the north-west, known as **The Gloup** (ON *glup* – hollow, ravine), is filled with sea-water which feeds in through a subterranean passage under the cliffs. This is a particularly fine example of this type of feature. Just north of the gloup are the remains of an Iron Age fort [ND350785].

An automatic weather station was built on Stroma in 2010 to provide hourly records for the engineers concerned with tidal power trials in the Pentland Firth.

* * *

Access: The owner who lives in Gills near John o' Groats runs boat trips to Stroma most weekends.

Anchorages:
1. Small harbour on S coast most of which dries. Good shelter and easy entrance at slack water but rocky bottom and slight swell in outer basin. Inner basin recommended, sandy bottom. Tie up in SE corner just inside pierhead.

2. Normally comfortable anchorage out of tide midway between harbour and Mell Head off the sandy beach, 3m, sand with weed patches.

10.3 Swona

(ON svín-øy or Swenfy-øy–Sweyn's or swine island). Old records call it 'Swinna'. The Norse was sometimes used perjoratively – 'a swine of an island'.

OS Maps: 1:50000 Sheet 7 1:25000 Sheet 461
Admiralty Charts: 1:50000 No.2162 1:26000 No.2581

Area: 92ha (227 acres)
Height: 41m (134 ft)

Owner: Cyril Annal and his brother. His family has owned Swona since 1910.

Population: 1841–54 (8 houses). 1881–47. 1891–42 (7 houses). 1931–6. 1961–3. 1971–3. Abandoned 1974 and uninhabited since.

Geology: Weathered Middle Old Red Sandstone.

History: In spite of the difficulty of access – Swona is surrounded by vicious tides – archaeological evidence would suggest that Swona was probably first occupied 5000 years ago.

In the 12th century this was the home of Grim, father of two of Sweyn Asleifsson's close friends.

Wildlife: A small herd of feral cattle still survive. The original herd, which was abandoned in 1974, consisted of a mixture of black Aberdeen Angus and Beef Shorthorns. The cattle eat seaweed during the grassless winter months, shelter from the cold in derelict buildings, and the young bulls fight for dominance in the spring. The size of the herd is usually about seventeen animals. Such herds of feral cattle are very rare and this herd which can be aggressive, is being studied with interest by scientists. It is now officially recognised as a separate breed.

Thousands of rabbits breed unchecked, crop the rich grasslands which the cattle need and provide an occasional meal for the seagulls.

There is a wealth of birdlife including greylag geese and nesting seabirds and waders, and, thanks to the lack of sheep, many wildflowers including some rare ones. Grey and common seals frequent the rocky shoreline. Swona is a Site of Special Scientific Interest (SSI).

* * *

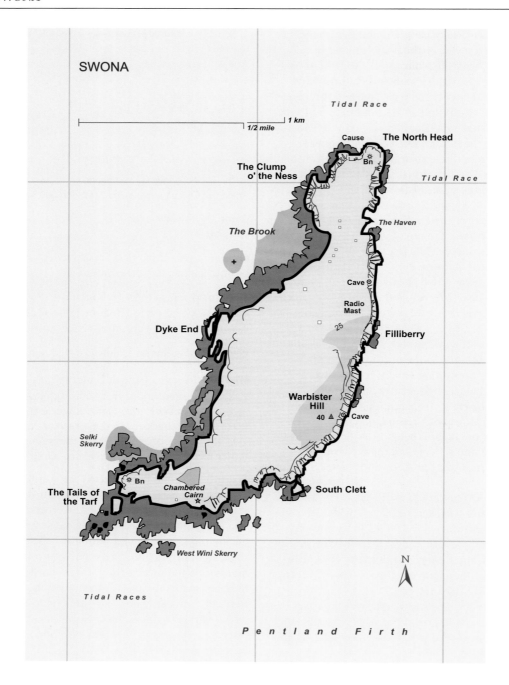

SWONA lies in the south approach to Scapa Flow. The Tails of the Tarf (?N – the end of the seaweed) is the most southerly point marked by the small white tower of **Swona Light**. The east side of Swona is mainly cliff with the rounded green summit of **Warbister Hill** (41m) rising close above the cliffs midway along the east coast and a cave further to the north.

The settlement on Swona was in the lowest-

lying part near the north end of the island. On the east side is a little cove called the **Haven**, Swona's best attempt at a harbour and on the west side is the **Brook**, an indentation with a wide stretch of shallow, treacherous rock and reef.

Associations with the distant past include a prehistoric chambered cairn [ND384837] in the extreme south of the island, an early Christian burial ground, and Viking remains.

In the 19th century the islanders' main occupation was line-fishing for cod. This was supplemented on occasion by piloting ships through the treacherous waters of the Pentland Firth – waters which they knew so well. Crofting was a marginal existence. The islanders built similar structures to the St Kildan 'cleits' in order to dry and salt their fish. They were built of the local flagstones and called 'skeows' [pron: skewse].

By 1932 only one family remained on the island. The last inhabitants in 1974 were Jim Rosie and his sister Violet. They had to leave when he developed Parkinson's disease. Now the solid stone and slated buildings have fallen into disrepair and old agricultural machinery rusts among the nettles.

Throughout history Swona has been the scene of many shipping disasters mostly on the west side during the east-going tidal stream. The tide is deceptive and can carry a boat on to the northern skerries with accelerating speed. By the time the danger is recognised it can be too late.

Martin Martin's (1695) solution should not be taken too seriously: '... Swinna isle, remarkable only for a part of Pentland Firth lying to the west of it, called the Wells of Swinna. They are two whirlpools in the sea, which run about with such violence, that any vessel or boat coming within their reach, go always round until they sink. These wells are dangerous only when there is a dead calm; for if a boat be under sail with any wind, it is easy to go over them. If any boat be forced into these wells by the violence of the tide, the boat-men cast a barrel or an oar into the wells; and while it is swallowing it up, the sea continues calm, and gives the boat an opportunity to pass over.'

*   *   *

Access: No normal access but, weather and tides permitting, try Explorer Fast Sea Charter, Kirkwall, 01856-871225.

Anchorage: Swona is surrounded with very tricky tides and it is often impracticable to approach the island. There are tidal races at both N and S ends of the island and the west coast is particularly dangerous.

1. The Haven, a small cove on the NE side of the island, 2c S of North Head is the best landing place on Swona when an approach can be made at slack water.

10.4 Swdtha

Derivation uncertain but may be (ON sviv-øy – island that appears to be floating or swinging).

OS Maps: 1:50000 Sheet 7   1:25000 Sheets 461 or 462
Admiralty Charts: 1:50000 No.2162   1:26000 No.2581

Area: 41ha (101 acres)
Height: 29m (95 ft)

Population: No record of any habitation.

Geology: Well-weathered Old Red Sandstone of the Middle period.

Wildlife: There are many storm-petrel burrows in the light soil and barnacle geese winter here. There is no written record of **SWITHA** ever having been inhabited in historic times and the Norse sagas make no mention of this little island. But Neolithic man lived here or, at least, visited the island for religious purposes, because he left two standing stones as evidence. The remarkable seamanship of these men in their flimsy craft never fails to astonish!

Sheep are grazed on Switha and probably have been for centuries. Every June, for at least a few days, the island echoes to the sound of human voices when shepherds, and occasionally members of their families, land on the island to shear the sheep.

Switha lies on the west side of the Sound of Hoxa amid tidal races beside the southern approach to Scapa Flow. Its most southerly point is called **The Ool** and between it and **The Kiln**, a point halfway along the south-east side, the cliffs reach a height of 29m. This is the highest part of the island and the ground falls away behind the cliffs except for a small hill (24m) to the north with one of the standing stones on its summit. A shallow cove in the south-west, **The Pool**, lies between the Ool and a low promontory, Point of the Pool.

*   *   *

Access: No normal access but, weather and tides permitting, try Explorer Fast Sea Charter, Kirkwall, 01856-871225.

Anchorage: Approach from N if possible to avoid dangerous tides at SE entrance to Cantick Sound, or time the passage carefully.
1. Temp. anchorage in the Pool, at SW end of Switha off Cantick Sound, in suitable conditions.

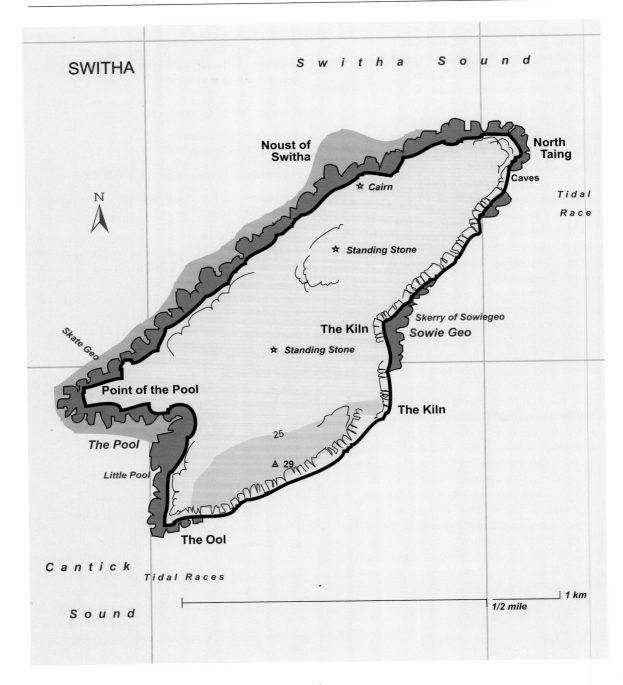

10.5 Flotta

(ON flott-øy – flat grassy island).

O S Maps: 1:50000 Sheet 7 1:25000 Sheets 461 or 462
Admiralty Charts: 1:200000 Nos.1942 or 1954 1:50000
No.2162 1:30000 No.35 1:26000 No.2581 1:12500
No.2568 oil terminal

Area: 876ha (2165 acres)

Height: 58m (190 ft)

Population: 1841–405 (82 houses).
1881–425. 1891–423. 1931–282. 1961–123.
1971–73. (1975– introduction of oil industry)
1981–178. 1991–126. 2001–81. 2011–80.

Geology: The whole island is Middle Old Red
Sandstone but the larger south-west portion is of
Rousay Beds weathered into low hills, whereas the

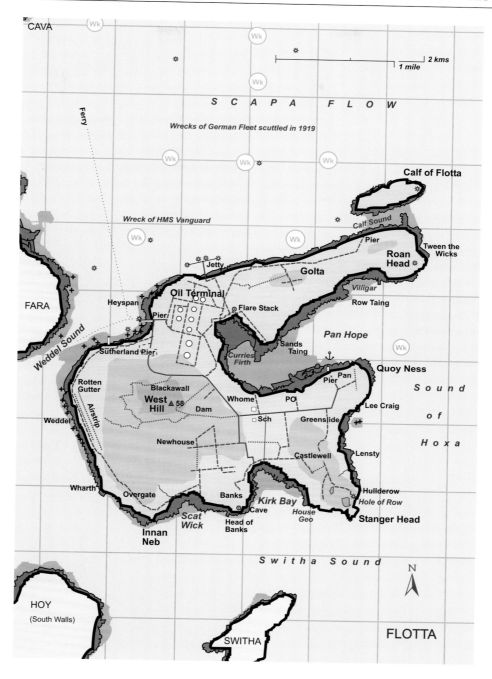

CAVA

Wk

Wk

☼

| 1 mile | 2 kms

Wk

S C A P A   F L O W

Ferry

Wrecks of German Fleet scuttled in 1919

Wk

Wk

Wk

Calf of Flotta

☼

Wreck of HMS Vanguard

☼

Calf Sound

Pier

Wk

Tween the Wicks

Wk

Roan Head

☼

Jetty

Golta

Villigar

FARA

Oil Terminal

Heyspan

⊙ Flare Stack

Row Taing

Pier

Pan Hope

Wk

Sutherland Pier

Sands Taing

⚓

Curries Firth

Quoy Ness

S o u n d

Rotten Gutter

Blackawall

Pier *Pan*

West Hill △58

Whome

PO

Lee Craig

o f

Weddel

Airstrip

Dam

□ Sch

Greenslide

+

H o x a

Newhouse

Castlewell

Lensty

Wharth

Overgate

Banks

Kirk Bay

Hullderow
Hole of Row

Scat Wick

⊙ Cave
Head of Banks

House Geo

Stanger Head

Innan Neb

S w i t h a   S o u n d

N

HOY

(South Walls)

SWITHA

FLOTTA

Golta peninsula and Quoy Ness are of Eday Beds – flagstones and sandstone of building quality.

History: An interesting sculptured stone slab from Flotta, thought to date from the 10th century, is in the Museum of Scotland in Edinburgh.

During the First World War Flotta became a naval base but after the war it returned to its former happy rural state. there were fields to be ploughed and lobsters to be caught in the rocky pools. Then the Second World War turned the island into an armed camp festooned with so many barrage balloons that it almost took off – the aim being to protect the southern entrance to Scapa Flow. Two new concrete piers were built with excellent access, and communication with Kirkwall and Stromness was improved. After the war the island once again slowly recovered from the shock, but, as with so many of the small islands, the population was decreasing and becoming more elderly. Improvement work was carried out, such as the laying of a water pipe in 1970 to bring fresh water from Hoy, but even so, the outlook was rather bleak.

Then Flotta, for the third time, was thrown irrevocably into the modern age because this flat little island, balanced near the edge of extinction, had the best-protected deep-water facilities in all of Orkney.

In 1974 the Occidental Group started construction of an oil terminal and linked it to the Piper and Claymore fields in the North Sea by 230km of pipeline. It became operational in December 1976. Many of the islanders were given employment but, inevitably, the work brought newcomers to the island and their assimilation was not always without problems. However, Flotta now has a thriving community with many young families and children, and, although the oil industry has passed its peak, there are still reasonable prospects for the foreseeable future.

The oil-terminal facilities are second only in size to those of Sullom Voe in Shetland but, unlike Shetland, practically all of the oil-related development, which copes with about 10% of all Britain's oil production, is confined to this one small island and has relatively little impact on the Mainland community.

Wildlife: Large number of Arctic tern, goodly population of Arctic skua and a compact seabird colony at Stanger Head.

*   *   *

Scapa Flow is no longer filled with men-of-war, iron-clads, or even sleek grey frigates of the modern fleet. The only continual signs of life and industry are the gas-flares of the huge oil terminal on **FLOTTA** sparkling on the water.

The island is almost rectangular except for the gaping mouth of **Pan Hope** in the east (the site of 17th-century salt pans). This wide bay cuts deep into the island with a northwards twist at Sands Taing. It then dries out in **Curries Firth**. Unfortunately all the inner part of the bay is too shallow to be of any use as an anchorage – but the waders don't mind.

In the pre-oil-terminal days the island was

mostly moorland with some grazing and cultivated land and most of the farms were small. Lobster fishing was needed to augment the meagre return from farming, yet there was always an air of vitality despite the number of old people. Now more than half the total land area is covered with all the paraphernalia of industry and houses. **West Hill** (58m), Flotta's highest point, is relatively clear but the airstrip lies below it by Rotten Gutter on the west coast. North-west of the terminal the **Golta** (ON – barren, sterile) peninsula is more open, but that is all there is now to be seen of the old Flotta. The south-east corner at **Stanger Head** is covered with the remaining derelict military installations of the Second World War – fascinating, or a suitable set for a disaster movie, depending on one's viewpoint. Most of the stone used came from the local quarry.

Calf of Flotta is a tiny island off Roan Head in the north. The water in Calf Sound which separates it from Flotta is very shallow with narrow navigable channel between the rock-like obstructions. These are, in fact, anti-submarine cables discarded after the Second World War.

*   *   *

Access: Daily ro-ro service by Orkney Ferries, 01856-811397, from Houton, 17km SW of Kirkwall, and Longhope or Lyness on Hoy. Bus service, Kirkwall/Houton and Stromness/Houton, 01856-870555.

Anchorages: (Orkney VTS on VHF Ch.16/11)
1. Sutherland Pier, 130m long. 3m depth on leeward side, 4m on seaward face. Used by work boats, fishing boats and tugs. (01856–873636).
2. Pan Hope, large bay on W side of Flotta. Good fair weather anchorage in 4–5m N of pier and clear of underwater cable.
3. Kirk Bay, on S side. Temp. anchorage but rocky and exposed in S winds.
4. West Weddel Sound, bay in NW of Flotta. Shallow and rocky but good anchorage in settled weather. Gibraltar Pier on E side, ferry priority (01856–873636).

10.6 Hoy

(ON há-øy – high island)

O S Maps: 1:50000 Sheet 7 1:25000 Sheet 462
Admiralty Charts: 1:200000 No.1954 1:75000 No.2249

north Hoy 1:50000 No.2162 south Hoy 1:30000 No.35 east coast

Area: 14318ha (35380 acres)
Height: 479m (1571 ft)

Owner: Sold in 1973 by the owner, Malcolm Stewart, to The Hoy Trust. After the passing of the Crofting Reform Act many crofters purchased their own land-holdings from the Trust which also sold 3237ha to the Royal Society for the Protection of Birds (including the Old Man of Hoy). The Trust hopes to encourage resettlement on the parts of Hoy which it still owns.

Population: 1841–1486 (294 houses). 1881–1380. 1891–1320 (271 houses). 1931–955. 1961–511. 1981–461. 1991–450. 2001–392. 2011–419.

Geology: Hoy is unique in being largely composed of Upper Old Red Sandstone although there are a few small volcanic intrusive dykes in the north-west and some small areas of exposed basalt. This particular type of sandstone – massive, hard, and red or orange-coloured – is to be found nowhere else in Orkney. Its mode of weathering has resulted in the fantastic precipices of the west coast.

The sandstone lies above a basalt lava layer which is about 120m thick. This has been exposed by erosion at, for instance, the foot of the Old Man of Hoy where it forms a pedestal. In the extreme north there is a small area of Lower Stromness Flags – a finely laminated Middle Old Red Sandstone which weathers to a good soil. The south-east of the island is also of Middle Old Red Sandstone.

History: It was on South Walls, according to the sagas, that Olaf Tryggvason, King of Norway from 995 to 1000, forced Sigurd Hlodvisson the Stout, Earl of Orkney and a fearless warrior, to submit to baptism on pain of death. The Earl duly became a Christian – but in name only.

Wildlife: Hoy is a treasure-house of plant life – by far the best in Orkney and including a number of rare alpines but there is also deep heather covering many of the hill-slopes. The only remaining fragment of native woodland is at Berriedale east of the Old Man of Hoy with willow, birch, aspen and rowan, and a few indigenous trees still growing in the clefts of

Ward Hill and Cuilags – rowan, hazel (only three survive) – *Corylus avellana*, aspen, birch – *Betula pubescens*, and sallow – *Salix atrocinerea*. Mountain hares are to be found in the north of Hoy and nowhere else in Orkney although the brown hare is quite common. This area is also said to support Orkney's only grasshoppers.

North Hoy is an RSPB Nature Reserve. Breeding species of bird to be seen – if you can survive the midges – are red grouse, golden plover, dunlin, snipe and curlew, with some hen harrier, merlin and short-eared owl. There is an important skua population – over 400 pairs of Arctic and 1500 great skuas (bonxies) were recorded in 1982 and the lochans support half the 110 pairs of red-throated divers recorded on Orkney. Stonechat, wheatear, some ring ousel and many twite are in evidence. On the cliffs there are huge numbers of fulmar, shag, kittiwake, guillemot, razorbill, puffin, black guillemot, and rock dove. There are also buzzard, peregrine and raven, and barnacle geese appear in late winter at South Walls.

May to July are the best bird-watching months.

* * *

THE OLD MAN OF HOY

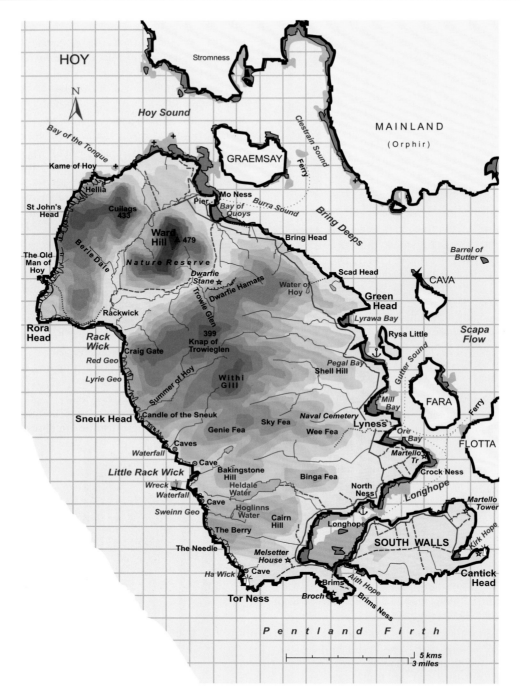

HOY is the highest and wildest and wettest (1500mm of rain) of all the Orkney islands. The high ground rises in three rugged masses, divided by 300m deep gaps, with **Ward Hill** in the middle. Ward Hill is the highest peak in Orkney (479m). Legend has it that on the steep north side of Ward Hill, where it hangs above the Hoy Outdoor Centre, there used to be a great

carbuncle which gleamed ruddy red in the dark but which disappeared whenever you approached it. There has never been an explanation for this.

The outstanding view of the Hoy cliffs from the Scrabster ferry gives newcomers a very misleading impression of Orkney. As can be seen from Table III, most of the Northern Isles are low-lying. Yet **St John's Head** on the NW coast is, at nearly

350m, one of the highest sea-cliffs in Britain with the world-famous rock pinnacle, the **Old Man of Hoy** (137m), to the south and the remarkable echoing valley of the **Kame** in the far north. In 1970, mountaineers spent two days descending St John's Head as it was almost impossible to abseil in the vicious sea-wind, and the subsequent hair-raising ascent took five days.

Many legends attach to the **Dwarfie Stane**, – a huge block of red sandstone (8.5m long x 4.3m wide x 1.8m high) lying within a natural amphitheatre – the Dwarfie Hamars (ON *hamars* – crags), south-east of Ward Hill [HY243004]. This is the only example in Northern Europe of a rock tomb similar to the rock-cut chamber tombs of the Mediterranean region. The tomb, which was probably cut in Neolithic or Early Bronze Age times c.2000-1600BC, consists of a passage and two chambers hollowed out of the stone. Martin Martin thought there was a domestic purpose – 'at one of the ends... there is cut out a bed and pillow capable of two persons to lie in, at the other end there is a void space cut out resembling a bed, and above both these there is a large hole which is supposed was a vent for smoke'. Martin said that the 'common tradition is that a giant and his wife made this their place of retreat'. Sir Walter Scott said that 'the necromantic owner may sometimes still be seen sitting by the Dwarfie Stone.'. He considered the owner to be a troll, rather than a giant. Certainly the mysterious **Trowie Glen** (ON *troll* – evil monster, ogre or goblin) is beside the Dwarfie Hamars.

Even the **Dwarfie Hamars** have their legend. They are named after the dwarfs who, as everyone knows, are excellent smiths and who were responsible for forging Thor's famous hammer.

The track of roadway running through this legendary valley and past the Dwarfie Stane comes from **Moaness Pier** and the village of Hoy and ends up on the Atlantic coast at **Rackwick**, west of Rora Head. This picturesque old fishing village, stretching up the glen from a pebble beach, is Orkney's most isolated spot. The school closed in 1954 and the population has faded away although some of the cottages are reinhabited by visitors in the summer months and the famous composer, Sir Peter Maxwell Davies, used to live and compose in a converted croft in the hills above the village. Many years ago the men of Rackwick were known as fine fishermen and even finer country dancers. They cheerfully walked

6km over the ghostly hills to Hoy village, danced the night through, and then walked back home again.

Most of the north of Hoy is now sadly depopulated. The main road runs down the east coast overlooking Scapa Flow, to **Lyness** opposite the island of Fara (No.10.7). During the Second World War Lyness was home to about 30,000 men when it was the headquarters for the Scapa Flow naval base. The village has never recovered from this invasion and the Navy left behind a desolate landscape of abandoned structures.

The secluded natural harbour of **Longhope** (ON – long bay) is south of Lyness. On each ness, guarding the harbour entrance like a Pictish broch, is a **Martello Tower** [ND324935 and 338913]. These were built for protection against U.S. privateers during the Napoleonic War (1813–15). As this was an assembly point for convoys, the Towers were each equipped with a 24-pounder canon on top, quarters for the gunners in the middle, and ammunition stores at ground level. A century later, they were armed once again for the First World War.

Melsetter House at the head of Longhope is one of Orkney's finest historic buildings [ND269893] set in a beautiful garden. It was a laird's house for the Moodie family until the late 19th century when it was bought by a wealthy Englishman, J G M Heddle, whose architect, W R Lethaby, enlarged it in the tradition of William Morris with furniture designed by Ford Maddox Brown and Dante Gabriel Rossetti. It can be visited by appointment.

The renowned **Longhope Lifeboat Station** is at Brims, in Aith Hope [ND291887]. This station has a remarkable record of daring rescues and will always be remembered for the loss of its entire crew when it went to the assistance of the Liberian cargo ship *Irene* in 1969. A force nine gale had raged for three days and the sea state was appalling. Eight men died including the coxswain and his two sons and the second coxswain and both his sons.

The south of Hoy is more green and mellow than the northern part and there is an active farming community on **South Walls**. South Walls was a tidal island until a narrow causeway – **The Ayre** – was constructed over the sandbank. The lighthouse on Cantick Head was built by David Stevenson in 1858.

Access: Orkney Ferries: every day passenger (and bike) service, Stromness/Graemsay/ Moaness, 01856-850624; ro-ro service Houton, Mainland/ Lyness (some via Flotta), 01856-872044; bus service, Kirkwall/ Houton; 01856-870555. No bus service on Hoy but car, taxi, mini-bus and cycle-hire available. Tourist information, 01856-872856.

Anchorages: (Orkney VTS on VHF Ch.16/11)
1. Mo Ness and Bay of Quoys. Ferry priority at pier steps or temp. anchorage in 3m, SE of pier.
2. Aith Hope, between Brims Ness and South Walls on the S coast. Reasonable anchorage in 4–11m, sand, off the former Longhope Lifeboat Station. Useful while waiting for a favourable tide.
3. Kirk Hope. Temp. anchorage in 7m in centre of bay beyond fish-farm. Exposed N and E.
4. Longhope, between S Walls and Hoy. Visitors' moorings E of pier. Apr–Oct. Anchor in 4–6m E of pier on S Ness avoiding fish-farm. There is 4m depth at outer end of pier but avoid obstructing ferry. Heavy squalls can occur with NW winds and use plenty of cable because of the weed. Snug anchorage in 7–10m about 2½c NW of South Ness beyond submarine cables.
5. Ore Bay and Mill Bay, opposite Fara, are not recommended as the bottom is foul with old hawsers and there are fish-cages. Temp. berth alongside concrete jetty but keep clear of ro-ro jetty (for access to Museum).
6. Pegal Bay, in Rysa Sound. Attractive anchorage with good holding but part obstructed by fish-cages and in W gales there can be violent squalls. Bottom shelves steeply.
7. Lyrawa Bay, S of Green Head is generally too deep and exposed for comfortable anchorage but excellent holding. Head of bay is shoal.

10.7 Fara

Possibly (ON vaer-øy – ram island). Previously called South Pharay.

OS Maps: 1:50000 Sheet 7 1:25000 Sheet 462
Admiralty Charts: 1:200000 Nos.1942 or 1954 1:50000 No.2162 1:30000 No.35 1:26000 No.2581 large scale No.2568

Area: 295ha (729 acres)
Height: 43m (141 ft)

Owner: S & J.D. Robertson Group Ltd.

Population: 1841–55 (10 houses). 1881–68. 1891–76 (15 houses). 1931–28. 1961–5. 1971–0. 1981–0. Uninhabited.

Geology: Rousay Flags of Middle Old Red Sandstone.

History: In the 19th century both Fara and Rysa Little were part of the Melsetter estate (Hoy and Walls) belonging to the Moodie family.

* * *

FARA has rich pastureland but, as with so many little islands, it was without an adequate pier. More and more of the inhabitants were attracted to secure centres of population and it became uneconomic to employ a teacher for the few remaining children. As numbers decreased further the pressure on the remainder increased. Eventually the number dropped below the critical minimum capable of manning a boat and carrying out similar communal tasks and the population collapsed. For Fara this point was reached in the 1960s yet the island lies close to the east side of Hoy and almost a stone's throw from Flotta, both populated areas. Today the ferry routes almost circumnavigate it, and neighbouring Flotta prospers.

The cultivated area was mainly on the north-east side and most of the abandoned houses are in the north. The summit, **Thomson's Hill** (43m), is in the centre of the island.

During World War II a rough narrow gauge railway was laid round the island to allow movement of ammunition and gas bottles to service the barrage balloons.

There are several jetties and a small pier with a windmill close behind it on the west coast south-west of Thomson's Hill. A track runs up the hill from the pier to Upper Quoy (ON *koie* – hut or shelter).

Peat Bay on the north-west coast is small and shallow with a stony beach.

In 2012 the owner applied for permission to erect seven 3Mw wind turbines on the island.

* * *

Access: Try a Hoy or Flotta boatowner or Explorer Fast Sea Charter, Kirkwall, 01856-871225.

Anchorages: Most areas foul with old tackle so tripping line essential.
1. SW of Peat Point in Gutter Sound. Occasional anchorage in 4–6m, sand and shingle. Peat Bay is foul but suitable for landing by dinghy.
2. SW of Thomson's Hill. Temp. anchorage S of small pier.

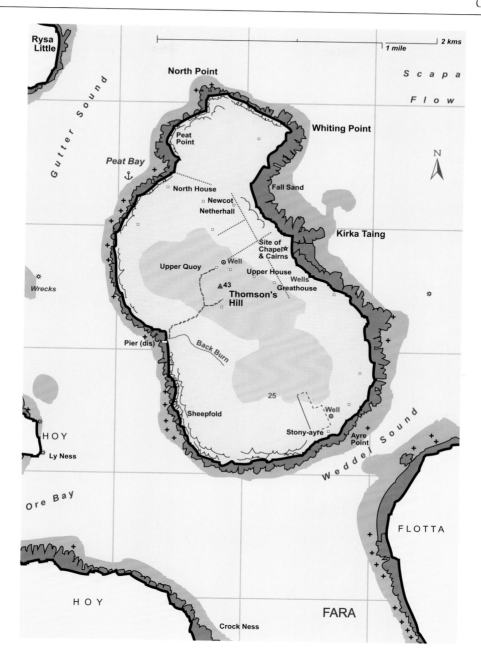

Beware rocks close in-shore further S.

3. The wind-farm proposal includes the provision of a pier with facilities but landing may be restricted.

10.8 Cava

(ON kálf-øy – calf island).

OS Maps: 1:50000 Sheet 6 or 7 1:25000 Sheet 462
Admiralty Charts: 1:200000 Nos.1942 or 1954 1:75000
No.2249 1:30000 No.35

Area: 107ha (264 acres)
Height: 36m (118 ft)

Population: 1841–23 (4 houses). 1881–25.
1891–13 (3 houses). 1931–14. 1961–0. 1981–2.
1991–2. 2001–0.

Geology: The underlying rock forms layers of flagstones and firm sandstones known as the Eday Beds of Middle Old Red Sandstone.

History: A notorious Orkney sailor, John Gow, who had become a pirate, returned to home

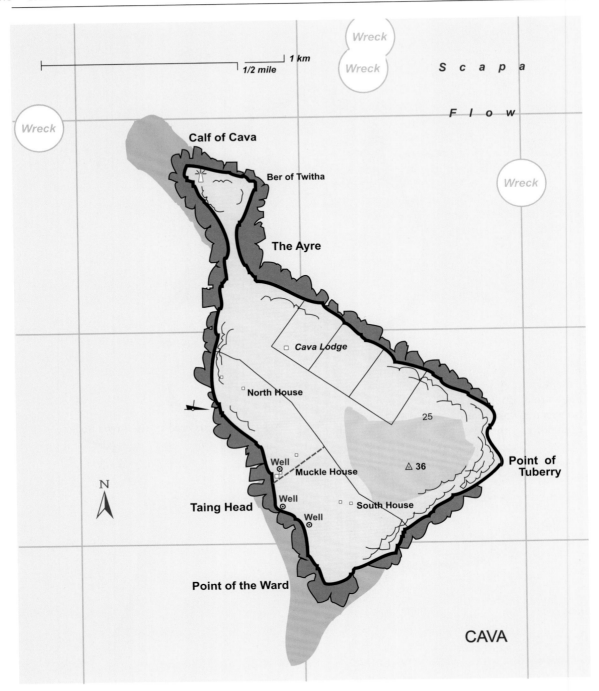

waters in 1725. Having unsuccessfully tried to rob Clestrain House opposite Stromness, he visited Cava and kidnapped two or three girls which he took aboard his ship. A few days later they returned home. One story claims that they were laden with riches while the other declares that they were badly beaten and that one later died.

Gow went on to raid Graemsay (No.10.10) and Eday (See No.10.22) but he was caught, tried, and sentenced to death by hanging. In life, Gow bungled every action and in death he was equally maladroit – or unlucky. The rope broke and he had to be hanged a second time. His total career in piracy lasted only six months.

A low grassy island with a stony shoreline, **CAVA** nowadays is mainly used for grazing.

Any small island lying off a larger island was often called Calf Island by the early settlers. Cava is distinct in being a Calf Island which has in turn its own Calf Island lying to the north – **Calf of Cava**. This is really a small peninsula which is joined to the north of Cava by a stony ridge. A small octagonal lighthouse stands on it.

A modest half-knot tide runs through the channel between Cava and **Rysa Little** (ON and E. – little heap of stones), an islet which does rise a little – 17m, to be precise. A small wrecked ship on this side of Cava lies to the north-west of a windmill standing near the shore. This is not exceptional as Scapa Flow is littered with wrecks.

After the German Fleet had surrendered to Admiral Beatty at the Firth of Forth on 21 November 1918, all the ships were transferred to Scapa Flow and held under the terms of the armistice. Most of the sailors were sent home and only skeleton German crews stayed aboard while the Allies argued about division of the spoils. The armistice was due to expire on 19 June 1919, with a return to hostilities so on the 17 June Admiral Von Reuter sent orders from his flagship *Emden* to make 'preparations for scuttling'. He was unaware that the armistice had been extended and the terms of a German surrender agreed.

On the 21 June 1919 – a quiet clear Saturday morning with the British Fleet away on exercise – all the mighty ships, some of the most modern fighting machines in the world, sank slowly beneath the waves. The entire fleet of more than 200 vessels was fully dressed with flags and the crews were in full dress uniform.

'Where they were sunk, they will rest and rust,' said the Admiralty in disgust. But in the following years many of the ships were salvaged or stripped of their valuable metal. The wrecks that remain are now protected, a great tourist attraction and seen by thousands of divers.

The wrecks lying nearest to Cava, taken clockwise from the north-west, are the light cruiser *Karlsrühe*, the 25,000-ton battleships *Bayern*, *Kronprinz Wilhelm* and *Markgraf*, the light cruisers *Köln* and *Dresden* and the battleship *König*.

Cava Lodge, which is a conspicuous white house standing in the middle of the north part of the island, is an interesting example of a traditional old Orkney house. Only a very few examples still survive in fair condition.

Barrel of Butter to the north-east of the collection of wrecks is a small rock showing just above sea-level but marked by a beacon. Its quaint name comes from early times when the people of Orphir paid an annual rent of a barrel of butter to the local laird in return for permission to kill seals on the rock.

Access: Try Explorer, Kirkwall, 01856-871225 or Roving Eye Enterprises, Stromness, 01856-811309 which has an ROV to study the wrecks.

Anchorage: No recommended anchorages.
1. Point of the Ward, S extremity of Cava. Temp. anchorage in settled weather on sand-spit about 1½c S of Ward Point, 3–6m, sand and shingle. Tides are weak in this area.

10.9 Copinsay

(ON kobbunge-øy – seal-pup island).

OS Maps: 1:50000 Sheet 6 1:25000 Sheet 461
Admiralty Charts: 1:200000 Nos.1942 or 1954 1:75000 No.2250

Area: 73ha (180 acres)
Height: 64m (210 ft)

Owner: Administered by the Royal Society for the Protection of Birds since 1972. Former lighthouse-keeper's cottage bought in 1991 by Paul Craig of Burston, Staffordshire as a holiday home. In 1993 he was very upset when Scottish Hydroelectric quoted nearly £1m to connect his house to the electricity mains.

Population: 1841–13 (1 house). 1881–5. 1891–9 (1 house). 1931–25. 1961–3 (lighthouse-keepers). 1981–0. 1991–0. 2001–0. 2011–0.

Geology: Tilted and eroded Rousay flags of Middle Old Red Sandstone with a top-skin of reasonable turf.

History: According to the sagas a great sea-battle was fought north of Copinsay, off the Mainland coast of Deerness. King Karl (there is some uncertainty who King Karl was but he might be King Duncan of Scotland, father of Macbeth) fought a battle with Thorfinn the Mighty. The ships were laid side by side and Earl Thorfinn leapt off his poop into the King's ship and struck out boldly. The King had eleven ships while Thorfinn only had five but his attack was so merciless that the King fled.

COPINSAY

Wildlife: Copinsay has its fair share of seals but it is best known nowadays for its bird life. The most interesting time for bird-watching is from May to July but there is also much to be seen in the autumn. Copinsay is a Nature Reserve which has been administered by the Royal Society for the Protection of Birds since 1972 as the James Fisher Memorial Island. There are about 10,000 pairs of kittiwake, 30,000 guillemot, 1,000 razorbill, and many fulmar, eider, ringed plover, rock dove, raven and twite breeding here and even a few corncrake. No gannets have nested here since 1860. The adjacent Holms – which are accessible at low tide – also have arctic tern, puffin and black guillemot, plus a few common tern. The

THE CLIFFS OF COPINSAY – GUILLEMOTS AND KITTIWAKES
SPRINKLED LIKE CONFETTI

Horse rock-stack is covered with birds including a
small colony of cormorant.

* * *

COPINSAY is a steeply-tilted green island which
reaches a height of 64m right at the edge of the
cliffs on its south-east side as though it had been
abruptly sliced with a giant knife. From this high
point the ground slopes steadily down to the west.
The cliff summit is dominated by the lighthouse, a
white tower standing 16m above the cliff-top and
in summer the rock ledges are heavily populated
with gulls, guillemots, razorbills, kittiwakes and
shags.

A track runs down the hill from the lighthouse
to the old farmhouse. This was still a working
farm after the Second World War and although its
isolation caused problems it was considered quite
a good productive farm.

The **Giant Stone** is a huge boulder which
according to legend was thrown at the island
by a giant who lived on the farm of Stembister
in Deerness on Mainland. The name Stembister
means stone farm.

Apart from the south-eastern cliff-face the
island is surrounded by reefs, holms and
skerries. The farmhouse stands on a small
peninsula with a long rock saddle, Isle Rough,
connecting Copinsay to **Corn Holm** in the
west. This divides North Bay from South Bay
and can be walked across at low water. There
was once a little chapel on Corn Holm but the
difficulty of access must have been a problem
for the islanders intending to worship in it.

Corn Holm is linked by drying reefs to
Ward Holm in the south and **Black Holm** in
the west. Ward Holm has a prehistoric cairn
on it.

Horse Sound which is about half a mile
wide separates the **Horse of Copinsay**, a
grass-topped rectangular stack 18m high,
from North Nevi (ON *nøv* – fist), the north-
east extremity of Copinsay. As with so many
small islands the demand for grazing was so
great that the islanders would carry sheep to
the top of the Horse, but it was said that it
could fatten one sheep and feed two, but that
three would starve. In the spring pigs were
also hoisted to the top to fatten on the huge
'crop' of sea-birds' eggs. The pigs' coarse hair
was used to make the strong rope needed for
fowling. 'Lee-running' was the local name
for the organised collection of seabirds' eggs
which was still practised on Copinsay until the
1940s.

A hole through the Horse is called **Blaster
Hole** because of the power of the water-jet which
is forced through it and 60m into the sky by
easterly gales.

* * *

Access: Boat trips by arrangement: *Verona*,
Deerness, 01856-741252; or Explorer Charter,
Kirkwall, 01856-871225.

Anchorage: No recommended anchorages but there is a
landing jetty.

1. Horse Sound. Temp. anchorage in 6–8m slightly E of the
line of the W coast of Copinsay (main island) and about
1½c offshore to avoid in-shore rocks.

10.10 Graemsay

(ON *Gríms-øy* – Grim's island).

OS Maps: 1:50000 Sheet 6 or 7 1:25000 Sheets 462 or 463
Admiralty Charts: 1:200000 No.1954 1:30000 No.35 large
scale No.2568

Area: 409ha (1011 acres)
Height: 62m (203 ft)

Owner: Arthur Ritch, a crofter at Fillets, bought the 360-acre Sandside estate in 1996 for £55,000. A. D. Johnston of Stromness is another owner.

Population: 1841–214 (48 houses). 1881–236. 1891–223 (47 houses). 1931–114. 1961–51.

1981–21. 1991–27. 2001–21. 2011–28.

Geology: Mostly Lower Stromness Flags, a finely laminated Middle Old Red Sandstone, which has eroded on the surface to a fine soil. Two major volcanic faults on a north-south axis roughly divide the island into three equal sections. Apart from the outcrops of ancient granites and schists through the Old Red Sandstone there is a larger

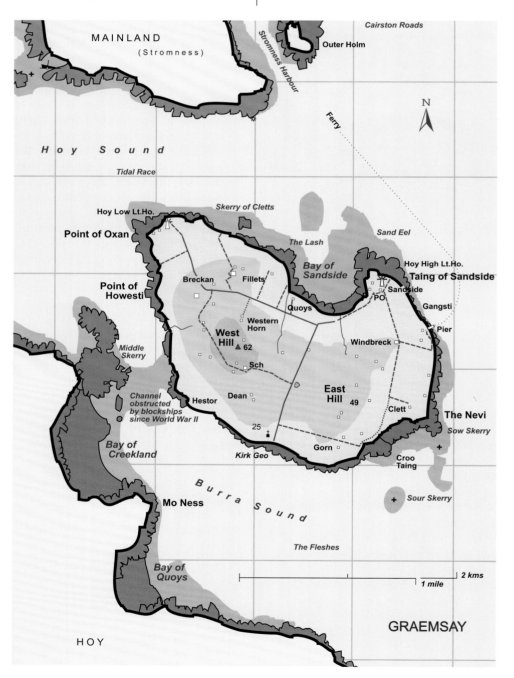

patch of granite-schist complex on the north coast – one of the few such outcrops to be found in Orkney.

History: Two early Celtic sites on Graemsay are dedicated respectively to St Bride and St Columba.

There are a number of crofts on the island but only one farm which is at Bu in Sandside. This was the original settlement of the natural son of Earl Robert Stewart when he was given the island by his father.

The 19th-century herring industry led to an increased interest in navigational safeguards and the construction of the two lighthouses, Hoy High and Hoy Low – both of which were built in 1851. Even so, on New Year's Day 1866, the *Albion*, en route to New York was wrecked off the Point of Oxan.

* * *

In Hoy Sound, off the comely island of **GRAEMSAY,** the tide can run so fast that the surface of the sea forms high ridges with whirlpools in the troughs. The ridges slowly but constantly move, like sand dunes during a sandstorm. These areas of violent turbulent water are called 'roosts' (ON *rost* – maelstrom) and Hoy Sound is a good example.

Graemsay is a green refuge with fertile soil encompassed by savage reefs, wrecks and shoals. It has two low hills, **East Hill** (49m) and **West Hill** (62m), the summit. The small lighthouse, **Hoy Low**, is on the north-western extremity, Point of Oxan, and a coastal battery was built beside it in the Second World War. The big lighthouse, **Hoy High** (33m), has an upper balcony supported on Gothic arches and keepers' houses built like Assyrian temples! It is in the north-east on the Taing of Sandside (ON – Sandside point) next to the island's only bay, the **Bay of Sandside**. This is also known as **The Hap** and it is shallow and rocky and guarded by the **Skerry of Cletts** and a dangerous reef called **The Lash**.

The small fishing pier and the ferry pier are east of Hoy High lighthouse. Further south a projection called **The Nevi** (ON *nøv* – promontory or fist) ends in the dangerous Sow Skerry.

A road runs across the island between the Bay of Sandside and a church at Kirk Geo on the south coast. Other roads feed off to the scattered dwellings and there is a small school beside West Hill. In 1996 Orkney Council decided to close the school as there was only one pupil. (This was sad news but the few children now go daily by boat to

Stromness – weather permitting.)

The islanders own a number of boats. These are mainly used for lobster fishing but they are sometimes needed for last-minute shopping at Stromness as, although it has a post-office, Graemsay has no shop. The islanders are good innovative farmers and fishermen. It was Patrick Honeyman of Graemsay who first introduced the Scots plough to Orkney. He even risked buying two of them at a time when only single-stilted ploughs were in general use.

Access: Orkney Ferries every day passenger and cycle service (by request), Stromness/ Graemsay/ Hoy, 01856-850624. Stopover time to visit Graemsay is usually possible.

Anchorage: There is no recommended anchorage and there are many hazards. Alongside pier ferry has priority at outermost steps. (Orkney VTS on VHS Ch. 16/11).

10.11 Mainland

(ON megenland – mainland) An alternative Norse name was 'Hrossey' – the island of horses. 16th century Latinist George Buchanan mistakenly called Mainland 'Pomona' and for a time the name was widely used but never by the islanders themselves. To Orcadians the Scottish mainland is simply 'Scotland'.

South Ronaldsay

(ON – Rognvald's island).

Burray

(ON borgr-øy – fort or broch island).

Hunda

(ON hund-øy – dog island).

O S Maps: 1:50000 Sheet 6 1:25000 Sheets 461 and 463. Admiralty Charts: 1:200000 No.1954 1:75000 Nos.2249 and 2250 1:30000 No.35 part S coast 1:25000 No.2584 part NE coast 1:12500 Kirkwall large scale No.2568 Stromness
Area: 58308ha (144079 acres)
Height: 271m (889 ft)

Owner: Multiple ownership.

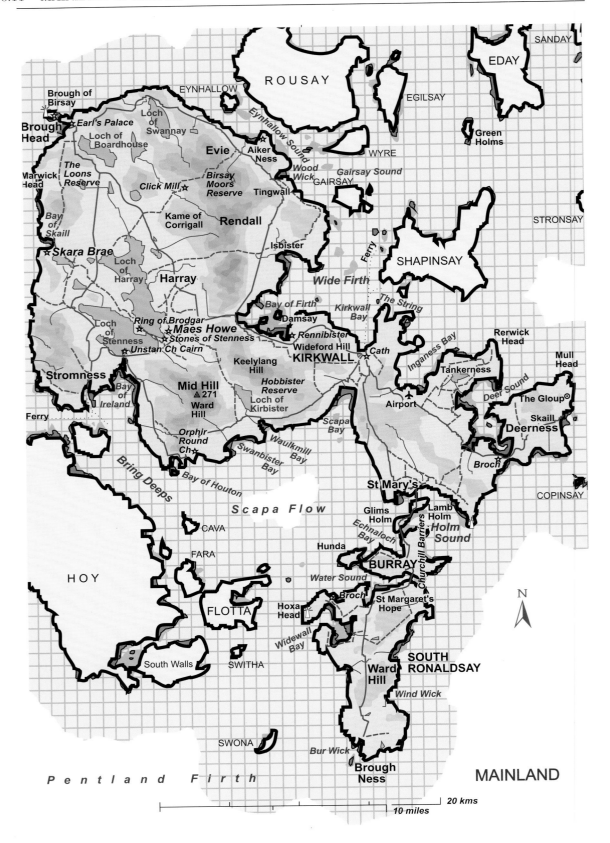

SANDAY

EDAY

ROUSAY

EYNHALLOW

Brough of
Birsay

Earl's Palace

**Brough
Head**

Loch
of
Swannay

EGILSAY

Green
Holms

Loch of
Boardhouse

Evie

Aiker
Ness

WYRE

Marwick
Head

The
Loons
Reserve

Click Mill

Birsay
Moors
Reserve

Wood
Wick

Gairsay Sound

GAIRSAY

Tingwall

Bay
of
Skaill

Kame of
Corrigall

Rendall

STRONSAY

Isbister

Skara Brae

Loch
of
Harray

Harray

Ferry

SHAPINSAY

Wide Firth

Bay of Firth

Damsay

Kirkwall
Bay

The String

Loch
of
Stenness

Ring of Brodgar

Maes Howe

Stones of Stenness

Unstan Ch Cairn

Rennibister

Wideford Hill

KIRKWALL

Cath

Inganess Bay

Rerwick
Head

Mull
Head

Stromness

Keelylang
Hill

Hobbister
Reserve

Tankerness

Deer Sound

The Gloup

Bay
of
Ireland

Mid Hill
▲ 271
Ward
Hill

Loch of
Kirbister

Airport

Skaill

Deerness

Ferry

Orphir
Round
Ch

Scapa
Bay

Broch

COPINSAY

Swanbister
Bay

Waulkmill
Bay

Bay of Houton

Bring Deeps

St Mary's

Scapa Flow

Glims
Holm

Echnaloch
Bay

Lamb
Holm

Holm
Sound

CAVA

FARA

Hunda

Water Sound

Churchill Barriers

HOY

Broch

BURRAY

St Margaret's
Hope

FLOTTA

Hoxa
Head

South Walls

SWITHA

Widewall
Bay

Ward
Hill

SOUTH
RONALDSAY

Wind Wick

N

SWONA

Bur Wick

Brough
Ness

MAINLAND

Pentland   Firth

20 kms

10 miles

Population:

	1841	1881	1891	1931	1961	1991	2001	2011
Mainland	16022	17165	16498	13352	13495	15123	15315	17164
S'th R'say	2331	2557	2315	1312	980	943	854	909
Burray	532	685	681	379	262	363	357	409
Hunda	6	8	7	0	0	0	0	0
G's Holm	0	0	0	0	0	0	0	0
L'b Holm	?	12	8	7	0	0	0	0
	18903	20423	19508	15043	14737	15174	16429	18482

Geology: As with all the Orkney islands, Mainland is sedimentary rock of Devonian (Old Red Sandstone) age except for some small patches of granite-schist complex. One of these is Brinkies Brae above Stromness which is the oldest place, geologically, in Orkney. The Dalradian foliated-granite rock was once an island in a great freshwater loch.

The sandstones in the west of Mainland are Upper and Lower Stromness Flags separated by a Fish Bed. These Stromness Beds are finely laminated and account for the dramatic cliff scenery in this area. The sandstones of the east are of the Rousay type although the Scapa Flow coastline, the Kirkwall area, Deerness and most of South Ronaldsay are Eday Beds, which are fine building stone. Deerness has some thick lava intrusions and the Gloup of Deerness on the east coast is a great rock hole connected to the sea by an underground fissure.

History: Mainland Orkney has so many notable relics dating from the late Stone Age that one must assume there was an advanced social structure on the island and considerable relative prosperity.

This age was followed by that of the broch-builders and the Picts (who may or may not have been the same people) but the Norsemen were not far behind them and some time in the 9th century the Earldom of Orkney was established. A dynasty followed which is well chronicled in the Norse Sagas and this reached its zenith in the 11th century under Earl Thorfinn the Mighty. Thereafter there was much infighting between rival descendants culminating in the death of Earl John in a drunken brawl in Thurso in 1231. He was the last of the Norse earls.

The succession passed to a son of the Earl of Angus, and various pale shadows followed him. King Haakon died in Kirkwall in 1263 and the Norse hold became ever more tenuous.

In 1379 Henry Sinclair of Roslin inherited the earldom and was formally invested by the King of Norway. He was a great sailor-adventurer and there is good evidence that he sailed to America and established settlements there long before Columbus.

In 1468 King Christian of Norway and Denmark included Orkney and Shetland as part of Margaret, Maid of Norway's, dowry but subject to a cash redemption. The total cash failed to be paid so Scotland wasted no time in annexing the islands in 1471.

Wildlife: Mainland has over 600 species of flowering plant, including wild lupins, daffodils and fourteen species of wild orchid. At places near the water's edge the rare Oyster Plant, *Mertensia maritima*, can be seen but the cliff-top home of the extremely rare magenta-coloured Scottish Primrose, *Primula scotica*, is kept secret. Underwater, the uncommon flame-shell mollusc has been found in Scapa Flow.

Brown hares are very common on Mainland and so are rabbits. There are no frogs but there are toads. The otter is not nearly so common here as it is in Shetland, probably due to the amount of cultivation.

West of Kirkwall there are three areas of heather moorland providing one of the finest moorland bird communities in Britain. Moor breeders include hen harrier, short-eared owl, red grouse, merlin, arctic and great skua, golden plover, dunlin, snipe, curlew, reed bunting, wheatear, stonechat, sedge warbler, twite, kestrel, woodpigeon and hooded crow. Lochan breeders are the red-throated diver, wigeon, teal, red-breasted merganser, eider and shelduck. On the lochs and wetlands are mallard, shelduck, wigeon, teal, pintail, shoveller, tufted duck, red-breasted merganser, dunlin, snipe, redshank, corncrake, sedge warbler and reed bunting. On the coasts there are kittiwake, guillemot, fulmar, razorbill and a few puffin. The Loch of Harray can sometimes hold 10,000 wintering duck and it is one of Britain's most important sites for pochard. Particular sites are: Birsay Moors and Cottascarth RSPB Reserve; Loch of Banks; The Loons RSPB Reserve; Loch of Boardhouse; Brough of Birsay; Marwick Head RSPB Reserve; Loch of Harray and Loch of Stenness; Binscarth Wood; Hobbister RSPB Reserve; and Stromness Harbour.

Particular sites noted for migrants with many rare ones being recorded. Particular sites are: Graemeshall Loch; Deer Sound; Scapa Bay; Kirkwall Harbour; Loch of Tankerness; The Churchill Barriers; and Echnaloch Bay.

The biggest trout ever caught in Britain (13kg) was taken from Stennech Loch.

* * *

A narrow neck of land divides east and west **MAINLAND**. This is the strategic site of Orkney's 'capital' – Kirkwall.

Kirkwall (ON *kirkjuvagr* – church bay) was established by the Norse in the 11th century but reached prominence and city status in the 12th century thanks to its harbour and its new **Cathedral of St Magnus**. This massive edifice in early Norman style, founded in 1137 by Magnus's nephew, Rognvald III, contains the remains of both its founder and its saint built into the great piers in the central bay. The transepts, part of the choir and part of the nave with its interlacing wall-arcades are the oldest parts. It is almost surprising to find this magnificent Gothic structure in a town of less than 7000 inhabitants but, I suppose, this is a true picture of what a medieval cathedral city was really like. The small houses clustered like chickens round the mother-hen cathedral. The building was completed in the 15th century and was saved by the townsfolk from destruction during the Reformation but when Cromwell's men arrived they used it as a prison and for stabling their horses. After that only the choir continued to be used as a parish church and the neglected structure deteriorated. It was restored in 1913–1930 and again in the 1980s.

Close to the cathedral is the **Bishop's Palace** which is mostly a 16th-century reconstruction of the original 12th-century building. It was here that King Haakon died in 1263 after his defeat by the Scots at Largs. Across the road is the **Earl's Palace** which has been called the finest structure of 16th-century Scotland. This magnificent building was built with forced labour by Earl Patrick, known as 'Black Pate', a man who was so ignorant that his sentence of death was delayed for a week to allow him to 'better inform himself'.

When entering the harbour from the sea, after passing the little islet called **Thieves Holm**, it is difficult to appreciate that much of the inner

Haswell-Smith .   St. Magnus Cathedral, Orkney

part of the bay, sheltered by The Ayre and called the **Peerie Sea**, was filled in during the 1800s to allow the town to expand to the west. Originally the cathedral and the Bishop's Palace would have dominated the harbour as well as the town. The shallow Peerie Sea must have provided excellent protection for Norse longboats.

For Orkney history it is worth visiting the Orkney Library in Laing Street and **Tankerness House Museum**, a well-restored example of a merchant's house.

Kirkwall was made a royal burgh by James III in 1486 when he also gifted the cathedral to the citizens. The main street is Albert Street, irregular and narrow, known simply as **The Street**.

East of Kirkwall and south of Inganess Bay is **Kirkwall Airport** set in an area of fertile fields and fat cattle, and beyond the airport is *Mine Howe*, a mysterious underground structure. The road continues to the eastern extremity of Mainland – Deerness parish – the old Norse hunting ground where the bones of red deer are still to be found in the peat bogs. Beside the road that crosses the narrow Deerness isthmus are the remains of the broch of Dingieshowe, and, to the north, the wide sands of St Peter's pool, covered with wading birds. At the **Brough of Deerness**, after passing The Gloup (ON *gljúfr* – hollow or ravine) [HY592079], a growling subterranean sea-vent caused by the sea breaking through the roof of a large cave, a rough walk of about 1km brings you to the remains of an ancient monastery which was a place of pilgrimage until the 17thC [HY595088]. Male pilgrims walked

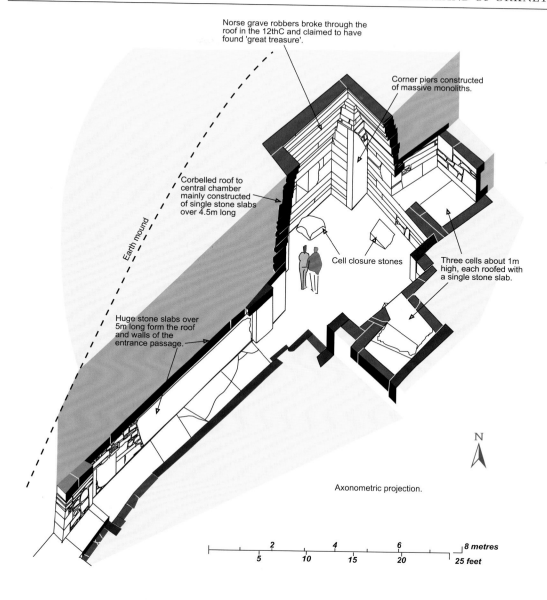

Norse grave robbers broke through the roof in the 12thC and claimed to have found 'great treasure'.

Corner piers constructed of massive monoliths.

Corbelled roof to central chamber mainly constructed of single stone slabs over 4.5m long

Earth mound

Cell closure stones

Three cells about 1m high, each roofed with a single stone slab.

Huge stone slabs over 5m long form the roof and walls of the entrance passage.

N

Axonometric projection.

2   4   6   8 metres
5   10   15   20   25 feet

MAGNIFICENT MAES HOWE

barefoot round and round the holy building chanting and scattering water and sharp stones behind them.

The road running due south from Kirkwall reaches the pleasant village of St Mary's in the parish of Holm [ham]. Here there is the first of the **Churchill Barriers**.

On 14 October 1939 a German submarine slipped past the blockships in the eastern approaches to Scapa Flow and torpedoed *HMS Royal Oak*. 833 men were lost. Britain had only been at war for one month and the disaster had a serious effect on morale. Churchill later ordered barriers to be built between the eastern islands and Italian prisoners-of-war provided the labour for this task. The Italians handled the engineering with skill and supported their faith by converting two Nissen huts into the delightful little **Italian Chapel** on Lamb Holm [HY488006]. This pious work was so appreciated by the Presbyterian Orcadians that in 1960 Signor Chiocchetti, and others who had done the original work, were invited to return to Orkney and restore the chapel paintings and interior to its wartime glory. Domenico Chiocchetti died in 1999.

Churchill Barrier No 2 crosses from **LAMB**

HOLM to **GLIMS HOLM**, an islet which provides peat for local use, and the next Barrier reaches Burray. The old blockships can still be seen beside these causeways.

BURRAY has a great stretch of beach in its eastern bay, and the Reef linking it to **HUNDA**, which is particularly rich in birdlife, on its west coast. Burray is remembered for its colourful Jacobite laird, Sir James Stewart, who, in 1725, was involved in a murder in Kirkwall. He fled into exile and twenty years later joined the battle at Culloden. He survived the defeat and considered it safe after all these years to return home to Burray. But on arrival who should he meet but the son of his murder victim who promptly handed him over to the authorities. He died in a London prison.

Cross the 4th Barrier to **SOUTH RONALDSAY**. This was the first area to see if commercial electricity could be produced from Orkney's great power source – wind – but the early design of wind turbine was not particularly successful due to the high cost of maintenance.

Nearby is **St Margaret's Hope** where there once was a chapel dedicated to Malcolm Canmore's Queen Margaret. (It is sometimes wrongly claimed that the Hope is named after Margaret, Maid of Norway, who died in 1290.) King Haakon's huge fleet of 120 ships anchored here at the start of August 1263 – the largest fleet in history ever to enter Scapa Flow before the 20th century. There was an eclipse of the sun that day which some would claim foretold the disaster that awaited him at Largs and his subsequent death in Kirkwall.

To the west is the Hoxa peninsula with a ruined broch where, according to the *Orkneyinga Saga*, Thorfinn Skull-splitter is buried [ND425940].

Travelling southwards down the island the road passes **Ward Hill**, the summit of which is only 118m high but is a memorable viewpoint. From this distance tidal rips and treacherous seas fade into a vast expanse of untroubled ocean. But it was off this coast in 1969 that the

THE ITALIAN CHAPEL – A WARTIME WORK-OF-ART

Longhope lifeboat was lost with all on board while attempting to reach the wreck of the *Irene*.

In the south-west there is another 'Gloup' [ND472856] and a burned mound [ND465841]. These are both worth seeing, but they lie about a kilometre from the nearest road. Near here the 5000-year-old chambered cairn known as the **Tomb of the Eagles** was discovered in 1958. It contained around 16,000 human bones with their skulls lining the walls and the remains of at least eight sea eagles. Nearby there is another newly-discovered tomb.

St Mary's Kirk at Burwick contains a penitent's stone, a block of whin with two foot-shaped hollows [ND439842]. One story claims that a man called Gallus prayed to the Virgin Mary for help when his ship sank. She sent a porpoise, who carried him ashore and then immortalised the poor beast by turning it into stone. Gallus built the church in gratitude.

The larger part of **MAINLAND** lies to the west of Kirkwall. The southern road from Kirkwall (A964) runs along the shores of Scapa Flow and through the **Hobbister Hill Nature Reserve**, where raptors can be seen while waders frequent the shores of Waukmill Bay. The next bay, Swanbister, was renowned in the 1830s for having a monster similar to the one which is reputed to inhabit Loch Ness (See also No.11.5).

Mainland's highest peak, **Mid Hill** (271m), is north of here and the last battle on Orkney soil was fought in the valley to the east of it.

That was in 1529 when William Sinclair tried to wrest the earldom from his uncle, Sir William Sinclair. He raised an army with the support of the Earl of Caithness and sailed into Scapa Flow but his cousins raised a local army which defeated him.

This is the parish of Orphir (ON *or-fjara* – 'out of' low water) and beside **Orphir Bay** is a tiny church probably built by Earl Haakon Paulsson, the murderer of St Magnus [HY335044]. He must have done penance by a pilgrimage or crusade to the Holy Land, because the design echoes that of the Holy Sepulchre in Jerusalem. Only the apse now remains (the rest was demolished in 1757 for a Presbyterian preaching box) but the church is mentioned in the sagas as a 'magnificent church' facing the 'drinking-hall'. The Vikings had very clear priorities!

The car ferry to Hoy sails from **Houton Bay** and the road then turns north up the coast of Clestrain Sound.

The northern road out of Kirkwall crosses a causeway and skirts **Wideford Hill** (225m) which is another marvellous view-point with a chambered cairn on its slopes [HY409121]. At **Rennibister** there is a good example of a souterrain or earth-house discovered in 1926 when a plough broke through the roof [HY397126]. The road continues along the south shore of Bay of Firth in which there are two small islands. The **Holm of Grimbister** is farmed, and **Damsay** (ON – pond island), which has several small pools on it, is mentioned in the sagas. It was in the days when Erlend and Sweyn were at war with Earls Rognvald and Harald. Erlend celebrated Christmas on Damsay with his men and then, dead-drunk, he returned to his ship to sleep. Although it was a full moon he and his men were taken by surprise and slaughtered. Tradition says that there was a nunnery on the island at one time and that no rats or mice are able to survive there.

This area of central Mainland is littered with prehistoric monuments but possibly the greatest concentration is around Lochs Harray and Stenness. By Tormiston Mill, a 19th century watermill, there is the green tumulus of **Maeshowe** (ON – great mound), Britain's largest chambered cairn and an example of truly breathtaking megalithic craftsmanship [HY318127]. A long, low, narrow passage leads into a large chamber with corbelled walls and

smaller side chambers. The passage is accurately aligned to take advantage of the configuration of the hill silhouette on Hoy. This means that sunlight enters the chamber not only at the winter solstice but also with brief flashes of light on 11 November, 1 December, 11 January and 31 January. The work has a flavour of Egyptian design and constructional similarity to the Treasury of Atrius in Greece although the proportions are more modest. The smaller chambers are floored and roofed with single massive stones. Maeshowe was raided by the Vikings – howebreaking was a very popular pastime – and they also indulged in graffiti in the form of runic inscriptions. One comment refers to a great treasure but does not make it clear whether it was Norse or Neolithic treasure. The longest inscription has been translated as 'These runes were incised by the best runester in the west, using the axe that Gauk Thrandilsson once owned in south Iceland.' Other comments are timeless in character – 'Thorny was bedded; Helgi says so,' and 'Ingigerd is the best of them all.'

Close to Maeshowe are the **Standing Stones of Stenness** (ON *steine-nes* – promontory of the stones) [HY307125]. One of the remaining four stones is over 5m high and nearby is the, even higher, Watch Stone. Only 1½km north, on the narrow isthmus between Lochs Harray and Stenness, is the dramatic **Ring of Brodgar**, with twenty-seven of the original sixty stones still standing [HY294133]. I remember seeing it at dawn washed with pale sunlight against an ominous dark sky surrounded by grey lochs and windswept grassland. And now, between Stenness and Brodgar in a new exciting project, archaeologists are excavating a massive 5000-year-old structure of a kind never before seen in Britain.

Further west, where Loch Stenness spills into the Bay of Ireland is **Unstan Cairn** [HY283117], an important chambered cairn first excavated in 1844. It produced the largest collection of Stone Age pottery found in Scotland (now housed in the Royal Scottish Museum, Edinburgh) as well as two seated human skeletons.

Stromness was a prosperous port for many centuries. It has less than 2000 inhabitants but has a very long waterfront dating back to the time when it was overcrowded and busy with ships on the northern sailing routes. From 1670 to 1891 it was a base for the Hudson Bay Company, in the 18th and 19th centuries it was a supply base

THE RING OF BRODGAR

for the Davis Strait whaling fleet, and for a short time it was involved in the North American rice trade. The ships of Captain Cook were serviced here after his last ill-fated Pacific expedition as also were those of Sir John Franklin off to look for the North-West Passage. **Login's Well**, which provided the ships with fresh water, can still be seen, and both the **Natural History Museum** and the Orkney Wireless Museum have many interesting exhibits. As for the future, a European Marine Energy Centre was opened here in 2004 making Orkney a world leader in the testing of wave and tidal power devices.

Stromness was also the home of the poet and writer, George Mackay Brown.

Some 10km north of Stromness on the west coast at the Bay of Skaill is possibly Orkney's most exciting archaeological site, **Skarabrae** [HY230187]. This astonishing prehistoric village dating from c.3100BC only came to light when it was exposed by a storm in 1850. A sandstorm buried the original village in about 2450BC, thus preserving a moment of time for posterity, and 5000 years later another storm revealed it. It was conscientiously excavated in 1928 and this has given us a marvellous chance to spy on the everyday domestic life of our ancient ancestors. The tiny individual 'houses' are closely linked by passages and each contains items of primitive Stone Age furniture – beds, dressers, lockers, hearth, fish-larder pools – and personal effects made of pottery, stone and whalebone. To the north of the Bay of Skaill a great Viking treasure was found in 1858 – the Skaill Hoard – enormous

brooches, rings, ingots of silver, and coins. The Vikings were anything but parochial – some of the coins had been minted in Baghdad!

Further north the coast road passes between **The Loons**, an area of pools and swamps and breeding waders, and **Marwick Head**, whose cliffs support vast numbers of seabirds. Both are Nature Reserves.

Marwick Head is the site of the **Kitchener Memorial** [HY227251]. Field-Marshal the Earl Kitchener of Khartoum was invited by the Czar to visit Russia and discuss the progress of the First World War. He travelled to Thurso by night-train, crossed the Pentland Firth in a destroyer, lunched with Admiral Jellicoe on the *Iron Duke* in Scapa Flow and then boarded the cruiser *Hampshire*. It was 4 June 1916. In spite of a severe gale the *Hampshire* left by Hoy Sound and turned north. Then in very heavy seas off Marwick Head she struck a German mine and sank immediately with only twelve survivors. Local Orcadians were forbidden to assist in a rescue attempt or speak to the press and the official Government report was obscure. Naturally, this encouraged talk of a cover-up and many wild stories circulated that there was gold aboard, Kitchener was still alive, or even that he had been deliberately executed. This is still a war-grave and diving is forbidden.

The north-west corner of Mainland is Brough Head (ON *borg* – broch, or the island at the end of a tidal isthmus) in the parish of Birsay (ON – broch island). **Brough of Birsay** is a drying or tidal island with extensive remains of a Viking settlement and an early medieval chapel [HY240285]. The chapel is built on the remains of an earlier, 6th or 7th-century, chapel. The settlement may have been part of a well-garrisoned fortress. This island well repays a visit but avoid being trapped by the incoming tide covering the causeway.

Overlooking Brough of Birsay is **Earl Stewart's Palace** [HY248279]. The palace was rebuilt in 1574 but this is the site where the earls of Orkney had their palace before moving to

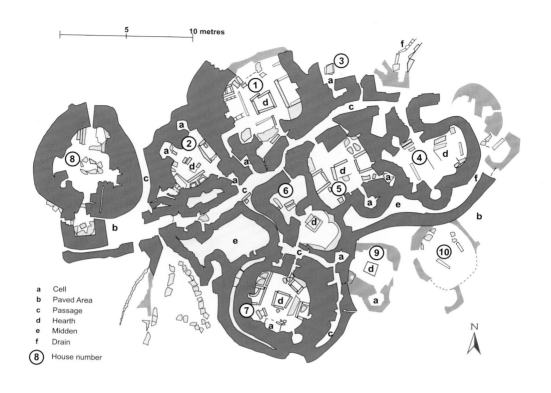

a   Cell
b   Paved Area
c   Passage
d   Hearth
e   Midden
f   Drain
⑧   House number

N

PLAN OF SKARA BRAE (C. 2800BC)

Kirkwall in the 12th century. The present ruin shows little of the original splendour.

The north coast road passes Loch of Swannay (thought by some to be the best trout-fishing loch on Mainland), and skirts Eynhallow Sound in the parish of Evie (ON – swirling tide). Here, like a sentinel on windswept Aiker Ness, stands **Gurness Broch** [HY382268]. This is the best-preserved broch in Orkney but there is a great complex of ruins surrounding it which are also fascinating to explore.

About 6km south-west of Gurness Broch by an undulating minor road is Orkney's last surviving example of a **Click Mill** [HY325228]. These were old horizontal watermills, once common in Scandinavia and still to be found in North Pakistan. South of here is the parish of Harray (ON – hunting territory), the only land-locked parish in Orkney.

*   *   *

Access: NorthLink ro-ro, 0845-6000-449;

Scrabster/ Stromness several daily, (2hrs): or Aberdeen/ Kirkwall, several weekly. Pentland Ferries ro-ro, 01856-831226, Gill's Bay/ St Margaret's Hope (1hr) several daily. John O'Groats Ferries, 01955-611353. John O'Groats-Burwick, S.Ronaldsay. Passenger only. By air: scheduled flights most days to Kirkwall from Aberdeen, Edinburgh, Glasgow, Shetland, Inverness, 0871-7002-000. Kirkwall airport, 01856-886210. There is a good bus service on Mainland, 01856-870555 or 08457-740740. Tourist information, 01856-872856.

Anchorages: Considerable care and experience is needed due to the many erratic tidal conditions. Eynhallow Sound is particularly hazardous. (Orkney VTS on VHF Ch.16/11)
1. Stromness Harbour. Enter by buoyed channel using leading lights. All-year marina (07810-465825) beyond the harbour, excellent shelter. Anchorage between South Pier and Lighthouse Pier or centre W of Inner and Outer Holm.
2. Bay of Ireland. Anchorage 4c NE of Bu Point in 5–6m, sand. Exposed to S.

3. Bay of Houton. Enter E side of Holm of Houton and follow leading lights, depth 3.5m. Anchor in centre of bay, 4–5m, sand. Good shelter and holding but restricted space. Pier has ferry priority. Tel: 01856-873636.

4. Swanbister Bay. Occasional anchorage in off-shore winds, NE of pier in 5–8m, sand and mud.

5. Waulkmill Bay, E of Ve Ness dries out 3c from head. Not recommended.

6. Scapa Bay (about 2km S of Kirkwall). Approach as sailing directions. Visitor's mooring Apr–Oct. No births inner S side of pier. Anchor mid-bay off the stone pier, clear of commercial traffic. Good anchorage, except in S'lies, which bring a swell. Untenable in SW gales.

7. Bay of Ayre (village of St Mary's on N shore with two piers). One visitors' buoy in centre. Good anchorage off village in 2–6m, or lie alongside pier. Keep well clear of Barrier and fish-farm.

8. Echnaloch Bay on NW side of Burray. Sandy beach at head with small pier on NE side. Visitor's mooring Apr–Oct or temp. anchorage in S'lies.

9. Hunda Sound. Excellent in any weather but many fish cages. Best mid-sound, in 7–11m, sand over clay, very good holding. Head and sides are shoal.

10. Water Sound. Good anchorage just W of Barrier in 2–6m or end of Burray pier, 2m.

11. St Margarets Hope (bay on S side of Water Sound). Approach with care on leading line. Fairway only 2.7m depth. Anchor in centre in 6m avoiding fish-farm and ferry. 100m-long pier on W side has 3m at end. Head and shores are foul.

12. Widewall Bay. Bottom sandy and shelves gradually. Give Herston Head a 2c berth. Useful when awaiting slack water for passage S.

13. Sand Wick is shallow and exposed.

14. Bur Wick is fringed with reefs but has a sandy beach at its head. Temp. anchorage off beach in 5–7m. Ferry pier with floating link-span. Tel: 01856-873636.

15. Wind Wick, between Hesta and Halcro Heads. Temp. anchorage in light W'lies, 5–10m.

16. Holm Sound. Temp. anchorage well off the sandy beach which heads the bay on the NE side of Burray, in 6–7m, sand, good holding but if wind is between NE and SE leave at once.

17. E Weddel Sound, SW Holm Sound. Excellent anchorage in centre of Bay, E of blockship, E of Barrier and clear of fish-farm, 2–4m, sand. Best anchorage in this area.

18. Kirk Sound. Anchorage in Mainland bay N of E end of Lamb Holm, close in-shore, avoiding fish-farm, 3–6m, sand and rock. Exposed SE. (*Visit Italian Chapel, Lamb Holm.*)

19. Deer Sound. Take care when entering and give shores a reasonable offing. Good shelter, good holding and very few squalls. Anchor off the stone pier on NW side of the Sound, below Hall of Tankerness, or off Mirkady Point, mid-channel in 4–5m. St Peter's Bay is not recommended.

20. Inganess Bay (Shapinsay Sound). Good anchorage with shelter from W and S and good holding in 6–8m, sand and shells. There are reefs and shallows off both entrance points.

21. Bay of Meil, W of Head of Holland. Visitors moorings. Good anchorage in centre of S part of bay clear of fish farm, 6–8m, sand.

22. Bay of Carness. Fringed with reefs but good anchorage in centre. Avoid fish-farm.

23. Bay of Kirkwall. All-year marina within the harbour (07810-465835), excellent shelter. Harbourmaster's permission required to berth alongside the quays. Anchor between Hatston Boat Slip and the CG lookout near W side of bay. SW side of bay is shoal. Exposed to N winds but these do not raise a heavy sea. Good holding but bottom foul.

24. Bay of Firth, shallow and many hazards. With care and local knowledge can offer good anchorage.

25. Bay of Isbister. Anchor 3½c ENE of Wald Taing in 8–10m, mud.

26. Wood Wick (Eynhallow Sound) dries out 3c from head. Temp. anchorage Tingwall pier has ferry priority. Tel: 01856-873636. 1½c S of Scara Taing, 6–8m.

27. Aiker Ness (Eynhallow Sound). Temp anchorage in bay SE of Aiker Ness, SE of Aikerness House, 1c off-shore in 5–6m, mud. Beware extensive shoal in centre and S of bay.

28. Sands of Evie (Eynhallow Sound). Rocky bottom, poor holding and not recommended.

29. Bay of Skaill. Centre of west coast of Mainland. Approach with caution. Temp. anchorage if calm and no swell (*to visit Skarabrae*). Exposed to W.

10.12 Auskerry

(*ON østr sker – east skerry*)

OS Maps: 1:50000 Sheet 5 1:25000 Sheets 461 or 465
Admiralty Charts: 1:200000 Nos.1942 and 1954 1:75000 No.2250

Area: 85ha (210 acres)
Height: 18m (59 ft)

Owner: Bought in 1973 or 1974 by Michael Holgate and Simon Brogan. Simon Brogan and his partner Teresa Probert have lived on the island since the 1970s and have brought up (and educated) their three sons there.

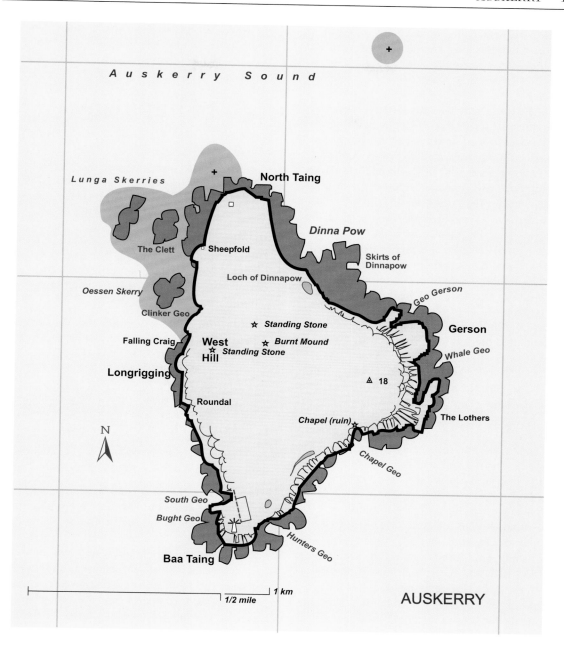

AUSKERRY

Population: 1881–8. 1891–7 (2 houses). 1931–4 (lighthouse-keepers). 1961–3. 1971–0. 1981–0. 2001–5. 2011–4.

Geology: Middle Old Red Sandstone in the form of weathered Rousay Flags.

History: This small island was more-or-less uninhabited for several decades (the lighthouse was made automatic in the 1960s) but it has an ancient history with standing stones making an abrupt statement on the wind-blown landscape,

a burned mound, and the ruins of a medieval chapel [HY677160] and evidence of Bronze and Iron Age dwellings. This is just the type of lonely outpost sought by the early Celtic Christians in their search for peace. It is a place to forget the passage of time. With only the sheep for company, the solitude is accentuated by the crashing of the surf and the screaming of the wind and seagulls.

Wildlife: A commercial flock of 300 North Ronaldsay seaweed-eating sheep. This is a Special

Protection Area with a large colony of storm petrel, and a breeding site for puffin, arctic tern, common and black guillemot and razorbills.

*   *   *

AUSKERRY is a flattish grassy islet with a rocky shoreline and a conspicuous white lighthouse at **Baa Taing** (ON – tongue or promontory at the sea-rock). To sailors it could be easily confused with Muckle Skerry in the Pentland Firth which is very similar in appearance except that Muckle Skerry has two light towers.

Auskerry is about three miles south of Stronsay (No.10.14) and is separated from it by Auskerry Sound – a turbulent reef-rimmed stretch of sea. The food and mail at one time were delivered by a local fishing boat from Whitehall village on Stronsay but in the last years of lighthouse occupation the keepers provisions came from Kirkwall. Nowadays, once again, the owners depend on a monthly visit from the Stronsay boat – weather permitting.

The inlet called **Hunters Geo** (ON *gja* – gully, creek) beneath the lighthouse on Baa Taing dates from the time when this was a favourite spot for seal-hunters. It is still a favourite spot for the grey seal, *Halichoerus grypus*, with its Roman nose, sad eyes (and halitosis) – known throughout the islands as the 'selkie'. In the late autumn many congregate on the skerries to pup and sing together.

Simon Brogan, Teresa Probert and their three home-taught sons have lived here in comparative isolation for many years. There are three small wind-turbines and some solar panels for electricity, and peat and driftwood provide heating but there is no plumbing. They have steadily extended the house which now has four bedrooms. Mr Brogan, who tends the sheep, first moved to Auskerry in 1974 after travelling with a rock band. The co-owner Michael Holgate, his wife Fiona – a former television presenter, and their son Adam have joined them on the island occasionally. The lighthouse was built in 1866 by David and Thomas Stevenson. It has two flats adjoining it, one of which is used as a store.

*   *   *

Access: Try Explorer Fast Sea Charter, Kirkwall, 01856-871225, a local boatowner in Kirkwall or Groat's Charters, Shapinsay, 01856-711254. The distance is 15 miles and the sea usually turbulent.

Anchorage: No safe anchorage. Many hazards and strong tides. Landing place in South Geo.

10.13 Shapinsay

Possibly (ON hjalpandis-øy – helpful island) – because of a good harbour?

O S Maps: 1:50000 Sheet 6 1:25000 Sheet 462
Admiralty Charts: 1:200000 Nos.1942 or 1954 1:75000 Nos.2249 or 2250 1:25000 No.2584

Area: 2948ha (7285 acres)
Height: 64m (210 ft)

Owner: Multiple ownership. The Balfour family owned the entire island until the early 20th century, when they sold the freehold to their tenant farmers.

Population: 1798–730 (and about eighty boats). 1841–935 (199 houses). 1881–974. 1891–903 (179 houses). 1931–584. 1961–421. 1981–329. 1991–322. 2001–300. 2011–307.

Geology: This is a fertile island due to the breakdown of the Rousay Beds sandstone which covers all of it except the south-east corner. Here is extruded basaltic lava and Eday Beds of Middle Old Red Sandstone, which is a much better building stone than the Rousay Beds variety.

History: In 1263 King Haakon assembled his large fleet of galleys in Elwick before sailing south to Largs but the island itself is hardly mentioned in the sagas.

Always agriculturally fertile and reasonably prosperous, Shapinsay also enjoyed the kelp boom in the 18th century. The island produced over 3000 tons of burned kelp every year, which brought in about £20,000 of income for the inhabitants.

Wildlife: In 1805 the minister on Shapinsay first noted that the Orkney vole was a unique sub-species of the European vole, *Microtus arvalis*. This little creature is a puzzle as it is found nowhere else in the British Isles, including Shetland. It is of Spanish origin but did not come from an Armada wreck because its DNA shows that it reached Orkney about 6000 years ago. And anyway, unlike rats, voles hate ships!

The best time for bird-watching on Shapinsay is in the winter. Oystercatcher, lapwing and

curlew nest on the farmland, and there are a few skua, gulls and terns in the south-east moorland. Inland is generally disappointing. In winter there are shelduck on The Ouse, an inlet on the north coast, and whooper swan on the Mill Dam, which is an RSPB Nature Reserve. Breeding waders such as redshank and snipe can be seen in spring and also various duck species. Balfour Castle woodland has many breeding birds and a variety of migrant species although the trees are generally small and stunted by the wind.

* * *

Intensively cultivated and close to Kirkwall, **SHAPINSAY** is a suburban sort of island. It is relatively low-lying with centrally situated **Ward Hill** (64m), its highest point flanked by two hummocks. The east coast has modest cave-riddled cliffs between **The Fit O'Shapinsay** in the south-east and **Ness of Ork** (pre-Norse – *orc* – boar) in the north-east. There is another minor escarpment flanking the north-west peninsula called **The Galt** (ON – boar) or Galt Ness. The rest of the coastline has little in the way of distinctive features with the exception of **Helliar Holm** (ON – holy island), a green tidal island with a lighthouse protecting the entrance to Elwick, and the remains of a broch, a chapel and a cairn.

Elwick (ON – holy bay) is another of the long line of famous anchorages used by King Haakon's fleet in 1263. As a harbour it was described by Rev Cruttwell's Gazetteer in 1798 as 'excellent for its extent as almost any one in this country. On the west side of it is a fine beach, with abundance of excellent fresh water'. The west side now has a ferry pier and a village with shops and a post-office. Cruttwell, incidentally, made an interesting claim: 'In this harbour it is high water at three quarters of an hour after nine o'clock, when the moon is new and full.'

Beside Elwick is the Victorian extravaganza of **Balfour Castle** [HY475164], with the only patch of woodland on Shapinsay. The building was completed in Scottish Baronial style in 1848 and is now run as a hotel.

The family of Balfour of Trenabie on Westray (No10.26) has a long association with Shapinsay. In the 18th century John Balfour made a fortune in India and then married the widow of a certain Colonel Mackennan. The Colonel had lent money to the Rajah of Tanjore and a number of other British expatriates were also caught in the same trap. The Rajah failed, or refused, to repay the loans so the lenders appealed for help from the British Government. They eventually received compensation, but only after John Balfour, by then (1790) MP for Orkney and Shetland, actively promoted their claim. Of course his wife, being Colonel Mackennan's widow, gained a substantial benefit from the settlement which contributed handsomely to John Balfour's fortune. Balfour bought estates on Shapinsay and several neighbouring islands and started building Balfour Castle.

But it fell to his son, Colonel Balfour, to complete most of the present structure with David Bryce as his architect. Colonel Balfour had raised a troop of volunteers and promoted himself to the status of colonel. The kelp industry had collapsed so he set about reforming the island's agriculture – squaring the fields into 10-acre units separated by open drains. He also built the attractive little village of **Balfour** populated with imported craftsmen such as joiners and weavers and the watermill which can be seen 1km north of the castle. A natural marsh beside it was dammed in the 1880s to provide the water. This is the **Mill Dam**. Balfour's improvements were generally of great benefit to the island but he himself is remembered as a petty tyrant. This is perhaps unfortunate as it was an age when many other landlords were clearing their islands for sheep.

Soon after the Second World War an expatriate officer of the Polish Lancers who had escaped the Katyn massacre, Tadeus Zawadski, bought Balfour Castle and the Balfour estate on Shapinsay. Like Balfour, he farmed it successfully, and he was a popular laird and resident of the island. He died in 1979.

Quholm in the north-east of Shapinsay [HY521218] was the family home of the parents of the American author, William Washington Irving. He was famous in his time and has been called the 'father of American literature' but is now often only remembered for his story of Rip Van Winkle. His father emigrated to the States in 1783 and set up shop as a hardware merchant in New York and his son was christened in honour of the first President.

* * *

Access: Ro-ro service by Orkney Ferries from Kirkwall, several sailings every day, 01856-872044. Balfour Castle Tour and cruise round Hellier Holm, 01856-711282. Tourist Office, 01856-872856.

Anchorages: There are turbulent tides in The String off Helliar Holm.
1. Elwick Bay. Visitors moorings on W side. Anchor anywhere suitable in the

COLONEL BALFOUR'S CASTLE

bay, but note that shores are fringed by a shallow bank. Bottom sand. Pier on W side at village. Avoid obstructing ferry. Good shelter.

2. Veantrow Bay. Exposed to N and uncomfortable. Best on E side, 6–9m, sand and coral, avoid fish farm.

3. Helliar Holm. Temp. anchorage E of Helliar Holm and clear of prohibited area, sand.

10.14 Gairsay

(ON Gáreksøy – Gárekr's island). Gárekr is a man's name.

OS Maps: 1:50000 Sheet 6 1:25000 Sheet 461
Admiralty Charts: 1:200000 Nos.1942 or 1954 1:75000 Nos.2249 or 2250 1:25000 No.2584

Area: 240ha (593 acres)
Height: 102m (335 ft)

Owner: Bought in 1971 by Val and David McGill of Cornwall, who are resident on the island and farm it.

Population: 1841–71 (15 houses). 1881–33. 1891–33 (5 houses). 1931–5. 1961–0. 1971–7. 1981–6. 1991–3. 2001–3. 2011–3.

Geology: Fertile soil over Rousay type Middle Old Red Sandstone.

History: Gairsay will always be remembered as the home of the boisterous Sweyn Asleifsson, one of the last of the great Vikings. (His story would make a great opera but there is only space here for a 'potted' version.)

In the 12th century, Sweyn's father, Olaf Rolfsson of Gairsay, had supported Earl Paul of Orkney in a sea-battle off Deerness against Olvir Rosta in which Olvir was defeated. Seeking revenge Olvir set fire to Olaf's home and Olaf and five of his men were burned to death. Sweyn was fishing in the Pentland Firth at the time but when the young man returned and saw the carnage, he crossed to Orphir on Mainland to tell Earl Paul what had happened.

It was the night of the Yule feast. A big surly man called Sweyn Breastrope, the Earl's favourite and foremost fighter, was belligerent with drink. After the Earl had gone to bed there was a quarrel and in the ensuing fight Sweyn Asleifsson killed him. Fearing Earl Paul's anger Sweyn ran for cover and appealed to Bishop William of Egilsay for help and advice. The Bishop was sympathetic and suggested that he lie low for a while. He sent

him to stay with friends on the island of Tiree (No3.10).

The following spring Sweyn visited Earl Maddad in Atholl and there learned that Earl Paul had declared him an outlaw. Maddad was married to Margaret, the beautiful but scheming sister of Earl Paul. She reckoned that both her son Harald, and her nephew Erlend, had a justifiable claim to the Orkney Earldom. Sweyn promised to support Harald's claim and in return he was paid compensation for the death of his father and given a merchant-ship with a crew of thirty men. Sweyn promptly sailed to Orkney, kidnapped Earl Paul (see Rousay No.10.21), and delivered him unharmed to Atholl. The Earl was never seen again and Margaret is reputed to have had her brother blinded and then murdered.

Sweyn sailed back to Orkney and went openly to the assembled Parliament at Kirkwall. In a meeting with Bishop William, Kol, and Kol's son Rognvald – the good-natured earl-presumptive – he explained what had happened. His explanation was accepted and after the meeting Parliament acknowledged Rognvald's authority as Earl of Orkney.

Sweyn inherited his father's lands including Gairsay and persuaded Earl Rognvald to lend him two ships. He then sailed to Scotland and landed at Helmsdale. He failed to capture Olvir Rosta, which was his intention, so he plundered and burned Rosta's homestead. Turning south, Sweyn then spent two years fighting and pillaging in the Irish Sea and followed this by marrying Ingrid, the rich widow of the chieftain of the Isle of Man.

Back in Orkney, after a further successful cruise, the volatile Sweyn fell out with Earl Rognvald, and after a nominal revolt, slipped away to Edinburgh and the court of David I, King of Scots. There he persuaded David to intercede on his behalf with Earl Rognvald. Rognvald duly forgave him and Sweyn returned to Gairsay.

Earl Rognvald meanwhile went on a crusade to the Holy Land and was absent for over two years leaving Harald in charge. Earl Maddad of Atholl had died and Harald was furious to discover that his widowed mother Margaret was having a child by Gunni, a brother of Sweyn Asleifsson. Harald outlawed Gunni but this enraged Sweyn. However Margaret by this time had already tired of Gunni and fallen instead for a handsome young Shetlander who carried her off to Mousa (No.11.2).

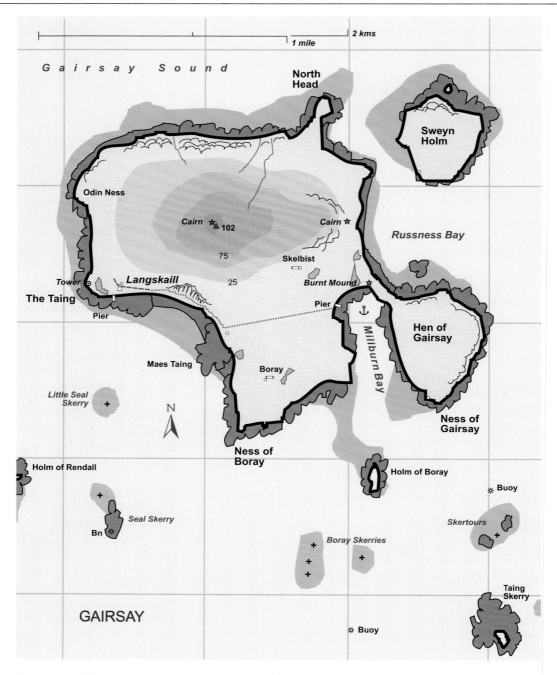

GAIRSAY

When Rognvald returned home he found Harald absent in Norway raising a force, possibly to usurp him. Sweyn and Erlend were jointly running his earldom. He sent Sweyn and Erlend north to defend Shetland against Harald and they captured three of Harald's ships. Taking advantage of Sweyn's absence in the north Harald approached Rognvald and asked for reconciliation. He explained that Rognvald had put him in charge during his absence but that Sweyn had turned against him. The easy-going Rognvald accepted this so he and Harald joined forces with a fleet of ships and lay in wait for Sweyn. As Rognvald and Harald had fourteen ships while Sweyn and Erlend had only seven Sweyn did not try to gain access to Mainland Orkney for supplies and assistance but chose instead to wait. Winter approached and Rognvald's fleet sheltered in Scapa Bay. It was a cold, dark, night with storm-force winds, poor visibility and gusts of sleet.

Suddenly out of the spray Sweyn's ships appeared and his men leapt aboard the anchored ships. Rognvald was ashore and Harald escaped, but nearly everyone else was caught off-guard and slaughtered.

Strangely, in spite of all this bloodshed, Rognvald the peacemaker eventually arranged a reconciliation between Harald and Sweyn who, thereafter, became close friends.

Sweyn returned to his buccaneering exploits which included a raid on Port St Mary in the Scillies but a few years later, in 1158, Rognvald, the good-hearted warrior-poet, died in a skirmish in Caithness and Earl Harald succeeded him.

Sweyn continued to live on Gairsay. He farmed in the summer, drank away the winter in his drinking hall with his eighty men-at-arms, and went a-viking every spring and autumn. In one exploit, about 1171, with a fleet of five ships off Dublin he captured two English ships with a cargo of wine and cloth. They let the sailors go, stitched the brightly coloured cloth to their sails for show, and drank so much that they could not remember how they sailed home to Orkney. They called it their Cloth Cruise.

The days of Viking raids were over, so eventually Sweyn decided to have one last cruise before retirement. He sailed south again to Dublin which was then held by the English. Fearless as ever, he stormed the city, captured it and held it to ransom. But the next day on his way to collect the ransom he was ambushed and killed.

One translation of the saga says: '… it is the judgement of men that he has been the greatest man in every way in the lands of the west, both in days present and days past…'

Wildlife: Arctic and great skuas breed on the heather-covered moorland and arctic terns, sandwich terns and cormorants frequent the surrounding skerries.

* * *

Although **GAIRSAY** is much the same size as Wyre, its neighbour to the north, it has a distinctive summit (102m) with a cairn on top whereas Wyre is low-lying. The south-east corner of Gairsay, which is over 20m high and is called **Hen of Gairsay**, is only attached to the rest of the island by a narrow neck of land. It shelters a cove on its west side which is the island's only anchorage. The sea south of Gairsay has many deceptive rock patches and skerries, and there are

three tiny islets – **Holm of Boray**, **Grass Holm**, and **Holm of Rendall**. North of Hen of Gairsay is a more substantial islet – **Sweyn Holm** (ON – Sveinn's or servant islet) – is probably named after Sweyn Asliefsson.

Near the end of the 17th century Gairsay was bought by Sir William Craigie, a wealthy merchant who had been a tacksman of the Earl. There was an existing house on a prominent site opposite the shores of Rendall and he developed this into the imposing small mansion of **Langskaill**. Langskaill or Skaill was the name given to a Viking drinking-hall although in Norway it usually refers to a farmhouse or store. This particular Langskaill is probably sited on top of the remains of Sweyn's drinking-hall.

The front of the mansion courtyard has a curtain wall with a walkway along the parapet and there is an arched doorway with an armorial shield above it. A bowling green used to be between the house and the sea with access to a solid stone pier. After Craigie's death the house was deserted and eventually part of the decaying building was used as a farm steading. New owners renovated and occupied the building but after the Second World War it was once more abandoned and neglected for a period until it was again renovated by the present owners.

Gairsay provides good pasturage for sheep under a tenancy agreement but this may not help the economics of running an island farm.
Access: Arrangements may be made at Tingwall or try Explorer, Kirkwall, 01856-871225.

Anchorages:
1. Milburn Bay, on S coast beside Hen of Gairsay. A submerged ridge (1.5m) joins W side of Milburn Bay to Holm of Boray. Shores are shoal. Anchor in centre, 6m mud.
2. Langskaill, by The Taing. Stone pier for owner's use.

10.15 Stronsay

Possibly (ON strjóns-øy – good fishing and farming island) – the inference being 'profitable property'.

O S Maps: 1:50000 Sheet 5 1:25000 Sheet 465
Admiralty Charts: 1:200000 Nos.1942 or 1954 1:75000 No.2250 1:25000 No.2622 Papa Sound

Area: 3275ha (8093 acres)
Height: 44m (144 ft)

Owner: Multiple ownership.

Population: 1798–887. 1841–1234 (250 houses). 1881–1274. 1891–1275 (269 houses). 1931–953. 1961–497. 1981–420. 1991–382. 2001–343. 2011–349.

Geology: Most of the island is the Rousay type of Middle Old Red Sandstone weathered into good soil and low hills but the south-west side of the Bay of Holland and a patch at Links Ness in the north-west is of the Eday variety of sandstone.

History: Two flint arrowheads found in 2007 are thought to be 10–12,000 years old. If this dating is confirmed they would be the earliest prehistoric artifacts found in Scotland. From the early 17th century to 1914 Stronsay was a fishing centre of constant importance. It was first exploited by the Dutch and built up to such an extent that by 1900 it had become the capital of the herring industry. This then declined but was revived for a time in the 1920s and 1930s. At one stage Whitehall had fifteen fish-curing stations (and forty pubs!) operating during the season, with a constant traffic of ships delivering the catch and exporting the cured and salted herring, mainly to Baltic markets. About 1960 there was an attempt to revive the industry with the formation of a co-operative to process white fish for export to the USA, but the great days are over.

Wildlife: In common with most of Orkney, this is a treeless landscape but the rich pastures have many wildflowers in spring and summer and examples of the rare blue-flowered oysterplant can be found near the shoreline at Lea Shun and on the shingle on the south side of St Catherine's Bay. A large area of naturalised Patagonian Ragwort (from south Chile) grows beside the path to The Pow, while Frog Orchids and Adder's Tongue can be found west of the beautiful Sand of Rothiesholm.

There is an enormous winter population of wildfowl including whooper swan and Greenland white-fronted geese, plus dabbling and diving duck and visiting shore-birds.

This is an excellent place for spotting rare migrant birds. American golden plover, tawny pipit, pied wheatear, Radde's, marsh and sub-alpine warblers, rustic bunting, Arctic redpoll and scarlet rosefinch have all been recorded. The lochs and wetlands are breeding haunts for redshank, snipe, shoveller and pintail and there are still a few corncrake and corn bunting nests and the

occasional quail. Fairly large seabird colonies occupy the area between Odness and Lamb Head on the west coast.

Recommended bird-watching sites are: the Rothiesholm Peninsula, where there are breeding skua, gull, tern and various wildfowl and waders on the moorland, and also red-throated diver and twite. This is one of the best moorland sites in the Northern Isles. The cliffs are tenanted by shag, guillemot, razorbill, fulmar and black guillemot and there are also many rare and interesting shells to be found on the beautiful beach.

Mill Bay and Meikle Water, which are good for observing migrant passerines, sea-duck, divers, and waders. White-fronted and greylag geese frequent the area in the winter together with whooper swan, many duck and waders.

* * *

STRONSAY is a low-lying island of rich green pastures and wide beaches. **Burgh Hill** (44m) in the south-east is the highest of several rounded hills scattered across the island, all of similar height. Many typical maritime heath plants grow on its slopes.

Whitehall is the main settlement and ferry port. Its name comes from a house built in the 1670s by Patrick Fea, a retired privateer. For over two centuries, up to the outbreak of the Second World War, this was the most active herring port in the northern Orkney Isles and the large two-storeyed houses are a reminder of days of prosperous fishing, large families, and many lodgers. Today, Whitehall is a modest little place, with a fish factory, post-office, and hotel, and a few fishing boats in the harbour. At one time there was a fleet of 300 boats in Papa Sound, fifteen fish-curing stations, and 1500 'fishwives'. Occasional whaling occurred when there was the opportunity. A school of fifty whales was driven into Mill Bay in 1834 and slaughtered, yielding £100 worth of whale oil.

The road from Whitehall joins a road which runs north and south down the spine of the island, with a separate branch across the neck of land between St Catherine's Bay and Bay of Holland to the **Rothiesholm** [**row**sum] peninsula.

The airstrip is in the far north beyond John's Hill near the tidal wetland of **Oyce of Huip**, and across Huip Sound is **Holm of Huip** with five cairns on it, a tiny lochan and many Atlantic grey

STRONSAY

seals. It was up for sale in 2002 for £110,000. To the north-west is rocky Links Ness and the islet of **Little Linga** (ON – heather isle).

Wardhill with its village and school is in the geometric centre of the island and immediately west of **Mill Bay**. There is a long beach round Mill Bay with a rock seat in the middle called the **Mermaid's Chair** [HY655262]. Scota Bess, one of Orkney's storm witches, would sit here casting

evil spells until finally the fisherfolk could stand no more of it. They beat her to death and buried her body but in the morning the corpse was found lying on the ground beside the grave. This happened several times so, in desperation, the islanders flung the body into **Meikle Water** (S. – little water), the loch south of Wardhill and it was never seen again. But it is said that any girl who sits in the Mermaid's Chair will be able to foretell the future.

Stronsay has long been a place of progressive farming and relatively large landholdings although there has been a natural change of character of the farming through the years. The kelp industry also played its part in the 18th century and circular, stone-lined kilns for burning the kelp can be seen dotted about the shores. James Fea of Whitehall started the industry in 1722 but the islanders feared the vengeance of *Nuckelavee*, a sea monster who hated smoke. Even forty years later they blamed the kelp industry for bad harvests and poor fishing and brought a case against James Fea, which they won. However, the next generation had a different attitude and the smoke from Stronsay's kelp kilns could be seen for miles.

The waters of Stronsay's **Well of Kildinguie** [HY654273] have long held the reputation for curing everything except the black death provided they are mixed with dulse from the adjoining sea-shore. However, close examination of the water may persuade one that the sickness is better than the cure.

Balanced on top of each of three rock-stacks

VAT OF KIRBISTER

in Odin Bay, – **The Malme**, **Tam's Castle**, and **Burgh Head**, – are the precarious ruins of anchorite cells. Here too is **Vat of Kirbister**, a dramatic 'gloup', boasting the finest natural rock arch in Orkney [HY686239].

The southern cliffs of Stronsay, on each side of the **Bay of Holland** (probably derived from the Old Norse for 'high land'), are rich in birdlife. It was from here that the islanders would collect the seabirds and eggs which were once an essential part of their normal diet. The Norse considered the area important because the adjoining Bay of Houseby indicates a farm which was an administrative and tax-collecting centre (ON *husabyr* – royal administrative farm). This also appears to have been a favoured area in prehistoric times as there are a number of tumuli, and on **Lamb Head**, the southern extremity, there are cairns and a small broch with a stone construction beside it which may be a Pictish or Norse pier [HY690214]. Here too is Hell's Mouth, a narrow, rocky, chasm in which breaking seas make a frightening sound.

* * *

Access: Orkney Ferries ro-ro ferry, daily except Tues. and Sun. 01856-872044. Scheduled daily air service Kirkwall, Sanday and Westray, 01856-872494 and 0345-222111. Tourist information 01856-872856.

Anchorages: (Orkney VTS on VHF Ch. 16/11)

1. Whitehall Harbour. Good anchorage but many reefs and shoals. Use N entrance and anchor where suitable S of Papa Stronsay. There is water both sides of both piers but avoid obstructing ferry. E side of W pier recommended. Visitors' moorings Apr–Oct. Alternatively anchor about 1c W of red can buoy in Jack's Hole.

2. Linga Holm (St Catherine's Bay). Occasional anchorage out of tide E of SE extremity in 6–10m. In E winds temp anchorage off W side of Linga Holm in 9–10m. Midchannel rock reported, LD 0.4, in Linga Sound.

3. Bay of Holland. Good anchorage in 3–8m, sand. W side best. Well sheltered except from S.

4. Mill Bay. Fringed by shoals and bottom foul, not recommended, but temp. shelter in N'lies.

10.16 Wyre

Or Weir [wYr] (ON vigr – spear head) – derived from shape of island? There is a Norwegian island with a similar name and shape – and another off Iceland.

OS Maps: 1:50000 Sheet 5 or 6 1:25000 Sheet 464
Admiralty Charts: 1:200000 Nos.1942 or 1954 1:75000
No.2249 or 2250 various No.2562 plans

Area: 311ha (768 acres)
Height: 32m (105 ft)

Population: 1841–96 (20 houses). 1881–80.
1891–67 (14 houses). 1931–44. 1961–47.
1991–28. 2001–18. 2011–29.

Geology: Middle Old Red Sandstone of the same
variety as neighbouring Rousay which weathers
to a good fertile soil.

History: Wyre is noted for what is possibly the
earliest stone castle to have survived in Scotland.
This was built by Kolbein Hruga, remembered
affectionately as 'Cubbie Roo', a mid-12th-century
chief and descendant of Earl Paul I. He was born
in Sunnfjord, Norway, and was established by
Thorfinn the Mighty as a *gøding*, or best man.

Cubbie Roo's son was Bjarni (1188–1223).
He became Bishop of the See of Orkney in about
1190 and he probably prevailed upon his father
to build the delightful little Romanesque chapel on
Wyre. Bjarni was also a poet who composed a lay
about the legend of the Jomsvikings which is the
only contribution to Norse literature to have come
from the Scottish islands.

Cubbie Roo's castle is
where Snaekoll Gunnason
and fellow rebels sought
refuge after killing Earl
John, the last of the Viking
earls, in 1232.

Wildlife: A large number
of divers and sea-duck
winter in the shelter of the
adjoining sounds.

*   *   *

The flat little island of
WYRE with its famous
castle ruin is mentioned
in the Norse Sagas. The
Orkneyinga Saga speaks
of 'Kolbein Hruga – the
most haughty of men...
He had a good stone
castle built there that was
a safe stronghold.' And
King Haakon's Saga, eight
years later, refers to the

last Norse earl, Earl John, being slain in a Thurso
cellar and how his murderers took refuge in Wyre
castle. They were besieged, but as the castle was
easily defended a truce was arranged.

Cubbie Roo's castle ruin is in the centre of
the island just north of the only hillock (32m)
[HY442263]. The castle is a stone keep about
7½m square surrounded by a deep stone-faced
ditch. The stonework is of high standard and
there is evidence of at least one upper floor. A
water tank is cut into the stone floor at ground
level. The entrance was from the east with a
door at the upper level so that a ladder could be
lowered for visitors. There are other ruins just
visible around the castle but their purpose is
uncertain.

North-east of the castle is the home farm, **The
Bu of Wyre** [HY443264]. The farm buildings
may have been built on top of Cubbie Roo's
original farmhouse where Bishop Bjarni spent his
boyhood.

Close to the castle ruin and farm buildings is a
rectangular roofless chapel standing in a burial
ground [HY443263]. The chapel dates from the
late 12th century and was dedicated to either St
Mary or St Peter. It has been partially restored and
is of Romanesque design showing the influence of

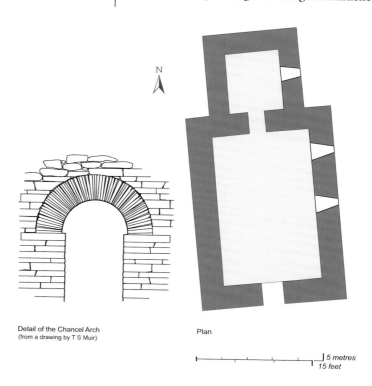

Detail of the Chancel Arch
(from a drawing by T S Muir)

Plan

5 metres
15 feet

THE 12TH-CENTURY CHAPEL ON WYRE

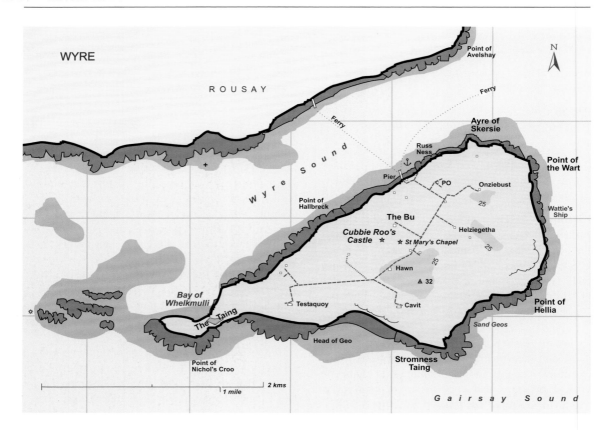

architectural ideas introduced to Orkney by Kol and Rognvald. The Vikings travelled widely and absorbed a remarkable amount of culture when they were not engaged in piracy.

In the centuries after the demise of 'haughty' Kolbein Hruga island folklore ascribed to him the character of a lumbering, well-meaning giant who could step from island to island. It was said that he tried to build bridges and causeways between the islands but the stones kept breaking his kishie (a straw basket normally used for carrying peat) which is why there are now so many rocks and skerries.

The renowned Orcadian poet, Edwin Muir, who was a contemporary and friend of the Orcadian painter, Stanley Cursiter, was born on Wyre in the late 1880s, and lived for a time in The Bu. 'I'm an Orkneyman, a good Scandinavian,' he said. In his autobiography he recalls his happy childhood on the island.

* * *

Access: Orkney Ferries ro-ro several sailings daily, Tingwall/ Rousay/ Egilsay/ Wyre, 01856-872044. Kirkwall/ Tingwall bus, 01856-870555.

Anchorage: Negotiate W end of Wyre Sound with care.
1. Wyre Sound. Reasonable anchorage E of the pier and close in-shore out of the tide. Ferry priority at pier.

10.17 Linga Holm

(ON lyng-øy, OE holm – heather island islet). Locally, sometimes called Midgarth Holm after the adjoining farm on Stronsay.

OS Maps: 1:50000 Sheet 5 1:25000 Sheet 465
Admiralty Charts: 1:200000 Nos.1942 or 1954 1:75000 No.2250

Area: 57ha (141 acres)
Height: 10m (33 ft)
Owner: Bought by the Scottish Wildlife Trust (SWT) in 1999 for £37,000 as a nature reserve.

Population: 1841–6 (1 house) 1891–0. Uninhabited since.

Geology: Middle Old Red Sandstone of the Rousay type.

Wildlife: More than 2300 grey seal pups are

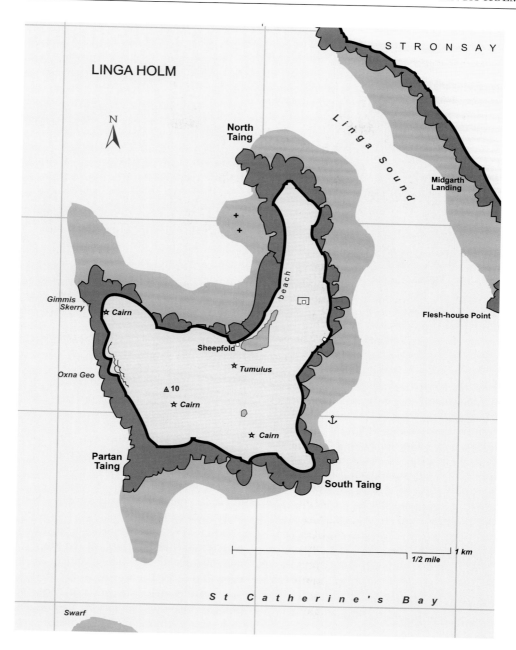

LINGA HOLM

N

STRONSAY

North
Taing

Linga Sound

Midgarth
Landing

Gimmis
Skerry

☆ Cairn

beach

Flesh-house Point

Sheepfold

Oxna Geo

☆ Tumulus

△ 10

☆ Cairn

☆ Cairn

⚓

Partan
Taing

South Taing

1 km

1/2 mile

St Catherine's Bay

Swarf

born here annually – about 7% of the total world population. Bird life is prolific with red-throated diver, skylark, several colonies of endangered ground-nesting birds, and Greenland white-fronted geese in winter.

The last owner's North Ronaldsay sheep have gone but the SWT use some sheep as 'woolly lawnmowers' to maintain an open habitat for rare wildflowers such as adder's tongue fern.

*   *   *

Stretching open its arms to try to block the north-west winds which blow at intervals into St Catherine's Bay, **LINGA HOLM** is rather unsuccessful as this small island is only 10m high at its highest point. It has had a long association with Mid Garth on Stronsay which is only separated from it by narrow Linga Sound. The Sound can look deceptively peaceful but can suddenly become turbulent with very little warning.

The eastern arm of the island which stretches

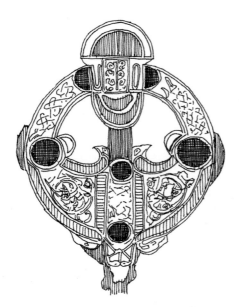

THE WESTNESS BROOCH OF ROUSAY

10.18 Papa Stronsay

(ON – priest's island of Stronsay.) The Norse called it Little Papey (ON papøy hin litli) and to the local people it is just 'Papy.'

OS Maps: 1:50000 Sheet 5 1:25000 Sheet 465
Admiralty Charts: 1:200000 Nos.1942 or 1954 1:75000
No.2250 1:25000 No.2622

Area: 74ha (183 acres)
Height: 13m (43 ft)

Owner: Bought in 1999 for a reputed £250,000 by a Catholic community of priests, the Transalpine Redemptorists, from Charles Smith who had been the owner and resident since buying the island in 1988.

Population: 1841–28 (5 houses). 1881–23. 1891–27 (4 houses). 1931–18. 1961–4. 1971–3. 1981–0. 1991–0. 2001–10. 2011–0.

Geology: Middle Old Red Sandstone of the Rousay Flags variety.

History: Following the occupation of the island by prehistoric man, Papa Stronsay became a hermitage for Culdee monks.

In the early years of the 11th century fair-haired Earl Rognvald Brusason – gallant but unprincipled – arrived from Norway to take his share of the Orkney earldom granted to him by King Magnus of Norway. This Rognvald should not to be confused with the later Earl Rognvald of St Magnus cathedral fame. The incumbent Earl Thorfinn of Orkney accepted the division of power and agreed that two-thirds of the revenue should go to Rognvald but asked, in return, for Rognvald's support and friendship. Rognvald agreed.

For several years Thorfinn and Rognvald enjoyed themselves rampaging up and down the west coast, fighting and laying waste parts of the Hebrides, Ireland, Galloway and the north-west of England.

Then Kalf Arnison, a relative-in-law of Thorfinn who had fallen out with King Magnus, asked for refuge and hospitality in Orkney for himself and his men. Thorfinn agreed but Rognvald would not and a quarrel ensued. The two Earls prepared for battle and their fleets eventually met in combat off the west coast of Hoy. Only when Kalf's six ships joined the fray was the issue decided and the defeated Rognvald fled to Norway. But later, in mid-winter, Rognvald

in a narrow tongue up the side of Linga Sound to North Taing has a building on it which has been in use as a boathouse. West of it is an extensive shallow pond beside a beach. The rest of the island is mainly open grassland rising gradually to its highest level in the south-west where there are the walls of a ruined house. Sometimes Shetland ponies have been seen grazing here. Prehistoric cairns in this area are evidence of the presence of early man but the most noteworthy archaeological item is the excellently preserved Pictish House.

Partan Taing (G. – edible crab, ON *taing* – point) is a reef on the south-west side which runs out towards the **Swarf** (ON *svarf* – grit), a dangerous skerry in the middle of the entrance to St Catherine's Bay.

*   *   *

Access: Enquire at Whitehall, Stronsay. The SWT (0131-312-7765) may run controlled tours to the island or try Explorer, Kirkwall, 01856-871225.

Anchorage: Midchannel submerged rock reported in Linga Sound and beware Swarf south of Linga Holm.
1. St Catherine's Bay. Occasional anchorage E or NE of South Taing (SE extremity) in 6m out of tidal stream. In light E winds temp. anchorage off W side of Linga Holm beach in 9–10m.

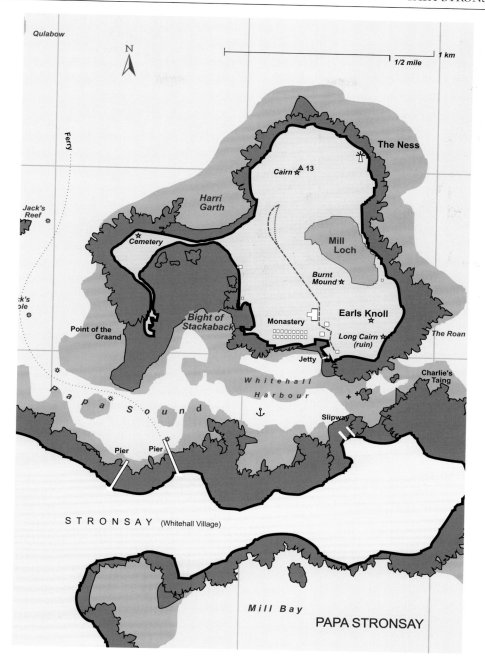

returned in a single ship and caught Thorfinn unprepared in a house in Orphir and set fire to it. Thorfinn escaped by leaping through the flames carrying his wife Ingibjorg and disappeared into the night. In a tiny skiff he then rowed across the Pentland Firth to safety.

Rognvald went to Papa Stronsay to obtain malt barley, which was grown on the island, probably by the Culdee monks, as he planned to brew ale for Christmas and hold a victory celebration, but while he and his men huddled by the fire in bitter December weather Thorfinn suddenly encircled them in flames. It was now Rognvald's turn to leap through the flames like Thorfinn, but he was carrying a lap-dog instead of a wife. He hid among the rocks and seaweed on the shore but the dog yapped and he was caught and slain by Thorkel Fosterer, one of Thorfinn's men.

And so Papa Stronsay played an important part in the history of Orkney for this episode led to

FAMOUS EGILSAY LANDMARK – THE 12TH-CENTURY CHURCH OF ST MAGNUS

a long period of peace and prosperity under the magnanimous rule of Thorfinn the Mighty.

Wildlife: Whooper swans winter on Mill Loch. Both the previous and present owners banned shooting and there are now a variety of birds including breeding arctic terns and visitors such as snow bunting.

*   *   *

For many centuries **PAPA STRONSAY** was known for its fertility and its luxuriant crops of grain. And from the early 17th century until 1914 it also prospered from the fishing industry as, in spite of limited acreage, it had no less than five fish-curing stations. These worked in co-operation with the fifteen stations at Whitehall, just across the harbour on Stronsay and much of the produce went for sale to the Baltic ports. In the 1950s the farm was producing excellent crops of oats, turnips and potatoes.

Papa Stronsay is low and flat, only reaching 13m above sea-level but it has an ample water supply from the marshy Mill Loch which covers about 5% of the surface area. Most of the buildings are in the south of the island overlooking Whitehall Harbour and close to a mound (8m high) known as **Earls Knoll** [HY668292] which contains a Neolithic chamber tomb and a local tradition that the 'skeely skipper' Sir Patrick Spens is buried there. Two noteworthy

cairns and a burnt mound are in the centre of the island and the excavated 12th century remains of St Nicholas Chapel have been found on the site of an 8th century Pictish church by the sea. Reminders of Papa Stronsay's popularity in the heady days of the herring boom are everywhere. A stone quay and a number of old piers are south of the house but only one curer's hut remains.

The original laird's house, now the Golgotha Monastery, is rambling and comfortable and the monks have built cells, a library, a small church and a cloister. They have a milking herd of cows and a further herd on Housebay farm (bought 2003) on Stronsay. In the words of Father Michael Mary: 'Commercial cheese production creates local jobs and gives us a financial infrastructure – after all, we can't just survive on prayers'.

A thin tongue of land curls out to the west and then southwards to **Point of the Graand** (ON *graand* – spit or sand bar). The whole area is very shallow and tidal and encloses the **Bight of Stackaback**. The light beacon at **The Ness** in the north-east is a white tower which is automatic and only 8m high.

It is well known in Orkney that when there is a spring tide on a Midsummer Night the grey seal or 'selkie' strips off his skin and becomes human and dances for sheer joy. A Papa Stronsay woman once fell in love with a selkie. The proof? Her children had thick horny skin on their hands and feet and always smelled of fish.

*   *   *

Access: No regular access but visits can be arranged with prior agreement from the owners. Enquire at Stronsay Hotel Hotel, 01857-616473.

Anchorage:

1. Whitehall Harbour. Good anchorage but many reefs and shoals. Use N entrance and anchor where space and depth available S of Papa Stronsay. Tidal stream slight.

10.19 Egilsay

(G. eaglais or El ecclais, ON -øy – church island) or possibly
(ON – Egil's island). In 1529 described as 'insularum ecclesia'.
The possible Celtic derivation, very unusual in Orkney, is
supported by the drying island at the north extremity being
called Kili Holm which could be (G. cille – chapel or cell islet).

OS Maps: 1:50000 Sheet 5 or 6 1:25000 Sheet 464
Admiralty Charts: 1:200000 Nos.1942 or 1954 1:75000
Nos.2249 or 2250 various No.2562 plans

Area: 650ha (1606 acres)
Height: 35m (115 ft)

Population: 1795–210. 1841–190 (35 houses).
1881–165. 1891–147 (33 houses). 1931–85.
1961–54 (15 houses). 1981–23. 1991–46.
2001–37. 2011–26.

Geology: Middle Old Red Sandstone similar to that
on Rousay.

History: Erlend's son, Magnus, reluctantly
accompanied King Magnus of Norway when he
plundered Wales in 1098 but he refused to fight,
although to prove he was no coward he stood on
the poop-deck singing psalms during the battle.
Needless to say this was not a popular gesture and
soon after the battle was won young Magnus had
to make a quick exit. He took refuge for a number
of years at the court of Edgar, King of Scots (the
son of Malcolm Canmore) avoiding all contact
with King Magnus. The Norwegian King was
by then known as Magnus Barelegs presumably
because he chose to wear a kilt. In 1103 Magnus
Barelegs was killed in Ireland so young Magnus
returned to Orkney in 1106 and claimed his
earldom and half the Orkney revenues. The other
half belonged to Earl Haakon, his cousin.

In spite of his piety Magnus was a fairly
unpredictable character but nevertheless he
had the popular support of many Orcadians.
He married a girl called Ingigerd but never
consummated the marriage. Apparently cold water
helped him to maintain a state of chastity. After
some years he lost interest in marital life and
travelled south to stay at the court of King Henry
I of England. Henry was married to King Edgar of
Scotland's sister.

Haakon took advantage of Magnus's absence
to assert his complete authority in Orkney when
suddenly Magnus reappeared with five warships.
Haakon rushed to arms but the Althing, or

Parliament, counselled peace and arranged a
parley on the island of Egilsay during Easter week,
1117. Both parties were to take no more than two
ships and equal numbers of men. Magnus landed
first, but then saw Haakon approaching with eight
ships and many men.

Magnus refused to let his men defend him and
spent the night praying in a small chapel while
Haakon camped on the shore. With Magnus was
a Celt called Holdbodi who recorded what then
happened.

In the morning Magnus came out of the chapel,
met Haakon on the shore and offered, for the sake
of peace, to go into exile – to Rome or the Holy
Land – but Haakon dismissed the idea.

Magnus then said he would accept imprisonment,
but this too was rejected. He next offered to be
maimed or blinded and to this Haakon agreed, but
Haakon's men objected as they did not wish Orkney
to continue to be divided between two earls. They
said they would prefer to kill either cousin outright
– no matter which. Haakon is then reported to have
said: 'I like my Earldom better than death, so kill
him.' But no one was keen to strike the fatal blow
in such a cold-blooded fashion.

Magnus said nothing, knelt, prayed, and then
commanded Lifolf, (who was Haakon's cook), to
use his axe to hew a great wound in his head.
This Lifolf did, and also struck a second time.

Holdbodi's account has since been supported by
the discovery in 1919 of what is almost certainly
Magnus' skeleton entombed in St Magnus'
cathedral in Kirkwall. The skull has been pierced
with an axe and the upper jaw severed.

Wildlife: A number of corncrake nest in the rich
farmland. Breeding ducks, waders and black-
headed gulls frequent the small lochs and in
winter the coastline supports many waders, purple
sandpiper and turnstone with numerous divers
and sea-duck in the sounds. But rats have become
a serious and growing problem.

* * *

EGILSAY is a spearhead-shaped island with a
low central ridge rising to 35m. Conspicuous on
the ridge is the great round tower of **St Magnus'
Church** [HY466304]. From the distance it could,
unromantically, be a factory chimney or grain silo
but closer inspection reveals the beautiful masonry
of this well-preserved 12th-century tower. The
style is unique in Orkney and follows an Irish

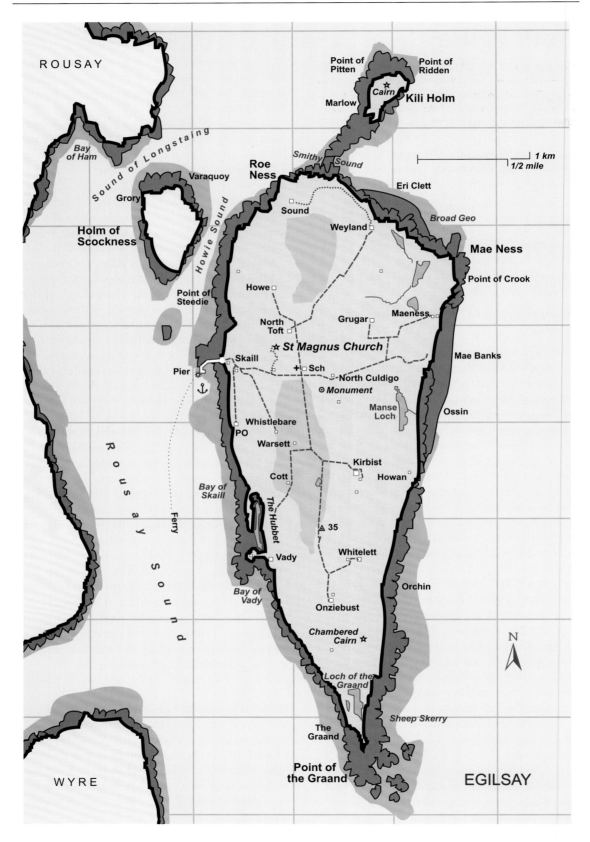

ROUSAY

Bay
of Ham

Sound of Longstaing

Varaquoy

Grory

Holm of
Scockness

Howie Sound

Point of
Steedie

Point of
Pitten

Point of
Ridden

Marlow

Cairn

Kili Holm

Roe
Ness

Smithy Sound

Eri Clett

Broad Geo

Sound

Weyland

Mae Ness

Point of Crook

Howe

North
Toft

Grugar

Maeness

★ St Magnus Church

Mae Banks

Pier

Skaill

✝ □ Sch

North Culdigo

⊙ *Monument*

*Manse
Loch*

Ossin

Whistlebare

PO

Warsett

Kirbist

Howan

Rousay Sound

Ferry

*Bay of
Skaill*

Cott

The Hubbet

△ 35

Whitelett

Vady

*Bay of
Vady*

Orchin

Onziebust

*Chambered
Cairn* ★

1 km
1/2 mile

*Loch of the
Graand*

Sheep Skerry

N

The
Graand

Point of
the Graand

EGILSAY

WYRE

ecclesiastical style of the 11th century. Even on mainland Scotland there are only a limited number of examples. The tower was reduced in height in the 19th century to improve its stability but it is still nearly 15m high. Originally, it was probably about 20m high and included several storeys. Its internal diameter at ground level is about 3m and the walls are over 1m thick.

The church nave, originally covered with Orcadian stone slabs,is now roofless but the church was in use until well into the 19th century. The walls are almost complete but they are dotted with 'put-log' holes, possibly for scaffolding, and there used to be a second storey above the chancel, roofed with a barrel vault.

This is not the church where St Magnus kept vigil before his death although it is dedicated to him and quite probably stands on the site of the earlier chapel. The place where the saint was murdered is not far away and marked by a stone cenotaph which was erected in 1938.

The name of this island with its probable Celtic connections, the design of the church and even the presence of a Celt as witness to the death of St Magnus leads one to wonder whether this may have been the site of an early Celtic monastery set in the heart of Norse territory?

There is a good little road running from the pier at **Skaill** (ON *skáli* – hall), on the west side of Egilsay, up to the schoolhouse (sadly unused in 2009) near St Magnus' Church. Here a road runs along the spine of the island serving the dozen or so small farms. Apart from a chambered cairn [HY474278] near the southernmost tip, **Point of the Graand** (ON – spit or sandbank), there are few other known prehistoric relics.

At the north of Rousay Sound which separates Egilsay from Rousay there is a small island like a stepping stone, **Holm of Scockness** (ON – islet of the crooked headland). **Kili Holm**, the islet to the north of Egilsay, is tidal. Both are used as rough grazing for sheep.

* * *

Access: Orkney Ferries daily ro-ro service, Tingwall/ Rousay/ Egilsay/ Wyre, 01856-872044. Kirkwall/ Tingwall bus, 01856-870555.

Anchorage:

1. Ferry priority at Skaill pier, anchor in Rousay Sound off the pier, 3–6m, sand. (Piermaster: 01856-872636) or shelter from W but subject to swell in S'lies and NE'lies.

10.20 Eynhallow

[**Yn**-*hal-oa*] (ON *øyin helga* – holy island)

OS Maps: 1:50000 Sheet 6 1:25000 Sheets 463 or 464
Admiralty Charts: 1:200000 Nos.1942 or 1954 1:75000 No.2249

Area: 75ha (185 acres)
Height: 30m (98 ft)

Owner: Owned by Duncan Robertson (an ornithologist) and subsequently by his daughter, Jean Robertson. She died in 1979 and Eynhallow was then bought from her estate by Orkney Islands Council for £60,000.

Population: 1841–26 (4 houses). 1891–0. 1931–0. 1981–0. Uninhabited.

Geology: Middle Old Red Sandstone of the Rousay variety.

History: This was probably the site of one of the earliest monastic settlements in Orkney and may only have been preceded by Christ Church on the Brough of Birsay. Although it was established after Earl Thorfinn's period of rule at the height of Norse dominance, it almost certainly had Celtic antecedents.

The *Orkneyinga Saga* records that Sweyn Asleifsson and his men once hid in the sea-cave (at Cave Geo?) on Eynhallow when being pursued by Earl Harald. The tide rose above the cave entrance, concealing it and leaving Earl Harald mystified by their disappearance, but the fugitives survived in the pocket of air trapped at the back of the cave.

Eynhallow is another of the small group of islands which is allowed to issue its own postage stamps.

Wildlife: It used to be claimed that rats and mice could not live on this enchanted isle but rats, in fact, prospered so well that they had to be eradicated. Not so the many common seals as these may be Fin Folk. Their enchanted summer home is called Hildaland and some think Hildaland is really Eynhallow.

On a more practical note this is a sea-bird sanctuary run as a Nature Reserve by Orkney Islands Council. Thirty-three species nest regularly on the island, including the fulmar (the 'malliemak'), whilst many others come as visitors. The fulmar, many of which live for over 40 years, is now quite common but was unknown in Orkney before 1900.

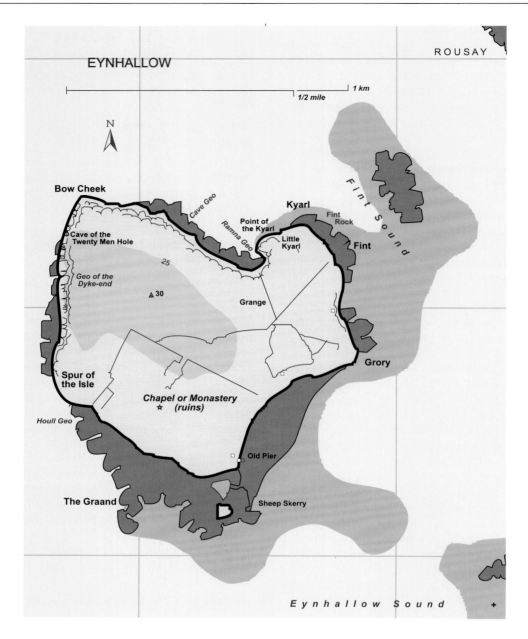

EYNHALLOW

ROUSAY

1 km
1/2 mile

N

Bow Cheek

Cave Geo

Ramna Geo

Kyarl

Point of
the Kyarl

Fint
Rock

Cave of the
Twenty Men Hole

Little
Kyarl

Fint

Geo of the
Dyke-end

25

△ 30

Grange

Spur of
the Isle

Grory

Chapel or Monastery
☆ (ruins)

Houll Geo

Old Pier

The Graand

Sheep Skerry

F i n t   S o u n d

E y n h a l l o w   S o u n d

*   *   *

With the exception of the exposed west side
EYNHALLOW is surrounded by reefs, shoals and
dangerous tides which must have required expert
seamanship by the early Christians when they
chose to settle here. The island has a compact
shape with the highest ground (30m) being just
north-west of the centre and a gently sloping
valley called the **Grange** divides the island. The
ruins of a small medieval church in what may

be a Cistercian monastery site can be seen facing
across Eynhallow Sound to the parish of Evie on
Mainland [HY359288]. Evie means 'swirl' and
the Reef of Burgar opposite the church creates
the dangerous Burgar Rost, a vicious tidal rip
that has to be treated with great respect. On the
other side of the island is the even more turbulent
Cutlar Rost.

The relatively recent history of the ruined
church is of interest because it was only
rediscovered by David Balfour, the island's
owner, in 1851. The owner cleared the island

when a virulent disease – possibly typhoid from a contaminated well – killed several of the crofters living in the small interconnected settlement of houses. When the tenants had gone the houses were set alight as a safety-precaution and it was only when the thatched roofs and timber partitions had burned away that it was seen that the stone walls formed parts of old monastic buildings – church, cloisters, refectory and dormitories. It is probable that the domestic occupation occurred at the time of the Reformation.

The church itself is thought to be early 12th-century and is a solidly constructed Romanesque structure. It is almost certainly part of the Orkney monastery to which Abbot Laurence was appointed in 1117 according to the records of Melrose.

The ruined bothy by the south shore is in fact the old 19th century schoolhouse and 'The Lodge', a summer residence clad with corrugated-iron sheet, was built near the landing beach by the then owner in the late 1800s. It is now used as a research centre by Aberdeen University, mainly for the study of fulmars.

The west coast is steep with cliffs of piled up sandstone slabs and its **Cave of the Twenty Men Hole** recalls the days when it was imperative for all the able-bodied men to hide from the naval press-gangs.

Eynhallow is an island rich in tradition and mystery and in the past was known as the enchanted island. It has, for instance, been known to vanish as one's boat approaches it. The only way to avoid this navigational disaster (so they say) is for the helmsman to keep his eyes resolutely fixed on the island while clasping an iron object.

* * *

Access: Excursions may be arranged at Tingwall or try Explorer Charter, Kirkwall, 01856-871225.

Anchorage: Local knowledge is essential. The tidal stream (Burgar Rost) S of island is very strong, unpredictable, and conditions can change suddenly. Tidal stream on NE side is dangerous. Temp. anchorage off beach in SE bay only when conditions are favourable.

10.21 Rousay

(ON Hrólfs-øy – Hrolf's island).

O S Maps: 1:50000 Sheet 6 1:25000 Sheet 464
Admiralty Charts: 1:200000 Nos.1942 or 1954 1:75000 No.2249

Area: 4860ha (12009 acres)
Height: 250m (820 ft)

Owner: Multiple ownership.

Population: 1841–982 (225 houses). 1881–873. 1891–774 (187 houses). 1931–468. 1961–237. 1991–217. 2001–212. 2011–216.

Geology: The Middle Old Red Sandstone of which Rousay is almost entirely composed has been adopted as a standard for its particular type – it yields greyish-coloured flagstones. These underlie the peat-covered uplands.

History: In the on-going struggle for control of Orkney, Earl Rognvald had landed and mustered his forces on Westray (No.10.26) and Earl Paul, known as Paul the Silent, who was effectively in control, had established his defences on Mainland. Battle seemed imminent until Rognvald asked Bishop William to mediate. The Bishop agreed, and a fortnight's truce was declared.

Paul decided that a few days' holiday would do him good so he sailed over to Rousay to stay with his friend Sigurd of Westness and early in the morning he, and a group of his men, went down to the shore to hunt otters.

The wild card in this idyllic scenario, however, was young Sweyn of Gairsay (No.10.14) – Sweyn Asliefsson – who had been rather unjustly outlawed a year before by Earl Paul. Sweyn had stayed on the Scottish mainland with Earl Maddad of Atholl and his wife, Margaret, whose son Harald also had claims to the Orkney title. He promised to support Harald's claim and Margaret's uncle provided him with a merchant ship and a crew of thirty men.

When Paul failed to return to the house for his morning ale, Sigurd sent out a search party, which found the bodies of Paul's men and six strangers. There had obviously been a fight but no trace of Paul could be found. It was only discovered later that Sweyn had sailed his new ship through Scapa Flow, up the Atlantic coast of Mainland, and into Eynhallow Sound – waters which he knew well from his life on Gairsay.

There he had surprised and kidnapped Paul and slain his followers.

Paul was taken to Atholl and given a friendly reception although held as a prisoner but later, when Sweyn had returned to Orkney, the ruthless Margaret had him blinded and then murdered.

*　*　*

Wildlife: There is a lot of angelica to be seen on Rousay – the plant which the Norsemen are said to have introduced which looks something like hogweed. The rare Primula scotica, alpine saw-wort, alpine bearberry and dwarf willow can all be seen and scarce plants such as serrated wintergreen and shady horsetail can only be found here. Muckle Water has a unique pondweed and some scarce species of plant life found nowhere else in Orkney. The elusive great yellow bumble-bee has a number of colonies on Rousay.

The brown hare is fairly common although the enormous population of rabbits is most in evidence and there are more families of otters on these coasts than elsewhere in Orkney.

The brown hare is fairly common but the enormous population of rabbits is most in evidence. There are more families of otters on these coasts than elsewhere in Orkney.

Bird-watching on Rousay is probably best from May to July. Inland and on the RSPB Reserve at Trumland there are many breeding species such as the red-throated diver, hen harrier, merlin, curlew, golden plover, red grouse, stonechat, wheatear, twite, short-eared owl and five gull species. The common sandpiper can be seen here although it is generally uncommon in Orkney.

Brings Heath and Quendale in the north-west have some 4000 pairs of arctic tern, many arctic skua and some great skua. Many fulmar, kittiwake, guillemot and razorbill can be found on the cliffs.

Great northern diver, eider, long-tailed duck, velvet scoter and red-breasted merganser winter in Eynhallow Sound.

*　*　*

ROUSAY is a hilly island and the sandstone strata have given the hills a terraced appearance. From the summit of **Blotchnie Fiold** (250m) in the south-east it is possible to see Foula (No.11.6) on a clear day nearly 100km distant on the Atlantic horizon.

This is possibly the most interesting of all the Orkney Islands and one of the best of the Northern Isles for anyone interested in prehistory. It has the added advantage that some of the best sites are quite near the ferry pier on the south coast. West of the pier are three remarkable burial cairns: **Taversoe Tuick** [HY426276] has two storeys and separate entrance passages, **Blackhammer** [HY414276] has seven divisions in the chamber (in 1936 two skeletons were found in it), and **Knowe of Yarso** [HY405280], a stalled cairn with four compartments. When this latter cairn, which is about 3km from the pier, was excavated in 1934 a large collection of mixed bones were discovered including the remains of twenty-one humans, several sheep, thirty deer, and a dog.

The pier and village settlement were built in the 1870s by General Traill Burroughs who is sometimes given the dubious distinction of being Orkney's most-detested 19th-century landowner. His home, **Trumland House,** was designed in a truly Victorian Scottish Baronial style by David Bryce in 1873 [HY428278]. The General made his money in India and married the heiress to the Traills of Rousay. She took an interest in the landscaping around the house – which has resulted in a pleasant patch of woodland – and chose a knoll for a viewpoint and on which to place a seat. This led to the discovery that the knoll was a 5000-year-old burial cairn with an adjacent earth-house (Taversoe Tuick).

The Traill family home was at **Westness** [HY383289], a couple of kilometres beyond Knowe of Yarso. It was burned down when John Traill, a Jacobite supporter, was hiding in the Gentleman's Cave on Westray (No.10.25) but was rebuilt later in the 18th century.

Excavations were started in 1978 on a number of Viking buildings beyond Westness. According to the *Orkneyinga Saga* this was the home of Sigurd where Earl Paul was kidnapped while hunting otters although there is some dubiety because not far away, at **Skaill** (ON *skáli* – hall), a farmer in 1963 started digging a hole to bury a cow and broke into a Norse grave. A young woman was buried in it with three magnificent silver brooches dating from about the 9th and 10th centuries. There is an old church at Skaill which may be pre-Reformation [HY374302].

Without doubt, the most significant archaeological site on Rousay is **Midhowe** [HY372306] which is just beyond Skaill and

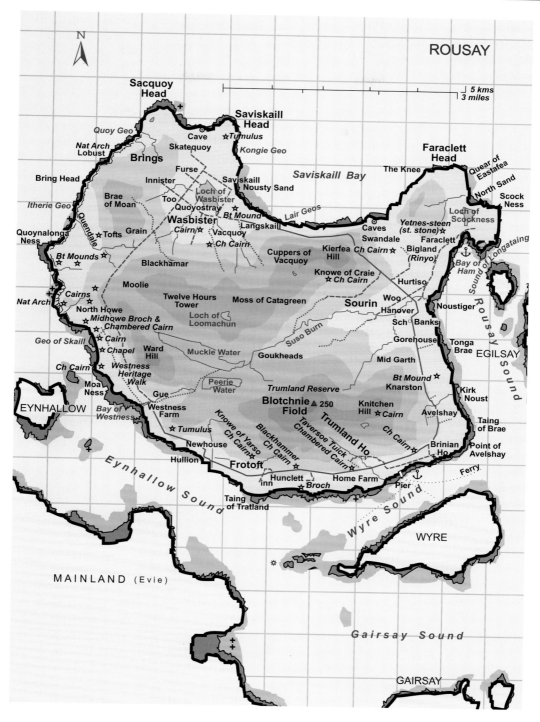

opposite Eynhallow (No.10.19). Here there is an enormous chambered cairn which predates Maeshowe on Mainland. The Midhowe chamber is 23m long and over 2m wide with 12 burial stalls arranged along each side. Unstan type pottery was found here and the remains of twenty-five individuals. There were also the remains of cattle, deer, sheep and even an Orkney vole. The original chamber height would have been about 2½m. Midhowe was excavated in the 1930s having been discovered, and the work paid for, by W G Grant who had bought Trumland House and much of the south-west of the island. It was Grant's forebears who founded the Highland Park whisky distillery at Kirkwall.

Near the tomb is an Iron Age broch [HY370307] which is over 9m in diameter and with walls over 4m high and clustered by it are the remains of later buildings like a small village. During excavation many domestic implements were revealed, some of which were of Roman origin.

Rousay is littered with the relics of prehistory. There are two more brochs in the immediate vicinity of Westness, at least fifteen brochs on the shores of Eynhallow Sound, and any number of cairns and burned mounds.

After the road turns northwards it crosses Quendale where the old mansion of **Tofts** stands – said to be the oldest two-storeyed domestic house in Orkney. The site is south of Brae of Moan [HY373326]. There is interesting cliff scenery all along this coastline due to the regular rock strata, with caves, geos, and a natural rock arch.

The place names by Saviskaill Bay on the north coast confirm associations with the Norse period, **Wasbister** (ON – west farm), Langskaill (ON – longhouse drinking-hall) and a number of 'quoy' suffixes (ON *koie* – shelter or enclosure), often applied to hillcrofts.

The north-east corner of the island forms a protuberance ending at Faraclett Head. Here, on the farm of Bigland, there is a fine example of a Stone Age village of the Skarabrae type called **Rinyo** [HY438321]. This has been dated to about 3700BC from pottery shards discovered at foundation level and this, in turn, has assisted the dating of Skarabrae. It also shows that these dwellings were contemporary with the chambered cairns.

On Faraclett Farm nearby there is an enormous standing stone called **Yetnes-steen** (ON *jötna-steinn* – the male giant's stone) [HY447327]. To prove there is no discrimination, at Swandale to the west, some rock-outcrops are called the **Gyro-stones** (ON *gyger* – a female giant).

There are a number of lochs on Rousay all rich in birdlife, such as **Loch of Wasbister** in the north-west, and in the desolate centre of the island where there is marvellous hill-walking, **Muckle Water** (big), **Peerie Water** (little) and **Loomachun** (ON – lochan of the red-throated diver or loon).

Although Rousay supported about 1000 people

at the start of the 19th century it has always been restricted by its lack of agricultural land. Only the coastal strip can be profitably worked.

Access: Orkney Ferries daily ro-ro service, Tingwall/ Rousay/ Egilsay/ Wyre, 01856-872044. Kirkwall/ Tingwall bus, 01856-870555. Rousay History Tour by mini-bus, 01856-821234. Tourist Office, 01856-872856.

Anchorages: (Orkney VTS on VHS Ch. 16/11)
1. Bay of Ham, N of Rousay Sound, good shelter from N and W. Anchor in 3½-6m. Avoid fish-farm. *(Access to the Stone Age village of Rinyo)*.
2. Saviskaill Bay. Avoid. Rocky bottom, exposed.
3. Wyre Sound. Trumland pier, ferry priority at hard ramp berth. Visitors' mooring, or anchor E of Rousay ferry pier. Close inshore out of the tide .Reasonable shelter. *(Access to Taversoe Tuick, etc.)*

10.22 Eday

[ee-day] (ON *eid-øy* – isthmus island.) Eday has a narrow waist.

O S Maps: 1:50000 Sheet 5 1:25000 Sheet 465
Admiralty Charts: 1:200000 Nos.1942 or 1954 1:75000 No.2250

Area: 2745ha (6783 acres)
Height: 101m (331 ft)

Owner: Multiple ownership since 1925. Previously owned by the Hebden family. Most small farms are owner-occupied.

Population: 1841–944 (193 houses). 1881–730. 1891–647 (138 houses). 1931–430. 1961–198. 1981–147. 1991–166. 2001–121. 2011–160.

Geology: Most of Eday is of an eponymous type of Middle Old Red Sandstone which is an excellent and attractive building stone. The fine yellow sandstone used in St Magnus Cathedral was quarried here. This is a true sandstone which is stratified in distinct slabs that are easily fashioned into blocks. It over-lies the Rousay type of sandstone except in a small patch at Backaland where Rousay Beds reach the surface.

The ridge of hills running down the spine of Eday is covered with peat. Only the narrow coastal strip is suitable for cultivation. The islands of Sanday (No.10.25) and North

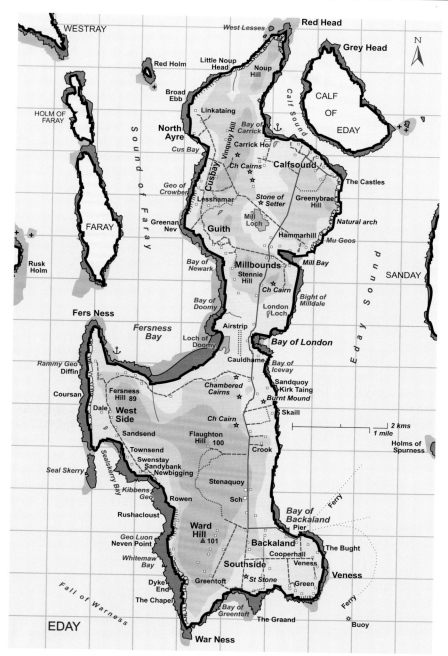

Ronaldsay (No.10.28) obtained most of their fuel requirements from Eday and the peat was also exported to a number of whisky distilleries throughout Scotland.

History: Near the start of the 17th century the youthful John Stewart, second son of the Earl of Orkney, was accused of poisoning his brother Patrick. It was claimed that he had colluded with a witch called Alysoun Balfour. Alysoun was tortured but John was acquitted and in 1628 was created Earl of Carrick. In 1632 he was granted the island of Eday and immediately set about building a home in the pleasant Bay of Carrick overlooking Calf Sound. The date 1633 is still to be seen inscribed over the courtyard gateway at Carrick House.

In 1725 the notoriously inept pirate, John Gow, after raiding Cava (No.10.8) and Graemsay (No.10.10) decided to raid Carrick House on Eday. He sailed into Calf Sound unaware that the fast tides could set him onto the Calf of Eday shore. Sure enough his ship *Revenge* got into difficulties and ran aground. He spent some time in full view of the House struggling for control and by the time he came ashore his old schoolmate James Fea, the owner of Carrick House, was waiting for him. He was arrested and handed over to the authorities. His ship's bell is still in Carrick House.

Wildlife: This is the only Orkney island on which bog myrtle, *Myrica gale*, can be found and yet it is so common in the highlands. The hills are used for rough grazing for sheep and are regularly burned to encourage the growth of young heather.

A number of otters, fairly uncommon in Orkney, frequent these coasts, particularly in the south-west between West Side and War Ness. There are lots of rabbits but no hares.

Eday has some special treats for bird-watchers, particularly from May to July. On Mill Loch there are several pairs of red-throated divers, probably representing the densest concentration of these fine birds in Britain (a bird hide is provided), and a few pairs of whimbrel nest on the moors which is a rare sight on Orkney. The moors also harbour arctic and great skua, curlew, snipe and golden plover. Fulmar and herring gull breed on Red Head in the extreme north and black guillemot can be seen on the shore. There are many migrants in the woodland at Carrick House particularly in spring and autumn.

* * *

EDAY can be dark and bleak with hills clothed in a deep layer of peat moorland. Only the southern part is cultivated and although there are many farms they are mostly small and owner-occupied. This is a long island with a low narrow waist where the airstrip is sited beside the shallow Loch of Doomy.

The north extremity is called **Red Ness**, or **Red Head**, and the islet beside it in the Sound of Faray is **Red Holm**. These names are explicit – the red rock colour is distinctive, and because Red Ness is so much higher (70m) than its surroundings it is a useful landmark clearly indicating the entrance to Calf Sound. **Carrick House** [HY567385] was built in 1633 by the Earl of Carrick, younger son of the unpopular Earl Robert Stewart. Carrick Farm and the village of Calfsound look north across the narrow tide-rippled sound to Calf of Eday (No.10.24). The Bay of Carrick is sheltered by the western ridge of Noup Hill (ON *gnupr* – headland crag), Muckle Hill of Linkertaing, and Vinquoy Hill. The remains of chambered cairns in these hills can be seen but the best example, although little remains, is at **Huntersquoy** (ON *koie* – shelter or enclosure) [HY563377]. This, like Taversoe Tuick on Rousay (No.10.21), has two storeys with separate entrances. **The Stone of Setter**, almost 5m high, stands proudly between Huntersquoy and Mill Loch, where red-throated divers can be seen among the reeds [HY564372].

A road runs southwards for the entire length of the island, from Calfsound to the standing stone at Southside. There are more chambered cairns and other evidence of early man, particularly among the moorland hills – Fersness, Whitemaw, Flaughton, Leeniesdale, and **Ward Hill** (101m), the highest on the island. Although the ferry route leads through Calf Sound in the north the ferry pier is at **Backaland** in the south-east.

The thick layers of peat on Eday were its salvation in the 18th and 19th centuries as it provided much-needed fuel for the other islands and prosperity also came from its quarries which supplied Kirkwall with slate. But increasing imports of coal destroyed the peat trade in the 1860s and the island took a long time to fully recover its self-esteem.

South-west of Warness, across the Fall of Warness where North Sea gales stir up fierce tidal rips, are **Muckle Green Holm** and **Little Green Holm**. They are occupied by a small cormorant colony and a number of nesting shags while Otter Pool on Muckle Green Holm still shelters a family of otters. The islet was called Hellisay (cave island) by the Norse and it was another hiding place used by Sweyn Asliefsson.

Access: Orkney Ferries ro-ro service every day from/to Kirkwall and most days from/to Stronsay/ Sanday, 01856-872044. Scheduled air service from Kirkwall, usually Weds. only, 01856-872494 or -873457. Tourist information, 01857-622248 or -622260.

Anchorages: (Orkney VTS on VHF Ch. 16/12)
1. Bay of Carrick, Calf Sound. Follow the white sectored light identifying the fairways in the Sound. Bay of Carrick is SE of Calf Sound Light-tower. Good shelter. Visitors' moorings Apr–Oct or anchor below Carrick House off the stone jetty close in-shore out of the tide in 3–4m sand. Avoid lobster boat moorings.

2. Fersness Bay. Shelter from all S'lies. Anchor off S shore in 3½–7m, sand and weed. Good holding.

3. Bay of Backaland, an indentation on the E coast ½M N of Veness. Pier has ferry priority but check for lying alongside. Temp. anchorage in suitable conditions 2c NW of pier, bottom stony.

4. Bay of London, small inlet at centre of E coast. Temp. anchorage at entrance to bay.

5. Mill Bay, small inlet on the E coast ¾M SSW of Greeny Brae. Temp. anchorage at entrance to bay.

10.23 Faray

(ON vaer-øy – ram island). Previously called North Pharay.

OS Maps: 1:50000 Sheet 5 1:25000 Sheets 464 or 465
Admiralty Charts: 1:200000 No.1942 or 1954 1:75000 No.2249 or 2250

Area: 180ha (445 acres)
Height: 32m (105 ft)

Population: 1841–67 (14 houses). 1871–83. 1881–72. 1891–58 (8 houses). 1931–40. 1961–0. 1971–0. 1981–0. 1991–0. No permanent habitation.

Geology: Middle Old Red Sandstone of the Rousay type with the exception of a small area of Eday type sandstone on the south-east coast.

History: A lone chambered cairn near Lavey Sound is the only apparent historic artefact on the island.

Wildlife: Holm of Faray and Faray itself are favourite breeding grounds for grey seals which can often be seen lying in great numbers on the wet rocks like over-cooked giant sausages. The two islands are jointly a Special Site of Scientific Interest (SSSI) because this is the second-largest breeding colony in the UK, with 9% of all British grey seal pups. Rusk Holm, the island due west of Faray, has its own flock of wild native sheep.

*   *   *

FARAY is part of a ridge which almost connects Fers Ness on Eday to Weather Ness on Westray. There is a wider gap to the south through which the Kirkwall Ferry sails into the Sound of Faray and a narrower gap at the north forming Weatherness Sound. In the middle, Faray is separated from Holm of Faray by Lavey Sound which dries out at low water but through which it is possible to sail after half-tide.

Faray rises to a height of 32m near the centre of the island.

A road still runs up the central axis serving the scattered empty houses. It was reported that during the General Election of 1992 three voters on Faray were unable to deliver their votes because the rudder of their boat was broken. Democracy was saved by the use of a pet homing skua which carried their voting papers to Mainland.

One of the crofts on the ridge is called 'Holland' – a name which is quite common throughout Orkney. Although the Dutch were well-known to the Orcadians the name is, in most cases, actually derived from (ON *há-land* – high land).

In the late 1930s there were eight families living on the island. They had crofts and supplemented their income by a spot of lobster-fishing. Then the Second World War intruded and a new world opened up. Comparisons were drawn and the simple but strenuous island life seemed less than perfect. By 1947 the last hard-working family had left and the island was deserted except for occasional summer occupation.

The only man-made relic of note is the chambered cairn beside Lavey Sound but it has been proposed that the rich peat bogs of both Faray and Holm of Faray should be made Special Areas of Conservation (SACs).

*   *   *

Access: Try Pierowall Charters, Westray, 01857-677493 or Eday Tourist Information, 01857-622248.

Anchorage: There are no recommended anchorages but temp. anchorage may be found using the chart. In S'lies anchor in Fersness Bay, Eday and in N'lies anchor by Weatherness, Westray to await suitable conditions for an approach to Faray. Avoid shoal area SW of Faray, and Lavey Sound which dries.

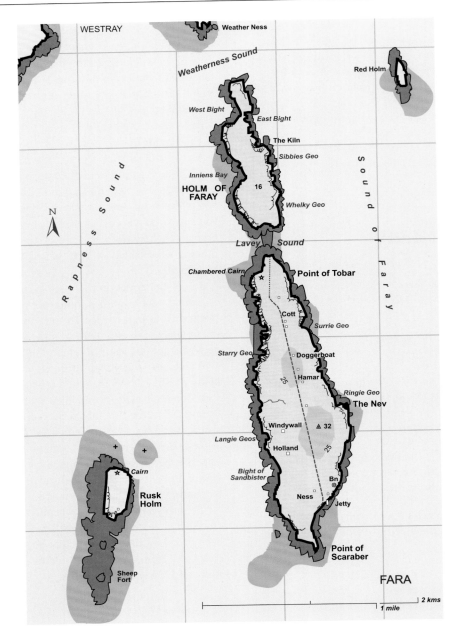

10.24 Calf of Eday

See Eday (No.10.22.) 'Calf' refers to a satellite of a larger island.

OS Maps: 1:50000 Sheet 5 1:25000 Sheet 465
Admiralty Charts: 1:200000 No.1942 or 1954 1:75000 No.2250

Area: 243ha (600 acres)
Height: 50m (164 ft)

Population: 1841–0. 1891–0. 1931–0. 1981–0. 1991–0. Uninhabited.

Geology: The island is composed of Middle Old Red Sandstone, mostly of the Eday variety but there is a thin intersection of Rousay flags on the north-south axis.

History: In the 18th and 19th centuries most of Orkney's salt came from the salt pans on this small island.

Wildlife: On Grey Head and the eastern cliffs there are large colonies of guillemot, razorbill and kittiwake, with black guillemot around the shores and moorland-nesting black-backed gulls on the

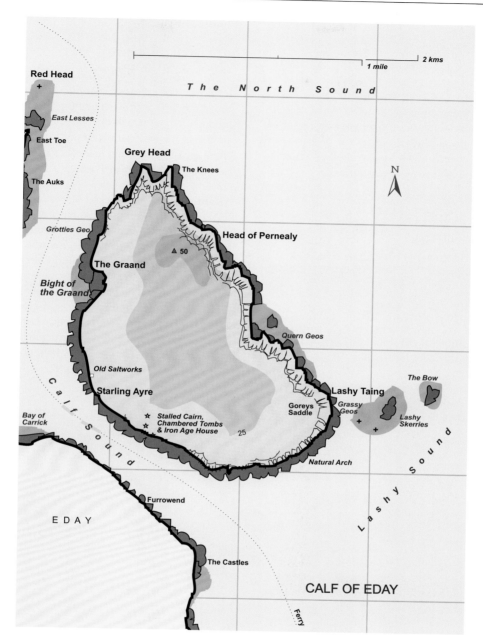

The North Sound

Red Head

East Lesses
East Toe

The Auks

Grey Head
The Knees

Grotties Geo

Head of Pernealy

△ 50

The Graand

Bight of
the Graand

Quern Geos

Old Saltworks

The Bow

Starling Ayre

Lashy Taing

Bay of
Carrick

Goreys
Saddle

Grassy
Geos

Lashy
Skerries

★ Stalled Cairn,
Chambered Tombs
& Iron Age House

25

Natural Arch

Furrowend

EDAY

The Castles

CALF OF EDAY

Ferry

heather top. A large cormorant colony thrives on the south side of the island.

* * *

Narrow Calf Sound between Eday and **CALF OF EDAY** is scenically attractive. The approach by sea from the north lies between the imposing **Red Head** of Eday and **Grey Head** of the Calf. The stone colours are subtle and dramatic.

The savage spring tide runs through the sound at six knots at both flood and ebb and in gales is whipped up into a turbulent race but at slack water in fine weather the sea becomes idyllic.

Among the group of chambered cairns on the heather slopes opposite Calfsound village, one is of particular interest as it has been built above an even earlier stone structure – whether a tiny dwelling or a tomb it is hard to say [HY579386].

Nearby [HY575390] is one of the finest examples of ancient saltworks in Britain.

* * *

Access: Try Pierowall Charters, Westray, 01857-677493, or ask Eday Tourist Information, 01857-622316.

Anchorage:

1. Bay of Carrick, Calf Sound. Follow the white sectored light identifying the fairways in the Sound. Bay of Carrick is SE of Calf Sound Light-tower on Eday. Good shelter. Anchor below Carrick House off the stone jetty close in-shore out of the tide in 5m sand. Avoid lobster boat moorings. Cross the sound *only* at slack water for dinghy landing.

10.25 Sanday

(ON sand-øy – sand island).

O S Maps: 1:50000 Sheet 5 1:25000 Sheet 465
Admiralty Charts: 1:200000 Nos.1942 or 1954 1:75000 No.2250

Area: 5043ha (12461 acres)
Height: 65m (213 ft)

Owner: Multiple ownership. Most of the farms are owner-occupied.

Population: 1798–1772. 1841–1892 (372 houses). 1881–2082. 1891–1929 (402 houses). 1931–1160. 1961–670. 1981–525. 1991–533. 2001–478. 2011–494.

Geology: Well-weathered Middle Old Red Sandstone with a greyish colour. This is mostly of the Rousay type which accounts for the good soil but the south-western extremity is of the firmer Eday type of sandstone. A fault crosses the island from Ness of Brough to Tresness.

Wildlife: The Site of Special Scientific Interest (SSSI) at North Loch includes Early March and Frog Orchids. Seaweed is plentiful around the coasts and *Laminaria digitata*, *L. cloustonii* and wracks such as *Fucus nodosus* and *F. serratus* are collected for alginate processing.

Sanday has prolific birdlife with colonies of Arctic tern, large numbers of ringed plover, and some corncrake and corn bunting. Many waders settle on the shoreline in winter including grey and golden plovers, bar-tailed godwit, dunlin, and

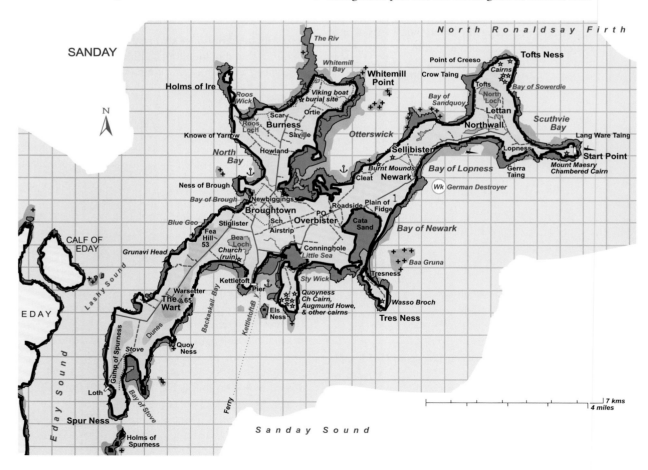

turnstone. Rats have been a problem but were, hopefully, eradicated in 2007.

Lady Parish has many spring and autumn migrants and breeding wildfowl such as teal, widgeon, shoveller, tufted duck, red-breasted merganser, eider and some breeding waders. At Gump of Spurness there are Arctic skua and short-eared owl.

*   *   *

Eric Linklater thought that, from the air, **SANDAY** looked like a fossilised, gigantic bat but we can be sure that the Norsemen never saw it from this angle. There are three peninsulas projecting from a common central base. The island is low-lying, the highest point being **The Wart** (65m) (The Ward or lookout point) and the peninsulas divide the long coastline into a large number of fairly shallow and exposed bays with beautiful wide white sandy beaches. These are usually deserted except for multitudes of wading birds. From a comparison with old maps it is possible that the sand-banks are slowly being extended by the sea and that the island is growing although in Otterswick the remains of a submerged willow forest dating from 5000BC show that the sea-level has risen by three metres.

In dark misty weather this low sprawling island is virtually invisible from the sea. Consequently, as there is no peat on the island, wrecks of wooden ships were very welcome and it is even said that prayers in church asked for the Lord's assistance in this respect.

The light, sandy soil is very fertile. It is tied in at the coasts by the roots of marram grass although thousands of rabbits do their best to disturb this delicate balance. A golf course spreads across the dunes of the Plain of Fidge at Newark. Kelp was the major industry in the 18th century with one quarter of Orkney's total production coming from Sanday. When the kelp boom died it was of little concern as during the 19th century the farms here were the most prosperous in Orkney. It is still productive but nowadays the farming is possibly more relaxed and supplemented by lobster-fishing and seaweed-gathering for alginate.

Although there are a few small lochs, the sandy soil is not good at retaining moisture, and as the rainfall is sometimes low water shortage can be a problem.

For many centuries agriculture took precedence over the preservation of ancient monuments on Sanday so there are few visible ruins although almost every ness has the faint trace of a broch. **Els Ness**, which at one time would have been a separate island but is now connected by an ayre, is on the south coast overlooking Sanday Sound. It has escaped the plough and is spattered with cairns like convex craters on the surface of the moon. Here there is a very interesting chambered cairn (central chamber and six cells) at **Quoyness** (ON – hut or shelter headland) which is the largest such cairn yet excavated in Orkney (key available at Lady post-office). Bones found in it were radiocarbon dated to about 2900BC [HY676378].

Stone Age burial mounds were treated with fear by the old crofters. This was because every mound had a resident hogboon. Hogboons are bad-tempered and untrustworthy and can cause a lot of trouble. At Hellihowe on Sanday one hogboon created so much trouble that the desperate farmer sold the croft and moved out. But as he carried his possessions into his new crofthouse the hogboon stuck its head out of a kirn and said: 'We're gettan a fine day tae flit on, guidman.'

Maybe the most interesting relic yet found is that of a Viking ship-burial north-east of **Scar** (ON – cleft) on the north-central peninsula of Burness [HY678458]. This was discovered in 1991 when about half the boat (6.5m long) had already been washed away by the sea. But the remaining – lengthwise – half contained a compartment with the skeletal remains of a man, a woman and a child. Beside the man was a sword, a quiver of arrows and some bone gaming pieces. Beside the woman were two spindle whorls, a pair of shears and some iron objects which might be parts of a wooden box. There was also a decorated whalebone plaque, a sickle, a brooch and some other remains possibly of textiles.

Scar itself is the site of the **Saville Stone**, a 20-ton block of Scandinavian gneiss – an obvious glacial erratic. It is said that this was thrown by a furious witch on Eday at a man on Sanday with whom her daughter had eloped. She missed, and the couple lived happily ever after.

At the eastern extremity of Sanday, the lighthouse stands above Tobacco Rock on the tidal island of **Start Point**. First built in 1802 by Thomas Smith, it was fitted with the first revolving light in Scotland by his stepson, Robert Stevenson, in 1806. The tower was rebuilt in 1870.

* * *

Access: Orkney Ferries daily ro-ro service, Kirkwall/Eday/Sanday, 01856-872044. Scheduled air service from Kirkwall, 01856-872494 or -873457.

Anchorages: (Orkney VTS on VHF Ch.16/12)
1. Kettletoft Bay. Check berth availability to lie alongside ferry pier on W side of bay, 3.5m depth at head, or anchor in bay in 4m. Approach bay using leading line. Very exposed. SE and S'lies bring in a swell.
2. Otterswick, on N coast. Large shallow bay. On entering give shores a wide berth. Good shelter but quite uncomfortable in N and E winds. Anchor to suit wind direction.
3. North Bay, on W coast, S of Holms of Ire. Enter from NW. Anchor in 3–5m. Exposed to W'lies.
4. Loth. Local ferry priority. Check berth availability to lie alongside pier.

10.26 Westray

(ON vestr-øy – western island).

O S Maps: 1:50000 Sheet 5 1:25000 Sheet 464
Admiralty Charts: 1:200000 No.1942 or 1954 1:75000 No.2249 1:37500 No.2622 NW coast

Area: 4713ha (11646 acres)
Height: 169m (554 ft)

Owner: Multiple ownership. Most of the larger farms are owner-occupied. Westray has a policy of giving local Orcadians first refusal when farms are for sale.

Population: 1841–1791 (387 houses). 1881–2200. 1891–2108 (433 houses). 1911–1668. 1931–1269. 1961–872. 1981–701. 1991–704. 1998–600. 2001–563. 2011–588.

Geology: Westray is entirely composed of Middle Old Red Sandstone of the Rousay Beds variety. The harder bedrock has a bluish colour, but most of the rock is a greystone flag which used to be used for building and slating. There is only a limited quantity of poor-grade peat and most of the island is fertile soil.

History: Earl Rognvald landed on Westray in 1136 on his second expedition to Orkney and gained the submission of the two local chieftains, Kugi of Rapness and Helgi of Hofn (Hofn – 'haven' – was the old name for Pierowall).

During the Reformation, in the mid-16th century, the last Catholic Bishop of Orkney, Adam Bothwell, followed the example of many of his brethren at the time and bestowed part of the Church lands, the island of Westray, on his sister Margaret and her husband. Margaret was married to Gilbert Balfour, scion of an ancient Fife family and one who, as Master of the Household to Mary Queen of Scots, had been involved in the murder of Mary's husband, Darnley, in 1567. (He had previously been implicated in the murder of Cardinal Beaton in 1546.) Gilbert, who was also Sheriff of Orkney and Captain of Kirkwall Castle, immediately set about building a magnificent castle in his new domain. It is possible that the ground-work was already there in the form of an unfinished castle started by Bishop Thomas Tulloch a century earlier. However, in due course Noltland Castle was completed and after Mary had married the Earl of Bothwell she instructed Gilbert to make it ready for the reception of herself and her new husband. At the same time she created him Duke of Orkney.

Mary was deposed before her visit could take place but Bothwell fled north to Orkney hoping for refuge. Gilbert, though, refused to let him stay and as he also failed to find shelter in Shetland, he had to sail on to Bergen, where he was arrested and given a life sentence in a Danish prison.

Gilbert Balfour meanwhile joined an uprising in favour of the exiled Queen but it was defeated and he was found guilty of treason. He fled to Sweden but could not resist being involved in a plot against the Swedish King for which he was arrested and executed.

In spite of all Gilbert's unfortunate conspiracies and Lord Robert Stewart's occupation of Noltland Castle for a time, the Balfour family held on to Westray and their ownership of the island continued for many generations. This might be attributed to the fact that Bishop Bothwell after his deposition as a Catholic Bishop suddenly chose to become a staunch Protestant.

Wildlife: Common plant species are bird's-foot trefoil, lady's smock, bog orchis, grass of parnassus, butterwort, eyebright and scabious. In the spring there are primroses everywhere including examples of the rare *Primula scotica*.

SEABIRDS GALORE AT THE NOUP

can be seen on the rocky foreshore, with sanderling in the sandy bays. The most interesting time is possibly mid-May to mid-July.

Other sites of interest are Stanger Head for puffin, Aikerness Peninsula for black guillemot and Loch of Burness near Pierowall which is the northernmost habitat of the little grebe. Here also are mute swan, teal, shoveller, tufted duck, moorhen, coot, snipe and redshank.

Although the hills and sea-cliffs of **WESTRAY** are not as high as others in the Orkneys, they are very impressive and beautiful. In fact there is such a diversity of scenery that this is often called the 'Queen of the North Isles'. The inhabitants are also noted for their own distinctive brand of 'bloody-Mary' humour.

In the south-west are three cairn-pimpled hills, Knucker Hill, Gallo Hill and **Fitty Hill** which is the highest point on the island at 169m. South of Fitty Hill on the road to Inga Ness is the deserted village of Netherhouse, a favourite of artists and photographers; and beyond it, at the Bay of Kirbist, is a stimulating cliff-top walk all the way to **Noup Head** (ON *gnupr* – craggy headland) which projects into the Atlantic and towers above the swell – when it can be seen through the clouds of wheeling seabirds. (Allow 3½hrs walking time.)

To the east is Bay of Noup and Rack Wick culminating at **Bow Head**, the northern extremity of a dangerous but dramatic coastline. Near Bow Head are **The Querns of Aikerness** which is a huge cauldron surrounded by rock pillars and arches.

South of the airstrip at Aikerness and overlooking the tidal race in Papa Sound is **Bay of Skaill** (ON *skáli* – hall).

The cliffs in this region and on the west coast in particular are riddled with caves. One of the most famous of these is **Gentlemen's Cave** on the south side of Noup Head [HY398486]. The Westray islanders are said to have been the only Orcadians who supported the Jacobite cause and after the defeat at Culloden in 1746 a number of the local lairds are thought to have hidden in this cave throughout the winter to avoid Hanoverian vengeance. Among them was one of the Balfours

Mice, and the Orkney vole, are common but otters are only occasionally to be seen. The first rats only appeared on the island during the Second World War after an enemy grain ship ran onto the rocks.

The seabird colonies on the west coast are probably the main interest for bird-watchers. The cliffs between Noup Head RSPB Reserve and Inga Ness are packed with birds including some 60,000 guillemot, 3000 razorbill, and 30,000 pairs of kittiwake, as well as shag, puffin, black guillemot and occasional continental migrants. On the inland heath near the cliffs there are about 2000 pairs of arctic tern, fifty pairs of arctic skua, and eider, oystercatcher, ringed plover and four species of gull. On the lochs and wetland areas there are breeding wildfowl and waders many of which over-winter here. A few corncrake can be heard. In winter, purple sandpiper and turnstone

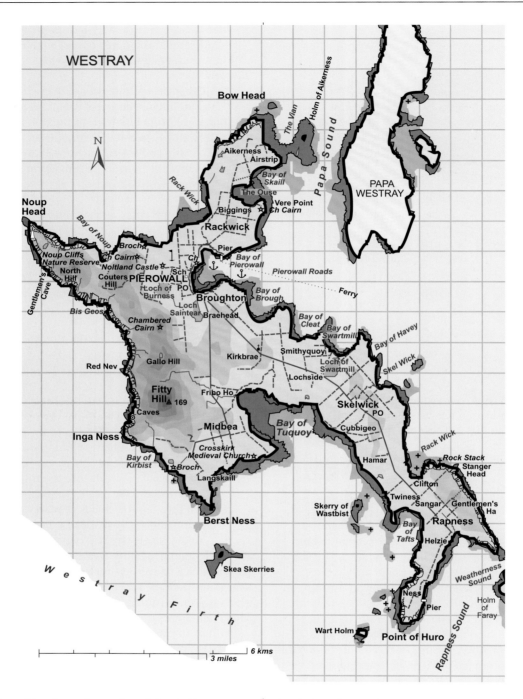

WESTRAY

N

Bow Head

Holm of Aikerness

Papa Sound

The Vian

Aikerness
Airstrip

Bay of
Skaill

The Ouse

Vere Point
Ch Cairn

Biggings

Rackwick

PAPA
WESTRAY

Noup
Head

Rack Wick

Pier

Bay of
Pierowall

Pierowall Roads

Bay of Noup

Broch

Ch Cairn

Noup Cliffs
Nature Reserve

North
Hill

Noltland Castle

Couters
Hill

Ch

Sch

PIEROWALL

PO

Ferry

Gentlemen's
Cave

Loch of
Burness

Loch
Saintear

Broughton

Bay of
Brough

Bis Geos

Braehead

Bay of
Cleat

Chambered
Cairn

Bay of
Swartmill

Bay of Havey

Red Nev

Gallo Hill

Kirkbrae

Smithyquoy

Loch of
Swartmill

Skel Wick

Lochside

Fitty
Hill △ 169

Fribo Ho.

Skelwick
PO

Caves

Cubbigeo

Inga Ness

Midbea

Bay of
Tuquoy

Rack Wick

Rock Stack

Crosskirk
Medieval Church

Hamar

Stanger
Head

Bay of
Kirbist

Broch

Clifton

Langskaill

Twiness

Sangar

Gentlemen's
Ha

Skerry of
Wastbist

Rapness

Berst Ness

Bay of
Tafts

Helzie

Skea Skerries

Weatherness
Sound

Ness

Holm
of
Faray

Pier

Westray Firth

6 kms

3 miles

Wart Holm

Point of Huro

Rapness Sound

of Trenabie whose descendant John Balfour
became landowner of a large part of Shapinsay
(No.10.12) in the 18th century. For many years
after the uprising supporters would meet in the
cave to drink the health of the 'King over the
Water'. For the inexperienced it is a fairly risky
climb down to the cave.

The principal village is **Pierowall** tucked in to
the sheltered Bay of Pierowall. Viking graves dating
back to 800 have been found here and there are
the remains of an ancient church, **Lady Kirk**.
Another church ruin, **Cross Kirk**, also of the
Norse period, is about 6km to the west, at Tuquoy.

On the slope of a hill west of the village is
mysterious **Noltland Castle** [HY429487].
Mysterious, because it is unclear why such a

mammoth structure was ever built by Gilbert Balfour. It stands alone like a man-of-war, a great stone fort with walls 2m thick pierced with tiers of gun-loops. It could have withstood a massive siege – but who would want to attack it? Gilbert Balfour, of course, had the character of a robber-baron so possibly he and his brother-in-law, the Bishop-about-to-be-deposed, had dreams of starting up their own mini-kingdom in Orkney using the combined fortresses of Noltland and Kirkwall.

A menacing inscription is over the arched doorway – 'When I see the blood I will pass over you in the night.'

On a lighter note, the length of festivity following a wedding in the Northern Isles is renowned. The longest wedding party on record was held at Noltland Castle. It continued from Martinmas to Candlemas without a break – three months!

Another Skarabrae-type Stone Age village was excavated, on the shore near the golf course at Links of Noltland. Further excavation in 2009 discovered a tiny crude sandstone figurine – Orkney Venus – carved about 4,800 years ago, a further broken one was found in 2010 and another in 2012. These are the earliest known representations of a human in Scotland. The site has been backfilled to protect it. Nearby are the Queen o' Howe broch and the Lum Head chambered tomb. Further south, at **Knowe of Skea** near Inga Ness, the discovery of a large well-preserved 5,000-year-old Stone Age tomb similar to Maes Howe (see No.10.11) is also proving of great interest.

A road runs the length of Westray from the airstrip in the north to near the southern extremity of **Point of Huro**, where the tiny islet of **Wart Holm** lies near Rull Rost, a frenetic tidal rip in the middle of the Westray Firth.

Westray plans to go entirely 'green' and use nothing but energy from wind, wave, tide, solar panels, methane from waste and, possibly, fuel made from rapeseed and sugar beet. The first large wind turbine, nearly 70m high, was erected in 2009.

*   *   *

Access: Orkney Ferries daily ro-ro services Kirkwall/ Westray, 01856-872044. Scheduled air service Kirkwall/ Westray and Papa Westray, 01856-872494 or -873457.

Anchorages:

1. Bay of Swartmill, Papa Sound. Occasional anchorage in off-shore winds but holding unreliable.
2. Bay of Cleat. As above.
3. Bay of Brough. As above but sheltered from SE'lies if Pierowall uncomfortable.
4. Pierowall Harbour. Easy access, well-sheltered 17-berth marina (07810-465784), 1m to 3m, depth. May–Sept. only. VH Ch. 14 for piermaster. Anchor SE of pier off S shore in 5m, sand and weed. Also possible clear of pier but restricted space.
5. Bay of Skaill. Shallow and not recommended.
6. Bay of Tuquoy on S coast. Temp. anchorage in settled weather, sand, 3–6m. Exposed, but negligible tidal stream.
7. Rapness Sound. Useful anchorage in N'lies only. Good holding. Alongside pier possible VHF Ch. 14 for piermaster.
8. Rack Wick too deep and Skel Wick has rocky bottom. Neither is suitable.

10.27 Papa Westray

(ON papøy meiri – big Papay or priest's island.) Known as 'Papay' to the Orcadians.

O S Maps: 1:50000 Sheet 5 1:25000 Sheet 464
Admiralty Charts: 1:200000 No.1942 or 1954 1:75000 No.2249 or 2250 1:37500 No.2622

Area: 918ha (2268 acres)
Height: 48m (157 ft)

Owner: Belonged to the Traill family for three centuries but now in multiple ownership.

Population: 1841–340 (69 houses). 1881–345. 1891–337 (76 houses). 1931–237. 1961–139. 1981–92. 1991–85. 2001–65. 2011–90.

Geology: The geology of Papa Westray is similar to that of Westray – Middle Old Red Sandstone of Rousay Beds with a fertile soil.

History: According to the *Orkneyinga Saga*, after Earl Rognvald Brusasson was murdered by his uncle in 1046 he was buried on Papay, but the location of his grave is a mystery. It is thought by some to be in the vicinity of Munkerhoose because an ornate cross with a gilt finish was found there in the St Boniface churchyard.

In 1567 Gilbert Balfour, Master of the Queen's Household, Captain of Kirkwall Castle and Sheriff of Orkney, and Margaret, his wife, were granted both Papa Westray and Westray by Margaret's brother, Adam Bothwell, Bishop of

Orkney. The Westrays belonged to the Catholic church but with the Reformation came a rapid disposal of church lands. Gilbert (together with his two brothers) had been implicated in the murder of Cardinal Beaton in 1546 and also the later murder of Darnley, Mary Queen of Scots' husband.

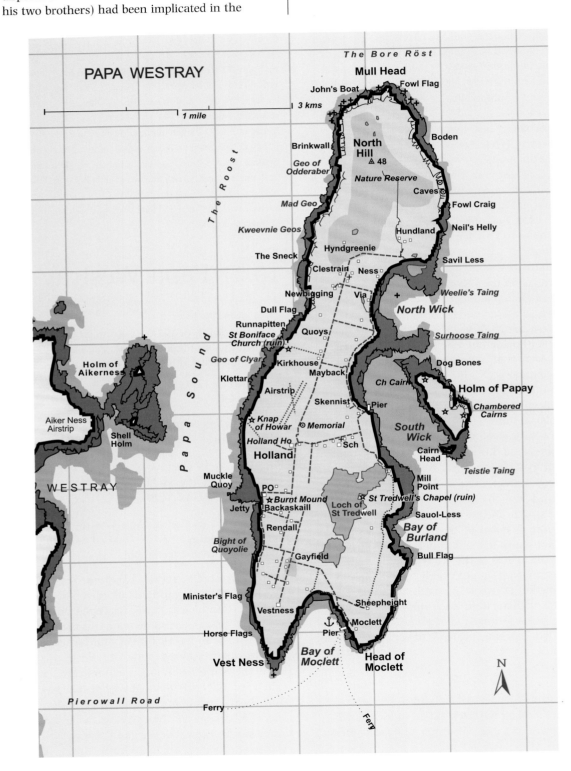

Wildlife: The dwarf shrub-heath in the north of the island is rich in herbs and specialised plants which will only grow on Old Red Sandstone. Among them is the Scottish primrose, *Primula scotica*, which has a purple flower with a yellow eye.

The low cliffs on the east coast were possibly one of the last breeding sites of the great auk before its extinction. Early in the 19th century a pair nested here, but the female died or was killed and the male bird was shot in 1813.

Some rare migrants have been recorded on Papa Westray particularly during easterlies in spring and autumn.

The best sites are: North Hill RSPB Reserve. This is the largest ternery in Europe with about 100,000 Arctic tern and some common and sandwich tern. There are also arctic skua (constantly nagging the terns), eider, four gull species, several wader species, and colonies of guillemot, kittiwake, razorbill, puffin and some black guillemot. Sooty shearwater and long-tailed skua can be seen at sea.

Holm of Papa: here there is, possibly, the largest breeding colony of black guillemot in Britain – some 130 pairs at the last count. There are also gulls, terns and some storm petrel.

Loch of St Tredwell: this was a former breeding site of the red-necked phalarope and many varieties of wildfowl and waders breed here.

Mid-May to July, and August to mid-October, are the best bird-watching times.

* * *

The attractive 'priest' island of **PAPA WESTRAY** has a long association with early Christianity. In fact it is claimed that this was the fountainhead of Christianity in Orkney.

But it has a much longer association with early man. The **Knap of Howar** on the west coast is a settlement that has been dated to about 3700BC [HY483518]. Two solidly built stone houses, which are thought to be the oldest preserved domestic dwellings in northern Europe, stand side by side, facing the turbulent 'Rôst' of Papa Sound. They are near the airstrip and the **House of Holland** (ON *há-land* – high land), former home of the Traills of Holland, past owners of the entire island [HY488515]. **Beltane House** is a nearby group of cottages which has been converted to a Youth Hostel, guest accommodation and a shop.

The flight across Papa Sound from Westray is the shortest scheduled air-flight in the world according to the *Guinness Book of Records*. It normally takes 96 seconds but was once accomplished in fifty-eight seconds; the distance between the two airstrips is less than the length of Glasgow's main runway.

North of the airfield is Munkerhoose religious site where the early Christian anchorites probably set up camp. The beautifully-restored pre-Reformation **Church of St Boniface** is built on the site of a much earlier building [HY488527]. Boniface was known as the 'German Apostle' for as a missionary bishop he converted much of Germany to Christianity. Several stone Celtic crosses from the graveyard can now be seen in the Tankerness Museum at Kirkwall and the Royal Scottish Museum at Edinburgh. A Viking grave remains on the site with a carved hog-backed gravestone of Red Sandstone. Nearby, a roundhouse (c.900BC) has recently been excavated where the cliffs are being eroded by the sea.

Papa Westray's fertile soil supports a number of active smallholdings, although some are now owned by absentee Westray farmers. To encourage tourism the islanders have constructed a 9-hole golf course with an old bath, flagless greens and lots of sheep as hazards. Players then hop over to Westray by air to finish the challenging 18-hole game.

The north of the island is devoted to the RSPB's famous **North Hill Nature Reserve**, a wonderland for bird-watchers. **North Hill** is the island's highest point at 48m. Beneath the low cliffs of the northern tip, Mull Head, there is a notoriously dangerous tidal race called 'The Bore'. During gales even the sea bottom 40m below the surface is savagely scoured by the cross-currents, and erosion is almost continuous.

The large expanse of the Loch of St Tredwell, with many wildfowl nesting on its shallow shores, is at the opposite end of the island. On a small peninsula on its east bank is a tiny ruined chapel, the **Chapel of St Tredwell** [HY496509]. Triduana or Tredwell was a devout 8th-century Celtic girl who is said to have lived alone on this little peninsula. Nechtan, King of the Picts, told her that he was aroused to passion by her beautiful eyes and attempted to rape her but his ardour was quickly dampened when she plucked out her eyes and handed them to him. It is said that this proves that spiritual attributes are more

important to a true Christian than physical ones.
The blind girl was later rewarded by being made
abbess of a nunnery at Restalrig in Midlothian
and in due course she was canonised.

The chapel, which is dedicated to her, became
by the 12th century a place of pilgrimage for
anyone with eye troubles. There used to be a
spring beside it where pilgrims would bathe
their eyes. Bishop John of Caithness claimed to
have regained his sight here in 1201 after being
blinded by Earl Harald.

The east coast has two large bays, North and
South Wick, which are separated by an islet,
Holm of Papay. Even this tiny piece of Orkney
has its remnants of prehistory for there are
several cairns and the largest is a chambered
cairn, 20m long [HY509518]. The walls are as
thick as those of Midhowe (See Rousay No.10-
21). There is a narrow central chamber with
compartments at each end and small cells
opening off it – ten single and two double cells.
On the walls are unusual 'eyebrow' decorations.
The cairn was first opened in 1849 but no
human remains were found in it. However, it is
contemporary with the houses at Knap of Howar
– older than Maeshowe on Mainland – and may
have been the place where these people buried
their dead.

* * *

Access: Orkney Ferries ro-ro service from
Kirkwall and Westray, Tues., Fri., 01856-
872044. Several daily passenger ferry crossings,
01857-677216. Scheduled air services Kirkwall/
Westray/ Papa Westray, 01856-872494. Papay
car hire, 01857-644202. Tourist Information
01856-872856.

Anchorages: (Orkney VTS on VHF Ch. 16/11)
1. Bay of Moclett, on S coast. Ferry priority at outermost
steps of pier. Visitors' mooring. Excellent anchorage, sand.
Avoid submarine cable and ferry approach. Good holding
but exposed S.
2. South Wick, on E coast, W of Holm of Papa. Very
shallow, sandy bay, 2m and less in depth. Visitor's buoy
near pier or anchor off pier on E side or off Holm of Papa
ESE of the pier. Exposed SE.
3. North Wick. Occasional anchorage, sand and stones,
4–5m. Best approach at LW to avoid reefs. Beware rock and
shoal in NW area.

10.28 North Ronaldsay

*The name is of uncertain derivation. The Norse name was
Rinansøy (?Ringa's isle) so it is almost certainly not derived
from (ON Ragnvalds-øy – Ronald's island).*

OS Maps: 1:50000 Sheet 5 1:25000 Sheet 465
Admiralty Charts: 1:200000 No.1942 or 1954 1:75000
No.2250

Area: 690ha (1705 acres)
Height: 20m (66 ft)

Owner: Multiple ownership. Bought by James
Traill, an Edinburgh lawyer, for £2222 in 1727
and held by the Traill family until quite recently
when some of the tenants purchased their
properties and became owner-occupiers.

Population: 1841–481 (92 houses). 1881–547.
1891–501 (86 houses). 1931–298. 1961–161.
1981–109. 1991–92. 2001–70. 2011–72.

Geology: Old Red Sandstone of Rousay Flags
mainly greyish or bluish in colour. The south
and east coasts have wide sandy beaches, north
and west is more rocky. There is no peat and a
shortage of fuel has always been a problem.

History: In spite of its remote location the island
has been continuously occupied since prehistoric
times.

King Harfagar of Norway had a son called
Halfdan Highlegs who fought a sea-battle against
Earl Einar (Torf Einar – 'the first man to cut peat
for fuel') in North Ronaldsay Firth. Halfdan lost
the battle and swam ashore but Einar followed
and slew him.

Rinansøy (North Ronaldsay) is mentioned on a
number of other occasions in the Norse sagas.

In November 1983 North Ronaldsay was
connected to the national grid and received
electricity for the first time.

Wildlife: The range of habitat and lack of
human interference encourages a wide selection
of wildlife – everything from breeding seals to a
wealth of botanical varieties.

Apart from the usual Orkney plant life there are
rare examples of the Arctic sandwort, *Arenaria
norvegica*, and skull-cap, *Scutellaria galericubata*.

The island is noted for its primitive, and
intelligent, sheep which exist on a diet of seaweed

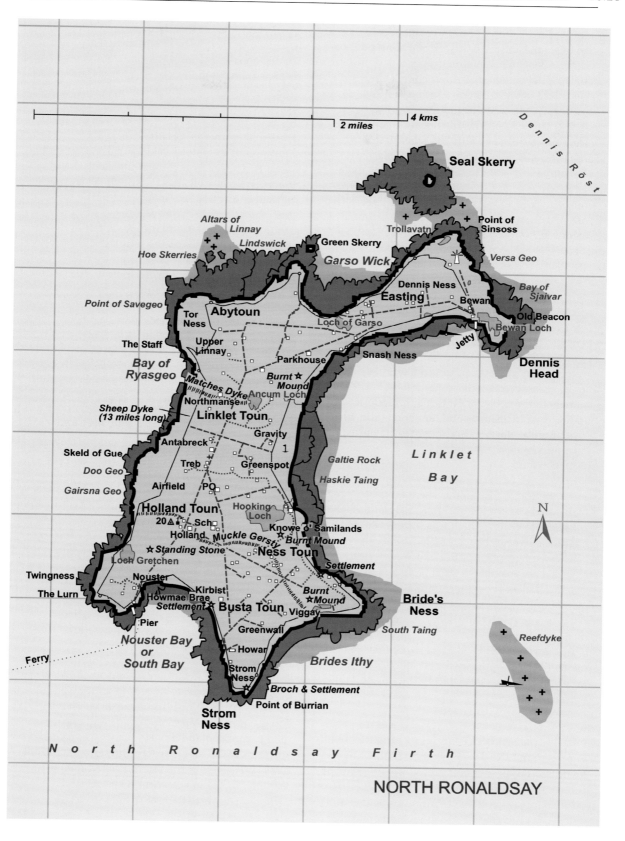

4 kms

2 miles

Dennis Röst

Seal Skerry

Altars of Linnay

Point of Sinsoss

Trollavatn

Lindswick

Green Skerry

Hoe Skerries

Garso Wick

Versa Geo

Dennis Ness

Easting

Bay of Sjaivar

Point of Savegeo

Bewan

Abytoun

Tor Ness

Loch of Garso

Old Beacon

Bewan Loch

The Staff

Upper Linnay

Jetty

Dennis Head

Snash Ness

Parkhouse

Bay of Ryasgeo

Burnt Mound

Matches Dyke

Northmanse

Ancum Loch

Sheep Dyke (13 miles long)

Linklet Toun

Gravity

L i n k l e t

Antabreck

1

B a y

Skeld of Gue

Doo Geo

Treb

Greenspot

Galtie Rock

Gairsna Geo

Airfield

PO

Haskie Taing

Holland Toun

Hooking Loch

N

20△ Sch

Holland

Muckle Gersty

Knowe o' Samilands

Burnt Mound

★ *Standing Stone*

Ness Toun

Loch Gretchen

Nouster

Settlement

Twingness

Kirbist

Burnt Mound

The Lurn

Howmae Brae

Settlement ★

Busta Toun

Viggay

Bride's Ness

Pier

Greenwall

South Taing

Nouster Bay or South Bay

Howar

Brides Ithy

Reefdyke

Ferry

Strom Ness

Broch & Settlement

Point of Burrian

Strom Ness

N o r t h   R o n a l d s a y   F i r t h

NORTH RONALDSAY

except when lambing. They are small, goat-like in shape, and variously coloured, and they produce very fine wool and delicious dark mutton. They are descendants of the original Orkney sheep, well adapted to the environment and producing their best mutton in mid-winter just when it is most needed. The flock is maintained at around 4000 head with each family having an agreed allocation according to an elected committee – The Sheep Court. Because of their diet of seaweed, an oil-spill could have disastrous consequences, so there is a flock on Auskerry (see No. 10.12) and a small flock kept in England as a safeguard.

This remote island also has wonderful birdlife – in many ways equal to Fair Isle (No.11.1) and a bird observatory was therefore established here in 1987. There are records of fifty-one breeding species of which thirty-four are regular and there is a colony of about fifty pairs of cormorant on Seal Skerry. Mute swan, shelduck, teal, gadwall, pintail, mallard, eider, shoveller, coot, moorhen, water rail, oystercatcher, ringed plover, lapwing, snipe, curlew, redshank, common and herring gulls, rock dove, sandwich tern, skylark, meadow and rock pipits, pied wagtail, wren, blackbird, hooded crow, starling, house sparrow, reed bunting, twite, raven, and the rare corncrake are all to be found.

Hedgehogs were thoughtlessly introduced in 1972 (although fortunately there are still no rats) with a consequent loss of many ground nests but a scheme to remove them was introduced. Many migrant birds can be seen including continental passerine migrants. Rarities which have been recorded are the olive-backed pipit, Spanish sparrow, Pallas's rosefinch, snowy owl and the pine bunting. At sea, Sabine's gull, long-tailed skua, Leach's petrel and sooty shearwater may be seen.

Apart from birds, Seal Skerry – Orkney's most northern rock – supports large colonies of both grey and common seals during the breeding season.

*   *   *

NORTH RONALDSAY has many similarities with Papa Westray (No.10.27), in size, population and land use, but its situation is even more remote. It is low-lying – nowhere is the ground higher than 20m above sea-level – extensively cultivated and studded with cottages. The inhabitants make up a closely-knit and competent community, well able to cope with their isolated situation. The County Library apparently has a full-time job keeping them supplied with books, while even the average Orcadian has quite a struggle understanding the local dialect. This contains many similarities to the traditional Norn dialect which was at one time the language of Orkney.

Because of its unique, primitive, seaweed-eating sheep the entire island is surrounded by the **Sheep Dyke**, a wall about 2m high. This great construction which was completed in the mid-19th century ensures that the sheep stay on the seashore because, although they survive well on seaweed, they would eat the local agricultural produce for choice. It is only when they are lambing that they are allowed to vary their diet.

Normally the dyke is maintained by the islanders as a matter of course, but in 1993 the worst storms in fifty years knocked down more than 3km of the 20km of wall allowing the scruffy little sheep to wander all over the farmland. The island community was much too small to undertake such a massive repair by itself so the Royal Navy, financially assisted by Prince Charles's Prince's Trust, came to the rescue and helped to rebuild the wall and save the crops.

The meat of these sheep has a unique flavour which is a delicacy much sought after by some of the top London restaurants. The wool also has special qualities and the islanders now spin their own fleeces in a mini-mill set up in the redundant lighthouse buildings in 2004.

The New Lighthouse in the north, overlooking Seal Skerry and now automatic, is the tallest land-based lighthouse in the British Isles. It is 42m (139ft) high and was built in 1854 to replace the Dennis Head Old Beacon built in 1788 and abandoned in 1809. Yet at Dennis Head on 11th March 1926, three German ships ran aground one after another!

In the past, communal farms or groups of smallholdings in Orkney were defined by boundary walls which have, in general, long since disappeared. But this is not so on North Ronaldsay, where many farming traditions can still be identified and two old boundary dykes, **Matches Dyke** and **Muckle Gersty** stretch right across the island in the form of raised mounds, dividing the island into three roughly equal portions. They are thought to be over 3000 years old.

Another old tradition is the use of 'plantiecruives'. miniature walled gardens outside the sheep-dyke by the seashore. These are used as cold frames to bring on the young kale plants, wind-proof and relatively frost-free.

North Ronaldsay was first occupied in the remote past and the first settlers have left much evidence of their activities. There is a standing stone near **Loch Gretchen** which is about 4m high and pierced by a hole [HY752529]. Two hundred years ago the islanders still danced round this stone on the night of the New Year but the meaning of the ritual has been forgotten.

The remains of a settlement at **Kirbist** [HY758523] may be another Skarabrae (see No.10.11) and there is also an unusual ruin near Hooking Loch which could be a primitive house.

At **Strom Ness**, the southern tip of the island, **Burrian Broch** has walls 4½m thick and four concentric ramparts on the side facing the land [HY762514]. Objects inscribed with Pictish symbols have been found in it and there are the remains of a settlement alongside. Unfortunately this site is in some danger of being damaged by the sea.

A hazardous patch of rocks called **Reef Dyke** lies off Bride's Ness in the south-west. Many ships have been wrecked here including, the wreck of an armed merchant ship of the Swedish East India Company, the *Svecia*, which went down in 1740 with two-thirds of its crew and a valuable cargo of silks and spices. It was investigated by marine archaeologists in 1975.

*   *   *

Access: Car-ferry return service Tues. and Fri. by Orkney Ferries, 01856-872044. Scheduled daily air service from Kirkwall, 01856-872494. Accommodation at N. Ronaldsay Bird Observatory, 01857-633200.

Anchorages: (Orkney VTS on VHF Ch. 16/11)
1. Nouster or South Bay. Ferry priority at outermost steps. Sufficient depth to lie alongside pier but also subject to swell. Two visitors' moorings April–Oct. Temp anchorage in middle of bay, 7m, sand. Exposed S to W and liable to swell.
2. Linklet Bay, S of Dennis Head. Occasional anchorage in 7m–9m, sand. Best W of jetty at N of bay. Exposed E to S.

Haswell-Smith.

THE SEAWEED-EATING SHEEP OF NORTH RONALDSAY

Fair Isle and the Shetland Islands

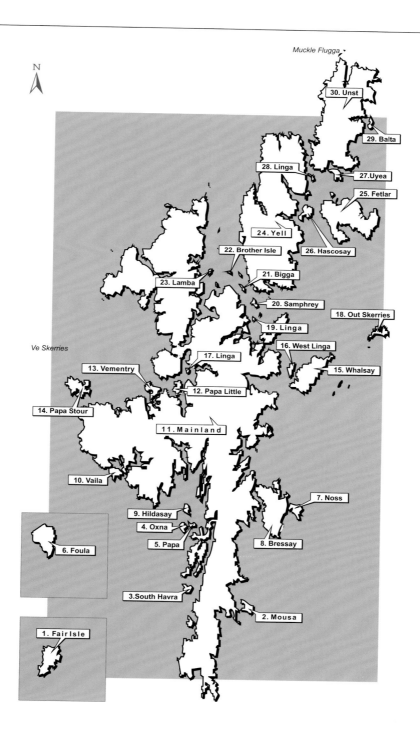

Muckle Flugga

N

30. Unst

29. Balta

28. Linga

27. Uyea

25. Fetlar

24. Yell

26. Hascosay

22. Brother Isle

21. Bigga

23. Lamba

20. Samphrey

18. Out Skerries

19. Linga

Ve Skerries

16. West Linga

17. Linga

15. Whalsay

13. Vementry

12. Papa Little

14. Papa Stour

11. Mainland

10. Vaila

7. Noss

9. Hildasay

4. Oxna

5. Papa

8. Bressay

6. Foula

3. South Havra

2. Mousa

1. Fair Isle

SECTION 11, Table 1: Arranged according to geographical position

No.	Name	Latitude	Longitude	Table 2* No.	Table 3** No.	Area in Acres		Area in Hectares
11.1	Fair Isle	59° 32N	01° 38W	48	30	1898		768
11.2	Mousa	60° 00N	01° 10W	88	112	445		180
11.3	South Havra	60° 02N	01° 21W	139	132	146		59
11.4	Oxna	60° 07N	01° 22W	132	137	168		68
11.5	Papa	60° 07N	01° 21W	140	149	146		59
11.6	Foula	60° 08N	02° 04W	37	13	3126		1265
11.7	Noss	60° 09N	01° 01W	62	38	848		343
11.8	Bressay	60° 09N	01° 05W	26	29	6931		2805
11.9	Hildasay	60° 09N	01° 21W	108	151	267		108
11.10	Vaila	60° 12N	01° 36W	63	73	808		327
11.11	Mainland	60° 15N	01° 20W	2	9	239388	96879	
	Muckle Roe	60° 22N	01° 25W			4381	1773	
	West Burra	60° 05N	01° 20W			1836	743	
	East Burra	60° 04N	01° 19W			1273	515	
	Trondra	60° 07N	01° 17W			680	275	
	Uyea	60° 37N	01° 25W			111	45	100230
11.12	Papa Little	60° 20N	01° 23W	80	82	558		226
11.13	Vementry	60° 20N	01° 28W	60	76	914		370
11.14	Papa Stour	60° 20N	01° 42W	46	79	2046		828
11.15	Whalsay	60 21N	00° 58W	31	57	4868		1970
11.16	West Linga	60° 22N	01° 02W	101	117	309		125
11.17	Linga (Olna Firth)	60° 22N	01° 22W	130	93	173		70
11.18	Housay (Out Skerries)	60° 25N	00° 46W	81	115	403	163	
	Bruray	60° 25N	00° 45W			136	55	218
11.19	Linga (Yell Sound)	60° 26N	01°09W	165	136	104		42
11.20	Samphrey	60° 28N	01° 09W	135	154	163		66
11.21	Bigga	60° 30N	01° 11W	123	146	193		78
11.22	Brother Isle	60° 31N	01° 13W	163	160	105		42
11.23	Lamba	60° 31N	01° 17W	154	144	114		46
11.24	Yell	60° 35N	01° 05W	9	34	52412		21211
11.25	Fetlar	60° 36N	00° 54W	22	43	10077		4078
11.26	Hascosay	60° 37N	00° 59W	70	153	680		275
11.27	Uyea	60° 40N	00° 54W	83	119	507		205
11.28	Linga (Bluemull Sd)	60° 40N	00° 59W	159	159	111		45
11.29	Balta	60° 45N	00° 47W	121	128	198		80
11.30	Unst	60° 46N	00° 52W	12	23	29820		12068

*Table 2: The islands arranged in order of magnitude
**Table 3: The islands arranged in order of height

Introduction

It is extremely rare to find a map of the British Isles in which the Shetland archipelago is shown in its true position. Almost invariably it is squeezed into a small inset. The result is that nearly everyone on mainland Britain fails to appreciate that Shetland, as the northern outpost of the British Isles, is closer to Bergen than to Aberdeen – and that Muckle Flugga is further from the Scottish/English border than Lands End.

Shetland was to the Norsemen what Gibraltar was to the British – a key naval base conveniently situated where world sea-routes converged. When the North Atlantic is seen from the correct viewpoint it is clear why the Vikings used Shetland as their first landfall, whether to raid Ireland, trade with the Isle of Man, or cross the Atlantic to Iceland, Greenland or beyond.

Although they had no magnetic compasses these remarkable navigators could not only use a crude sextant and gnomonic (sun/shadow) compass by day, and follow the stars at night, but they also knew how to read the Atlantic swell – a method still known to the Polynesians – and follow natural indicators such as the drift of seaweed and the flight of seabirds.

Take the story of 'Raven' Flokki and his two beautiful daughters. Long ago there was said to be a Land of Ice and Volcanoes beyond the Færoes and Flokki wanted to find it and make it his home. So he set sail from Norway but when he had reached Shetland one of his daughters, Geirhild, died and he buried her beside the loch which still bears her name, Loch of Girlsta. Flokki then sailed on to the Faeroes where his second daughter met and married an islander and would travel no further. Flokki was determined to continue although no one could tell him how to reach the land of Ice – only that they thought it was in the direction of the setting sun. So Flokki captured three ravens and sailed west. After a few days he released the first raven and saw it fly back the way he had come. The next day he released the second raven, but it flew ever higher and was lost to sight. The following day he released his last raven which flew high, but then set course to the north-west. He followed it and reached his chosen land, and that is how Flokki became the first Icelander.

In the Icelandic sagas, which were put in writing in the 13th century, Shetland is consistently called *Hjaltland* and that is still the Icelandic name. This has led to all sorts of scholarly assumptions regarding the derivation of the Norse name although in the Faeroe Islands and West Norway it was known

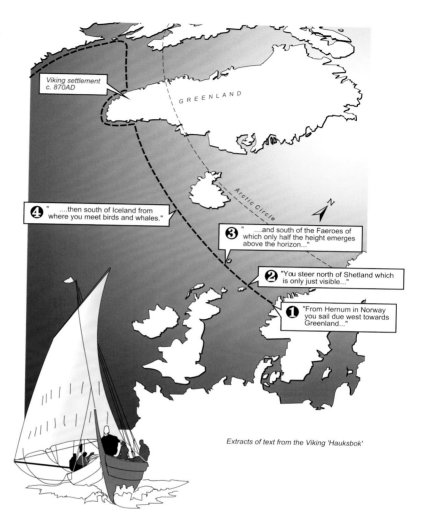

Viking settlement c. 870AD

GREENLAND

Arctic Circle

❹ "....then south of Iceland from where you meet birds and whales."

❸ "....and south of the Faeroes of which only half the height emerges above the horizon..."

❷ "You steer north of Shetland which is only just visible..."

❶ "From Hernum in Norway you sail due west towards Greenland..."

Extracts of text from the Viking 'Hauksbok'

THE VIKING ROUTE TO GREENLAND AND BEYOND

as *Hetland*. In 1221 one of Henry III's clerks at Westminster called Shetland *Heclandensis* and the pope's clerk in 1226 called it *Ihatlandensis*. But in 1289 the Norwegian king in a letter to the English king called it plain *Shetland* although in 1299 in Shetland itself it was written as *Hiatlandi*.

The pre-Norse name for Shetland was *Inse Catt* according to early Irish documents, i.e. the islands of the Catt tribe, whose totem was a cat. This was the same tribe that gave its name to Caithness – Catt Cape. The equivalent name for Orkney was Inse Orc – islands of the tribe of Orc, whose totem was an *orc* or boar.

The Icelandic, and assumed early Norse, name of *Hjaltland* has been variously interpreted by the experts as meaning 'high land', 'land shaped like

the hilt of a sword', or 'Hjalti's land' (– whoever Hjalti may have been). I am sure these are all carefully considered and learned interpretations but the Norwegian historian, A W Brøgger, has suggested that the Norsemen were merely talking of the land of Catt, or Cattland. As they would have pronounced Catt as 'chat', i.e. chatland – this seems to me to be an absolutely brilliant piece of common sense. It is the hardest task in the world to reach a simple solution!

In spite of its northern situation Shetland's winter climate is only marginally colder than that of mainland Britain thanks to the North Atlantic Drift. This is an extension of the Gulf Stream. Summers are certainly cooler but the very long hours of daylight tend to compensate. In fact in midsummer the Simmer Dim (the summer gloaming) is an unforgettable experience. Wind speeds can be high, and sometimes very high, but rainfall is not excessive and less than that of many areas of the British mainland.

Shetland's geology is very different from that of Orkney, although there are some large areas of Orkney's ubiquitous Old Red Sandstone. Generally, though, the rocks are Precambrian and of the Dalradian group giving an undulating rather than a slab-shaped profile. These rocks do not decompose into fertile soil. Consequently, there are large areas of blanket peat and few rock outcrops. The coastlines have been eroded to form high cliffs and whereas Orkney's cliffs are mainly limited to its Atlantic coast – Shetlands intrude everywhere.

Shetland, like the south of England, and the Outer Hebrides to a lesser degree, is sinking and at a rate sufficient to make a marked difference in the last few centuries. A mere century ago one could walk from Muckle Roe to Mainland at low water.

The geology and poor soil combine to create a landscape which is more primitively picturesque than that of Orkney but in spite of the poverty of much of the soil there is a feeling of affluence which is not entirely due to the oil industry. Perhaps it can be attributed to the rich character and open generosity of the Shetland Islanders themselves.

11.1 Fair Isle

Referred to in the sagas as (ON frioar-øy – fair isle) but a derivation from (ON feoer-øy – far off isle) seems more plausible.

O S Maps: 1:50000 Sheet 4 1:25000 Sheet 466
Admiralty Charts: 1:200000 No.1942 or 1119 1:25000 No.2622

Area: 768ha (1898 acres)
Height: 217m (712 ft)

Owner: Acquired by the National Trust for Scotland (NTS) in 1954 from Mr George Waterston with the help of Lord Bruntisfield.

Population: In 1701 the population was decimated by smallpox but it recovered and in 1790 was 220. 1841–232 (35 houses). 1861–380. 134 emigrated to Nova Scotia in 1862.

1881–214. 1891–223 (34 houses). 1931–108. 1955–about 50. There was talk of evacuation but the NTS improved amenities and encouraged repopulation. 1961–64. 1981–58. 1991–67. 2001–69 2011–68. There are many applications when a vacant house is advertised.

Geology: Red sandstone cliffs and natural sandstone arches and stacks surround the island. The highest cliffs are in the north but Sheep Rock in the south-east has some of the finest arches. There is copper ore on Fair Isle at Copper Geo.

History: In the Norse saga of *Burnt Njal*, Kari the viking came from Iceland and landed on Fair Isle. He spent the winter there, staying with his good friend David the White. And in the *Orkneyinga Saga* Earl Rognvald sent Uni to Fair Isle in preparation for his invasion of Orkney. When the time was due, Uni soaked a warning beacon with water so that it could not be lit and the Earl was able to pass Fair Isle and land on Westray (No.10.26) unopposed.

In 1588 the 38-gun *El Gran Grifon*, a Spanish fleet auxiliary flagship was wrecked at Fair Isle. After the Armada's defeat she had withstood an attack in the English Channel by Sir Francis Drake's *Revenge* but managed to escape northwards. Then on a night in late summer there was a severe squall and she ran onto the rocks in Sivars Geo, on the south-east side of Fair Isle. About 200 men survived the catastrophe and struggled ashore. They had already been without food for days and were weak and starving. The islanders supplied what little food they had but found it difficult to support such a large number of extra mouths. As the rations were small the men set about raiding the winter stocks, killing poultry and slaughtering the few precious cattle and sheep until, in desperation, the islanders managed to round them up and ship them off to Shetland. There they were well fed and well treated until they were repatriated. In 1984 a Spanish delegation dressed as conquistadors dedicated an iron cross in the island's kirkyard to those who had died.

This was just one wreck out of many. A survey has shown that, up to the advent of radar, there was a major shipwreck on the rocks of Fair Isle every four to five years on average.

In 1630 Fair Isle became part of the Shetland estates of Sinclair of Quendale and it was held by his family until 1750. They obtained rent

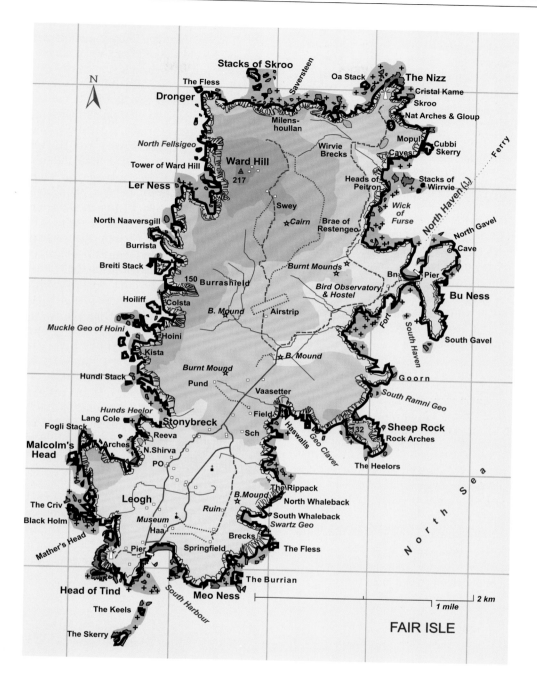

FAIR ISLE

from twenty-four households in four townships and a 'Hamburg Merchant's' booth by the south harbour.

For several centuries the Dutch had turned herring fishing into a very profitable industry. Their fishing boats or 'busses' crowded the waters of Orkney and Shetland protected by naval men-of-war and the catches were exported to Europe, the Mediterranean, and even South America. The French cast covetous eyes on this wealth and in a famous sea-battle in 1702 their navy attacked Dutch men-of-war off Fair Isle with some success.

In 1770 Fair Isle was purchased by Stewart of Brough in Sanday, Orkney, and in 1866 was sold to J. Bruce of Sumburgh.

Wildlife: About 240 different species of flowering plant have been recorded, including juniper, which is rarely found elsewhere in Shetland. White campion and reed grass are widespread with swathes of blue spring squill and thrift. There are also examples of the rarer orchids. Heather and cranberry are common, and dwarf willow and alpine bistort can be found in the hilly moorland.

Like Hirta (No.9.1), Fair Isle has its own distinctive sub-species – the Fair Isle wren (*Troglodytes troglodytes fridarienis*) and the Fair Isle fieldmouse (*Apodemus sylvaticus fridarienis*). The rabbits are so multi-coloured that some could be wearing Fair Isle jerseys, but they have not yet achieved the status of a separate sub-species.

The Bird Observatory was founded in 1948 by George Waterston, a well-known ornithologist, who bought the island because of its exceptionally interesting birdlife. Over 373 species of bird have been recorded, which is more than anywhere else in Britain, and well over 220,000 birds of about eighty different species have been ringed such as puffin, pipit, wheatear, brambling, fieldfare, redwing, crossbill, siskin and sometimes, Lapland bunting, barred warbler and pied woodpecker.

There are large colonies of seabirds including great and arctic skua. Other breeding species are eider, oystercatcher, ringed plover, lapwing, and snipe. Curlew, whimbrel and dunlin occasionally breed here and breeding passerines include raven, wren, starling, house sparrow, twite, wheatear, white and pied wagtail, skylark, and rock and meadow pipit.

The best all-round months for bird-watching are April, late June to early September, and late October. The best time to spot rare migrants is between mid-September and late October when the wind is from the east.

*   *   *

FAIR ISLE lies twenty-four miles south-west of Shetland's Sumburgh Head which is roughly half-way between the two northern archipelagoes. It has a distinctive outline with high red sandstone cliffs in the north sloping down to a low, bare southern coastline. **Ward Hill** (217m) in the north-west is the highest part of the island. The Hill Dyke and the ancient Feelie Dyke separate the northern hill-grazing land from the southern fields.

The majority of the inhabitants live in the south where there is a limited amount of ground suitable for cultivation. Here, the scattered settlement of **Stonybreck** (ON *brekke* – hillside) includes a post-office, general store, school, museum, Church of Scotland kirk, and Methodist chapel (each used on alternate Sundays).

The airstrip is centrally situated and to the east of it is the **Bird Observatory and Hostel**. East again, **Bu Ness** (ON – home headland) is only joined to the island by a very narrow isthmus dividing two relatively sheltered bays, North and South Haven. **North Haven** is the port for the passenger ferry, *The Good Shepherd*. Rough roads continue north from the airstrip and the Bird Observatory (roads south of the airstrip are macadamed). One road leads to the radio mast by Ward Hill, and the other serves the lighthouse on **The Nizz** (ON *nes* – the headland). Both the island lighthouses were built by Stevenson in 1892. In this area, known as **Skroo** (ON – stack of oats built to withstand winter gales), the cliffs have been savagely bent by primeval forces and perforated with caves and natural arches by the sea. But this is in keeping with the whole north of the island which is generally wild and barren. In summer the Ward Hill area becomes a test of nerve as the great skua, or 'bonxies', dive-bomb all intruders.

Once again long sea crossings obviously did not deter early man for there are a number of tumuli which date back to about 3500BC (Houlalie is the largest) and an Iron Age fort is at Landberg near the Observatory [HZ226722].

The population decline was halted thanks to the timely intervention of the ornithologist George

FAIR ISLE POST OFFICE, SHIRVA. A POST OFFICE WAS OPENED AT SOUTH HARBOUR IN 1877. IT MOVED HERE IN 1948.

Waterston who gained international recognition for the island by publicising its varied birdlife. He had visited it regularly since 1935 but while a prisoner-of-war in Germany he dreamed of purchasing the island and setting up a bird observatory. After the war he realised his dream and in due course he also enabled the National Trust for Scotland to continue the good work. The Trust improved the mail-boat pier, good communications being the essential ingredient for a viable island community, and also improved much of the property. A new £4 million Bird Observatory and Hostel was built in 2010 with accommodation for thirty visitors.

All the buildings are connected to a mutually owned electricity generating station. The electricity previously came solely from diesel generators but since 1982 two wind turbines have contributed 70% of the power.

The school has probably the highest pupil-to-staff ratio in Britain with – in 2007 – eight staff (some part-time) for eight pupils. As so often with small island schools the results are exceptional. At the age of twelve pupils go to a boarding school in Lerwick for their secondary education. The school hall, built in 1980, is a popular community hall in the evenings.

Apart from those directly involved with the Nature Reserve or in community service, the main occupation is crofting, supplemented by some fishing, and the knitting of traditional jerseys. The distinctive, brightly-coloured and non-repetitive geometric patterns of Fair Isle knitwear are sometimes said to have been introduced by the shipwrecked Spanish sailors from *El Gran Grifon* but it is almost certain that they were an insular development from traditional Nordic designs.

In 1941 a German Heinkel bomber on a weather reconnaissance flight was attacked by RAF Hawker Hurricanes from Sumburgh and crashed on Fair Isle, killing two of the five crew members. The wreckage is still there.

Although this rocky island would seem to be a climber's paradise, with the semi-detached headland of **Sheep Rock** south of Bu Ness considered a prime test of climbing ability, the stone is reported to be of poor quality and unreliable. However as the top of Sheep Rock provided four hectares of valuable pasture the islanders used to climb it with chains and then used ropes to raise and lower the sheep.

A few examples of the traditional Shetland boat – the 'yoal' (yawl) – can still be found at Fair Isle.

She is a lightweight craft with a raked stem and stern, clinker-built, and very similar to the Danish Gokstad ship of 1000 years ago. In 2008 the exciting and spectacular six-hole golf course by the south lighthouse which has fallen into disuse was reinstated by a keen American.

The Thief's Hole in the cliff-face of **Malcolm's Head**, behind Fogli Stack, was the traditional smugglers' or press-gang hideout. Another feature of interest is an 80m subterranean passage, the **Kirn of Scroo**, at the North Light which ends in a 'gloup' or borehole.

* * *

Access: Passenger ferry: Grutness (by Sumburgh), (booking essential); three times a week; Lerwick alternate Thurs. in summer, 01595-760222. Air service from Tingwall, Shetland: Mon.,Wed., and Fri., 01595-840246. Air service from Kirkwall, Orkney: Thur. and Sun., 01856-872494. Bird Observatory Lodge, 01595-760258. There are NTS volunteer work parties in the summer to restore buildings, etc., 0131-243-9300.

Anchorages:
1. North Haven, Bu Ness. Small secure harbour (built 1992) but limited space for lying alongside or rafting. Small pontoon for visitors or anchorage possible but occasional swell and very restricted space, sand and weed. Follow leading marks for entry. Mail-boat pier was built 1958 and slipway 1981.
2. South Haven, Bu Ness. Temp. anchorage in N'lies but poor holding due to rocky bottom. Anchor in 4m. Careful entry required.
3. South Harbour, a small bay at the S end between Meo Ness and Head of Tind. Recognised anchorage and landing place but many dangers.

11.2 Mousa

[moo-să] (ON *mós-øy* – moor or mossy island).

OS Maps: 1:50000 Sheet 4 1:25000 Sheet 466
Admiralty Charts: 1:200000 No.1119 1:75000 No.3283

Area: 180ha (445 acres)
Height: 55m (180 ft)

Owner: George Bell

Population: 1774–11 families. 1841–12. 1861–0 and uninhabited since.

Geology: The old quarry on Mousa was the source of many of the flagstones used for the streets of Lerwick.

Copper ore is to be found at Sand Lodge on Mainland, just opposite Mousa.

History: Mousa, and its famous broch, are best remembered for their part in the sagas.

According to the Icelandic *Egil's Saga* about 900AD a young man in Norway, Bjorn, fell in love with a girl called Thora Jewel-hand. They eloped from her family home and he took her to his mother's house on the Sogne fjord where she stayed throughout the winter, virtue intact. In the spring Bjorn's father gave him a trading-ship and suggested that he make for Dublin where business was good. His parents wanted Thora to remain with them until his return but the couple would not be separated and Thora sailed with him. A violent storm blew up and they were in grave danger but they managed with difficulty to run the ship aground on Mousa. The young lovers married and made the ancient broch into their honeymoon home for the winter. Meanwhile the crew set about repairing the ship.

The following spring news came that Thora's family had persuaded King Harald of Norway to outlaw Bjorn. As his ship was now ready for sea Bjorn and Thora sought refuge in Iceland. It was another stormy voyage but they were given a very friendly welcome on arrival. Not long after, Thora produced a daughter called Asgerd and they all lived happily ever after.

In the Norse *Orkneyinga Saga* the story is told of Margaret, wife of Earl Maddad of Atholl, daughter of Earl Haakon and mother of Earl Harald. After the death of her husband, the mature but beautiful Margaret, wasted no time in moving in with Gunni, brother of the buccaneering Sweyn Asleifsson of Gairsay (see No.10.14). She soon became pregnant but Margaret was mercurial, oversexed and not really made for motherhood. She gave birth to the child in 1153 but, growing tired of Gunni, she turned her attention to a handsome young man from Shetland, Earl Erland Ungi son of Harald the Fair-spoken. She was of course only too delighted to be carried off to Shetland by Erland and taken to the broch on Mousa. There the couple established their love nest and, although the broch does not look particularly cosy by present-day standards, no doubt love overcame all discomforts. At least

THE BROCH OF MOUSA

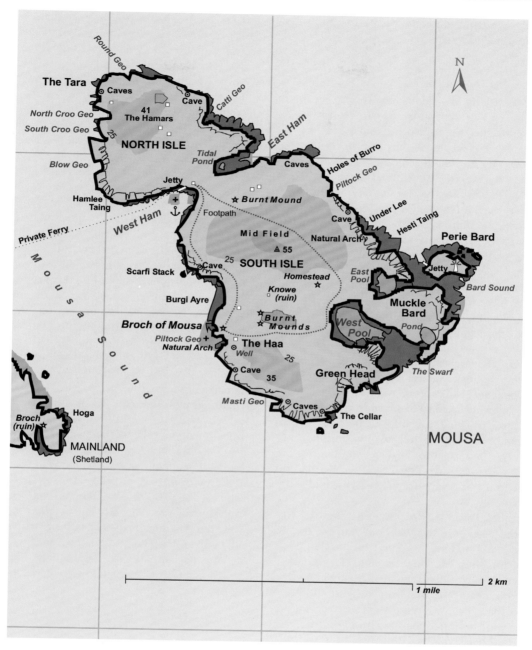

The map shows MOUSA with labels: Round Geo, The Tara, Caves, Cave, Catti Geo, North Croo Geo, 41 The Hamars, South Croo Geo, 25, NORTH ISLE, East Ham, Tidal Pond, Caves, Holes of Burro, Blow Geo, Piltock Geo, Jetty, Footpath, Burnt Mound, Cave, Under Lee, Hesti Taing, Hamlee Taing, West Ham, Mid Field, Natural Arch, Perie Bard, Private Ferry, △ 55, SOUTH ISLE, Jetty, Mousa Sound, 25, Cave, Homestead, East Pool, Bard Sound, Scarfi Stack, Knowe (ruin), Muckle Bard, Burgi Ayre, Burnt Mounds, West Pool, Pond, Broch of Mousa, Piltock Geo, The Haa, Green Head, The Swarf, Natural Arch, Well, 25, Cave, 35, Caves, The Cellar, Masti Geo, Hoga, MOUSA, Broch (ruin), MAINLAND (Shetland). Scale: 2 km / 1 mile.

the chosen spot was private and defensible, which was important as it was not long before Margaret's twenty-year-old son, Earl Harald Maddadson, besieged it. He was enraged by his mother's behaviour but her hide-out proved 'an unhandy place to get at'. So, in the end, after a long siege he agreed to forgive her provided she married Erland. This she did and after the ceremony Harald sailed them over to Norway for a legitimate honeymoon.

Wildlife: The most noticeable life-forms are sheep, seals and sea-birds. The seals, both common and grey, particularly favour East and West Ham.

Botanically the island has an interesting mixture of moorland and salt-water plants.

This is an RSPB reserve. Breeding species of birds include great and arctic skuas, eider, storm petrel, fulmar, many arctic tern and black guillemot. A colony of storm petrel and a few rock doves nest in the broch's dry-stone walls and migrant waders frequent the lochans.

*   *   *

Two men fishing in a small boat off **MOUSA** in September 1779 were surprised when a strange ship approached from the south and asked for help. They climbed aboard only to discover that it was a French warship wanting to be piloted into Lerwick harbour. They immediately lied to the French saying that two powerful British warships were waiting in Lerwick. They were able to describe the ships because they had seen them sailing south some months before. This persuaded the French not to attack Lerwick but they refused to release the two fishermen. Months later the French man-of-war – still with its two prisoners aboard – was captured by a British ship, and strangely enough it turned out to be one of the actual British ships which the men had lied about! So nearly a year after their abortive fishing trip the two well-travelled fishermen returned home.

To the Vikings an island was a piece of land which a boat could circumnavigate but the term 'circumnavigation' included transporting a boat across dry land. It was for this reason that the Mull of Kintyre was judged to be an island. Similarly little Mousa counted as two islands, **North Isle** and **South Isle**, because it has a narrow waist or isthmus which a boat could be carried across.

North Isle is the smaller part and rises to a height of 41m. It is divided from South Isle by two bays, **West Ham** (ON *ham* – harbour) and East Ham. South Isle's highest point is **Mid Field** at 55m and there is a further small hill in the south which rises to 35m. The south-east is indented to form what are almost two drying islands with saltwater pools separating them, **Muckle Bard** and **Perie Bard** (ON – big and subordinate sandbar or reef). A lighthouse stands on Perie Bard.

There are two tiny lochans on Mousa, one on each 'island', with ancient tumuli beside the southern loch. The remains of old farm-buildings are on an attractive site above this loch and nearer the east coast is a ruined water mill. There is also an old two-storeyed building known as **The Haa** [HU458236]. On the east coast itself the wreck of the first *St Sunniva* can be seen. She ran aground in 1930 in thick fog.

On the western shore, the world's finest, best-preserved and most complete broch can be clearly seen from Mainland across the Mousa Sound. The **Broch of Mousa**, dating from the Iron Age, has lost its upper courses but is still some 13m tall. It is a very fine example of the craft of the ancient builders. Unlike many other brochs there is no sign of a surrounding settlement – the broch of Mousa appears to stand alone. The external diameter at ground level is about 15m with the walls gracefully curved inwards so that the upper diameter is about 12m. The circular internal courtyard is approximately 6m in diameter and contains a wheelhouse which was possibly added in the 2nd or 3rd century. The stairs between the double walls lead upwards through six galleries.

Many brochs have been built in tandem facing each other over a stretch of water, and this broch is no exception as on a headland projecting into Mousa Sound there are the remains of its sister Broch of Burraland. The real purpose of these structures, possibly built before the Roman invasion of British waters, is still a mystery.

Mousa's broch is built of small stones of a local schistose slate meticulously laid dry to give a smooth exterior. The workmanship is quite remarkable when one remembers that timber was an exceptionally scarce commodity and the curved walls were probably built without templates and to a line depending on the eye of the stonemason. This skill and accuracy has resulted in a building, possibly 1000 years old at the time of the Vikings and now 1000 years older still, appearing today as though the builders had just laid the last stone and gone home for the night.

*   *   *

Access: Regular summer boat trips from Leebitton pier, Sandwick. No dogs. Weather permitting so check first, 07901-872339. Also late night storm petrel trips in season (booking essential).

Anchorage: Near the broch the bottom is rock and unsuitable for anchoring.
1. West Ham, Mousa Sound – a bay ½M N of the broch. There is a cottage and boat slip. Anchor in 4m, sand. Sheltered from NW through N to E. Fresh S'lies cause a swell.

11.3 South Havra

(ON hafr-øy – ewe island.) Less probable alternatives are (ON havari-øy – shipwreck island) or (ON – Halvor's island). Formerly written as Halvera and Hevera.

OS Maps: 1:50000 Sheet 4 1:25000 Sheet 466
Admiralty Charts: 1:75000 No.3283 1:25000 No.3294

Area: 59ha (146 acres)
Height: 42m (138 ft)
Population: 1841–37. 1881–35. 1891–24 (4 houses). Uninhabited since 1923.

Geology: Soil with no peat deposits over an area of epidotic syenite, undifferentiated schist and gneiss.

History: South Havra was the home of the Foud (Magistrate) of all Shetland, Olaf Sinclair, in the 16th century. He was also laird of the great odal estate of Brew.

South Shetland occasionally suffered raids by men from Lewis (No.8.14). There was one such raid which ended in a pitched battle at Sumburgh in which sixty men died. It is said that Olaf

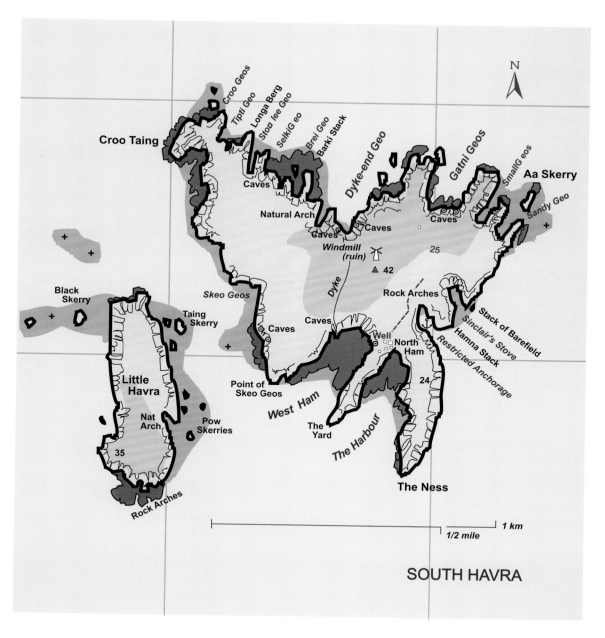

SOUTH HAVRA

Sinclair only escaped death by diving off the high cliffs at Sumburgh Head.

*   *   *

SOUTH HAVRA could easily be called the island of shipwrecks as it lies directly across the southern approach to the comparatively sheltered waters of Clift Sound and the Burras. The east side is steep-to but elsewhere there are reefs and skerries galore particularly in the channel between South Havra and Little Havra and also stretching north from Little Havra to the west of Croo Taing. The cliffs and broken shoreline of both islands are made up of a tumble of interesting rock formations perforated with caves and arches.

Eight families were living on the island until May 1923 when they all decided to leave. Up to that time it seems to have been a viable small community with a full-time schoolteacher and eight pupils. The ground was fertile and productive and, although there was no peat for fuel, this could be found at Deepdale on the Mainland shore. However, the operation was not easy as the peat had to be brought down the hillside on a sledge, controlled by ropes to stop it falling over the cliff and into the sea. It then had to be manhandled across the slippery rocks and into a heaving boat. It must have been difficulties such as these which persuaded the islanders to abandon their homes.

The settlement was on the cliff-top to avoid obstructing the agricultural land. This however meant the young children and the livestock always had to be tethered.

The island's summit is 42m high and on top of it stands the conspicuous ruin of a **windmill** which itself is nearly 8m high. This was, strangely, the only corn-grinding windmill in Shetland, a land of wind-whipped islands with a long association with the Dutch. This windmill was built by the islanders in the middle of the 19th century to grind their corn as there was no stream to operate a water mill. The ruin is worth visiting and the island is an exciting place to explore.

The two larger coves on the south coast are optimistically called the Harbour and West Ham (ON *ham* – harbour). Both bays are exposed and partly filled with drying rocks.

The Havra rock formations are repeated on the adjacent Mainland with a tiny rocky islet, **Holm of Maywick**, in the centre of the separating channel.

*   *   *

Access: By arrangement: MV Cycharters, Scalloway, 01595-696598. Tourist Office, 01595-693434.

Anchorage:
1. In the S inlet on the E coast. (There are two narrow inlets close together but the N inlet is foul with rocks). Anchor in middle of pool in 2m with warps ashore.

11.4 Oxna

(ON yxn-øy – ox island).

OS Maps: 1:50000 Sheet 4   1:25000 Sheet 466
Admiralty Charts: 1:75000 No.3283   1:25000 No.3294

Area: 68ha (168 acres)
Height: 38m (125 ft)

Population: 1841–19 (2 houses). 1871–29. 1881–30. 1891–31 (5 houses). 1901–36. 1931–0. Uninhabited since.

Geology: Much of the rock is epidotic syenite, which is like a dark granite.

History: At the end of the 19th century a young Oxna boy was playing with his friends near a skarf's (cormorant's) nest. The topsoil had been scalped away by the islanders to add to the soil in the arable areas and consequently the ground was bare. Something glinted in the sunlight and with some difficulty the boy prised the object from the roots and took it proudly home. A visiting schoolteacher from Burra was shown the find and he informed the museum authorities in Edinburgh. I hope the bright-eyed lad or his family were paid 'treasure trove'. They deserved it because he had unearthed an exquisite example of Norse jewellery – a solid gold armlet about 7cm (3 inches) in diameter, plaited from four heavy gold wires.

*   *   *

OXNA has a compact shape, uneven surface and a number of small lochans. Its summit to the south of the centre is 38m high. Extending for a considerable distance to the north is a broken line of islets and skerries. Joined to Oxna by a drying reef are the **Hoggs of Oxna** with a narrow channel, Bulta Sound, separating them from the

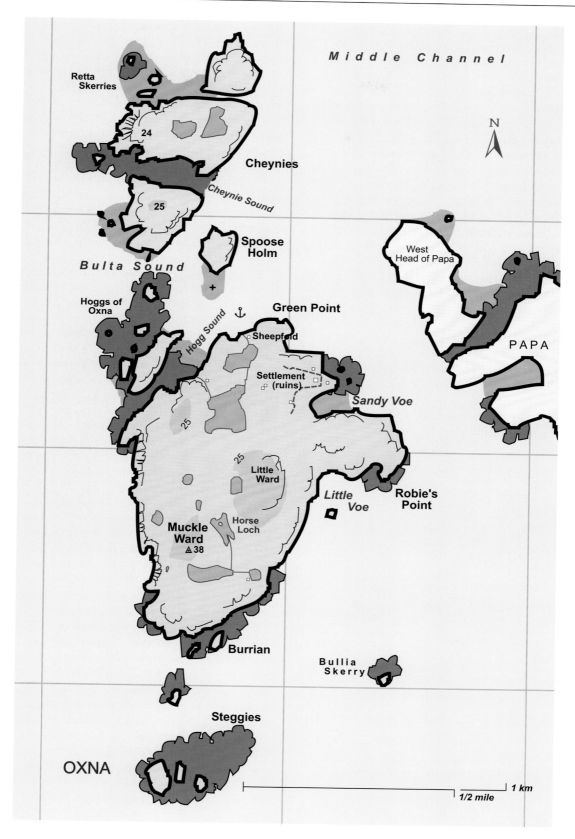

OXNA

next group called the **Cheynies**. Bulta Sound is navigable, but only 100m wide.

The Cheynies are a group of three drying islets forming a single unit and to their south-east is a further little islet called **Spoose Holm**.

When Oxna was inhabited the main settlement was beside the narrow inlet called **Sandy Voe**, facing the island of Papa (No.11.5). It seems that the First World War was the beginning of the end for Oxna. With the menfolk away it was virtually impossible for the women and children to maintain a viable community in such a demanding environment. Difficulties of transport and communication, fishing and subsistence crofting, hard enough at the best of times, must have become insurmountable. And even when the war was over many of the islanders never returned – mere statistics among the losses on the Somme or at sea.

*   *   *

Access: By arrangement: MV Cycharters, Scalloway, 01595-696598. Tourist Office, 01595-693434.

Anchorage:
1. Anchor NNE or SSE of Spoose Holm, 6–9m, sand over rock. Area partly obstructed by fish-cages. Beware reef close S of Spoose Holm. Reasonably sheltered except from the NE.

11.5 Papa

(ON pap-øy – priest or hermit island).

OS maps: 1:50000 Sheet 4 1:25000 Sheet 466
Admiralty Charts: 1:75000 No.3283 1:25000 No.3294

Area: 59ha (146 acres)
Height: 32m (105 ft)

Population: 1841–21. 1881–14. 1891–23 (2 houses). 1931–0. Uninhabited since.

Geology: Much of the bedrock is epidotic syenite, which is similar to a coarse granite.

Wildlife: The island is said to be infested with rats but if so, they are well concealed.

*   *   *

All Shetland's holy islands are clustered in the south-west of the archipelago and it has been suggested that by the time the early Irish Christians had sailed in their currachs all the way to Shetland they were only too content to settle down where they had landed and go no further.

Why the first missionary chose **PAPA** and not Oxna or Langa (an islet to the north) will never be known but maybe Oxna was already inhabited and the poor chap was just too tired to sail over to Langa. Certainly Papa has a lot to commend it. It has some pools of fresh water, enough land to cultivate for food, and reasonable proximity to Mainland.

Before the island was vacated in the 1920s it supported three or four crofts.

There is a deep and narrow channel separating Papa from Oxna and the coast of Papa is indented with a series of small inlets. Off the north-east headland is the **Hogg of Papa** – to balance the Hoggs of Oxna at the opposite side of the group – and the west side of the island has a tidal channel joining it to the fair-sized islet called **West Head of Papa**. This tidal islet alone is actually larger than the aforementioned **Langa** (ON – long island) and yet Langa supported one croft and a population of nine souls in 1841 and thirteen in 1881 although it was deserted by the 1890s. Papa has a goodly stock of peat and the Trondra (Mainland) islanders have the right to cut it as they have none of their own.

Even smaller islets lie to the east of Papa in the centre of the shipping route into the port of Scalloway – **Green Holm** with **Merry Holm** and a scattered group of skerries beside it. To the north is **Burwick Holm** by the Ness of Burwick.

In May 1903 the crew of *Adelong* fishing near Papa reported that a sea-monster, known locally as a 'sifan', had ruined ten of their nets.

A similar report from the other side of Shetland had been given in a sworn account by six men crewing the *Bertie* in June 1882. They had been fishing south-east of Fetlar for two days. Their holds were full of fish and they were hauling in their lines to return home when they saw a sifan heading for their boat. It was 150 feet long with a huge head covered with barnacles, a square mouth with bright green whiskers – 'probably of seaweed' – and it had humps and a long neck. They fired at it at close range and threw ballast stones at it but that only infuriated it and it followed the boat for three hours.

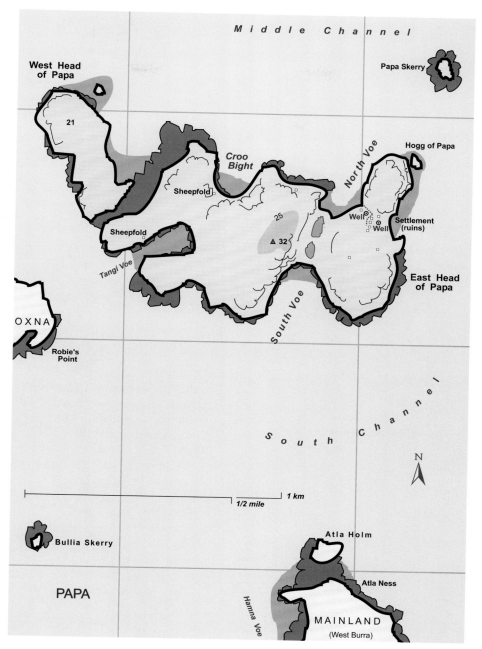

Access: By arrangement: MV Cycharters, Scalloway, 01595-696598. Tourist Office, 01595-693434.

Anchorages: A tripping line is advised.

1. North Voe. Temp. anchorage in 6m in centre of gut.

2. West Head of Papa. Temp. anchorage in 5m in bay between Papa and West Head of Papa. Beware rocks on Papa shore and keep nearer the West Head of Papa shore. Head of bay is shoal.

3. NNE of Spoose Holm. (See Oxna, No.11.4). Safest anchorage except in NE'lies but a considerable dinghy distance from Papa.

4. Temp anchorage in South Voe in centre of gut, 6m.

11.6 Foula

*[**foo**-lë] (ON fugl-øy – bird or fowl island.) Sometimes called Uttrie – the outer isle.*

○ S Maps: 1:50000 Sheet 4   1:25000 Sheet 467

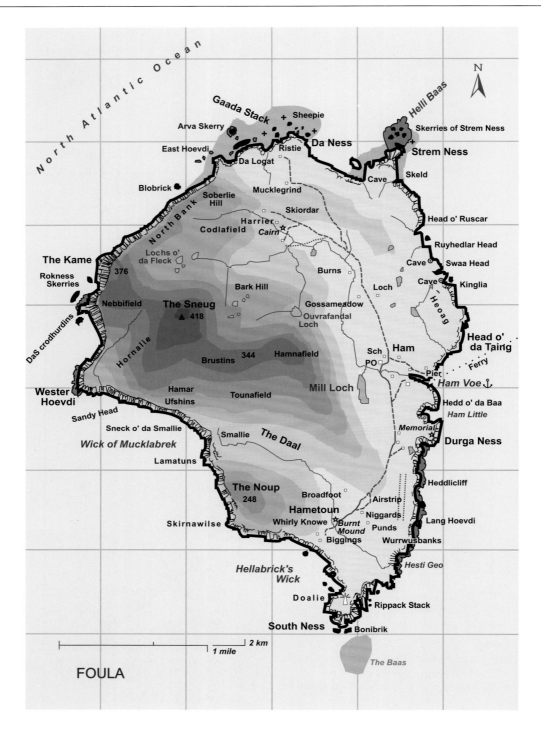

FOULA

Admiralty Charts: 1:75000 No.3283 1:75000 No.3281 NE
part only.

Area: 1265ha (3126 acres)
Height: 418m (1371 ft)

Owner: The family of Professor I Stoughton

Holbourn of Pendre, Brecon, Wales have owned
Foula since 1900. There is an interesting
viewpoint of an absentee landlord. In 1914
before leaving after a lecture tour in the United
States the Professor said that Foula was the
Romans' Ultima Thule, that he was 'King of

Thule' and that the Foulans '...are some of the most delightful people I ever knew,' but that they are, 'a little queer in their notion about property. Until quite recently they spoke Norse and as a rule they are 200 years behind the rest of the world. The only wheeled vehicles on the island are wheelbarrows and even they are regarded with suspicion.'

Population: In 1720 the 'Mortal Pox', (smallpox) killed about 200 out of the population of only 220. Numbers were later replenished from Mainland. 1841–215. 1881–267 (and 7 fishing boats or 'sixareens'). 1891–239 (47 houses). 1901–222. 1931–118. 1951–70. 1961–54. 1971–33. 1981–39 (15 occupied houses). 1991–40. 2001–31. 2011–38 (20 households).

Geology: The west and centre is sedimentary (Old Red Sandstone) and the land terminates abruptly with high sandstone cliffs of variegated colours. The north-east side is metamorphic, consisting mainly of schists and gneiss. Foula has some of Shetland's best arable land.

History: In 1490 Foula became the possession of Alv Knutsson. Previously it had belonged to the Norwegian family of Ciske. When the last Queen of Foula, Katherine Asmunder, died in the late 17th century Norse udal law was still recognised by the islanders who were unaware of the advent of Scots Law in the rest of Shetland.

About this time, according to tradition, a ship's surgeon named Scott persuaded the islanders to hand over their old Norse title-deeds on the pretext that they needed to be registered in Edinburgh. They never saw them again and the family of Scotts of Melby, owners of Vaila (No.11.10) and various estates on Shetland Mainland, thereby acquired possession of the island. As a result the crofters lost their udal rights, under which they were freemen land-owners. Instead they became tenants and virtual bondsmen subject to the whims of their landlords. Luckily, as fishermen, the islanders were more rent-productive than those depending solely on crofting and this saved them from clearance for sheep-farming. But their insecurity continued until 1882, when they gained some protection under the Crofting Acts.

Until 1800 Norn was still the normal tongue of this isolated community although it was no longer spoken anywhere else in Britain. Even in 1894,

Jacobsen, the Færoese linguist, was surprised at the similarities with Færoese.

Modernisation has been slow. Wireless telegraphy was installed in 1937, the first telephone in 1954 and there was no piped water supply until 1982.

Foula still uses the old Julian calendar which most of the rest of Britain (see Jura No.2.6) discarded in 1753 and Christmas on the island is therefore still celebrated on the 6th of January. And New Year's Day, or 'Nuerday', is on 13 January. According to the islanders this is neither old-fashioned nor heathen, but just downright independent.

Wildlife: Foula is yet another island with its own variety of sheep although they are not as distinctive as the Soay (No.9.2) sheep of the St Kilda group or even the seaweed-eating sheep of North Ronaldsay (No.10.28). They are known as 'hardback' sheep and, in common with all primitive sheep, they have exceptionally hairy fleeces. They were possibly introduced by the Vikings. Recently the sheep have been found to have a carnivorous streak – they bite the heads off young arctic tern and skua nestlings. Red deer on Rum (No.4.3) have a similar habit. The RSPB has suggested that the sheep should be given minerals as they are probably trying to compensate for a deficiency in the vegetation. On the other hand they may have just discovered a new gastronomic treat.

Foula, like Fair Isle (No.11.1), has its own sub-species of field mouse, *Apodemus sylvaticus thuloe* – a charming little creature with big feet. Foula also has rabbits, hedgehogs and house mice.

The Viking name of Foula is still apt for this is an internationally recognised seabird station with over 125,000 breeding birds (twelve species) including the rare Leach's petrel. It is the most prolific breeding site in the North Atlantic for that ponderous pirate, the great skua or 'bonxie'. In the 19th century bonxies bred nowhere else in Britain except Foula and Unst (No.11.29) but, thanks to the attention of egg-collectors, only about fifteen pairs were left by the late 19th century and only *three* pairs by 1920. However, with protection, it has made a remarkable recovery and there are about 3000 breeding pairs on Foula's cliffs and boulder fields. The great skua – large, dark brown and heavily built – will attack even a gannet or black-backed gull forcing it to vomit up its catch. During the nesting season it will fearlessly attack men or dogs yet, strangely, the smaller arctic skua, or 'scootie-allan', shows no fear of it.

Parts of the sheer northern cliffs provide no foothold for nesting birds but elsewhere the narrow ledges are packed with noisy activity. The south-east of the island, which is almost bare of peat, has high densities of nesting oystercatcher, ringed plover, arctic skua and arctic tern. Unfortunately, there are now greatly reduced numbers of puffin (or 'Tammy Norie'). This may be due to a reduction in sand-eels caused by over-fishing or it may be a result of the increased numbers of bonxies. After all, a bonxie will even take an occasional lamb so, puffins are an easy meal.

*   *   *

FOULA is the most westerly of the Shetland group, lying a lonely fourteen miles out in the Atlantic. Not so long ago bad weather could cut off the island for up to six weeks at a time. There can still be delays but since the residents built the airstrip in the 1970s there have been regular scheduled flights and with broadband internet and adequate power supplies Foula is no longer quite so remote.

The land rises from east to west with low, broken cliffs and some small coves on the east coast, but a west coast of precipitous cliffs rising to a height of 150–365m. There are five distinct peaks all leaning to the north; the **Sneug**, which is the highest at 418m, just west of centre; **Hamnafield** or Hamnafjeld (344m) at the centre; the **Noup** (248m)(ON – precipitous crag) on the south-west coast; the **Kame** (376m) on the west coast; and **Soberlie Hill** (221m) on the north-west coast. The Noup is separated from the other peaks by a glacial valley called the **Daal** (ON *dal* – valley).

At one time the menfolk of Foula were almost entirely engaged in fishing but nowadays crofting has had to take precedence. All the crofts are on the east side with about half the population settled in **Hametoun** (S. – home town) in the south-east and the remainder living at **Ham** near Ham Voe (ON – harbour inlet). Here there is a post-office, a school (rebuilt at considerable expense), a church and a chapel. The 'smiddy' sells items made by the islanders like colley lamps, ram's head knives, sheepskin rugs and items made from copper salvaged from the *Oceanic*, sister ship

to the *Titanic*. She was wrecked off Foula in 1914.

Ham Voe is the best that Foula can provide in the way of harbour facilities. The island's only 'beach' is at the head of the narrow little voe and the fishing boats have to be drawn well up to clear the big waves which tumble in, particularly when the wind is in the east. Even the small mailboat/ferry, after it has had all the goods and equipment off-loaded by the islanders, has to be power-hoisted onto a concrete pad at the pier for security. A monthly mailboat service began in 1879, when the local minister wrote to Queen Victoria and received a reply from Disraeli. But 'monthly' was an optimistic term as there was no harbour and passengers and goods had to be landed on the rocks. It was not until 1914, after thirty years of petitioning, that a tiny concrete pier was built using local labour and shingle from the back of Smell Geo. It included a step for a gun because of the advent of the First World War. The officials chose to site the pier alongside the only skerry in the Voe so consequently one side of the pier is inaccessible. Many years later a power-driven crane and winch was fitted to allow the mailboat to be lifted out instead of being manhandled. The winter service from Walls is entirely dependent on the weather and there have been many problems after 1990 as a new ferry was built which was found to be unable to cope with the severe conditions.

The strong sense of community in this gaunt and beautiful outpost is very evident. For about a century the population was slowly disintegrating and in 1965 Eric Linklater claimed that this 'old folks' home remote in the pitiless Atlantic will not survive much longer as a human habitation'. Yet today the population has stabilised, shows signs of increasing, and new houses and a school for the next generation have been built. There is no doubt that this is the result of better communications; access to an airstrip, a telephone, and a radio transmitter. But a different attitude by mainlanders is also helping to save the last few populated islands from complete desolation. Local authorities have at last realised that island schools may be uneconomic but that they are an essential element in maintaining a population, and that this also applies to improved harbours and services.

Foula has many physical similarities to Hirta, St Kilda (No.9.1). Both these Atlantic islands have high mountains, skyscraping cliffs and little land suitable for cultivation. In both cases an essential source of food was seabirds and eggs collected from the terrifying cliffs. But there the similarity ends because the St Kildans were basically crofters who had virtually no concept of private property. All decision-making had to be communal following the tenet that the community is more important than the individual.

On Foula, on the other hand, the islanders were fishermen rather than crofters and like all sailors they were intensely independent and self-assured. They believed in private enterprise and standing on their own feet. The community was important, but only as a collection of individuals. Even the houses on Foula stand apart whereas on St Kilda they cling together.

Is there a lesson to be learned? The St Kildans have gone, but Foula is still a thriving community.

Foula's stacks are not as high as those of Hirta but they are just as interesting. For instance, near **Hellibaas** (ON – flagstone rocks on which the sea breaks in bad weather) on the north coast there is a high square-topped stack with a natural arch at its base which looks like a ruined castle. And Foula's cliffs are unequalled in dramatic impact even if they just fail by 2m to match the height of the awesome St Kildan cliffs. There is a narrow chimney on top of **Hamnafjeld** (ON – harbour mountain) which is so deep it is said to go straight down to Hell; and at the head of the Daal in the **Wick of Mucklabrek** is the Sneck of the Smallie, another secret chimney which plunges down between the sea-cliffs in a narrow slit until only the sky is visible 60m above.

Relics of the quaint Norn language still linger in the dialect on Foula, noticeable in place names such as Hedd o' da Baa (head of the underwater rock) and Wester Hoevdi (western height). Linklater recalled how when the menfolk had finished fishing they would dance the Foula Reel to the tune of *The Shaalds of Foula* (shaald – shoal) – 'Up wi' da lines and link it awa, awa, ta da shaalds o Foula.'

One of these famous, but dangerous, shoals – **Hoevdi Grund** (ON – high ground) – which were once rich in cod, haddock, mackerel, halibut, saithe and ling, lies only three miles east of South Ness.

* * *

Access: Mail boat/ passenger ferry, May to Sept. weather permitting, from Walls, 2 or 3 times per week, 07881-823732, or 01595-743976 for information. Advance booking essential.

Scheduled flights from Tingwall, weather permitting, Mon., Tue., Wed., and Fri. 01595-840246. Day trips, Cycharters Ltd., 01595-696598.

Anchorage: There is no adequate harbour. Local boats are hauled out and even the mailboat/ferry is lifted out by crane each trip.
1. Ham Voe. Very restricted. Beware rocks on N and S sides of Ham Voe and on E side of pier. Approach with care on a WNW course to just off the SW corner of the pier. The stone pier is 27m long with steps halfway along its NW side and a depth of 1.8m at its head and on its west side. Anchor in corner of Voe with warp to hold stern off. No turning room for boats of over 36'. Best to leave promptly if bad weather likely.

11.7 Noss

(ON nos – nose, or high rocky promontory) or (ON nes – headland.)

OS Maps: 1:50000 Sheet 4 1:25000 Sheet 466
Admiralty Charts: 1:75000 No.3283 1:17500 No.3291 excludes E coast.
Area: 343ha (847 acres)
Height: 181m (594 ft)

Owner: John Hamilton Scott of Garth and Wendy Scott. Noss is part of the Garth Estate.

Population: 1841–24 (3 houses). After 1871 partly cleared by Walker, the owner's factor. 1881–3. 1891–3 (1 house). 1931–4. Only summer habitation since. 1961–0. 1971–3. 1981–0. 1991–0. 2001–0. 2011–0.

Geology: Old Red Sandstone cliffs stratified and eroded in horizontal slabs which provide perfect shelves for nesting birds with occasional traces of volcanic vents.

History: A small chapel existed in front of the old homestead at Gungstie (now the SNH visitor centre) in 1633, built by 'shipwrakt' persons. The walls were still standing in 1774 and the burial ground beside the Sound was used until the middle of the 19th century. There is good reason to believe that the chapel site was originally Celtic and pre-Norse but, unfortunately, the burial ground is now being eroded by the sea. In 1969 the tenant found an underground passage beside the house.

The homestead was built some 400 years ago

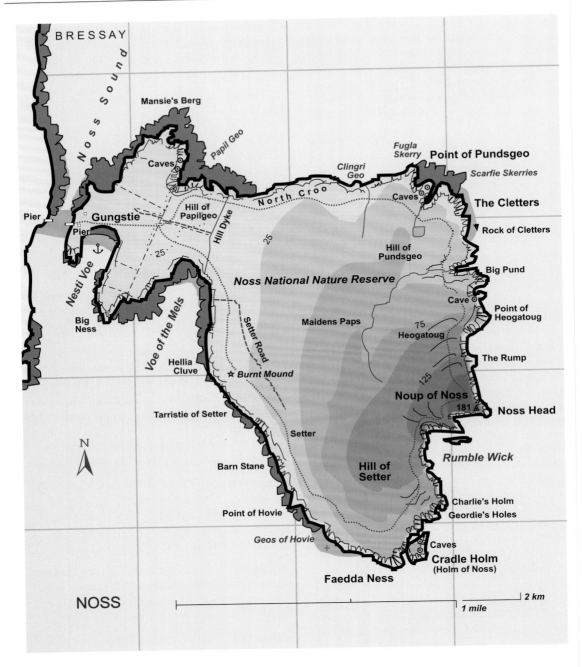

NOSS

and for a time was the only inhabited house on Noss. In the early 19th century the farm was reputed to produce the best butter and milk in Shetland. The tenant farmer at the time was the father of Dr James Copland who published the *Dictionary of Medicine* in 1832.

In 1869 the Marquis of Londonderry leased the island and turned it over to pasture for his prize breed of Shetland stallions. These were used in his Durham coal mine as a substitute for child labour. The mares were kept on Bressay to allow controlled breeding.

Since 1900 Noss has been used for sheep-farming providing pasturage for about 420 Shetland ewes.

Wildlife: The island, which has been a National Nature Reserve since 1955, is managed by Scottish Natural Heritage. Explanatory leaflets are available at the visitors' centre. Visitors are required to keep to the cliff-top path and no camping is permitted.

There are 150 species of flowering plants here including the semi-parasitic Lousewort or 'Sookie Flooer', but Noss is best known for its seabirds, more than 160,000 of them. The first gannet colony only became established on Noss in 1911. Now there are over 5,000 pairs nesting on the headland with over 10,000 pairs of kittiwake and 65,000 pairs of guillemot. Twenty pairs of arctic skua and 300 pairs of great skua (bonxie) nest inland. There are also many fulmar, eider (dunter), great black-backed gull, razorbill, puffin, shag and black guillemot (tystie).

The best bird-watching period is mid-May to July.

*   *   *

The isle of **NOSS** is a veritable metropolis of seabirds and the cacophony of sound from their cries is so loud that it can sometimes be heard far to seaward when even the island itself is out of sight. The cliffs of Noss are made up of narrow horizontal beds of sandstone which the sea has carved into thousands of attractive ledges. These are ideal sites for seabirds' dream-houses and competition is intense in Bird City.

The **Noup of Noss**, towering 180m above the waves, is the highest point on Noss and the 'city centre'. Every precipitous dormitory suburb has a suitable name which rolls off the tongue delightfully: to the north – the Cletters, Whiggie Geo, Point of Heogatoug, and the Rump; and southwards – Rumble Wick, Geordie's Holes, Feadda Ness and Holm of Noss. The best viewpoint is from the sea.

Holm of Noss, also known as Cradle Holm, is a stack standing 48m high and considered now to be almost impossible to climb. It is separated by a 20m gap from the cave-riddled cliffs of Feadda Ness. This used to provide a handy anchorage for small boats until a rockfall blocked it. In the 17th century a crofter was wagered a cow that he could not reach the top of the Holm and he won the wager, reputedly by climbing a ship's mast for part of the way. While on the top he fixed stakes in the turf and constructed a replaceable rope railway which could support a box cradle large enough to carry a man and a sheep. Unfortunately, after completing the work he slipped and fell to his death. It was of little consolation to him that his engineering was

faultless and that his famous 'Cradle of Noss' was used every summer for over 200 years to graze sheep on the top of the Holm. It was dismantled in 1864 by Mr Walker, the laird's factor, who considered it unsafe. He had a safety wall built along the cliff-head.

Noss Sound is shallow, rocky and narrow (less than 200m) and wind and tide can funnel through, making it decidedly unpleasant at times. It has been the scene of many shipwrecks. An old track along the south shore ends at **Setter** where there are still the ruins of a settlement. In Norse times there were five settlements along this south coast according to the records. The visitors' path continues from here and circumnavigates the island.

The old house at Gungstie was restored as staff accommodation in 1986 and includes a visitor information room. The Pony Pund – the stables building built by the Marquis of Londonderry in 1870 – was converted at the same time and contains an interpretative display.

The name of **Papil Geo** (G. – priest's inlet) on the north coast below the **North Croo** might be a reminder that an early Christian hermit once lived on Noss – possibly in the caves which open on to the Geo, or it may be related to the chapel site at Hametoun.

From the landing place at Gungstie the ground climbs towards the west, gently at first and then quite steeply. The 'Hill Dyke' crosses the island's neck and during the lambing season this separates the lambs from the nesting bonxies. The ground cover is mostly heather and coarse grass but the grazing was once fine grass pasture for the Marquis of Londonderry's ponies. In the nesting season when climbing up the slopes to the cliff-head the bonxies dive-bomb with determination. This is rarely dangerous but is certainly intimidating. On the cliff-top path expect also to have your senses assaulted. The sight of prolific birdlife is unbelievable, the noise is deafening, and the smell overpowering.

*   *   *

Access: Lerwick to Bressay (See No.11.8) then car, bus, taxi or walk (5km) to Noss Sound. For crossing to Noss by inflatable from Bressay (summer only, and no dogs) hail the Scottish Natural Heritage warden at Gungstie on Noss, 01595-693345. For wildlife trips round Bressay and Noss try Alluvion Trips, 01595-692577 or contact Tourist Office, 01595-693434.

Anchorages: Noss Sound is shallow, rocky and has a strong tidal current. Passage requires a shallow-draught and local knowledge.

1. Nesti Voe, at S end of Noss Sound. Occasional anchorage. Enter mid-channel and anchor in the middle, sand. Exposed S.

2. Voe of the Mels, W of Nesti Voe. Occasional anchorage. Approach E of mid-channel and anchor near head of voe in 4m sand. Exposed S.

3. Noup of Noss, steep-to. There are mooring rings on the rocks below the Noup for use in quiet weather to watch the birds.

11.8 Bressay

In 1490 called (ON Brús-øy – Brusi's island) from a proper name, but in 1263 was possibly referred to as (ON breid-øy – broad island).

O S Maps: 1:50000 Sheet 4 1:25000 Sheet 466
Admiralty Charts: 1:75000 No.3283 1:17500 No.3291
Area: 2805ha (6931 acres)
Height: 226m (741 ft)
Owner: Mr John Hamilton Scott of Garth, Lord Lieutenant of Shetland, who farms Maryfield Farm, is the principal landowner. He inherited the Bressay estate from his uncle, Mr Norman Ogilvie Mouat Cameron of Garth.

Population: 1841–904 (167 houses). 1881–847. 1891–799 (166 houses). 1931–448. 1961–269. 1981–334. 1991–352. 2001–384. 2011–368 (174 households).

Geology: Almost entirely composed of Middle and Upper Old Red Sandstone with a few volcanic outcrops and some thin bands of tuff between the flagstones on the east coast. Much of Shetland is roofed with 'slates' – thin flagstone slabs – from Bressay, and building stone was quarried at Aith.

History: A selection of prehistoric remains are scattered across Bressay but the best-known early historical artefact is probably the Bressay Stone which was found near Culbinsbrough churchyard and which can be seen in the Scottish National Museum of Antiquities in Edinburgh. It is a Pictish cross-slab with an ogam inscription which includes two Gaelic words and one Norse word which might indicate that the early inhabitants were co-operating peacefully. It is exquisitely carved with a Celtic cross, representations of priests, a horseman, some animals and, possibly, Jonah and two whales.

In the 11th century Harald Hardrada's ships lay in Bressay Sound (ON *Breideyjarsund*) before sailing south to a Viking defeat by Harold Godwinsson at Stamford Bridge. In the 13th century King Haakon's fleet also sheltered in the Sound before meeting a similar fate at Largs.

From the 15th to the mid-17th century most of Bressay was owned by Sigurd Jonsson, a Norwegian nobleman. John Neven the Younger of Unst became owner of the estate in 1660 and then it passed to the Hendersons, who were also of Norwegian origin. Most of the remainder of the island belonged to the Bolts of Cruister, Magnus Bult being 'Foude' of Bressay in 1612. The Bolts lived in the Haa of Cruister but the building was abandoned – it is now a ruin – when the Mouats of Garth acquired the Bolts' estate in the early 19th century.

In 1640 ten Spanish men-of-war sailed into the Sound and attacked four Dutchmen, two of which were sunk. Later, an English fleet of ninety-four ships commanded by Admiral George Monk anchored here for several days in 1653 while searching for Van Tromp and the Dutch fleet.

In the early 18th century French privateers sailed through and 'pillaged like gentlemen' and a French fleet in a fishing war with the Dutch burned 150 busses anchored in the Sound. The area was a favourite fishing ground for the Dutch and in 1774, for instance, over 400 busses – mostly Dutch – anchored in the Sound. It was said that Amsterdam was built 'oot o' da back o' Bressa'.

During the Peninsular War, naval press-gangs raided the area and removed numerous young Shetlanders, magnificent seamen whom the islands could ill-afford to lose, for service with Nelson's fleet.

1871 was 'da year 'at Walker made da uproar'. The laird at that time was Miss Mouat and her factor, Walker, cleared many of the crofts for sheep. He built Maryfield House for himself and named it after his wife. The site, opposite Lerwick, was previously a croft called Troubletoon.

The German High Seas Fleet visited the Sound in the early years of the 20th century and Bressay boasted gun emplacements in both World Wars.

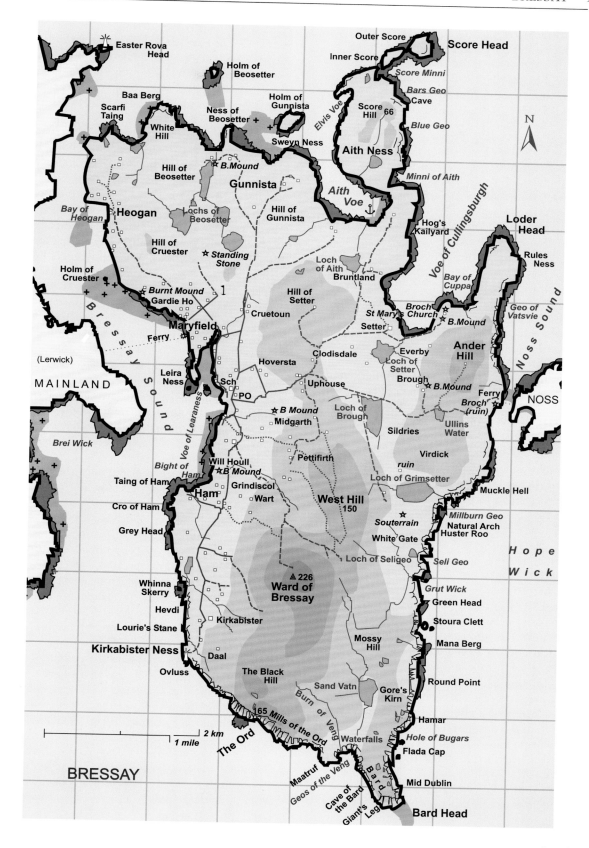

Easter Rova Head
Holm of Beosetter
Outer Score
Inner Score
Score Head
Score Minni
Bars Geo Cave
Baa Berg
Scarfi Taing
Ness of Beosetter
Holm of Gunnista
Elvis Voe
Score Hill 66
Blue Geo
White Hill
Sweyn Ness
Aith Ness
Hill of Beosetter
B.Mound
Gunnista
Minni of Aith
Bay of Heogan
Heogan
Lochs of Beosetter
Hill of Gunnista
Aith Voe
Hog's Kailyard
Loder Head
Hill of Cruester
Loch of Aith
Bruntland
Voe of Cullingsburgh
Rules Ness
Standing Stone
Bay of Cuppa
Holm of Cruester
Burnt Mound
Gardie Ho
Hill of Setter
Broch Church
B.Mound
Geo of Vatsvie
1
Cruetoun
St Mary's Church
Setter
Ander Hill
Maryfield
Ferry
Clodisdale
Everby
Loch of Setter
Brough
B.Mound
Noss Sound
(Lerwick)
MAINLAND
Leira Ness
Sch
PO
Hoversta
Uphouse
Loch of Brough
B.Mound
Sildries
Ullins Water
Ferry
Broch (ruin)
NOSS
Bressay Sound
B Mound
Midgarth
Pettifirth
Virdick
ruin
Voe of Learaness
Brei Wick
Will Houll
B Mound
Loch of Grimsetter
Muckle Hell
Bight of Ham
Taing of Ham
Ham
Grindiscol
Wart
West Hill 150
Souterrain
Millburn Geo
Natural Arch
Huster Roo
Cro of Ham
White Gate
Hope
Grey Head
Loch of Seligeo
Seli Geo
Wick
Grut Wick
Whinna Skerry
Ward of Bressay
226
Green Head
Hevdi
Kirkabister
Stoura Clett
Lourie's Stane
Mossy Hill
Mana Berg
Kirkabister Ness
Daal
The Black Hill
Sand Vatn
Gore's Kirn
Round Point
Ovluss
Burn of Veng
Hamar
Hole of Bugars
165
Mills of the Ord
Waterfalls
Flada Cap
2 km
1 mile
The Ord
Maatruf
Geos of the Veng
Bard
Mid Dublin
BRESSAY
Cave of the Bard
Giant's Leg
Bard Head

N

Wildlife: Many migrant birds reach the crofts in the west of the island. Waders and whooper swans can be seen at the Loch of Grimsetter on the east coast. Further south, bonxies nest near Sand Vatn, seabirds nest on the cliffs and a colony of arctic skua nests near Bard Head.

*   *   *

Lerwick and **BRESSAY** are symbiotic. Lerwick could not exist if it were not for the protection which the island gives to its excellent harbour; Bressay owes much of its livelihood to close proximity to Lerwick.

The merits of an anchorage in Bressay Sound were known by the Vikings but it was the Dutch fishermen in the 15th century who turned it into a port. The Dutch busses – two-masted craft of over 80 tons – and their accompanying men-of-war which would now be called 'fishery protection vessels' would crowd into the Sound in vast numbers. At times it was said one could cross from Mainland to Bressay by stepping from boat to boat. For the Dutch this was a great government-protected industry with more than 2000 busses exporting their catch of Scottish herring to countries throughout the western world. James VI (James I of England) tried to introduce a licensing system to control them but it was ignored. Later Charles I enlisted the help of the Navy and after an exchange of fire the Dutch agreed to pay an annual fee and obey the rules. One such rule was that fishing could not begin before the Feast of St John the Baptist (Johnsmas – 24 June). By mid-June the Sound would fill with boats preparing for the start and the Shetlanders meanwhile would make what profit they could from the event by setting up booths and bars on the shore.

By 1798 a few Shetland boats had succeeded in joining the bonanza. According to the Rev. Cruttwell: 'The inhabitants of Bressay fit out about twenty-six large fishing boats.'

It is a sad historical fact that the social structure in the Scottish islands denied most of the inhabitants the chance to own an ocean-going fishing boat with the result that the vast wealth of the northern seas was largely exploited by foreigners. It is only in very recent times that Scottish fishermen have had the opportunity to participate.

The south and east coasts are high, barren and precipitous whereas the north and west coasts are lower with rocky foreshores and productive crofts. **Ward of Bressay** – 'Da Wart' – is a pyramid-shaped hill in the centre of the southern part of the island. It is the highest point on the island at 226m but its interesting silhouette is not appreciated by the inhabitants of Lerwick as on sunny winter mornings it casts a shadow across the town.

On the south coast above the cliffs there is another hill called **The Ord** which reaches a height of 165m. East of here is the bleak expanse of **Sand Vatn** and the most southerly point of Bressay, **Bard Head**. The sandstone cliffs which stretch round this point and up the west coast are composed of interesting rock formations. Beside the aptly-named **Giant's Leg** is the Cave of the Bard, better known as **Orkneyman's Cave** [HU514360]. No one is certain now who the Orkneyman was: he might have been a Jacobite, or a fugitive from the naval press-gangs, or the name might come from an earlier age. The cave is only accessible by boat but is well worth the trouble. The entrance is a symmetrical archway which is wide enough for several boats to enter abreast and the water within is clear and deep with extraordinarily beautiful variegated colours on the roof and walls. The cave then narrows but opens up again into a spacious hall with stalactites. It is possible to go in by dinghy for a considerable distance.

Bressay has had its brochs but only traces of these remain. In Culbingsbrough Voe (ON Kolbeinsborg) in the north-east, called Cullingsburgh by the Ordnance Survey, there is one on a small promontory [HU521423]. Beside it is the ruined wall of a chapel, **St Mary's Church**, which is claimed to have been the only cruciform church in Shetland and which may date back to the Norse era. In the burial ground is a stone commemorating a Dutch captain, Claes Bruyn, who was master of a merchantman *Amboina*. In 1636 after a foray with Portuguese ships off Mozambique, he took on a cargo of Persian silk at Surat in India, was delayed by violent gales off the Cape of Good Hope, lost twenty-nine of his crew from disease, and then at last, months later, reached Bressay Sound. He dropped anchor thankfully and promptly dropped dead.

St Mary's is overlooked by **Ander Hill** which has a derelict lookout tower on top of it built by the Admiralty before the First World War. Ander Hill has a similar profile when viewed from every point of the compass.

Gunnista was also the site of an early church dedicated to St Ola or Olaf and the parish church until 1722. It was demolished by the laird, William Henderson of Gardie, despite the minister's protests, to use the materials for a new church to be built nearer Gardie House. **Aith Voe**, between Gunnista and twisted Aith Ness, is a fair anchorage with its entrance guarded by two islets, **Holm of Beosetter** and **Holm of Gunnista**.

A third early church existed at **Kirkabister** in the south-west dedicated to St John, but it has long since disappeared. **Bressay Lighthouse** is close by, at Kirkabister Ness, marking the southern entrance to Bressay Sound. It was built in 1858 and is now automatic.

The ferry docks by **Maryfield**, the main house for Maryfield Farm (452ha). To the north is the charming little mansion, **Gardie House**, the laird's house, which was built in 1724 but had its facade remodelled about 1900.

* * *

Access: Frequent daily ro-ro ferry from Lerwick, (voicebank) 01595-743974. Tourist Office, 01595-693434.

Anchorages:

1. Visitor berths in marina (2m least depth) at Voe of Leiraness.
2. Lerwick Harbour, (Mainland). Berth in Small Boat Harbour or Albert docks subject to HM's agreement or temp. anchorage S of Small Boat Hr.
3. Bard Head. Mooring rings for use while visiting the Cave of the Bard (Orkneyman's cave) by dinghy in settled conditions.
4. Aith Voe, N coast. Enter E of Gunnista Holm. Anchor in 5½–7m. Good shelter but fish cage obstruction.

11.9 Hildasay

Possibly (ON hildis-øy – battle island). Hild was the battle goddess of Norse mythology. The Vikings liked to settle a quarrel by single combat on an uninhabited island in order to avoid interference by spectators. The island name is sometimes spelt Hildesay. Alternatively (ON Hildis-øy – Hildir's island). Hildir is a man's name.

OS Maps: 1:50000 Sheet 4 1:25000 Sheet 466
Admiralty Charts: 1:75000 No.3283 1:17500 No.3294
Area: 108ha (267 acres)
Height: 32m (105 ft)

Owner: Mr & Mrs John Griffiths.

Population: 1881–7. 1891–30 (5 houses). 1901–0. Uninhabited since.

Geology: The high-quality red-green 'granite' on Hildasay – actually an epidotic syenite – was quarried for many years and was even said to have been exported to Australia but with the advent of concrete the quarry became uneconomic and closed down.

History: Hildasay was bought by an American with Shetland family connections in 1897.

* * *

HILDASAY is an oval island, shaped like a yeti's footprint. It reaches a height of 32m near its north end. There are rocky escarpments on the west and north coasts and the south coast has three 'toes' formed by two narrow inlets, Cusa Voe and Tangi Voe (ON – seaweed inlet). A large loch, **West Loch**, with several small islets covers a considerable part of the west side of the island.

Hildasay has a satellite island – the yeti's big toe – called **Linga** (ON – heather island). It is close to the south-east coast and it was a separate croft in the 19th century.

To the north-west, but separated by a deep navigable channel, is a long reef of skerries and holms including **North Score Holm**, **Easter Score Holm** and **Sanda Little**. It culminates in **Sanda Stour** (ON – big sandy island) at its south end. This little islet is 19m high and the sea has carved its rocks into a natural arch.

The ruins of Hildasay's small settlement, which reached its maximum size of five houses towards the end of the 19th century, is on the hillside in the north. At that time the island was going through a relatively prosperous stage. Apart from three or four crofts there was a curing-station for herring and a granite quarry. The quarry had a small railway track to carry the cut stone down to the landing place – the only such railway track in Shetland. The owner allowed islanders from Burra and Trondra to cut peat on the island as they had none on their own islands. The peat on Hildasay was of particularly good quality and the peat-cutting visits were always a good excuse for a social occasion.

Unfortunately, the good times came to an end. The quarry closed down when the sale of its stone became uneconomic and almost simultaneously the curing-station was closed because of the

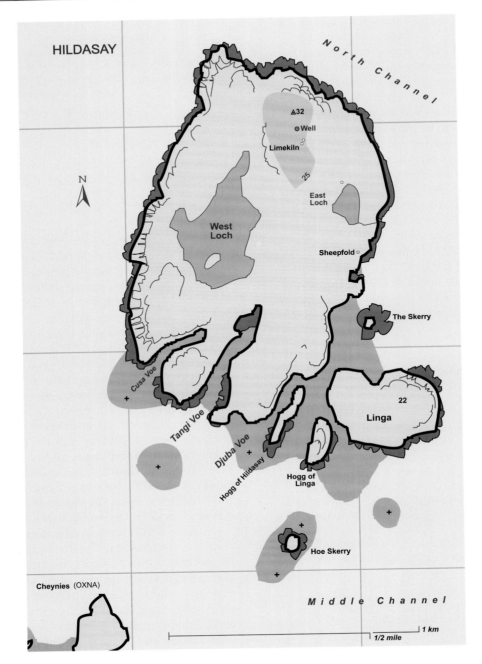

HILDASAY

North Channel

△32
⊙Well
Limekiln

25

East
Loch

West
Loch

Sheepfold ▫

The Skerry

N

Cusa Voe

+

Tangi Voe

Djuba Voe
+

Hogg of Hildasay

22

Linga

Hogg of
Linga

Hoe Skerry

+

+

+

Cheynies (OXNA)

Middle Channel

1 km
1/2 mile

decline in the herring industry. Only sheep remained. The island was abandoned about 1900 but it was determined not to be forgotten and in the latter years of the last century issued its own postage stamps.

A brief interruption to its isolation occurred during World War II when it was used occasionally for marine training purposes.

* * *

Access: By arrangement: MV Cycharters, Scalloway, 01595-696598. Tourist Office, 01595-693434.

Anchorage: There is no recommended anchorage and temp. anchorage by The Skerry (N of Linga) is risky owing to the proximity of fish-cages but there is an old pier for a landing place.

11.10 Vaila

Probably (ON val-øy – falcon island) but could also be horse island, battlefield island or round island.

OS Maps: 1:50000 Sheets 3 and 4 1:25000 Sheet 467
Admiralty Charts: 1:75000 Nos.3283 or 3281 1:25000 No.3295

Area: 327ha (808 acres)
Height: 95m (312 ft)

Owner: Dorota Rychlik and Richard Rowland, of London. Purchased in 1993 from Mr Henry Anderton. The owners have restored Vaila Hall.

Population: 1841–29 (4 houses). 1881–9.

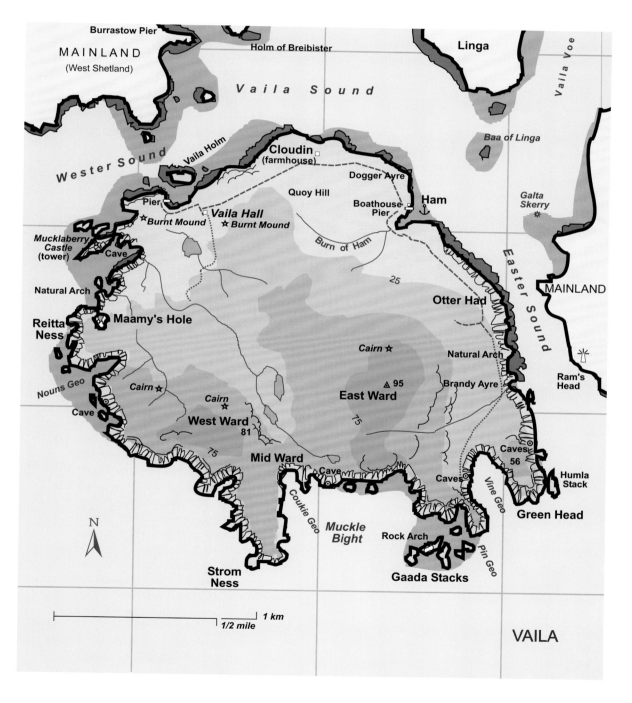

1891–19 (2 houses). 1901–30. 1931–5. 1961–9.
1971–5. 1981–0. 1991–1. 2001–2. 2011–2.

Geology: Fine, dark-grey sandstone typical of
the Walls region. It was deposited about 400
million years ago but has since been folded and
metamorphosed and subsequently glaciated. The
south-east corner has an intrusion of complex
Sandsting granite seen in the red cliffs by the
Gaada Stacks.

History: A Neolithic house site has been
discovered and there are Bronze Age burned
mounds in the fertile north-west of the island.

In 1490 the estates of the Norwegian family of
Ciske were divided and Vaila and Foula (No.11.6)
became the possession of Alv Knutsson. Gorvel
Fadersdatter 'of Geskie' succeeded to the title in
1537 and she leased Vaila, and Walls, to Robert
Cheyne of Ury (later to become Commissioner
of Zetland) in 1576 with permission to build a
fortress for safety from 'Heland men, perattis and
utheris invasionis'. There was some confusion
concerning national ownership of all the
Northern Isles at this time as they had been
mortgaged to Scotland for Princess Margaret
of Norway's dowry in 1468 and Scotland had
later foreclosed on the unpaid debt and annexed
them. Consequently, Andrew Hawich of Scatsa
contested Cheyne's claim to Vaila but Cheyne was
able to produce proof of title from the Scottish
king. Two years later (1582) Gorvel transferred
all her estates to the King of Denmark but he too
confirmed Cheyne's right to lease the property for
66 'good dollars' a year.

The Scandinavian claim became more and
more tenuous and by 1661 the Danes were
complaining that the rent was seldom received.

In 1696 the Cheyne's sold Vaila to James
Mitchell, a Scalloway merchant and he built a
house on the island which now forms part of
the south wing of Vaila Hall. In 1736 the island
was inherited by James Scott of Melby (see also
No.11.6) and it was the Scott family who leased it
to the notable Shetlander, Arthur Anderson.

Arthur Anderson was born in Shetland in
1792. He was a beach-boy (fish-drier), who
acquired some education and volunteered to
join the Navy. He became a midshipman and, in
due course, a Captain's clerk. He then left the
Navy and obtained employment with a London
shipowner, Willcox, who eventually offered him a
partnership. This gave him time to travel during

which he intervened successfully in a civil war
in Portugal and founded a Liberal newspaper in
Shetland. In 1837 he and Willcox started the
Peninsular Steam Company which, three years
later, became the Peninsular and Oriental (P & O),
running regular mail services to India and China
with a strict discipline that almost matched the
Royal Navy.

Meanwhile Anderson continued to take a great
interest in Shetland's welfare. He presented Queen
Victoria with a fine knitted Shetland shawl which
made these shawls instantly popular in fashion-
conscious London society and created a new
cottage industry. Also in 1837 he leased Vaila
and established the Shetland Fishery Company
– breaking the existing feudal system by which
all catches, and most of the boats, belonged to
the laird. And in the following year he started a
regular steamship mail-service to Shetland, which
existed until recently in the form of the P & O
Ferries serving the Northern Isles.

This untiring and benevolent man was Member
of Parliament for Orkney and Shetland for several
years – establishing a Liberal tradition which has
remained part of the philosophy of the islands.
But his outlook was far from insular: for instance,
he suggested the cutting of a Suez Canal long
before de Lesseps. He was philanthropic, founding
the Widows' Homes in Lerwick for widows of
seamen and fishermen, never priggish, and always
retained a great sense of humour.

Arthur Anderson, who died aged seventy-
seven, may have had only a passing connection
with the island of Vaila but the island gains
much by association with one of the truly great
Shetlanders.

In 1893 Herbert Anderton, a rich Yorkshire
mill-owner on a wool-buying business trip to
Shetland, fell in love with Vaila and bought it.
He immediately carried out a massive building
programme with similarities to the Bullough
developments on Rum (No.4.3). Anderton
used Vaila Hall as a summer residence and
accommodated large house parties. His brother,
Francis Swithin, a Royal Academician, assisted
with other developments on the island and his
brother-in-law and fellow mill-owner, Colonel
Foster, bought nearby Burrastow House on
Mainland.

During the depression Mr Anderton's fortune
largely disappeared as he tried to maintain full
employment for his mill-workers. He retired to

the island in 1933 and lived there in virtual isolation until he died in 1937. Colonel and Mrs Foster then inherited Vaila but they had both died by 1953 and their daughter was confined to the deteriorating building with multiple sclerosis. Meanwhile, the farm also fell into disrepair so that when, on Miss Foster's death in 1969, Herbert Anderton's great-nephew inherited the island, it was almost too late for him to take remedial measures to stop further serious deterioration of the property. He sold Vaila to the present owners in 1993. Burrastow House (built 1759) on Mainland is a hotel with a well-regarded restaurant and can usually organise a boat to Vaila.

Wildlife: Over 100 different species of wildflower have been recorded on Vaila.

The blue (mountain) hare was introduced in the 20th century and the peat and heather moorland and cliff fringe provide nesting sites for many seabirds. The skeleton of a sperm whale which died on the shore has been cleaned and assembled by the island's owners for visitors to view.

Green fertile ground on the north of **VAILA** slopes upwards to moorland in the south. Here there are two cairn-topped rounded hills, West Ward (81m) and **East Ward** (95m), the island summit. The moor has some scattered pools and lochans and on the south-east coast it falls abruptly to the sea in red granite cliffs which rear up again in arches and rocky stacks like Dracula's teeth where they are split by narrow geos.

On the west coast the cliffs are of more modest height but they also have a natural arch and the explosive **Maamy's Hole**, where the waves are forced under pressure through a fissure into a 'gloup' [HU221464].

Vaila is separated from Mainland by Wester Sound and Easter Sound, which form entrances to **Vaila Sound** with its good natural harbour of Walls. This used to be a port of call for ships from Aberdeen and Leith, and for the Shetland deep-sea fishing fleet, and is still the terminus for the Foula passenger ferry (No.11.6). The islet of **Linga** (ON – heather isle) which lies in the middle of Vaila Sound had a population of nine in 1841. This increased to thirteen in 1881 and there were still two inhabitants in 1931.

On the narrow peninsula running parallel with Wester Sound, **Mucklabery Castle** [HU221468], is an ancient two-storey watch tower of unknown origin but which may have been of use to smugglers watching for excisemen. The tower was restored by Herbert Anderton with added crenellations and an angle turret.

West Pier in Voe of Vaila is sheltered by **Vaila Holm** (Gluibuil) at this north-west corner. It is the landing point for the boat from Burrastow House on Mainland which crosses the narrows of Wester Sound, passing the **Holms of Breibister** and **Burrastow**.

There is another pier at **Ham** (ON – harbour) in the north-east – the **East Pier**. The boat-house with studio above was possibly the first reconstruction project undertaken by Anderton. Both he and his wife were keen artists and his brother was a member of the Royal Academy. Anderton's work had often taken him abroad and among the many artefacts he brought back was a Buddha from Japan. With true Victorian abandon he constructed a small Buddhist temple beside the studio. (This is quite unique for Shetland but not for Scottish islands in general. Both Eilean Righ (No.2.9) and Holy Island (No.1.3) also have Buddhist connections). Unfortunately, the temple and studio later fell into serious disrepair but the gardens at Ham, which Herbert Anderton created, still shelter his tomb.

The fertile ground in the north supported a productive farm and **Cloudin Farmhouse** was built in 1894. When Lord Londonderry's famous stud of Shetland ponies on Noss (No.11.7) was sold Anderton bought foundation stock and built up a large herd. He also had sheep, Clydesdale horses and a small herd of dairy cows.

Work started on **Vaila Hall**, which is the largest house of its kind in Shetland, in 1895. The south wing incorporates James Mitchell's laird's house as well as the original entrance doorway with the Mitchell coat-of-arms above it inscribed with the date 1696. The north wing of the hall was reconstructed from various outbuildings with a central courtyard which became the hall itself. Some of the stone and skilled labour for the work was imported from England and many of the ornaments and contents came from further afield. The stone griffons flanking the entrance steps, for instance, are thought to have come from Germany.

As befitted an island laird, a brass cannon made in Yorkshire was ceremoniously fired from the terrace whenever the Andertons arrived on Vaila.

*   *   *

INSIDE AN IRON AGE WHEEL-HOUSE AT JARLSHOF

Access: Crossing from Burrastow pier only by prior arrangement at Burrastow House Hotel, 01595-809307.

Anchorages:
1. Ham (Boathouse Pier). Reasonable shelter in all winds. Anchor off pier but beware old moorings.
2. Burrastow Pier (on Mainland). Anchor off pier. Sheltered W–N.

11.11 Mainland

(ON megenland – mainland).

Muckle Roe

(S. and ON – big red island).

West *and* East Burra

(E. and ON – west and east broch island).

Trondra

Probably (ON – boar island) but may be from the man's name (ON – Prondr's isle) or, improbably, the Norse tribe's name (ON – Praendir island), from which Trondheim in Norway derives.

O S Maps: 1:50000 Sheets 1, 3 and 4 1:25000 Sheets 466 to 470 inclusive.
Admiralty Charts: 1:500000 No.219 1:200000 Nos.1119 and 1233 1:75000 Nos.3281, 3282 and 3283 1:30000 No.3298 Yell Sound 1:17500 No.3291 approaches to Lerwick various scales: No.3294 Clift Sound, Scalloway, Sand and Hos Wick, Seli, Sandsound and Weisdale Voes: No.3295 Vaila Sound, Gruting, Dales and Ronas Voes, Bay of Quendale, Swarbacks Minn, Olna and Ura Firths 1:12500 No.3297 Sullom Voe

Area: 100230ha (247668 acres)
Height: 450m (1476 ft)
Owners: Multiple ownership. Shetland Council owns a large area in the north.

Population:

	1841	1881	1891	1931	1961	1991	2001	2011
M'land	20572	20821	19741	15172	13282	17562	17550	18765
E/W B'a	586	642	695	767	653	889	819	852
M'e Roe	214	230	213	154	103	115	104	130
Trondra	244	133	154	91	20	117	133	135
	21616	21826	20803	16184	14058	18798	18683	19882

Geology: Mainland is formed from a ridge of very old rocks made up of granite, schist, and gneiss. The southern leg or promontory is mainly of dark blue and grey slates and mica-schists but with a band of Old Red Sandstone on the east coast. North of here the ridge of stratified metamorphic rocks continues in more crystalline forms of schist and gneiss interrupted by long bands of limestone as far north as Laxfirth. West Mainland is generally of Old Red Sandstone but North Mainland is a very complex structure with granites and diorites predominating and basaltic lavas and tuffs on the west side.

On top of the ancient core of igneous and metamorphic rocks great beds of sediment (Old Red Sandstone) were laid down in geologically recent times. There were occasional volcanic intrusions of lava forming layers of igneous rock.

During the last Ice Age the Scandinavian ice sheet spread across Shetland and scoured the surface, removing much of the 'new' Old Red Sandstone from the central spine and smoothing the topography into rounded hills, wide valleys and many small lochs. The ice brought debris with it. There is a two-ton boulder of laurvikite in the roadside wall of Dalsetter croft in Boddam

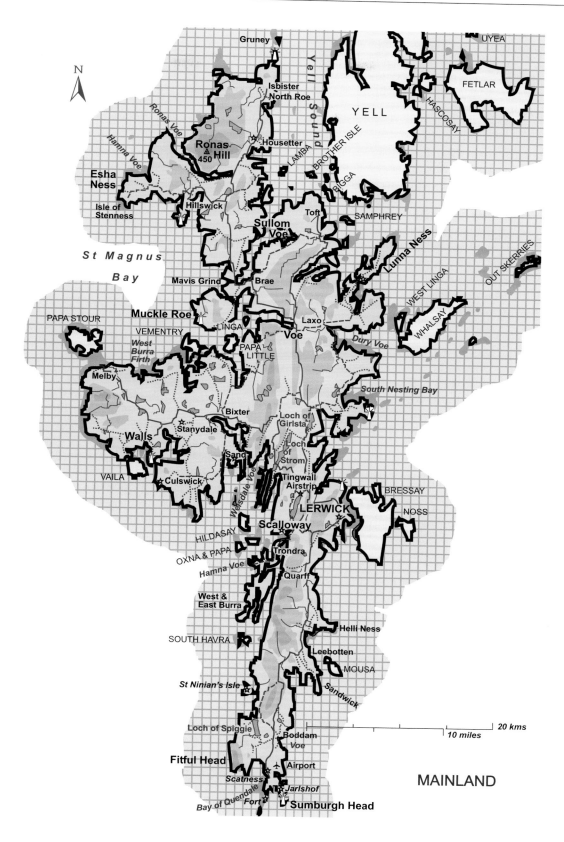

N

Gruney

UYEA

Isbister
North Roe

FETLAR

Yell Sound

YELL

HASCOSAY

Ronas Voe

Housetter

Ronas
Hill
450

LAMBA

BROTHER ISLE

Hamna Voe

BIGGA

Esha
Ness

Hillswick

Toft

SAMPHREY

Isle of
Stenness

Sullom
Voe

Lunna Ness

OUT SKERRIES

St Magnus

Mavis Grind

Brae

WEST LINGA

Bay

PAPA STOUR

Muckle Roe

Laxo

Voe

WHALSAY

VEMENTRY

LINGA

Dury Voe

West
Burra
Firth

PAPA
LITTLE

South Nesting Bay

Melby

Bixter

Loch of
Girlsta

Walls

Stanydale

Loch
of
Strom

VAILA

Sand

Culswick

Tingwall
Airstrip

BRESSAY

LERWICK

NOSS

HILDASAY

Scalloway

OXNA & PAPA

Trondra

Hamna Voe

Quarff

West &
East Burra

Helli Ness

SOUTH HAVRA

Leebotten

MOUSA

St Ninian's Isle

Sandwick

Loch of Spiggie

Boddam
Voe

20 kms

10 miles

Fitful Head

Airport

MAINLAND

Scatness

Jarlshof

Bay of Quendale

Fort

Sumburgh Head

(near Sumburgh), which was deposited there by the ice. It has come from just south of Oslo.

History: There are none of the Orkney-style chambered cairns on Shetland which could lead one to suppose that these islands were inhabited by a different prehistoric race or, at least, a people with its own distinctive social and religious code.

Christianity filtered north into Shetland slightly later than to Orkney which is understandable and the islands played a lesser part in Norse history. This is possibly due to their geographical position as a staging post on the route to the Faeroes, Iceland, Greenland, western Scotland and Ireland. In general terms, however, the history of Shetland in the Norse period was similar to that outlined for Mainland Orkney (No.10.11).

In 1468 King Christian of Norway and Denmark mortgaged both Shetland and Orkney to the Scottish Crown as part of Margaret of Norway's marriage dowry. As the cash redemption was not forthcoming, Scotland foreclosed and annexed the islands in 1471.

Apart from a few churchmen there were virtually no Scots living in Shetland at that time but the next one hundred years saw a considerable influx of land-hungry Scots. It was in this period also that the Lowland Scots dialect started to mingle with the native tongue. The Sinclair family was there well before 1469 and by 1600 Sinclair was the commonest surname among the one-third of the population which used Scottish surnames. The native Shetlanders still used Norse patronymics.

In 1564 Mary, Queen of Scots, granted the feu of Orkney and Shetland in perpetuity to her half-brother, Lord Robert Stewart. By 1568 Lord Robert had forced the Bishop to resign, gained the right to all crown, church and earldom property together with the right to claim revenue from every islander, and had made himself the chief magistrate. No Norse earl had ever held such power.

By 1571, Lord Robert had installed his half-brother, Laurence Bruce, as foud (chief magistrate) and Bruce used and abused this position to confiscate land on every excuse. He soon lost his position as chief magistrate but, nevertheless, by 1638 the Bruce family held one-eighth of all the lands of Shetland.

In 1581 Lord Robert was made Earl of Orkney and in 1591 his son, Earl Patrick Stewart,

succeeded him. He built the castle at Scalloway, and the house at 'Jarlshof' and as chief magistrate he nominally supported the Norse legal forms, but would confiscate land readily. However, his main interest was in reducing the land-holdings of the entrenched landowners such as the Bruce family of Muness and this made him many powerful enemies. He was imprisoned in 1609 and executed in Edinburgh in 1615 by James VI. Norse law was superseded by Scots law; udal was replaced by feudal. The landowning families had now gained enormous power and fought among themselves to divide the spoils.

A very few items of udal law have survived to the present day in Shetland and Orkney such as the right of a crofter to own the foreshore down to the low-water mark. In the rest of Scotland the foreshore, with a very few exceptions, belongs to the Crown Estates. Understandably, the islanders insist that there should be no further erosion of their few remaining udal rights.

Wildlife: There are very few trees to be found, but the largest plantation in Shetland is at Kergord, north of Weisdale. Many interesting alpine plants grow on Ronas Hill including dwarf specimens of willow, *Salix herbacea*. Shrubs generally are heather and juniper as much of the landscape consists of upland peat bog, grass, and moorland, with many small lochs, but about 680 flowering plants and ferns, and nearly 1000 varieties of fungi, have been recorded. The Alpine Mouse-Ear Chickweed, *Cerastium arcticum edmondstonii*, can be found nowhere else in the world but the Shetland Isles and there are also a number of unique microspecies of Hieracium, or Hawkweed. White water lilies, *Nymphaea alba*, flourish in some of the lochans.

Native domestic mammal species are the small, hardy, Shetland ponies (about 1m high) and the distinctive black and brown Shetland sheep which are thought to be identical to Siberian wild sheep. Arctic hares, introduced for sport about 200 years ago, are common.

There is good fishing in many of the lochs but in Loch of Spiggie the fish are said to be 'dour'.

Mainland Shetland is of ornithological interest throughout the year with the great asset of nineteen hours of summer daylight. East and south-east winds bring in migrants with May, September and October being best for unusual sightings. The red-necked phalarope and the

Slavonian grebe are scarce and the black-throated diver can probably not be found.

Sites: Sumburgh and Fitful Head for breeding seabirds. About 2500 moulting eider off-shore in autumn and long-tailed skua occasionally seen.

Pool of Virkie, north of Sumburgh has intertidal sand and mud flats for wintering and migrant shore-birds.

Quendale Bay, sand-dunes and machair. Wintering divers and sea-duck with Loch of Hillwell to the north an important breeding site for wildfowl. Corncrake sometimes heard here.

Loch of Spiggie RSPB Reserve is the most important winter wildfowl site in Shetland. Shelduck, teal, oystercatcher and curlew nest here. Great and arctic skuas, kittiwake and arctic tern are often present, and whooper swan, sometimes, in autumn. Greylag geese, wigeon, tufted duck, pochard, goldeneye and long-tailed duck in spring.

At Boddam Voe, on east coast opposite Loch of Spiggie there are wintering divers, grebe, sea-duck, gulls and waders. Great skua and raven are attracted by the nearby slaughter-house.

Scalloway and Lerwick Harbours, gulls and black guillemot. Migrant passerines in town gardens. Loch of Clickhimin on west side of Lerwick is a wintering wildfowl site.

Lochs of Asta and Tingwall, pochard, tufted duck, and possibly the only mute swans in Shetland.

Weisdale, Sandsound, and Tresta Voes for goldeneye, sea-duck, grebes and wintering divers.

Kergord woodland, north of Weisdale, gives cover for nesting birds, rook, tree sparrow, goldcrest, and migrant species.

Sandness, west extremity of Mainland, wintering wildfowl and sea-birds.

Lunna Ness, red-throated diver on the lochans, migrants in the sycamore trees.

Sullom Voe, wintering great northern diver, Slavonian grebe, eider, long-tailed duck and velvet scoter. Also ravens, waders and gulls.

Esha Ness, guillemot and kittiwake colonies in Old Red Sandstone cliffs. Nearby breeding terns, whimbrel and skuas.

* * *

MAINLAND, the principal island of the Shetland group, lies at about the same latitude as the south of Greenland. It has a landscape of hills which are mostly smooth, low and covered with rough grass, heather and upland peat bog. The highest point is the massive barren crest of **Ronas Hill**, or Rønies Hill, at 450m (1476ft). This is also the highest point in all Shetland.

The long leg of land stretching from **Sumburgh** in the south to Lerwick in the north is undulating peat moorland with a border of neat meadows. The great tilted wedge of Sumburgh Head is set between Grutness Voe and West Voe of Sumburgh with busy **Sumburgh Airport** straddling the connecting isthmus.

Grutness Pier on the east is the departure point for *The Good Shepherd* on its trips to Fair Isle (No.11.1) and south-west, facing **Horse Island** and Scat Ness with its substantial ruined Iron Age Fort on **Ness of Burgi**, are the world-famous ruins of Jarlshof.

Jarlshof [HU397096] was given its fanciful Viking name by Sir Walter Scott in his novel *The Pirate* but it is rather misleading because the site covers at least five distinct archaeological periods over a span of some 3000 years. The ruins are complex and fascinating. There are Bronze Age huts and farm buildings, earth-houses from the

SCALLOWAY CASTLE

Iron Age with a broch and wheel-houses (1st–8th century), a variety of Norse long-house remains (9th–14th centuries), the foundations of a medieval farmhouse (14th–16th centuries), and the walls of the house belonging to Earls Robert and Patrick Stewart (16th century). In 1997 some equally remarkable ruins were discovered by chance at **Scatness**, only one mile from Jarlshof. These are also now open to the public and well worth seeing.

BODDAM CROFT MUSEUM. THE SMOKESTACK OF THATCH AND TIMBER IS CALLED A 'TEØFI'.

The land stretches west to the awesome heights of **Fitful Head** (ON – *hvitfugla* – white birds). It encloses the wide sandy sweep of Bay of Quendale, scene of the 1993 *Braer* tanker disaster. South of the bay are two islets, **Lady's Holm** and **Little Holm**.

East of the main road by Gallow Hill and south of the village of **Boddam** is the **Croft House Museum** which portrays croft life in the 19th century beside a working horizontal water-mill of original Norse design [HU399147].

Although the main road continues north to Channer Wick, a more interesting secondary route branches west at Boddam by the eutrophic **Loch of Spiggie** (Sc *spigg* – stickleback), rich in water-plants, fish and wildfowl. Beyond, the bleak Bay of Scousburgh shelters behind the island of **Colsay** with its prehistoric cairn.

St Ninians Isle is Shetland's answer to Mont St Michel but most of the remains of the early-Christian monastic settlement have now disappeared. Only the lower courses of a 12th-century chapel [HU367209] can be seen amid the bare sheep-grazed downs where a sandy isthmus crosses to the island. But in 1958 excavation revealed the remains of an earlier (pre-Norse) church, and a hoard of 8th-century Celtic silver was found under a stone slab in a box made of Norwegian larch. This may have been hidden by the monks before a Viking raid. South of the chapel is a Holy Well – a spring of crystal-clear water.

North of St Ninians Isle the tiny islet of **Griskerry** lies close to the Ness of Ireland with a road running up the Ness to Maywick.

Back on the east coast after rejoining the main road a number of scattered settlements surround Sand Wick and the pier at **Leebotten** where the boat leaves for Mousa (No.11.2) on pre-arranged visits.

Hollanders Knowe is where a secondary road cuts off to the west through the hills to Scalloway while the main road continues to Lerwick. This was once a Dutch trading post.

Scalloway [skalaway or -awa] (ON *skallivaagr* – voe of the booths) is on the west coast and only 8km from Lerwick. It was the capital of Shetland until Lerwick claimed that title about two centuries ago but it is still an important little village port and a centre for the fish-processing industry. The pier was built in the 1830s for the export of salt cod to Spain and it was extended in 1896. The most prominent feature is **Earl Patrick's Castle**, built with forced labour in 1600 to a medieval design which was already out-of-date. It was abandoned only fifteen years later when its owner was executed. A resident told me that the lime mortar was mixed with 'the hair of maidens'.

In 1942 Prince Olaf, later, King of Norway, visited Scalloway in recognition of the many Norwegians who were carrying out clandestine wartime operations. Fascinating information on these operations (and the 'Shetland Bus') can be found in Scalloway Museum on the waterfront.

* * *

Mainland is now connected by bridges with the long, narrow islands of **TRONDRA**, **WEST BURRA** and **EAST BURRA**. The busy fishing port of **Hamna Voe** is on West Burra.

The main road to Lerwick passes Sandy Loch Reservoir and as it enters the town, the Loch of Clickimin is on the left – unfortunately now surrounded by new housing. In it, but connected to the shore by a causeway, is possibly Lerwick's most memorable feature [HU464408], the massive structure of **Clickimin Broch** [klich-imin]. The broch is 20m in diameter, has walls 5½m thick and 4½m high, and the entire structure stands on a great stone platform with a gateway leading into an enclosure. The site is thought to have been occupied from the 6th century BC up to possibly the 7th century AD and to have been in turn a dun, a broch and, latterly, a wheelhouse. There are a number of inexplicable features and the ruin is so tidy that one must wonder whether the Victorian lady who carried out the excavation was occasionally overcome by idealism. (Such questions, however, should not be allowed to spoil your appreciation.)

LERWICK (ON *leir vik* – mud creek) is a cosmopolitan town built round a lively waterfront and harbour. The harbour is being extended to cope with a growing fleet as well as oil-industry vessels. Although Norsemen probably founded the town and appreciated the safe anchorage in Bressay Sound, it was the Dutch who developed it in the early 17th century by using Lerwick as a base for their fishing activities. The Shetlanders were glad to sell their wares to the visiting sailors and consequently a shanty town of booths, shacks, bars and brothels grew up leading to 'great abominatioun and wickednes'. In 1640 ten Spanish warships sailed into Bressay Sound and sank two of the four Dutch men-of-war who were there to protect the fishing 'busses'. In 1653 Cromwell, instead of knocking Lerwick about, tried to impose an English claim to the fishing grounds by sending Admiral George Monk with ninety-four ships to search for Van Tromp. He landed an army of troops to build what is now **Fort Charlotte**, possibly Lerwick's first permanent building. But twenty years later the Dutch returned, set fire to it and carried on fishing. Then the French took an interest and in 1702 their privateers attacked the Dutch and sailed around the Shetlands which they 'pillaged like gentlemen'. They burned 150 busses off Lerwick.

Strangely, neither Shetland, nor for that matter, Scotland, seem to have had much to say in these Continental battles over the local fishing grounds. In 1798 the Rev Cruttwell reported that: 'The herring fishery is carried on almost wholly by foreigners, 200 busses from Holland, 50 from Denmark, 40 from Prussia, 20 from Dunkirk and about the same from the Netherlands.'

Flagstoned **Commercial Street**, Lerwick's main street, meanders behind the waterfront buildings, attractively irregular and criss-crossed with narrow alleys and dark wynds. **Fort Charlotte** at its north-west end was first repaired after the Dutch attack and then it was thoroughly renovated and a barrack block added in 1781. It is, today, the only Cromwellian military structure which survives intact in Scotland.

The district of Hillhead, a chaotic composition of old stone gables and slated roofs, is above Commercial Street. It contains the **Town Hall**, 1882 Scottish baronial with fine stained glass windows and a Victorian interpretation of a Viking drinking hall. Nearby is the interesting and comprehensive **Shetland Museum**. Both of these are certainly worth visiting. The Fort is rather uninspiring but provides commanding views from its ramparts. The town itself has intriguing corners to explore and a replica Viking longship which makes trips around the bay (information at the Tourist Office) provides a very different view of Lerwick.

A winter visit to Lerwick should be timed for the last Tuesday of January when the nostalgic Viking fire festival of Up-Helly-aa is celebrated with great gusto by the locals. There are 'guisers', lighted torches, songs, revelry and a burning longship.

North of Lerwick Harbour the town fades away into rough land round the Bight of Vatsland. A small group of rocks called the **Holms of Vatsland** lie in the bay. The road runs to the head of Dales Voe and then turns north to the scattered community of Veensgarth and **Tingwall Airfield** where a route strikes off to Weisdale and the west Mainland. Near the **Tingwall Agricultural Museum** a secondary road runs south to Scalloway and passes Loch of Tingwall. This is an interesting diversion as the Viking parliament and law court, the Althing, used to meet here in the valley. The actual site is thought to be **Law Ting Holm** [HU418434], a small promontory at the north end of the loch which was an island in Norse times. There is a standing stone at the foot of the loch and, on **Gallow Hill** to the west, a mother and daughter were burned as witches in the early 18th century.

North of Tingwall the road runs alongside the **Loch of Girlsta** named after a Norse maiden,

Geirhilda, who is said to be buried on the island in the loch. The districts of North and South Nesting, a remote area of low hills skirted by the loop of a secondary road, lie to the east. Off their indented coastline are the **North** and **South Isles of Gletness** with **Green Holm** far to the south, **Hoo Stack**, **Eswick Holm**, **Cunning Holm**, **Holm of Skellister**, **Hog Island** and **Green Isle**. A line of skerries called the **Stepping Stones** runs far out to sea punctuated by **Muckla Billan** and **Muckle Fladdicap**.

Near the head of Dury Voe (South Voe) at **Laxo** (ON *lax* – salmon) is the pier of the car ferry to Whalsay (No.11.15). A secondary road skirts the Voe and becomes unclassified as it turns north. Halfway up the Ness is **Lunna Kirk** which was built in 1753 [HU486691].

West Lunna Voe is remembered as the anchorage for the 'Shetland Bus', small fishing boats which courageously dodged the Germans to assist the Norwegian resistance during the Second World War. This was a lifeline for supplies, rescuing refugees and transferring agents, but in the end, fuel shortages in Norway so reduced the local fishing fleet that the Shetland boats became more and more conspicuous. German patrols also became more efficient with the result that many brave men and their ships were lost. **Lunna House** (1660), now a summer hotel, was the headquarters for the operation. For cover, most of the trips had to be undertaken in the long, dark, sub-Arctic nights of winter when the weather was at its worst. Lt-Com David Howarth (in *The Shetland Bus*) recalled five days of November storm with winds of over 100mph. 'At Lunna the salt water snatched from the wave crests in Vidlin Voe streamed over the isthmus and over the house to a height of a hundred and fifty feet. From the upper windows the spray looked as solid as streamers of grey silk...'

Just beyond Lunna, at Grut Wick, the Ninian oil pipeline to Sullom Voe makes its first landfall after 103 miles on the seabed. **Lunna Holm** marks the extreme end of Lunna Ness.

The main road divides again at **Voe**. One branch leads north up Dales Voe to **Booth of Toft**, where the car ferry leaves for Yell (No.11.24). The other takes a north-westerly direction along the shore of the Olna Firth, scene of the last whaling station in Shetland, and up to the uninspiring village of **Brae** (ON *breio eio* – broad neck) on Busta Voe. Here, a road

turns off for **Sullom Voe**. These sheltered waters supported an active flying-boat base during the Second World War and they are now the setting for giant tankers visiting Europe's largest oil and gas terminals. Part of the area is reclaimed land where excavated material was dumped in Orka Voe. The Ninian and Brent pipelines – both of nearly one metre diameter – discharge their oil here.

Beyond Brae, a road crossing a bridge to the south-west links the round, hilly island of **MUCKLE ROE** with Mainland. Almost completely encircled with high cliffs of red granite there are some crofts in the south-east but the rest of the island is of broken high moorland – wild walking country.

At **Mavis Grind** (ON *maev eids grind* – gate of the narrow isthmus) Mainland almost splits into two islands [HU340684]. To the right of the road are the head waters of Sullom Voe, to the left is a small sea-loch and the waters of St Magnus Bay. **Egilsay**, a group of drying islets, lies off-shore, and further north, **Isle of Gunnister** and **Isle of Nibon** with **Oe Stack** and a rock arch. This is the district of Northmavine, an area of scenic beauty. After about 8km the road divides with the left fork heading for **Hillswick** (ON *hildiswik* – battle bay) on the shores of the Ura Firth. The Ness of Hillswick is a peninsula with many multi-coloured rock formations. Off its west coast is **Isle of Westerhouse**, **Isle of Niddister** and **The Drongs** – spiky stacks and grotesque shapes carved by the sea out of the Old Red Sandstone with one huge perpendicular column over 30m high. Hillswick was developed in the 18th century as a haaf fishing station by Thomas Gifford of Busta. A haaf (ON *haf* – sea) is a deep-sea fishing ground in the Northern Isles. Gifford provided all the equipment and the fishermen provided all the fish – a somewhat inequitable arrangement, but normal practice at that time.

A secondary road continues westwards into the forbidding landscape of **Esha Ness** eventually reaching Stenness (ON – stone headland) where there was also a small haaf fishing-station partly sheltered by **Isle of Stenness** which has a natural arch on it. In 1933 Joan Grigsby camped on the isle and wrote a successful book about the experience called *An Island Rooin*. Nearby stack-shaped **Dore Holm** (ON – doorway islet) has a flying buttress on its north-west side making a natural arch 21m high and the islet is completely perforated by a cavernous passage which looks like a giant doorway. The Esha Ness area has many prehistoric relics and interesting walks. Moorland lochans sprinkle the ground above the western cliffs which are broken into fantastic shapes, weathered and tilted and a home for many seabirds. There are arches, caves and subterranean passages and the precipitous view north from the lighthouse track to **Grind of the Navir** (ON – gateway of the giants) is particularly dramatic.

The north side of Esha Ness is indented by **Hamna Voe** (ON – harbour bay), an anchorage and one-time whaling station with a narrow rocky entrance which is difficult to identify from the sea. Luckily three islets lie to the north, **Muckle Ossa**, **Little Ossa** and **Fladda**, and Muckle Ossa has a hole right through it. A line of sight through the hole leads directly to the voe entrance.

A certain John Williamson who was born here in 1740 became known as Johnny Notions. He was a blacksmith, clock repairer, weaver, joiner and bonesetter at different times in his life but he became renowned for protecting people from smallpox when the disease was rife and the medical profession could only advocate leeches. He is said to have collected vesicles from victims of the disease, dried them by a peat fire and buried them for several years. These were then inoculated under his patients' skin and the wound was dressed with a cabbage leaf.

An unclassified road near Hillswick leads to the headwaters of lovely **Ronas Voe**. Beside the

voe is a knowe called **Hollanders' Grave** where Dutch seamen were buried in 1674 [HU299804]. They were on a crippled Dutch East-Indiaman, the *Wapen van Rotterdam*, which sheltered here during the war with the English. She was discovered by the frigate *Newcastle* and taken after a fight.

Another Dutch East-Indiaman, the *Wapen van Alkmaar* carrying ivory from Ceylon foundered in a Shetland storm in 1689. (These ships took the long route past Shetland in order to avoid the English Channel.) In the early 1930s a fishing boat dredged up two tusks thirty miles north-east of Shetland which were sent to Aberdeen University for identification. The University claimed they had come from a Shetland mammoth and this myth was not dispelled until they were radio carbon-dated in 1993.

Across Ronas Voe is Shetland's highest hill, **Ronas Hill** (450m), with a chambered cairn at the summit. An invigorating hill-walk to the top is rewarded by a striking panoramic view stretching from the Atlantic, with the little islets of **The Cleiver** and **Gruna Stacks** beyond the entrance to the cutlass-shaped Ronas Voe, Foula (No.11.6) on the horizon, Sullom Voe to the south-east, Yell Sound to the east with the **Holms of Burravoe**, and **Muckle** and **Little Holm**. Beyond the northern tip of Mainland lies **Gruney**, **Outer Stack**, **Scordar**, **Turla**, **Fladda**, and assorted skerries collectively known as **Ramna Stacks** – a group designated as a 'Special Protection Area' on account of its prolific birdlife. The district of North Roe lying at the foot of Ronas Hill and west of the road is a huge expanse of trackless wilderness peppered with lochs and bog pools. Heading north the road skirts Colla Firth and passes the **Loch of Housetter**. Beside the road are two standing stones [HU361855] and chambered cairns. The road ends at Isbister by Sand Voe. Mainland tapers away at **Point of Fethaland**, 4km to the north, while to the north-west is the drying island of **Uyea** [oe-yë]. Climbers consider the cliffs and stacks in this region offer

OLD LODBERRIES SOUTH OF LERWICK HARBOUR

a worthwhile challenge but, whether climbing or not, it is a place of extraordinary beauty.

Taking the left fork where the road divides at Veensgarth and passing west of the Tingwall Airstrip the road climbs **Wormadale Hill** with its magnificent view down **Whiteness Voe**. There is a workshop here (called Hjaltasteyn) making, and selling, handmade jewellery from Shetland's own gemstones. **Loch of Strom** has the ruin of a medieval castle on a crannog-like islet [HU396475]. This may have been a residence of the Sinclairs before the castle at Scalloway was completed.

Weisdale Voe has a strange claim to fame. It was the birthplace in 1786 of John Clunie Ross who was recognised by Queen Victoria as 'King' of the Cocos Islands. Far down the voe, off the shores of Strom Ness are the islands of **Flotta** (ON – flat island) and **Hoy** (ON – high island).

The road crosses the hills and runs along the shore of Tresta Voe and **The Firth** to **Bixter**. Here a secondary road meanders northwards for 16km eventually meeting the main north road at Voe on the Olna Firth. At the head of Bixter Voe another minor road runs south to Sand, where there are the arched remains of **St Mary's Chapel**, which is said to have been built by the crew of a wrecked Spanish Armada galleon but is actually of Norse origin [HU346472]. At the entrance to the voe are two tiny islets, **Fore Holm** and **Kirk Holm** with the latter, surprisingly, having the remains of an ancient settlement on it. This road continues through Easter Skeld to the south coast at Culswick where, 2kms away beside a cave, are some remnants of the **Broch of Culswick** [HU254448]. The islet of **Giltarump** lies to the south and **Muckle Flaes** is near the broch. A hermit is reputed to have lived at one time on the storm-lashed **Burgi Stack**.

A more interesting archaeological site, well sign-posted, is to the north at **Stanydale** – a large heel-shaped cairn on the open moors. It dates from about 1600BC and is thought to have been a Neolithic temple or meeting place of religious significance. The nearest known similar structure is in Malta. The walls

are nearly 4m thick and they enclose an oval chamber with stalls. The floor has post holes in which are traces of spruce. Live spruce was almost certainly only introduced to Scotland in the 16th century so driftwood is the most likely explanation. There are many settlement remains round about indicating that this windswept moorland once supported a sizeable community.

An abandoned village at **West Houland** is reminiscent of the cleared settlements in the Western Isles – thankfully a rather uncommon sight in this part of the world.

Near here an unclassified road runs north to West Burra Firth where the ferry sails to Papa Stour (No.11.14). **Galta Stack** is in the middle of the firth and at the entrance are **The Heag** and **Isle of West Burrafirth**.

Walls (ON – voes) is a little township with a snug harbour which once knew a certain prosperity providing barrels of salted fish for export to Aberdeen and Leith. The Foula ferry (No.11.6) sails from here. The mapmakers thought the Shetlanders' pronunciation, which sounded like Wa's, was a Scottish form of 'walls' so they anglicised the name accordingly. It actually comes from the Norse *vágar*, or *voes*, the 'v' being pronounced as a 'w'.

Unclassified roads from Walls service a fairly large area of crofts but to the north the landscape is wild and barren. The road ends at Melby which looks past the **Holm of Melby** in the Sound of Papa to Papa Stour (No.11.14) and the North Atlantic.

* * *

Access: Ro-ro service by NorthLink Ferries daily between Aberdeen and Lerwick (via Kirkwall, Orkney), 0845-6000-449.

Sumburgh Airport, 01950-461000, scheduled air services daily to/from: Aberdeen, 08700-

CLICKIMIN FORT, BLOCKHOUSE AND BROCH

400006; Edinburgh, 08700-400007; Glasgow, 08700-400008; Inverness, 01667-462280; Kirkwall (Orkney), 01856-886210. Also scheduled flights, Bergen, Norway.

Ro-ro weekly ferry service (summer) by Smyril Line between Lerwick, Færoe Islands, Norway, Iceland and Denmark, 08704-201267.

Shetland bus services, 01595-744219.

Inter-island ferries, 01806-244219. General information, 01595-743970.

Shetland Islands Tourist Information publish an Inter-Shetland Transport Timetable, 01595-693535.

Anchorages:

1. Grutness Voe, 1½M N of Sumburgh Head. Well sheltered except that NE'lies and E'lies bring a swell. Beware shallows in S half of entrance. Noisy due to airport (but convenient for Jarlshof visit). Concrete pier has depth of 2.7m alongside but avoid obstructing it. Anchor off pier in 6m. The small boat marina, behind breakwater, has 1m depth.

2. Voe Bay. Reasonable shelter in NE'lies. Head and N shore are shoal and also avoid S headland. Anchor off SW shore in 6m sand and heavy weed.

3. Leven Wick. Good shelter from S and W. Anchor in SE corner ¾c off beach in 6m sand.

4. Hos Wick. Good shelter from N and W. Anchor at NW corner but beware rocky patches. Head is shoal. Alternative anchorage in bight N of Broonies Taing south of derelict pier. (Sea-cave with blowhole to explore on Ness of Cumliewick.)

5. Sand Wick. Anchoring not advised due to abandoned submarine cables.

6. Wick of Sandsyre (N Mousa Sound). Rocky ridge extending 1c from SE side affords some shelter for occasional anchorage. Anchor mid-bay off small stone pier on S side.

7. Aith Voe is shallow, narrow and partially obstructed with rocks. Temp. anchorage when conditions allow.

8. Gulber Wick. Holding good but exposed SE. Anchor near head.

9. Voe of Sound. Foul ground and submarine cables restrict anchorage. Best avoided.

10. Brei Wick. Anchor in NW where depth permits. Avoid rocks in SE.

11. Lerwick Small Boat Harbour with 70m pontoon (easy access to town centre). Contact the Port Controller on Ch. 12 before entering harbour. Office opposite Victoria Pier. Berthing alongside breakwater not recommended.

12. Lerwick Harbour. For berth in Albert Dock contact HM on Ch.12.

13. Lerwick Harbour at Gremista Marina, 2km N of Lerwick. Run by Users Association. Possible but first contact Port Control Ch 12 for details.

14. Dales Voe. Reasonable shelter except from NE. Beware entrance dangers, keep mid-channel, and avoid fish-farm. Anchor just beyond Muckle Ayre promontory in centre, 6m mud.

15. Lax Firth. Good shelter. Enter on W side. Anchor at head in 6m off stone pier. Anchor at head beyond the ayre on E shore in 5–6m.

16. Wadbister Voe. Excellent shelter in SW winds. Beware centre rock at entrance.

17. Cat Firth. Excellent shelter but holding unreliable. Anchor N of Little Holm in 6m between the burns and W of mid-channel. Beware two wrecks which cover.

18. Vassa Voe. Excellent shelter but little room. Follow sailing instructions closely.

19. South Voe of Gletness. Temp. anchorage in fair weather off W side of South Isle of Gletness in 4m sand. Many dangers.

20. North Voe of Gletness. Exposed N and E. Approach with care. Anchor near head of voe in 4m sand.

21. Dock of Ling Ness (South Nesting Bay). Good anchorage for draft of less than 1½m. Numerous rocks to be avoided.

22. Grunna Voe, S side of head of Dury Voe. Excellent anchorage in 5–10m, black mud, good holding. Approach keeping towards N shore of Dury Voe and turn into Grunna Voe when fully open. Keep 1c off both shores.

23. Vidlin Voe. Sheltered anchorage in pool off pier in 4m, mud. If insufficient room anchor S of Vidlin Ness clear of fish-cages in 6–10m, mud but in NE and E gales a swell sets in to this area. Careful attention to charts needed. Avoid ro-ro terminal. Visitors' berths at marina have depth at LWS of 1.7m.

24. Boatsroom Voe, at head of Hamna Voe, W side of Lunna Ness. Excellent anchorage in SW or NE corner but partly obstructed by fish cages. Good holding. On approach keep over 1c off Lunna Ness.

25. West Lunna Voe (Shetland Bus anchorage). Excellent anchorage about ½c off-shore below the tower, 10-12m or in N centre of pool 4-8m. There are several rocks to avoid. Follow sailing instructions carefully for approach.

26. Swining Voe. Good anchorage but most parts too deep for small craft, mud and shingle.

27. Dales Voe, beyond Colla Firth. Excellent holding and free of swell but subject to violent gusts in W'lies. Keep ¾c off when passing Scarvar Ayre and anchor in 5–15m, mud.

28. Firths Voe. Temp. anchorage in summer weather. Both sides clear beyond ½c and head dries 2c.

29. Garths Voe, off Sullom Voe. Tug and boat harbour for oil terminal. Avoid.

30. Sullom Voe. Excellent anchorage anywhere above the Ness of Haggrister narrows in depth to suit. For approach through Yell Sound to Sullom Voe it is essential to contact Harbour Control (Ch.14) and follow sailing instructions. The head of Voxter Voe is shoal.

31. Gluss Voe. Good sheltered anchorage in pool at head of voe in 4–12m, sand. W end of pool dries. Easy approach up centre of voe.

32. Bay of Ollaberry. Occasional anchorage with good shelter from W. Anchor at head of bay in 5m.

33. Quey Firth. Temp. day anchorage only.

34. Colla Firth. Good shelter from W. Best anchorage off pier in Voe of the Brig. On approach keep 1c off shores. Pier is 32m long with 4m at its head. It is used by trawlers. Marina has visitors' berth (2m),

35. Burra Voe (North Roe). Drying rocks at middle of entrance. Keep less than ½c from Burgo Taing when entering. Good anchorage centrally off N shore in 4–6m, sand. Temp anchorage in SW opposite the houses but holding poor.

36. Easter Wick of Fethaland. Temp. anchorage in good weather.

37. Sand Voe on N coast. 60° 36.2N 01° 20.0W. Good sheltered anchorage close to W side of inner part of Sand Voe in 4–5m but difficult to get out in NW'lies. Good anchorage in outer voe in depths over 7m but exposed to NW.

38. Ronas Voe, NW Mainland. Subject to violent squalls. Secure anchorage at head of voe in 4–10m but winds fitful. Enter mid-channel till S of Burries Ness then tend towards the NE shore, moving into mid-channel once above the narrows. Dramatic scenery. (Access to climb Ronas Hill.)

39. Hamna Voe. Tricky entrance only 65m wide needs careful attention to sailing instructions. Reasonably sheltered anchorage in E of the voe where it shoals rapidly or in S. Temp. anchorage off the beaches on SE side. Good holding but bottom may be foul.

40. Brae Wick and Sand Wick. Coast foul but with local knowledge temp. anchorage possible.

41. Hills Wick, Ura Firth. Good shelter except from S, 4–10m, sand, holding unreliable.

42. Ura Firth, at head N of Cro Taing. Good shelter in 4–10m sand, but holding unreliable.

43. Hamar Voe, Ura Firth. Excellent shelter and holding good. The head of the pool at the head of the voe is shoal but has no hidden dangers. Anchor where depth suitable.

44. Mangaster Voe. Good anchorage near the head in 4–6m but north of the moorings. Partly obstructed by fish cages.

45. Roe Sound. Approach with care and avoid in W'lies. Good anchorage just W of islet, Crog Holm, but exposed W.

46. Busta Voe, Swarbacks Minn. Fair anchorage off Brae in 6m but bottom mainly seaweed. Visitors' berths available at 54-berth marina. 2m at MLWS.

47. Olna Firth, Swarbacks Minn. Excellent shelter. Anchor in 4–8m above the narrows. Centre of firth clear for approach but avoid mussel farms. Small marina behind pier/breakwater. Visitors welcome.

48. Gon Firth. Well-sheltered anchorage in bight at SE corner but weedy.

49. Sound of Houbansetter. Good shelter in N'lies. Anchor at any suitable depth.

50. Aith Voe. Well sheltered. Anchor anywhere to suit. Aith Marina has 2 visitor berths but only 1.2m depth. Good access and shelter at pier berth.

51. Uyea Sound, S side of Swarbacks Minn. Good shelter and holding in bay on N side, 4–8m, but fish cages and many weedy patches. Approach with care. Landing possible at pier in tiny harbour on S side. Passage through to Cribba Sound best tackled at near HW. MLWS depth 1m.

52. Vementry Sound. Many sheltered anchorages but the entrance to the sound is not well defined and there are many dangers. Interesting area to explore but not for the faint-hearted.

53. West Burra Firth, St Magnus Bay. Occasional anchorage subject to a heavy swell. Anchor about 2c beyond narrows towards W shore in 9–12m sand. Approach needs care. Pier for Papa Stour ferry (built 1992) affords good shelter but avoid ferry berth.

54. Voe of Snarraness, St Magnus Bay. 60° 17.7N 01° 34.7W. Clear of dangers beyond ½c off-shore. Excellent holding, and more sheltered than West Burra Firth. Anchor in 9–14m in pool centre (fish cages), mud, or in shallow bay on E side, sand.

55. Lera Voe, Vaila Sound. Approach through Easter Sound. Anchor N of pier on S side of voe. Several hazards and fish-farm.

56. Walls, pier and spacious anchorage. Marina (built 1995).

57. Vaila Voe. Many moorings N of Saltness in 4–5m, mud. Good holding and more room off Skeo Taing. Better anchorage than Lera Voe. Beware Baa of Linga NW of Galta Skerry beacon, otherwise approach is relatively simple.

58. Gruting Voe. Small marina and well-sheltered anchorages in any of the voes leading off Gruting Voe: Browland Voe, Scutta Voe, or Seli Voe. Olas Voe is shallow. Keep mid-channel but at entrances to Browland Voe and Scutta Voe keep N of mid-channel. Mud generally.

59. Skeld Voe, The Deeps (W of Hildasay). 60° 09N 01° 27W. Marina with 8 visitors' berths in depths up to 2.5m. Secure anchorage in pool S of marina in 5.5m but can be subject to swell in S'lies.

60. Rea Wick, Seli Voe and Sand Voe. Best visited at LW. Temp. anchorages in quiet off-shore winds.

61. Sandsound Voe. Pier at Omunsgarth suitable for boats at all times. Anchor in bight N of Omunsgarth or wherever suitable in The Firth, Bixter Voe or Tresta Voe. Beware Billy Baa off Fora Ness on first approach and there are several reefs and shoals to be avoided at Salt Ness and the upper reaches. Holding good.

62. Weisdale Voe. Good anchorage N of narrows at Hellister Ness sheltered except for S'lies. Head of voe is shoal. In S'lies use Bay of Haggersta.

63. Stromness Voe. Restricted entrance with rocks and strong tide but attractive anchorage in 8m on E side after the narrows.

64. Whiteness Voe. Temp. anchorages in quiet off-shore winds.

65. Scalloway harbour. Approach with care. Well sheltered. Visitors' pontoon near Scalloway Boating Club (SBC) at Port Arthur, on W side of outer harbour. Alternative berths by arrangement with SBC or anchor off the town on a line between Blacks Ness and Gallow Hill, 6–10m, soft mud. Below the castle there is a quay with depths exceeding 3m alongside, but contact HM.

66. Scalloway Bay. Anchor off W side of bay, 8m, soft mud. Use anchor buoy. Better shelter in East Voe in SW'lies, 4m, well NE of fish quay.

67. West Burra Firth, S of Scalloway entrance. Good shelter and holding. Approach mid-firth and anchor in centre N of bridge in 10–12m sand.

68. Hamna Voe, NW extremity of West Burra. Good shelter and fairly easy approach but restricted room, and bottom can be foul with moorings. There is a 75m long jetty at the head of the voe with 3.4m depth alongside its head. Small marina planned.

69. West Voe leading to South Voe. Small marina behind breakwater at Bridge End but shallow and bottom foul.

70. Clift Sound. Good shelter except from strong S'lies in entrances to Voe of North House and Stream Sound and West Voe of Quarff avoiding submarine cables.

71. May Wick. Occasional anchorage off pleasant sandy beach in 3m, sand. Extensive shoal.

72. Bigton Wick, St Ninians Isle. Good shelter except from N. Anchor on W side as near the isthmus as possible, sand. Some swell possible. (Visit St Ninian's Isle.)

73. St Ninians Bay. Good shelter except from S. Anchor on W side as near the isthmus as possible, sand. Some swell possible. (Visit St Ninian's Isle.)

74. Bay of Scousburgh. Temp. anchorage in quiet conditions.

75. Bay of Quendale not safe except as temp. anchorage in very settled weather.

11.12 Papa Little

(ON pap-øy litla – little island of the priest.) Shetlanders call it Papa Litla.

OS Maps: 1:50000 Sheet 3 1:25000 Sheet 469
Admiralty Charts: 1:75000 Nos.3281 and 3282 1:25000 No.3295

Area: 226ha (558 acres)
Height: 82m (269 ft)

Population: 1841 – 11 (1 house). Uninhabited since.

Geology: Papa Little lies at the junction of two faults: the Walls Boundary Fault (which may be an extension of the Great Glen Fault), and a lesser fault running westwards to Sandness Hill. Most of the island is Old Red Sandstone but the west is peat-covered metamorphic schists and phyllite.

History: Although this was obviously recognised by the Norsemen as a 'papar' island it is not known whether it was associated with any specific religious figure. It is, in fact, possible that at that time it was part of the religious lands of Papa Stour. It was inhabited, possibly for centuries, by some farmers and fisherfolk, but abandoned or cleared in the mid-19th century. The islanders of Papa Stour (No.11.14) have a traditional right to cut peat on Papa Little and this became essential in the 1870s when their own stocks ran out.

* * *

The south-west side of **PAPA LITTLE** is steep with low cliffs surrounding the projection of Moo Ness (ON – headland like a heap of stones). These dwindle to Green Banks in the south. There are several small hills with the highest being **North Ward** (82m), and South Ward (also 82m) topped with a cairn.

The large deep bay on the west coast is defined by two projecting entrance points. The southerly of these is called **Point of Hamna-ayre** (E. and ON – point of the shingle-spit of the harbour), where boats were once drawn up on the shingle beach when the island was inhabited. There are vivid patches of sea pinks in the grass round the shore – a plant known locally as 'banksflooer.'

Papa Little no doubt served its early inhabitants well with its bare but pleasant slopes, generous

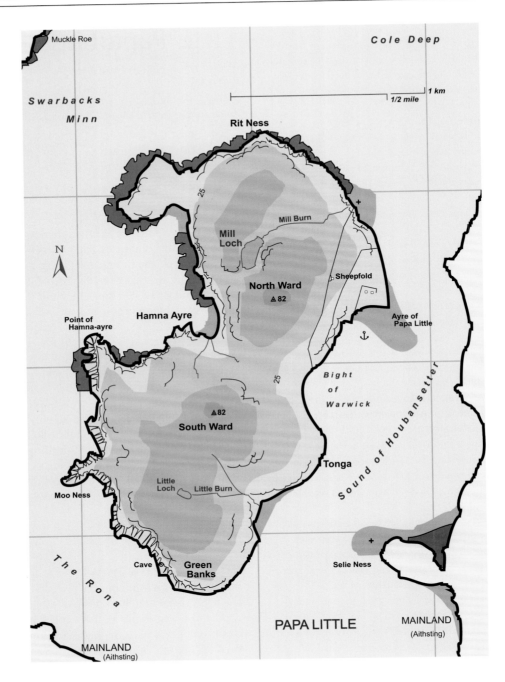

PAPA LITTLE

stock of peat for fuel, relatively sheltered position, and two little lochans, one in the north and one in the south, to provide fresh water.

The advantage of having peat on one's doorstep cannot be overestimated. To collect it from the mainland or another island required an enormous amount of toil and trouble and even an element of danger. After the peat blocks had been cut and dried they were loaded into each individual's 'kishie' – a large basket slung on the back – to bring them to the shore, or to a steep-sided rock which a boat could approach. There they were stacked up in preparation for the loading, which often had to be carried out fairly promptly because of weather and tide. If the boat lay off a beach the people would wade out to it while the skipper or one of the crew stowed the peats neatly. As the boatload increased the boat had to

MAA LOCH, VEMENTRY

be moved further out into deeper water making access more difficult.

If the boat could come alongside a rocky shore distance was less but the work was just as back-breaking and unpleasant. Controlling the boat in a swell, or if the weather was poor while the peats were being emptied into it and stowed, required skilful seamanship. And carrying a full kishie over slippery seaweed-covered rocks could be difficult and dangerous.

After the heavily laden boat had arrived at its destination the whole procedure began all over again but in reverse, and even when the peats were finally delivered to each croft door the work was not over, for they still had to be stacked expertly to keep each precious particle dry and safe from winter storms. It is little wonder that some said there was more heat generated by the peat-gatherers than by the peat itself.

* * *

Access: No regular access but try St Magnus Bay Charters, Aith Marina, 01595-810378 or Shetland Marine Charters, Brae, 01806-522447.

Anchorage:
1. Bight of Warwick, Sound of Houbansetter. Anchor off E shore of Papa Little in the bight S of the drying sand-spit in 7–10m. Good holding and well sheltered except, possibly, from N–NE.

11.13 Vementry

(ON Vémundar-øy – Vémundr's island) Vémundr is a man's name.

OS Maps: 1:50000 Sheet 3 1:25000 Sheet 467
Admiralty Charts: 1:75000 No.3281 1:25000 No.3295

Area: 370ha (914 ft)
Height: 90m (295 ft)

Population: 1841 – 2 (1 house). No permanent habitation since.

Geology: Although the area is predominantly of undifferentiated schist and gneiss, Vementry has a large intrusive sheet of coarse granite on the north-west side composed mainly of pink orthoclase, felspar, and quartz – but with very little mica. Across the Cribba Sound near Clousta there are volcanic rocks and Old Red Sandstone.

History: Swarbacks Minn was an important naval anchorage during the First World War and Vementry was fortified with two six-inch guns to protect it.

* * *

VEMENTRY, in the parish of Aithsting, is a good example of a typical small Shetland island with a broken landscape of lochs, voes, rocky shoreline, windy heath, and some relics of man's ancient past. Old records mention a chapel on Vementry but its site is uncertain.

Swarbacks Head (ON and E. – headland of the black-backed gull) in the north, guards the entrance to the large irregular area of sheltered water called Swarbacks Minn. Above its rocky bluff and skerry there is an emplacement of two six-inch guns from the 1914–18 war [HU290619]. **Northra Voe** (ON – northern creek), the small inlet beside Swarbacks Head has a chambered cairn on its west side beside a small burn [HU290612].

There are several small hills on Vementry. The highest, **Muckle Ward** (90m), has a magnificent, circular (8m diam.), stone-faced cairn on its summit [HU295609]. It stands on a heel-shaped platform made of big stone blocks with an 11m-wide facade. A passage with some of its lintels still in position leads to a trefoil-shaped chamber. This type of tomb is to be found only in Shetland and has its chambers laid out like the heel of a shoe. These cairns are usually built in a prominent position, such as at the top of a hill, but the size varies and may depend on the importance of the interred individuals. This tomb on Muckle Ward is a large one and the best preserved in Shetland – probably because its situation is not readily accessible. It is also

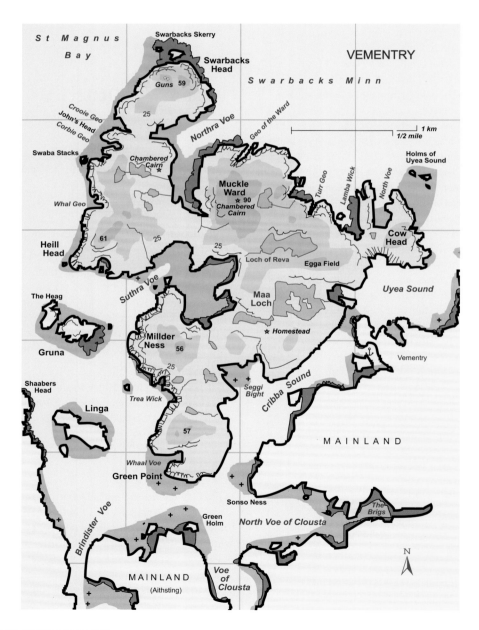

unusual because it has no entrance and was presumably closed after the last burial.

The west coast is divided by shallow, rocky, Suthra Voe (ON – southern creek), which penetrates into the heart of the island. Two islets almost obstruct the entrance, **The Heag** and **Gruna** (ON – green island), while **Linga** to the south spreads halfway across the sound. Only a shallow, narrow channel separates Vementry from Mainland as a neck of land projecting out of Mainland divides Cribba Sound from Uyea Sound. Vementry House stands, white-walled, at the root of this peninsula with its snug little harbour beside it.

* * *

Access: A boat-owner in Vementry harbour (Mainland) may take you across or try St Magnus Bay Charters, West Mainland, 01595-810378.
Anchorages: Vementry Sound has a number of suitable anchorages but passage is difficult with many rocks and dangerous reefs. Proceed with great care using large-scale chart and sailing instructions.
1. Uyea Sound. Reasonable shelter. Anchor in bay on N side in 4–8m, good holding when not in weed, but restricted by fish cages. Narrow passage through to Cribba Sound has minimum depth of 1m.
2. Cribba Sound. Good shelter in NW half. Fish cages.
3. Suthra Voe. Approach with great care as both sides foul with rocks. Well-sheltered anchorage in centre of NE bay, 8m.

11.14 Papa Stour

(ON papøy stóra – big island of the priests).

O S Maps: 1:50000 Sheet 3 1:25000 Sheet 467
Admiralty Charts: 1:75000 No.3281

Area: 828ha (2046 acres)
Height: 87m (285 ft)

Owner: Multiple ownership.

Population: 1841–382 (66 houses). 1871–351. 1881–254. 1891–244 (44 houses). 1931–100. 1961–55. 1991–33. 2001–23. 2011–15.

Geology: Formed from volcanic lava and ash and then sculpted by the sea resulting in some of the finest sea caves in Britain. These, however, are only accessible in fine weather. There are also many interesting skerries, stacks and voes.

History: Papa Stour, with its fertile soil, is thought to have been first settled about 3000BC. When the Norsemen came they presumably found monks or hermits in residence but they settled here themselves nevertheless. A fascinating piece of archaeological detective work by Dr Barbara Crawford of St Andrews in the early 1980s has revealed what is almost certainly the 13th-century residence of Duke Haakon, later King of Norway, who had a farm on the island beside Housa Voe.

In the early 16th century merchants from Hamburg and Bremen considered the island of sufficient importance to build a summer trading booth to buy fish and fish oil from the islanders and exchange various commodities. But the haaf (ON deep-sea) fishing decreased and herring fishing had taken its place by the mid-19th century. A herring station was constructed at Hamna Voe and curers and gutters came from far afield, even from Ireland. Fuel was so scarce and the fishermen so busy that the islanders started burning the turf and even today large areas lie scalped and bare. By the 1870s the situation was so bad that people started to leave.

In 1970 the school closed because there were no more young children. In fact the total population by then was only sixteen fairly elderly people. Although the Sound of Papa is relatively narrow, tides rage through it and the island can be isolated for days at a time. But after an advertisement was placed in *Exchange and Mart* mentioning that crofts would be granted free together with five sheep each, young people started to flood in from all over Britain. It was a refuge from the rat-race – a place for 'human values' and flower-power. Shetlanders started calling it the 'Hippy Isle'. Most of the incomers gave up quickly when they discovered the rigours of island existence but a few remained and they gave the island new life. The population rose to about thirty. By 1992, however, numbers were once again falling and a new search was on.

As a result the Primary School was able to reopen in 2003 with pupils enjoying the undivided attention of the teacher who had previously taught the three pupils on Foula (No.11.6). But peace was short-lived for in 2005 a serious dispute between families again threatened the stability of the island.

Wildlife: This is a fertile island and it is said that fishermen can locate the island in a summer haar by the pungent smell of the wild flowers – 'Fir da scent o flooers in Papa leds wis aa da wye.'

VOLCANIC SEA-CAVES BY BREI HOLM, PAPA STOUR

Papa Stour and Foula (No.11.6) were the last refuges of the primitive and goat-like Shetland sheep. These were classified as an endangered species.

The stacks and inlets support many sea-birds and there are quite large colonies of cormorant and Manx shearwater. It is interesting to learn that although the fulmar is relatively widespread now, in 1890 an ornithologist visiting Papa Stour noted with delight that he had seen one.

Common seals breed on the skerries.

*   *   *

Each volcanic island being formed today off the coast of Iceland will become a **PAPA STOUR** tomorrow. Already their soft ash is being eaten away by the sea from its hard volcanic base leaving tunnels and arches and weird, grotesque, tortuous shapes. On the surface, where the sea cannot wash it away, seeds dropped by the seabirds take root and the ash is converted into fertile soil, rich in essential nutrients.

Papa Stour is one of the most fertile of the Shetland Islands, its only failing being a total lack of fuel in the form of peat. It has exciting volcanic forms and a precipitous coastline, indented and eroded, above a tumble of detached rocks, stacks and skerries – a wonderland for climbers and potholers. In the north-west there is an immense cliff with a natural tunnel, the **Hole of Bordie**, penetrating it for nearly 1km (½M)! **Virda Field**,

the highest hill (87m), sits above it. Beyond the narrow cleft of Akers Geo are the **Fogla** (ON *fugl* – bird) and **Lyra** (ON *lyrie* – Manx shearwater) **Skerries**. They also have subterranean passages through which the tide surges. Here too a great column of rock, the **Stack of Snalda**, reaches skywards, and far out to sea the **Ve Skerries** (ON – suffering skerries), a favourite seal-hunting ground in days gone by, lie low and menacing among the Atlantic waves.

Probably Britain's finest sea-cave, **Kirstan's** (or Christie's) **Hole**, is on the south-west side of the island [HU152606]. It is at the head of a narrow creek and confined between vertical rock faces about 30m high. A columnar stack stands like a sentry beside the 27m-wide natural arch forming the cave entrance. Within there is an enclosed space with glistening walls standing open to the sky. The cave then continues for about another 70m, ending at a beach.

John Tudor, a Victorian traveller, raved about the caves of Papa Stour. His favourite was **Francie's Hole** nearer Hamna Voe. This is smaller than Christie's Hole, but in his view more beautiful. The entrance is perfectly arched and inside you are 'in fairyland, so exquisite is the colouring of the roof and sides, and so pellucid is the water'. Caves branch off on one side and at the back is a small pink beach above which 'are alcoves or recesses like stalls in a church'.

Hamna Voe (ON – haven or harbour creek)

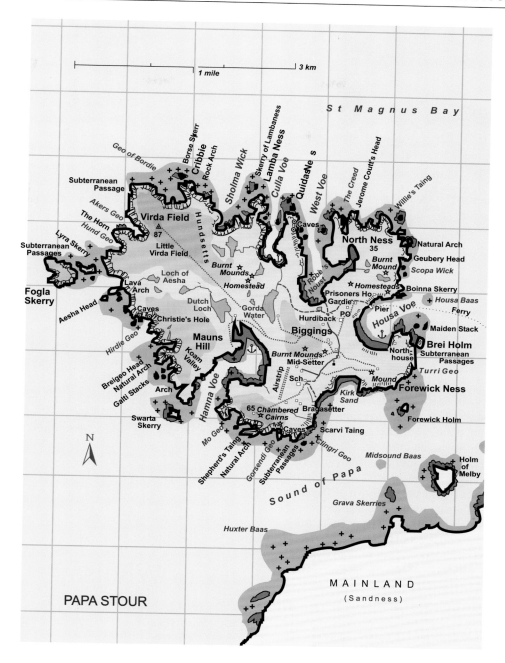

St Magnus Bay

PAPA STOUR

MAINLAND
(Sandness)

is an almost land-locked lagoon. Red cliffs on the east side by the entrance conceal the modest island airstrip and the school. There is a natural rock arch in these cliffs with the remnants of two chambered cairns above it. The church is above a small beached cove known as **Kirk Sand** and there are more cairns and burned mounds nearby. The odds are that the church, which looks across the Sound of Papa to Melby on Mainland, was built on the most sacred pagan site. **Forewick**

Holm lies off-shore.

All the habitation is in the east, mainly around **Housa Voe** (ON – voe of the houses). Although more exposed than Hamna Voe, Housa Voe has a pier for the small ferry-boat from West Burra Firth on Mainland. Off the headland between Kirk Sand and Housa Voe there are many interesting rock formations and a small islet, **Brei Holm**, joined to the ness by a drying reef. Said to have been the precarious site of a leper colony in the

BENIE HOOSE – A NEOLITHIC RETREAT

which blew the ship far out to sea.

* * *

Access: Ro-ro ferry from West Burrafirth, daily except Tues. and Thur., 40 minutes, 01957-722259, weather permitting and prior booking essential. Scheduled air service from Tingwall, two flights Tues. only, 01595-840246.

Anchorages: Passage in the Sound of Papa requires great care as there are strong tides and many off-shore dangers. There are severe overfalls off the NW coast.

1. Hamna Voe. Shelter from all weather but entry impossible in strong S'lies. At the narrows there is only 2m depth at LWS, and 20m width. Follow instructions for entry, which requires care. Anchor N or S in 4–6m.

2. Housa Voe. Reasonable shelter in 4–6m, sand. There is a new pier/breakwater with alongside depth of 2.5m. Enter from N 1c off and parallel to NW shore to avoid Housa Baa.

3. West Voe. In E bay which dries at head, 4–6m, sand. No shelter from N'lies.

4. Culla Voe. Good holding and shelter from all weather. Approach mid-channel to avoid sunken rocks at entrance. Anchor near head of Voe in 3m.

18th century recent excavations have shown that it might first have been an early Norse monastic community.

Near Brei Holm is an isolated stack with the vestige of a stone house to be seen on its narrow top. This is the **Maiden Stack**, or Frau Stack. In the early 14th century Lord Thorvald Thoresson is said to have built this for his daughter to live in to ensure that she would not be in the company of men. But it was all to no avail for when he released her she was found to be pregnant.

The group of houses which cluster behind the post office at Housa Voe is known as **Biggins** (ON *byggja* – buildings) and is probably the island's earliest settlement. At the start of the 19th century the Hon Edwin Lindsay was sent here in disgrace by his family for refusing to fight a duel. They had him declared insane and he was kept under guard on the island for twenty-six years. It was a Quaker preacher, Catherine Watson, who arranged his escape and he was then able to claim his inheritance. There is a spring at the south of the island called Lindsay's Well, where he was allowed to bathe.

Papa Stour's mood changes with the weather and at times it has either a magical or a sinister quality. This is particularly noticeable on the north coast when a haar creeps in and blankets the wicks and geos. But even Housa Voe is not immune. The islanders tell of a strange ship that sailed into the voe on a sunny day long ago. The crew were seen to be preparing to attack the village so the local witch, Minna Baaba, immediately created a storm,

11.15 Whalsay

(ON hvals-øy – whale island).

O S Maps: 1:50000 Sheet 2 1:25000 Sheet 468
Admiralty Charts: 1:75000 No.3282

Area: 1970ha (4868 acres)
Height: 119m (390 ft)

Owner: Multiple ownership.

Population: 1841–628 (112 houses). 1881–870. 1891–927 (167 houses). 1931–900. 1961–764. 1991–1041. 2001–1034. 2011–1061.

Geology: The bedrock is almost entirely of gneiss with granite veins. There are good stocks of peat which the Out Skerries islanders are entitled to cut.

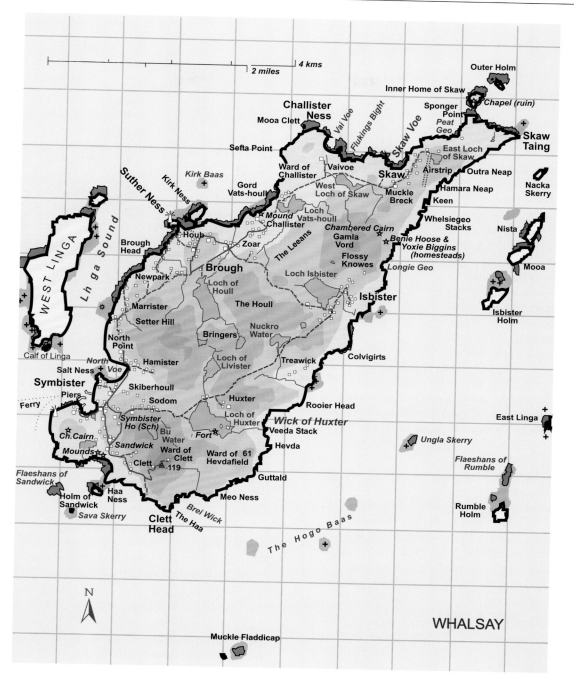

History: The Bruces of Muness in Unst gained possession of Whalsay from its crofter-owners and brought in a period of harsh rule. In the 19th century the punishment for any small misdemeanour was exile from the island.

Naval press-gangs valued the sailing ability of Whalsay men and would sometimes remove them from their 'sixerns' when they were out fishing.

The families were not informed.

The recent history of Whalsay is the 'boom and bust' history of fishing for this is an island of fishermen. In 1832 many lost their lives when there was a great storm at sea but fishing continued and 1834 was the peak year for herring catches. Second-hand 'half-deckers' were bought on the Scottish mainland to replace the native sixerns and improve the Whalsay fleet. But this optimism was followed in 1839 by a slump in the herring market followed in 1840 by another violent storm in which many men were drowned. Bankruptcy and poverty were rife.

By the late 19th century, however, the industry had recovered and bigger boats were introduced. For a time all was well, and then steam drifters created new problems as the Whalsay men lacked capital to compete.

BREMEN BÖD – A 17TH CENTURY HANSEATIC TRADING POST

Between the two World Wars Whalsay fishermen survived by catching what herring they could in the summer and supplementing this with in-shore haddock-fishing in the winter, but after the Second World War conditions improved when Government grants and loans assisted the purchase of superior dual-purpose vessels.

This 'mini-boom' continued until 1965 when 200 Norwegian ships appeared fitted with power tackle and sonar and swept the seas of fish. The Shetlanders tried to follow the Norwegian example and for a few years there were huge catches but by 1977 the stocks had disappeared and herring-fishing was banned. Since 1983 there has been limited intermittent fishing, complicated by the predation of foreign fleets and the requirements of the European Union.

Wildlife: The Shetland record brown trout – 9lb 4oz – was caught in Whalsay's Loch of Huxter.

Small colonies of kittiwake and puffin nest at the south end of the island and whimbrel, arctic tern and arctic skua nest on the moors and by the lochans. A few red-throated diver, known as 'rain geese' in Shetland, may also be seen. This is an important staging-post for migrant birds; unusual species such as the red-rumped swallow, hoopoe, and Pallas' warbler, have been recorded.

* * *

WHALSAY is the 'Bonny Isle'. Pleasant green pastures could easily support livestock but few do, for the islanders are fishers not farmers and the economy revolves round fish. Off-shore there are rocks, reefs and skerries with fascinating names like the **Hogo Baas** and **Rumble Holm** which give shelter to lobsters, prawns, and a surprising number of white fish. It takes a local to know all these sand-banks and crevices. Furthermore, Whalsay's millionaires – and it is said there are more than twenty of them – now own some supertrawlers which search the distant oceans for fish. As a result, there is an expanding and relatively prosperous population, a fish-processing plant, and a desire by every young man to get to sea in his own boat. Why waste time milking cows when there are fish in the sea? Lerwick can supply all the milk required. Recently, however, the European Union has cast a dark shadow over this idyllic scenario and the future is uncertain.

Ward of Clett, a well-defined hill in the south of the island, is the highest point at 119m. It rises south-west of the **Loch of Huxter** (ON – prehistoric-mound farm) with its Iron Age holm fort [HU559620]. This is thought to be one of the earliest versions of a broch – the idea from which the later versions evolved. Unfortunately, many of the stones were removed to build cabbage enclosures or 'plantiecruives', but sufficient remains to be of interest.

Generally, the island has an attractive rolling landscape of low hills and small lochs, with activity mainly centred around the small port at **Symbister** in the south. The airstrip is at the other end, at **Skaw** (ON – point) in the north. There are two islets off Skaw Taing, **Outer** and **Inner Holm of Skaw**, with a ruined chapel on Inner Holm.

The lighthouse on **Symbister Ness** in the south-west is close to the busy little harbour, which is in the most southerly of two small voes. **Bremen Böd**, near the Symbister pier, has an old wooden windlass beside it. This is a Hanseatic store set up by German merchants in the 17th century to trade brandy, tobacco, linen, muslin, fruit, and salt for haddock, fish oil, cod and other fishy delicacies. It is the only complete surviving example in Scotland of such a building. It was rescued from dereliction and is now used as a visitors' interpretative centre.

Symbister House is an extravagant solid-granite Georgian mansion sited east of the harbour, which has served as a Junior High School since 1940 [HU543622]. It was built in 1823 by the head of the distinguished Shetland family of Bruce at great cost (£30,000), not because he needed a second home – he already had a fine house on Mainland – but for the rather petty reason that he did not wish to leave the money for his heirs to enjoy. The grounds, incidentally, are reputed to be haunted by an old sailor who was murdered by the gardener for winning a game of cards.

Between Symbister and Loch of Huxter is the ruined cottage where the poet Christopher Grieve (Hugh MacDiarmid) lived from 1933 to 1942. The place name is **Sudheim** (ON – south home) but the Ordnance Survey had anglicised this to **Sodom**! – much to MacDiarmid's amusement.

A shallow bay on the south coast, Sand Wick, has Bronze Age burned mounds beside it. Several skerries and an islet, **Holm of Sandwick**, obstruct entrance to the bay.

Halfway up the north-west coast the village of **Brough** (ON – stronghold) is beside Kirk Ness with a narrow isthmus leading to a church [HU555655] and at Suther Ness there is another lighthouse. Directly across on the other side of the island is **Isbister** (ON – east farm), a settlement of houses clustered beside a loch and looking south-east over two strings of islets. Nearby are the delightfully named **Nista** (ON – northmost isle), **Mooa** (ON – narrow isle), and **Isbister Holm** with **Nacka Skerry** to the north, and further out are **East Linga** and the **Grif**, **Swarta**, **Longa** and **Rumble Skerries** (ON – beside the deep sea, black, long and round-rocks skerries respectively). The Grif Skerry was a haaf fishing station where the boats could be beached in bad weather while the men sheltered in primitive huts.

Some of these names can be very confusing. For instance, the Admiralty Chart attaches names to the rocks south of Whalsay which are incorrect according to the Whalsay fishermen. They say that a sailor should read **Muckla Fladdacap** as Muckle Fladdacap, **Muckla Billan** as Peerie Fladdacap, **Litla Billan** as Haerie, and **Haerie** as Ooter Vooder!

Midway between Loch Isbister and Loch of Huxter is pewter-coloured **Nuckro Water** (ON *nøkk* – water monster). This is the home of a vicious water demon, known in Shetland as the 'njuggle', which usually appears in the form of a beautiful, friendly, horse. But once seated on its back the human victim is carried into the water and drowned. The njuggle can also appear in other forms and it is most dangerous after sunset. Another njuggle lives in Njugals Water near Tingwall on Mainland.

Between Isbister and Skaw the **Yoxie Biggins** may date from about 3000BC. This is a heel-shaped structure somewhat like Staneydale on Mainland. It was first assumed to have religious significance but now it is thought more likely to have been a Neolithic farmhouse. A ruin from the same period, **Bunzie** (or **Benie**) **Hoose**, is adjacent and it has a clover-leaf layout [HU587652].

Access: Frequent daily ro-ro ferry service from Laxo or Vidlin, Mainland, (½hr), 01806-566259. Scheduled flights Tingwall/Out Skerries, Mon., Wed., Thurs., lands at Whalsay on request, 01595-840246. Tourist Information, 01595-693434.

Anchorages:
1. Symbister Harbour. Sheltered but busy fishing-boat harbour on W coast. Tie alongside S breakwater/jetty, 102m-long, provided those already berthed are agreeable or try the marina which has depths of 2m.
2. North Voe. Only use as a last resort. Bottom foul with old moorings.

11.16 West Linga

(E. and ON – west heather-island).

OS Maps: 1:50000 Sheet 2 1:25000 Sheet 468
Admiralty Charts: 1:75000 No.3282

Area: 125ha (309 acres)
Height: 52m (171 ft)

Population: Uninhabited.

Geology: Coarse micaceous and hornblendic gneiss with granite veins. There is a raised beach above Croo Wick (ON – sheep-pen bay) at the south extremity.

History: Liv Schei in her fascinating book, *The Shetland Story*, notes that on the 7 August 1485

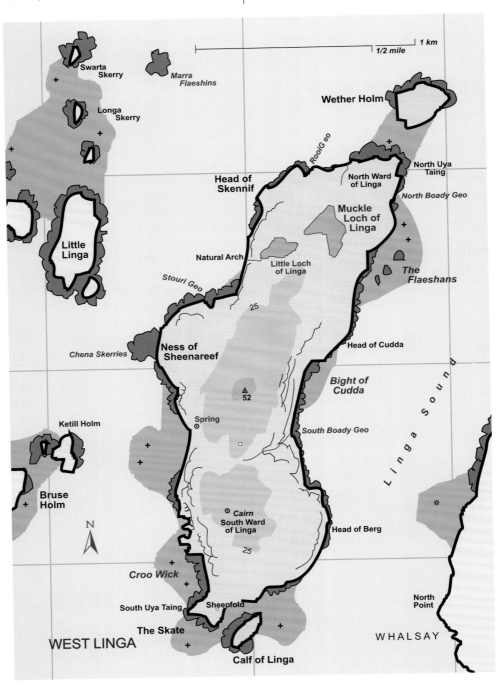

WEST LINGA SEEN FROM SODOM (HUGH MACDIARMID'S COTTAGE) ON WHALSAY

at Korskirken in Bergen a meeting was held to discuss an illegal purchase of various lands in Shetland. The most important piece of land listed was ten merks on 'Liungøuo i Hwalsøyo.'

WEST LINGA is a long narrow island covered in rough heath with its highest point (52m) almost in the exact geometrical centre. There is a further minor hill in the southern part with a cairn on it and two small lochans in the northern half. It is somewhat surprising that an island of this size with a supply of drinkable, if brackish, water has so little sign of human habitation but this is probably due to the lack of an anchorage. There is not even a suitable place to beach a boat easily for any length of time. However, in spite of such difficulties the island seems to have been inhabited intermittently until, possibly, the end of the 18th century.

It is said that while the Bruce family were 'acquiring' Whalsay the udaller of West Linga went out fishing. While he was absent his young son got his head stuck in a large jar and his mother was frantic with worry. The Bruce representative happened to land on the island during this incident and the mother appealed to him for help. He refused until the mother signed over the land, whereupon he calmly broke the pot. This story may have grown with the telling but it no doubt had some basis in fact.

The **Calf of Linga** is a drying islet off the Skate (ON – a rock or sand-shelf) at the southern extremity. At the opposite extreme in the north there is another islet called **Wether Holm**. This is separated from West Linga by a narrow 3m-deep channel.

West Linga divides the sea area between Whalsay and Mainland into two Sounds, Linga and Lunning. Both have fierce tides but Lunning Sound is broken up with many islets and skerries which create swirls and eddies understood only by the Whalsay fishermen. The islets are **Hunder Holm** according to the Ordnance Survey but known locally as 'Unerim' (ON – Arnorr's holm), **Bruse Holm** or 'Brusim' (ON – Brusi's holm), **Ketill Holm** or 'Kettlim' (ON – Ketill's holm), **Score Holm** or 'Skurim' (ON – Skori's holm) and **Little Linga**.

The poet and author, Hugh MacDiarmid, who lived in a Whalsay cottage which overlooked West Linga, claimed in *The Uncanny Scot* to have spent three days on the island. He said that he asked a boatman to leave him there and not to look for him for three days and that he had with him only a good stock of matches, some thick black tobacco, and two books. He slept in a cave in the rocks and caught four sillocks with a bent pin on a string. It transpired later that the story was entirely imaginary – although he had spent part of a day on the island with the man who grazed his sheep there.

* * *

Access: No regular access. Try the Tourist Office, 01595-693434 or ask at Symbister on Whalsay.

Anchorage: No recommended anchorages.

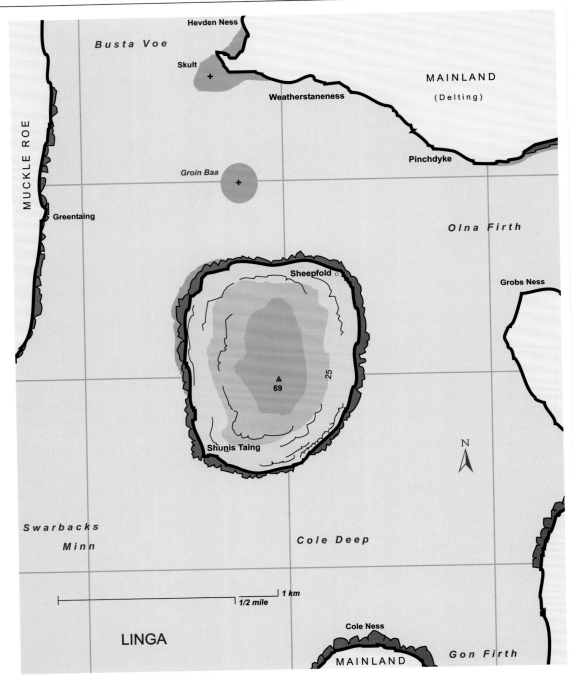

11.17 Linga

(ON lyng-øy – heather island).

OS Maps: 1:50000 Sheet 3 1:25000 Sheet 469
Admiralty Charts: 1:75000 Nos.3281 or 3282 1:25000
No.3295

Area: 70ha (173 acres)
Height: 69m (226 ft)

Population: Uninhabited and no Census records.

Geology: Gneiss, schists and some quartzite and pelite.

* * *

A circumnavigation of **LINGA** reveals all. From every viewpoint its rounded surface of rough grass and heather resembles a well-cooked pudding in a rock-encrusted pie-dish. There are no coves or caves or crags, no hidden secrets, no ancient ruins. To its credit the view from the top of the dumpling (69m) is striking and worth the effort of achieving a landing, and to be fair, Linga is not unwelcoming to visitors – merely indifferent.

Access: No regular access but try St Magnus Bay Charters, West Mainland, 01595-810378.

Anchorage: No recommended anchorages. Beware Groin Baa in the north channel.

1. Possible temp. anchorage, if conditions are suitable, off NE side in 12–15m but use tripping line.

11.18 Housay
or West Isle (ON hús-øy – house island).

Bruray

or East Isle (ON brúar-øy- island forming a bridge) – together with

Grunay

(ON – green island). These are known as the Out Skerries (ON út-skeri – outer skerries) or just 'The Skerries' (ON austrskeri – eastern skerries).

OS Maps: 1:50000 Sheet 2 1:25000 Sheet 468
Admiralty Charts: 1:75000 No.3282
Area: 218ha (539 acres)
Height: 53m (174 ft)

Owner: Housay, Bruray and the nearby stacks and skerries are owned by Cussons Estate. They were bought by A S Cussons (of Imperial Leather fame) in 1967 excluding the crofting rights. These are presently owned by the South African Frank Cussons. The only exception to this is Laurence Anderson who owns his own property of 'Sunnyside' beside Da Stripe.

Grunay changed hands many times in the 20th century. The present owner, Torquil Johnson-Ferguson of Dumfriesshire also owns Lunga (No.2.12). He put Grunay up for sale in 1993, but is possibly still the owner.

Population:

	1841	1881	1891	1931	1961	1991	2001	2011
Housay		71	86	68	71	58	50	50
Bruray		59	54	34	34	27	26	24
Grunay		25	25	6	0	0	0	0
Total	122	155	165	114	105	85	76	74

Geology: The Mio Ness peninsula (joined to Housay by The Steig which is a collapsed cave) is granite. Apart from a strip of fragmented limestone which stretches from the southern coast of Housay through the centre of Housay and Bruray the rest of the islands are of gneiss and schist. Grunay has granite bedrock.

History: The extent of settlement by early man still awaits scientific investigation. Norse habitation is much more clearly recorded by the hundreds of Norse place-names. These could never have arisen from a few transitory visits and point to continuous settlement over a long period of time.

But the real history of the Skerries is the history of the sea that surrounds them because through the centuries many ships have foundered on these treacherous rocks and the people of the Skerries have had to live with, and understand, the sea in all its moods. One of the earliest recorded wrecks was a Spanish Armada horse-carrier which was said to have sunk in the narrow channel called The Rett.

With the outbreak of the second Anglo-Dutch war in 1664 Dutch East-Indiamen, being merchant ships, avoided the English Channel

THE SKERRIES SHORELINE – A GRAVEYARD FOR SHIPS

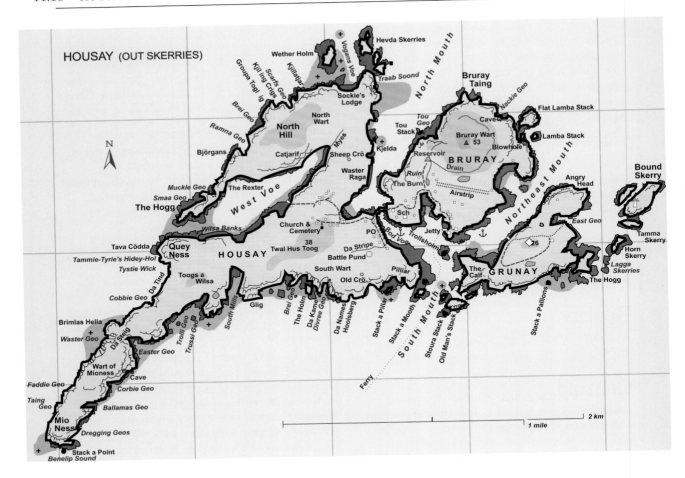

and preferred to take the longer route ('Achter Om') round the north of Scotland. Although, following the accession of a Scottish King to the English throne in 1603, Scotland and England had a shared monarchy, both countries still had independent Parliaments and the Scots were not at war with the Dutch. On the night of the 11 December 1664 the *Kennermerland,* bound for the Cape of Good Hope ran hard on to Stoura Stack and broke up in the South Mouth. The foremast fell ashore and three men in the rigging survived. The rest were swept out to sea and drowned. The only body washed ashore, a drummer-boy, is buried near the old fish factory. The Earl of Morton, who owned the islands at that time, recovered about 120,000 guilders by promptly setting up a primitive salvage operation but King Charles II stepped in and claimed ownership. There was a court case in Edinburgh which the King won and the Earl lost both the guilders and his Orkney and Shetland estates. The islanders also got nothing, but at least enough barrels of

spirits came ashore to keep them inebriated for weeks and it is still said that a chest of gold was hidden on the seashore. It is also said that the first hens on Out Skerries came from this wreck.

The *De Liefde,* one of a convoy of ships laden with gold and silver coins to pay for exotic goods in Java, ran into Mio Ness on 8 November 1711 and was lost with all hands except for the look-out in the crow's-nest who was thrown onto the grassy top of the cliff. He reported that there were millions of guilders and several chests of gold coins on board. Most of the money may still be somewhere on the seabed. Occasional coins turn up and an official dive in 1967 recovered a chestful of silver coins and some gold ducats. Diving to these wrecks, however, has to meet official guidelines.

More recently, in 1906, the wreck of the *North Wind* with a cargo of wood provided the islanders with wooden floors in every house – a great luxury.

But shipwrecks only brought occasional and limited prosperity. Fishing is the historic means of livelihood and in the 19th century Out Skerries provided a valuable haaf fishing station and intermittently throughout the 20th century it was a centre for the industry.

Wildlife: Very well placed to receive continental migrants when the wind is in the east so, apart from islanders' relatives, divers and island-hoppers, the majority of visitors are bird-watchers. The islands support small breeding colonies of gulls, terns, eider and black guillemot but, otherwise, there is only limited birdlife on the cliffs which are not high enough to provide attractive nesting sites.

HOUSAY and **BRURAY** are linked by a concrete bridge built in 1957, replacing the first bridge built in 1899 and a subsequent 'improvement', and they are nowadays the only inhabited islands in the Out Skerries group. Although this cluster of little islands and skerries, exposed and isolated, reach tentatively into the vast inhospitable wastes of the North Sea they are considered to be one of the happiest and most flourishing parts of Shetland. On approach by sea the cliffs, which are not particularly high, still look forbidding and impregnable. But on a close approach a gap appears and once through the narrow 'mouth' a different picture presents itself. In between the three main islands of the archipelago, Housay, Bruray and Grunay, is a landlocked haven and a pier, completed in 1986, where the ferry docks. Neat, trim and colourful cottages scattered around deep-green miniature fjords create a Nordic flavour. Behind, low grassy hills are used for grazing. There is a little cultivation on a belt of relatively fertile soil but generally the people are fisherfolk, not farmers.

The Skerries is a world in miniature with about 1500 tiny geographical features, each of which is specifically named by the islanders. Housay has a long precipitous leg stretching south-westwards and ending at **Mio Ness** (ON – narrow headland). It humps up like a bent knuckle to a height of 48m near its south extremity. The island itself has a hill on each side of **West Voe**, a deep inlet on the west coast and a modest settlement with a post-office and a cemetery in the middle. At the northern extremity is **Wether Holm**.

North Hill is covered with mounds of stones like 2m-long upturned boats. These are said to be prehistoric graves. There is other evidence of early man – lengths of walls built of Cyclopean masonry,

'skeos' round West Voe (a 'skeo' is the Shetland equivalent of a St Kildan 'cleit', or stone larder), and a mysterious stone rectangle of large boulders called **Battle Pund**. This has some similarity to Hjaltadans on Fetlar (No.11.25). There are varying explanations for both it and its name.

Across the bridge, on Bruray there are more houses, a school overlooking the harbour, and the airstrip beyond. North of the airstrip is the highest point on the archipelago at 53m where a much-needed fresh-water collection system was installed in 1957. Even so, water sometimes has to be brought over by tanker from Mainland.

As ever in such small communities, the school is a vital requirement for stability and the islanders insisted that their children should be fully educated on the island. Consequently a new school was built in 1965. With two teachers it provides both primary and secondary education – including a course in computer graphics! It is the smallest secondary school in Britain. The old school was converted into a church and a new Community Hall was built in 1981. Sadly the Council narrowly voted to close the secondary school in 2014. With only three pupils at the time, this was a devastating blow to the island's viability. The primary school, also with three pupils in 2014, remains open.

There is about a mile of surfaced road which can be quite busy as, since the introduction of the ro-ro ferry, there are about twenty cars. Every family owns a boat, and a fish-processing factory was built here in the productive early 1970s but fish is no longer such a prolific commodity.

The small island of **Grunay** on the east side of the harbour is separated from the others by South Mouth and Northeast Mouth. The entrance to South Mouth is guarded by both **Stoura Stack** – cause of the *Kennermerland* (or *Carmelan*) disaster – and **Old Man's Stack**, while **Lamba Stack** stands by Northeast Mouth. East of Grunay is **Bound Skerry** with a lighthouse which is now automatic. It was twice bombed by the Germans in the Second World War as they thought it was a munitions factory! The lighthouse was built in 1857 for £21,000 and the keepers were housed on Grunay. Robert Louis Stevenson's signature is in the visitors' book. Since the war the house on Grunay has been in ruins and the island is reputed to be rat-infested.

In July each year there is a rod-fishing competition and yacht racing in August. On its route to Out Skerries the ferry passes a group of islets and skerries stretching south from Mio Ness – **Benelip**, consisting of linked islets – **North and South Benelip** and **Easter Skerries** – the largest – while the ferry is named after **Filla**, which lies immediately to the south.

*   *   *

Access: Ro-ro ferry daily except Tues. and Thurs., on prior booking from Vidlin, (90 mins), Fri., Sat., Sun., Mon., or Lerwick on Tues. and Thurs. (150 mins), 01806-515226. Flights from Tingwall, 01595-840246. Tourist info., 01595-693434.

Anchorages:
1. Between Housay and Bruray. Berth at pier usually available (charge) with good facilities, in small boat marina, or anchor in Bod Voe towards bridge, abreast school if possible, 6m, but many moorings. Use tripping line. Good shelter.
2. Between Bruray and Grunay. Anchor in 4m in entrance to bight on Bruray shore central between the rocks. Use tripping line. Reasonable shelter but NE'lies bring an uncomfortable swell.
3. North Mouth, pool N of bridge (Stringa Voe). Sheltered but not recommended as room very restricted.
4. West Voe on W side of Housay. Mouth obstructed by the Hogg, a rocky islet 2c long. The narrow difficult entrance is at S end of the Hogg where a bar restricts least depth to only 0.6m. Inside the depth increases and there is excellent shelter but the entrance at HW or in any swell is tricky.

11.19 Linga

(ON lyng-øy – heather island)

OS Maps: 1:50000 Sheet 2 or 3 1:25000 Sheet 468
Admiralty Charts: 1:75000 No.3282 1:30000 Nos.3292 or 3298

Area: 42ha (104 acres)
Height: 40m (132 ft)
Population: No census records and uninhabited
Geology: Mainly schists with some quartzite and pelite covered by a thin soil.

Wildlife: Common seals and occasionally a grey seal or two haul out on the rocky shore at the north end of Linga.
Relative to the size of island, few sea birds breed here. Neighbouring **Fish Holm** which is managed by the RSPB as a bird sanctuary is

much more popular. But on the sea round about when the tide is running there are occasional large concentrations of feeding shags, seaduck and black guillemot or 'tysties' to be seen. Eider, long-tailed duck and cormorant are also fairly common.

*   *   *

For a 'heather isle' **LINGA** certainly has heather but it has no drama: just a single rounded hill grazed by a scattering of sheep.
The small light beacon at the north end [HU467739] does not appear to disturb the common seals which favour the shoreline here, but they use the island only for relaxation. They pup elsewhere.

*   *   *

Access: Try Northmavine Charters (Colla Firth pier), 07765-907818. Tourist information, 01595-693434.

Anchorage:
No recommended anchorages. The entire sea area between Linga and Fish Holm should be avoided.
1. Temp anchorage in suitable weather off the centre of the south coast. Gravel and rock, 5m, holding uncertain.

11.20 Samphrey

(ON Sandfridar-øy – Sandfridr's island) Sandfridr is a woman's name.

OS Maps: 1:50000 Sheet 2 or 3 1:25000 Sheet 468
Admiralty Charts: 1:75000 No.3282 1:30000 Nos.3292 or 3298

Area: 66ha (163 acres)
Height: 29m (95 ft)
Population: 1841–36 (6 houses). 1881–0. Uninhabited since then.
Geology: Coarsely crystalline gneiss with occasional granite veins.

History: In late 1832 a terrible storm blew up unexpectedly and caught six Samphrey men out fishing on the haaf. Their sixern was blown through mountainous seas until it eventually ended up on a Norwegian beach. It suffered only minor damage and the men were given accommodation and treated very hospitably by the Norwegians. In the spring they returned home, none the worse for their holiday abroad, to a great welcome from their families who had believed they were dead.

Wildlife: The grazing is reasonably good for sheep but wildflowers are scarce, not only because of the grazing but also, because the island is so flat, it catches the worst of the salt-spray.

A number of sea-birds breed here and both Samphrey and neighbouring Fish Holm are managed by the RSPB as a bird sanctuary.

*   *   *

SAMPHREY defensively straddles the southern entrance to Yell Sound. The tides can run fast past its shores. It is low-lying, shaped something like the jaw-bone of an ass, and the highest ground in the centre of the island is only 29m above sea-level.

Samphrey is relatively clear of rocks in the surrounding sea except for the shallow **Bunglan** promontory on the west side. A large pool or lochan on this headland is only cut off from the sea by narrow margins of land on two sides.

Many of the remnants of human occupation have already disappeared but there is a wee kirkyard. It is reputed to have very few men buried in it as according to tradition: 'Samphrey men are always taken by the sea.' Such certainty could only have arisen in a community dedicated to fishing and the sea which, in the end, may have taken too many, for slowly during the 19th century the number of fishermen and their families dwindled until the island was entirely depopulated. Samphrey is now merely habitation for seabirds and sheep.

On Hogmanay 1941 a Gloster Gladiator N5642 of 152 squadron flying over Yell Sound, had engine failure, made a forced landing in a bog on Samphrey, somersaulted and finished upside

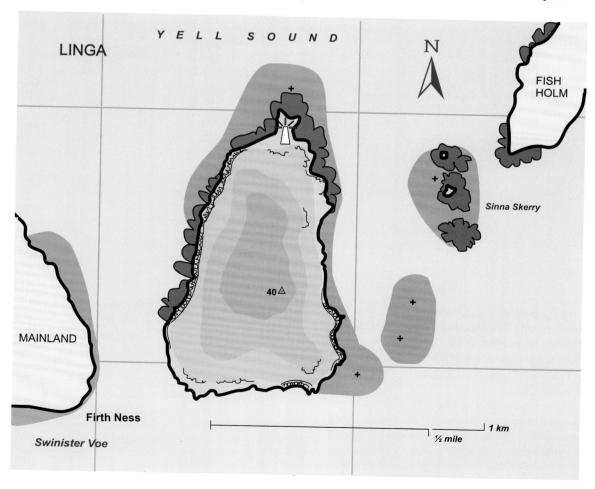

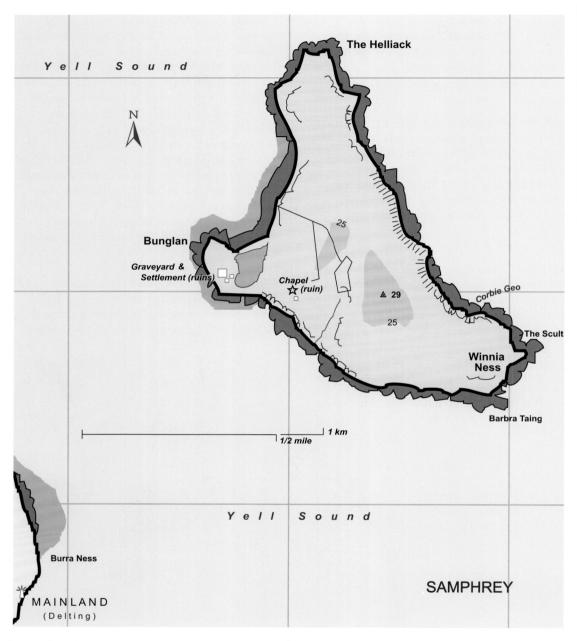

down. The pilot, Sgt. Makin, unhurt, climbed out nonchalant. This was the second time that he had made such a landing. South-east of Samphrey there is a small island, **Fish Holm**, whose name may have originated from its fish-like shape.

A rock outcrop, The **Rumble**, north-east of Samphrey is marked by a beacon. Orfasay (ON *orfyrisøy* – tidal island) is across the sound and linked to the south coast of Yell (No.11.24).

* * *

Access: Try Northmavine Charters (Colla Forth pier), 07765-907818.
Tourist Information 01595-693434 for recommended boatmen.

Anchorage:
1. Temp. anchorage in suitable weather in the bight N of Bunglan, the W promontory. Approach with care and anchor in 5m. Use tripping line. Beware submarine cable which is on a line between the W extremities of the two headlands.

11.21 Bigga

(ON bygd-øy – island of the building).

OS Maps: 1:50000 Sheet 2 or 3 1:25000 Sheet 470
Admiralty Charts: 1:75000 No.3282 1:30000 No.3298
Area: 78ha (193 acres)
Height: 34m (112 ft)

Population: 1841, 1881 and 1891 – no separate
Census records. 1931 – 1. Since uninhabited.

Geology: Moine bedrock of coarsely crystalline
gneiss and quartzite.

Wildlife: Storm petrel and puffin occasionally
breed here. Uynarey, to the north, is a nature
reserve managed by the RSPB.

*   *   *

BIGGA is now a 'sheep isle' but it appears to
have been inhabited until the 1930s. It is long
and narrow with a head and torso. The neck is
between two bays, Easter and Wester Hevda Wick
(ON – east and west bays of seaweed or manure).
The torso rises to a central height of 34m and
there is a small hill at the north extremity or head
with a prehistoric cairn on its eastern slope.

In the south of the island there is a house
which is used as a shepherd's bothy. The local
newspapers reported the story of two sailors
from Yell, who were given home leave during the
Second World War. They were home-sick and
desperate to rejoin their families in time for Yule.
The weather was very wild and the ferry from
Mainland refused to sail so they borrowed a small
open boat from a friend and set off. The snow-
covered hills of Yell could just be seen through
the spume over the wind-whipped open Sound
and the tide was in full racing flood but they
were accomplished sailors and knew the waters
well. However, they could make no headway as
the storm increased in strength and it was many
hours later before they managed to struggle
ashore on Bigga. They sheltered in the bothy but
it was so cold that they spent the night playing
the fiddle and dancing Shetland reels to keep
warm. The next day they were given assistance by
a passing drifter and arrived on Yell just in time to
join their family celebrations.

There is a reef at the north end of Bigga which
crosses the narrow sound separating Bigga from
Uynarey. Uynarey (ON – venerated island) is

slightly higher than Bigga with steeper sides.

Access: Try Northmavine Charters (Colla Firth
pier), 07765-907818 or the Yell ferryman may
advise. Tourist Information, 01595-693434.

Anchorage: Strong tides and a number of rocks make this
area hazardous.
1. Temp. anchorage when conditions suitable in Wester
Hevda Wick. Beware rock with less than 1.8m over it ½c
off NW extremity.

11.22 Brother Isle

*(ON breidare-øy – broad beach island.) The alternative (ON
brodur-øy – brother island), is improbable.*

OS Maps: 1:50000 Sheets 1, 2 or 3 1:25000 Sheet 469
Admiralty Charts: 1:75000 No.3282 1:30000 No.3298

Area: 40ha (99 acres)
Height: 25m (82 ft)

Population: Uninhabited and no Census records.

Geology: Undifferentiated Moine gneiss and
quartzite.

Wildlife: Occasional site for breeding storm
petrel.

*   *   *

BROTHER ISLE does not extend a welcome to
visitors. If an anchorite or hermit monk ever did
live on it, he must certainly have enjoyed solitude
for Brother Isle like a pirate ship repels boarders
on all sides. The shallow depression on the north
side, known as **The Pool**, is full of hidden rocks
and there is an evil drying rock called Stoura Baa
lurking a short distance away. The southern tip
has a long reef of rocks extending to the south-
east amid vicious tidal rips. There are also tidal
rips off the east and west coasts.

When gales are blowing against the tides in Yell
Sound the surface of the sea is whipped into a
demonic frenzy. It is then that the South Yell folk
refer to the tides familiarly as 'bitin' grices' – or, in
other words, swine.

The island itself is unremarkable. There is a
central hillock of 25m height and a dent on the
east side called **Tungli Geo** (ON – gloomy inlet).
Nearby is a substantial cave, which could, I

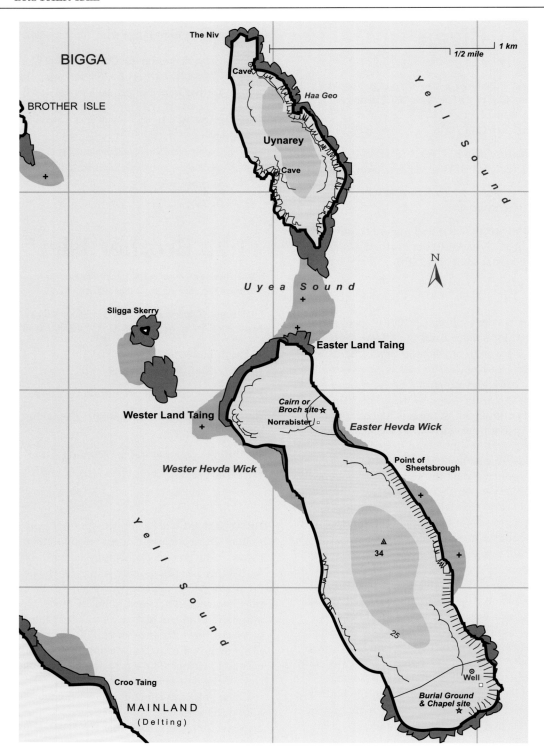

suppose, have provided some shelter for a hermit.

To the west of Brother Isle, the ugly head of **Tinga Skerry**, rears 5m above the dark waters of Yell Sound and, like an iceberg, conceals most of its body beneath the surface.

* * *

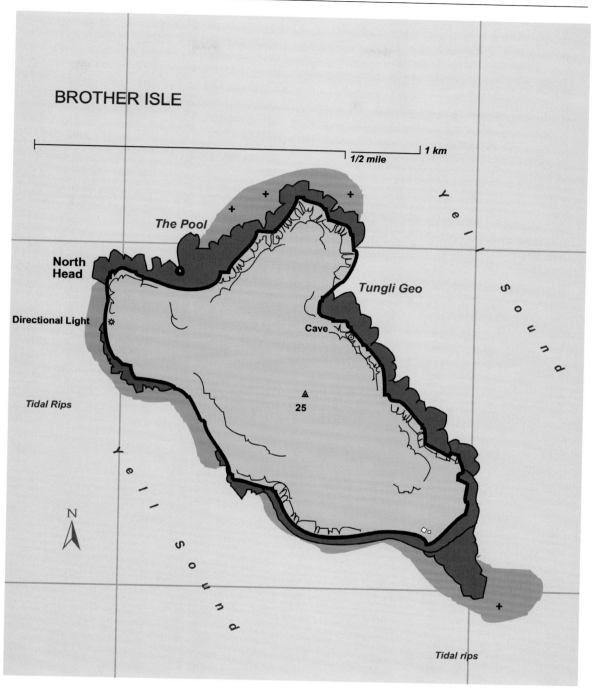

BROTHER ISLE

1/2 mile   1 km

The Pool

North
Head

Directional Light

Tidal Rips

Tungli Geo

Cave

Yell Sound

25

N

Yell Sound

Tidal rips

Access: Try Northmavine Charters (Colla Firth pier), 07765-907818 or the Yell ferryman may advise. Tourist Information, 01595-693434.

Anchorages: No recommended anchorages.

11.23 Lamba

(ON – lamb island).

OS Maps: 1:50000 Sheets 1, 2 or 3 1:25000 Sheet 469
Admiralty Charts: 1:75000 Nos.3281 or 3282 1:30000
No.3298

Area: 43ha (106 acres)

Height: 35m (115 ft)

Population: Uninhabited.

Geology: Intrusive igneous rocks – mainly granite and syenite.

Wildlife: Sometimes a whole family of otters can be seen in the cleft on the north-east side beside the eponymous Otter Had.

Storm petrel and puffin usually take up residence in the nesting season.

* * *

LAMBA's main claim to distinction is the tall (27m) light tower at its southern extremity, **South Head**. This helps to define the entrance to busy Sullom Voe oil terminal.

There are caves in the steep bluff beside the light tower and a cleft called **Hesti Geo** (ON – horse inlet). On the east coast a wider indentation called the **Wick of Lamba** (ON – Lamba Bay) is at least partly sheltered from the tidal currents in this area. These are clearly seen in the turbulence which builds up off both South Head and North Point. There is another bay on the north-west side but it is full of rocks and dries out at low water.

Lamba is surrounded by low escarpments which means that access can be something of a scramble but once above the shore the ground rises more gradually to a height of about 35m at the centre.

An interesting wreck of a Norwegian steamer – the *SS Robert Lee* – lies near Lamba in a depth of

THE 'BONXIE', OR GREAT SKUA, LORD OF THE SKIES

only 10 metres but divers should be very wary of the strong currents.

Near the entrance to Sullom Voe is another, smaller, island with a light beacon. This is **Little Roe,** which in 1841 was inhabited by eleven people sharing a single house.

* * *

Access: Try Northmavine Charters (Colla Firth pier), 07765-907818.

Anchorages: No recommended anchorages.
1. Temp. anchorage in suitable weather conditions in Wick of Lamba, 7–10m.

11.24 Yell

(ON gjall – barren) but some think the name may be Pictish. The early Norse name was 'Jala' or 'Jela' which might mean white island (i.e. sandy beaches?).

O S Maps: 1:50000 Sheets 1 and 2, or 1 and 3 1:25000 Sheet 470.
Admiralty Charts: 1:75000 No.3282 1:30000 Nos.3292 and 3298 1:12500 No.3293 Basta Voe

Area: 21211ha (52412 acres)
Height: 205m (672 ft)
Owner: Multiple ownership, including the RSPB, A Cunningham-Brown, J Ballantyne, Wilson, and L H Johnson.

Population: 1841–2611 (550 houses). 1881–2529. 1891–2511 (525 houses). 1931–1883. 1961–1155. 1981–1191. 1991–1075. 2001–957. 2011–966.

Geology: Pre-Cambrian rocks under a thick blanket of peat. Most of the island is of garnetiferous mica plagioclase gneiss but the north-eastern coast and the south-east corner have an underlay of striped granulitic oligoclase gneiss and some bands of calc-silicate rock. The central highland is thick lenticular quartzite and the western cliffs are muscovite biotite gneiss with some silvery mica schists.

History: Early prehistoric remains are scattered around the coasts of Yell with hardly any to be found inland and there are a number of Iron Age structures such as the important broch at Ness of Burraness, overlooking Fetlar. About twelve broch sites have been identified and at least fifteen sites of ancient chapels.

Yell moorland was possibly of less interest

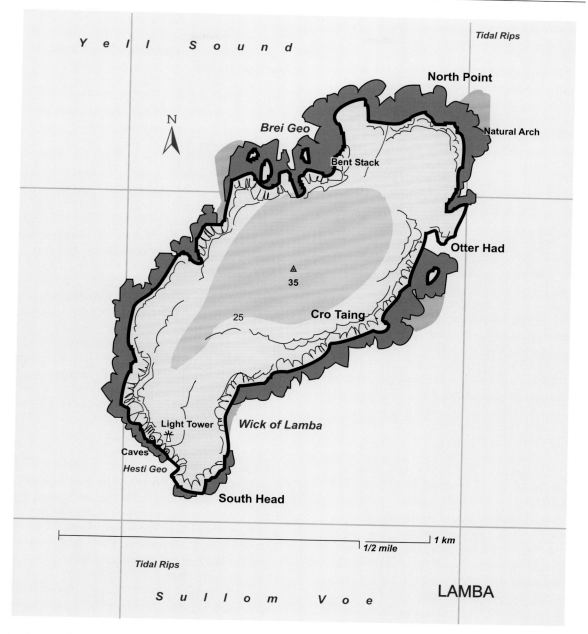

to the past landowners because it was never formed into really large estates and has always had multiple ownership. The largest landowners in the 19th century were Mouat in the north, Leask in the west and MacQueen in the Burravoe district.

Wildlife: The moors and heaths of Yell provide a habitat for most of Shetland's eight species of orchid with the heath spotted orchid by far the most common.

The coasts are otter territory and the lochans are well-stocked with brown trout. The west coast in particular is favoured by grey seals but a bearded seal, a stray from the Arctic drift ice, was recorded here in 1977.

At the Lumbister RSPB Reserve in the north-west near Whale Firth there are typical breeding species for the Shetlands – red-throated diver, red-breasted merganser, golden plover, eider, merlin, curlew, snipe, lapwing, arctic and great skuas, dunlin, great black-backed gull, raven, twite and wheatear. Oystercatcher, black guillemot, puffin and ringed plover breed on the coast.

Generally speaking, the waters of Yell Sound offer an important wintering area for divers, eider, and long-tailed duck.

The ferry to **YELL** docks at Ulsta. As you cross the Sound, what appears to be a reef at the southern extremity of the island turns out to be the lonely remains of a broch built precariously on a skerry. Yell itself has a gloomy appearance – low-lying hills blanketed in peat bog – yet for many this is the real Shetland. The peat of course has its merits as the Rev. Cruttwell pointed out in the 18th century: 'The inhabitants have plenty of fuel, catch immense quantities of small fish and live comfortably.' On the other hand, Buchanan in the 16th century claimed that Yell was 'so uncouth a place that no creature can live therein, except such as are born there'. By the 1960s Yell's danger of serious depopulation became a matter of grave concern. Some said that part of the problem was the islanders' 'social egalitarianism,' which denied anyone the opportunity to be a leader or entrepreneur. This is unlikely but airing the matter seems to have helped because the numbers now appear to have more or less stabilised. Yell is quite a large island – half the size of Arran – but it has such a bleak landscape that human settlement, and attitudes, tend to cling to the edges.

Two roads run north from **Ulsta**, the main road on the west coast and a secondary, more scenic and interesting, road following the south and east coasts.

This secondary road skirts Hamna Voe (ON – harbour voe) and runs into **Burravoe** (ON – broch voe) in the extreme south-east. The whitewashed crow-stepped **Old Haa of Burravoe**, built in 1637, is the oldest surviving building on the island [HU522796]. It is used as a local museum and craft centre. Burravoe has a tiny well-protected harbour which discourages visitors by its welter of skerries surrounding the islet, **Green Holm**, at its entrance.

The east coast has pleasant hamlets and crofts and touches of cultivation to relieve the dark peat mosses on the slopes of Yell's highest hill, **Ward of Otterswick** (205m). Beyond the cliffs the expanse of steel-blue sea is broken by Fetlar (No.11.25) and when the weather is favourable Out Skerries (No.11.18) can be seen on the horizon.

In 1924 a German 3-masted barque, *Bohus*, ran aground and broke up here with the loss

of two of its crew. The figurehead lay for many years on the shore until it eventually rotted and disintegrated but not before a fibreglass reproduction had been made and set up on the shore as a monument. This is known as the 'White Wife of Queyon' [HU529853].

The only settlement of note on the main road up the west coast is **West Sandwick**, a pretty spot with houses clustered round the sandy beaches of Southladie Voe [HU440887]. The remains of a broch on a drying islet on the coast look across to the **Holm of West Sandwick** which has a rock arch through which the sea breaks. A challenging walk along these west coast cliffs past the prehistoric settlement at **Birrier** [HU438913] beside **Sweinna Stack**, and **Ern Stack** (which was the last recorded nesting-place of the sea-eagle in Shetland) leads to Stuis of Graveland at the entrance to **Whale Firth**.

Yell is almost bisected where the west- and east-coast roads rejoin at **Mid Yell**, the island's main settlement. It is here that the narrow twisted Whale Firth nearly meets the sheltered anchorage of **Mid Yell Voe**, a suitable venue for many sailing regattas. The lonely haunted **Windhouse** at the head of Whale Firth is on a site which has been occupied since Neolithic times.

The ruined herring curing station halfway up Whale Firth at **Grimister** closed shortly after the Second World War – and apart from a few crofts the firth is deserted. The Germans claimed that their U-boats often sheltered here during the First World War and one could hardly imagine a better hiding-place! The whole west-coast area beyond Whale Firth to North Neaps at the remote northern extremity of Yell is an untouched wilderness of peaty heath and mire with many small lochans rippled by the continual wind. Yet this desolate expanse containing the **Lumbister RSPB Reserve** has some of the most interesting scenery and hill-walks on the island. The coast is wildly indented with green hollows, great rock arches, caves and tumbled cliffs.

The main road continues beyond Mid Yell – with its islet of **Kay Holm** hidden by a headland – round the length of Basta Voe, and ends at **Gutcher**, which is the ferry terminal for Fetlar (No.11.25) and Unst (No.11.30). But before jumping aboard at this point remember that the best of Yell lies north where a secondary road continues up the shores of attractive Bluemull Sound through the rural village of **Cullivoe**.

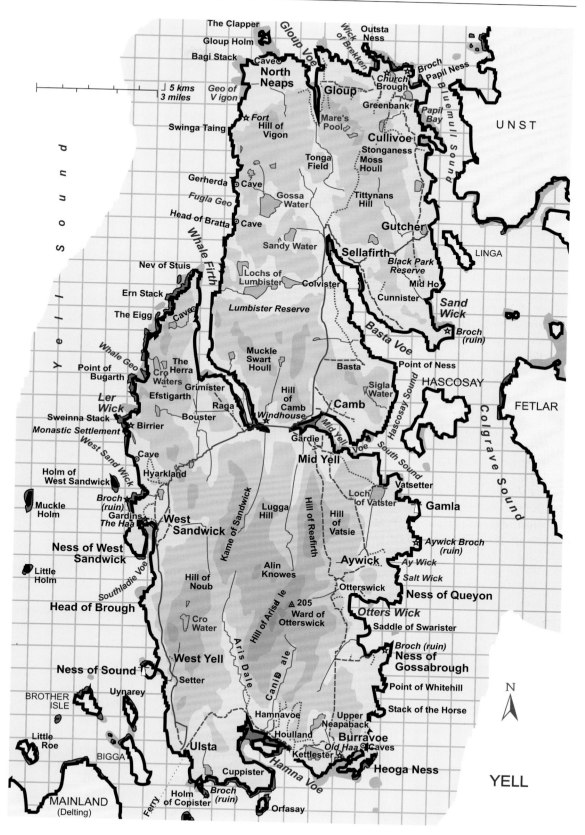

The Clapper
Gloup Holm
Bagi Stack
Geo of Vigon
North Neaps
Gloup Voe
Wick of Brekken
Outsta Ness
Broch
Papil Ness
Cave
Church Brough
UNST
5 kms
3 miles
Fort
Hill of Vigon
Mare's Pool
Greenbank
Gloup
Papil Bay
Bluemull Sound
Swinga Taing
Cullivoe
Stonganess
Moss Houll
Tonga Field
Gerherda
Cave
Tittynans Hill
Fugla Geo
Gossa Water
Head of Bratta
Cave
Gutcher
Sandy Water
Sellafirth
Black Park Reserve
LINGA
Nev of Stuis
Lochs of Lumbister
Colvister
Mid Ho
Ern Stack
Cunnister
Sand Wick
The Eigg
Cave
Lumbister Reserve
Broch (ruin)
Whale Geo
Muckle Swart Houll
Basta
Point of Ness
HASCOSAY
Point of Bugarth
Cro Waters
The Herra
Basta Voe
Efstigarth
Grimister
Sigla Water
FETLAR
Ler Wick
Raga
Hill of Camb
Camb
Windhouse
Colgrave Sound
Sweinna Stack
Bouster
Monastic Settlement
Birrier
Mid Yell Voe
Gardie I
Hascosay Sound
Cave
South Sound
Hyarkland
Mid Yell
Vatsetter
Holm of West Sandwick
West Sand Wick
Loch of Vatster
Gamla
Muckle Holm
Broch (ruin)
Lugga Hill
Hill of Reafirth
Hill of Vatsie
Aywick Broch (ruin)
Gardins
The Haa
West Sandwick
Ness of West Sandwick
Kame of Sandwick
Alin Knowes
Aywick
Ay Wick
Salt Wick
Little Holm
Southladie Voe
Ness of Queyon
Otterswick
Hill of Noub
Otters Wick
Head of Brough
Cro Water
Hill of Arisd le
205
Ward of Otterswick
Saddle of Swarister
Ness of Sound
Aris Dale
West Yell
Setter
Cani le
Broch (ruin)
Ness of Gossabrough
BROTHER ISLE
Uynarey
Point of Whitehill
N
Little Roe
Hamnavoe
Stack of the Horse
Upper Neapaback
Ulsta
Houlland
Burravoe
BIGGA
Old Haa
Caves
Cuppister
Kettlester
Heoga Ness
MAINLAND (Delting)
Ferry
Holm of Copister
Broch (ruin)
Hamna Voe
YELL
Orfasay

As the road passes the priests' loch on Papil Ness, and turns along the north coast at **Brough**, the roofless **Kirk of Ness** [HP532049] can be seen by the west shore of Kirk Loch. This medieval parish church was dedicated to St Olaf but has been deserted since 1750. There is no historical proof but legend claims that it is from here that Leif the Lucky set off on his expedition to America. The rough wilderness is, incomprehensibly, covered with the remains of ancient settlements which have never yet been adequately investigated. To the west on the cliff top is the broch which has given the area its name [HP540051]. There is a delightful walk along these cliffs and the views are stunning but it is important to keep clear of the edge which is brittle and crumbles easily.

Skeletons have been found in the sands of the **Wick of Brekken** which may once have had a settlement like Jarlshof.

The road ends at **Gloup Voe** (ON – ravine creek), although there is a track continuing round the head of the voe to West-a-Firth on the far side. The **Fishermen's Memorial** [HP507044] here on the hillside above the voe commemorates yet another devastating island disaster. The entire male community in this remote northern haven (ten sixerns with fifty-eight fishermen on board) was lost in a savage storm on 20 July 1881.

A track leading north from Gloup connects with the Coastguard Lookout Station which is set on the cliffs between two wicks. To the west is **Gloup Holm** with jagged **Eagle Stack**, **Whilkie Stack** and **The Clapper**. To the east, Muckle Flugga lighthouse is on the horizon – convincing proof that this is the end of the road.

*   *   *

Access: Several daily ro-ro ferries from Toft, Mainland to Ulsta, Yell, (20 mins), 01957-722259. Also daily frequent ro-ro from Belmont, Unst to Gutcher, Yell (10 mins), and from Hamars Ness, Fetlar to Gutcher, Yell (20 mins), 01957-722259. Tourist Information, 01595-693434.

Anchorages:

1. Hamna Voe on S coast. Exposed SE–S. Anchor W of Ness of Galtagarth, good holding. Head is shoal. Approach on central course and beware Burga Skerry 3c S of Green Holm. Ulsta has a shallow-draft marina.
2. Burra Voe at SE extremity of Yell. Approach from S and enter with great care following directions. There are many dangers in the approach. Berth at pier or anchor near head of bay in 4-6m. Bottom foul.
3. Wick of Gossabrough on E coast. Small stone pier on S side. Easy access but beware Wick Skerry at entrance. Exposed N to E. Anchor off beach in SW bay. Holding unreliable.
4. Otters Wick has many rocks and careful use of chart required. Exposed E to SE.
5. Mid Yell Voe, mid E coast, good secure anchorage. Head dries for ½M. Approach on mid-channel course. Berth at pier in depth of 3m or anchor north of pier in 2½–10m, mud and sand. Gusty in N winds. Small marina for shallow draft boats.
6. Basta Voe. Good shelter. Both sides clear to ¾c from shore. Shingle bank off point on NE shore. Anchor beyond the shingle bank in 5–15m, clay, good holding mostly.
7. Wick of Gutcher, small bay in Bluemull Sound with ferry terminal. Berthing reserved exclusively for ferry.
8. Culli Voe, in Bluemull Sound, is shallow but concrete pier at entrance to voe projects 42m from shore and has 3.5m depth at head. Fair anchorage as far into the voe as depth permits or temp. anchorage south of pier in 5m, holding good, sand and shells. Small marina for shallow draught boats at head of voe.
9. Wick of Breckin (Breakon) on N coast. Temp. anchorage in S or E winds, holding poor (Lunda Wick on Unst is better).
10. Gloup Voe, not recommended. Mostly too deep, heavy sea with N–NW winds, and voe dries out halfway to head.
11. Whale Firth on W coast. Quiet, secluded anchorage. Beware sunken rock 2c NE of Nev of Stuis at entrance and rocks off S shore at Grimister. Otherwise clear of dangers.
12. Southladie Voe, close E of Ness of West Sandwick. Good anchorage except in S'lies. Limited anchorage in the pool at head, 1½m, soft mud. Keep to W side at narrow passage off Urabug ayre where there is only 1m depth.

11.25 Fetlar

(ON – fat/prosperous land). Intriguing suggested alternative derivation (ON fetill – a strap or tie) with (ON -ar) as the plural form. See below.

O S Maps: 1:50000 Sheet 1 or 2 1:25000 Sheet 470
Admiralty Charts: 1:75000 No.3282 1:30000 No.3292 west part
Area: 4078ha (10077 acres)
Height: 158m (518 ft)
Owner: Most of the island was inherited by Mrs Borland, Edinburgh, on the death of her aunt, Lady Nicolson (c.1980). Fetlar has been owned by Nicolsons since the early 1800s but the recent owners were not direct descendants of Sir Arthur Nicolson.

Population: 1841–761 (137 houses). 1881–431. 1891–363 (70 houses). 1931–217. 1961–127. 1981–101. 2001–86. 2008–48. 2011–61.

Geology: There is gneiss in the west including Lambhoga. East of a fault line there are magnificent serpentine outcrops which are only equalled by those of Cornwall and which account for the interesting cliff formations. There is also metagabbro and phyllite. The sand in the Wick of Houbie is magnetic and at Moo Wick at the tip of Lambhoga there is a residual deposit of kaolin. At Hesta Ness in the north-east the serpentine has been altered to antigorite and steatite. Here too there are bands of pure talc, which was mined at one time.

History: The story of Fetlar goes back a long way. Yet Fetlar, in spite of its great contrast to its neighbour, the rather desolate Yell, has never achieved a distinctive place in Shetland history, probably due to its lack of a safe harbour. The first Norse settlers are thought to have landed here, and swashbuckling King Harald the Fair-haired landed on Fetlar during his pursuit of 'Vikings' in the 9th century but he swiftly moved on to a secure anchorage at Unst.

The first large-scale clearances in Shetland started here on the Lambhoga peninsula in 1822 when the landowner, Sir Arthur Nicolson, evicted the crofters to make room for sheep. By 1858 he had emptied the whole of the north and west part of the island and cleared nearly 30 townships. He built himself the three-storey tower folly at Grutin using stone from the crofters' houses.

A serious drop in population during the 1980s and again in 2008 led to the local community council advertising for settlers. The two biggest drawbacks are that older children have to travel to Yell for schooling and there was no adequate harbour. However a new pier and breakwater and the reopened primary school have worked wonders and virtually doubled the population.

Like so many Shetland islands, Fetlar has a history of shipwrecks. An incomplete list illustrates this:

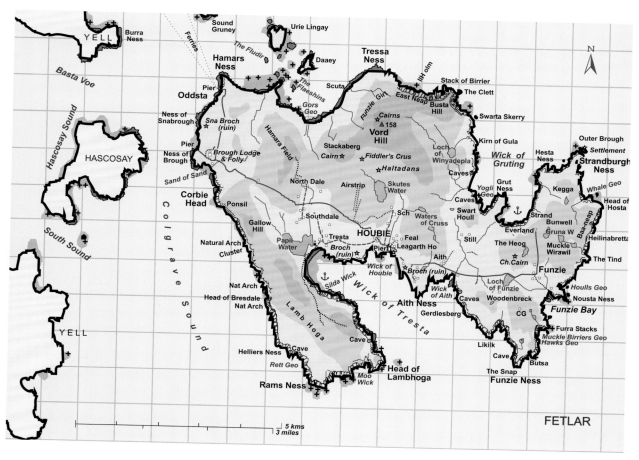

1601– a Danish vessel. 1699– a packet, wrecked at Hamars Ness. 1710– a vessel from Emden. 1737– *Wendela*, Danish. 1765– a vessel at Whale Geo. 1773– *James*. 1794– a vessel at Aith. 1799– *Good Intent*. 1811– *Stadt Memel*. 1847– *Clarenden*. 1848– *Neptune*. 1870– *Johan Caesar*, Hamburg. 1882– *Lizzie*. 1897– *Flosta*. 1897– *Anna*. 1900– *Hedevig*, Norway. 1962– *Maia*, Russian trawler.

Wildlife: More than 200 different species of wildflower have been recorded on this verdant isle. Rarer species include frog orchid and northern gentian, but the rarest are members of the sedge family. In the sheltered area at Leagarth House there used to be a number of quite exotic trees.

There are many grey and common seals around the coasts and otters can often be seen, particularly between Brough Lodge and Urie.

The lochs, some with restricted access, offer fly fishing for brown trout.

Fetlar is an outstanding bird sanctuary, especially for breeding waders of which there is the highest density in Britain. All visitors should first contact the RSPB warden. Lapwing, oystercatcher and ringed plover breed on the crofts, and golden plover, dunlin, curlew, and many whimbrel nest on the moorland. Snipe, redshank and red-necked phalarope breed on the lochans and wetlands. There are also breeding seabirds. Manx shearwater, shag, kittiwake, guillemot and puffin are to be seen on the cliffs, particularly on the Lamb Hoga peninsula which also has Britain's largest colony of storm petrels. There are common tern and about 4500 pairs of arctic tern.

Fetlar is probably most renowned for the snowy owls, which were found nesting at Stakkaberg in 1967. This is the extreme southern limit of their breeding range. Unfortunately the old male, having driven off all competitors, died of old age in 1975 leaving several morose females without a mate. Consequently, there are now no resident snowy owls although they still occasionally make an appearance.

Other breeders on the island are red-throated diver, eider, raven and twite and recorded migrants include two-barred crossbill and greenish warbler. In the autumn there are many fieldfare and redwing.

*   *   *

Let your imagination take over for a moment and think of **FETLAR** in the dark ages of prehistory – a fair and fertile land populated by Mesolithic farmers.

Now let us suppose that two tribes live on the island and because the grass is always greener next door they engage in intermittent feuding and fighting. The wars go on for years until at last someone decides to call a truce. There is a meeting at which, after argument, they agree to a division of land, and so that there can be no further dispute whatsoever, they join forces and build a big wall right across the centre of the island. With their territories now clearly defined, they live happily ever after.

This idyllic state continues until the 7th or 8th century AD and then the unexpected happens. Land-hungry Norwegian settlers, following in the wake of the first marauding Vikings, come to Shetland. Their first landfall is Fetlar, which is about as near to Norway as you can get and here they see a land of milk and honey. History does not record the viewpoint of the original islanders but we can be sure the land was acquired while they were slaughtered, enslaved or merely absorbed.

The Norsemen would be surprised to find Fetlar divided by a huge wall and, as they lacked a scientific definition for an island, they thought of it as two islands. This is much the same as their view that a mountain barrier divided Lewis and Harris into two separate islands or a narrow isthmus turned the Mull of Kintyre into an island. At this point an element of fact creeps into our reconstruction because early Norse records always spoke of Fetlar as Est Isle and Wast Isle. Fetlar, as a name for the whole island, is first found in a document dated 1558 although an earlier document in 1490 talks of Foetilør. As 'fetill' means a strap or a tie in Norse one might guess that they thought of Fetlar as two islands tied together.

Meanwhile, the ancient wall itself took on an aura of mystery. 'Who had built it?' the settlers wondered. And as time passed their descendants attributed its creation to the Finns, magical figures in Norse folklore, who might have been Laplanders, or giants, or trolls, or all three rolled together. It was said that the Finns built the wall in a single night in exchange for a farmer's best cow.

Today, the one-metre wide wall, or what little is left of it, is still called **Funzie Girt** [fin-ee girt] which means the Finns' dyke and it cuts round the west side of Vord Hill but disappears near Whilsa Pund. It then reappears south of Skutes Water, crosses the Vallahamars and ends by the Stack of Billaclett where there is a cave in which the trolls lived. It divides Fetlar into two almost equal sections.

There are other mysteries too in this mid-island region. Between Vord Hill and Skutes Water, are the **Fiddler's Crus** [HU618927]. These are three mysterious stone circles set in a triangular pattern and almost touching each other. Each circle is about 13½ metres in diameter. Nearby, about 200 metres north of Skutes Water, there is another strange monument called **Haltadans** (or Hjaltadans) which means 'limping dance' [HU622924]. This is an outer circle of thirty-eight serpentine stones, about 11½ metres in diameter, with an internal, low and concentric earth bank. Two stones lie at the centre. Both these structures seem to be related but archaeologists have no satisfactory explanation of their purpose. The local explanation is that a fiddler and his wife were dancing in the moonlight one night with trolls and all were enjoying it so much that they failed to notice the dawn. Everyone was instantly petrified by the light of the rising sun. The stone circles are the dancing trolls and the two prostrate central stones are the fiddler and his wife. This is a typical Norse legend with trolls as creatures of the night coupled with a Christian flavour of retribution for ungodly pleasures.

Fetlar is Shetland's most fertile island and it is still known as the Garden of Shetland although it is not quite as well tended as it once was. It is quite hilly with **Vord Hill** (ON – watch hill) at 158m being the highest point. Two Neolithic heel-shaped cairns on the hill are possibly 5000 years old. The shelter in the southern cairn was built during the First World War [HU622936].

It is a pity that such an attractive island has no secure anchorages, although it is usually possible to find shelter provided there is no sudden change of wind. The survival of any island's population today depends on reliable communications and on-site education. In Fetlar's case, the former criterion was satisfied in 1974, when a regular vehicle ferry service to a pier at Oddsta was inaugurated, but the island still lacks the facilities for secondary education which Out Skerries, (No.11.18) with a similar population, had.

Fetlar's single road runs west to east across the island. To the south there is the great **Lamb Hoga** (ON – sheep pasture) peninsula with its steep gneiss cliffs. Shetland ponies sometimes graze here on the open moorland. The lairds of **Brough Lodge** [HU580926], the Nicolsons, crossed the native stock with Norwegian to achieve an improved breed. Beneath the stretch of **Papil Water** (ON – priests' water) is the magnificent sweep of beach at **Tresta**, well sheltered from the prevailing wind.

The adjoining cove at **Houbie** (ON *hopr* – light), with the airstrip to the north of it, also has a pleasant, but much smaller, beach. Prominent **Leagarth House**, by the small pier, was built by Sir William Watson Cheyne in 1900. He was a Houbie lad who became a famous surgeon after assisting Joseph Lister in his development of antiseptic surgery in 1867. Sir William died in 1932. The **Fetlar Interpretive Centre**, almost opposite Leagarth House, should not be missed. It is a treasure trove of island history.

The road continues through pleasant green valleys to the east coast settlement, and old haaf station, of **Funzie** [fin-ee], a picturesque collection of cottages, many of which are unfortunately deserted. As the name suggests, it was here that the very first Vikings are said to have settled. The land in summer is swathed in wildflowers and on almost every rocky headland there is a lichen-covered ruined broch. The cliffs here are not as high as elsewhere but their rugged serpentine rock-faces are full of colour. **Funzie Bay** was the site of a haaf fishing station in the 19th century.

Under Baa-naap is a rocky point called **Heilinabretta** where the Danish ship, *Wendela*, ran aground and sank in 1737 [HU675911]. She was carrying a large quantity of unspecified silver currency, most of which was immediately salvaged by the islanders. A diving team in the 1970s investigated the wreck and collected a number of silver coins in the area. Unauthorised diving is forbidden.

Broken cairns top Vord Hill and, below, the landscape is dotted with ancient mounds. The view from here is magnificent. The whole island can be seen stretching from The Snap, a headland beneath the Coastguard Lookout-point in the south-east, to **Hamars Ness** near the ferry pier in the north-west; and from **Rams Ness** in the south to **Strandburgh Ness** in the east. The latter has a tiny islet, **Outer Brough**, beside it with the remains of a broch and ancient settlement. Great natural arches in the Wick of Gruting (ON – stony area) flank **Kirn of Gula**, a blowhole, where fishermen took refuge in the 18th century when the press-gangs called [HU645931]. Beneath the cliffs of East Neap are rock-stacks, including the remarkable shape of **The Clett** [HU641944] off Busta Pund with, believe it or not, a hermitage perched on it! The sea between Fetlar and Bluemull Sound is sprinkled with low-lying islets including **Daaey**, **Urie Lingey** and **Sund Gruney** (ON – south green island).

* * *

Access: Ro-ro ferry several times daily from Gutcher, Yell, or Belmont, Unst. 01957-722259. Tourist Information, 01595-693434.

Anchorages:
1. Vehicle-ferry terminal at Oddsta, Hamars Ness, has a small pier and new breakwater.
2. Brough Lodge, W coast. Convenient temp. anchorage except in W'lies. Anchor off the pier and below the tower, N of Ness of Brough, in 4–6m. Good holding.
3. Wick of Tresta. Good shelter if wind W or N, but swell comes in with W gales. Open to SE. Head shoals. Anchor in 6–8m sand, good holding. Approach on central course and beware rock 2c E of Head of Lambhoga. Magnetic anomalies.
4. Wick of Gruting. Good shelter in S winds. Open N. Keep 1c off all shores. Anchor centre-bay E or W of Ness of Gruting in 10m sand, good holding.

11.26 Hascosay

[ha-skoa-say] (ON huskot-øy – cottage or cottages island) or (ON haf-skogen-øy – sea-wood or driftwood island).

OS Maps: 1:50000 Sheet 1 or 2 1:25000 Sheet 470
Admiralty Charts: 1:75000 No.3282 1:30000 No.3292

Area: 275ha (680 acres)
Height: 30m (98 ft)

Owner: Part of the Nicolson of Fetlar estate inherited in the 1980s by Mrs O Borland of Edinburgh, a niece of Lady Nicolson.

Population: 1841–42 (6 houses). 1851–13. 1861–0 Uninhabited since.
Geology: The bedrock is a coarse micaceous gneiss.

History: A branch of the Edmondston family once owned the island and a James Edmondston is named as laird of Hascosay in 1645.

Hascosay was home to a small but thriving community until it was bought by Sir Arthur Nicolson, the laird who cleared much of Fetlar for sheep in the mid-19th century. His house on Fetlar, Brough Lodge, overlooked Hascosay and this may have been why the islanders decided to leave before they were forcibly evicted. On the other hand, the trouble may merely have been lack of a good supply of fresh water and nothing to do with Sir Arthur.

Wildlife: Hascosay is an RSPB reserve and a Special Area of Conservation on account of its blanket bog. So, although it is reputed to have magic soil which keeps mice away, removing its soil would not be appreciated.

The BBC cameraman, Hugh Miles, visited Hascosay with the renowned Shetland ornithologist, Bobby Tulloch, in 1979, to make a BBC *Wildtrack* programme on otters. Hascosay is noted for its otters but on this occasion they failed to appear and the film was eventually shot on Fetlar and (Basta Voe) Yell. Nevertheless, Tulloch's books include many of his beautiful photographs of the Hascosay otters.

* * *

HASCOSAY has an undulating surface, the highest point being 30m above the south-west bluff. The island is criss-crossed with burns or rivulets fed by several small pools, none of which is large enough to merit the title of lochan and none of which provides a supply of good drinking water. Even when the pools are filled with rainwater they quickly turn brackish with the salt-spray and there is only one rather inadequate well. **Housa Wick** (ON – house bay) is an attractive rocky inlet which cuts deep into the island in the south-west. On a shallow isthmus behind it are the walls of the Edmondston's old hall which they vacated before 1800. There is also the site of a chapel but it is not known to whom it was dedicated.

A smaller bay on the north side is used for fish-farming. It is called **Djuba Wick** (ON – deep bay) but with a depth of less than 10m according to the Admiralty Chart the derivation of the name is open to conjecture.

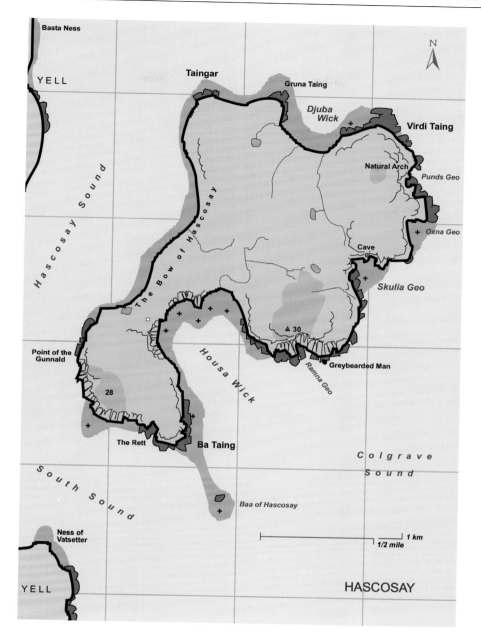

The broken cliffs in the south fall away to **The Rett** (ON – the straight) and **Ba Taing** (ON – point of the underwater rock). On the opposite headland of Housa Wick there are more cliffs and an off-shore stack called **Greybearded Man**. Continuing up the east coast there is **Skulia Geo** (ON – hiding-hole inlet) with a submerged rock concealed in the middle of the geo and a fair-sized cave to explore on its shore. Nearby the rocks form a natural arch. There are a number of fine caverns on Hascosay.

* * *

Access: No regular access. Try Muckle Flugga Charters, Burrafirth, Unst, 01806-522447, or Northmavine Charters (Colla Firth pier), Mainland, 07765-907818. Tourist Information, 01595-693434.

Anchorages: No recommended anchorages.
1. The Bow of Hascosay, Hascosay Sound. Temp. anchorage at N end of Bow in 5–10m. Avoid fish farm.
2. Housa Wick. Temp. anchorage in centre of Wick, 8–10m. The head is foul. Beware Baa of Hascosay 3½c SSE of Ba Taing.

11.27 Uyea

[yoo-ay] Possibly (ON ve-øy – home island or island of the sacred place).

OS Maps: 1:50000 Sheet 1 1:25000 Sheet 470
Admiralty Charts: 1:75000 No.3282 1:30000 No.3292

Area: 205ha (507 acres)
Height: 50m (164 ft)

Owner: Sold by Jim Smith, a local farmer, in 1990 for about £100,000 including the livestock (320 sheep) and the islet of Wedder Holm. It was bought by Peter Hunter of Uyeasound on Unst, a crofter and salmon-farmer.

Population: 1841–23 (3 houses). 1881–5. 1891–8 (1 house). 1931–12. 1961–0. 1981–0. 1991–0. 2001–0. Uninhabited.

Geology: Hornblende-schists in the west, mica-schists in the east.

History: Uyea Hall was the five-bedroom home of Basil Neven-Spence who was the Member of Parliament for Orkney and Shetland from 1935 until he was defeated in 1950 by Jo Grimond. Sir Basil is buried in the chapel cemetery.

Wildlife: Although mice are plentiful on Unst, there are none on Uyea we are told. Maybe some of Hascosay's magic soil is responsible (see No.11.26).

Otters can be seen by the shores, and many seals.

* * *

UYEA is only two-thirds the size of Vaila (No.11-10) but is similar in respect that it is dominated by a single large house originally built by the owner. On Uyea **The Hall** stands amid a group of structures on the central ridge near the middle of the island and is therefore fairly conspicuous. The highest point on the ridge is 50m.

Farm roads or tracks lead to the main house from a bay on the north coast with a rough jetty on the foreshore.

There are a number of antiquities which mirror those just across the sound on Unst. Part of the old chapel beside **Brei Wick** (ON – broad bay) dates from the 12th century [HU608985], while **Tur Ness**, just north of Brei Wick, is the site of an ancient settlement. At the northern end of the island there is a chambered cairn representing even earlier times.

Quite close to **Hawks Ness**, the southern extremity, is an islet called **Wedder Holm** (ON – ram islet) and further away to the east is the small island of **Haaf Gruney** (ON *hafgroenøy* – green island in the fishing grounds). This island is now classified as a national nature reserve on account of its colony of breeding storm petrel. The remains of a disused chromate mine are on it and its green pastures have for long been used for grazing.

In the early 18th century two young girls from Uyea rowed themselves over to Haaf Gruney to milk the cows. On their return a storm blew up and increased in fury. For several days they could do nothing but bail and hang on until they were at last cast ashore on the island of Karmøy off the south-west coast of Norway. The superstitious islanders at first took fright but when one of the girls made the sign of the Cross they helped them. In any case there was a severe shortage of women on Karmøy at the time so, needless to say, before long the girls were happily married and their descendants still live there today.

Access: No regular access. Try Muckle Flugga Charters, 01806-522447, a boat-owner in Uyeasound, or Tourist Information, 01595-693434.

Anchorages:
1. Skuda Sound, bay W of Scarfa Taing. Anchor off the jetty in 5–6m, mud and sand. Reasonable shelter and holding. Beware Cliva Skerries, W of the bay.
2. Bay on S side between Winna Ness and Hawks Ness. Temp. anchorage in suitable conditions. Approach and anchor centrally towards the head in 5–6m.
3. Brei Wick. Avoid. Shallow and foul.

11.28 Linga

(ON lyng-øy – heather island).

OS Maps: 1:50000 Sheet 1 1:25000 Sheet 470
Admiralty Charts: 1:75000 No.3282 1:30000 No.3292

Area: 45ha (111 acres)
Height: 26m (85 ft)

Owner: The island was bought in the 1980s by a Mr Renwick who started building a pseudo-Norman castle at North Booth, but was refused planning permission. He abandoned the project (and many unused concrete blocks) and sold out to Charles Henderson of Yell. He, in turn, sold Linga to an American lady but kept the crofting rights and uses the land for grazing sheep.

Population: No Census records and uninhabited.

Geology: A bedrock of coarse mica-schist and gneiss.

Wildlife: In spite of its name, very little heather is to be found on Linga. Many seabirds breed here – particularly guillemot – and there are resident otters. Seals breed in the season.

* * *

LINGA is a long narrow island lying roughly parallel to the coast of Yell, and separated from it by Linga Sound. This is a fairly secluded corner of Shetland – if anywhere in this part of the world can truly be called secluded. Yell holds out two tentative arms, Head of Gutcher and Burra Ness (with a ruined broch on it) to shelter the waters of Linga Sound. There is often little in the way of

activity here except for the ferry between Yell and Fetlar, but further north is Bluemull Sound, busy with underwater tidal turbine trials.

The long low ridge of Linga reaches a maximum height of 26m near its southern end. It has few known antiquities but there is the site of an old chapel [HU559986], which would indicate that it might have had a number of inhabitants at

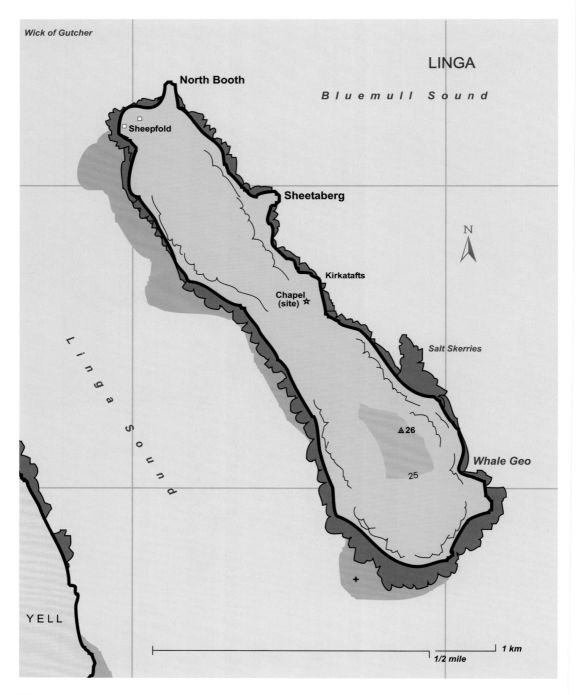

some time. The source of an adequate supply of fresh water is a puzzle although it may have been brought over by boat from neighbouring Yell. The island is now used for grazing sheep.

There is said to be a ring of green turf on the island (although its position is elusive!) called the **Bear's Bait**. An ancient Norse tale says that Jan Tait of Fetlar killed one of the King of Norway's men after an argument and the King had him brought to Norway to answer for the crime. After the King had spoken to Jan he was so impressed by his courage and candour that he promised to grant him his freedom provided he captured a giant bear that was causing trouble in the district. Jan put out a barrel of drugged butter for the bear to eat and had no trouble capturing it and taking it to the King. The King kept his promise and granted him his freedom but he was surprised that Jan had not killed the bear. He ordered him to do so and then to leave Norway forthwith. Jan, however, was proud of his capture and wanted to show it to his friends so he brought the bear back to Shetland and kept it tethered on Linga. The ring marks the spot where the poor old bear walked round and round its stake for the rest of its days.

Access: No regular access. Try Muckle Flugga Charters, 01806-522447, or Tourist Information, 01595-693434.

Anchorages: No recommended anchorages.
1. Linga Sound. Temp. anchorage in suitable conditions just N of the mid-point of the W coast in 3–6m. Approach with caution and use tripping line.

11.29 Balta

Perhaps (ON Balti-øy – Balti's island) from the man's name.

OS Maps: 1:50000 Sheet 1 1:25000 Sheet 470
Admiralty Charts: 1:75000 No.3282 1:12500 No.3293

Area: 80ha (198 acres)
Height: 44m (144 ft)

Population: No Census records and uninhabited now.

Geology: Metagabbros interspersed with some hornblende-schist. Covered with the most extensive area of dune grassland in Shetland. Unfortunately this is being steadily eroded by

rabbits, intensive sheep grazing and strong winds.

History: The remains of a broch at South Sail at the top of the northern cliffs may once have had a 'brother' broch across the Sound on Swinna Ness – they often came in pairs – but there is no record of it. It does suggest, however, that Balta was inhabited at that time.

Wildlife: The island provides a playground for thousands of rabbits. The eastern cliffs provide residential sites for nesting seabirds. A Glaucus gull nested for several years on nearby Huney during the 1980s.

*   *   *

BALTA is a long narrow island like Linga (No.11.28) but with a more complex shape. It has three hills spaced along its length, the central one at **Muckle Head** (S. – big head) being the highest (44m). The southern hill is 38m high.

The east coast, facing the stormy North Sea, consists of steep cliffs broken by fissures and rocky coves and with tumbled half-submerged rock-falls close to the foot where they have not slipped away down the steep submarine slopes. There is a shallower patch, **Salta Skerry**, at the southern extremity of the island. Heavy seas break over this area when the wind is in the south-east. The whole of this east coast is slowly being eroded by the sea which pounds against it relentlessly.

The rock strata tips the whole island up towards the east while the west side is low-lying with a short stretch of sandy beach extending up the slope at South Links. Balta has the best dune grassland in Shetland but it is steadily deteriorating due to wind erosion, rabbit damage and, possibly, overgrazing. The shallow western bay protects Shetland's most northerly fish farm.

Apart from the broch ruin at **South Sail** [HP660089], another site of archaeological interest is that of an ancient chapel dedicated to the popular Norse saint, St Sunniva.

Balta Sound was a busy and popular harbour in the early 1900s and the island must have seen a lot of activity as hundreds of brown-sailed luggers of the Scottish fishing fleet bustled in and out to off-load their herring catches.

In 1917 a Royal Navy submarine, E49, struck a mine and sank in Balta Sound. The wreck, which lies at a depth of thirty-five metres, is classed as a 'war grave' and permission to dive must be obtained from the Ministry of Defence.

On the west side of South Channel is the small uninhabited island of **Huney** which has a flat grassy top about 19m high. There is a narrow channel called the Yei between Huney and the coast of Unst which is full of rocks and sand-banks but which the local fishermen negotiate with ease (at the right state of the tide).

*   *   *

Access: Try Muckle Flugga Charters, 01806-522447, a boat owner at Baltasound or Tourist Information, 01595-693434.

Anchorages: Approach mid-channel by S Channel when entering Balta Sound. The N Channel is tricky and requires great care.

1. Mid E-side of Balta. Good anchorage and well sheltered except for S–SW in which case move to the Unst side. Best spot with Buness House, Unst, in line with Skeo Taing but may be obstructed by fish cages. Anchor as near Balta as depth permits, sand.

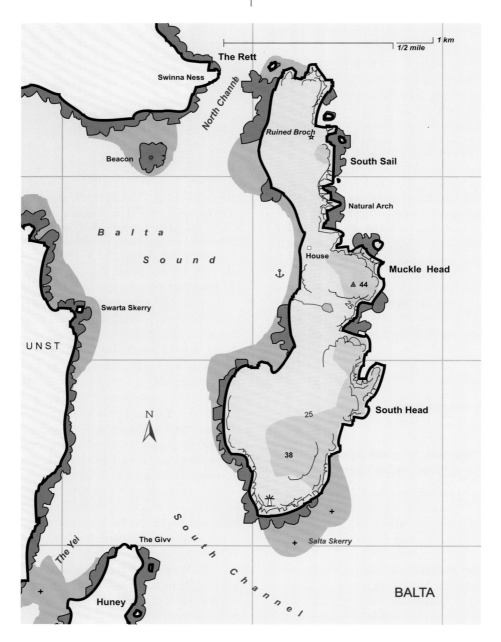

11.30 Unst

[unst – not oonst] Derivation obscure and may be of Pictish origin, but possibly (ON ørn-vist – home of the eagle or erne).

O S Maps: 1:50000 Sheet 1 1:25000 Sheet 470
Admiralty Charts: 1:75000 No.3282 1:30000 No.3292
southern part only 1:12500 No.3293 Balta Sound only

Area: 12068ha (29820 acres)
Height: 284m (932 ft)
Owner: Multiple ownership. Family descendants of Saxby (who wrote *Birds of Shetland*) and Edmonston (*A Flora of Shetland*) still have sizeable land-holdings, as do John and Wendy Scott of Garth.

Population: 1798–1688 (300 houses) approx. 1831–2730. 1841–2808 (517 houses). 1881–2173. 1891–2269 (470 houses). 1931–1326. 1961–1148. 1981–1140. 1991–1055. 2001 –720. 2011–632.

Geology: Unst has a complex but fascinating geology. The western side, defined by Loch of Cliff and the Loch of Watlee by Valla Field is coarse-grained gneiss, sometimes studded with tiny garnets, under peat moorland, which is very similar to that of adjacent Yell. The eastern side is composed of metagabbro and serpentine interspersed with schists. The serpentine has veins of iron chromate, and black and green jasper. A complex dislocation zone divides these two zones.

Limestone can be found in the south and talc at Haroldswick in the north-east. Unst has the only surviving talc mine in Britain.

History: Harolds Wick is named after King Harald Haarfagr (Fair-hair) who anchored here in 875 after first visiting Fetlar (No.11.25). Norway was being harassed by Viking, or pirate, raids from Shetland and Orkney so the king visited the islands and annexed them in the name of Norway. The pirates were, in any case, probably descendants of Scandinavian settlers.

Wildlife: This was the home of Thomas Edmonston, who published *A Flora of Shetland* in 1845, when he was still in his teens. He discovered the Norwegian Sandwort here in the Keen of Hamar which is found nowhere else in Britain but North Ronaldsay (No.10.28) and Rum (No.4.3), and protected by law since 1981, and the Shetland Mouse-ear Chickweed, which is unique to Unst. Edmondston was killed accidentally by a musket during an Amazon expedition when he was still a young man.

The Keen of Hamar is now a National Nature Reserve and the Warden's permission is needed to enter, 01463-239431. It is a remarkable site of broken serpentine scree with many unusual and rare plants such as fragrant and frog orchids, which can also be found occasionally elsewhere on Unst. An excavated Viking longhouse is nearby.

Small groups of Shetland ponies, whose numbers are in decline elsewhere, can still be seen on Unst. There are no bats, weasels, frogs, toads, hedgehogs or adders but there are plenty of rabbits. Rats were first recorded in 1903, and otters are common.

Hermaness National Nature Reserve is one of the few breeding sites of a rare moth and the cliffs of this, Britain's most northerly peninsula, hold one of our largest seabird colonies. 10,000 pairs of fulmar, the same of gannet, 5000 pairs of kittiwake, 16,000 pairs of guillemot, 2000 pairs of razorbill, and some 25,000 pairs of puffin have been recorded. There are a small number of arctic skua and, this being with Foula the last stronghold of the bonxie (great skua) when it was nearing extinction, now boasts at least 800 pairs.

It is also at Hermaness that the famous black-browed albatross returned each spring from the early 1970s to the late 1990s. A vagrant from the South Seas and trapped in the northern hemisphere, it kept hoping to find a mate. It occasionally winked at a passing gannet but was always violently rebuffed.

Many seabirds visit Bluemull Sound, particularly in winter and early spring, when eider and tysties (black guillemot) breed here.

*   *   *

Britain's most northerly inhabited island, **UNST** is one of the most interesting in the Shetland group. It has its share of dreich peat moorland, particularly in the west, but the cliff scenery is spectacular.

The ferry from Yell (No.11.23) docks at the chunks of serpentine which make up Belmont pier. The shell of **Belmont House**, a Lowland-style mansion built in 1777, can be seen across the fields [HP565010]. The main road branches off to Uyeasound, past standing stones, and on to **Muness Castle** [HP629011]. This desolate ruin in a desolate landscape could have been devised by Edgar Allen Poe for *The Fall of the House of*

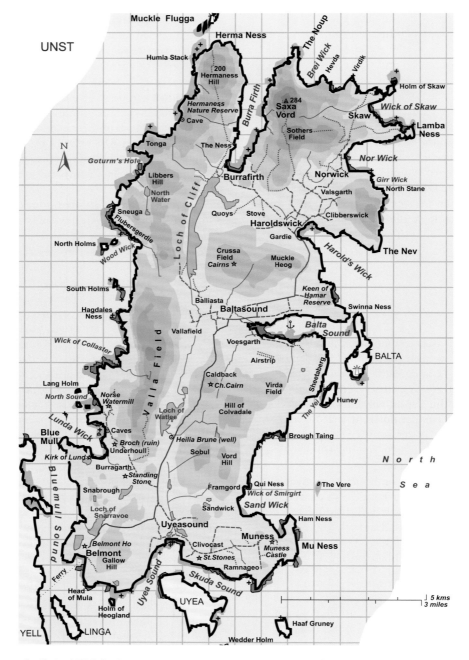

UNST

Muckle Flugga

Herma Ness

The Noup

Humla Stack

Brei Wick

Hevda

Virdik

Holm of Skaw

200
Hermaness
Hill

Saxa
284
Vord

Wick of Skaw

N

Hermaness
Nature Reserve

Cave

Sothers
Field

Skaw

Lamba
Ness

Burra Firth

Tonga

The Ness

Nor Wick

Goturm's Hole

Burrafirth

Norwick

Girr Wick

Libbers
Hill

Valsgarth

North Stane

North
Water

Loch of Cliff

Quoys

Stove

Clibberswick

Sneuga

Haroldswick

Flubersgerdie

Gardie

Harold's Wick

North Holms

Wood Wick

Crussa
Field
Cairns ☆

Muckle
Heog

The Nev

South Holms

Keen of
Hamar
Reserve

Hagdales
Ness

Balliasta

Baltasound

Swinna Ness

Wick of Collaster

Vallafield

⚓ Balta
Sound

BALTA

Valla Field

Voesgarth

Airstrip

Lang Holm

Caldback

Virda
Field

Sheetaberg

North Sound

Norse
Watermill

☆ Ch.Cairn

Huney

The Yel

Blue
Mull

Loch of
Watlee

Hill of
Colvadale

Brough Taing

North

Caves

Sea

Lunda Wick

Broch (ruin)
Underhoull

● Heilia Brune (well)

Sobul

Vord
Hill

Kirk of Lund ☆

Burragarth

Framgord

Qui Ness

● The Vere

Standing
Stone

Wick of Smirgirt

Snabrough

Sandwick

Sand Wick

Loch of
Snarravoe

Bluemull Sound

Uyeasound

Ham Ness

Muness

Belmont Ho ☆

Clivocast

Mu Ness

Belmont
Gallow
Hill

☆ St.Stones

Muness
Castle

Ferry

Uyea Sound

Ramnageo

Skuda Sound

Head
of Mula

5 kms
3 miles

UYEA

Holm of
Heogland

YELL LINGA

Haaf Gruney

Wedder Holm

Usher. It was built in 1598 by Lawrence Bruce of Cultmalindie in Perthshire, an evil man and a relative of the notorious tyrant Earl Patrick. Bruce also built the castle at Scalloway on Mainland (No.11.11). Muness is a handsome ruin, a high stone rectangle with circular towers and similarity of detail to the Earl's Palace in Kirkwall (No.10.11) built in the same period. Above the entrance is inscribed (the Shetland phonetics are unmistakable):

'List ze to knaw yis bulding quha began Laurence the Bruce he was that worthy man quha ernestly his airis and ofspring prayis to help and not to hurt this vark aluayis – the zeir of God 1598'

In spite of this urgent plea, the work at Muness Castle was soon destroyed, for the castle burned down in the 17th century. The history of the disaster is confused. One story in Norn verse claims it was a certain Hakki of Dikkeram, possibly in response to the abduction of a girl called Helga and the murder of her father by one of the Bruce family. Another story claims the castle was sacked and torched by French privateers.

Beside Mu Ness (ON – maiden headland) is the islet of **Hunts Holm** and to the north a Norse settlement has been excavated at **Sandwick**.

A branch to the west off the main spinal road leads to a track which passes **Bordastubble**, Shetland's largest standing stone [HP579034], and arrives at **Lunda Wick**. Here there is the ruin of the 12th-century **Lund Church**, last used for worship in 1785 [HP566041]. In the cemetery are the 16th-century graves of two Bremen merchants, probably representatives of the Hanseatic trade. (See Whalsay, No.11.15.) Lund Church – or St Olaf's Chapel – is built on **Blue Mull**, the headland which gives its name to Bluemull Sound. The mull is best admired from the sea, where it has a distinct blue colour when seen from the distance. On the opposite side of Lunda Wick at **Underhoull** are grass-covered earthworks surrounding the ruin of a broch [HP575044]. A 9th-century Viking longhouse, excavated in the 1960s, was built on an earlier Iron Age site. Further north, where the road crosses a burn, there is a restored Norse-type horizontal click mill.

Islets are scattered about North Sound, north of Lunda Wick, called **Lang Holm**, **Round Holm**, **The Vere** and **Brough Holm**. As expected, this latter islet has the remains of yet another broch on it. Further north up this dramatic coastline are two more groups, **North Holms** and **South Holms**, which has a subterranean passage.

The main road continues over a relatively featureless landscape with the ridge of **Valla Field** (ON – hill of mythological battle) to the west reflected in the brown waters of **Loch of Watlee**. The wishing well of **Helia Brune** [HP594046] is beside the loch and there are a few scattered chambered cairns. It is interesting, by the way, to note a resemblance between the map of Unst and Robert Louis Stevenson's map of Treasure Island. RLS visited Unst after his Uncle David had built Muckle Flugga lighthouse. Not long after the visit he began writing *Treasure Island*.

Baltasound is Unst's 'capital' with two hotels and an airstrip. The Swedish Church was built in 1910 and used by Scandinavian fishermen until the 1950s. The Sound used to be the centre of the northern herring industry and in its heyday had a seasonal population of 10,000, but its main use as a port today is for the export of talc. It is also a collection point for the oil industry – hence the busy little airfield.

To reach the large scattered settlement of **Haroldswick** the road skirts **Crussa Field** and **Muckle Heog**, hills which have clusters of ancient cairns on them. One is called Harald's Grave and is supposed to be the burial site for King Harald the Fair-haired. Haroldswick has the most northern post-office in Britain and is always happy to frank your letters accordingly.

Nor Wick, a bay with a glorious sweep of beach and weathered rocks, is an old haaf fishing station site. In 1700 a sea-eagle stole a baby girl, Mary Anderson, from the croft on the hill above the wick and carried her off to its eyrie on the cliffs of Fetlar. This was seen by a Fetlar islander and a young boy, Robert Nicolson, was lowered down to the nest by rope. He rescued the baby

225 Tern Watching at Nor Wick

TERN WATCHERS AT NOR WICK

and she was returned unharmed to Unst and, according to the story which is sworn to be true, when Mary grew up, Robert married her and the happy couple settled in Yell and raised a family.

At **Wick of Skaw**, Britain's most northerly dwelling, a croft farmhouse, nestles among marsh marigolds in a small valley by the beach. One of the outhouses is made from an old upturned boat [HP658164], – normal island practice where nothing is wasted.

A visit to the summit of **Saxa Vord** (ON – Saxa's lookout), Unst's highest point at 284m is no mountaineering feat as there is a road climbing the one thousand feet or so to the top. The view is breathtaking. The furthest outpost of the British Isles, **Out Stack** – or 'Oosta' – is only 3km further north. Lady Franklin landed on this bare rock in 1849 and prayed for her husband when he failed to return from his North West Passage expedition. Out Stack may be in the lead but **Muckle Flugga** with its lighthouse, built by David Stevenson in 1858 for £32,000 and surrounded by wheeling seabirds, is close behind. (It was automated in 1995.) Beneath one's feet are some of Shetland's most spectacular cliff-scenery and the deep, beautiful, but ominous, cleft of **Burra Firth**. At the entrance to Burra Firth there is a 100m-long natural tunnel through the rock at **Hol Hellier** through which a dinghy can sail on a calm day. Looking back, to the south, the firth almost meets the long and narrow Loch of Cliff, which in turn leads to a distant valley stretching the length of Unst, splitting the island longitudinally. Across the Burra Firth, the **Herma Ness** peninsula is a wild area almost uncontaminated by man. It is a Nature Reserve run by Scottish Natural Heritage.

The Ministry of Defence has had radar and other installations on and around Saxa Vord since the 1950s but these were closed in 2005 with devastating consequences for the island population. This is a windy place. In 1962 an unofficial all-British wind speed record of 177mph was recorded on top of Saxa Vord. It may have reached a higher speed but the anemometer blew away.

Saxa was a giant who lived on Saxa Vord and Herma was another giant who lived on Hermaness Hill and they were always quarrelling; or so the story goes. One day, Herma, using a ship's mast as a fishing rod, caught a whale for supper and asked Saxa to boil it for him in his kettle. (Saxa's Kettle is a huge rock-cup in Nor Wick in which the tide boils and gurgles.) Saxa agreed provided he could keep most for himself but Herma objected to this. The giants started throwing stones at each other and one of the stones which Herma threw can be seen on the west side of Saxa Vord and a stone which Saxa threw is a skerry on the west shore of Burra Firth called **Saxa's Baa**.

I suppose it is fitting that the end of the world should be a land of giants, for there is nothing beyond here but the icy wastes of the Arctic.

*   *   *

Access: Frequent daily ro-ro ferry service from Gutcher, Yell (10 mins), or Hamars Ness, Fetlar, 01957-722259. Tourist Information, 01595-693434.

Anchorages:

1. Uyea Sound. Fairly good shelter except from S'lies.There is a pier on NW side at head of sound. Anchor NE side in suitable depth, mud and sand. If caught by S'lies try Skuda Sound. See Uyea (No.11.27).

2. Sand Wick, Ham of Muness. Exposed NW–N–E. Temp. anchorage towards head of bay in 3–6m. Head shoals to shingle beach. Approach needs care.

3. Balta Sound, only safe all-weather anchorage on Unst. Pontoon berth W of main pier (charge) is accessible at all states of the tide or anchor where suitable but best SW of pier,4-8m, mud. Good holding.

4. Harolds Wick. Exposed SE–E. Temp. anchorage near E side of head but holding uncertain. Approach mid-channel. *(Visit Unst Boat Haven marine museum.)*

5. Nor Wick, on NE coast. Unsafe in E'lies. Temp. anchorage near centre of head, 8–10m, good holding in stiff grey sand.

6. Wick of Skaw. Dangerous due to tidal roost. Best to avoid this area by at least 1M.

7. Burra Firth. Exposed N. Sides high and steep-to but wide sandy beach 2½M up firth at head. Easy access. Temp. anchorage off beach, holding good. *(Hermaness Visitor Centre.)*

8. Muckle Flugga. No anchorage and landing only possible in fine weather at steps cut in rock.

9. Lunda Wick, just E of Blue Mull. Sheltered S and E, otherwise exposed. Anchor in SE towards head, sand and mud, holding good. Approach with care S of mid-channel.

10. Wick of Belmont, off Bluemull Sound. Vehicle ferry terminal at head with berthing reserved exclusively for ferry. Rocky bottom.

The East Coast

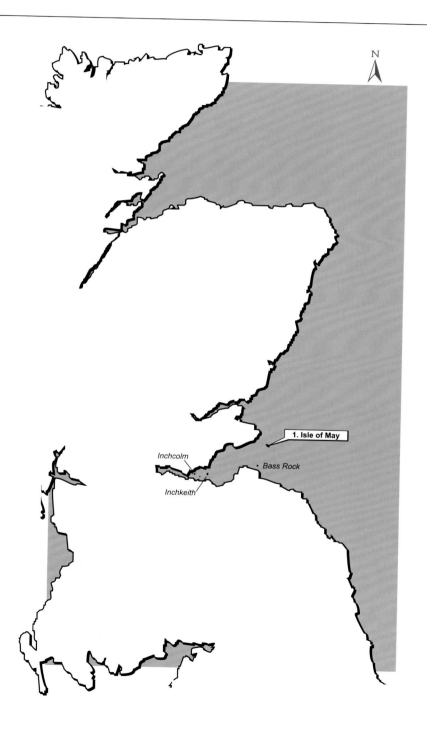

1. Isle of May

Inchcolm

Inchkeith

Bass Rock

SECTION 12, Table 1: Arranged according to geographical position

No.	Name	Latitude	Longitude	Table 2* No.	Table 3** No.	Area in Acres	Area in Hectares
12.1	Isle of May	56° 11N	02° 33W	157	120	111	45
12.A	*Bass Rock*	56° 05N	02° 38W			19	8

*Table 2: The islands arranged according to magnitude
**Table 3: The islands arranged according to height

Introduction

It is remarkable that over the entire length of the east coast of mainland Scotland, from John o' Groats – or more accurately, Duncansby Head – to the border north of Berwick-upon-Tweed, there is only one island which comes within the terms of classification for this book by having an area of forty hectares or more. And even this single example – the Isle of May – only just meets the conditions as it is a mere forty-five hectares (111 acres) in area.

There are no islets really worth mentioning north of the Tay except, possibly, the **Halliman Skerries** off Branderburgh and Lossiemouth – a mere line of seaweed-covered rocks; a few broken shards of land at the extreme head of the Cromarty Firth; **Keith Inch** which is part of the docks at Peterhead; and **Inchbroach** which is part of Montrose.

In the Firth of Tay itself there is only the quaintly named **Mugdrum Island** (G. – hog-back island) while out in the open sea beyond the Firth is the lonely and infamous **Bell Rock**. During the 1980s, radio broadcasts had to drop Bell Rock readings from the inshore shipping forecasts when a fire gutted the interior of the lighthouse. The Bell Rock, incidentally, was originally known as **Inchcape** (G. – island stumbling-block), which is understandable as this tiny rock chip with some skerries around it is only just large enough to support a lighthouse and seems to be there for no logical reason. It was certainly the cause of many shipping tragedies (an average of six ships each year) before Robert Stevenson built the famous lighthouse which marked its position in 1811.

We have to look to the Firth of Forth to find every other islet on the east coast. The Isle of May has been mentioned. The Bass Rock, although below the classified size, is of such historic interest that it has been included as an appendix to this section. But the remaining little islands also have fascinating histories.

To the west of the Bass Rock is the rugged island of **Fidra** (ON – feathered arrow shape) owned by the RSPB. On the Briggs of Fidra which is a broken reef spanning between Fidra and the shore are the remains of a Cistercian Hermitage which belonged to a Nunnery founded at North Berwick in the 12th century. At the time of the Dissolution of the Monasteries in Scotland (1561) the North Berwick and Fidra sisterhood consisted of eleven nuns, each drawing an annual income of £20. Although this was a very comfortable income, and they came of good families, not one of them could sign her name. It is possible to anchor on the east, west or south sides of Fidra, although there is often an uncomfortable swell. On the east side there is a landing jetty for the lighthouse. The south anchorage is tricky because of the rocks and submarine cables.

Two smaller islets lie between Fidra and the Bass Rock – **Craigleith** and **Lamb**. The Lamb has a Dog guarding each side of it (they are skerries) while Craigleith's claim to fame is that it was used as a rabbit warren. Craigleith is owned by Sir Hew Hamilton-Dalrymple and managed by Scottish National Heritage. Lamb was owned by a Brazilian-born internet entreperneur who, after a disagreement with the American financial authorities, sold the island to Uri Geller in 2009 for £30,000. Geller said he bought it for its 'mystical association' with the Pyramids of Giza.

Further up the Forth, standing conspicuously foursquare in the middle of the seaway opposite the Port of Leith is **Inchkeith**. It is about half the size of the Isle of May but slightly higher and also has a lighthouse on the summit. It is now unkempt but it once supported a viable small farm with good pasturage and there are several springs providing drinking water. The geology, apart from a few beds of sandstone, is chiefly sheets of igneous rock separated by thin strata of sedimentary deposits – shale with many fossils, coal, and limestone.

The plant life is varied and I can vouch for the virility of the birdlife. During the nesting season the gulls strafe visitors relentlessly.

Some time between 679 and 704 St Adomnan, abbot of Iona, founded a 'school of the prophets' on the island and it was here that he met St Serf who had just arrived in Scotland from Rome. In 1010 Malcolm II rewarded Robert de Keth of the Catti (Chattan) clan from Caithness (Cattiness) for his assistance in repelling the Danes and gave him large estates which included Inchkeith and Dalkeith. This is the probable derivation of the name of the island although there are other possibilities. In 1497 the sufferers from a contagious disease called 'grandgore' were shipped from Edinburgh to a Hospital on Inchkeith. The crew of a plague-stricken ship was also quarantined here in 1580; more plague-victims were sent over in 1609; and in 1799 many Russian sailors who had died of an infectious disease were buried on the island.

In 1547 after the battle of Pinkie Cleugh, the victorious English general – the Duke of Somerset – landed marines on Inchkeith and ordered them to fortify the island. A large square fort with corner towers was accordingly built on the summit (site of the present lighthouse). Italian mercenaries held the fort for the English until 1549 when D'Essé, a French general, led a joint Scottish and French force in a brilliant manoeuvre which recaptured the island. The Queen Regent, Mary of Guise, landed on Inchkeith the following day to see the 'three and four hundred of her dead foes still unburied'. As the date of capture was June 29th – the day of *Fête Dieu* in France – she renamed the island *L'Ile de Dieu*. D'Essé demolished the fort and built a larger and stronger one on the same site with an outer surrounding wall and a moat crossed by a drawbridge. Mary, Queen of Scots inspected the French garrison of this fort in 1564 and the commemorative stone from the original gateway with the inscription 'M.R. 1564' can still be seen where it has been built into a wall beside the lighthouse.

After Mary's deposition the Castle of Inchkeith was ordered to be 'raisit' but ended up instead being used as a prison. However, it was refortified during the Cromwellian Wars and, even when the ubiquitous Dr Johnson visited Inchkeith with Boswell in 1773, Boswell noted that the fort was strongly built. It was not until 1808 that it was at last 'raisit' to make room for the lighthouse.

In 1878, after twenty years of deep thought, the Admiralty realised that Inchkeith had a commanding position in the Forth and decided to fortify it once again. They installed elaborate batteries at the three corners of the island designed by the Royal Engineers as three separate fortresses. Each battery is partly underground and these magnificent fortifications can still be explored today. In fact Inchkeith is an island so rich in history that it is surprising that it has not received more detailed archaeological study, particularly before all its valuable artefacts disappear. It also has, incidentally, Scotland's *lowest average rainfall* (21.75ins). Dr Johnson said: 'I'd have this island: I'd build a house... A rich man of an hospitable turn here, would have many visitors from Edinburgh'. When the lighthouse was made automatic, Inchkeith was purchased from the Lighthouse Commissioners by Sir Tom Farmer, a well-known Edinburgh businessman, but he has not yet followed Dr Johnson's advice.

Inchmickery (G. *innis na bhicaire* – isle of the vicar) is an insignificant islet lying between **Cramond Island** (which is a drying island, accessible at low water) and Inchcolm. It probably had some past connection with the abbey on Inchcolm. The story goes that James IV, who had an enquiring mind, wanted to discover the 'Original Language' of the human race. So he sent two newly born infants with a dumb nurse to live on uninhabited Inchmickery. After a year or two he and his courtiers seriously agreed that the children 'spak extremely guid Ebrew'.

The remnants of various Second World War fortifications make Inchmickery today an interesting piece of abstract sculpture.

Inchcolm (G. – island of St Columba) was named in the 12th century in memory of Columba's visit to it in about 567. Its old name was Aemonia or Emona. It is best known for the monastery which dominates its skyline and which was founded in 1123 by Alexander I. A century earlier when a Danish force under King Sueno entered the Firth of Forth and pillaged Fife with the support of an English force sent by Sueno's brother King Canute, Macbeth drove them off. In return for 'a great summe of gold' Macbeth agreed that the defeated invaders could bury their dead on St Colme's holy island (Shakespeare put the price at 'ten thousand dollars').

Naturally, as a well-endowed monastery, Inchcolm was fair game for plunder and an English ship first raided it in 1335 carrying off all the treasures including a famous image of St

Columba. A storm almost wrecked the ship on Inchkeith so the sailors vowed to return the image if they survived. In due course they landed at Kinghorn, sent the image back to Inchcolm, and then sailed for home with the rest of the booty, a clear conscience, and a fair wind. There was another English raid in 1384 and this time the raiders tried to burn down the monastery, but St Columba sent a change of wind which put the fire out.

In 1547, after the battle of Pinkie Cleugh, the Monastery was fortified, and there were occasions when it was, like the Castles of Inchkeith and Inchgarvie, also used as a state prison. Euphemia, mother of Alexander, Lord of the Isles, was imprisoned here, as was Patrick Graham, Archbishop of St Andrews. But there were dark secrets too, as revealed in the 1880s, when a human skeleton, standing upright, was found built into one of the walls.

The various buildings on Inchcolm are too extensive to discuss in detail here but they form a most interesting group and some parts of the monastery are remarkably well preserved. The site is maintained by the Government and has a resident custodian. There are boat excursions from South Queensferry and for yachtsmen the best anchorage is in the north bight.

The island beneath the Forth (Rail) Bridge – **Inchgarvie** (G. – rough island) – also has a long and interesting history but as the bridge has destroyed its insularity it is not a subject for this book. Like Inchkeith it had its castle fortification which was considered an important stronghold and was also used as a state prison on occasions, and even a hospital for the quarantine of infectious diseases. It was demolished by Cromwell but rebuilt in 1779 for protection against John Paul Jones. In the end stone from the castle was used to help build the bridge caissons in 1883.

For the defence of the bridge a gun emplacement was maintained on Inchgarvie during the Second World War.

12.1 Isle of May

(ON maa-øy – gull island). In 13th century recorded as 'Maeyar' leading to a comparison with (G. machair – level land) because of the island's plateau-like structure but this is not convincing.

OS Maps: 1:50000 Sheet 59 1:25000 Sheet 59
Admiralty Charts: 1:75000 Nos.175 or 190 1:25000 No.734

Area: 45ha (111 acres)
Height: 50m (164 ft)

Owner: The Commissioners of Northern Lights. Scottish Natural Heritage (SNH) manage it as a National Nature Reserve.

Population: 1881–22. 1891–27. 1931–10. 1961–7. 1971–10. 1981–2. 1991–0. 2001–0. 2011–0.

Geology: The rock is mainly hard fine-grained basalt of a dark-grey colour with tinges of green and greenstone. There are fewer sea-caves than there are on the Bass Rock as the rock here is harder.

History: The island became a celebrated place of pilgrimage after St Adrian, first Bishop of St Andrews, was discovered and murdered when attempting to shelter here from the Danes in about the year 870. He was buried on the island but half his stone coffin is supposed to have miraculously floated over to Anstruther and ended up

INCHCOLM ABBEY

Haswell-Smith

in Anstruther Wester churchyard. Six thousand Fife Christians are said to have been slaughtered in this attack, including another saint – Monance.

David I (1124–53) gifted the May to the Benedictine Monastery of Reading in Berkshire on the promise that nine priests would say mass for his soul and that of his successors in perpetuity. He built a chapel on the island dedicated to St Adrian for the new Priory.

The May was sold by the abbot of Reading privately to William Wishart, archbishop of St Andrews c.1270. This may have been encouraged by Alexander III, who disliked the idea of the May being under English control, and certainly the brethren in Reading tried to rescind the deal when they learned of it.

When Edward I installed John Balliol on the throne of his 'vassal kingdom' of Scotland in 1292, the very first Parliament was asked to return the May to the Benedictines of Reading. Bishop Fraser of St Andrews, however, appealed to the Pope for a ruling and this delayed any settlement. The Battle of Bannockburn in 1314 eventually resolved the matter, although the Scottish monks had meanwhile deserted the island and established themselves in more comfort at Pittenweem. For the next two centuries the monks continued to till the island but live elsewhere while the English demolished the island Priory during many incursions. Later, however, a small Hermitage was built among the ruins.

In 1549 the Provost of St Andrews took a feu on the island which was described then as waste land providing no income, due to the rabbit warrens having been destroyed by the English. It was agreed that a chaplain should stay in the Hermitage and continue to conduct services in the chapel 'out of reverence to the relics and tombs of the saints buried in the island; and for the reception of pilgrims...' Two years later a feu charter was conferred on the Balfours of Montquhanny and in

1558 it passed to the family of Forret of Fyngask. Then sometime before 1636 the island was bought by the Cunynghames of Barnes and it was agreed that together with James Maxwell of Innerwick they could levy an 'impost' on ships for erecting and maintaining a Light on the Isle of May. Parliament ratified this in 1641 and again in 1645 for the 'true and thankful service done to his hieness... Be his Majesty's Lovitt Johne Cunnynghame of Barnes In bigging and erecting upoun the yle of Maij belonging to him Lyand in the mouth of the firth Of ane Lighthous...'

In 1672 the Earl of Kellie is recorded as the owner but he sold it to the Scotts of Scotstarvet. The Marquis of Tichfield, 4th Duke of Portland, inherited it from the Scotts by marriage in 1795 and the Duchess eventually sold it to the Northern Lighthouse Commissioners for the sum of £60,000 in 1815. In the 20th century the island played an important part in anti-submarine defense during both world wars.

Wildlife: A number of interesting plant communities are to be found and over sixty varieties of seaweed have been recorded here.

The Scottish Seabird Centre in North Berwick has a direct video link to the Isle of May similar to its remote interactive cameras on the Bass Rock and Fidra. This allows visitors to watch the birds and other wildlife such as seals throughout the year without disturbing them. By individual control of the cameras they can pan the area and zoom in on points of interest.

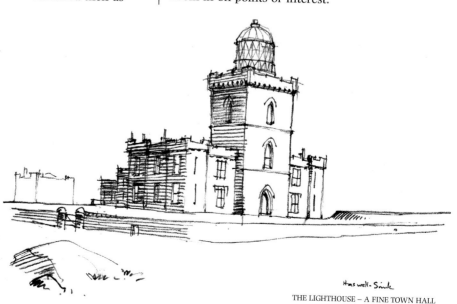

THE LIGHTHOUSE – A FINE TOWN HALL

Renowned for its birdlife, in early summer the Isle of May is a wonderful nesting place for many seabirds but, unlike the Bass Rock, there are no gannets. April/May and August/October are the most interesting periods for bird-watching.

Breeders: Large numbers of shag, kittiwake, guillemot, razorbill, puffin, and also, fulmar, herring gulls and lesser black-backed gulls, eider, oystercatcher and a few common and arctic terns, wheatear and rock pipit.

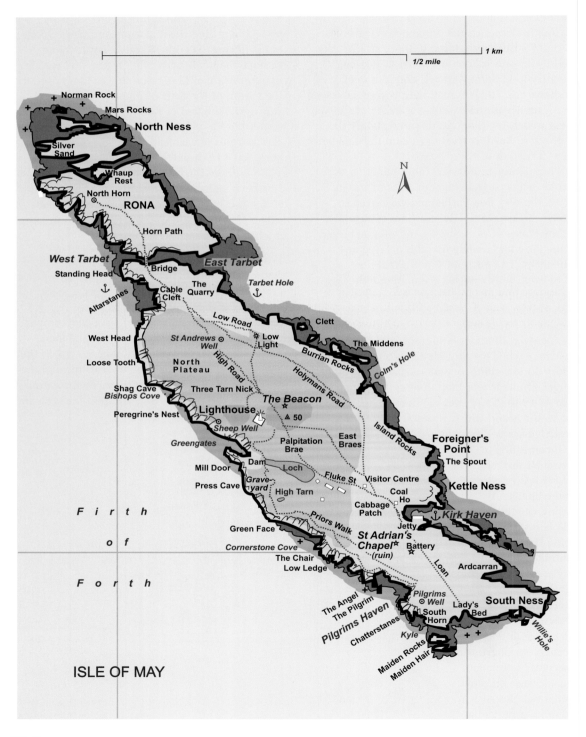

ISLE OF MAY

Over 240 bird species have been recorded and in autumn there are often enormous numbers of relatively common birds. Other species seen include wryneck, bluethroat, icterine, barred and yellow-browed warblers, great grey and red-backed shrikes, red-breasted flycatcher, Lapland and ortolan buntings, and scarlet rosefinch. Rarities recorded include the red-footed falcon, spoonbill, Pallas's sandgrouse, Daurian redstart, Siberian thrush, pied wheatear, Pallas's-, paddyfield-, melodious-, olivaceous-, and subalpine warblers, red-throated pipit, yellow-breasted and rustic buntings, and pine grosbeak. At sea: divers, shearwaters, sea-duck, petrels and skuas.

*   *   *

The verdant islet May,
Whose fitful lights amid surrounding gloom,
. . . from danger warns the home-bound
mariner.

Fergusson, 1772.

The **ISLE OF MAY** is well known for three diverse reasons – its archaeological interest, its historic lighthouse and its birdlife. The island itself is a long narrow slab of hard basalt with a grassy and reasonably fertile surface partly surrounded by cliffs. The highest point at 50m is near the centre with the lighthouse on it.

Most of the antiquities are at the southern end not far from **Kirkhaven**, where there is a jetty and crane built for the lighthouse keepers. The main ruin is of a rectangular building nearly 10m long with two Norman-style window openings in the west wall [NT658990]. The building is on a north-south access and has had several alterations such as the addition of a defensive tower. The north part of the structure, defined by a partition wall, may have been a chapel but about 1600 a small smithy and forge were constructed inside the ruins of the church which had probably been abandoned years before. Although this building was joined to **St Ethernan's Priory** (c.1140), the Priory itself was demolished in a succession of English invasions. However, during archaeological excavations in 1992, a monastic church was uncovered. The cloister garth and numerous graves were investigated in 1995 and excavation under the 13th-century Benedictine church has revealed signs of an earlier building. Large quantities of pottery included a 13th, or 14th, century decorated jug which probably came from

A CHAPEL IN THE CLIFFS NEAR ST ADRIAN'S PRIORY

Scarborough and shards of Iron Age and Beaker vessels.

David I was the son of the saintly Queen Margaret and he was determined to substitute the Roman faith for the Culdee faith of St Columba and the other early Christians. He spent money lavishly on abbeys, cathedrals, and churches, gave generous donations to Augustinians, Cistercians, and Benedictines and was profligate in his distribution of Crown lands to the Church. His friendship with the Benedictines of the House of Reading on the Thames came about through his marriage to Henry I of England's sister. His endowment made the Priory of May one of the kingdom's wealthiest establishments.

There are records that shortly after David had founded the Priory Sweyn Asliefsson (See Gairsay, No.10.14), the likable buccaneering Orcadian, plundered it and then sailed up the Firth of Forth to Edinburgh to be received by King David with great honour. It seems that he proudly told David of his exploits and was severely reprimanded so he promptly sailed back down the Forth, restored all the plunder to the monastery, and then sent his greetings to David whereupon he was restored to his position of honour.

A creek at the south-west corner of the island is known as the **Pilgrims' Haven**. It has two outlying rock-stacks (one of these isolated pinnacles is 24m high and supposed to look like a bishop's mitre but I found that to be somewhat imaginative) and a shingle beach in the cove on which a small boat can rest. In the 14th and 15th centuries a steady stream of pilgrims landed here and flocked up the slope to pay their respects at St Adrian's shrine. On the way they would stop to drink brackish water from the **Pilgrim's Well** [NT659989], which was reputed to cure many ailments and bring about remarkable miracles. One of these pilgrims was Mary of Gueldres, *en* *route* from the Netherlands in 1449 to marry James II. Another was James IV who made the pilgrimage on a number of occasions – 1490, 1503, 1505 and 1513. James V may also have visited the May in 1540.

In the 17th century there was a small village just south of the Priory and there is a tradition that the inhabitants lived by ship-wrecking and smuggling. Contraband was kept in the cave near the **South Ness** which the excisemen were told was inhabited by a colony of kelpies. The May caves were also used by Fife fishermen to avoid the press-gangs and one well-concealed cave is still called 'Press Cave'. Archaeologists are investigating the village remains.

In a hollow near the cliff-edge is a solitary tombstone for a John Wishart who died in 1730. This was probably the site of the village cemetery.

West of the lighthouse-keepers' cottages and outbuildings there is a deep gorge which has been dammed to provide a water supply. Prior to this there was no satisfactory source of fresh water as, although there are several wells, they are either brackish or dry out at intervals. The lighthouse is now automatic but on an earlier visit to the island a keeper proudly showed us his walled garden, well protected to keep out the rabbits and full of superb vegetables.

The lighthouse is a handsome structure which would make a fine town hall but is quite out-of-keeping with the landscape. It was started in 1816 and contains a square light-tower with mock battlements and a spacious two-storey building with accommodation for the superintendent keeper.

The track running past the lighthouse and on to **Altarstones Landing** in the north-west is called **Holyman's Road** because it was the path customarily taken by the Prior.

In the centre of the island and not far from the modern lighthouse is a platform-like structure which is all that remains of the original lighthouse or **Beacon** [NT657994]. When Alexander Cunningham had it built in 1635 it was the first and only lighthouse in Scotland – a mere platform 12m high with a burning beacon on it. When Cunningham's son, John, together with James Maxwell, obtained permission to charge ships an impost for the light, they improved the design by raising the beacon platform to 18m and constructing the tower like a Border keep. This was in 1656. The impost

was four Scots shillings a ton for foreign ships and two shillings for home vessels collected by Customs officers on the Fife coast and bringing in about £280 sterling per year. The light came from burning a ton of coal each night in a grate or chauffer at the top of the tower. In gales, up to three tons of coal were consumed.

The architect for the beacon tower was drowned when his boat capsized while on a supervision visit. Several old ladies of Pittenweem were blamed for the tragedy and burned as witches.

The lighthouse was rather unsatisfactory, particularly as in a gale very little light could be seen on the dangerous windward side. In January 1791 the light was out for two nights during a severe storm. It was found that the lighthouse-keeper, his wife, and five children, had been asphyxiated by the fumes although a baby survived. There were many shipwrecks and complaints but nothing was done until two Royal Navy frigates, *Pallas* and *Nymph*, were wrecked on the rocks near Dunbar in 1810. The pilots said they thought a limekiln at Broxmouth was the May light, and that the May light was the Bell Rock. At last the Government acted. The Commissioners of Northern Lights bought the island in 1815 and started construction of the present lighthouse – using the latest design of oil lamps and reflectors.

Maiden Hair Rock, near the Pilgrims' Haven, is supposed to be named in honour of St Thenaw. King Loth of Lothian was reputed to have been gifted his kingdom by King Arthur of the Round Table. The legend claims that in the year 516, Princess Thenaw, Loth's young unmarried daughter, was found to be pregnant. The king was furious and ordered her to be cast headlong from Traprain Law (then known as Dunpender) as punishment for fornication. After praying for forgiveness the girl was thrown from the height, but she landed on soft ground and suffered no injury. King Loth was convinced that only a witch could have had such a remarkable escape and decreed that she be put to death by drowning. So she was rowed out from Aberlady and cast into the water near the Isle of May. She managed to clutch on to the seaweed on Maiden Hair Rock for a time but after crying for help from God she was swept away by the tide far up the Forth. She was at last washed ashore beside the Monastery at Culross and it was here, lying on the beach, that she gave birth to her son, Kentigern, later known as St Mungo, patron saint of Glasgow. Soon after, mother and son were discovered by a monk and St Serf, Abbot of Culross, looked after them.

Access: Information on boat trips from Anstruther and Crail, 01333-311073. Scottish Natural Heritage, Fife, 0334-54038.

Anchorages: Use plenty of chain as holding is poor.
1. Altarstones Landing, W side. Subject to surge and exposed to all W'lies. Occasional anchorage in 5m, opposite the steps. Moored dinghies subject to damage except in flat calm. Hoist inflatables clear of sea.
2. Kirkhaven, E of S Ness. Long, narrow gut entered from SE with jetty at head. Pleasant in calm weather but subject to surge in S–SW winds and dangerously exposed to E'lies and breaking seas. Depth only 1.2m but with space for small yacht to tie to rings. Very narrow, but mid-channel approach under power is straightforward.
3. East Tarbet or Tarbet Hole. Subject to swell and exposed to E. Awkward landing on rocks. Occasional anchorage in 4m.

12-Appendix Bass Rock

Derivation uncertain. Possibly named after a man named Bass mentioned in the Book of Lecain (Chronicles of Picts and Scots). In Old Norse 'Baa' is a sunken rock on which the sea breaks in bad weather – maybe this is an inaccurate application meaning 'a dangerous rock'; or (ON berserk – in a bear's shirt) meaning 'a wild warrior'.

O S Maps: 1:50000 Sheet 66   1:25000 Sheet 351
Admiralty Charts: 1:75000 No.175   1:50000 No.734

Area: 7½ha (19 acres)
Height: 107m (350 ft)

Owner: Sir Hew Hamilton-Dalrymple.

Population: (Lighthouse-keepers) 1961–5. 1971–3. 1981–0. 1991–0.

Geology: A volcanic plug of phonolite rock.

History: Most of the rock belonged to the Bishopric of St Andrews when Malcolm Canmore is said to have granted the remaining part of it to the Lauder family in 1056. The Lauders became known as the Lauders of the Bass and they held it until the mid-17th century. In 1706 it became the property of Sir Hew Dalrymple and it is still in the ownership of his family.

St Baldred, an Irish missionary may have been the first inhabitant. He died in 606.

THE BASS ROCK FROM THE RAMPARTS OF TANTALLON CASTLE. THE ISLE OF MAY LIES ON THE HORIZON.

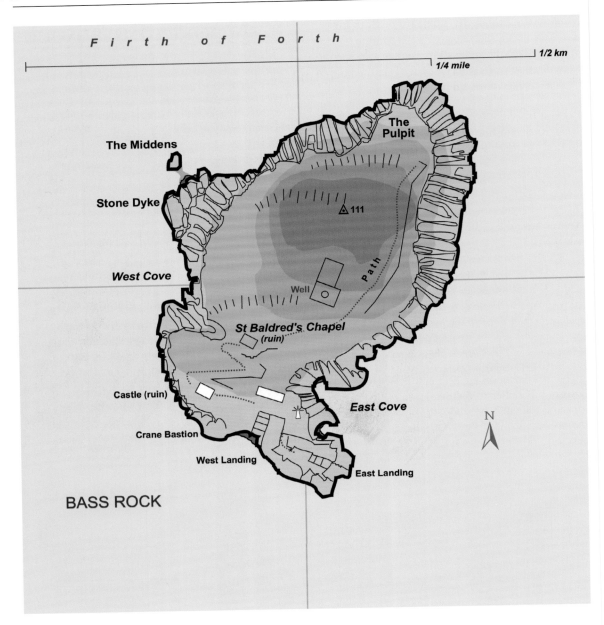

Firth of Forth

1/2 km
1/4 mile

The Middens

The Pulpit

Stone Dyke

△ 111

West Cove

Path

Well

St Baldred's Chapel
(ruin)

Castle (ruin)

East Cove

Crane Bastion

N

West Landing

East Landing

BASS ROCK

In 1338, the siege of Dunbar Castle by the English was broken because the Bass Rock was able to provide Black Agnes, Countess of March and Dunbar, with provisions.

The date when the fortress was built, probably by the Lauders, is not on record. It is first mentioned in 1405 when Prince James, the twelve-year old son of Robert III, later to become James I, was sent here for safety by his father until a vessel could be found to take him to France, as the king's brother, the Duke of Albany, had designs on the throne. Albany tipped off the English who intercepted James' ship, and imprisoned the prince in the Round Tower at Windsor for nineteen years. When James was eventually ransomed for £400,000 he, understandably, decided to get his own back and imprisoned the son of the Duke of Albany in the fortress on the Bass Rock.

In 1542 the crude little chapel which had been built about 1491 was consecrated and dedicated to St Baldred.

When Cromwell stormed north and defeated the Presbyterians at Dunbar (they had offered allegiance to Charles II), there was an attempt to send the Church Records over to the Bass Rock for safe-keeping. But the Rock surrendered to Cromwell's forces in 1651, the Records were removed to London, and it is thought they were lost in the fire at the House of Commons in 1834.

When Charles II was restored as monarch in 1660 he set about destroying the Church of Scotland, but the Covenanters fought back with secret 'conventicles'. Many Presbyterians were arrested and in 1671, the Bass Rock was bought (for £4000) and used as a prison for the recalcitrant Covenanters. It was not until 1688 that many of these men were released when James VII was relieved of the Crown and William of Orange proclaimed king. Much of Scotland however remained faithful to James until the Battle of Killiecrankie after which the only remaining Jacobite stronghold was the Bass Rock. It held out for nearly two years under its Governor, Sir Charles Maitland, but was eventually starved into submission in 1690.

It was now the turn of four Jacobites to be held prisoner. But not for long, because while the new Governor, Fletcher of Saltoun, was away they captured the garrison and with only a gunner and sixteen friends from Lothian to help them they held the Bass Rock from 1691 until 1694. Even then they only surrendered because they were granted an amnesty.

In 1701, the fortress was dismantled and the island was sold to Sir Hew Dalrymple, whose family still own it. Its main use at this time was for grazing sheep and collecting gannets to eat.

In 1902 the lighthouse was constructed and the island was once again temporarily inhabited.

Wildlife: Forty-eight species of wildflower have been recorded here. This includes the tree mallow, *Lavatera arborea*, a tall biennial with attractive rose-coloured flowers. It was introduced to the Bass Rock by sheep farmers in the 17th century (its woolly leaves make good bandages). It is thriving in the milder winters and as its seeds can survive in water for more than three months it is invading surrounding islands and destroying the puffin burrows. Another unusual plant is the Pheasant's-eye Daffodil, *Narcissus poeticus*, which comes from central Europe. Examples can also be found of the native Sea Beet, *Beta vulgaris maritima*.

Birdlife is prolific. There are common inland species such as blackbird, hedge sparrow and rock pipit, while seabirds are packed onto every steep rock-ledge. The island is most famous for its huge gannet colony of over 40,000 pairs and the bird is even named after the island – *Morus bassanus*. There are also large numbers of kittiwake, razorbill, shag, fulmar, herring gull, guillemot and puffin. These, together with the birdlife on St Kilda and the Isle of May, can all be viewed live by remote video at the Scottish Seabird Centre in North Berwick.

* * *

The **BASS ROCK** can be thought of as the Ailsa Craig (No.1.1) of the East Coast but it is very much smaller. There was a fortress on it for centuries and most of the materials were brought over from the mainland. Considering the difficulty of landing in even comparatively quiet conditions, one marvels at the dogged determination of the builders.

There is a huge cave which cuts right through the base of the Bass Rock from east to west. The sea – and the seals – slip through, and it can be explored by dinghy in calm weather. Its least height is about 10m, length 170m, and there is a patch in the middle where there is a small gravel beach.

Sailing around the rock is an unforgettable experience. The view of the cave may be beautiful and fascinating but it is the assault on all the senses which is beyond belief. The eyes are dazzled by clouds of wheeling and diving birds set against rock formations draped in guano and deep shadows of caverns and overhanging ledges. The ears are deafened by the high-pitched cries of the seabirds as a descant to the surging bass tones of the sea growling in the rock clefts – what a subject for Mahler! And the nose really suffers. The smell is overpowering.

The rock itself appears from the mainland to slope gradually down to the sea but this slope is in fact divided into three rough terraces. The lowest terrace with the landing place has the remains of the fortress on it which was purchased by the Government in 1671 as a state prison. On the second terrace are the ruins of **St Baldred's Chapel**, probably built on the site of his original anchorite cell. The highest terrace has what was once a walled garden and a well – although this is no more than a catchment for surface water. There is a cairn at the summit (111m).

* * *

Access: There are boat trips from North Berwick in the summer months and controlled landing. Contact the Scottish Seabird Centre.

Anchorages: No anchorages.
1. Landing jetty on S side, below lighthouse. Unless flat calm (very rare), advisable to lie off and approach in dinghy. Even then, landing can be difficult due to the swell.

Table 2:
The islands arranged in order of magnitude

NO.	NAME	TABLE I NO.	AREA IN HECTARES	NO.	NAME	TABLE I NO.	AREA IN HECTARES
1	Lewis/Harris	8.14	220673	52	Mingulay	7.2	640
2	Mainland (Shetland)	11.11	100230	53	Ronay	7.16	563
3	Mull	3.3	87794	54	Muck	4.1	559
4	Uists/Benbecula	7.14	74540	55	Shuna	2.11	451
5	Islay	2.4	61956	56	Graemsay	10.10	409
6	Mainland (Orkney)	10.11	58308	57	Sandray	7.4	385
7	Arran	1.4	43201	58	Wiay	7.15	375
8	Jura	2.6	36692	59	Island of Stroma	10.2	375
9	Yell	11.24	21211	60	Vementry	11.13	370
10	Hoy	10.5	14318	61	Ceann Ear (Monach Isles)	7.18	357
11	Bute	1.8	12217	62	Noss	11.7	343
12	Unst	11.30	12068	63	Vaila	11.10	327
13	Rum	4.3	10463	64	Little Cumbrae Island	1.5	313
14	Tiree	3.10	7834	65	Wyre	10.16	311
15	Coll	3.13	7685	66	Tanera Mór	6.8	310
16	Barra	7.6	6835	67	Handa	6.10	309
17	Raasay	5.7	6405	68	Isle of Ewe	6.2	309
18	Sanday	10.25	5043	69	Fara	10.7	295
19	Rousay	10.21	4860	70	Hascosay	11.26	275
20	Westray	10.26	4713	71	Seaforth Island	8.12	273
21	Colonsay	2.7	4617	72	Eilean Mór (Crowlin Islands)	5.6	270
22	Fetlar	11.25	4078	73	Inchmarnock	1.7	266
23	Stronsay	10.15	3275	74	Lunga	2.12	254
24	Eigg	4.2	3049	75	Holy Island	1.3	253
25	Shapinsay	10.13	2948	76	Pabbay	7.3	250
26	Bressay	11.8	2805	77	Calf of Eday	10.24	243
27	Eday	10.22	2745	78	Gairsay	10.14	240
28	Scalpay	5.3	2483	79	Fuday	7.11	232
29	Ulva	3.7	2415	80	Papa Little	11.12	226
30	Lismore	3.9	2351	81	Housay (Out Skerries)	11.18	218
31	Whalsay	11.15	1970	82	Carna	3.14	213
32	Luing	2.14	1543	83	Uyea	11.27	205
33	Taransay	8.9	1475	84	Berneray	7.1	204
34	Scarba	2.10	1474	85	Boreray	8.1	198
35	Gigha	2.3	1395	86	Gruinard Island	6.3	196
36	Canna	4.4	1314	87	Ensay	8.3	186
37	Foula	11.6	1265	88	Mousa	11.2	180
38	Kerrera	3.2	1214	89	Faray	10.23	180
39	Great Cumbrae	1.6	1168	90	Killegray	8.2	176
40	Scarp	8.13	1045	91	Isle Martin	6.4	157
41	Soay	5.1	1036	92	Shuna	3.12	155
42	Rona	5.9	930	93	Sanda	1.2	151
43	Papa Westray	10.27	918	94	Wiay	5.5	148
44	Iona	3.1	877	95	Garbh Eilean (Shiant Islands)	8.8	143
45	Flotta	10.5	876	96	Hellisay	7.9	142
46	Papa Stour	11.14	828	97	Garbh Eileach	2.16	142
47	Pabbay	8.4	820	98	Eilean nan Ron	6.12	138
48	Fair Isle	11.1	768	99	Little Bernera	8.20	138
49	North Ronaldsay	10.28	690	100	Longa	6.1	126
50	Hirta (St Kilda)	9.1	670	101	West Linga	11.16	125
51	Egilsay	10.19	650	102	Eilean Iubhard	8.11	125

TABLE 2

NO.	NAME	TABLE I NO.	AREA IN HECTARES	NO.	NAME	TABLE I NO.	AREA IN HECTARES
103	Mealista Island	8.15	124	136	Eilean Dubh Mór	2.15	65
104	Pabay	5.2	122	137	Eilean Macaskin	2.8	64
105	Priest Island	6.5	122	138	Isay	5.8	60
106	Eorsa	3.6	122	139	South Havra	11.3	59
107	Rona (North)	9.4	109	140	Papa	11.5	59
108	Hildasay	11.9	108	141	Floddaymore	7.17	58
109	Cava	10.8	107	142	Linga Holm	10.17	57
110	Pabay Mór	8.19	101	143	Eileach an Naoimh	2.13	56
111	Ailsa Craig	1.1	99	144	Inch Kenneth	3.4	55
112	Soay	9.2	99	145	Horse Island	6.7	53
113	Gighay	7.10	96	146	Tahay	7.21	53
114	Swona	10.3	92	147	Longay	5.4	50
115	Little Colonsay	3.5	88	148	Eileanan Iasgaich	7.12	50
116	Eilean Righ	2.9	86	149	Scotasay	8.7	49
117	Auskerry	10.12	85	150	Stockinish Island	8.6	49
118	Vuia Mór	8.17	84	151	Texa	2.1	48
119	Fuiay	7.8	84	152	Shillay	8.5	47
120	Lunga	3.8	81	153	Switha	10.4	47
121	Balta	11.29	80	154	Lamba	11.23	46
122	Muldoanich	7.5	78	155	Eilean an Ròin Mòi	6.11	45
123	Bigga	11.21	78	156	Soay Mór	8.10	45
124	Boreray	9.3	77	157	Isle of May	12.1	45
125	Eilean Kearstay	8.16	77	158	Stuley	7.13	45
126	Eynhallow	10.20	75	159	Linga (Bluemull Sound)	11.28	45
127	Papa Stronsay	10.18	74	160	Vacsay	8.18	43
128	Copinsay	10.9	73	161	Eilean Dubh	6.6	43
129	Hermetray	7.20	72	162	Muckle Skerry	10.1	42
130	Linga (Olna Firth)	11.17	70	163	Brother Isle	11.22	42
131	Gunna	3.11	69	164	Eilean Trodday	5.10	42
132	Oxna	11.4	68	165	Linga (Yell Sound)	11.19	42
133	Tanera Beg	6.9	66	166	Flodday (Loch Madday)	7.19	42
134	Cara	2.2	66	167	Flodday (E Barra)	7.7	42
135	Samphrey	11.20	66	168	Nave Island	2.5	40

Table 3:
The islands arranged in order of height

NO.	NAME	TABLE I NO.	HEIGHT IN METRES	NO.	NAME	TABLE I NO.	HEIGHT IN METRES
1	Mull	3.3	966	52	Handa	6.10	123
2	Arran	1.4	874	53	Little Cumbrae	1.5	123
3	Rum	4.3	812	54	Sanda	1.2	123
4	Lewis/Harris	8.14	799	55	Tanera Mór	6.8	122
5	Jura	2.6	785	56	Isle Martin	6.4	120
6	Uists/Benbecula	7.14	620	57	Whalsay	11.15	119
7	Islay	2.4	491	58	Ronay	7.16	115
8	Hoy	10.6	479	59	Crowlin Islands	5.6	114
9	Mainland (Shetland)	11.11	450	60	Garbh Eileach	2.16	110
10	Scarba	2.10	449	61	Rona (North)	9.4	108
11	Raasay	5.7	443	62	Fuiay	7.8	107
12	Hirta	9.1	430	63	Gruinard Island	6.3	106
13	Foula	11.6	418	64	Coll	3.13	104
14	Eigg	4.2	393	65	Lunga	3.8	103
15	Scalpay	5.3	392	66	Wiay	7.15	102
16	Boreray	9.3	384	67	Gairsay	10.14	102
17	Barra/Vatersay	7.6	383	68	Eday	10.22	101
18	Soay	9.2	378	69	Gigha	2.3	100
19	Ailsa Craig	1.1	338	70	Iona	3.1	100
20	Holy Island	1.3	314	71	Lunga	2.12	98
21	Ulva/Gometra	3.7	313	72	Eorsa	3.6	98
22	Scarp	8.13	308	73	Vaila	11.10	95
23	Unst	11.30	284	74	Gighay	7.10	95
24	Bute	1.8	278	75	Luing	2.14	94
25	Mingulay	7.2	273	76	Vementry	11.13	90
26	Mainland (Orkney)	10.11	271	77	Shuna	2.11	90
27	Taransay	8.9	267	78	Fuday	7.11	89
28	Rousay	10.21	250	79	Papa Stour	11.14	87
29	Bressay	11.8	226	80	Eilean Dubh	6.6	87
30	Fair Isle	11.1	217	81	Tanera Beg	6.8	83
31	Seaforth Island	8.12	217	82	Papa Little	11.12	82
32	Canna/Sanday	4.4	210	83	Eileach an Naoimh	2.13	80
33	Sandray	7.4	207	84	Shillay	8.5	79
34	Yell	11.24	205	85	Hellisay	7.9	79
35	Pabbay (Sound of Harris)	8.4	196	86	Priest Island	6.5	78
36	Berneray (Bishop's Isles)	7.1	193	87	Mealista Island	8.15	77
37	Kerrera	3.2	189	88	Eilean nan Ron	6.12	76
38	Noss	11.7	181	89	Eilean Iubhard	8.11	76
39	Pabbay (Bishop's Isles)	7.3	171	90	Isle of Ewe	6.2	72
40	Westray	10.26	169	91	Shuna	3.12	71
41	Carna	3.14	169	92	Longa	6.1	70
42	Shiant Islands	8.8	160	93	Linga (Olna Firth)	11.17	69
43	Fetlar	11.25	158	94	Pabay Mór	8.19	68
44	Muldoanich	7.5	153	95	Vuia Mór	8.17	67
45	Colonsay/Oronsay	2.7	143	96	Longay	5.4	67
46	Tiree	3.10	141	97	Sanday	10.25	65
47	Soay	5.1	141	98	Eilean Macaskin	2.8	65
48	Muck	4.1	137	99	Tahay	7.21	65
49	Great Cumbrae	1.6	127	100	Copinsay	10.9	64
50	Lismore	3.9	127	101	Shapinsay	10.13	64
51	Rona	5.9	125	102	Eilean an Ròin Mòr	6.11	63

TABLE 3

NO.	NAME	TABLE I NO.	HEIGHT IN METRES	NO.	NAME	TABLE I NO.	HEIGHT IN METRES
103	Graemsay	10.11	62	136	Linga (Yell Sound)	11.19	40
104	Little Colonsay	3.5	61	137	Oxna	11.4	38
105	Wiay	5.5	60	138	Eilean Kearstay	8.16	37
106	Inchmarnock	1.7	60	139	Soay Mór	8.10	37
107	Horse Island	6.7	60	140	Cava	10.8	36
108	Flotta	10.5	58	141	Gunna	3.11	35
109	Scotasay	8.7	57	142	Egilsay	10.19	35
110	Boreray	8.1	56	143	Hermetray	7.20	35
111	Cara	2.2	56	144	Lamba	11.23	35
112	Mousa	11.2	55	145	Vacsay	8.18	34
113	Eilean Righ	2.9	55	146	Bigga	11.21	34
114	Eilean Dubh Mór	2.15	53	147	Nave Island	2.5	34
115	Housay/Bruray	11.18	53	148	Wyre	10.16	32
116	Stroma	10.1	53	149	Papa	11.5	32
117	West Linga	11.16	52	150	Faray	10.23	32
118	Calf of Eday	10.24	50	151	Hildasay	11.9	32
119	Uyea	11.27	50	152	Eynhallow	10.20	30
120	Isle of May	12.1	50	153	Hascosay	11.26	29
121	Ensay	8.3	49	154	Samphrey	11.20	29
122	Inch Kenneth	3.4	49	155	Switha	10.4	29
123	Texa	2.1	48	156	Isay	5.8	28
124	Papa Westray	10.27	48	157	Floddaymore	7.17	28
125	Killegray	8.2	45	158	Pabay	5.2	28
126	Eilean Troday	5.10	45	159	Linga (Bluemull Sound)	11.28	26
127	Stronsay	10.15	44	160	Brother Isle	11.22	25
128	Balta	11.29	44	161	Flodday (Loch Maddy)	7.19	25
129	Stockinish Island	8.6	44	162	Eileanan Iasgaich	7.13	23
130	Fara	10.7	43	163	North Ronaldsay	10.27	20
131	Flodday (E Barra)	7.7	42	164	Muckle Skerry	10.1	20
132	South Havra	11.3	42	165	Ceann Ear/Iar	7.18	19
133	Swona	10.3	41	166	Auskerry	10.12	18
134	Little Bernera	8.20	41	167	Papa Stronsay	10.18	13
135	Stuley	7.13	40	168	Linga Holm	10.17	10

Appendices

Islands permitted to issue their own postage stamps

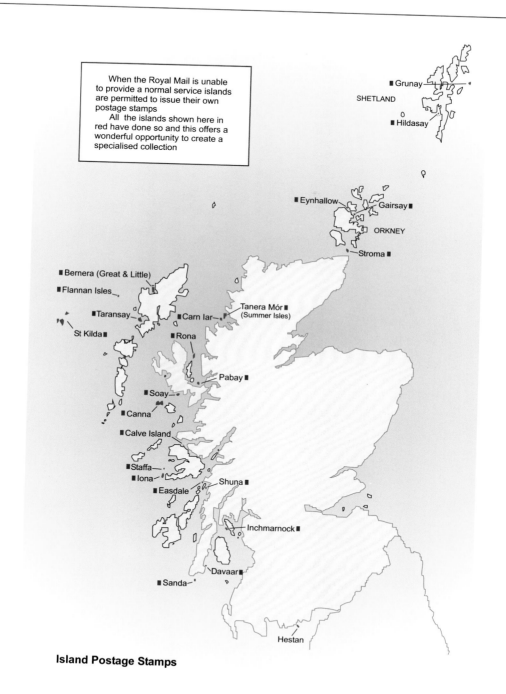

When the Royal Mail is unable to provide a normal service islands are permitted to issue their own postage stamps

All the islands shown here in red have done so and this offers a wonderful opportunity to create a specialised collection

■ Grunay

SHETLAND

○ Hildasay

■ Eynhallow   Gairsay ■

ORKNEY

Stroma ■

■ Bernera (Great & Little)

■ Flannan Isles

■ Taransay   ■ Carn Iar   Tanera Mór ■ (Summer Isles)

St Kilda ■   ■ Rona

Pabay ■

■ Soay

■ Canna

■ Calve Island

■ Staffa
■ Iona   Shuna ■
■ Easdale

Inchmarnock ■

Davaar

■ Sanda

Hestan

Island Postage Stamps

00x-stampC4

THE SCOTTISH ISLANDS   [517]

Island whisky distilleries

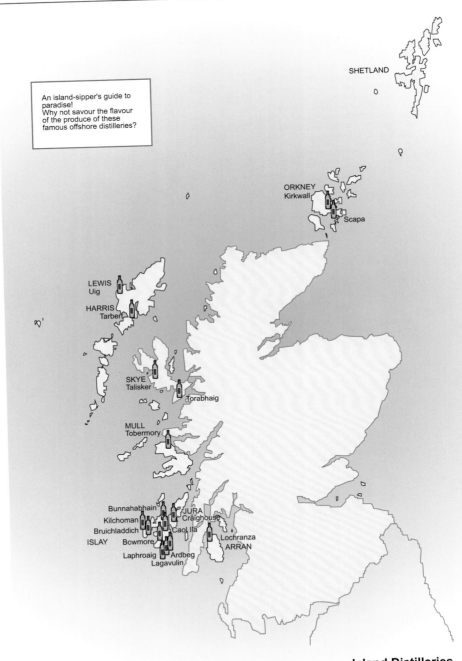

An island-sipper's guide to paradise!
Why not savour the flavour of the produce of these famous offshore distilleries?

SHETLAND

ORKNEY
Kirkwall
Scapa

LEWIS
Uig

HARRIS
Tarbert

SKYE
Talisker
Torabhaig

MULL
Tobermory

Bunnahabhain
Kilchoman   JURA
Bruichladdich   Craighouse
ISLAY   Bowmore   Caol Ila
Laphroaig   Ardbeg   Lochranza
Lagavulin   ARRAN

Island Distilleries

Island golf courses

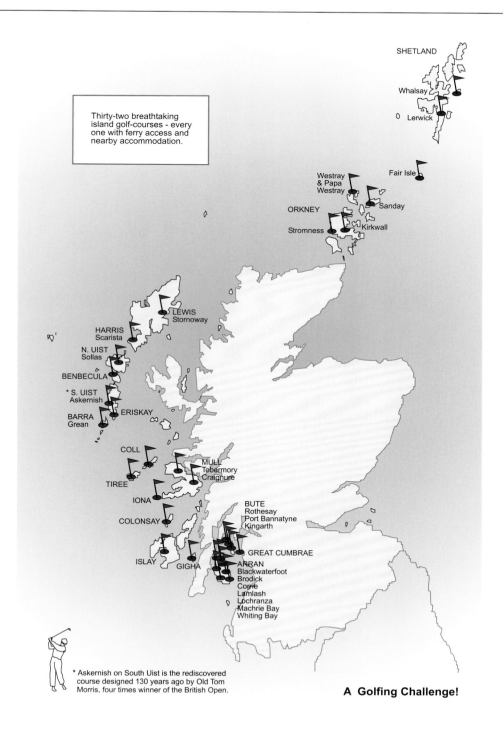

Thirty-two breathtaking island golf-courses - every one with ferry access and nearby accommodation.

SHETLAND

Whalsay

Lerwick

Fair Isle

Westray & Papa Westray

Sanday

ORKNEY

Kirkwall

Stromness

LEWIS
Stornoway

HARRIS
Scarista

N. UIST
Sollas

BENBECULA

* S. UIST
Askernish

BARRA
Green

ERISKAY

COLL

TIREE

MULL
Tobermory
Craignure

IONA

COLONSAY

BUTE
Rothesay
Port Bannatyne
Kingarth

GREAT CUMBRAE

ISLAY

GIGHA

ARRAN
Blackwaterfoot
Brodick
Corrie
Lamlash
Lochranza
Machrie Bay
Whiting Bay

* Askernish on South Uist is the rediscovered course designed 130 years ago by Old Tom Morris, four times winner of the British Open.

A Golfing Challenge!

Island lighthouses

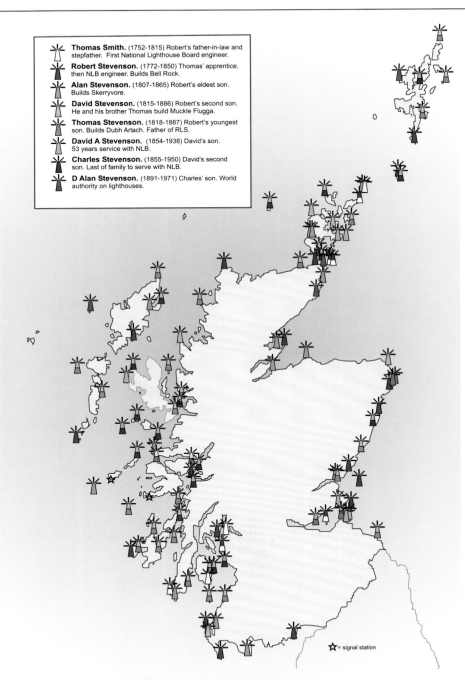

Thomas Smith. (1752-1815) Robert's father-in-law and stepfather. First National Lighthouse Board engineer.

Robert Stevenson. (1772-1850) Thomas' apprentice, then NLB engineer. Builds Bell Rock.

Alan Stevenson. (1807-1865) Robert's eldest son. Builds Skerryvore.

David Stevenson. (1815-1886) Robert's second son. He and his brother Thomas build Muckle Flugga.

Thomas Stevenson. (1818-1887) Robert's youngest son. Builds Dubh Artach. Father of RLS.

David A Stevenson. (1854-1938) David's son. 53 years service with NLB.

Charles Stevenson. (1855-1950) David's second son. Last of family to serve with NLB.

D Alan Stevenson. (1891-1971) Charles' son. World authority on lighthouses.

☆ = signal station

The Stevenson Lighthouses

Bibliography

The relevant section(s) are in square brackets after each entry. [G] = general

Admiralty Hydrographer. *North Coast of Scotland Pilot.* [G]
----------*West Coast of Scotland Pilot.* [G]

Allen, J Romilly, *The Early Christian Monuments of Scotland.* 1903. [G]

Anderson, A O, and M O, *Adomnan's Life of Columba.* 1961. [G]

Anderson, Joseph (ed), *The Orkneyinga Saga.* 1873. [10,11]

Anderson, R S G *The Antiquities of Gigha.* 1978. [2]

Arbman, H *The Vikings.* 1961. [G]

Atkinson, George Clayton, *Expeditions to the Hebrides in 1831 and 1833.* David A Quine (ed). 2001. [5,8,9]

Atkinson, Robert, *Island Going.* 1949. [G]
----------*Shillay and the Seals.* 1980. [7,8]

Bailey, Patrick, *Orkney.* 1971. [10]

Barclay, R S, *The Population of Orkney 1755–1961.* 1965. [10]

Barry, G, *History of the Orkney Islands.* 1805. [10]

Bathurst, Bella, *The Lighthouse Stevensons.* 1999. [G]

Blaeu, Joan, *The Blaeu Atlas of Scotland.* 1654. Reprinted 2006. [G]

Blake, George, *The Firth of Clyde.* [1]

Booth, C Gordon, *A Guide to Islay and Jura.* 1984. [2]

Boswell, James, *The Journal of a Tour to the Hebrides.* 1785. [G]

Botanical Society of the British Isles. *Proceedings.* [G]

Bray, Elizabeth, *The Discovery of the Hebrides. Voyagers to the Western Isles 1745–1883.* 1986. [G]

Brøgger, A W, *A History of the Norse Settlements in Scotland.* 1929. [G]

Brown, G M, *An Orkney Tapestry.* 1969. [10]

Brown, P. Hume, *Early Travellers in Scotland.* 1891. [G]

Budge, Donald, *Jura, an Island of Argyll.* 1960. [2]

Butler, David, *Isle of Noss.* 1990. [11]

Buxton, Ben, *Mingulay. An Island and Its People.* 1995. [7]

Caldwell, David H., *Islay, Jura and Colonsay. A Historical Guide.* 2001 [2]

Campbell, A J, *Fifteen Centuries of the Church in Orkney.* 1938. [10]

Campbell, J F, *Popular Tales of the West Highlands.* 1860–2. [G]

Campbell, John Lorne, *Canna: the Story of a Hebridean Island.* 1984. [4]

Carmichael, Alasdair, *Kintyre.* [G]

Carmichael, Ian, *Lismore in Alba.* 1947. [3]

Childe, V Gordon, *Prehistory of Scotland.* 1935. [G]
----------*Skara Brae: A Pictish Village in Orkney.* 1931. [10]

Clouston, J Storer, *A History of Orkney.* 1932. [10]

Clouston, J Storer, *The Orkney Parishes.* 1927. [10]

Cluness, A T, *The Shetland Isles.* 1951. [11]

Clyde Cruising Club Publications Ltd.
----------Sailing Directions (with annual updates):
Clyde Area. [1]
Kintyre to Ardnamurchan. [2,3]
Ardnamurchan to Cape Wrath. [4,5,6]
Outer Hebrides. [7,8,9]
North and North-East Coasts and Orkney. [6,10]
Shetland. [11]

Cooper, Derek, *Hebridian Connection.* 1977. [G]
----------*Skye.* [5]
----------*The Road to Mingulay.* 1985. [7,8]

Council for Scottish Archaeology.
Discovery and Excavation in Scotland. [G]
Scottish Archaeological News. [G]

Cowan, E J, McDonald, R A, et al, *Alba: Celtic Scotland in the Medieval Era.* [G]

Cruttwell, Clement, *The New Universal Gazetteer.* 1798. [G]

Craig, David, *On the Crofters' Trail.* 1990. [G]

Craig, G Y, *Geology of Scotland.* 1991. [G]

Cummins, W A, *The Age of the Picts.* 1995. [G]

Cursiter, J W, *List of Books relating to Orkney and Shetland.* 1894. [10,11]

Darling, Dr Frank Fraser, *Island Farm.* 1944. [6]
----------*Island Years.* 1942. [3,6,9]
----------*A Naturalist on Rona.* [9]
----------*West Highland Survey.* [G]

Darling, F Fraser and Boyd, J Morton, *The Highlands and Islands.* 1969. [G]

Dasent, G W, *The Orkneyingers' Saga.* 1894. [10]

Dawson, Alan, *The Relative Hills of Britain.* 1992. [G]

Delaney, Frank, *The Celts.* 1989. [G]

Dey, Joan, *Out Skerries.* 1991. [11]

Dickson, John, *Emeralds Chased in Gold.* 1899. [12]

Donaldson, M E M, *Wanderings in the Western Highlands and Islands.* 1920 [G]
----------*Further Wanderings – Mainly in Argyll.* 1926. [G]

Drever, W P, *Udal Law in the Orkneys and Zetland.* 1914. [10,11]

Drummond, Maldwin, *West Highland Shores.* 1990. [G]

Duncan, Angus, *Hebridean Island: Memories of Scarp.* 1995. [8]

Edmonston, T, *Glossary of Shetland and Orkney Dialect.* 1866. [10,11]

Fabian, D J *et al. The Islands of Scotland including Skye.* [G]

Faux, Ronald, *The West.* 1982. [G]

Feacham, R, *A Guide to Prehistoric Scotland.* [1963]

Fenton, Alexander, *The Northern Isles: Orkney and Shetland.* 1978. [10,11]

Fenton, Alexander and Palsson, Hermann, *The Northern and Western Isles in the Viking World.* [G]

Forth Yacht Clubs' Association Pilot Handbook. *Berwick-on-Tweed to Peterhead.* 1974. [12]

Garms, Harry, *The Natural History of Europe.* 1967. [G]

Gear, Sheila, *Foula. Island West of the Sun.* 1983. [11]

Gordon, Seton, *Highways and Byways in the West Highlands.* 1935. [G]

----------*Afoot in Wild Places.* [G]

Gorrie, D, *Summers and Winters in the Orkneys.* 1868. [10]

Graham, Henry Grey, *The Social Life of Scotland in the Eighteenth Century.* 1899. [G]

Grant, I F, *The Lordship of the Isles.* 1982. [G]

Grant, James Shaw, *Discovering Lewis and Harris.* 1987. [8]

Gregory, D, *History of the Western Highlands and Islands.* 1881. [G]

Grieve, Symington, *The Book of Colonsay and Oronsay.* 1923. [2]

Grigsby, Joan, *An Island Rooin.* 1933. [11]

Grimble, Ian, *Highland Man.* 1980. [G]

----------*Scottish Islands.* 1985. [G]

Groome, F Hindes, *Ordnance Gazetteer.* 1900. [G]

Gunn, J, *The Orkney Book.* 1909. [10]

Harker, Alfred, *The West Highlands and the Hebrides.* 1941. [G]

Heddle, J G F M and Mainland, T., *Orkney and Shetland.* 1920. [10,11]

Henderson, Isabel, *The Picts.* 1967. [G]

Hewison, James King, *Bute in the Olden Time.* 1893. [1]

Hewitson, Jim., *Clinging to the Edge.* 1996. [10]

Higgins, L R, *A Tangle of Islands.* 1971. [G]

Hogg, Garry, *The Far Flung Isles.* 1961. [G]

Hossack, B H, *Kirkwall in the Orkneys.* 1900. [10]

Howarth, David, *The Shetland Bus.* 1953. [11]

Jakobsen, Jakob, *Old Shetland Dialect and Place-Names of Shetland.* [11]

----------*Etymological Dictionary of the Norn Language in Shetland.* [11]

Jamieson, Peter, *Letters on Shetland.* 1949. [11]

Johnson, Samuel, *Journey to the Western Isles of Scotland.* 1775. [G]

Knox, John, *Tour of the Highlands of Scotland and the Hebride Isles in 1787.* 1787. [G]

Lacaille, A, *The Stone Age in Scotland.* 1954. [G]

Lamont, W D, *The Early History of Islay.* 1966. [2]

Lawrence, Martin, *Clyde to Colonsay.* 2001. [1,2]

----------*Crinan to Canna.* 2004. [2,3,4]

----------*Skye and Northwest Scotland.* 2002. [5,6]

----------*Western Isles.* 2003. [7,8,9]

----------*North and East Scotland.* 2003. [6,10,12]

Lawson, Bill, *The Teampull on the Isle of Pabbay.* 1994. [8]

Linklater, Eric, revis. J R Nicolson. *Orkney and Shetland.* 1990. [10,11]

Linklater, Eric, *The Ultimate Viking.* 1955. [G]

Loder, J de V, *Colonsay and Oronsay in the Isles of Argyll.* 1935. [2]

Love, John A., *Rum. A Landscape Without Figures.* 2002 [4]

MacCaig, Norman, *Collected Poems.* 1988. [G]

MacCormack, John, *Island of Mull.* 1923. [3]

MacCulloch, J, *The Highlands and Western Isles of Scotland.* 1824. [G]

Macdonald, Donald, *Lewis. A History of the Island.* 1978. [8]

MacDonald, James, *General view of the agriculture of the Hebrides or Western Isles of Scotland: with observations on the means of their improvement, together with a separate account of the principal islands.* 1811. [G]

McEwen, John, *Who Owns Scotland.* 1981. [G]

MacGregor, Alasdair Alpin, *Searching the Hebrides with a Camera.* 1933 [7,8]

Mackenzie, Compton; Campbell, J L; Borgström, Carl, *The Book of Barra.* 1936. [7]

McKerral, Andrew, *Kintyre in the Seventeenth Century.* 1948. [1,2]

MacKillop, Donald, *Sea-Names of Berneray.* 1990. [7,8]

Mackintosh, W R, *Around the Orkney Peat Fires.* 1914. [10]

Maclean, Charles, *The Isle of Mull. Placenames, Meanings and Stories.* 1997. [3]

McKirdy, A., Gordon, J. and Crofts. R., *Land of Mountain and*

Flood: The Geology and Landforms of Scotland. 2007. [G]

McLellan, Robert, *The Isle of Arran.* 1970. [1]

Maclennan, John, *Place-Names of Scarp.* 2001 [8]

Macnab, P A, *Mull & Iona.* 1982. [3]

McNeill, F Marion, *Iona.* 1959. [3]

Madders, Michael, and Welstead, Julia, *Where to Watch Birds in Scotland.* [G]

Marshall, David, *The Story of Inchkeith.* [12]

Martin, Martin, *A Description of the Western Isles of Scotland.* 1703. [G]

----------*A Late Voyage to St Kilda.* 1698. [8,9]

Marwick, H, *Ancient Monuments of Orkney. Official Guide.* 1952. [10]

----------*Orkney.* 1951. [10]

----------*Orkney Farm Names.* 1952. [10]

----------edit. Nicolaisen, W F H, *The Place-Names of Birsay.* 1970. [10]

----------*The Place-Names of Rousay.* 1947. [10]

Mercer, John, *Hebridean Islands: Colonsay, Gigha, Jura.* 1982. [2]

Millman, Lawrence, *Last Places.* 1992. [7]

Mitchison, Rosalind, *A History of Scotland.* 1982. [G]

Mooney, J, *Eynhallow. The Holy Isle of the Orkneys.* 1923. [10]

Morton, Tom, *Hell's Golfer – a good walk spoiled.* 1995. [7,8,10,11]

Muir, Edwin, *Autobiography.* [10]

Munro, Dean Sir Donald, *Description of the Western Isles of Scotland.* 1549. [G]

Munro, Neil, *Children of the Tempest.* [7]

----------*The Clyde River and Firth.* [1]

New Statistical Account of Scotland. 1845. [G]

Murray, Frances, *Summer in the Hebrides.* 1887. [G]

Murray, W H *The Islands of Western Scotland.* 1973. [G]

----------*The West Highlands of Scotland.* 1988. [G]

Newton, Norman S, *Colonsay and Oronsay.* 1990. [2]

----------*Islay.* 1988. [2]

Nicolaisen, W F H, *Scottish Place-Names.* 1976. [G]

Nicolson, A, *History of Skye.* 1930. [5]

Nicolson, Adam, *Sea Room. An Island Life.* 2001. [8]

Nicolson, James R, *Traditional Life in Shetland.* 1990. [11]

O'Dell, A C and Watson, Kenneth, *The Highlands and Islands of Scotland.* 1962. [G]

O'Dell, Andrew, *Historical Geography of the Shetland Isles.* [11]

Orkney Antiquarian Society. *Proceedings.* [10]

Pennant, T, *A Tour in Scotland, and Voyage to the Hebrides.* 1776. [G]

Perrot, David, *Guide to the Western Isles.* 1986. [G]

Philip, Kathleen, *The Story of Gigha.* 1979. [2]

Rea F G, *A School in South Uist.* 1964 [7]

Reed, Laurence, *The Soay of Our Forefathers.* 2002 [5]

Rendall, R, *Orkney Shore.* 1960. [10]

Robson, Michael, *Rona, the Distant Island.* 1991. [9]

Royal Commission on the Ancient and Historical Monuments of Scotland.

    Argyll. 1971–92. [1,2,3]

    Orkney. 1946. [10]

    Outer Hebrides, Skye and Small Isles. 1928. [4,5,6,7,8]

Sawyer, P H, *The Age of the Vikings.* 1962. [G]

Schei, Liv Kjørsvik and Moberg, Gunnie, *The Orkney Story.* 1985. [10]

----------*The Shetland Story.* 1988. [11]

Scott, M A, *Island Saga. The Story of North Ronaldsay.* 1968. [10]

Scottish Mountaineering Club. District Guide Books, *Islands of Scotland* *Munro's Tables*

Shaw, Frances J, *The Northern and Western Islands of Scotland: their Economy and Society in the Seventeenth Century.* 1980. [G]

Shaw, Margaret Fay, *From the Alleghenies to the Hebrides.* 1993. [G]

Sharpe, Richard, *Raasay: a Study in Island History.* 1982. [5]

Sheddon, Hugh, *The Story of Lorn.* [3]

Simpson, W Douglas, *The Ancient Stones of Scotland.* 1965. [G]

----------*The Celtic Church in Scotland.* 1935. [G]

Simpson, Sir James Y, *Inchcolm.* [12]

Sinclair, Andrew, *The Sword and the Grail.* 1993. [10]

Sissons, J B, *The Evolution of Scotland's Scenery.* 1967. [G]

Skene, W F, *Celtic Scotland.* 1876. [G]

Smout, T C, *A History of the Scottish People.* 1985. [G]

Smith, G Gregory, (ed.) *The Book of Islay: Documents Illustrating the History of the Island.* 1895. [2]

Society of Antiquaries of Scotland. *Proceedings.* [G]

Steel, Tom, *The Life and Death of St Kilda.* 1975. [9]

Steven, Campbell, *The Island Hills*. 1955. [G]

Storrie, Margaret C, *Islay: Biography of an Island*. 1981. [2]

Teignmouth, Lord, *Sketches of the Coasts and Islands of Scotland*. 1836. [G]

Tennent, Norman, *The Islands of Scotland*. [G]
The Statistical Account of Scotland. 1791–99. 1800. [G]
The Third Statistical Account of Scotland. 1961. [G]

Thompson, Francis, *Harris and Lewis, Outer Hebrides*. 1968. [8]
----------*Northern Scotland & the Islands*. [G]
----------*The Uists and Barra*. 1976. [7]

Tranter, Nigel, *Argyll & Bute*. 1977. [1,2,3]

Tulloch, Bobby, *Bobby Tulloch's Shetland*. 1993. [11]

Tulloch, Vie, *The Isle of Gigha*. 1988. [2]

Wainwright, F T (ed.) *The Northern Isles*. 1962. [G]
----------*The Problem of the Picts*. 1955. [G]

Walker, John, edit. McKay, Margaret M., *The Rev Dr John Walker's Report on the Hebrides of 1764 and 1771*. 1980. [G]

Watson, W J, *The History of the Celtic Place-Names of Scotland*. 1926. [G]

West, R G, *Pleistocene Geology and Biology*. 1968. [G]

Westwood, Jennifer, *Albion. A Guide to Legendary Britain*. 1985. [G]

Whitehouse, G K, *The Wild Goats of Britain and Ireland*.

1972. [G]

Whittow, J B, *Geology and Scenery in Scotland*. 1979. [G]

Wightman, Andy, *Who Owns Scotland*. 1996. [G]

Williams, Ronald, *The Lords of the Isles: the Clan Donald and the Early Kingdom of the Scots*. 1984. [G]

Williamson, Kenneth and Boyd, J. Morton, *Mosaic of Islands*. 1963. [G]
----------*St. Kilda Summer*. 1960. [9]

Wilson, Neil, *Scotch and Water: an Illustrated Guide to the Hebridean Malt Whisky Distilleries*. 1985. [G]

Youngson, Peter, *The Long Road: a Driver's Guide to Jura*. 1987. [G]
----------*Jura. Island of Deer*. 2002 [2]

JANDARA

Index of Islands

The section and island reference number is given for each entry. Int = Introduction. Ap = Appendix

INDEX OF ISLANDS